TEXTILES for RESIDENTIAL and COMMERCIAL INTERIORS

TEXTILES for RESIDENTIAL and COMMERCIAL INTERIORS

5th Edition

MaryPaul Yates
Adrienne Concra

FAIRCHILD BOOKS

NEW YORK · LONDON · OXFORD · NEW DELHI · SYDNEY

FAIRCHILD BOOKS
Bloomsbury Publishing Inc
1385 Broadway, New York, NY 10018, USA
50 Bedford Square, London, WC1B 3DP, UK

BLOOMSBURY, FAIRCHILD BOOKS and the Fairchild Books
logo are trademarks of Bloomsbury Publishing Plc

Third edition published 2009

Fourth edition published 2014

This edition first published in the United States of America 2019

For legal purposes the Acknowledgments on pp. xii–xiii
constitute an extension of this copyright page.

Cover design: Sam Clark / ByTheSky Design
Cover image: Courtesy Getty Images

A catalog record for this publication is available from the Library of Congress.

ISBN: PB: 978-1-5013-2651-6
         ePDF: 978-1-5013-2652-3

Typeset by Lachina Creative, Inc.
Printed and bound in China.

To find out more about our authors and books visit
www.fairchildbooks.com and sign up for our newsletter.

CONTENTS

UNIT FOUR
FLOORCOVERINGS

UNIT FIVE
HOUSEHOLD AND
INSTITUTIONAL TEXTILES

EXTENDED CONTENTS

UNIT TWO
UPHOLSTERY

UNIT THREE
WINDOW TREATMENTS
AND WALLCOVERINGS

PREFACE

The fifth edition of *Textiles for Residential and Commercial Interiors* reflects the suggestions of professors who used earlier editions of the book, and benefits from the expertise of numerous generous professionals in all segments of the interior fabric industry. Many of these professionals read sections of the manuscript related to their expertise and contributed comments, updates, and corrections. Some of the college instructors and professors shared invaluable comments offered by their students. The organization, pedagogy, and scope of the book reflects all this input.

The book is written as a textbook, directed to interior design students and educators in higher education, but it is also a useful reference for practicing interior designers, architects, retailers, and consumers with a professional or personal interest in textile furnishings.

Changes for the fifth edition include:

- New illustrations that feature current market trends
- Outline of current performance and sustainability standards, guidelines, and codes for multiple products
- Simplified organizational structure, minimizing redundancy
- Examination of current and new finishes and fiber preferences
- More illustrations of and performance information about fibers and fabrics suitable for outdoor use

- Extensive discussion of environmental and health issues related to the manufacture and use of interior textiles and their relationship to governmental codes, requirements, and trends

To achieve a greater understanding of interior textiles requires examining and studying fabrics as well as the information included in the textbook. This text can be used in conjunction with *Swatch Reference Guide for Interior Design Fabrics* by Deborah Young, also available from Fairchild Books. Direct access to fabric swatches can enhance understanding of essential details of woven, printed, and nonwoven fabrics.

Because readers will have different levels of knowledge about textiles, the text begins with a focus on textile fundamentals. As requested by users of the earlier editions, all aesthetic, durability, appearance retention, comfort, and health and safety properties are examined in greater depth at the end of each section that relates to the relevant end-use. All levels of manufacturing and processing, from fiber to yarn, to fabrication, to dyeing and finishing, are discussed in detail. Newly developed fibers and new processing techniques are covered.

For the benefit of the instructor and the student, key terms and review questions are offered at the end of each chapter. The appendices include a list of generic manufactured fiber names, established performance guidelines for contract fabrics, a bibliography, and an extensive glossary. The text is richly illustrated, with line drawings and full-color, detailed photographs of fibers, yarns, fabrics, equipment used in manufacturing, coloring and finishing processes, end products and end-use settings.

The text is presented in five units, with Unit One having a focus on textile fundamentals. Units Two through Five are divided by end-product category. Unit Two includes discussion of upholstered furniture coverings and fillings; Unit Three focuses on window coverings, drapery linings, and textile wallcoverings; Unit Four covers soft floorcoverings and cushions; and Unit Five presents material on both functional and decorative bath and bedding textiles used in residential and commercial settings.

In larger institutions with extensive offerings, *Textiles for Residential and Commercial Interiors* is appropriate for a course to follow completion of introductory textiles and interior design courses. It can be used in either textiles or interior design departments. In smaller institutions where course offerings may be more limited, the text would be useful in an introductory course with an expansive scope (e.g., apparel textiles and interior textiles, or housing and interior textiles). The book's organization permits the selection of units or chapters dealing with topics in the order preferred by the instructor.

Instructor Resources

An Instructor's Guide and PowerPoint presentations for each chapter accompany the text to assist in planning, presenting, and evaluating content found in the text and in the STUDIO.

Textiles for Residential and Commercial Interiors STUDiO

Fairchild Books has a long history of excellence in textbook publishing for design education. Our new online STUDIOs are specially developed to complement this book with rich media ancillaries that students can adapt to their visual learning styles. *Textiles for Residential and Commercial Interiors* STUDIO features online self-quizzes with scored results and personalized study tips, and flashcards with terms and definitions, to help students master concepts and improve grades. STUDIO access cards are offered free with new book purchases and also sold separately through www.fairchildbooks.com.

ACKNOWLEDGMENTS

We are pleased to have been asked to participate in the well-established franchise of *Textiles for Residential and Commercial Interiors*. For several decades, this book, in its previous four editions, has been a fixture in the educational protocol for many interior designers and textile professionals. We are both industry professionals who also teach college courses in our field and care deeply about contributing to the knowledge and professionalism of our future colleagues. We appreciate the opportunity to build on that goal through this platform.

First and foremost, thank you to all our friends and colleagues, both companies and individuals, who shared images, illustrations, and information so that we could make *Textiles for Residential and Commercial Interiors*, fifth edition, attractive, informative, and accurate. Max Concra, Judy Juracek, and Jim Koch stand out as photographers who were always willing to help us fill in missing slots with beautiful images.

We thank the experts and specialists who spent precious free time reviewing sections of the book and sharing their vast knowledge and expertise so that we could fine-tune the manuscript and improve accuracy: Alan Dean, Duvaltex; Brian Fogg, Carpet Cushion Institute; Bob Peoples, Carpet America Recovery Effort (CARE); Janan Rabiah, Association for Contract Textiles; Marie Rich, Stevens Enterprises; Ken Salyer, Tri-Kes; Richard Turner, Carpet and Rug Institute; and Thomas Woller.

For advice and help of all sorts, thanks to Patti Annis, University of Georgia; Michael and Maureen Banner; Sandra P. Clarkson; Chandler Crawford; Edouard A. Daunas, Martin Patrick Evan; Margaret Dunford, Sage Automotive; Lisa Farasiano, Kravet; Joe Foye, Mohawk; Nancy Green; Nat Harrison; Meredith Hoefle, Standard Textiles; Thom Houser, University of Georgia; Jeff Irwin, Lady Fabrics; Beth James, Mohawk; Glen Kaufman; Brooke Kuhlmann, Earthbound Brands; Mark Pollack; Declan Redfern; Rebecca Saletan; Julie Shapiro; Troy Virgo, Shaw Industries; and David Yates.

We would like to thank our acquiring editor Noah Schwartzberg, development editor Amy Butler, and art development editor Edie Weinberg, for their can-do attitudes and good spirits throughout this project. We further offer our admiration to the numerous previous authors of this volume, and especially thank Amy Willbanks, who has allowed the use of her numerous informative photographs to be used in this edition.

We would each like to thank our actual and virtual families for cheering us on. We are blessed to have grown children who think their mothers are awesome professionals, and offer us moral support at all turns. Thank you Max Concra, Lindsey Concra, Bryan Weisgal, and Leah Weisgal!

Last but not least, we would like to acknowledge each other. Partnerships are not always easy; writing books is definitely a trial. We have been close friends and mutually admiring colleagues for a long time, and this project proved to be not a wedge, but a wonderful collaboration. We enjoyed the partnership—and the shared accomplishment of completion.

MaryPaul Yates
Adrienne Concra

Bloomsbury Publishing wishes to gratefully acknowledge and thank the editorial team involved in the publication of this book:

Acquisitions Editor: Noah Schwartzberg
Development Editor: Amy Butler
Art Development Editor: Edie Weinberg
Editorial Assistant: Bridget MacAvoy
In-House Designer: Eleanor Rose
Production Editor: Claire Cooper
Project Manager: Courtney Coffman, Lachina

The publisher also wishes to thank the following reviewers for their contributions to this edition:

Ruth Beals, Converse College
Cheryl Gulley, Watkins College of Art and Design
Amy O'Dell, Lanier Technical College
Jessica Royale MacKenzie, Northern Arizona University
Victoria Runge, University of Tennessee, Chattanooga
Angela Stephens, Central Piedmont Community College
Sharon Ting, UCA Farnham, United Kingdom

UNIT ONE
THE FUNDAMENTALS OF TEXTILES FOR INTERIORS

1

The Interior Textile Industry

Facing page: Photo © Koch Studio, Inc., www.jk-gallery.com; Photo courtesy of Fabricut Fabrics, www.fabricut.com.

Fabric for interior furnishings is produced in every corner of the world. With international trade, instant electronic communication, and increasingly efficient worldwide transportation of goods, a wider range of beautiful fabrics is available, at more reasonable prices, to the consumer than at any other time in our history. The volume and diversity of choices makes a designer's job easy—in some ways. It also makes the selection process more challenging, as the aesthetic and performance features of offerings and the sheer range of availability can be overwhelming. This text aims to offer designers parameters and considerations that are critical to making wise choices and successful specifications of fabrics for interior furnishings.

Several levels and segments make up the fabric-production industry, whether the intended market is interior furnishings, apparel, or industrial application. Each operation in the manufacturing process is an equally important link in the chain of production and distribution. These mutually dependent entities, composed of many independent firms, all need reliable suppliers and all serve the ultimate customers. Furniture producers, for example, must have a supply of fillings, linings, and finished fabrics. In turn, they depend upon product designers to guide their product offerings, distributors and sales agencies to sell their product, and interior designers and architects who are willing to recommend their upholstered products to clients and retailers who then offer their products to purchasing customers.

Sharing a common goal—to operate profitably—all members of the industry work cooperatively to ensure that the **end products** offered are widely accepted by consumers. To secure this acceptance and realize their goal, suppliers, producers, and distributors often support and seek assistance from outside consultants for product development, marketing, and branding; trade associations; independent testing authorities; and other providers. While such groups are not directly involved in the manufacturing sequence, they have a major influence on quality, awareness, and selection of the industry's goods.

Although consumer acceptance or rejection of the products available primarily determines the economic health of the industry, the fabric industry is directly affected by environmental issues and economic factors, as are all other industries. Fiber and fabric executives are aware of, and respond to, many variables in order to keep their firms financially viable.

Major Segments of the Industry

Fiber Suppliers and Producers

Fabric starts with **fiber**, the chemically distinct raw material of which fabric is made. Is it cotton? Polyester? Wool? Fiber is fabricated into yarn, or sometimes, directly into fabric. Natural fiber harvesters and processors and **manufactured fiber producers** initiate the work of the fiber industry, which culminates in products used by the residential and commercial consumer.

Natural fiber suppliers recover naturally formed fibers, principally from animal fleece (such as sheep), from silk-producing caterpillars, or from plants (such as cotton bolls and flax plants). These suppliers focus on production of high yields of quality fibers while balancing the concerns of the environment, business needs, and the marketplace. Except for silk, these materials naturally occur as short lengths called **staple**. Staple fiber is combed, cleaned, and aligned to make long lengths that can be woven or knitted. The staple fiber supplier usually handles the first part of the yarn-making process, and then ships the fiber in a loose, rope-like form called **tow** to the yarn producers.

Natural man-made fiber producers utilize natural materials such as wood chips, cotton linters, bamboo, sugar beets, glass, and corn, which they process chemically to generate fibers including rayon, PLA (polylactic acid), fiberglass, and acetate.

Synthetic manufactured fiber producers manufacture acrylic, nylon, polyester, polypropylene (olefin), and PVC (polyvinyl chloride, also known as vinyon) from synthetic polymers derived from petroleum. Synthetic fiber is extruded from a liquid (much like toothpaste from a tube) into a continuous length, which is referred to as **continuous filament** form.

Filaments also may be cut, texturized, brushed, and combed to simulate staple form for aesthetics, in order to more closely mimic natural fibers. Silk naturally occurs as a filament, other than bits of scrap silk fiber, which are typically handled as staple and are used for spinning.

Yarn Producers

Yarn producers combine fibers into usable yarn structures. **Spinners** align, spin, and twist staple-length fibers into spun yarns, and **synthetic yarn producers** combine filament-length fibers into untwisted or twisted multi-filament yarns, and add texture to the filament yarns. Yarn producers frequently employ multiple twisting or plying operations to expand the assortment of yarns available to fabric manufacturers.

Fabric Manufacturers

Fabric manufacturers use **weaving, knitting, knotting and twisting, braiding,** and **tufting** to form fabric structures from yarns. Others use **felting, spunbonding,** and **needle punching** to produce **nonwovens**, which are fabrics made directly from fiber, bypassing a need for yarn. They extrude polymer to produce **film**—or sheeting made directly from solutions—bypassing both fiber and yarn stages, thereby functioning as the fabric manufacturer.

Fabric producers and textile machinery engineers work cooperatively to develop new equipment and devise more efficient fabrication techniques, continually striving to fulfill two major goals. First, they work to engineer fabric structures that will be appealing to and perform satisfactorily for the consumer. Second, they strive to operate as efficiently as possible. Manufacturers are profitable when they work efficiently and produce desirable products at appropriate prices.

Dyers, Printers, and Finishers

Dye, which chemically bonds with fiber to change its color, can be incorporated before the fabric is made. Manufactured fiber producers may incorporate dye pigments within filaments as they are extruded (**solution-dyed**); dyers may immerse fibers (**stock-dyed**) or yarns (**yarn-dyed**) in a solution of dyestuff.

Some fabrics that are dyed using one of these three methods are ready to go to the consumer once they are woven, but other fabrics require extra processes, or **finishes**, to achieve the final result that professionals and consumers want. Additionally, some fabrics will have color applied after the fabric is woven, either through **piece-dyeing** (the entire bolt of fabric is immersed in a dye bath) or through **printing** (dye is applied only to certain areas of the surface of the fabric). Before such unfinished fabrics are dyed or printed, they are called **greige goods**. Piece-dyed fabrics and most printed fabrics need to be finished—at the least washed, dried, pressed—before they are usable.

In addition to performing simple processes like washing and drying fabric, **finishers** apply mechanical and chemical treatments to alter a cloth's appearance. For example, pile-yarn orientation and luster can be adjusted. Performance characteristics such as water- and soil-repellency, wrinkle recovery, and shape retention can be improved. By applying coatings and laminating other fabrics to the backs of carpet and to fabric wallcoverings, finishers can improve the functional characteristics and stability of these structures and facilitate their efficient installation.

It should be noted that fabric production is a **vertical** process. Producing and handling fiber, spinning yarns, weaving fabrics, applying color, converting greige goods, and constructing end products are all part of reaching the end-user. Though becoming more rare, some producers, called **vertical manufacturers**, undertake several of these processes. For example, dyers, printers, and finishers may all be parts of one company, or may be completely separate, or may also be part of a fiber, yarn, or fabric manufacturer. They may be an independent operation that simply performs a service to another operation, not ever taking ownership of the material. Whether performed under one roof or several, many steps and teams of collaborators are needed to make every fabric.

Converters and Distributors

Converters take ownership of fabric that is unfinished, add value to it, for example, by having it dyed or printed, and then resell it. These companies employ designers who create original designs and signature collections. They may also commit to large runs of fabric from mills and resell the fabric in smaller lots, usually by the **piece** (approximately 60 yards/meters). Converters do not generally cut-to-order for small quantity sales. Converters sell to furniture manufacturers and wholesalers/distributors, functioning as a mill does. They may also act as a distributor to segments of the industry that purchase in large quantities, such as the hospitality segment.

Distributors, commonly called wholesalers, or jobbers, are the main suppliers to the interior designer and architect marketplace. Distributors work with mills all over the world to develop products that create a brand identity for the wholesaler, and conform to their clients' aesthetic preferences, serviceability requirements, and budgets. The distributors adopt these fabrics into their own lines and sell them under their own labels. These companies maintain showrooms in major design centers, produce marketing material such as brochures, advertisements, and samples, and retain a large sales staff who visit designers in their offices to show the latest product offerings. A designer may order the fabric from the distributor and resell it to a customer, or the professional may **specify** the fabric and have the customer (the end-user) purchase the fabric. Also, a firm that makes furniture, fabricates window coverings, or installs wallcoverings may purchase the material and then invoice the end-user for the finished, or installed, product. (The term *end-user* is commonly used to describe a corporate purchaser, while *consumer* refers to a retail customer.) Although distributors do not manufacture fabric, they often present themselves as "**mills**." This is a term-of-art in the industry as shorthand to the designer/specifier/customer.

Especially in small cities and remote areas, an upholstery or drapery workroom, a wallcovering installer, or an interior designer may maintain a product showroom. These businesses are often geared to the trade (to professional interior designers and architects) and also sell to retail consumers. Designers receive a **trade discount** off the price sold to retail customers.

In decades gone by, the best sources were available only to the trade. Increasingly, designers and consumers alike have a vast array of available interior products, through multiple channels. The quality and diversity of retail products at affordable prices and the general public's increasingly high level of aesthetic intelligence challenges today's interior designer to hone marketing skills, professional practices, and to offer a high level of expertise.

Fabric Designers, Colorists, and Creative Directors

Every stage in the sequence of making fabric necessitates aesthetic choices. Fabric designers are responsible for ensuring that the company's line is ready, on time, in the proper form, starting from a scrap of yarn, a few colors (Figure 1.1), and some ideas, all the way to having samples ready to ship on the date of the product's release.

Well in advance of production, **fabric designers** identify and forecast the aesthetic features preferred by current and future consumers. By studying sales reports, company records, and the general market patterns, they remain alert for slight shifts in the selection of fashion-related qualities such as color, fabric weight, textural characteristics, and drapability. Designers tally the relative popularity of woven patterns and printed patterns; simple or elaborate design motifs; small-scale or large-scale patterns; and fiber, yarn, and fabric color

Figure 1.1 Designers research future color trends. Photo courtesy Color Association of the United States, www.colorassociation.com.

choices. They interpret and forecast trends and anticipate variations and evolution of the ideas, while considering suitability for production operations.

Additionally, each fabric must meet requirements and expectations for quality, price, performance, suitability for being produced efficiently, and environmental impact. To these ends, designers work closely with all operations, whether outside vendors or in-house production, in order to engineer the best possible qualities through yarn choices, structural development, and finishing.

Fabric designers may focus on structure (weave, knit, how the fabric is made), surface pattern, or color, or in several areas of the process. **Design directors**, or **creative directors**, manage the entire creative team. **Colorists** are designers who specialize in color development of patterns in process, but the term can also describe personnel of dyers who develop dye formulas and match colors.

In some market segments, design personnel are termed **stylists**, which can carry a variety of job descriptions. A stylist may be a creative director in some companies, or someone who arranges displays for photo-shoots, or one who merchandises, purchasing products from a variety of sources to build a product line. European designers, merchandisers, and wholesaler/distributors are often referred to as **editors**.

End-Product Producers and Market Segments

End-product producers fabricate and construct items that are ready for immediate use or for installation in an interior setting. Fibers, yarns, and finished fabrics are among the many materials used to make upholstered furniture, drapery and window treatments, wallcoverings, carpet and padding, and household and institutional textiles.

Some interior products are specifically produced for use in privately owned (**residential**) interiors. Other products are specifically designed and constructed to withstand the higher levels of anticipated use in public (**contract**) interiors—offices; hospitals and other medical facilities, including nursing homes and other long-term care facilities (healthcare); hotels, motels, and restaurants (hospitality); schools, colleges, and dormitories (education); stores and shopping centers (retail); libraries and public buildings; religious buildings; high-traffic public spaces (such as airport terminals); and theaters.

The upholstered furniture market includes chairs, sofas, ottomans, and the like, each covered by a fabric, vinyl, or leather; most have a combination of fiber, foam, or feather filling. Window coverings range from sheer curtains to blinds and shades containing grasses or metal slats. Wallcovering offerings range from elegant moiré taffetas to rough burlap cloths made of jute, vinyls, and high-performance woven fabrics. Floorcoverings range from scatter rugs to wall-to-wall carpet to exquisite Turkish or Persian rugs. Carpet backing can be jute or olefin, and rug padding may be animal hair, rubber, or polyurethane.

Household textiles (**domestics**) used in residential interiors include beddings, towels, and tabletop accessories; similar such products designed for use in hospitality or healthcare facilities are referred to as **institutional textiles**, which are required to conform with performance criteria and life-safety codes.

Among the assortment of products included in each of these categories, fiber content, yarn features, fabric structure, color styling, finishes, and product design differ. In most cases, fabric and **end-product designers** work cooperatively with producers and marketing specialists to plan necessary combinations that meet a variety of consumer desires and that conform with specific requirements set by the design professional and agency with jurisdiction over a given installation.

At every level, producers must continually refine products and develop new and unique items. They must offer design, composition, and performance characteristics that spark enthusiasm from interior designers, architects, end-users, and consumers.

Design Professionals

Design professionals, who are primarily licensed, registered, or certified interior designers and architects, select fabrics for many categories of installation, as previously discussed. Professional interior designers have endeavored to require that designers be licensed, registered, or certified by passing, for example, the National Council for Interior Design Qualification (NCIDQ) examination. Design professionals may operate their own firms, partnerships, or be employed by independent firms, schools, banks, or many sorts of large corporations. They normally provide services in accordance with the terms of a contractual agreement made with their clients. Most importantly, contracts establish legal responsibility between client and design professional.

Interior designers and architects serve as critical links between the industry and end-users and consumers. These professionals have a positive economic effect on the industry by selecting new products and by recommending and specifying products that are consistent with their clients' selection criteria. To do their jobs well, they must be familiar with the industry's array of products in order to assess the anticipated aesthetics and performance features needed for specific end-use conditions. Distributors' representatives play a critical role in providing information to the designer and architect who are specifying products. Designers and architects must be aware of codes governing the selection and installation of products in a facility or in a particular location within a facility. Ultimately, the accuracy with which interior designers and architects recommend or specify products helps determine their professional reputations and that of their suppliers. Customers will ultimately return to the designer, and to the product suppliers, only if they are satisfied with completed jobs.

Consumers and End-Users

The **consumer** or end-user pays for the end product; thus, the consumer may be a person, a group, a corporation, an agency, or an institution. Consumers may prefer to use their own talents and judgment when selecting products, or they may elect to contract for the services of an interior designer or architect for this task. In the latter case, functioning as consultants, the professionals select, recommend, or specify products; their clients, who pay for the merchandise, are the consumers.

An end-user is, likewise, the party that pays for, and uses, the product, but, as previously noted, the term **end-user** is also specifically used to refer to corporate purchasers. For example, a hotel chain, a large corporation, or a hospital may be the purchaser and end-user, and is a corporate entity rather than an individual.

Selecting Interior Textiles

In most cases, the residential or commercial consumer determines the relative importance of several fabric attributes, personally deciding which compromises can be made. For certain commercial products, however, the fabric is expected to meet specific product standards, and, in some cases, compliance with certain regulations and building codes is required.

Challenges to Design Professionals and Consumers

In order to provide the best solution for the function and aesthetics of the interior, consumers and design professionals, such as interior designers and architects, should be informed when making their interior textile product selections. They must, for example, consider the factors affecting the apparent color of textiles to ensure that the color characteristics chosen will look the same when seen in the interior setting. A basic understanding of fiber properties, yarn and fabric features, factors affecting color retention, and finishing treatments is helpful. The designer should consider the environment where the fabric will be installed and any unusual needs the fabric will need to fill, as well as the maintenance that will be needed. These several product and end-use variables will be discussed in detail throughout this book.

The task in design is especially challenging because residential and commercial consumers have widely varying and constantly changing aesthetic preferences and performance needs. Designers, architects, and suppliers must be knowledgeable of market trends. They must be aware of the resources available for reliable information, including trade publications, professional journals, and the Internet, and especially from valued, reputable suppliers.

When contract designers and architects are selecting interior textile products for commercial use, they must ascertain which, if any, agency has jurisdiction over the project, and they must identify all applicable codes affecting their selections. In turn, they must confirm that their planned product selections conform to all mandated selection criteria. Interior designers and architects are, in fact, legally and ethically responsible for choosing textiles that meet all applicable industry and government standards and codes, particularly performance standards and life safety codes. It may be necessary for the design professional to educate the consumer, explaining that codes and safety requirements may preclude the choice of certain aesthetic or structural features with a textile product.

Aesthetic Considerations

Several aesthetic or sensory characteristics are considered in the selection of interior textile products (see Table 1.1). These include **design elements** such as color, line, texture, and form, and **design principles** such as emphasis, rhythm, contrast, and harmony. Although the initial visual impact of these features is a primary concern, consideration must also be given to variables such as the effects of end-use lighting on the apparent color, the availability of matching items, and the life expectancy of the fashion features.

Performance and Safety Factors

Among the selection criteria held by consumers are several variables pertaining to performance (see Figure 1.2 and Table 1.2). For some consumers, functional attributes such as indoor air quality, glare reduction, and acoustic control may be critical; for others, texture retention may be of paramount importance; and for still others, durability and wear-life may be high on the list. At the same time, many consumers are increasingly demanding fabrics that are highly stain resistant and very easy to clean. For some applications within a commercial interior, certain flame resistance codes may be mandated.

Maintenance Considerations

Products are selected for their appropriateness for an environment, as well as for the enjoyment they will provide during their expected use-life. The most common reasons that an end-user replaces fabric is that the current item in use has become dirty. Moreover, the

TABLE 1.1
AESTHETIC PRODUCT SELECTION CRITERIA: SOME EXAMPLES

	Variable Characteristics
Design Elements	Form: 3D form of upholstered furniture, pillows
	Color characteristics: hue, value, and intensity
	Texture: smooth or rough resulting from the fiber, yarn, or fabric structure or from an applied finish
	Pattern: detail, size, and repetition of motifs
	Light: level of reflectance, level of transmittance
Design Principles	Scale: size of motifs, fullness of window coverings
	Emphasis: dominant visual characteristic
	Rhythm: repetition of elements
	Contrast: differentiates items in the visual field
	Harmony: pleasing arrangement of parts
Styling Features	Color styling: heather, multicolored, solid-colored
	Texture styling: nonpile, cut pile, uncut pile, level, multilevel
	Hand: warm, cool, smooth, rough, soft, harsh
	Drapability: fluid, stiff
	End-product styling: trimmed, plain, traditional, contemporary
	Availability of matching and/or coordinated items
	Coordination with existing interior and current furnishings
	Life expectancy of fashion features

Figure 1.2 Color development tools. Photo courtesy Color Association of the United States, www.colorassociation.com.

most common complaints that suppliers hear about field failures (when the fabric no longer looks good) turn out to be that the fabric is dirty, or that it was improperly cleaned. Therefore, the type and level of maintenance required is a critical aspect of a satisfactory specification or selection. Proper maintenance of textiles affects their serviceability, in terms of appearance retention, wear, durability, and safety. Dirt that is not removed from carpet, for example, will facilitate an abrasive action between traffic and the carpet fibers, as well as affect the apparent color. Concomitantly, the aesthetic value of the floorcovering will be diminished.

Both the end-user and design professional should be aware of proper maintenance, including the cleaning agents and equipment needed (Table 1.3). Maintenance procedures should be examined prior to installation to determine that the practices are both feasible and affordable. With commercial installations, interviews with the maintenance personnel are helpful in determining any deficiencies in equipment. Insufficient or incorrect maintenance may lead to premature replacement of a product and greatly add to the long-term cost. Careful consideration should be given to the selection of nontoxic cleaning products that contribute to improved indoor air quality and that do not require dumping contaminants or chemicals into the wastewater system. Together with the cost of utilities, the energy efficiency of a product will result in long-term savings or long-term expense.

Cost and Installation Factors

Product costs for a given project may be categorized by **initial cost** and **life-cycle cost**. Initial cost starts with the cost of the product, as well as the cost incurred for installation, including site preparation, labor, and any accessories that are needed (see Table 1.4). A detailed **project bid** provides prices for each of the products chosen, together with the installation charges, thus

TABLE 1.2
PERFORMANCE AND SAFETY PRODUCT SELECTION CRITERIA: SOME EXAMPLES

	Variable Characteristics
Functional Properties	Insulation, glare reduction, static reduction, fatigue reduction, acoustic control, mobility improvements, safety enhancement
Appearance Retention	Color retention, texture retention, resistance to pilling and snagging, soil hiding, soil repellency, soil shedding, soil release
Durability and Wear-Life	Resistance to tear and surface disturbance, dimensional stability, fuzzing, fiber loss, repairability, warranty availability
Structural Stability	Tuft bind strength, delamination strength, stability of yarn twist
Flame Resistance	Natural characteristics, chemically manipulated in fiber state ("inherent") or in yarn/fiber state ("applied"), treatment durable to cleaning
Design and Performance Mandates	Flame resistance, indoor air quality, structural stability, colorfastness, wear resistance, functional properties (acoustical value, static reduction)

TABLE 1.3
MAINTENANCE PRODUCT SELECTION CRITERIA: SOME EXAMPLES

	Variable Characteristics
Cleanability	Washable, dry-cleanable, need for vacuuming, need for brushing, ease of stain removal, appearance after cleaning
Cleaning Location	On-site versus off-site cleaning
Level of Ironing Required	None, touch-up, extensive
Frequency of Cleaning	Daily, weekly, monthly
Cleaning Products Required	Toxic, biodegradable, readily available

enabling the client and designer to determine affordability of the project. If necessary, the project can usually be completed in phases.

Life-cycle cost is comprehensive and is listed in a formal **project specification**. Consideration is given to several factors, including the initial cost, installation expenses, ongoing maintenance costs, and the anticipated life-span of the product. With life-span in mind, the initial costs may be amortized; for example, an expensive textile product that is expected to be serviceable for ten years could, in fact, be less costly than one whose initial cost was less but whose life expectancy was shorter.

Challenges to the Industry

As in any industry, interior products businesses must offer desirable product to their customers in order to generate the necessary volume of sales to support cash flow, cover their operating expenses, pay their suppliers, and realize an adequate profit. End-product producers and fabricators will not survive without a flow of viable fabric and fiber supply. Likewise, reductions in end-product sales result in reductions in the quantity of fiber, yarn, and finished fabric needed, and thereby threaten the financial stability of upstream firms. Moreover, low profit margins limit the ability of firms at all level to expand and develop new product.

To remain profitable, firms in the industry must constantly monitor consumer selections and quickly respond to changes in consumer preferences. Products must offer desirable aesthetic features, meet any mandated design and performance specs, and be functional within available maintenance and service guidelines. Additionally, installation procedures must be practical, and the price of the product, along with any charges for assembly, delivery, and installation, must not exceed the ability or willingness of the consumer to pay.

TABLE 1.4
COST AND INSTALLATION PRODUCT SELECTION CRITERIA: SOME EXAMPLES

	Variable Characteristics
Initial Cost	Product price, accessories prices, fees for design professional, delivery charges, installation charges
Life-Cycle Cost	Maintenance costs, including equipment, cleaning agents, and labor
	Warranty costs, insurance costs
	Energy costs
	Interest charges
	Disposal
Installation Factors	Site preparation
	Labor, tools, and level of skill needed; permanence: movable, removable, permanent

Economic Factors Affecting the Industry

All businesses must cope with the variable economic climate. When consumers' wages are high and unemployment is low, business for discretionary spending on items such as furniture or carpet is obviously more robust than when consumers are missing paychecks. Likewise, furnishing purchases increase during cycles of robust commercial and residential building. The cost and availability of components impact pricing and sales opportunities, as do the number and success of competitors. Rising costs of labor and workers' compensation; maintaining appropriate working conditions; surviving shifts in cost of goods, equipment, utilities, and in transportation; and changing tastes of customers create unpredictability and challenges for every enterprise.

Challenges to Fiber and Fabric Producers

Fiber and fabric producers face additional financial and environmental hurdles that would not be of direct concern to, say, a retail business. Growers and producers of natural materials are at the mercy of weather, pests, and plant and animal diseases. Commodity markets dictate raw material costs and availability. Fabric manufacturers must respond to environmental concerns such as water pollution and consumption, avoid pesticide and fertilizer runoff into water supplies and depletion of nonrenewable resources (such as oil), utilize renewable resources, and create and utilize recycling opportunities for their products. Animal-fiber suppliers must use humane treatment for the fiber-producing animals in their care.

Imports and Tariffs

As previously mentioned, fabrics are produced all over the world. Manufacturers in specific countries and areas specialize in particular types of fabrics or techniques. Often, the component parts of a fabric—from the fiber to the dyestuff to the weaving—are sourced from many countries. The United States' fabric-making capabilities have been increasingly diminishing for many decades; labor is in short supply and expensive for factory jobs. But low tariffs and strong currency have led to offerings of diverse product in both high-priced and volume interiors markets. American manufacturers import yarn and machinery, and export interior furnishing fabrics to many countries. Prices and availability of materials and labor at all points along the supply chain impact the end product.

Government Regulations and Consumer Protection

Businesses must also satisfy national and regional governmental requirements, put in place to protect the environment and the health and safety of the populace from overzealous business practices. Companies must pass the costs incurred on to consumers. These protections dictate working conditions, compensation restrictions, waste disposal, and environmental protection, among other issues. For example, in the United States and Europe, textile producers are legally required to minimize utilization of water and purify what is used before returning it to the environment. In most of Asia this is not required, thereby reducing manufacturing costs in those areas.

Associate Members of the Industry

Trade associations, publishers, advertising and public relations firms, and service organizations provide valuable assistance to the interior furnishings industry. Some are for-profit and others nonprofit; in either case, to be viable, they must be profitable for themselves and for the industry. Many of these firms focus on education and dissemination of news related to the industry.

Publishers

Writers and publishers provide members of the industry, students, educators, practicing professionals, retailers, and consumers with a wide assortment of books, websites, newsfeeds, print and online magazines, and technical journals that focus on products for and other developments relevant to interiors. Some of these publications are for the professional preparation of students; some apprise industry professionals of new techniques, new products, research findings, marketing plans, and consumer preferences; some exist to inform the consumer.

Media exposure of styles, materials, and decorating trends, as seen in print, television, and cyberspace, impacts the demand for goods and services provided by the fabric industry. Although magazines related to the decorative arts have been around since the early twentieth century, especially since the advent of online publications a proliferation of material directed toward the consuming public has flooded the market. Magazines targeting specific styles, regions of the country, socioeconomic levels, housing types, materials, and even well-known personalities have raised the consumer's aesthetic awareness and expectations.

Television has brought building and furnishing products into even more homes. The popularity of television programming about home construction, remodeling, and decorating has increased rapidly, resulting in the introduction of entire television networks devoted to home decor, gardening, and lifestyle.

Trend Services

Various color and trend forecasters offer color and trend information via presentations, conferences, online services, access to reference material, and actual samples of color and material. Color Association of the United States (CAUS), Color Marketing Group (CMG), Trend Union, Pantone, WGSN, and Fashion Snoops are a few examples.

Advertising and Public Relation Firms

Industry members use advertising firms and advertisements to promote their brands and corporate identity. They utilize the media to introduce and promote new products, new equipment, and new materials. Upstream firms direct their advertisements to downstream firms and to end-users and consumers; end-product producers direct their advertisements to members of the trade, to retailers, and to consumers; retailers direct their advertisements to retail consumers. In some cases, the cost of a promotional campaign is shared; for instance, a fiber producer shoulders a portion of the charges assessed for promotions run by an end-product manufacturer.

Service Organizations for Maintenance

In contrast to promoting the sales or improving the safety of a fabric product, some organizations focus on the efficient, proper, and economical maintenance of the goods. The Association for Linen Management (ALM), for example, has members in textile care and environmental services (e.g., hospitals, nursing homes, educational institutions, hotels, motels, and so on), and it also has member businesses such as chemical manufacturers and textile manufacturers. The Dry Cleaning and Laundry Institute International provides education, research, legislative representation, and industry-specific information to its members on dry-cleaning and care procedures related to dry-cleaning.

Trade Associations

Trade associations are organized to represent, protect, and promote the interests of their members, who provide financial support for the operation and activities of the association. Trade associations in this field usually have very few paid personnel, and most of their work is done by volunteers from the associations' member firms. The personnel establish liaisons between their members and various federal and state agencies and often lobby legislative bodies. They maintain websites that offer detailed educational material and technical literature. They devise marketing programs and conferences that increase the recognition and acceptance of their members' products. Some associations even maintain testing laboratories to evaluate and certify the quality of these products.

Some trade associations are composed of firms that compete with one another in the marketplace but also share a common goal. The American Fiber Manufacturers Association, for example, is supported by several independent firms, each of which is competing for sales orders for raw fiber. At the same time, however, these producers recognize the value of cooperating to provide information about manufactured fibers and to extend their use. Other trade associations are made up of firms belonging to different segments of the industry but having a vested interest in the marketing and widespread use of a particular category of products. The Textile Exchange, for example, operates internationally and is committed to expansion of textile sustainability.

The Carpet and Rug Institute works to increase the use of soft floorcoverings, Cotton Incorporated strives to increase the use of products containing cotton,

Australian Wool Innovation works to increase the long-term success of Australian woolgrowers, and the Business and Institutional Furniture Manufacturers Association (BIFMA) represents business and institutional furniture manufacturers.

Trade organizations often establish guidelines or standards to help their memberships' customers better understand the materials in which they specialize. For example, the Upholstered Furniture Action Council (UFAC) is made up of upholstered furniture industry firms that collaborated to establish a test that would measure an upholstered furniture's resistance to catching fire from burning cigarettes, which is the top cause of fires in the United States.

The Association for Contract Textiles (ACT) (Figure 1.3) was established to address a variety of issues related to contract fabric manufacturing and distribution of fabric for commercial building interiors. Among many other endeavors, the organization developed the ACT Voluntary Performance Guidelines to make specification easier for designers. ACT's icons on a contract fabric's marketing materials indicate that the cloth meets or exceeds these guideline requirements. (These registered certification marks are shown in Appendix B, p. 427.) Furthermore, ACT's **Facts**, based on the NSF/ANSI 336 standard, is the definitive sustainability certification program for contract fabrics (see Chapter 3).

Interior designers form the core membership of American Society of Interior Designers (ASID) and International Interior Design Association (IIDA), organizations that strive to advance the interior design profession, primarily through education, outreach, and advocacy.

Key Terms

braiding	natural fiber supplier
colorists	natural man-made fiber
consumer	producers
continuous filament	needle punching
contract (commercial)	nonwovens
interiors	piece
converter	piece-dyeing
design director	printing
design elements	project bid
design principles	project specification
design professional	residential interiors
end product	solution-dyed
end-product designer	specify
end-product producer	spinner
end-user	spunbonding
fabric designer	staple fiber
Facts	stock-dyed
felting	stylists
fiber	synthetic manufactured
film	fiber producers
finishers	synthetic yarn producers
finishes	tow
filament	trade associations
greige goods	trade discount
initial cost	tufting
institutional textiles	vertical
knitting	vertical manufacturers
knotting and twisting	weaving
life-cycle cost	yarn-dyed
manufactured fiber	
producer	
mill	

association
for contract
textiles

Figure 1.3 A service mark registered with the U.S. Patent and Trademark Office and owned by the Association of Contract Textiles, Inc. Courtesy the Association of Contract Textiles, Inc.

Review Questions

1. Identify the major segments of the interior textile industry and discuss their interconnectedness.
2. Discuss the environmental challenges that face natural fiber suppliers and manufactured fiber producers.
3. Why is it critically important that members of the industry monitor slight shifts in both the aesthetic features and the functional expectations of interior textile products?
4. Identify several interior textile products used in residential and commercial interiors. What interior textile products are used in hospitality settings, for example?
5. What challenges face design professionals in selecting and specifying interior fabrics?
6. What challenges face fabric and fiber producers, and why must they meet these challenges?
7. Discuss the consequences of offering interior textile products that do not coincide with the wants and needs of the consumer.
8. Discuss the role of interior designers and architects in choosing textiles. What legal ramifications are associated with their decisions?
9. Why would competing firms work cooperatively in a trade association?
10. Discuss the external factors that affect the economic health of the industry.

Trade Association Links

American Association of Textile Chemists and Colorists (AATCC)
http://www.aatcc.org

American Fiber Manufacturers Association (AFMA)
http://www.afma.org

American Institute of Architects (AIA)
http://www.aia.org

American Society of Interior Designers (ASID)
http://www.asid.org

American Society of Testing and Materials (ASTM)
http://www.astm.org

Association for Contract Textiles (ACT)
http://www.contracttextiles.org

Business and Institutional Furniture Manufacturers Association (BIFMA) International
http://www.bifma.org

Decorative Fabrics Association (DFA)
http://www.dfa.info

Industrial Fabrics Association International (IFAI)
http://www.ifai.com

Institute of Inspection, Cleaning, and Restoration Certification (IICRC)
http://www.iicrc.org

International Code Council (ICC)
http://www.iccsafe.org

International Interior Design Association (IIDA)
http://www.iida.org

Merchandise Mart Properties, Inc. (MMPI)
http://www.mmart.com

National Association of Decorative Fabric Distributors (NADFD)
http://www.nadfd.com

National Council of Textiles Organizations (NCTO)
http://www.ncto.org

National Fire Protection Association (NFPA)
http://www.nfpa.org

NSF International
http://www.nsf.org

International Casual Furnishings Association
https://www.icfanet.org/

Wallcovering Association
http://www.wallcoverings.org

2

Fabric Performance
and Evaluation

Standards, Certifications, Ratings, and Guidelines

Specifiers hear a lot about performance features, ratings, and standards for fabrics coming across their desks. Most of this data is driven by marketing efforts, in attempts to offer information that might suggest one product is better than another, or that a given product has unique features. In the process, our industry has unintentionally made performance data more muddled.

When the design-driven contract market was first evolving in the 1950s, innovative suppliers felt an imperative to convince users that the newer, more attractive fabrics they were offering would perform as well as the less-attractive, but very durable, fabrics that were then successful in the market. In the process, suppliers barraged the architect and design community with test data, standards, and ratings, with suppliers trying to outdo one another with higher test data. Specifiers began asking for higher and higher ratings, under the misconception that higher test result ratings would ensure additional protection.

Please note that very few codes or standards apply broadly to interior fabrics; the codes that do apply almost entirely apply to commercial interiors, and generally to flammability ratings, many of which are applicable only to certain states, cities, or specific types of buildings. *The simple fact is that fabrics from reputable suppliers, if used for the application of the normal use for which they are marketed, are unlikely to need additional performance assurance or extra test data.*

Furthermore, established suppliers stand behind their products. Fabric and furniture marketers offer up-front information on their products, are willing to answer endless questions, and can suggest products that are designed for a specific situation or unusual code. Manufacturers pretest their fabric to be sure it is appropriate for the intended market, and to maintain lot-to-lot quality control. They test yarns and dyestuffs to be sure the quality is maintained. By the time fabric from an established supplier crosses the specifier's desk, labeled with its intended market, it is very well vetted.

For these reasons, understanding test data on soft materials is virtually irrelevant for interior designers and architects. Nonetheless, the current climate dictates that design professionals now customarily expect performance and sustainability features to be verified. Since designers and specifiers will come across this data, it is important to highlight the differences between standards, certifications, and ratings, although its detail is of limited relevancy to the design community.

While understanding the difference between standards, codes, and ratings related to fabrics provides context for information that crosses designers' desks every day, delving into fabric test methodology and precise processes that leads to ratings on a given standard is the fabric producer's realm, and is outside the scope of a specifier's work. Additionally, specifications for standards are constantly evolving. For these two reasons, this text refers to only the most common standards, and in simple terms as to the performance feature to which each refers. Specific details for any standard can be found on the internet, or in the voluminous books of standards published by the standard-setting organizations.

Standards describe specific material performance, behaviors, and attributes. Some record the product's reaction to a specific event, such as having a cigarette left on it. Together with other informed and interested persons, many members of the textile industry participate in the work of trade associations, nonprofit, and governmental scientific and technical associations that develop standards pertaining to areas such as definitions, recommended practices (including for life cycle analysis), methods of testing, classifications, design specifications, or performance specifications. Participants in these groups share their expertise and opinions, usually on a voluntary basis, to help establish standards that are fair and meaningful. Producers throughout the industry may elect to use these standards when they evaluate their components and end products. A standard that is adopted by a governmental **regulatory agency** becomes legally binding and is called a **code**. Codes refer to the standard that was adopted in order to define the requirements for meeting the code.

Certifications are given to products, processes, and services (even entire buildings) that have met criteria based on standards. Some certifications identify safety features; others signify environmentally desirable features within single or multiple life-cycle assessment categories. Some certifications are based on evaluation of a single property or attribute, such as the release of a certain chemical, and others are based on multiple attributes and analysis of several criteria. In particular, products that meet certification requirements are often awarded a mark or label. Certification claims by manufacturers and service providers may provide useful information, but **third-party certification** is the gold standard of evaluations, because it requires results from an impartial third-party tester that has no connection to the product or service being tested and receives no benefit from the sale or use of the product or service. Some certification agencies also develop standards.

Ratings refer to how a product, service, or method ranks based on a given scale, guidelines, or standards. For example, a higher lightfastness rating would logically be desirable for a fabric to be used outdoors compared with one that will be used indoors. Ratings are also measurements used in evaluations of a fabric's or building's sustainability attributes.

Guidelines are not codes, and are not mandated in any way, but are recommendations established by a professional organization or other entity that suggest helpful standards. A code, which is a legal mandate, is, for example, something a physician must do to legally practice medicine, whereas a guideline might be adopted by the American Medical Association, in which case physicians will probably comply as members in good standing.

Similarly, the Association for Contract Textiles (ACT) suggests that if a fabric meets or exceeds all of its Voluntary Guidelines (which reference various standards) for general contract upholstery, it should perform satisfactorily in a typical contract application for a reasonable period of time. The ACT Guidelines are highly regarded as meaningful, though they are in no way legally required, warrantied, or mandatory. They are a recommendation for satisfactory end-use performance. (See http://contracttextiles.org/performance-guidelines/.)

Standard Methods of Testing

A **standard test method** prescribes specific procedures to be followed when making a given measurement. A test method details the selection, size, number, and preparation of the test specimens; describes the test apparatus; specifies test conditions, including the controlled atmospheric conditions required; sets forth test procedures; lists the observations and calculations to be made in analyzing and reporting the test results; and is carried out in a controlled atmosphere. Test methods attempt to simulate the conditions to which materials may be subjected in actual use. Such small-scale laboratory techniques minimize the need for large-scale, long-term, and more expensive evaluation procedures so that producers can efficiently and economically check quality control, and attempt to predict their products' viability for a given end-use. In order to produce reproducible results, textile researchers and quality-control personnel must strictly adhere to all details included in a standard test method, as performance comparisons can be made only among specimens tested in a like manner. As mentioned previously, the full text of standard test methods is available online or in the publications of the entity that established the standard.

Manufacturers use standards to assure lot-to-lot continuity of their own product, and that of their own suppliers. Manufacturers may also use test results as the basis for claims that their products exhibit specific functional and use-life characteristics, and may analyze test results to determine whether or not to put their name or other identifying mark on the product label.

Suppliers provide assurance that marketed fabrics comply with stipulated specifications, and may also provide evidence of its performance on a given test. Sometimes specifiers or end-users request samples so that they may test them on their own initiative.

Organizations That Establish Standards

Among the many scientific and technical associations involved in establishing standards, only a few are of particular interest to producers and consumers of furnishing fabric. The following are some of the better-known textile-related organizations that provide standards, certification/labeling (some use their own standards, others use outside standards), and whole-building rating programs.

ISO (International Organization for Standardization, www.iso.org), based in Geneva, Switzerland, is the world's largest nongovernmental developer and publisher of international standards. ISO is composed of national standards institutes from 157 countries (one member per country). Some member institutions are part of their countries' governments; others are from the private sector. The ISO 9000 standard, for example, attempts to define, establish, and maintain an effective quality assurance system for manufacturing and service industries, while its 14000 series of standards pertains to ways in which an organization can minimize its operation's negative impact on the environment.

ANSI (American National Standards Institute, www. ansi.org) is a private, nonprofit organization that oversees the development of voluntary standards for products, services, processes, and systems. ANSI undertakes the development of standards only when commissioned to do so by an industry group or a government agency, and accredits standards developed by organizations, government agencies, consumer groups, and businesses. ANSI and ISO work together to develop and publish American and international standards.

ASTM International (formerly the American Society for Testing and Materials, www.astm.org) is a global standards organization that develops and publishes voluntary consensus technical standards covering a wide range of products, systems, and services for any imaginable material, from fabric to metals, concrete, and acoustical board, and beyond. Standards developed at ASTM International are the work of more than 30,000 members. The Society publishes the ***Annual Book of ASTM Standards***, which consists of 72 volumes and is divided among 16 sections, with each focusing on a limited variety of materials, products, or processes. Included in each volume are all proposed, tentative, and formally adopted standards, guidelines, and performance specifications developed for use with the specific materials or processes covered.

ASTM International's 132 committees carry out its work. Each major committee is given a letter and number, followed by a general product designation. For instance, D-13 is the Committee on Textiles. Further numerical designations are used for subcommittees, for example, D-13.21 Subcommittee on Pile Floor Coverings or D-13.56 Subcommittee on Performance Standards for Textile Fabrics. Standards developed by ASTM International committees are described as **full-consensus** standards; that is, ASTM International members and nonmembers who have an interest in a standard or who would be affected by its application are encouraged to participate in the development of the standard. Each committee and subcommittee has the participation of both producers and users of the products in question, to ensure a balanced representation of all biases and opinions.

Most of the physical property standards to which the ACT Guidelines refer are ASTM standards. For example, pilling, breaking strength, abrasion resistance, and seam slippage are commonly measured with ASTM standards, and ASTM E84 offers a standard for one of the most common flammability tests (used primarily in direct-glue wallcoverings). Environmentally related ASTM standards relate to various aspects of building systems, though not to interior materials.

AATCC (American Association of Textile Chemists and Colorists, www.aatcc.org), along with ASTM, has established the most frequently cited standards relevant to interior fabrics. Founded in 1921, AATCC is an international technical and scientific nonprofit society that establishes standard methods of testing dyed and chemically treated fibers and fabrics. Fabric makers, dyers, and dyestuff manufacturers use AATCC standards to measure and evaluate colorfastness—to light, washing, shrinkage, water resistance, flammability, and other exposures. AATCC does not set standard performance specifications, but producers and retailers use the test methods to help predict performance of fabrics' colorfastness.

AATCC maintains a technical center that serves as a test demonstration and training center and laboratory equipped with all of the testing apparatus used in AATCC test methods. The organization publishes the ***AATCC Technical Manual***, which includes all of its standard test methods, and a monthly journal, the ***AATCC Review***, which covers recent developments in dyeing, finishing, equipment, and current research in the field of textiles.

Revisions of Standards

As mentioned, standards are revised periodically. An organization's publication will list the year of original adoption or of the last revision of every standard, along with the year of the last re-approval. The latest edition of a standard is used in quality-control and research activities.

Standards developed by one scientific association are often shared with, and cross-listed by, other associations. For example, several ASTM flammability tests are cross-referenced by the NFPA (National Fire Protection Association.) Cross-listing may indicate widespread acceptance of a standard, but it does not change its voluntary status. Only when adopted by a government agency does a standard become mandatory.

Codes

Codes are governmental regulations; that is, they are mandatory practices and performance specifications. Code writers and champions aim to assure the safety and well-being of the general population. Codes are laws—or regulations—enacted by federal, state, and local governments. Individual jurisdictions may write their own laws or rely on the work of government agencies or on model building codes. Frequently, a regulatory agency will adopt a **standard performance specification** as a code, in effect turning a recommendation into a requirement. Several state-level fire marshals' offices, for example, have adopted selected NFPA standards as code.

Because codes are legally dictated, the design professional is legally responsible for selecting products that comply with all applicable codes. This is a fairly straightforward requirement, since quality suppliers are also liable for claims that they make about the features of a product that they market.

Facilities and installations usually follow consistent requirements. For example, requirements for a health-care facility, corporate office, or a residence rarely deviate from the standard for its category. However, any end-user can decide to require a particular code that is not typically mandated. Designers must check with the architects/code compliance expert on every job to determine relevant requirements, and with suppliers to assure that all specified materials meet or exceed the customer's needs.

Building Codes and Regulations

In an effort to protect citizens, local, state, and national governments adopt standards into law. For example, building codes specify standards for plumbing design, mechanical features, quantity of sprinklers needed for fire safety, and many other requirements. Each state, city, or county could have different codes, which makes an architect, builder, or engineer's job very complicated. In an effort to establish some uniformity from region to region, several organizations establish **model codes**. That is, they develop a list of standards set by the organizations previously discussed, and they lobby to have the model code adopted, perhaps with slight variations, in many jurisdictions.

Organizations That Establish Model Building Codes

Of codes that apply to interiors, the International Code Council and the National Fire Protection Association have developed those that are most widely used in the United States. The relevant codes for soft materials focus on fire safety.

In 1994, the three regional model codes organizations joined forces to create the **International Code Council (ICC)**. The U.S. government has no national building codes, but the goal of the ICC is to develop a single, nationally recognized, coordinated set of codes that address all aspects of building construction. The ICC is also responsible for updating (on a three-year cycle) and publishing these international codes, or I-codes. (Although they are called *international* codes, they are the most widely used set of model building codes in the United States.) States, counties, or city governments adopt and then modify the adopted codes to better serve their communities, and are responsible for enforcing the building codes within their jurisdictions.

ICC's **International Building Code (IBC)** has been adopted and is used as a base code standard throughout the United States. Individual states' building codes are typically listed as IBC, with the year of the version in use, and with a suffix connoting the state's specific amendments. The ICC's **International Energy Conservation Code (IECC)** addresses the design of energy-efficient buildings and their mechanical, lighting, and power systems. Generally speaking, these codes relate to the building envelope (mechanical and electrical systems, window ratings, insulation) and not to fabric and interior furnishings.

The **National Fire Protection Association (NFPA)** is an international nonprofit organization established in

1896. Through the creation of over 300 consensus codes and standards, and through research, training, and education, the association strives to decrease the potential for the development of, and devastation from, fires. Most of the fire safety codes utilized in the interiors market are based on NFPA standards.

Regulatory Agencies

In certain circumstances, **governmental regulatory agencies** have the power to oversee the selection of interior products. Some cities have stringent flammability mandates, and virtually all states have established criteria related to the flammability of products used in commercial interiors. Again, meeting these requirements is a simple matter, because suppliers for these markets are well aware of the requirements and market their products accordingly. Nonetheless, jurisdictions, responsibilities, and mandates of all regulatory agencies change frequently. Interior designers and architects must verify current jurisdictions and requirements.

The following federal agencies proscribe requirements for fabric and surface materials in limited facilities. These generally endorse the normal requirements for the type of facility and therefore do not generally necessitate special attention. Currently, federal agencies are under extreme revision and realignment. Regulations are being abolished and revised at an astounding rate. Current status is best evaluated on each agency's website.

- FHA (**Federal Housing Administration**), a division of Department of Housing and Urban Development (HUD)
  - Jurisdiction: public areas of public housing project interiors, some structures insured by FHA
  - Use of Materials Bulletin 44d stipulates carpet specifications
- **Social Security Administration (SSA),** a division of Department of Health and Human Services
  - Jurisdiction: fire safety and acoustics regulations for hospitals and extended-care facilities that receive reimbursement from Medicaid and Medicare
- **General Services Administration (GSA)**
  - Jurisdiction: all federal facilities

- Government facilities select from GSA pre-approved products
- Has its own body of test specifications
- **Federal Aviation Administration (FAA) and National Highway Traffic Safety Administration (NHTSA),** divisions of Department of Transportation (DOT)
  - Jurisdiction: commercial airplanes and automobiles, respectively
  - Regarding fabric and furnishings, mainly pertains to fire safety regulations
- **Consumer Product Safety Commission (CPSC)**
  - Jurisdiction: consumer products
  - Prohibits initial introduction of highly flammable products so as to prevent selection
  - Does not set standards for product selection
  - Currently working on a furniture flammability standard

Key Terms

AATCC Review	International Building
AATCC Technical Manual	Code (IBC)
American Association of	International Code Council
Textile Chemists and	(ICC)
Colorists (AATCC)	International Energy
American National	Conservation Code
Standards Institute	(IECC)
(ANSI)	International Organization
Annual Book of ASTM	for Standardization
Standards	(ISO)
ASTM International	model codes
certifications	National Fire Protection
codes	Association (NFPA)
Consumer Product Safety	National Highway Traffic
Commission (CPSC)	Safety Administration
Federal Aviation	(NHTSA)
Administration (FAA)	ratings
Federal Housing	regulatory agency
Administration (FHA)	Social Security
full-consensus standards	Administration (SSA)
General Services	standard performance
Administration (GSA)	specification
governmental regulatory	standard test method
agencies	standards
	third-party certification

Review Questions

1. What purposes do standard performance specifications have for manufacturers?
2. Distinguish between standard methods of testing and standard performance specifications, and between standards and codes.
3. What is a certification? A third-party certification?
4. Name some organizations that establish standards, and explain how they work. Explain the meaning of *full-consensus* standards.
5. Characterize the work (that pertains to interior furnishings) of such regulatory agencies as the EPA, the FAA, and the CPSC.
6. Explain how organizations that develop test methods for evaluating textiles function.
7. What are model building codes?

3

Fabric and Sustainability

Consumers and professionals in many industries are increasingly conscious of environmental concerns; with awareness, consumers and manufacturers alike are voluntarily reducing the consumption of components and finished goods, reusing materials, and recycling resources. Most consumers are accustomed to recycling common materials such as glass, plastic, paper, and consumer electronics. Awareness of the environmental impact of human action is at an all-time high.

The American fabric industry, which has routinely exceeded governmental regulations and guidelines related to health, safety, and resources, has much to be proud of in prioritizing and protecting our environment; for example, heavy metals that are used in massive quantities in electronics were eliminated from fabric manufacturing decades ago. Fiber producers have been successfully recycling post-consumer product—such as drink bottles becoming yarn—for over two decades. Carpet producers, leaders in reclamation of their product at the end of its normal life, continually evolve new ways to recycle the material and use manufacturing byproducts. (One example: shredded carpet fibers used in a concrete mixture for reinforcement.) Preserving available raw materials and eliminating landfill waste is a major, industry-wide, and industry-driven goal.

Nonetheless, consumers and textile industry professionals are seeking additional ways to reduce the consumption of raw materials and processing agents, to recycle existing products into a second product, and to reuse existing products in alternative ways. More manufacturers have, for example, increased their use of recycled materials for product packaging. In the industry, every aspect of production and processing is frequently evaluated and refined, from minimizing or eliminating pesticides in the growing of natural fibers and improving treatment of fleece-producing animals, to the recycling of plastic for fiber conversion. Some practices are industry-wide and some are quality practices developed by individual companies. Numerous companies have made sustainable practices the focus of their missions.

Sustainability

Many products are advertised as being "green," "sustainable," or "environmentally friendly" in order to attract environmentally conscious consumers. What do these terms mean, anyway?

Sustainability requires that three pillars—the environment, social, and economic facets of a product or process—are all in good order so that our biological systems are able to remain diverse and productive indefinitely. "Environmentally friendly" is a casual term; for example, pesticide-free crops are less harmful to the environment than are pesticide-laden crops, but the overall question of sustainable farming is not addressed simply by eschewing insecticides. "Green" colloquially characterizes an action, or a product that results from an action, that reduces environmental impact.

The goal of environmentally sensitive manufacturing is to create a **cradle-to-cradle**, or *closed-loop*, system, in which all materials are reclaimed and reused. A closed-loop system is currently perceived to be the highest bar, rarely attainable with current systems, and therefore **cradle-to-grave** is more than likely the assessment used to evaluate how an item or method affects the environment throughout its life, from the time of creation to disposal. With closed-loop as the goal, manufacturers, consumers, regulators, and trade organizations strive to create environmentally preferable products and services.

Environmentally Focused Design Considerations

International Environmental Awareness

In order to make sensitive product decisions with regard to environmental concerns, a specifier or purchaser must consider that the manufacturing cultures of countries varies considerably. Some countries have rules and regulations about water use and waste water disposal, use of carcinogenic and hazardous materials in manufacturing, treatment of workers, and the like. Other cultures and countries do not prioritize these factors in their manufacturing.

This section focuses on the issues at stake, and on U.S. governmental structure and regulations. However, most product offered to the interiors market is made abroad. EU nations, largely, have an admirable record in environmental concerns and regulations; some are more rigorous than those of the United States. Many Asian manufacturers do not prioritize conservation-minded natural resource use, although this is rapidly changing. Therefore, when making a product selection, a critical issue related to environmental impact is to understand the maker's standards, and whether they were met or exceeded.

Finishes and Aftertreatments

Fabrics are often treated with flame retardant, antimicrobial, and stain resistant agents, as well as with other compounds for a wide variety of aesthetic and functional purposes. Natural fibers, even those that are organically grown, may have chemicals applied during cleaning, and for conveniences such as mothproofing and stain resistance. Some of the chemicals that provide these added performance features are considered possible carcinogens and toxic to varying degrees. Consequently, pushback and controversy surrounds their use in fabrics, but the finishes, and the performance features they provide, are nonetheless in demand. Furthermore, certain finishes may limit or inhibit recyclability or reuse of the material.

Indoor Air Quality

Some finishes, and the material itself, may emit toxic fumes, which reduce **indoor air quality (IAQ)**. With regard to cleaning agents, water-based products offer lower toxicity than do petroleum-based products, and the problem of IAQ is reduced when fewer chemicals are used in the growth of fibers or in fabric production. Nonetheless, IAQ is a serious issue and is consistently ranked in the top five concerns by the EPA. Because the average American spends 90 percent of his or her time indoors, sufficient fresh air circulation throughout interior spaces and limitation of indoor pollutants is a critical public health issue. Pollution, in gas form, may be generated from new furnishings and finishes and the chemicals with which they are treated. For this reason, most manufacturers recommend an **off-gassing** period, which allows the gases emitted from furnishing materials to be dissipated through the air while the space is still vacant. These gases are referred to as **volatile organic compounds (VOCs)**.

VOCs are chemicals that contain carbon, which, during evaporation, give off gases, and can cause health problems. The rate at which the materials off-gas depends on their molecular makeup and how quickly they vaporize. The amount of volatile material emitted is given a VOC number, VOC rating, or description of VOC content, either in pounds per gallon or grams per liter or as a percentage by mass. Some of the thousands of natural and manmade VOCs have a distinct smell, while others are odorless. Many are harmful to humans and the environment. The EPA reports that the quantity of volatile material in indoor VOCs can be ten times higher than that found outdoors. Materials and finishes that contain no or low harmful VOC levels contribute to the public's health and welfare.

Carpet, wallcovering, and paint are the largest potential contributors to VOC in an interior, in part because they are present in large quantities. As a result, some manufacturers of these products have lead the way in testing for environmental impacts, exploring less-toxic materials, and pursuing recycling efforts.

Reuse of Textile Products

Reusing a product is one way to minimize material destined for a landfill. Many carpet producers, for example, are seeking new ways to use byproducts from carpet manufacturing. Any reused material reduces waste quantity and also preserves available raw materials.

Recycling of Textile Products

While **repurposing**, or *reusing*, takes an existing product and uses it in a different way (such as the carpet cut into strips and used to reinforce concrete mixtures), **recycling** returns a product to a previous state in the manufacturing cycle. That reclaimed material is then used to produce another product.

The Council for Textile Recycling (CTR) (www. weardonaterecycle.org) is a nonprofit organization dedicated to raising public awareness about the importance of textile recycling and the need to reduce the amount of used clothing and other post-consumer textile waste being sent to landfills. The organization cites the EPA statistics that textile waste occupies nearly 5 percent of all landfill space. Although nearly 4 billion pounds of post-consumer textile waste are recycled each year, 85 percent of such waste holds space in our landfills.

Many consumer-level reuse/recycling avenues are available for textile waste. For several decades, U.S. charities have worked with the recycling industry, repurposing and recycling billions of pounds of fiber material. More and more communities are setting up programs to participate in these initiatives.

Most textile manufacturers have long recycled **post-industrial** (or *pre-consumer*) materials, which are their own manufacturing waste, within their own facilities. The manufacturer can often recapture materials that end up on the factory floor, and reprocess it into the production process so that it is not wasted. An example of post-industrial fiber waste is the small amount of yarn or fiber that is left over after a large order is completed, or fibers that are too short to be processed through a given spinner's standard processing. Reprocessed wool, reprocessed polyester, and spun silk are all well-established and popular examples of yarn made from what is, essentially, post-industrial fiber waste.

Post-consumer materials are those generated by residential or commercial end-users—the final users of the products before they are disposed of. Post-consumer recycling is considered to have greater eco-benefits than recycling post-industrial content, because if it is not recycled, post-consumer waste will almost surely end up in a landfill. One of the most successful post-consumer recycling efforts is reclaiming **PET (polyethylene terephthalate)**, better known as polyester, from plastic drink bottles into usable polyester fiber, which is extensively used in interior fabrics and in apparel.

Recycling (and reusing) carpet fiber is another success story for the interiors industry. Virtually every commercial carpet company has a recycled product platform; some offer sustainability guarantees for at least some of their product lines. Most carpet tile is recyclable. The Carpet and Rug Institute (CRI, www.carpet-rug.org) and Carpet America Recovery Effort (CARE, www.carpetrecovery.org) provide information on recycling and reuse programs in the carpet industry (refer to Unit Four). (Most commercial carpet is made of nylon.)

Whether from drink bottles or used carpet, the material must be collected and taken to a central processing location. The fibers are then identified and sorted, shredded, crushed, and converted to fiber pellets. Such recycled fibers are most often used in industrial, automotive, or building materials, but many quality fabrics containing recycled fiber are indistinguishable from those constructed of virgin fiber, and are popular in the marketplace.

While polyester and nylon are both readily recyclable, several discouraging hurdles stifle increased efforts. Some of the reasons are:

- Material must be made of 100 percent of the fiber to be recycled. This may require, for example, that the material be not only "nylon," but a specific type, or configuration, of nylon.
- Fibers may be difficult to identify once they are in the field and have been in use for a period of time, though efforts are underway to "mark" different batches of fiber distinctly.
- Fiber recovery is difficult; for example, since upholstery fabric is part of something else, the furniture may need to be disassembled to reclaim the fabric. The challenge of recycling carpet begins with collecting the bulky, heavy floorcovering and delivering it to a central collection site.
- Significant infrastructure is required for collection, storage, and processing of the reclaimed material.
- All of these steps incur costs. While virgin fiber is of known quality, recycled fiber is less consistent. Therefore, if the recycled fiber is nearly as expensive, or even higher priced than virgin fiber, few users will pay a premium for the recycled material. Note that, because these fibers are petroleum products, the value of the material, whether recycled or virgin, depends on the price of oil. When oil prices are low, virgin fiber drops in price, while recycling costs remain fixed, resulting in an even steeper challenge for recycled fiber producers.

Fiber producers, carpet and fabric manufacturers, carpet and fabric distributors and installers, design professionals, and end-users are all critically necessary to developing more successful recycling programs. With demand, more supply will evolve. Design innovations must build recyclability into a product, so that in the future more fabric—and other materials—can avoid the landfill.

Figure 3.1 American manufacturers use state-of-the-art yarn packaging to reduce waste within factories. Photo courtesy Glen Raven, Inc., www.glenraven.com.

Organic Fiber

In an attempt to reduce chemicals used to grow natural fibers, researchers are experimenting with **organically grown** cotton. In this work, the cotton is cultivated on land that has been chemical-free for a minimum of three years and is nurtured without the use of chemical fertilizers or pest-control agents. Other advances include the development of genetically colored cotton that allows subsequent dyeing processes to be eliminated and reduces the chemicals that exist on the fibers. Similarly, other plant fibers (such as linen) can be organically grown. Ethical treatment of animals is an important part of sustainability; wool and other animal fibers can be organically and conscientiously raised.

Organically grown or raised fiber is a tiny fraction of the fiber used in the market. Its application is primarily in apparel and luxury bedding. Note that even organically grown fibers may have chemicals such as pest deterrents and wrinkle-resistant finishes added in the dyeing process or after it is made into fabric.

Environmental Impact Evaluation

Governmental Agencies

The U.S. government has no standardized national policy or strategy for sustainable consumption and production. Nonetheless, numerous U.S. federal laws pertain to the environment. Those that affect the textile industry

in some fashion are largely administered through the **Environmental Protection Agency (EPA)** or the **Federal Trade Commission (FTC)**. These agencies write and enforce regulations based on laws passed by Congress.

In our current political climate, these agencies, in particular the EPA, are under siege. By executive order, agencies charged with protecting air, water, land, natural resources, human health, and working conditions are being defunded, and regulations and data collection initiatives are being eliminated. Therefore, sadly, this discussion may be moot or significantly eroded in short order.

The EPA was established in 1970 to protect human health and safeguard the natural environment. Primary initiatives focus on maintaining air, water, and land quality. The EPA's sustainability programs address health and safety issues related to:

- Air, land, water
- Chemicals, substances, toxins, pesticides
- Climate change, ecosystems
- Human health and environmental emergencies
- Green living, sustainable practices
- Waste, cleanup

The FTC was established in 1914 to promote consumer protection and to eliminate unfair business practices, such as monopolies.

Agency Activities

Most federal agencies' websites provide extensive information and data on the subjects under their auspices. The EPA established and updates databases of environmental information for products and services. Anyone can check the following websites for the latest iteration of databases and endorsement, which are helpful in order to identify environmentally preferable products, services, standards, certification organizations, and environmental assessment tools.

For example, EPA's "Introduction to Ecolabels and Standards for Greener Products" (https://www.epa.gov/greenerproducts/introduction-ecolabels-and-standards-greener-products) offers extensive information on the federal government's initiatives. Its "Guidelines for the Assessment of Environmental Performance Standards and Ecolabels for Federal Procurement" endorses standards and ecolabels for specific categories, including sustainability assessments for carpet, commercial furnishings fabric, and furniture. In 2017, the General Service Administration (GSA) announced the addition of an EPA-recommended icon to its purchasing program. All government facilities select from GSA pre-approved products, and the U.S. government has, to date, prioritized environmentally responsible products.

- NSF/ANSI 140 Sustainability Assessment for Carpet
- NSF/ANSI 336 Fabric Sustainability Standard (Facts® certification)
- ANSI/BIFMA e3 Furniture Sustainability Standard

These are among the important standards for interior that are endorsed by the EPA and included in the list of recommended standards

(see https://www.epa.gov/greenerproducts/guidelines-assessment-environmental-performance-standards-and-ecolabels-federal).

EPA's **Environmentally Preferable Purchasing (EPP) Program** was originally designed to facilitate in the mandatory purchasing of products and services with reduced environmental impact by federal and state governments (see https://www.epa.gov/greenerproducts/about-environmentally-preferable-purchasing-program). Developed in conjunction with the EPA, FTC's **Green Guides** set forth definitions of terms and outline general principles that apply to environmental marketing claims for products and services. These are a valuable resource, although furnishing materials are barely mentioned (see https://www.ftc.gov/news-events/media-resources/truth-advertising/green-guides).

Environmental Regulations

Regulations cover a variety of activities and conditions that may be detrimental to the environment or human health, including treatment of employees, raw material procurement, manufacturing processes, packaging and shipping methods, waste disposal practices, and even the construction and operation of buildings and machinery. Very few of these regulations bear on an interior designer's job of selecting, or understanding, fabric.

As noted, while federal agencies do collect data and make recommendations on "green" attributes, guidelines, and standards, governmental regulation toward nationalized policy or strategy for sustainability are few. A small number of regulations, however, do apply to the fabric industry. (It should be noted that, likewise, most of the federal government's data collection does not include fabric, just as building codes do not pertain to furnishing materials.)

The FTC, with input from the EPA, developed Part 260, "Guides for the Use of Environmental Marketing Claims" as a revision to the **Code of Federal Regulation (CFR)** Title 16, which covers federal rules and regulations regarding commercial practices. The regulations covered in Part 260 prohibit deceptive acts or practices regarding environmental attributes of products and services. Claims made in advertising, labeling, product inserts, catalogs, and sales presentations must be substantiated through an evaluation and testing process performed by an independent national or international standards setting organization[1] (see https://www.ftc.gov/enforcement/rules/rulemaking-regulatory-reform-proceedings/green-guides). Unsubstantiated or misleading marketing or manufacturing claims about the environmental benefits of a product, service, or technology are known as **greenwashing**.

The EPA works closely with various other governmental agencies and consultants in the development of environmental standards. Several other federal departments are responsible for enforcing environmental standards and laws. These relate to fabric materials in marginal ways, primarily in manufacturing and material cultivation stages. The Department of Agriculture (USDA), Department of Commerce (DOC), Department of Defense (DOD), Department of Energy (DOE), and Department of Health and Human Services (HHS) are examples.

These agencies police federal laws that relate to everything from insecticides that are used on crops (the **Federal Insecticide, Fungicide, and Rodenticide Act**) to safety standards for all work environments; the latter is regulated by the **Occupational Safety and Health Administration (OSHA)**.

Health, safety, and environmental stewardship concerns about chemicals and processes have become important considerations when selecting and specifying textiles.

Safety Data Sheets (SDS) identify hazardous chemicals and health and physical hazards, including exposure limits and precautions for workers who may come into contact with these chemicals. Any chemicals, including cleaning chemicals, used in manufacturing processes that pose a potential hazard to workers are identified in SDS. Textile manufacturers routinely review the dyes and chemicals in their factories and processes, and utilize SDS in that process.

Fabric, as an "article," is typically considered to be exempt from the requirement for SDS with regard to specifiers and end-users. (Similarly, consumers do not typically ask for an SDS when purchasing a TV.) Although the form is not actually required for fabric, the demand for this protocol is widespread today. Design professionals review product SDS when specifying materials to evaluate potential VOC off-gassing problems, for example. SDS are also required to be available to local fire departments and local and state emergency planning officials.

Note that SDS were formerly MSDS (Material Safety Data Sheets). OSHA made a change to the Global Harmonized System (GHS) so that SDS are in a common format with other like protocols worldwide, and, in so doing, dropped the "M" (Material) from the name.

Environmental Regulations

Of the extensive list of laws tangentially related to the fabric market, the **Clean Air Act** (which stipulates standards for air quality and purity with an emphasis on controlling air pollution), **Safe Drinking Water Act** (which stipulates standards for water purity and groundwater protection), and **Clean Water Act** (which stipulates standards for water quality and purity) most directly reward the industry for safe manufacturing practices.

Additionally, the **Resource Conservation and Recovery Act** (which stipulates standards management of hazardous waste), the **Toxic Substance Control Act** (which authorizes the EPA to regulate certain toxic chemicals), the **Emergency Planning and Community Right-to-Know Act** (which polices companies' release of toxic chemicals), the **Pollution Prevention Act** (which promotes pollution prevention through hazardous substance reduction and increased efficiency),

the **Energy Policy Act** (which addresses energy production, energy efficiency, renewable energy, and climate change technology), and the **Energy Independence and Security Act** (which supports production of clean renewable fuels and research on greenhouse gas capture and storage options) all encourage responsible manufacturing and protect consumers and the environment.

Local Governmental Agencies

In addition to the U.S. federal laws pertaining to the environment that affect the textile industry, state laws and building codes can impact the entire life of any product, from its manufacture and use, to its end of life options. These include zoning for manufacturing facilities, use of municipal utilities, and fire codes related to end-use installation.

Environmentally Related Building Codes

Building codes, as discussed in Chapter 2, are most often developed by nationally recognized organizations (such as the **International Code Council**, or ICC) as model building codes and standards that may be subsequently adopted by state, county, or city governments, and then modified for their specific communities' needs. In addition to what might be considered "standard" building codes, green building codes address energy conservation, building component and system efficiency, sustainable products, materials and methods, and innovative technologies and design.

The **International Green Construction Code (IgCC)** and the **International Energy Conservation Code (IECC)** are model codes developed by the ICC in conjunction with other organizations as overlays to the IBC (International Building Code). These codes can apply to both commercial and residential construction for new and existing buildings, and aim to establish clear and specific requirements that promote safe and sustainable construction. These codes relate to building envelope and mechanical systems, and ongoing facility management. Interior furnishing fabric is not a part of either code.

The IgCC addresses sustainability attributes for entire construction projects and building sites, from design phase through to facility management. The IECC addresses energy-efficient design for building envelopes and mechanical and power systems. Because these codes apply to the building itself, soft materials are not generally regulated by these codes. IgCC does refer to carpet, however.

Life-Cycle Inventory

Marketing Claims

When comparing various fabrics' overall environmental impact, as with any other overall consideration in a choice about fabric, it is important to look at a comprehensive picture. Generally, producers and marketers highlight one particular feature of a fabric as testament that the fabric is the best choice for the environment. Perhaps it is organic or recycled fiber, or it can be (hypothetically) recycled, or the production of its fiber is not deleterious to the environment.

On the other hand, perhaps it is made half way around the world and requires considerable energy to harvest the material. For example, rayon is often touted as environmentally friendly because it is made from cellulose. However, dangerous, toxic chemicals used in its production (in particular carbon disulfide) have serious health impact on workers who produce it, and the chemicals are expelled into the environment from manufacturing processes. Bamboo is considered by some to kinder to the environment than are other fibers, but in fact it is transformed to a textile fiber with the help of the exact same chemicals; bamboo also uses rayon as a cellulosic starting point, rather than cotton or wood pulp. Furthermore, although bamboo is rapidly renewable, it is an invasive plant, so farming it in areas where it is not native could be environmentally dangerous.

Life-Cycle Inventory and Life-Cycle Analysis

The **life-cycle inventory (LCI)** is an analysis of flows to and from the natural environment into the product or service that is being evaluated. That is, each aspect of a product or service's life is assessed, with attention to raw material, flows of water and energy input, and releases into

the environment. The ultimate goal of environmentally sensitive manufacturing is to create cradle-to-cradle, or closed-loop, systems in which all materials—including energy and water—are reclaimed, with no degradation or harm, and can reused at the same quality level that was possible at the beginning. Cradle-to-cradle is the highest bar, and rarely met, but data accrued from the life-cycle inventory assessment process adds to a broad base of information so that relative cradle-to-grave environmental impact can be established within product categories.

Although most reputable certifications and individual interior fabric evaluations follow an LCI model, in order to complete a true **life-cycle assessment (LCA)**, databases must be available for comparative study of product performance. To date, because the fabric industry does not collect such data, the established databases have scant material on textiles. Therefore, true LCA of interior furnishing materials is not currently undertaken. Nonetheless, evaluating green product claims is simpler when viewed through the lens of a product's life cycle. (See the list of databases at the end of this chapter.)

An LCA aids in identifying products, processes, or services that are environmentally preferable, in order to compare which "have a lesser or reduced effect on human health and the environment when compared with competing products or services that serve the same purpose."[3] A range of methodologies, with slight variations, are available for use in LCAs. The EPA and numerous other environmental associations provide LCA guidelines and online programs for use by design professionals. Some can be used to evaluate products and methods, others are designed to consider entire buildings, and still others focus on specific life-cycle stage evaluation factors.

For most applications the life cycle can be divided into four stages: raw material acquisition, manufacture and transportation, use/reuse/maintenance, and recycle/waste management. Energy demands and environmental wastes associated with each stage are evaluated in the evaluation.

- Stage 1: Raw Material Acquisition
  - Extraction or removal of raw materials from mining or harvesting.
  - Transportation materials from acquisition to processing.

- Stage 2: Manufacture and Transportation
  - Converting of raw materials into a form that can be used to manufacture a finished product, including transportation.
  - Manufacturing a finished product ready for shipping.
  - Packaging and labeling of the finished product.
  - Transporting and distributing of the finished product.
- Stage 3: Use, Reuse, Maintenance
  - Product longevity and durability, taking into account frequency of necessary reconditioning, repair, or servicing, and any materials that are needed to accomplish the product's upkeep.
  - When no longer needed will the product be recycled or disposed?
- Stage 4: Recycle/Waste Management
  - Disposal or reuse.
  - Energy requirements to recycle or dispose the product.

The EPA identifies positive or negative impact based on a product's or service's LCA as "Environmental Attributes." The EPA's three basic attribute categories are natural resources use, human health/ecological stressors, and hazard factors associated with materials.[4]

- Natural Resources Use
  - Ecosystem Impacts—Adverse impacts on the ecosystem, endangered species, wetlands loss, fragile ecosystems, and erosion.
  - Energy Consumption—The total amount of energy consumed for product or service manufacture, use, and disposal. Often referred to as **embodied energy**. Different sources of energy are associated with different environmental impacts such as acid rain, climate change, air pollution, and other human health risks.
  - Water Consumption—Water resources that are consumed or used that affect water quality of aquatic ecosystems and drinking water.
  - Nonrenewable Resource Consumption—Resources that are not renewable within 200 years. Could produce acid rain, climate

change, air pollution, human health risks, and risks to endangered species or ecosystems.
  - Renewable Resource Consumption—Resources that are renewable in fewer than 200 years (timber-based products) to those that are renewable in under than two years (grain-based feed stocks). In most cases the use of renewable resources is preferable to use of nonrenewable resources; however, some products made from renewable resources may also have negative environmental impacts (e.g., ethanol is derived from a renewable resource, yet its manufacture can lead to releases of VOCs).
- Human Health and Ecological Stressors
  - Releases—The release of pollutants (chemicals, gasses, biologics, particulate matter) into the air, water, or soil. An example would be ozone depleting chemicals that impact global warming.
  - Indoor Environmental Releases—Potentially hazardous chemicals released during off gassing, mold, fungi, microbials.
  - Hazardous Waste—Toxic substances with immediate health or ecological impacts.
  - Nonhazardous Waste—Non-toxic substances with health or ecological impacts.
- Hazard Factors Associated With Materials
  - Human Health Hazards
    - Acute toxicity (poisoning)
    - Cancer
    - Neurologic, developmental, reproductive toxicities
    - Immunotoxicity, immune deficiencies, allergies
    - Sensitization, irritancy, reactivity
    - Corrosivity
    - Flammability
  - Ecological Hazards
    - Aquatic, avian, terrestrial species toxicities

There are, of course, other factors that must be considered when selecting products, processes, or services. In addition to environmental impact concerns, design professionals must address issues related to aesthetics, function, safety, cost, client preferences, and codes. The LCA is one of many tools used in the design process.

Textile Related Sustainability Standards, Certifications, Ratings

It has become customary practice for design professionals to expect verification of green claims concerning products, processes, or services. Claims can be confirmed in documentation presented via standards, certifications, and the ratings. When evaluating manufacturers' green product claims, look for compliance to standards, certifications, and test ratings issued by the organizations previously noted. (Standards, certifications, and ratings are defined in detail in Chapter 2.)

Standards describe specific performance, behaviors, attributes, or results. National conformity standards used to measure sustainability attributes are developed by both government and private sector organizations. Private standard setting organizations are typically required to meet any existing federal requirements confirming their qualifications to develop standards for particular industries. Unless adopted by government or industry and mandated by law, adherence to a given standard is voluntary.

Note that most ANSI third-party certifications are structured around meeting all the standard's prerequisites in order to achieve certification. Additional points earned by meeting extra criteria, which merit higher levels within the certification.

Certifications are given to products, processes, or services that have met criteria based on standards. Certification identifies environmental preference within single or multiple life-cycle assessment categories; some evaluate a single environmental attribute, such as the release of a certain chemical, and others analyze several criteria in order to evaluate multiple attributes. Products that meet certification requirements may be awarded a mark or label from the certifying body. Third-party certification programs are considered higher caliber than those claims made by the product's manufacturer or by other parties that have a stake in the product's success. An impartial third-party testing service has no connection to the product or service being tested, and receives no benefit from the sale or use of the product or service. Some certification agencies also develop standards. A manufacturer can produce a fabric and check itself against any of the third-party certification standards. However, when a certification is performed by an outside, approved tester, the certification or mark will hold more weight.

Ratings can refer to how a product, service, or method ranks on a specific scale, based on a guideline or standard. Many sustainability standards specify several tiers, which are based on how well the product meets the standard's requirements.

Ecolabels

Certifications for sustainability attributes are commonly referred to as **ecolabels**. In addition to the EPA's list of recommended standards for sustainability, numerous other associations and consortiums identify third-party certification and labeling organizations.

Global Ecolabelling Network, which is nonprofit, (www.globalecolabelling.net) and **Ecolabel Index** (www.ecolabelindex.com) are two organizations that maintain databases of ecolabels. The periodical **Ecotextile News** (www.ecotextile.com) publishes a biennial **Eco-Textile Labeling Guide**.

It should be noted that, while the manufacturers and distributors of interior furnishings products have dedicated vast financial and personnel resources to understanding sustainability features, developing standards, and striving to meet them, the design community and end-users are not yet dedicated to requiring products that meet these standards. Products that meet specific standards are most often required for state and federal government procurement, although individual specifiers or end-users may require them. Since standards are periodically updated and revised, the best resources for current requirements are the websites for the standard-setting organizations.

Organizations Establishing Sustainability Standards

Several organizations that were introduced in Chapter 2 are also involved in developing sustainability standards.

- **International Organization for Standardization (ISO)** is the world's largest nongovernmental developer and publisher of international standards. ISO developed its 14000 series of standards, which pertain to ways in which a manufacturing organization can minimize its negative impact on the environment, to evaluate a manufacturer's sensitivity to sustainability. Factories become ISO

14000 certified; the certification does not apply to products or services.

- **American National Standards Institute (ANSI)**, the private non-profit organization that oversees the development of voluntary standards for products, services, processes, and systems, accredits standards developed by organizations, government agencies, consumer groups, and businesses, and works closely with the ISO, NSF, and other organizations in the development and publications of standards for use in the United States and internationally. Currently, the most important sustainability standards for interior furnishings are ANSI-accredited standards, assuring that they are consensus-based and transparent.
- **ASTM International** develops and publishes voluntary consensus technical standards. To date, its environmentally related standards pertain to building construction and not to soft furnishings.[5]
- **NSF International**, an independent global organization committed to protecting public health and the environment, is accredited by ANSI to develop standards and guidelines. Through its National Center for Sustainability Standards, NSF International has developed sustainability standards for building products and materials; furniture; carpet and flooring; fabrics; wallcoverings; roofing membranes; green chemicals; and drinking water quality. NSF International and ANSI worked together with the **Association for Contract Textiles (ACT)** and with the Carpet and Rug Institute (CRI) to develop sustainability standards for contract fabric and carpet, respectively. More information on NSF International's sustainability standards and protocols can be found at http://www.nsf.org /services/by-industry/sustainability-environment/ sustainability-standards-protocols/.

Sustainability-Related Certifications and Certifiers

The following are some of the better-known organizations that provide certification/labeling related to fabrics for interiors and whole-building rating programs. Some developed, or collaborated on development of, the standards to which they certify; others are strictly third-party certifiers.

For example, SCS Global (https://www.scsglobalser-vices.com/) and UL Environment (http://industries.ul.com/ environment, part of Underwriters Laboratories) are not only exclusive certifiers of the two most popular certifications (SCS Indoor Advantage and Greenguard, respectively) for levels of VOCs in interior environments, but these companies are both accredited third-party certification bodies that evaluate a wide range of nationally and internationally recognized standards. Both agencies are approved certifiers for NSF/ANSI 336 Sustainability Assessment for Commercial Furnishings Fabrics (Facts certification), NSF/ANSI 140 Sustainability Assessment for Carpet, and ANSI/BIFMA e3 Furniture Sustainability Standard. These organizations perform auditing and testing services and develop standards in the areas of environmental protection, ethical and social responsibility, product quality and safety, and life-cycle assessment services.

Numerous providers offer a wide array of services that assist manufacturers and marketers in their quests for conscientious business practices. In the discussion below, several multifaceted players' roles are described. Another example is **Intertek**, which does not certify to or develop codes, but offers comprehensive eco-testing, supply chain audits, certification, and is especially known for assisting in developing life-cycle assessment solutions for a large number of industries and customers including textile retailers, manufacturers, and suppliers. More information on industries Intertek serves can be found at www.intertek.com.

Single-Attribute Third-Party Sustainability Certifications

In the early stages of sustainability awareness, concern and testing focused around the impact a product made on the environment. This trend evolved into several standards that were developed to measure IAQ, i.e., comparative levels of materials' VOC off-gassing into interior environments. More recently, a products' environmental impact is judged more heavily by what goes into the products, from raw materials, to processes, and to manufacturers' treatment of workers.

- Greenguard and **Greenguard Gold**, developed by the **Greenguard Environmental Institute**, certify (at two rating levels) that a product does not emit harmful levels of VOCs into an interior environment. The base-level certification, Greenguard, certifies to different standards, depending on the product type. Greenguard Gold certifies to California Department of Public Health test CA01350. Greenguard and Greenguard Gold are not specific to fabric or carpet; many interiors products can be certified to this single-attribute standard.

The Greenguard Environmental Institute was acquired by UL Environment, a division of UL (Underwriters Laboratories), in 2011, which is now the provider of the Greenguard certification program.

See www.greenguard.org for Greenguard Product Guides.

- **SCS Indoor Advantage Gold** certification, developed by **SCS Global** (Scientific Certification Systems Global Services) similarly represents that a material performs to a standard related to a single attribute, which is that the product does not emit harmful levels of VOCs into an indoor environment. SCS Indoor Advantage Gold, like Greenguard Gold, certifies to California Department of Public Health test CA01350.

SCS Indoor Advantage Gold, like Greenguard and Greenguard Gold, is not specific to fabric or carpet; many interiors products can be certified to the standard. A complete list of SCS Global's services and standards can be reviewed at www .scsglobalservices.com.

- **Green Label** and **Green Label Plus** certification, developed and administered by the **Carpet and Rug Institute**, similarly certify to California Department of Public Health test CA01350, and aim to encourage specification of carpet, adhesive, and cushion products with the lowest possible VOC chemical emissions. UL handles testing for Green Label Plus. See http://www.carpet-rug.org /green-label-plus.html

Life-Cycle-Based Third-Party Sustainability Certifications

Facts certifies to NSF/ANSI Standard 336 (Sustainability Assessment for Commercial Furnishings Fabric), which is presently the premier standard for furnishing fabric sustainability. This assessment addresses the environmental,

economic, and social aspects of furnishing fabrics, including woven, non-woven, bonded, and knitted fabrics used for commercial upholstery, drapery, wallcovering, system furniture panel fabric, and bedding applications (it excludes sheet sets and blankets). Facts certification requires a fabric to be evaluated across its life-cycle for

- Fiber sourcing
- Safety of materials
- Water
- Energy
- Air quality
- Social responsibility
- Recycling practices

Based on a point system, three levels (silver, gold, and platinum) of Facts certification are available. The maximum possible points are 100; of these, 50 percent address fabric composition and 50 percent address fabric manufacturing. To be compliant, a fabric must meet all prerequisites in the standard. If certified, manufacturers are allowed to use the NSF Sustainability Certified mark and the Facts Certified mark on the products and in related advertising. A more detailed overview of the standard is available on the Association for Contract Textiles website (http://contracttextiles.org/facts-sustainability-certification/#facts). Several independent certifiers are licensed to review compliance (see http://www.nsf.org /services/by-industry/sustainability-environment/ sustainability-standards-protocols/furnishings-fabric).

NSF/ANSI Standard 140 (Sustainability Assessment for Carpet) (adopted 2007, updated 2015) is used to evaluate the sustainability of commercial carpet products for office, education, government, healthcare, and hospitality settings (see http://www.carpet-rug.org/nsfansi-140-standard.html). Again, a point system is incorporated to indicate certification level on three performance levels (silver, gold, and platinum). The rating system considers performance and quantifiable metrics in:

- Public health and environment
- Energy and energy efficiency
- Biobased or recycled materials
- Manufacturing and reclamation and end of life management

LEVEL® certifies to ANSI/BIFMA e3-2010 (Furniture Sustainability Standard), which was developed by a joint committee of stakeholders formed by the **Business and Institutional Furniture Manufacturers Association (BIFMA)**, using the ANSI consensus process (see https://www.bifma.org/?page=e3standard for more information on ANSI/BIFMA e3 Furniture Sustainability Standard). The standard establishes performance criteria addressing environmental and social aspects throughout the supply chain, in order to promote increasingly sustainable furniture. The standard allows for multiple levels of achievement and addresses areas of

- Materials
- Energy usage
- Human and ecosystem health
- Social responsibility

NSF/ANSI Standard 342 (Sustainability Assessment for Wallcovering Products) is the current premier standard for evaluating and certifying sustainability of wallcovering products (see http://www.wallcoverings.org/?page=NSF342Info). Developed through an ANSI standards development process, the standard outlines a consistent approach to evaluating environmentally preferable wallcovering manufacturing and distribution processes. This multi-attribute standard includes relevant criteria across the product life cycle, from raw material extraction to manufacturing, distribution, use, and end-of-life reuse or disposal. Four ratings (conformant, silver, gold, or platinum) are possible, based on the point totals achieved through the third-party certification process. Certified manufacturers can use the NSF Sustainability Certified mark on products that meet the standard.

The **Cradle to Cradle Certified**™ program measures achievement in environmentally intelligent design in the following areas:

- Chemical inputs
- Energy
- Water
- Social equity
- Recyclability/compostability

Cradle to Cradle certifies to the C2C standard and is used not only for fabrics, but for a range of products. The evaluation process and the standard can be found on the **Cradle to Cradle Products Innovation Institute** website at http://c2ccertified.org. The C2C Certification mark is licensed by the Cradle to Cradle Products

Innovation Institute. This certification was met with raised eyebrows in its early days because the standard was not transparent and the C2C Institute was the only certifier. This has evolved into a respected system, with multiple certifiers. Although it is not an ANSI consensus standard, it is transparent and contains valid criteria, especially in material health categories, which have been validated by LEED (see the next section). In LEED's most recent version, Cradle to Cradle certified products can earn up to two points under LEED's Materials and Resources credit system.

OEKO-TEX®, based in Switzerland, offers a range of services to textile businesses that commit to responsible, sustainable management, including overseeing and certifying products for a number of standards. It also developed **OEKO-TEX Standard 100**, which focuses on health-related issues, especially evaluation for harmful substances in processed textiles that come into direct or near contact with the skin. The focus is on levels of chemical substances that may cause skin irritations, allergies, cancer, or harm to the nervous system, internal organs, or fertility, or which are suspected of causing such problems.

OEKO-TEX's STeP (Sustainable Textile Production) certification program evaluates manufacturing processes, from fiber production to manufacture of clothing. The list of substances that are prohibited or subject to restrictions in products bearing the OEKO-TEX label can be found at www.oeko-tex.com. Although OEKO-TEX standards are more relevant to apparel, they can be used to evaluate the dyes and pigments used in furnishings fabrics and carpet. This standard is more popular in the EU than in the United States.

Global Organic Textile Standard (GOTS) is the leading worldwide textile processing standard for organic fibers. GOTS covers the entire supply chain and sets high ecological and social requirements that a manufacturer must meet for a product to be certified, including use of appropriate dyestuffs and performance additives, mandatory wastewater treatment, and assurance of safety and ethical treatment of workers. The standard covers the processing, manufacturing, packaging, labeling, trading, and distribution of any textile made from at least 70 percent certified organic natural fibers. GOTS currently certifies to Version 5, which offers two certification levels: the GOTS "organic" label must contain a minimum of 95 percent certified organic fiber, whereas the "made with organic" label must contain a minimum of 70 percent certified organic fibers. GOTS organic labeling is more widely utilized in apparel than in interior furnishings. The full standard and a list of approved testing/certification agencies can be found at http://www.global-standard.org.

Whole-Building Environmental Standards

Fiber-based materials play only a small part in current whole-building environmental standards. The focus of these standards is on construction practices that result in energy-efficient and environmentally sustainable buildings that are conducive to human health. It is important to note that a fabric cannot be LEED certified or Green Globes certified. Certain fabrics can contribute in small ways to LEED certification, but, since fabrics are not buildings, they are not candidates for whole-building certification.

A few organizations develop standards and provide certification for environmentally responsible attributes of residential and commercial building types. Currently, the most prominent voluntary green building rating and certification program is **LEED (Leadership in Energy and Environmental Design)** developed by the **U.S. Green Building Council (USGBC)**. **Green Globes**, owned by the **Green Building Initiative (GBI)** is a strong contender in the whole-building assessment category. The **Living Building Challenge**, from the **International Living Futures Institute**, is also well recognized.

LEED

LEED (Leadership in Energy and Environmental Design) is a system created by the U.S. Green Building Council (USGBC) with the mission of encouraging sustainable building design and thereby encouraging market transformation that enables environmentally and socially responsible, healthful environments. The USGBC, a non-profit organization, provides green building resources, educational courses, research, and statistical information. USGBC also established the World Green Building Council to offer alternative compliance pathway for projects executed overseas, allowing for regional differences and issues.

Many state and local governments utilize LEED as a desired standard for publicly owned and publicly funded buildings. LEED highlights multiple building rating system categories, such as New Construction, Existing Buildings, Operations and Maintenance, Commercial Interiors, Core and Shell Construction, Schools, Retail, Healthcare, Homes, and Neighborhood Development.

LEED certification emphasizes state-of-the-art building in numerous credit categories. Currently, these are:

- Integrative process credits
- Location and transportation
- Sustainable sites
- Water efficiency
- Energy and atmosphere
- Materials and resources
- Indoor environmental quality
- Innovation
- Regional priority

Prerequisite requirements must be met initially, and optional environmental attributes are referred to as *credits*. Points are earned for the credits. Each prerequisite and credit includes a group of preferred attributes and explanations of overall goals or intent. Evaluations are based on a combination of national standards and LEED developed requirements. To achieve certification, projects must comply with all prerequisites and a sufficient number of credits to earn 40 or more of the available certification points. LEED offers four levels of certification: certified, silver, gold, or platinum.

LEED for Homes certification starts at 45 points. In some categories bonus points are available, which can raise the total possible points over 100. In LEED for Commercial Interiors, textiles are grouped under Materials and Resources and are included with Furniture and Furnishings. Credits for this group are worth up to 8 points out of the 100 total points:

- Reuse Furniture and Furnishings: 1 point
- Recycled Content: 1–2 points
- Regional (Locally Produced) Materials: 1–2 points
- Rapidly Renewable Materials: 1 point
- Low-Emitting Materials—Flooring Systems: 1 point
- Low-Emitting Materials—Systems Furniture and Seating: 1 point

Fabrics and furnishings rarely contribute more than a tiny percentage of LEED points to a building project. For example, in order to attain the 1 point allowed for reuse of furniture and furnishings, all of the furniture and furnishings in the building would need to be previously used.

LEED Certified Professionals

In addition to the LEED standard, the USGBC accredits design and building professionals who pass exams through the Green Building Certification Institute (GBCI). **LEED Accredited Professionals (LEED AP)** have a thorough knowledge of the LEED programs and have proficiency in a particular LEED rating system. **LEED Green Associates** have a current understanding of LEED's green building practices and principles. LEED adds other certification levels periodically.

Green Globes

The Green Building Initiative (GBI) is a nonprofit organization that promotes energy-efficient, healthy, and environmentally sustainable buildings. Its Green Globes certifications, based on its **Building Assessment Protocol for Commercial Buildings**, are tailored for a wide range of buildings from large and small offices, multi-family structures, hospitals, schools, and institutional and municipal buildings.

GBI is also an accredited standards developer under ANSI/GBI 01 Green Building Assessment Protocol for Commercial Buildings, upon which the Green Globes certification is based. Under Green Globes, fabrics are grouped under Materials and Resources and are included in the Interior Fit-Out Category (interior partitions, interior finishes, doors, millwork, cabinetry, furniture, window treatments, plumbing fixtures, light fixtures, and so on). There are two basic methods that can be used when comparing sustainability of textiles and other fit-out products under Green Globes:

- Path A: Performance Path identifies performance or objectives to be achieved (10 points maximum).
- Path B: Prescriptive Path identifies exactly how to comply with specific standards (16 points maximum). Depending on the assessment method

used, the total Interior Fit-Out Category is worth a maximum of 16.5 or 22.5 points out of the new construction total of 1,000 points, of which Reuse of Existing Furniture can equal 4 points and Low Floorcovering VOC (includes carpet) can achieve 2.5 points.

Green Globes Professionals

A **Green Globes Professional** is trained in the Green Globes building assessment and certification process and serves as consultants on Green Globes projects in order to facilitate the building certification process and provide project management for their own clients. A **Green Globes Assessor** is certified in the areas of GBI's sustainable design, construction, energy, and facility management protocols and requirements. After training, assessors are contracted by GBI to perform independent third-party assessments for Green Globes building projects.

Living Building Challenge

A third whole-building standard that is gaining popularity in the design community is the Living Building Challenge. Developed by the International Living Future Institute, which was founded by the Cascadia Green Building Council (a chapter of the USGBC together with the Canada Green Building Council), the system grants "Petals" for seven performance areas:

- Place
- Water
- Energy
- Health and Happiness
- Materials
- Equity
- Beauty

Living Product Challenge certification is based on LCA analysis and also synthesizes other hard data, but also measures features often deemed subjective, such as social justice and equality. To earn full program certification (Living Status), projects must meet all assigned imperatives and have proven performance through at least 12 consecutive months of operation, as the evaluation is based on demonstrated improvement over a short history. Projects will earn partial program certification (Petal recognition) if they meet the requirements of a minimum of three categories, one of which must be water, energy, or materials.

Key Terms

Association for Contract Textiles (ACT)
American National Standards Institute (ANSI)
ASTM International
Building Assessment Protocol for Commercial Buildings
Business and Institutional Furniture Manufacturers Association (BIFMA)
certifications
Clean Air Act
Clean Water Act
Code of Federal Regulation (CFR)
cradle-to-cradle
Cradle to Cradle Certified
Cradle to Cradle Products Innovation Institute
cradle-to-grave
Ecolabel Index
ecolabels
Eco-Textile Labeling Guide.
Ecotextile News
embodied energy
Emergency Planning and Community Right-to-Know Act
Energy Independence and Security Act
Energy Policy Act
Environmental Protection Agency (EPA)
Environmentally Preferable Purchasing (EPP) Program

Facts
Federal Insecticide, Fungicide, and Rodenticide Act
Federal Trade Commission (FTC)
Global Ecolabelling Network
Global Organic Textile Standard (GOTS)
Green Building Initiative (GBI)
Green Globes
Green Globes Assessor
Green Globes Professional
Green Guides
Green Label
Green Label Plus
Greenguard
Greenguard Environmental Institute
Greenguard Gold
Greenwashing
indoor air quality (IAQ)
International Code Council (ICC)
International Energy Conservation Code (IECC)
International Green Construction Code (IgCC)
International Living Futures Institute
International Organization for Standardization (ISO)
Intertek

Leadership in Energy and Environmental Design (LEED)
LEED Accredited Professionals (LEED AP)
LEED Green Associates
LEVEL certification
life-cycle assessment (LCA)
life-cycle inventory (LCI)
Living Building Challenge
NSF International
Occupational Safety and Health Administration (OSHA)
OEKO-TEX Standard 100
off-gassing
organically grown
PET (polyethylene terephthalate)

Pollution Prevention Act
post-consumer
post-industrial
recycling
repurposing
Resource Conservation and Recovery Act
Safe Drinking Water Act
safety data sheet (SDS)
SCS Global
SCS Indoor Advantage Gold
standards
sustainability
Toxic Substance Control Act
U.S. Green Building Council (USGBC)
volatile organic compounds (VOCs)

Review Questions

1. What is an example of a sustainability code for fabric? A guideline? A code?
2. What is Facts?
3. What is LEED?
4. What is greenwashing and how can it be prevented?
5. Discuss the environmental challenges that face natural fiber suppliers and manufactured fiber producers.
6. Why is it critically important that fabric manufacturers keep up to date on governmental regulations?
7. Discuss what is involved in a life-cycle assessment and life-cycle inventory. Why are LCAs not routinely undertaken for interior fabrics?
8. Explain importance of IAQ. How can the negative effects of interior textiles on the IAQ be reduced?
9. Identify ways the professional designer can strive to protect the environment when selecting textiles.
10. Discuss the benefits of building green.
11. Discuss the recycling of plastic bottles into textile applications.

Notes

1. U.S. Code of Federal Regulations (CFR) Title 16—Commercial Practices, Chapter 1, FTC Part 260—Guides for the use of Environmental Marketing Claims.
2. Executive Order 13101, Section 201—Greening the Government Through Waste Prevention, Recycling, and Federal Acquisition, 1998.
3. Environmental Protection Agency, "Life-Cycle Assessment: Principles and Practice," May 2006, page 11.
4. Environmental Protection Agency, EPA's "Final Guidance on Environmentally Preferable Purchasing, Appendix B (1)—Menu of Environmental Attributes," as published by the EPA on August 20, 1999, http://www.epa.gov/opptintr/epp/pubs/guidance/finalguidance.htm.
5. Environmentally related ASTM standards to date relate to buildings rather than to furnishing materials. These include a Guide for Life-Cycle Assessment of Building Materials (ASTM E1991), Standard Practice for Data Collection for Sustainability (ASTM E2129), Standard Practice for Measuring Life-Cycle Costs of Buildings and Building Systems (ASTM E917), Standard Guide for General Principles of Sustainability Relative to Buildings (ASTM E2432).

Environmental Feature Databases

- EPA.
- U.S. Life-Cycle Inventory Database (https://www.nrel.gov/lci/); from NREL (National Renewable Energy Laboratory), a government-owned, contractor-operated laboratory and research institution funded through Department of Energy (DOE).
- EIE (Environmental Impact Estimator; https://calculatelca.com/software/impact-estimator/); software for LCA in the construction industry from Athena Sustainable Materials Institute, a nonprofit research collaborative.
- BEES (Building for Environmental and Economic Sustainability, https://www.nist.gov/services-resources/software/bees) established by NIST (National Institute of Standards and Technology), under U.S. Department of Commerce. For building evaluations; does not include textiles.

4

Fiber Classification
and Properties

The goal of a design professional is to select a fabric that preforms well under the appropriate conditions. Fiber characteristics, along with yarn type, fabric structure or construction, and finish, impact the appearance, strength, cost, and hand (feel) of a fabric.

Fibers (Figure 4.1) are chemically distinct materials that can be manipulated in various ways. Fibers can be made into elongated forms (**yarn**), which are used to make woven and knitted fabric or melded into a film or a nonwoven. There are many different sources of fiber and cultures around the world have historically learned to harness local, natural resources that can be used in fabric production. The first synthetic fiber was invented in the 1930s and an explosion in the number of variations thereof followed. Chemists continue to manipulate these materials, striving to meet modern day demands for functional and aesthetically pleasing fabrics. In order for a fiber to have broad, modern-market appeal it must be plentiful, competitively priced, and able to be processed successfully and efficiently.

Whether a fiber is natural or manufactured, it is distinguished by its chemical composition and characterized by specific molecular structure and external physical features. Such characteristics are inherent features of natural fibers and are engineered features of manufactured fibers. In either case, these variables result in the specific appearance and performance properties of fibers. However, keep in mind that fiber is but one component of a fabric and any and all of these features can be offset in an actual fabric through construction choices and finishing. A review of fiber nomenclature will introduce the basic vocabulary for fiber labeling.

Figure 4.1 Fibers. Courtesy of Glen Raven, Inc.

Fiber Classification and Identification

Two broad categories of fiber are **natural** and **manufactured**. Natural fibers, obtained from plants, animals, or minerals, are classified according to their source. Plant, or **cellulosic**, fibers include cotton, flax, hemp, jute, and sisal. Animal, or **protein**, fibers include wool, silk, and fleece from other animals, such as **mohair** and **cashmere** from goats. Mineral fibers are found in the ground and include glass and asbestos. Manufactured fibers are produced from chemical compounds, are engineered for specific end-uses, and provide performance properties that cannot be achieved with natural fibers. They are versatile and quick to produce. Four subgroups of manufactured fibers are regenerated fibers, synthetic fibers, biopolymer fibers, and mineral fibers. These categories will be discussed in detail in Chapter 5.

Fiber Classification

Natural and manufactured fibers are identified by a **common name** (for natural fibers) or a **generic name** (for manufactured fibers) names for purposes of discussion and for sample and product labeling. Fibers grouped under the same name are chemically related and possess similar properties. Familiarizing yourself with these names and with the properties that typically characterize each group will assist you in making informed fabric selections.

A fiber classification system is presented in Table 4.1. Fibers are first classified on the basis of how they are produced, whether natural or manufactured. A few manufactured fibers, such as rayon, are produced from natural substances but are not categorized as a natural fiber because they are the product of an industrial process.

The Federal Trade Commission establishes **generic** names for manufactured fibers in accordance with congressional directive. Each class is defined in terms of specific chemical composition. An up-to-date listing of the generic class names set forth by the Federal Trade Commission is available at https://www.cbp.gov/sites/default/files/assets/documents/2016-Apr/icp040_3.pdf.

TABLE 4.1
TEXTILE FIBER CLASSIFICATION

Natural Fibers		
Protein (Animals)	**Cellulosic (Plants)**	**Mineral (Rock)**
Alpaca (alpaca)	Leaf	Asbestos
Angora (Angora rabbit)	Abaca (manila fiber)	
Camel (Bactrian camel)	Banana	
Cashmere (cashmere goat)	Henequen	
Cattle hair (cattle)	Piña (pineapple)	
Fur fibers (beaver, fox, mink, sable, etc.)	Sisal	
Llama (llama)	Seed	
Mohair (Angora goat)	Coir (coconut)	
Qiviut (musk ox)	Cotton	
Silk (silkworm)	Kapok	
Vicuna (vicuna)	Milkweed	
Wool (sheep)	Stem (bast)	
Yak	Hemp	
	Jute	
	Flax	
	Ramie (China grass)	

Regenerated Manufactured Fibers (Natural Polymer Based)		
Cellulosic	**Protein**	**Rubber**
Acetate	Azlon	Rubber (natural rubber)
Lyocell		
Rayon		
Triacetate		

Synthetic Fibers (Synthetic Polymer Based)				Mineral Fibers
Acrylic	Melamine	Olefin	Spandex	Glass
Anidex	Modacrylic	PBI	Sulfar	Metallic
Aramid	Novoloid	Polyester	Vinal	
Elastoester	Nylon	Rubber (synthetic)	Vinyon	
Fluoropolymer	Nytril	Saran		

Bio-Polymer Fibers (Both Natural and Synthetic Polymer Based)					

PLA

Acetate	Melts and fuses away from flame	Burns quickly with melting	Continues to burn rapidly with melting	Brittle, irregular-shaped black bead	Acrid (hot vinegar)
Rayon	Does not shrink away, ignites upon contact	Burns quickly without melting	Continues to burn, afterglow	Light, fluffy ash, small amount	Similar to burning paper
Lyocell	Does not shrink away, ignites upon contact	Burns quickly without melting	Continues to burn, afterglow	Light, feathery ash, light gray to charcoal in color	Similar to burning paper

Mineral

Glass	Shrinks away from flame	Melts and glows red to orange	Glowing ceases, does not burn	Hard bead, white	None
Metallic (pure)	May shrink away from flame or have no reaction	Glows red	Glowing ceases, does not burn, hardens	Skeleton outline of fiber	None

Synthetic

Acrylic	Fuses and shrinks away from flame	Burns with melting	Continues to burn with melting	Brittle, irregular-shaped bead, black	Acrid
Modacrylic	Fuses and shrinks away from flame	Burns slowly and irregularly with melting	Self-extinguishing[a]	Hard, irregular-shaped bead, black	Acid chemical
Nylon	Fuses and shrinks away from flame	Burns slowly with melting	Usually self-extinguishing[a]	Hard, tough, round bead, gray	Celery
Olefin (polypropylene)	Fuses, shrinks, and curls away from flame	Burns with melting	Continues to burn with melting, black sooty smoke	Hard, tough, tan bead	Chemical or candle wax
Polyester	Fuses and shrinks away from flame	Burns very slowly with melting	Usually self-extinguishing[a]	Hard, tough, round bead, black	Chemical
Saran	Fuses and shrinks away from flame	Burns very slowly with melting, yellow flame	Self-extinguishing[a]	Hard, irregular-shaped bead, black	Chemical
Spandex	Fuses but does not shrink away from flame	Burns with melting	Continues to burn with melting	Soft, crushable, fluffy, black ash	Chemical
Vinyon	Fuses and shrinks away from flame	Burns slowly with melting	Self-extinguishing[a]	Hard, irregular-shaped bead, black	Acrid

Bio-Polymer

PLA (polylactic acid)	Melts and shrinks away from flame	Melts and burns with slight white smoke	Usually self-extinguishing[a]	Hard tan or gray bead	Slightly acrid odor

[a]Self-extinguishing fibers stop burning when the source of ignition is removed.

Fiber Identification

In some instances, a professional or a consumer may encounter a fabric of unknown fiber content. The fabric may be, for example, a **customer's own material (COM)** and carry no labeling, or it may be commercial yardage that has become separated from its labels. Various testing and examination procedures can identify unknown fibers, although these require an adequately equipped laboratory. A **burn test** is easy for a novice to perform and can identifies the fiber's general chemical composition such as cellulosic, protein, or synthetic. This is the procedure for the burn test, which should be conducted with caution:

- Hold several fibers, or a yarn from a fabric, with metal tweezers over a fireproof surface that will safely catch ashes and drips.
- Strike a match away from the body.
- Observe the reaction of the specimen as it approaches the flame, when it is in the flame, and after the ignition source is removed. Note the odor and examine the cooled residue. Does it burn readily? Shrink from flame? Melt? Does it smell like plastic, firewood, or a cookout?

Cellulosic fibers, including rayon, burn quickly, smell like burning paper and have an ash residue. Protein fibers burn slowly and are often self-extinguishing. They smell like burning hair and have a harder residue than plant fibers. Synthetic fibers melt, smell like burning plastic, and have a hard bead residue. If a mixture of reactions is noted when a yarn is burned it is likely that the yarn is a blend of two or more fibers, a blend may be suspected. Visual characteristics may help the observer to separate different fibers in the yarn and repeat the test.

Fiber Composition, Molecular Structure, and External Physical Features

To understand fibers, we need to look at their physical structures, chemical compositions, and molecular arrangements. These factors contribute to the appearance, hand, and performance of an end product.

Fiber Composition

All fibers, whether natural or manufactured, are relatively fine and have comparatively high ratios of length to width. This structural feature ensures the flexibility required for both ease in the manufacturing process and serviceability of the end product.

Fibers are different, not only in their chemical compositions, but also in their molecular arrangement and the nature of their external physical features. These features occur naturally, but can be manipulated in some cases. Generic fibers vary in their properties according to their chemical compositions. For example, cotton and linen exhibit similar characteristics due to their shared cellulosic chemical composition but have very different molecular structures and physical features.

Molecular Structure

The various atoms present in each fiber are combined into distinctive molecular fiber-forming units known as **monomers**. Through a process known as **polymerization**, thousands of monomers are linked by strong chemical bonds into extremely long, chain-like units known as **polymers**. Within textile fibers, the polymer chains assume, or are made to assume, different types of arrangements. Four of these arrangements are schematically illustrated in Figure 4.2.

When polymer chains are aligned parallel to the long axis of the fiber, the arrangement is **oriented** (Figure 4.2b). When the chains are laterally or longitudinally parallel to each other and closely packed, a high number of chemical bonds or attractions, weaker than the main chain bonds, may form between adjacent chains. Such ordered regions are **crystalline** (Figure 4.2c and d).

Polymer chains that do not exhibit any orderly, crystalline structures are called **amorphous polymers** (Figure 4.2a). In amorphous arrangements, the molecular chains are random and disorganized. By contrast, in an oriented chain arrangement (Figure 4.2b) molecules are aligned parallel to the length of the fiber. These molecular arrangements create the fiber's **longitudinal configuration**, and contribute to a fiber's flexibility, strength, elasticity, and hand.

Fibers cannot have a totally oriented, crystalline interior arrangement because they would be brittle and

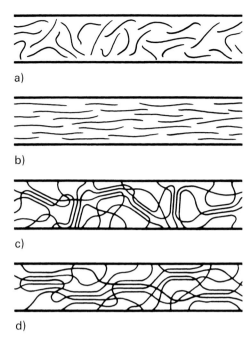

Figure 4.2 Molecular arrangements in fibers: (a) amorphous, (b) oriented, (c) nonoriented crystalline, (d) oriented crystalline. Fairchild Books.

inflexible and would snap under stress. Fibers that tend to be highly ordered, such as flax, are stiff, have relatively low elasticity and abrasion resistance, do not drape well, and also wrinkle more than most fibers.

External Physical Features

The external features of fibers include their cross-sectional shape, their surface texture, their longitudinal configuration, their length, and their diameter. These features, like molecular composition and arrangement, directly influence the properties of fibers. These features are inherent in natural fibers and can be manipulated in manufactured fibers.

Cross-sectional Shape

The **cross-sectional shape** of a manufactured fiber can take on many forms. In production, the **spinneret**, a nozzle with holes through which the chemical is extruded, controls the cross-sectional shape. The cross-sectional shapes of natural fibers are a reflection of the fibers' growth patterns. The cross-sectional shape of a fiber impacts luster, texture and the hand of a fabric.

Surface Texture

The **surface texture** of fibers may be smooth or wrinkled, somewhat rough, or otherwise irregular. Some typical textures and cross-sectional shapes are illustrated in Figure 4.3. Together with other external features, texture affects the luster and feel of fabric, aesthetic variables that are relatively important selection criteria for many consumers.

Longitudinal Configuration

Longitudinal configuration describes the outer surface contours of the fiber. Lengthwise, fibers may be fairly straight or twisted, or they may have a two- or three-dimensional **crimp** (compressed small folds or ridges) where a fiber bends or twists. Longitudinal configuration impacts aesthetic considerations like luster and hand as well as performance properties, such as elasticity and resiliency. Figure 4.3 illustrates the longitudinal configurations of wool, cotton, rayon, and a conventional manufactured fiber.

Length

Textile fibers range in length from a fraction of an inch or millimeter to several miles or meters in length. Cotton fibers measure less than 1 inch in length, silk filaments approach 2 miles in length, and manufactured fibers can be produced in any length desired. Fibers are classified as either staple or filament. Short fibers that are measured in inches are called **staple fibers**. All the natural fibers, excluding silk, are staple fibers. **Filament fibers** are long, continuous fiber strands of infinite length, typically measured in yards or meters. All manufactured fibers are originally produced as filament fibers; to better mimic natural fibers, filament is often cut into staple lengths and then spun into yarn. Filament yarns have greater **tensile strength** (how far a material can be stretched without breaking) than do yarns made from staple fibers. In addition, the longer the staple length of the fiber, the higher the tensile strength.

Diameter

The **diameter**, or width, of a raw fiber of which a yarn is comprised greatly affects the hand and performance

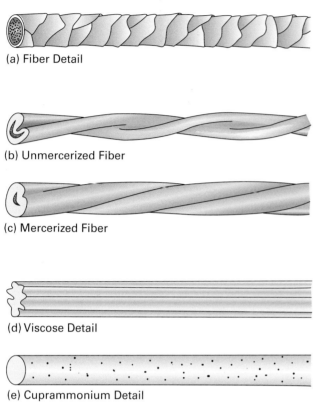

(a) Fiber Detail

(b) Unmercerized Fiber

(c) Mercerized Fiber

(d) Viscose Detail

(e) Cuprammonium Detail

Figure 4.3 Cross-sectional shape, longitudinal configuration, and surface textures of selected fibers: (a) overlapping surface scales of wool, (b) twisted configuration and wrinkled surface of cotton, (c) straight configuration and irregular surface of viscose rayon, (d) straight configuration and smooth surface of conventional manufactured fiber. Fairchild Books.

Aesthetic Properties

Luster

The **luster** of textile fibers depends on the quantity of light waves reflected from their surfaces and the direction in which these waves are traveling. Luster is determined by cross-sectional shape, longitudinal configuration, and surface texture. Fiber surfaces reflect some portions of incident light waves, transmit other portions, and absorb still other portions. Fibers with round cross sections and smooth surfaces typically reflect large quantities of light rays in one direction producing a very shiny, lustrous surface. Rayon, used in the tie back in Figure 4.4, is highly lustrous. Fabrics made with filament yarns, either from natural sources like silk or synthetic like polyester are more reflexive than fabrics made from staple yarns.

The natural irregular texture of cotton fiber gives cotton fabrics a low luster. The surface scales and three-dimensional crimp of wool scatters light rays, which results in a subdued, matte luster. Manufactured fiber producers can alter the amount of sheen by can adding a **delustering** agent to the chemical solution.

Hand

Hand refers to the tactile characteristics of a fabric. These characteristics include perceived temperature and the level of surface smoothness or roughness. Whether a fabric has a pleasant hand, or feel, is a subjective evaluation that often governs consumer selection. Among many other contributing factors, hand is influenced by the inherent structural features of the fiber.

Drape

Drape, as shown in Figure 4.5, is the manner in which a fabric hangs vertically and it is an important consideration when selecting fabrics for window treatments, slipcovers, table linens and bedding. Yarn type and fabric construction are the largest contributors to a fabric's drapability features, but the fiber's diameter and flexibility are also factors. Fibers of fine diameter and with high flexibility, such as microfibers, tend to drape easily.

characteristics of fabric. Smaller diameter fibers are more pliable, drapable, and softer than larger diameter fibers; larger diameter fibers are stiffer, crisper, and resist crushing. For example, fiber of fine diameter is used for sheer curtaining to create a light and opaque fabric, while large-diameter fiber is used in carpeting to lessen crushing, in order to reduce visible wear from normal traffic patterns.

Natural materials grow irregularly; the diameters of natural fibers are not uniform and cannot be controlled. Manufactured fibers can be produced in any thickness and can be uniform throughout the yarn, or engineered to alternate thick and thin areas. Microfibers and nanofibers are ultrafine manufactured fibers grouped together to form a yarn. Fabrics made from these complex yarns are highly drapable and have a soft hand and a silky appearance.

Figure 4.4 Aurelia tieback. Courtesy of Samuel & Sons, Inc.

Figure 4.5 Drapery panel. Courtesy of Cowtan & Tout, Inc.

Texture

Texture is the nature of the fiber's surface. Texture is due to the physical structure of the fiber and is identified by both visual and tactile senses. Texture can affect luster, appearance, and comfort. Natural fibers tend to have more texture than manufactured fibers because of their inherent growth irregularities. However, the cross-sectional shape of manufactured fibers can be changed to allow for differences in texture.

Appearance Retention Properties

Various features, which are described below, contribute to a fiber's ability to retain its original appearance over a period of time after exposure to use and adversarial environmental agents.

Abrasion Resistance

Abrasion resistance is the ability of a fiber to resist loss due to friction from another object. The inherent ability of a fiber to resist visible signs of surface abrasion depends largely on its strength and elongation. Abrasion from normal wear and tear eventually changes the textural features and apparent luster of a fiber's surface. In application, this is most often after the fabric has become unsightly for other reasons. Upholstery fabrics abrade most often from soil in the cloth that is not removed and, to a degree, from rubbing by and contact with other fabrics such as the clothes that people are wearing. A fabric that is laundered abrades by rubbing against itself.

While features such as luster and longitudinal strength are inherent properties of a fiber, abrasion resistance depends on interconnected attributes: yarn fabrication, weave structure, fabric construction, finish, and backing. A fiber's abrasion resistance is not normally measured independently, and tests for fabrics' abrasion resistance are highly questionable.

Fabrics that receive high marks on abrasion resistance tests are often flat with a course hand. Most commonly, upholstery fabrics become soiled and unsightly long before their surface abrasion becomes an issue. In real-life practice, fiber is only one of the many factors that impact a fabric's abrasion resistance, along with yarn and fabric construction, fabric finish, and appropriate cleaning and maintenance. Abrasion of floorcoverings comes from the movement of shoe soles or furniture across the surface. Toweling is abraded as it is moved over glassware or skin and through repeated laundering, which removes the weakened fibers and results in the fabrics becoming thinner.

Flexibility

Flexibility is the ability of the fiber to bend repeatedly without breaking. Fabrics need flexibility in order to drape, and to contour to upholstered furniture, panels, and walls. Fibers displaying low flexibility and elasticity, such as flax, may split and break along crease lines.

Tenacity

Tenacity, or strength, is related to the type of polymer arrangement and/or the length of the fiber. Fiber strength is measured through laboratory tests. Machines equipped to record the length of test specimens at the break point are also equipped to record the grams of force or load that caused the rupture. This information is used to calculate the strength, or breaking tenacity, required to rupture the fiber and is conducted both wet and dry.

Although nearly identical to cotton in chemical composition, flax is stronger than cotton because of its longer staple length and its molecular structure. Natural cellulosic fibers such as cotton exhibit high tenacity scores when wet, which makes them ideal for use in toweling. The strength exhibited by a fiber may not be the principal determinant of the strength of the fabric. Yarn type, fabric construction and structure, finish, and backing have more of an impact on a fabric's strength than does its fiber content.

Elongation

Elongation is the ability of a fiber to be stretched or extended without breaking. Elongation depends on the internal molecular arrangement and the external structural features of the fiber. Flax displays minimal **elongation**; by contrast, wool tends to exhibit high elongation. Fibers with a natural or engineered crimp have greater elongation than do fibers with an essentially straight, nontextured configuration.

The elongation of fiber is generally measured at the breaking point. Laboratory equipment used for this is engineered to exert a force while extending the specimen. The machine will then record the breaking load or force in grams and the length of the specimen at the point of rupture. After completion of the test, the elongation of the specimen is calculated and expressed as a percentage of the original length.

Cohesiveness

Cohesiveness is the ability of fibers to cling together during spinning. Cohesiveness is due to crimp, twist, or the surface contour of fibers. Cotton, one of the shortest fibers, can be made into very strong yarns and fabrics because of the cohesiveness of the fibers, which are due to convolutions in fiber structure. Fabrics made of cohesive fibers are more resistant to raveling and yarn slippage, although these characteristics are heavily dependent on the actual yarn configuration, as well as the structure and construction of the fabric.

Light Resistance

Light resistance is the ability of a fiber to resist degradation due to exposure light. All fibers are impacted by light, but some are degraded more rapidly than others. Over time, light alters the interior structure of synthetic fibers, breaking their chemical bonds and reducing the length of the polymer chain.

The rate and extent of fiber damage from light is influenced by several factors including fiber composition, length of exposure, type and intensity of the light, atmospheric conditions, the presence and type of colorants, and the use of polymer solution additives. Table 4.2 compares the light resistance of selected textile fibers.

Insect Resistance

Insect resistance is the resistance to insect damage, including moths, beetles, crickets, ants, and roaches. Natural fibers are susceptible to insect damage while synthetic fibers are inherently insect resistant. Moth larvae and carpet beetles are likely to attack wool carpet fibers unless they are treated for moth resistance. All domestic wool floorcoverings are treated to repel these insects, but imported products may or may not be treated. Crickets and silverfish can attack cellulosic fibers, which should be stored clean under dry conditions.

Resiliency

Resiliency is the ability of a fabric material to recover from folding, bending, crushing, or twisting and is directly related to wrinkle recovery. Animal fibers such as wool and silk are highly resilient, while cellulosic fibers are less so. Manufactured fibers can be engineered for resiliency. In general, synthetic fibers resist wrinkling but once the fabric is wrinkled, it can be difficult to remove. The resiliency of fibers is generally rated in relative terms: excellent, moderate, or poor. Table 4.3 rates commonly used fibers for resiliency.

Compression Resiliency

Compression resiliency, or **loft**, is the ability of a fiber to spring back to its original thickness after being compressed. Compression resiliency contributes to springiness, covering power, and resistance to flattening. It is an important property for end-uses such as carpeting, pile upholstery fabrics, and fiberfill applications. The more loft in carpeting (Figure 4.6), the less it will show wear in high-traffic areas. High compression resiliency in fiberfill batting will allow the air spaces to remain intact, creating insulation properties.

Elastic Recovery

Elastic recovery measurements indicate how completely a fiber returns to its original length after being elongated. Elastic recovery is measured as a percentage of the return to original length. Fibers having highly disoriented interior structures typically exhibit an inherent desire to return to their relaxed state. Those having crimp also tend to display better recovery than non-crimped fibers.

TABLE 4.2
LIGHT RESISTANCE OF SELECTED TEXTILE FIBERS

Fiber	Level of Resistance
Glass	Excellent
Acrylic	Excellent
Modacrylic	Excellent
PLA	Excellent
Polyester	Excellent
Lyocell	Moderate
Flax	Moderate
Hemp	Moderate
Cotton	Moderate
Rayon	Moderate
Triacetate	Moderate
Acetate	Moderate
Olefin (Polypropylene)	Moderate
Nylon	Poor
Wool	Poor
Silk	Poor

TABLE 4.3
RESILIENCIES OF SELECTED TEXTILE FIBERS

Fiber	Level of Resistance
Wool	Excellent
Polyester	Excellent
PLA	Excellent
Silk	Excellent
Nylon	Good
Acrylic	Good
Olefin	Good
Lyocell	Fair
Acetate	Fair
Rayon	Poor
Cotton	Poor
Hemp	Poor
Flax	Poor

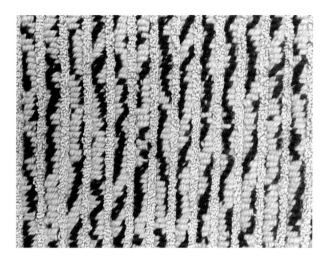

Figure 4.6 Carpet sample. Courtesy Martin Patrick Evan, Ltd.

Dimensional Stability and Shrinkage Resistance

Dimensional stability is the ability of a fiber to retain its original size and shape throughout use and care. A fabric may increase or decrease in size. For the most part, shrinkage or growth is related to a fiber's reaction to moisture or heat. The vertical yarns of a drapery fabric may lengthen when the humidity is high and may or may not return to the original length under normal levels of humidity. By contrast, wool may lengthen, but will return to its original size when humidity drops. **Shrinkage resistance** is the ability of a fiber to retain its original shape during cleaning.

Propensity to Pill

Pilling is the formation of tiny balls of entangled fibers on a fabric's surface. Pilling is most common with synthetic staple fibers. Fabrics composed of short staple yarns both natural and manufactured are more subject to pilling than fabrics composed of longer staple or filament yarns. High yarn twist and high yarn count can minimize pilling.

Oleophilic Propensity

Oleophilic fibers exhibit a strong attraction to oily stains. Oleophilic properties are due to a fiber's chemical composition. Synthetic fibers that have low moisture absorbency have a high attraction to oils and grease.

Soil Repellency

Soil repellency is the ability of a fiber to resist dirt and stains. Some fibers attract and retain soiling, while some tend to repel foreign matter. Wool has exterior scales along the fiber length that capture dirt and stains preventing them from seeping into the fabric. Nylon carpet fibers have been engineered to reduce initial attraction for soil and to retard the rate of soil accumulation. An innovative approach to soil hiding is the introduction of **microscopic voids** lengthwise within fibers. The interior voids deflect incident waves, obscuring the appearance of soil.

Comfort Properties

Absorbency

Absorbency is the ability of a fiber to take up moisture and it impacts end-use, static electricity, cleanability, and how well a fabric accepts dyes. Absorbency is expressed as a percentage of **moisture regain**, which is the amount of moisture a dry fiber will absorb from the air. Typical moisture regain values are listed in Table 4.4.

Fibers with high regain values, including the natural and regenerated cellulosic fibers, are referred to as **hydrophilic** fibers. These fibers easily absorb water, dye chemicals, and detergent solution. Due to their high moisture content they do not build up static electricity. Fibers with low regain values are **hydrophobic**, and absorb little or no moisture. These fibers are more challenging to dye, more difficult to clean with soap and water, and build up static electricity. **Hygroscopic** fibers, such as wool, absorb moisture without feeling wet. Wool is more hygroscopic than any other fiber, with a moisture regain of up to 16 percent.

Heat Conductivity

Heat conductivity and **heat transmittance** are synonymous terms used to refer to the rate at which a material conducts heat. Most fibers do not conduct heat and therefore are insulating. Natural cellulosic fibers tend to exhibit high heat conductivity, whereas natural protein fibers exhibit poor heat conductivity. Blankets made of wool fiber are known for their exceptional heat retention and insulating power.

TABLE 4.4
PERCENTAGE MOISTURE REGAIN OF SELECTED TEXTILE FIBERS

Fiber	Percentage
Wool	16.00
Rayon (viscose)	13.00
Rayon (HWM)	11.0
Lyocell	11.50
Flax	10.0–12.0
Cotton	8.50
Acetate	6.00
Nylon	4.00–4.5
Acrylic	1.3–2.5
Spandex	0.6
Polyester	0.4–0.8
PLA	0.4–0.6
Vinyon	0.50
Olefin (Polypropylene)	0.01–0.1
Saran	0.00
Glass	0.00
Acetate	1.32
Silk	1.25
PLA	1.24–1.25
Spandex	1.2
Acrylic	1.14–1.19
Nylon	1.14
Olefin (Polypropylene)	0.91

Covering Power

Covering power is the ability of a textile structure to cover or conceal an area relative to its weight. The effectiveness with which fibers cover a surface depends on structural features, such as cross-sectional shape and longitudinal configuration, along with loft.

Density/Specific Gravity

A fiber with a low **specific gravity** provides maximum cover with minimum weight. This is commonly referred to as **loft**. If the diameters of two fibers are equal, the fiber with the lower specific gravity will cover more area with less weight than will the fiber with higher specific gravity. For example, acrylic fiber's low specific gravity and relatively low cost make it popular for well-priced, lightweight, and warm blankets, as opposed to wool, which is heavier and more expensive. In terms of floorcovering, wool is perhaps the ideal fiber. Wool is resilient and abrasion resistant insuring that it will retain its appearance and perform well in use. It is, however, expensive. Nylon usurps wool's place as number one fiber used in the carpeting because it is less expensive and provides maximum cover.

Health, Safety, and Protection Properties

Chemical Resistance

Fibers come into contact with various chemicals during processing (dyeing and finishing) or during maintenance (soaps, bleaches, detergents, and dry-cleaning solvents). The chemical resistance of fibers helps determine end-use serviceability and care of fabrics and can be measured in the laboratory, following the procedures set forth in standard test methods.

Flammability Characteristics

Textile fibers burn at different temperatures and have different rates of **combustion**. Heat of combustion values specify the amount of heat energy generated that could cause burn injuries as well as maintain the temperature required for further decomposition and combustion. The heats of combustion, ignition temperature, and other pyrolytic characteristics of selected fiber groups are listed in Table 4.5.

Fibers are described as flammable, flame resistant, noncombustible, or fireproof. A **flammable fiber** is relatively easy to ignite and sustains combustion until it is consumed. A **flame-resistant fiber** may have, for example, relatively high decomposition and ignition temperature, or a slow rate of burning. **Noncombustible fibers** do not burn or contribute significant amounts of smoke. Noncombustible fibers are not fireproof, however, because they can melt and decompose at high temperatures. A **fireproof fiber** is unaffected by fire. Table 4.6 includes a listing of the relative flammability of several fibers.

Thermoplasticity

Thermoplasticity is the ability of fibers to be transformed through heat exposure. This property allows

TABLE 4.5

PYROLYTIC CHARACTERISTICS OF SELECTED TEXTILE FIBERS

FIBER	Temperatures				Heats of Combustion (Btus/Lb)	Limiting Oxygen Index
	Decomposition°		Ignition			
	°F	°C	°F	°C		
Natural						
Protein						
Wool	446	230	1,094 (self-extinguishing)	590	9,450	25.2
Cellulose						
Cotton	581	305	752	400	7,400	17–20
Mineral						
Asbestos			Fireproof			
Regenerated Manufactured						
Cellulosic						
Acetate	572	300	842	450	7,700	18.4
Rayon	350–464	177–240	788	420	7,400	18.6
Mineral						
Glass	1,500	815	Noncombustible			
Synthetic						
Acrylic	549	287	986	530	1,300	18.2
Aramid	Decomposes above 800°F (427°C)					
Modacrylic	455	235	Will not support combustion; self-extinguishing			
Novoloid	Decomposes (converts to carbon)	Resists over 5000°F (2760°C); does not burn				
Nylon	653	345	989	532	12,950	20.1
Olefin (Polypropylene)						18.6
Polyester	734	390	1,040	560	9,300	20.6
Saran	168	76	Will not support combustion; self-extinguishing			
Vinyon			Will not support combustion; self-extinguishing			

TABLE 4.6
RELATIVE FLAMMABILITY OF SELECTED TEXTILE FIBERS

Fireproof	Noncombustible	Flame-Resistant	Flammable
Asbestos	Glass	Aramid	Cotton
		Novoloid	Flax
		Wool	Hemp
		Modacrylic	PLA
		Vinyon	Lyocell
		Saran	Rayon
		Silk	Acetate
			Triacetate
			Acrylic
			Nylon
			Polyester
			Olefin (Polypropylene)

thermoplastic fibers to be **heat set**—for example, permanent creases and pleats can be made in fabrics of a thermoplastic material. It is a drawback when a thermoplastic fiber is heated to its melting point by such items as lit cigarettes and hot irons.

Heat Susceptibility

Although the natural fibers, along with rayon, lyocell, and PLA, are not thermoplastic, and thus cannot be permanently set with heat, they are nonetheless sensitive to heat. Exposing natural fibers to elevated temperatures, especially for prolonged periods, may cause degradation and discoloration. For example, excessively high ironing temperatures weaken and scorch cotton and linen fabrics.

Electrical Conductivity and Static Propensity

Static electricity is the electric charge caused by the rubbing together of two dissimilar materials. Carpeting is the largest contributor to static electricity in an interior. Static develops as soles of shoes rub against carpets. When a person touches the electrical conductor, such as a metal doorknob, accumulated electrons rapidly flow from the body to the conductor.

Electrical conductivity describes the relative ease with which a fiber conducts or resists the flow of electrons. Fibers that keep electrons flowing, minimizing their accumulation, are classified as **conductors**. Olefin, acrylic, and modacrylic are conductors; metal fibers are especially good conductors. Nylon, polyester, and wool are **insulators** and resist the flow of electrons.

Humidity in a room reduces static electricity. Controlling levels of relative humidity is a year-round practice in such interiors as computer rooms and medical facilities. For use in these sensitive areas, anti-static carpets are available. They are engineered either by adding compounds to the synthetic fiber or by including conductive material in the carpeting.

Key Terms

abrasion resistance	flammable fiber
absorbency	flexibility
amorphous polymers	generic name
appearance retention	hand
cashmere	heat conductivity
cellulosic	heat-sensitive fiber
cohesiveness	heat set
combustion	heat transmittance
common name	hydrophilic
compression resiliency	hydrophobic
conductors	hygroscopic
covering power	insect resistance
crimp	insulators
cross-sectional shape	light resistance
crystalline polymer chain	loft
customer's own material (COM)	longitudinal configuration
	luster
delustering	manufactured fiber
density	microscopic void
diameter	monomers
dimensional stability	natural fiber
drape	noncombustible fiber
elastic recovery	oleophilic fiber
electrical conductivity	oriented polymer chain
elongation	pilling
fiber	polymerization
filament fiber	polymers
fireproof fiber	protein
flame-resistant fiber	resiliency

shrinkage resistance	surface texture
soil repellency	tenacity
specific gravity	tensile strength
spinneret	texture
staple fibers	thermoplasticity
static electricity	yarn

Review Questions

1. Explain how generic classes are defined. Are there similarities among fibers within the same class? Are there differences, as well?

2. When will the burning test for fiber identification be useful? What is one distinctive reaction that will support the identification of protein fibers? Of cellulosic fibers?

3. Explain the difference between natural fibers and manufactured fibers.

4. What is one distinctive reaction that will support the identification of a thermoplastic fiber?

5. Identify some textural features of textile fibers that affect their hand, their luster, and their ability to adhere to one another.

6. Which fibers occur naturally in staple length? In filament length? Are manufactured fibers produced in staple or filament length?

7. Explain the types of manufactured fibers and how they differ.

8. Describe a procedure to identify the fiber content of an unknown fabric.

9. How do interior fiber voids obscure the appearance of soil?

10. How important is the *hand* of a textile product to consumers? Is hand largely subjective? What fiber features influence the hand of a textile?

11. How do the effects of abrasive forces on textile products show up to the consumer? How are abrasion and pilling related? How do fiber producers engineer fiber toughness? Why is it critical to select a fiber having relatively high abrasion resistance for use in soft floorcoverings?

12. How do the weight and cost of textile floorcoverings relate to the specific gravity of the fiber used?

13. Identify interior textile products whose serviceability is improved by having fibers exhibiting a high level of resiliency.

14. Discuss the influence of fiber stiffness on the resiliency and abrasion resistance of textile fabrics.

15. How can one predict fabric performance?

16. The breaking tenacities of cotton and flax are higher when the fibers are wet. Does this have an influence on their end-use performance?

17. Differentiate among these terms: flammable, flame resistant, noncombustible, and fireproof.

18. When is thermoplasticity of a fiber an advantage? When is it a disadvantage?

19. Can products composed of cotton be heat set? Explain your answer.

20. Distinguish between hydrophilic, hydrophobic, and hygroscopic fibers, and cite benefits and limitations of each fiber type.

5

Textile Fibers

Natural Fibers

Natural fibers are obtained from plants, animals, and minerals. Natural **cellulosic fibers** (plant fibers) are produced from the seeds, stems (bast), or leaves of plants. Cotton is a seed fiber, flax is an example of a bast fiber, sisal is a leaf fiber, coir is a husk fiber, and cork is taken from the bark of a tree. Natural **protein fibers** (animal fibers) are produced from animals. Wool fiber is obtained from the fleece of sheep and silk is harvested from silk cocoons. Mineral fibers are obtained from the earth; examples of these are glass and asbestos.

Natural Cellulosic Fibers

Plant fibers are primarily composed of **cellulose**, and therefore, as a class, are called cellulosic. As a group, they share some common properties including high absorbency, high moth resistance, low flame resistance, low resiliency, and low mildew resistance. Natural cellulosic fibers exhibit no static buildup and are stronger when wet. However, each fiber differs in the amount of cellulose, physical structure, and the type of molecular arrangement. These differences give fibers slight variations in properties and chemical reactions.

Cork

Cork is harvested by stripping the bark from the cork oak tree. After the tree matures the bark can be removed from the tree every nine years, making cork a renewable resource. The bark grows back and the tree can live up to 250 years. Cork is used in flooring, wallcovering, and furniture.

Cotton

Cotton fiber is the most widely used natural fiber in both the interior and apparel industries. It is generally believed that cotton was first cultivated in India and then spread to Egypt, China, Mexico, and Peru. Native American people grew cotton in the early 1500s and European colonists in the American south cultivated the crop by the late 1700s. For several hundred years, the time-consuming and tedious task of separating cotton fibers from the seed was done by hand. With the invention of the cotton gin in 1793 by Eli Whitney, the cotton fiber could be separated from the seed mechanically, making it possible to supply large quantities of cotton fiber to the fast-growing textile industry.

Cotton is grown in climates in which the growing season is long and hot, with adequate rainfall. Four varieties of cotton—Egyptian, Sea Island, American Pima, and Upland—are produced in the United States, China, India, Pakistan, Turkey, and Brazil. The United States produces primarily Upland cotton, a short staple variety. Egyptian, Sea Island, and American Pima are long staple cottons. Long staple fibers produce fabrics that are softer, smoother, and stronger with more sheen and a higher perceived value.

The cotton fibers grow inside the seedpod or boll of the plant, which splits open when the cotton fibers mature, exposing the fiber (Figure 5.1). Cotton fibers range in color from white to cream. The **ginning** process separates the fiber from the seeds and removes foreign matter. The ginned fiber, called **lint**, is sold to spinning mills for yarn production. The remaining seeds are covered with very short fibers called **linters**. The linters are separated from the seed and used in manufactured fiber production, such as rayon and acetate, paper, and plastic production. Linters are also processed into batting for padding mattresses, furniture, and automobile cushions. The seeds are used for livestock feed or processed into cottonseed oil, meal, and hulls.

Figure 5.1 Cotton boll. Courtesy of Amy Willbanks, www. textilefabric.com.

Cotton's staple length ranges from $1/2$ inch to $2^1/2$ inches, depending on the variety. Short staple fibers are **carded**, a manufacturing process that separates and aligns the fibers prior to spinning. Long staple fibers are carded and **combed**, a technique where the fibers are further aligned and the short staple fibers removed. Viewed under a microscope, the cotton fiber has ribbon-like twists that form a natural crimp, making it very cohesive and therefore easy to spin into yarn.

Cotton is relatively strong and has a soft hand. Cotton has excellent moisture absorption, is stronger wet than dry, and dries quickly—good features for apparel, household, and institutional textiles. Because twists in the fiber reflect light rays, the fiber has a matte luster. The luster, strength, and moisture absorption of the fiber can be increased with mercerization, a chemical treatment that can be applied to either the yarn or the fabric. Unlike wool, cotton lacks resiliency. Cotton is flammable and will decompose with prolonged exposure to sunlight. Cotton is resistant to moths but harmed by silverfish. Especially in humid climates, mildew can permanently damage cotton fabrics. Cotton is popular for draperies, bedding, towels, table linens, rugs, and upholstery fabrics. Figure 5.2 shows a collection of casual cotton stripes.

Compared to other plant fibers, the production of cotton has a negative impact on the environment. Twenty-five percent of all pesticides used in the United States are used on cotton crops. Some of these chemicals are among the most toxic as classified by the Environmental Protection Agency. In developing countries, where regulations are less stringent, the amount of pesticides and insecticides and their toxicity are often greater than in the United States. Cotton is also a very water-intensive crop, requiring a minimum of 15 to 20 inches per year. Cotton also depletes nutrients from soil.

Organic cotton is grown without synthetic chemicals and meets the standards established by certifying organizations to ensure fairness in the market. Organic cotton can be USDA certified (organically grown), but the processing of the fiber is not covered. **Natural-colored cotton** is grown in very limited shades of brown and green, eliminating the need for dyeing.

Cotton growers commonly use **genetically modified (GM)** cottonseeds. GM seeds are resistant to natural pests, which lowers the use of pesticides. Some experts

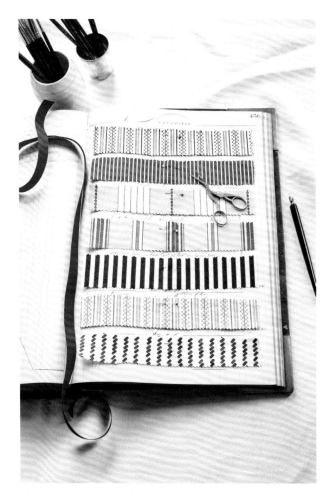

Figure 5.2 Collection of cotton stripes. Courtesy F. Schumacher & Co.

argue that this practice will contribute to the sustainability of cotton, but others argue that it is harmful to the environment. Cotton Incorporated is a U.S.-based company that promotes the use of cotton through education and marketing campaigns. The **Better Cotton Initiative (BCI)** is an organization whose members include retail stores, textile manufacturers, and cotton growers who promote environmental, social, and economical sustainable cotton production around the world.

Flax

Flax fiber is obtained from the stem of the flax plant and **linen** refers to cloth made from the flax fiber. It is the oldest of all domestically produced fibers. Flax is thought to have originated in the Mediterranean region of Europe. Remnants of linen have been found among the remains of the Swiss Lake Dwellers, who lived in the Stone Age. Linen cloth was used to wrap the mummies in the early Egyptian tombs. Medicinal uses for flax can be traced to the Ancient Greeks. Europe as well as the colonies had a vibrant flax industry up until the eighteenth century. With the invention of the cotton gin, cotton began to dominate the textile industry and flax production declined.

The flax plant grows to approximately 4 feet high and is usually planted very densely to minimize branching (Figure 5.3). Like all bast fibers, the fibrous strands are embedded longitudinally in the stem of the plant. The flax stalks are harvested by pulling them up by the roots then bundled and dried.

A series of steps follows which removes the seeds and breaks down the woody exterior separating the fiber from the stem and preparing the staple for spinning (Figure 5.4). The flax seeds are used in the food and feed industries and in the production of linseed oil. The majority of flax is grown in Belgium, France, the Netherlands, Ireland, Italy, and Germany.

Flax is a staple fiber that ranges from 12 to 24 inches in length. It is often used in its natural color, which ranges from a soft camel to taupe (Figure 5.5). Individual flax fibers are characterized by **nodes**, markings similar to those of bamboo, which givens linen fabrics a unique texture. The long fiber length gives flax more strength and more luster than cotton. Flax is stronger wet than dry and exhibits excellent absorbency, hence its use in table linens. Flax is highly resistant to damage from ultraviolet light and from insects, and more resistant to mildew than cotton is. Flax has extremely low elongation, low

Figure 5.4 Flax that has been hackled. Courtesy of CELC Masters of Linen.

flexibility, and low abrasion resistance. Its low flexibility is a problem, especially when linen fabrics are repeatedly folded on the same crease line for storage, as is the case with tablecloths and napkins (Figure 5.6).

Linen fabrics are appreciated for their crisp hand and textural interest. Due to poor elastic recovery, linen fabrics wrinkle. Flax is used in upholstery and drapery fabric, trimming, wallcoverings, toweling, bedding, and table linens. **Union**, a blend of cotton and linen, is a popular print ground cloth.

Flax production requires fewer chemicals and less water than does cotton, and therefore has less negative environmental impact. Because the flax plant is harvested by the roots soil erosion can be a problem. Significant amounts of water are used to process the fiber, but the water can be recycled.

Hemp

Hemp is another bast fiber with attributes similar to flax. The fiber comes from a tall shrub of the mulberry family

Figure 5.3 Flowering field of flax plants. Courtesy of CELC Masters of Linen.

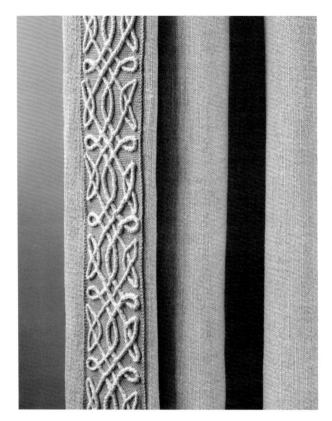

Figure 5.5 "La Terre Border" embellishes a linen drapery panel. Courtesy of Samuel & Sons, Inc.

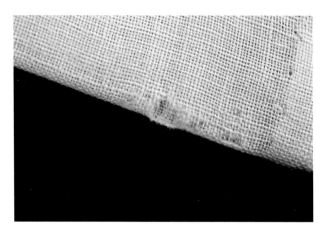

Figure 5.6 Folded linen fabric showing breakage. Courtesy of Amy Willbanks, www.textilefabric.com.

Figure 5.7 Hemp plant. Courtesy of CELC Masters of Linen.

that grow between 6 to 15 feet in height. The bark layer contains the long fibers that extend nearly the entire length of the stem (Figure 5.7). Hemp is fast growing and can be cultivated in many climate zones in a wide range of soils. Hemp fibers are separated from the stalk in much the same way that flax fibers are processed. By-products are hemp seeds and oil.

The use of hemp dates back the Stone Age, with hemp fiber imprints found in pottery shards in China more than 10,000 years old. Hemp has played a very important part in American history. In the early 1600s, hemp was considered such a vital resource that laws were passed ordering farmers to grow it. George Washington and Thomas Jefferson both grew hemp on their plantations. The Betsy Ross flag was made of hemp, and the Gutenberg Bible, the Declaration of Independence, and Lewis Carroll's *Alice's Adventures in Wonderland* were written on 100 percent hemp paper.

Hemp production has been the subject of a worldwide controversy. It is in the same plant family as cannabis; however, industrial hemp used for textiles has a very low content of THC (delta-9-tetrahydrocannabinol, the active hallucinatory ingredient in marijuana). Cultivation of hemp was illegal in the United States until legislation in the late 1990s allowed for minor production. Today, hemp production is allowed in many states with a few requiring licenses from the U.S. Drug Enforcement Administration (DEA). The majority of hemp in the United States is imported.

Because of its long fiber length, hemp exhibits high luster. Hemp fibers are similar to flax fibers in feel and texture. Like cotton and flax, hemp can withstand high temperatures. Hemp fiber is one of the most durable and strongest natural textile fibers. Hemp fibers are more absorbent and more mildew resistant, and they hold more insulation power than cotton does. Hemp withstands ultraviolet light rays and is less prone to fading than cotton fabrics are. Hemp fibers are easily damaged by strong acids, exhibit a high resistance to alkalis, and are difficult to bleach.

Hemp fiber has limited use in interior products such as bedding and rugs and as a print ground cloth. Anti-mildew and anti-microbial properties make hemp fibers very suitable for sails, awnings, and floorcoverings.

Jute

Jute is one of the least expensive fibers and is often used as a less expensive alternative to flax. It grows to a height of 15 to 20 feet and the fiber is extracted by the same basic method as for flax and hemp. Bangladesh is the world's largest producer and exporter of jute. Jute is grown throughout India, China, Pakistan, Nepal, Myanmar, and Thailand.

Jute is less uniform than flax and has a much rougher surface. Jute exhibits excellent absorbency, high covering power, poor flexibility, low elongation, and low elastic recovery. The majority of jute fiber goes into making rope, cordage, twine, and bagging. **Burlap** is a common fabric made from jute that is used for coffee and sugar bagging. Jute fiber is also used for carpet backing (Figure 5.8a), curtains, chair coverings, wallcoverings, and area rugs (Figure 5.8b). Jute has many advantages in residential and commercial textiles because of its sound and heat insulation and low thermal conduction. Its antistatic and fastness to ultraviolet light rays are also advantageous. As consumers demand more environmentally sensitive materials, the use of jute has been on the rise in interior products. It grows rapidly and requires modest amounts of fertilizer and pesticide. Jute products are 100 percent biodegradable and recyclable.

Figure 5.8 Jute products: (a) jute carpet backing, (b) jute rug.
Courtesy of Amy Willbanks, www.textilefabric.com.

Ramie

Ramie, a bast fiber from the ramie plant, is also known as grass cloth, rhea, or **China grass**. Ramie has been grown in China for thousands of years. Ramie is a tall perennial shrub that can be harvested several times a year. Ramie grows in hot, humid climates. The major producers of ramie are China, the Philippines, and Brazil. Ramie is a thin, pure white fiber with a cross-sectional shape similar to flax.

Ramie is higher in luster than flax because of its longer fiber length. It is also one of the strongest natural fibers and is highly resistant to mold, mildew, and insects. Like other bast fibers, ramie is stiff and will break if folded repeatedly. Ramie exhibits poor resiliency, poor elongation, poor elastic recovery, and has moderate abrasion resistance. Ramie is used for outdoor mats, in table linens, window treatments, and bath products.

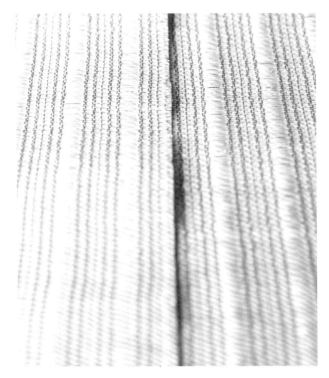

Figure 5.9 Sisal wallcovering. Courtesy Cowtan & Tout.

Sisal

Sisal is obtained from the leaves of the agave or yucca plant. The sisal plant consists of a rosette of sword-shaped leaves about 3 to 6 feet tall. The leaves are harvested and transported to a decortication plant that removes the non-fibrous parts of the plant. Mexico, Africa, South America, and Brazil are the leading producers of sisal.

Long a favorite carpeting material for porches and sunrooms, sisal can also be used creatively in more formal rooms. Sisal does not build up static, nor does it trap dirt. It is a strong, durable fiber and is resistant to seawater. Its outstanding weathering properties make it suitable for use in outdoor settings. Dyes are remarkably colorfast, but strong sunlight will fade the color over a period of time. Sisal fiber used for wallcovering (Figure 5.9) lends a naturally textured look to the walls in this bedroom.

Minor Natural Cellulosic Fibers

Abaca fiber comes from the leaf stem of the abaca plant, a member of the banana family. It has a natural luster because of its long fiber length. Strong and durable, abaca fiber is used for placemats for indoor/outdoor use, floorcovering, wallcovering, and production of wicker furniture.

Piña fiber is obtained from the leaves of a pineapple plant grown mainly in the Philippines. It is used to produce very lightweight, sheer fabrics. Piña fiber is used for placemats, embroidered tablecloths, and clothing.

Coir fibers are extracted husk of the coconut shell. Coir fibers are extremely stiff and are resistant to abrasion, water, and most weather conditions. These properties make coir suitable for indoor and outdoor mats, rugs, outdoor carpeting, and brushes. These products are extremely durable. Sri Lanka is the major producer of coir fiber.

Natural Protein Fibers

Natural protein fibers are obtained from animals. Wool and silk are the two major natural protein fibers. Because of their similar chemical composition, all protein fibers exhibit high resiliency, low density, high absorbency (hygroscopic), flammability resistance, and weaker wet strength.

Silk

Silk is a natural protein fiber discovered in China around 2700 B.C. The Chinese legend goes that Emperor Huang Ti, concerned about the imperial mulberry grove, appointed Empress Xi Lingshi to investigate the tiny white worms that were devouring the tree's leaves. Gathering a bundle of cocoons, the empress accidentally dropped a silkworm cocoon in her hot tea. She noticed that the cocoon separated into long, slender filaments. The empress learned to unwind the silk cocoon creating yarn. **Sericulture**, the production of cultivated silk, spread throughout China, and silk became a precious commodity highly sought by other countries. Today, the leading producers of silk are China, Japan, and India.

Silk is a natural animal fiber produced by the larvae of a silk caterpillar, often referred to as a silkworm. The larvae or caterpillar feeds on mulberry leaves, increasing in size until it begins spinning a cocoon (Figure 5.10).

In the process, the silkworm excretes both a protein material (silk) and a water-soluble gum called **sericin**. This substance keeps the stands of silk joined and

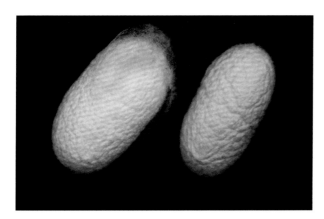

Figure 5.10 Silk cocoons. Courtesy of Amy Wilbanks, www
.textilefabric.com

provides a glue-like substance to hold the cocoon together. In order to harvest the silk, the sericin is softened in warm water, and skilled technicians collect the filament ends and unwind the cocoons. Filaments are combined to make a multifilament silk yarn.

Cultivated silk is the only natural fiber found in filament form. Silk fiber is long and thin and has a smooth surface. Silk has a triangular cross-sectional shape and is one of the strongest natural fibers, with medium elongation and moderate abrasion resistance. The silk fiber is weakened or **tendered** by sunlight. Silk is used in lined window treatments, for light upholstery, bedding, wallcoverings, and decorative table accessories. Silk is biodegradable and will decompose in landfills. Sustainable and eco-friendly silks that use low-impact and fiber-reactive dyes are available.

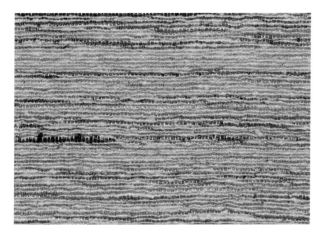

Figure 5.11 Tussah silk drapery fabric. Courtesy of Amy
Wilbanks, www.textilefabric.com

There are several varieties of silk. Staple-length silk, known as **noil**, is recovered and combined into spun silk yarns. If the sericin is left in place, the silk is marketed as **raw silk**. **Wild silk** is produced in a less controlled environment with the silkworms eating oak leaves instead of mulberry leaves. The cocoons are harvested after the moth has emerged, thus damaging the cocoon. Wild silk is only found in staple form, is much less uniform in texture and color. A common variety of wild silk is Tussah silk (Figure 5.11). **Dupioni silk** is a type of silk yarn that is a result of two silkworms spinning their cocoons together. The yarn has natural thick and thin areas and these variations give dupioni fabrics a subtle texture. This is a natural process and the amount and position of the thick and thin areas cannot be controlled.

Wool

Wool fiber comes from the fleece of sheep. Wool has many unique inherent properties, including flame resistance, thermal retention, and water repellency. Archeologists believe that wool fiber production began during the Stone Age, about 10,000 years ago. Primitive man had been using sheep for food and clothing for centuries. Between 3000 and 1000 B.C. the Persians, Greeks, and Romans distributed sheep and wool throughout Europe as they continued to improve breeds. The Romans took sheep with them as they built their empire in what is now Spain, North Africa, and the British Isles. Sheep were first introduced into what is now the southwest United States in 1519 by Spanish troops under Hernán Cortez.

Today, sheep thrive in all 50 states and in most countries of the world. Sheep can live on rough, barren land in high altitudes, converting vegetation to protein. The major producers of wool are Australia, New Zealand, China, and Argentina. **Shearing**, or removing the fleece from the sheep, is done once a year in the spring or early summer. The wool is then sorted and graded. Fiber length, diameter, luster, color, and age of the sheep determine the quality of wool. The grade of the fiber determines the type of product for which the wool will be used.

After shearing, the fibers are **scoured** to remove sand, dirt, plant material from the environment, and dried body excrement. A byproduct of scouring is grease or **lanolin** used in creams, soaps, lotions, cosmetics, and other pharmaceutical products.

Wool fibers range in length from 1/2 inch to 6 inches. The wool fiber is composed of three distinct parts. The center of the fiber contains hollow, honeycomb-shaped cells that give wool its excellent insulating power. The fiber has a natural **crimp** (bends and twists) along the length of the fiber. Crimp acts like a spring and increases the resiliency and elasticity of wool in fabrics and carpets. Traffic patterns are minimized in wool carpeting because the fibers exhibit high recovery to crushing; furthermore, its resiliency helps wool carpeting and draperies absorb sound and insulate against heat and cold. The outer structure is composed of over lapping scales. A thin, porous, wax-like **cuticle** that repels water as well as stains covers the scales. The outer scaly layer of the wool fiber also contributes to the wool's unique property of **felting**. In Figure 5.12, gray wool felt has been used as an applique. Under the mechanical action of agitation, friction, and pressure in the presence of heat and moisture, the scales on the edges of the wool fiber interlock. This process can be done in the fabric form or the fiber form, and adds weight and density to the fabric. The scaly structure also contributes to a scratchy hand that is disliked in warmer climates.

Wool fiber is hygroscopic, taking up moisture in vapor form. Tiny pores in the cuticle allow vapor to pass through to the center of the fiber. The high moisture content makes wool inherently flame resistant. Wool's crimp and scale structure lead to cohesive in the spinning process, producing very strong yarns. The fiber's high elongation and excellent elastic recovery also contribute to its high durability ratings.

Wool is a staple fiber and the fibers vary in length. Shorter fibers are cared and spun into woolen yarns. Fabrics made from woolen yarns exhibit more loft, or bulkiness; higher thermal retention, resulting in more warmth; and more covering power, for better insulation. **Worsted** yarns contain longer fibers that have been carded and combed, resulting in a finer, smoother, thinner fabric with a crisp hand.

Wool also stays cleaner longer than other fabrics. Because the high moisture content allows for less static, wool does not attract lint and dust. Wool's coiled fibers and their shingle-like structure also help keep dirt from penetrating its surface. Although wool fibers and products are relatively expensive, the positive characteristics make wool fiber highly desirable for upholstered furnishings, draperies, wallcoverings, blankets, and carpeting (Figure 5.13).

Wool fiber is often recycled for use by taking wool yarn or fabrics and converting them back to a fiber in a process called **garneting**. These wool fabrics made of recycled material must be so labeled according to the Wool Products Labeling Act. Recycled wools have been used in carpeting and apparel for decades and are

Figure 5.12 "Odette." Courtesy of Lori Weitzner.

Figure 5.13 Mulberry's "Bohemian Romance" collection.
Courtesy of Kravet Fabrics.

increasing in use because there is simply not enough wool for use on a worldwide scale.

Although it requires special production procedures and certification, **organic wool** represents a growing market in the wool industry. For wool to be certified as organic in the United States, it must be produced in accordance with federal standards for organic livestock production. Organic wool is in short supply; much of it comes from Australia and New Zealand. Organic wool is also getting attention from companies that produce bedding material. Several manufacturers produce organic wool blankets, and other manufacturers offer mattresses made from organic wool.

Minor Natural Protein Fibers

Minor protein fibers are obtained from animals in the goat, camel, and rabbit families (see Table 4.1). With the exception of mohair, these fibers have very limited use in interiors because of their high cost and limited supply. Many of these specialty fibers are blended with wool to add softness, texture, color interest, or to create a higher perceived value.

Alpaca fibers are obtained from the hair of a domesticated animal of the camel family. Alpacas are native to the Andes mountains. The fibers are soft, fine, and lustrous and are used in upholstery fabrics and rugs. Alpaca fibers are typically used in their natural colors, which include a range of whites, browns, grays, and blacks.

Mohair is the fiber of the Angora goat. The goats are sheared twice a year. Its smooth fibers up of to 12 inches in length give mohair a lustrous appearance. The fiber is very resilient and has fewer scales and less crimp than wool. Because it resists crushing, mohair is popular in upholstery fabrics, particularly pile fabrics, in spite of its high price tag (Figure 5.14). Its thermal retention properties help mohair blankets retain their heat. South Africa is the largest producer of mohair fiber, supplying more than half of the world's total production. Other major producers are the United States and Turkey. Even though mohair comes from an Angora goat, it is not called Angora.

Angora is the fur of the Angora rabbit. This domesticated rabbit is raised in the United States, France,

Figure 5.14 Mohair velvet upholstered on a chair. Courtesy of Joseph Noble, Inc.

Italy, and Japan. The fiber is obtained by plucking or shearing. Angora fiber is very soft and smooth. The smoothness of the fiber contributes to its low cohesiveness and for this reason; angora is often blended with sheep's wool. Angora fiber has a high thermal retention and is used in blankets and bedding products.

Camel's hair is the fiber of the two-humped Bactrian camel and provides the best insulation of all the specialty wools. The Bactrian camel originally came from North Afghanistan but today they are found living in Turkey, China, and Siberia. In the spring of every year, the fiber is gathered by hand, when the camels shed their outer hair and undercoat. A camel produces about 5 pounds of fiber per year. It is typically used undyed, in its natural state.

Llama fibers, like alpaca fibers, are also obtained from the hair of a domesticated animal of the camel family. Llama fibers are coarser and less strong than alpaca fiber. Llama fibers are used, on a limited basis, for rugs.

Cashmere fiber is the fleece of a cashmere goat and is one of the softest, most expensive fibers produced. The fiber is obtained by combing the domesticated animals during the molting season. Cashmere fibers are used for bedding, blankets, and for light upholstery. More than half of all cashmere fiber is produced by China, followed by Mongolia, Afghanistan, and Iran.

Manufactured Fibers

Manufactured fibers are made using raw materials derived from natural products, minerals, synthetic chemicals, or a combination of these. Currently, four major groups of manufactured fibers are produced: regenerated fibers, synthetic fibers, mineral fibers, and biopolymer fibers. Manufactured fibers are engineered for specific end-uses and are more versatile than natural fibers. Many different fiber profiles are offered under brand names by particular manufacturers, while the generic form of any fiber is a distinct chemical unit.

Production

The initial stage of manufactured fiber production involves preparing the fiber-forming solution. These substances can be regenerated or chemically altered cellulosic material extracted from plant matter, such as wood pulp or protein material taken from soybeans. Non-fibrous material such as natural gas, oil, and coal can be synthesized to form synthetic fibers. Inorganic compounds are used to from metal and glass fibers. Even though the substances used are natural, the process of chemically altering the solution to form fiber is highly polluting.

The second stage of spinning process is called **extrusion**. The fiber-forming substance, known as **dope,** is extruded, or forced through a device called a **spinneret**. As illustrated in Figure 5.15a, a spinneret is similar to a showerhead. In the same manner as pressure forces water through a showerhead, pressure forces the dope through the minute openings in the spinneret.

The cross-sectional shape and size of the spinneret can be adjusted to alter the fiber's physical and aesthetic properties. Improvements in hand, soil-hiding capacity, wicking, and absorbency can be produced. Thick and

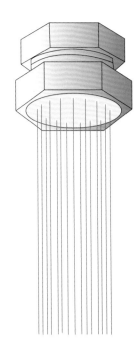

(a)

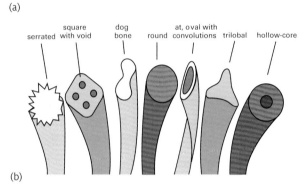

(b)

Figure 5.15 Fiber manufacturing process: (a) spinneret device for extruding manufactured fibers, (b) various cross-sectional shapes of manufactured fibers achieved by varying the shape of spinneret openings. Illustration by Andrea Lau/Fairchild Books; illustration by Lauren Rudd/Fairchild Books.

thin fibers can be created with variations in the diameter along their length, producing fabrics similar to linen or wild silk (Figure 5.15b).

Next the fiber is solidified using a variety of spinning techniques, depending on the fiber. The spinning process can be modified to produce crimp, which provides bulk or stretch and makes yarn spinning easier. Drawing stretches or lengthens the filament, reducing the diameter and further stabilizing the fiber. Filament can either be used as yarn or cut into short staple lengths, which are then spun into yarn.

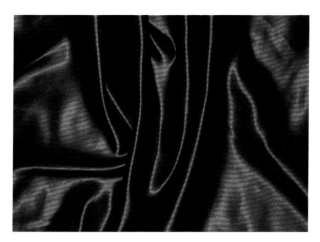

Figure 5.16 Satin fabric made from acetate fiber. Courtesy of Amy Willbanks, www.textilefabric.com.

Fiber Variants

Fiber modifications can be made in four general ways: the spinneret can be changed to produce fibers of different sizes and shapes, the fiber's molecular structure and orientation can be changed to enhance fiber durability, components (additives) including other fibers can be added to the fiber solution, and varied spinning processes can enhance fiber characteristics.

Manufactures develop fiber variations, even with fibers in the same generic class. These modifications impart particular features into a fiber and are often given **trade names** for marketing purposes. For example, among several polyester fibers, one may have a pentalobal cross-sectional shape, be inherently flame resistant, and dull; yet another may be inherently antistatic, have a relatively small diameter, and be bright. The availability of hundreds of **fiber variants** enables end-product manufacturers to be highly selective.

In turn, this helps them to offer a wide variety of products.

After the fiber forming solution is made, the producer may incorporate **additives** to engineer specific properties. Such additives include dye pigments for superior colorfastness, optical brighteners to improve apparent whiteness and brightness, ultraviolet absorbers to minimize light degradation, flame retardant agents to reduce flammability, **delusterants** to reduce light reflectance and hide accumulated soil, and antistatic agents to increase electrical conductivity.

Regenerated Cellulosic Fibers

In the 1800s and early 1900s, chemists sought to invent a fiber to substitute for the luxurious but costly silk. **Artificial silk** was created in the late 1800s, and the fibers were commercially produced in the United States in 1910. Because of negative connotations associated with the term artificial, fiber producers changed the name to rayon. Further work resulted in acetate's introduction to consumers in 1924. Regardless of the raw material used, **regenerated fibers** convert a natural substance that is not in fiber to a fiber. This is done through a lengthy and highly polluting chemical process.

Acetate

Acetate begins with cellulose, generally from trees, cotton linters, or bamboo. Fabrics of acetate have high drapability and the look and feel of silk, but are more reasonably priced (see Figure 5.16). A major problem is gasfastness. With exposure to such gaseous pollutants or air contaminants as oxides of nitrogen or sulfur, some dyed acetate fabrics permanently change color. This can be prevented with solution dyeing, as described in Chapter 9. Acetate is heat sensitive and consumers must be cautious with high temperatures to avoid melting.

Rayon

Rayon was the first regenerated cellulose fiber and is obtained from wood pulp and cotton waste. Rayon has a soft hand and is highly drapable. Short, staple-length fibers give a cotton-like look and feel to fabrics but with a smoother hand and more sheen. In filament form the fiber has luster similar to silk, and is often used in lieu of the more expensive fibers. Yarn used to create embroidery (Figure 5.17) is often composed of rayon. The sheen of the fiber adds a reflective quality to the fabrics.

Rayon has undergone many improvements over the years; however, it is not as strong as cotton and not dimensionally stable when wet. For this reason rayon is often blended with other fibers. It adds softness and luster to cotton fabrics used for upholstery, table linens, and blankets. For drapery, an acetate/rayon blend is popular. It also is used in trimmings such as cords and galloons. Rayon can also be identified as viscose. The following

Figure 5.17 Embroidered fabric. Courtesy of Kravet, Inc.

and antimicrobial properties, however, these properties are destroyed during the regeneration process. Bamboo rayon is soft, comfortable, absorbent, and wicks water away from the body faster than cotton.

Regenerated Protein Fibers

Regenerated protein fibers are made from naturally occurring protein polymers. These polymers do not occur naturally as fibers. Further processing is needed to convert them into fiber form.

Azlon

Azlon is a manufactured fiber composed of any regenerated naturally occurring proteins. **SoySilk®**, a registered trade name of SWTC, Inc., is an azlon fiber made out of soybean residue from the tofu manufacturing process. SoySilk exhibits good colorfastness and excellent absorbency and comfort. Soy products are found mainly as sheets in the interior furnishings industry.

Synthetic Fibers

Synthetic fibers are derived from such materials as natural gas, oil, and coal. Even though their chemical compositions vary, synthetic fibers have similar positive and negative attributes. They are wrinkle resistant and easy care. Known for their durability, synthetics also offer resistance to moths and mildew. Synthetics have a low moisture absorbency, which makes them excellent for end-uses that call for water repellency, such as outdoor furniture coverings. They collect static electricity, which can lead to pilling. Synthetics are widely used in upholstery, drapery, and carpeting, particularly in commercial interiors where performance and cost are determining factors. Synthetic fibers are continually being modified to improved performance.

Acrylic

Acrylic was developed to resemble wool. It has a low specific gravity and high bulkiness, which makes it successful in end-uses such as blankets that require warmth without the weight. Acrylic can be laundered rather than dry-cleaned; has an inherent resistance to

are variations of rayon that utilize unique material or are processed slightly differently. It cannot be overstated that these regenerated cellulosic fibers begin with an organic matter, however the chemicals used in processing the fiber are as polluting as those used to process rayon.

Lyocell is variation of rayon, marketed under Tencel®, a Lenzing AG trade name. The fiber-forming substance is the same as rayon, however, the spinning process employed is different, which gives lyocell higher tensile strength as well as higher wet strength. Almost all of the organic solvents used to make lyocell can be recycled.

Modal® is a registered trade name for a type of rayon derived exclusively from beech trees. Modal is very soft and is popular for household textiles, such as bedding, upholstery, and towels.

Bamboo rayon is a regenerated fiber obtained from the bamboo plant. It is fast growing, reaches maturity quickly and does not require the use of pesticides, herbicides, or fertilizers. Bamboo takes five years to mature but once mature can be re-harvested. China and Taiwan produce bamboo for fiber. The fiber is smooth, strong, durable, and long lasting. It also has antibacterial

moths, carpet beetles, and the outdoor elements; and has superior resistance to the damaging rays in sunlight. Foamed acrylic can be applied as a coating to drapery fabrics and linings for sound and heat insulation, temperature control, and room darkening features.

Acrylic has low abrasion resistance and cannot be treated for flammability, which make it a less-than-ideal choice for commercial interiors. Sunbrella®, a trade name for a solution-dyed acrylic from Glen Raven, Inc., has gained popularity for use in residential interiors for both indoor and outdoor use (Figure 5.18). With solution dyeing, dyes are added to the chemical bath before the fiber is extruded, locking the color to the fiber.

Modacrylic

Modacrylic was developed to offer a higher level of flame resistance than regular acrylic. To a great extent, modacrylic has been replaced in the marketplace by inherently flame resistant polyester.

Nylon

Nylon fibers were the first truly synthesized manufactured fibers. They were unceremoniously introduced into the consumer market in 1938 as a replacement for boar's bristles in toothbrushes. During World War II, when silk inventories were stockpiled for use in parachute manufacture, nylon moved into hosiery.

Figure 5.19 Nylon carpet samples. Courtesy of INVISTA Sarl.

Selected features can be engineered into the nylon fiber, such as a change in hand or luster and the ability to hide soil. Drawing and **heat setting** are controlled to engineer the desired amount of strength, elongation, abrasion resistance, and resiliency. Nylon has excellent resilience, making it the number one choice for carpeting in the United States (Figure 5.19). Fiber from nylon carpeting can be recycled and, unlike recycled polyester that degrades in the recycling process, nylon can be endlessly recycled. The strength and abrasion resistance of nylon fibers support their use upholstery fabrics. Nylon has poor moisture regain and sags quite badly when used on vertical applications such as wallcovering, panel cloths, or drapery.

Olefin

The **olefin** fiber is made from ethylene, a byproduct of the natural gas industry, and is also referred to as **polypropylene**. Of all of the synthetic fibers, olefin is the least toxic to produce and requires the least amount of energy. Like acrylic, olefin is lightweight and bulky.

Olefin is an excellent fiber choice for upholstery or carpeting where performance and low cost are a

Figure 5.18 Sunbrella fabric. Courtesy of Glen Raven, Inc.

Figure 5.20 Olefin upholstery fabric. Courtesy of Amy Willbanks, www.textilefabric.com.

consideration (Figure 5.20). It is moisture resistant and chemical resistant, stain resistant, abrasion resistant, colorfast, generates low static electricity. Its main drawback is that olefin can only be solution dyed, limiting the color range. Additionally, it cannot be treated to pass the most stringent flammability tests because of its moisture resistance.

Olefin has almost completely replaced jute in carpet backing because of its low cost, easy processing, and excellent durability. Olefin is also used for draperies, slipcovers, and automotive interiors. The first high-performance wallcoverings were made of olefin, which remains the dominant fiber in that market.

Polyester

Although **polyester** has been available in the domestic market since 1953, its importance has grown dramatically for both the apparel and interior textile industries. Polyester is the most widely used synthetic fiber. Manufacturers have the ability to engineer polyester's properties by controlling the shape and form of the fibers. With drawing and heat setting, the strength, elongation, abrasion resistance, resiliency, dimensional stability, and general appearance of the fiber can also be controlled.

Polyester is preferred for vertical surfaces such as drapery, privacy curtains in healthcare settings, and panel fabrics. For upholstery applications, polyester has excellent strength as well as abrasion resistance. In staple form, polyester is versatile and blends well with other fibers. Polyester's main sustainability advantage lies in its recyclability. Recycled polyester comes from two main sources: post-consumer (e.g., plastic bottles) and post-industrial waste (fiber, carpeting, or off-spec polyester products).

Inherently flame-retardant polyester is the preferred choice for vertical applications in public spaces that require the most rigorous flammability standards, such as window treatments in hotels or privacy curtains in hospitals. The flame-retardant properties do not degrade through cleaning or with age. Trevira CS®, a trade name of Trevira GmbH, is a brand of such a fiber. For the maritime sector, Trevira CS meets international fire safety standards.

Polyurethane

Polyurethane is a soft, durable, and highly versatile fiber that is the predominate material used in upholstery cushions and mattresses. In film form, polyurethane has gained popular as a replacement for vinyl. It is suppler than vinyl and requires a woven backing for dimensional stability. Polyurethane is more durable to abrasion and more puncture proof, however it is also a more expensive alternative. The hand of polyurethane and vinyl are very different with vinyl having a more plastic feel and polyurethane having a more rubber like feel. Heat and moisture weaken polyurethane causing flaking and peeling.

Spandex or Elastane

Spandex, also called **elastane**, is modified polyurethane engineered to be an elastomeric fiber. The term *spandex* is more commonly used in the United States, with *elastane* used more commonly worldwide. With superior strength and durability, it has replaced rubber as the number one elastic fiber. These fibers have high elongation, high elastic recovery, and high holding power. Lycra®, a trade name owned by Invista, is commonly used in apparel. In recent years, their superior elasticity supports the use of elastic fibers in upholstery fabrics that are applied to furniture with curved forms and convex and concave shapes.

PVC

PVC (polyvinyl chloride) is the name for the fiber-forming substance that in film form is commonly called **vinyl**.

Figure 5.22 "Bulldog vinyl" sample. Courtesy Joseph Noble, Inc.

Figure 5.21 "Ruin vinyl" upholstered on a chair. Courtesy Joseph Noble, Inc.

PVC was the basis for the very first man-made fiber; an early brand name was **vinyon**. PVC can also be extruded into a yarn and woven into fabrics. Chilewich uses this yarn to create washable placemats and outdoor fabrics. PVC fibers have excellent resistance to chemicals, bacteria, and insects. Vinyl used as wallcovering and as upholstery is a ubiquitous and practical choice for restaurants and hospitals where water repellency and easy cleaning is essential. A knit backing is applied to vinyl to make it more dimensionally stable. Vinyl can be embossed (Figure 5.21 and Figure 5.22) or printed. Vinyl has made strides in the flooring industry virtually, replacing linoleum for residential use.

Mineral Fibers

Mineral fibers, glass, asbestos, and **metallic fibers** are obtained from the ground. As a known carcinogen, asbestos is no longer used. Glass fabrics were popular as curtains in the 1960s as an early solution to flammability in public spaces but have since been replaced with flame retardant polyester. Fabrics made of glass fibers are heavy for drapery and irritating to the skin for upholstery. They have, however, found a use in mattresses as a flameproof barrier fabric. Precious metal threads made from silver and gold were used historically to adorn rich brocades. Today, less expensive metals such as aluminum replicate the same effect. Stainless steel fibers are incorporated into carpeting and upholstery to reduce static electricity.

Bioploymer Fibers

Biopolymer fibers are a type of regenerated fiber that offers the easy care and durability performance characteristics of synthetics, while claiming to incorporate the sustainability attribute of replacing a portion of the petrochemical makeup with natural, renewably sourced components.

PLA

PLA (polylactic acid) is a manufactured dextrose fiber produced from corn. PLA products have a combination of features similar to those of cotton: comfortable hand and excellent absorbency and resiliency. PLA is soil-resistant and exhibits high UV resistance, which promotes its use in outdoor furniture and furnishings applications, although at a higher cost than vinyl.

PLA gives off fewer toxic chemicals than petroleum plastics and uses less energy in the manufacturing process. However, environmental groups have questioned the eco-friendliness of PLA on several fronts. PLA uses genetically engineered corn seeds, which most developed nations have deemed unsafe. Products made from PLA are compostable, however, only at high temperatures used by commercial composters. Containers made from PLA included in recycling bins contaminate petroleum plastics, which are highly recyclable. Finally, a debate continues as to whether limited natural resources should be used for products or for food.

Fiber Developments

Today's new fibers and textile materials are coming into being thanks to new technologies. Compared to the wave of new fibers created in the latter half of the twentieth century, the emerging technologies of the last two decades may not be as broad in scope, but specialized solutions are being discovered to meet specific challenges and solve real problems. Textiles for commercial spaces demand durability along with more sustainable products. Fiber suppliers will continue to improve fibers used in athletic wear, safety clothing for industry, military, police, and firefighters, as well as for automotive.

Microfibers are superfine synthetic filaments that are grouped together to make a yarn that produces soft, fluid, silky fabrics with exceptional drapability. Although the filaments are fine, the strength is exceptional. Both heavyweight and lightweight fabrics can be sueded or sanded without affecting the strength. With more filaments comes more surface area as well. This allows printed fabrics to be vivid, with more clarity and a sharper contrast. A microfiber lets a comforter retain its loft, fullness, ample shape, and airiness. Window coverings drape exceptionally well. Manufacturers claim that microfibers have the comfort and feel of natural fibers with the strength and easy care of manufactured fibers. However, microfibers still have some of the undesirable characteristics of synthetic fibers, such as lack of breathability. Recently, environmentalists found an abundance of microfibers shed from clothing in rivers, lakes, and oceans. These plastic fibers make up the bulk of the debris along U.S. shorelines. The fibers are so small that fish readily consume them, creating a toxic food source.

Nanotechnology is the science and technology of manipulating individual atoms to enhance product performance. Traditional treatments coat the fiber, fabric, or product, affecting the hand, look, and color of the fabric. The molecules in nanotechnology permanently attach to the fiber without changing the feel and appearance. A permanent bond is established that does not affect the hand, look, or color of the product. This leads to superior performance characteristics for fabrics, such as increased resistance to spills, stains, microbes, and static. Moisture-wicking characteristics can also be improved using nanotechnology. Nanotechnology continues to grow in importance in the home furnishings industry. Developments in fiber engineering continue today. Other marketing tools, such as trade names and logos, are extensively used for the purposes of promotion and marketing (see Chapter 11).

Environmental Stewardship

Consumer awareness of the importance of **environmental stewardship** has led to increased demand for products manufactured with minimal impact on the world's well-being. The demand for textiles that have a green pedigree has grown even in the face of economic hardships endured by many consumers. Using recycled raw materials rather than virgin materials to make these products potentially conserves natural resources, reduces energy consumption, carbon dioxide and other emissions, and landfill waste.[1] Chapter 3 covers the industry approaches to evaluating and comparing sustainable initiatives. With the textile industry's increasing focus on sustainability, fibers are often the first consideration in the quest to make fabrics more eco-friendly. Every fiber has a footprint and an impact on the environmental. With the population set to increase to 9 billion by 2050, needs for fiber supply will be high, and increasing, in the next decades. Balancing environmental and economic sustainability to meet projected demand is key to any discussion or definition of sustainability across the home furnishings chain.[2]

Key Terms

abaca	lanolin
acetate	linen
acrylic	lint
alpaca	linters
Angora	llama
artificial silk	lyocell
asbestos	manufactured fiber
azlon	metallic fibers
bamboo	microfiber
Better Cotton Initiative	mineral fiber
(BCI)	minor protein fiber
biopolymer fiber	modacrylic
burlap	Modal®
camel's hair	mohair
carded	nanotechnology
cashmere	natural-colored cotton
cellulose	nodes
cellulosic fiber	noil
China grass	nylon
coir	olefin
combed	organic cotton
cork	organic wool
cotton	piña
crimp	PLA
cuticle	polyester
delusterant	polypropylene
dope	polyurethane
drawing	protein fibers
dupioni silk	PVC
environmental	ramie
stewardship	raw silk
extrusion	rayon
felting	regenerated fiber
fiber variant	scouring
flax	sericin
garneting	sericulture
genetically modified (GM)	shearing
ginning	silk
glass	sisal
heat setting	SoySilk®
hemp	spandex
jute	spinneret

synthetic fiber	vinyon
tendered	wild silk
trade name	wool
vinyl	worsted

Review Questions

1. Cite both positive and negative properties of wool.
2. Why is silk not vulnerable to moth attack (as long as the fiber is clean)?
3. Discuss the positive and negative features of genetically modified cotton.
4. Identify properties of cotton that support its use in residential and commercial textiles.
5. Distinguish among the following terms: flax plant, flax fiber, linen, and linens.
6. Why has the use of asbestos been discontinued?
7. Trace the production sequence of manufactured fibers. Explain how fiber engineering is accomplished during the production.
8. How does heat setting benefit the consumer? Are there concomitant challenges?
9. Acetate, rayon, and lyocell are cellulosic in nature. Why aren't these fabrics called natural cellulosic fibers?
10. What advantages do acrylic fibers offer over wool fibers?
11. What fiber features can be engineered by using a particular shape for the spinneret openings? Which fibers retain the shape of the openings?
12. What properties support the use of olefin and saran fibers in outdoor textile applications?
13. Why is hemp considered to be more environmentally friendly than cotton?
14. Define microfiber, and state the advantages of using microfibers in home furnishings.
15. Discuss the manufacture of PLA, and list negative and positive properties.

16. Discuss the differences in regenerated fibers and synthetic fibers.
17. List common properties of both natural protein fibers and natural cellulosic fibers.
18. What is a bio-polymer fiber? Identify a bio-polymer fiber, and discuss the positive and negative properties.

Notes

1. Janet Rodie. (2010). "From Waste to Worth." Textile World, November/December 2010, p. 24.
2. Maria Thiry. (2012). "Naturally Good," AATCC Review, Vol. 11, No. 3, p. 25.

6

Textile Yarns and Yarn-Like Structures

All textile yarns, like textile fibers, must be relatively long and thin to provide the flexibility required in manufacturing and use. However, yarns can have marked differences in their degrees of twist, textural characteristics, complexity, and relative fineness. The fineness of yarns can be measured and reported in numerical terms. These numbers, along with other notations, are used in designations of yarn construction.

Yarns can be divided into two categories: simple yarns, and novelty yarns that have slubs, loops, and other irregular textural effects that add tactile and visual interest. This chapter describes the production and qualities of a widely array of yarns.

Yarn Production

Yarns are produced as spun yarns, monofilament yarns, filament yarns, or textured filament yarns. Spinners produce spun yarns, fiber producers manufacture monofilament yarns, and **throwsters** produce filament and textured filament yarns.

Spun Yarns

Spun yarns are composed of staple fibers that are twisted together to form a yarn (Figure 6.1). The amount of twist, measured in twists per inch, can be manipulated. The greater the amount of twist, the stronger the yarn, however, the greater the amount of twists, the harder the hand of the textile. For example, yarns intended for sweaters have low twist, revealing more fiber and creating a soft, comfortable hand. Yarns used for commercial upholstery are highly twisted, creating strength over comfort. Because spun yarns have many fiber ends protruding from their surfaces, their level of light reflectance is less than that of multifilament yarns. Spun yarns are used to provide warmth, softness, and absorbency.

Spinning Spun Yarns

The spinning process is similar for all staple fibers. Fibers are aligned and twisted creating one continuous strand called yarn. Different fibers require different processing to prepare the fiber for spinning. Because natural fibers

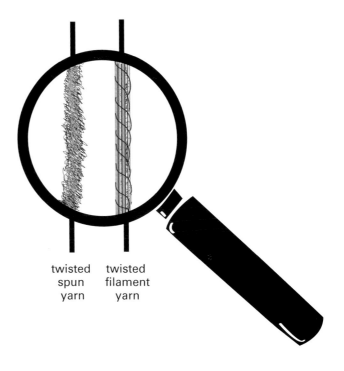

twisted
spun
yarn

twisted
filament
yarn

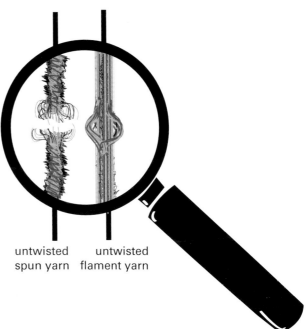

untwisted
spun yarn

untwisted
flament yarn

Figure 6.1 Spun yarn and filament yarn. Illustration by Lauren Rudd/Fairchild Books.

vary in staple length, each requires a unique spinning system. Manufactured filament fibers can be cut into staple lengths and spun using these same systems. To better understand the spinning process, the next sections take a closer look at the cotton, wool, and linen spinning systems.

Cotton System

The following summary identifies the basic procedures used in the cotton spinning system and describes the changes produced in each step:

- **Opening and cleaning**: Loosening, cleaning, and blending the cotton fibers.
- **Picking**: Fluffing the compacted fibers into a loose, disoriented mass.
- **Carding**: Initially aligning the fibers in a somewhat parallel fashion and forming a carded **sliver**, a long, loose strand that is approximately 1 inch in diameter.
- **Combing**: Further aligning the fibers and separating the shorter staples before forming a combed sliver.
- **Drawing out**: Reducing the diameter of the sliver to produce a **roving**, a long, fine strand that is approximately $1/4$ inch in diameter.
- Spinning and twisting: Reducing the diameter of the roving and twisting the resulting fine strand into a usable spun yarn.

The cotton system is used for spinning fibers that are approximately $1/2$ inch to $1 1/2$ inches in length. Not all cotton goes through the combing stage. Carded cotton is uncombed, has a combination of long and short fibers, and the fibers are less aligned. With combed cotton, the shorter fibers have been combed out, leaving longer fibers more highly aligned. This additional process creates a stronger, smoother, more lustrous yarn. Today, polyester and rayon staples, alone or blended with cotton, are frequently spun on the cotton system.

Woolen and Worsted Systems

Wool has two spinning systems, woolen and worsted. The basic equipment in the woolen spinning system is designed to handle fibers from 2 to 3 inches in length; in the worsted system it is designed to handle fibers from 3 to 5 inches in length. Spinners can adjust the equipment, however, to spin the longer staples frequently used in interior textile yarns. **Woolen yarns**, like carded yarns, have varied lengths of staples and less fiber alignment; **worsted yarns**, like combed yarns, contain only long staples that are highly aligned. Figure 6.2 is a single woolen yarn.

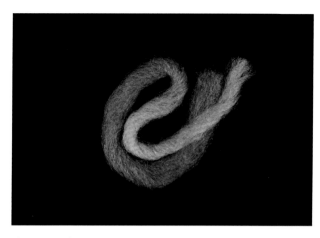

Figure 6.2 Singles woolen yarn. Yarn courtesy of Textile Fabric Consultants. Photo courtesy of Max Concra.

Linen System

The linen spinning system is designed to align and twist flax tow fibers, which are approximately 12 inches in length, and flax line fibers, which are approximately 24 inches in length. **Tow fibers** are spun into relatively heavy yarns for use in interior textile products such as wallcoverings, upholstery, and drapery fabrics, while **line fibers** are spun into fine yarns for use in such items as woven table linens and bed sheets.

Filament Yarns

Filament yarns, natural or manmade, are one continuous strand. Manufactured fibers are extruded directly from the spinneret. Silk is a naturally occurring filament fiber. Filament yarns from manufactured fibers can be monofilament or multifilament. Fiber producers produce **monofilament** yarns (Figure 6.3) that are composed of one single filament. For strength and stability, the filament has a relatively large diameter and is drawn and heat set. Monofilament yarns are often used in the production of lightweight, translucent window coverings (Figure 15.4, p. 200). They are also used as strong sewing thread in the construction of many interior textile products.

Throwsters produce **multifilament yarns**. Multifilament yarns are made from filament fibers and are typically referred to as simply **filament yarns** (refer to Figure 6.1). Long length of silk and manufactured filament are combined or thrown together into multifilament (Figure 6.4) yarn structures; no textile yarn spinning

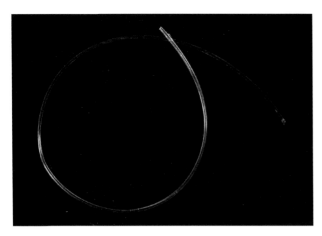

Figure 6.3 Monofilament yarn. Yarn courtesy of Textile Fabric Consultants. Photo courtesy of Max Concra.

process is required. The throwster needs only to gather and twist several of the fine strands.

Typically, filament yarns are more uniform, stronger, and more lustrous than spun yarns. There is less propensity for pilling in a filament yarn because there are no fiber ends protruding from the fabric surface. Filament yarns are used in fabrics where smoothness and luster are desired.

Textured Filament Yarns

Throwsters may use a texturing process to introduce such characteristics as bulk and cohesiveness to groups of filament. These yarns are designated as **textured filament yarns** or **bulk continuous filament (BCF)**. **Texturing**

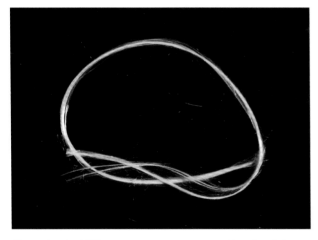

Figure 6.4 Multifilament yarns. Yarn courtesy of Textile Fabric Consultants. Photo courtesy of Max Concra.

processes introduce multidimensional configurations to otherwise parallel and smooth filaments. Such physical changes may decrease strength, but they can impart elasticity, create a softer, warmer hand, help to simulate a natural appearance, and increase fiber cohesiveness. They also increase the bulk or apparent volume of the grouped filaments to provide greater covering power, as shown in Figure 6.5. In use, fabrics composed of textured yarns conceal dirt and wear.

Some filament fibers are chopped into short staple fiber lengths and later processed into spun yarns. When filaments are to be reduced to staple lengths and spun into yarns, they are first grouped into a rope-like bundle known as **tow**. This untwisted bundle is then textured to impart the fiber cohesiveness required for the production of spun yarns. The textured tow is stretched or cut into staple fibers of the desired length, generally from 1 to 6 inches.

Yarn Twisting

Twisting must be used for all spun yarns, and while it is optional for multifilament yarns, it is generally used to stabilize the fine, parallel filaments. The amount of twist as well as the direction of the twist can be adjusted.

Level of Twist

The level or amount of twist used in yarn formation is denoted by the number of **turns per inch (tpi)**. The tpi affects the appearance and the durability of yarns. Multifilament yarns may have low twist (2 to 3 tpi) because twist does not increase the strength, but some twist is needed to keep the yarn together. Filaments can be made with high tpi to produce a pebbly, bumpy surface effect, referred to as **crepe filament yarns**.

Spun yarns require higher twist (30 to 40 tpi) to hold the fibers together. Low levels of twist create spun yarns that are bulky and soft, but weak. High twist produces stronger, smoother, more lustrous yarns. If too much twist is applied, kinks and ridges may form, reducing the elasticity and strength of the yarns.

Throwsters and spinners use a variety of techniques to control the aesthetic features and service-related qualities of yarns and expand the assortment of yarns available to producers and consumers. They may vary

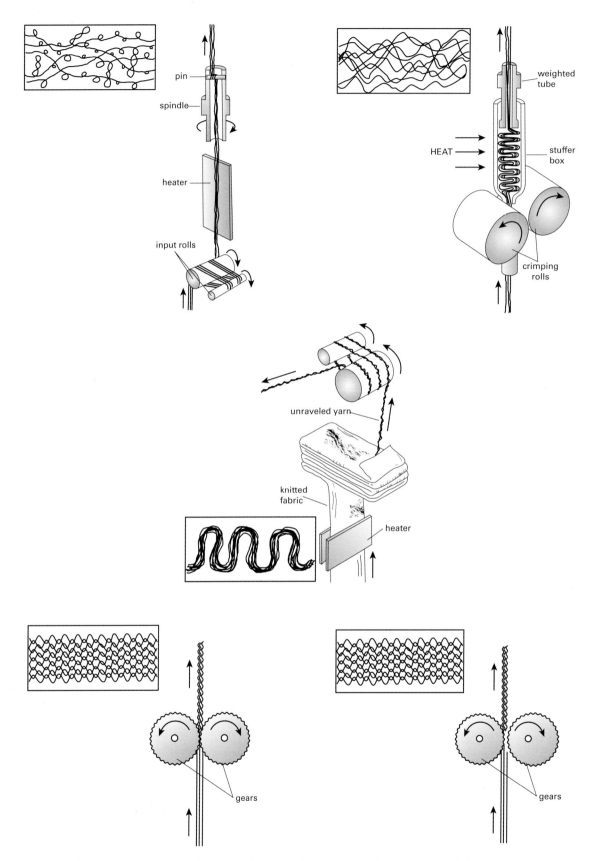

Figure 6.5 **Yarn texturing processes: (a) false-twist coiling, (b) stuffer-box crimping, (c) air jet, (d) knit-de-knit crinkling, (e) gear crimping.** Fairchild Books.

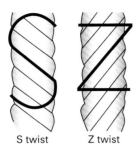

S twist · Z twist

Figure 6.6 Direction of twist in textile yarn. Illustration by Andrea Lau/Fairchild Books.

the level of twist used, introduce decorative effects, or combine various numbers and types of yarn strands. The resulting yarns are then classified and named on the basis of their structural characteristics.

Direction of Twist

In addition to the amount of twist in a yarn, the direction of the twist is also designated. The letters S and Z are used to describe the direction of twist in all textile yarns (Figure 6.6). A left-handed or counterclockwise twist is called an **S twist** and a right-handed or clockwise twist is termed a **Z twist**.

Yarn Classification and Nomenclature

Yarns produced by throwing or spinning textile fibers are classified and described by the number of their parts and their design features. A brief outline will serve to introduce the classification system used with textile yarns and the extensive number of names used for decorative yarns.

I. Simple yarns
   1. Single
   2. Ply
   3. Cord
   4. Cable
   5. Rope

II. Novelty yarns
   1. Slub
   2. Spiral
   3. Corkscrew
   4. Nub
   5. Seed
   6. Ratiné
   7. Bouclé

Simple Yarns

Yarns having a smooth appearance and a uniform diameter along their length are classified as **simple yarns**. Simple yarns may be composed of a single yarn or a number of single yarns twisted or plied together in various ways. Figure 6.7 shows a simple two-plied yarn.

Single, Ply, and Cord Yarns

Simple single yarns are produced in a single spinning or throwing operation, or, in the case of monofilament yarns, in a single extruding operation. Although simple multifilament yarns are composed of multiple filaments, they are classified as single yarns. Most single yarns are not strong enough to be used as warp yarns. For this reason, two or more single yarns are plied together, creating a stronger, more uniform yarn. Two singles of opposite twists, S and Z twist, naturally twist together. Figure 6.8 illustrates a single yarn, a plied yarn, and a rope. When two or more singles yarns are plied together, it is called a corded yarn (Figure 6.9).

Figure 6.7 Two-ply yarn. Yarn courtesy of Textile Fabric Consultants. Photo courtesy of Max Concra.

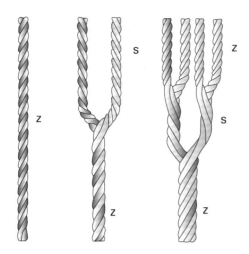

Figure 6.8 Simple yarns and yarn twist: (a) single yarn, (b) plied yarn, (c) rope. Illustration by Andrea Lau.

Figure 6.9 Cord. Yarn courtesy of Textile Fabric Consultants. Photo courtesy of Max Concra.

Cable and Rope

When simple cord yarns are plied, the resulting structure is called a **cable yarn**; when cable yarns are plied, the new structure is called **rope**. Rope structures composed of sisal or hemp fibers frequently appear in hand-woven chair seats. In comparison with complex yarns, simple yarns have minimal texture. Interest can be added by blending more than one fiber or by blending more than one color. **Heather** is used to describe yarns that combine multi-tonal or multicolored fibers.

Novelty Yarns

Yarns with variations in the level of twist used along their length, three-dimensional decorative features,

or components with different fiber contents are called **novelty yarns**. The unique combination of features characterizing each of these decorative yarns determines its yarn name.

Novelty yarns may be spun, filament, or a combination of both. A **slub** or **thick-and-thin** yarn has both fine and coarse segments along its length, created by varying the level of twist used in the final spinning operation (Figure 6.10). Because fewer twists per inch are used for the coarse areas, they are softer and weaker than the finer, more twisted areas. In filament yarns, the same effect can be achieved by varying the extrusion pressure during the formation of the manufactured fiber. The amount of slub and the distance between the slubs can be engineered to create different effects. Figure 6.11 shows a curtain fabric with a slub yarn. Figure 6.12 shows dupioni silk. Dupioni is a natural occurring thick-and-thin silk yarn. Two silk cocoons become affixed and the resulting yarn has an irregular texture.

Novelty yarns can be created by plying different types of yarns together in a variety of way to produce yarns with textural effects. These yarns typically have a base yarn, an effect yarn, and a binder yarn that secures all three yarn together. Plying two yarns of different thicknesses is called a **spiral** or a **corkscrew** yarn. Figure 6.13 shows thick, multi-colored slub yarn plied with a straight yarn.

Nub yarns have balls of fibers, occasionally of a contrasting color, added at irregular intervals along the base yarn's length. **Seed yarns** have a more compact nub. **Ratiné yarns** have uniformly spaced loops of equal size.

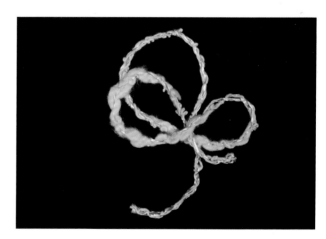

Figure 6.10 Slub yarn. Yarn courtesy of Textile Fabric Consultants. Photo courtesy of Max Concra.

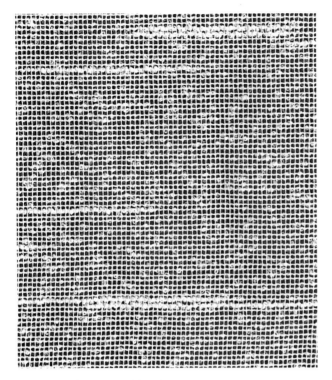

Figure 6.11 Filament slub in a leno weave. Yarn courtesy of Textile Fabric Consultants.

Figure 6.12 Dupioni silk. From *Swatch Reference Guide for Interior Design Fabrics* by Deborah E. Young, published by Fairchild Books.

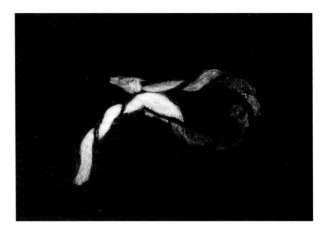

Figure 6.13 Spiral or corkscrew yarn. Yarn courtesy of Textile Fabric Consultants. Photo courtesy of Max Concra.

In their production, a fuzzy effect yarn is fed faster than the base during the plying sequence, producing small, tightly spaced loops that are almost perpendicular to the base. Ratiné yarns resemble rickrack. **Bouclé yarns** (Figure 6.14) have pronounced, closed loops that vary in size and spacing. Notice the core yarn wrapped with an effect yarn. Figure 6.15 shows a plaid fabric woven with a bouclé yarn.

Specialty Yarn Types

Core-spun and covered-core yarns are special types of yarns having a synthetic rubber or spandex filament as the core component.

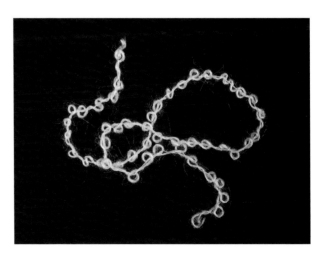

Figure 6.14 Bouclé yarn. Yarn courtesy of Textile Fabric Consultants. Photo courtesy of Max Concra.

Figure 6.15 Plaid with bouclé yarn. From *Swatch Reference Guide for Interior Design Fabrics* by Deborah E. Young, published by Fairchild Books.

Yarn Number

Yarn numbers designate the diameter or size of yarns. They are determined according to various yarn numbering systems, but the number or count of one system can be converted to its equivalent number in other systems.

Yarn Numbering Systems

Yarn numbering systems are based on either the mass per unit of length or the length per unit of mass. In both cases they are used to determine the thickness of the yarn.

Indirect Yarn Numbering Systems

In **indirect yarn numbering systems**, the yarn number or size is based on length per unit of mass (weight), and the yarn diameter decreases as the yarn number increases. These systems are traditionally used for spun yarns.

- Cotton Count (cc) System: The cc system is used to determine the yarn number of yarns spun on the cotton spinning system. The cc yarn number is equal to the number of 840-yard lengths or hanks of yarn produced from one pound of fiber.
- Linen Lea (lea) System: The lea system is used to determine the yarn number of yarns produced on the linen spinning system. In this system, the lea number is equal to the number of 300-yard hanks of yarn produced from one pound of fiber.
- Woolen Run (wr) System: The wr system is used to determine the yarn number of yarns produced on the woolen spinning system. The wr number is equal to the number of 1,600-yard hanks of yarn produced from one pound of fiber. Some spinners may choose to use the woolen cut (w/c) system instead of the wr system. In the w/c system, the yarn number is equal to the number of 300-yard hanks of yarn produced from one pound of fiber.
- Worsted Count (wc) System: The wc system is used to determine the yarn number of yarns on the worsted spinning system. The wc number is equal to the number of 560-yard hanks of yarn produced from one pound of fiber.

Core-Spun and Covered-Core Yarns

When staple-length fibers are spun around the elastomeric filament, the structure is called a **core-spun yarn**; when filaments are wrapped or braided around the filament, the structure is called a **covered-core yarn**. These types of yarns are used as stretch furniture coverings for commercial use.

Designation of Yarn Construction

ASTM D1244 Standard Practice for Designation of Yarn Construction includes recommendations for describing the structural features of simple yarns (the standard does not cover the description of novelty yarns). Three basic notations are used to designate the construction: yarn number, direction of twist, and number of components.

Direct Yarn Numbering Systems

In **direct yarn numbering systems**, the yarn number or size is based on mass (weight) per unit of length, and the yarn diameter increases as the yarn number increases. These systems are generally used with silk and manufactured filaments.

- Denier (den) System: In this system, the den number is equal to the weight in grams of 9,000 meters of a monofilament or multifilament yarn. A den number of 200, for example, means that 9,000 meters of yarn weighed 200 grams.

Because converting yarn numbers or counts determined in one system to equivalent numbers in other systems is laborious and time consuming, selected conversions are presented in Table 6.1.

Blended Yarns

Blended yarns are composed of fibers that are different in fiber type, length, diameter, or color and spun together into one yarn. Heather is used to describe yarns that combine multi-tonal or multicolored fibers. Fibers can be used in the same proportion or in varying proportions.

Blending is done to produce fabrics with better performance characteristics; obtain varying texture, hand, or fabric appearance; minimize fiber cost; or obtain unique color effects.

Blended yarns are more uniform when they are combined early in the processing stage. When a blended yarn contains both short and long fibers, the long fibers tend to move to the center of the yarn. The short outside fibers migrate of the outside of the yarn and contribute to pilling, poor abrasion resistance, and a harsher hand. A common blend in fabrics is a cotton and polyester yarn, which is used for upholstery fabrics, window covering fabrics, bedding, and toweling. The blending is done to combine the desirable properties of both cotton and polyester.

Formation of Yarn-Like Structures

Several components incorporated in interior textile products are yarn-like structures. While some of these strands are composed of textile fibers, and are generally referred to as yarns, they are produced with techniques other than throwing and spinning.

TABLE 6.1
YARN NUMBER CONVERSIONS

Cotton Count (840 yd per lb)	Linen Lea (300 yd per lb)	Woolen Run (1,600 yd per lb)	Worsted Count (560 yd per lb)	Denier (g per 9,000 m)	Tex (g per 1,000 m)
Coarsest					
0.357	1.000	0.188	0.536	14,890.0	1,654.0
0.667	1.867	0.350	1.000	7,972.0	885.2
1.000	2.800	0.525	1.500	5,315.0	590.5
1.905	5.333	1.000	2.857	2,790.0	310.0
3.333	9.333	1.750	5.000	1,595.0	177.2
3.810	10.67	2.000	5.714	1,395.0	155.0
40.00	112.00	21.00	60.00	132.9	14.80
50.00	140.0	26.25	75.00	106.3	11.80
60.00	168.0	31.50	90.00	88.58	9.84
531.5	1,488.0	279.1	797.3	10.00	1.11
Finest					

Courtesy of Celanese Corporation.

Chenille Yarns

Chenille yarns are actually narrow strips cut from a leno-woven fabric. In a leno-weave interlacing, illustrated in Figure 7.13, p. 90, pairs of warp (lengthwise) yarns are crossed in a figure-eight fashion around the filling or weft (crosswise) yarns. The warp yarns are simple and highly twisted, and the filling yarns are simple, low-twist strands. After weaving, the fabric is carefully cut lengthwise between the leno-entwined warp yarns, producing fuzzy, caterpillar-like structures (Figure 6.16).

Felted Wool Yarns

Research projects sponsored by the Australian Wool Innovation have led to the development of unique **felted wool yarns** for use in soft floorcoverings. One technique exposes loosely knitted strands of wool rovings to heat, agitation, and moisture, causing felting shrinkage and converting the strands into yarn-like structures. In this way—by capitalizing on the inherent tendency of wool fibers to shrink and mat together—manufacturers produce wool carpet yarns while avoiding the expense and time involved in conventional spinning, twisting, and plying. This helps to offset the relatively high cost of the fibers in the finished product.

Metallic Yarns

Metallic yarns are formed in various ways. Frequently, silver-colored foil is encased between clear polyester film sheeting. The roll is then cut into narrow strips or yarns. Yarns may be used alone or in combination with conventional textile yarns. Metallic yarns are typically used for decoration rather than functional purposes, and a wide range of types and colors are available.

Polymer Tapes

Polymer tapes are produced by extruding a polymer solution as a wide sheet of film, much like a sandwich wrap, but thicker. The film sheeting is then slit into long strands of the desired width. These structures, often referred to as fibrillated ribbons or fibrillated tapes, are usually composed of polypropylene (olefin) or saran. Fibrillated polypropylene (olefin) tapes predominate in backing fabrics produced for use with pile floorcoverings, and they are colored and used extensively as the face yarns in carpet designed to be installed outdoors and in laundry rooms, locker rooms, basements, and barns.

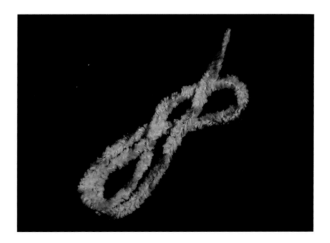

Figure 6.16 Chenille yarn. Yarn courtesy of Textile Fabric Consultants. Photo courtesy of Max Concra.

Key Terms

blended yarn	filament yarn
bouclé yarn	heather
bulk continuous filament (BCF)	indirect yarn numbering system
cable yarn	line fibers
carding	metallic yarns
chenille yarn	monofilament yarn
combing	multifilament yarn
cord	novelty yarns
core-spun yarn	nub yarns
covered-core yarn	opening and cleaning
crepe filament yarn	picking
direct yarn numbering systems	polymer tapes
	ratiné yarn
drawing out	rope
felted wool yarn	roving

S twist	thick-and-thin yarn
seed yarn	throwsters
simple single yarn	tow
simple yarn	tow fibers
sliver	turns per inch (tpi)
slub yarn	twisting
spinning and twisting	woolen yarn
spiral or corkscrew yarn	worsted yarn
spun yarn	yarn number
textured filament yarn	Z twist
texturing	

Review Questions

1. Identify the advantages textured filament yarns bring to textile end products.
2. Describe the techniques used to texture filament yarns.
3. Explain the importance of twisting spun yarns.
4. Differentiate between the types of complex yarns.
5. What yarn features are changed as the level of twist is increased?
6. Differentiate between indirect and direct yarn numbering systems.
7. Describe the production of chenille yarns. Would this process make these yarns more or less expensive than conventional yarns, and why?
8. Describe the differences in single, ply, and cord yarns.
9. Describe the differences in spun and filament yarns.
10. How does yarn twist affect the durability of both spun and filament fibers?

7

Fabricating Textiles for Interiors: Weaving

Fabrications are methods of producing fabric from fiber and yarn. Each method offers a unique structure and aesthetic features. The type of fabrication or construction also affects durability, application, and maintenance requirements. The method of fabrication also has a direct effect on the cost of the end product, an important criterion in the selection of most residential and commercial interior textile products. Most textiles are woven and produced by interlacing yarns.

Weaving

The majority of woven fabrics are made by **interlacing** two sets of yarns at right angles to each other. Lengthwise yarns, known as **warp yarns**, pass through the loom and are held under tension. One warp yarn is known as an **end**. Crosswise yarns, known as the **filling** or **weft yarns**, interlace with the warp. One weft yarn is known as a **pick**. Weft yarns pass over and under selected warp yarns creating a weave or pattern. Plain weave, where the weft travels over and under every other warp yarn, is the simplest of all weaves (Figure 7.1). Note that the warp and weft are at right angles to each other.

The complexity of the pattern reflects the type of loom used to produce the fabric. Basic interlacing patterns are executed on simple looms and include plain weaves, twill weaves, and satin weaves. Decorative interlacing patterns are executed on complex looms and include dobby weaves, leno weaves, Jacquard weaves, and pile weaves. In any case, all looms have some common features, and all woven fabrics have some common components.

Loom and Weaving Fundamentals

Weaving is done on a machine called a **loom**. Looms used in weaving operations vary in width and efficiency, as well as in complexity. Some looms are constructed to weave narrow trimmings, while others are fashioned to weave wide-width sheers or bedding.

To execute even a simple interlacing pattern, a loom must have components and control mechanisms to systematically raise and lower specific warp yarns, insert the filling yarns, align each successive filling yarn, and advance the warp yarns and woven fabric as the operation progresses.

Figure 7.1 Plain weave. From *Swatch Reference Guide for Interior Design Fabrics* by Deborah E. Young, published by Fairchild Books.

Parts of a Dobby Loom

The component parts of a simple loom are shown in Figure 7.2. **Yarn beams** hold the supply of warp yarns. The warp yarns are threaded through **heddles**, thin metal, nylon, or string strips with eye-like openings. The number of heddles required depends on the complexity of the pattern, the compactness of construction, and the fabric width. **Harnesses** house the heddles and move up and down, shifting the position of selected warp yarns. The **beater bar** (or **reed**), a comb-like device with openings called **dents**, helps to keep the warp yarns aligned and ensure grain straightness. The number of **dents per inch** in the reed determines the number of warp threads per inch. The **beater** moves forward and backward to push each new filling yarn into position on the cloth. A **cloth beam** holds the woven fabric.

On industrial looms, before each warp end is threaded through a heddle, it is threaded through a **drop wire**, a small, curved metal device. If a strained warp yarn breaks during weaving, its drop wire drops, immediately stopping the operation and preventing an unsightly flaw

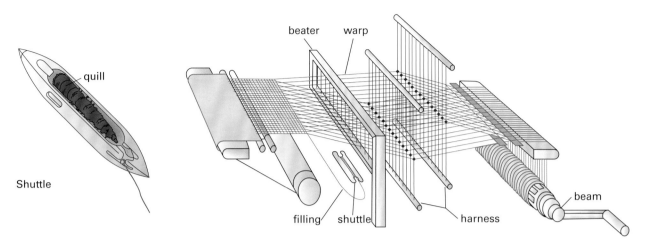

Figure 7.2 Basic parts of a simple shuttle loom. Fairchild Books.

in the fabric. On conventional looms, the filling yarn is wound on a **bobbin** that is carried by a **shuttle**, shown in detail in Figure 7.2. Faster, rapier looms are **shuttleless looms** and use pinchers to carry the weft across the width of the fabric. Air or water jet looms propel the weft across the fabric (Figure 7.3).

Basic Weaving Operation

Preparing a loom for weaving is a lengthy and time-consuming process. First, a warp has to be made. Large packages of yarn are mounted on a **creel frame** (see Figure 7.4) and warp yarns are wound onto a warp beam (Figure 7.5). The yarns are treated with a hot starch or sizing in an operation known as **slashing** to make the yarns smoother and stronger, enabling them better to withstand the weaving stresses. The warp beam full of slashed and dried warp yarns is placed on the loom and

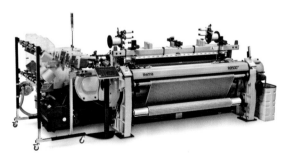

Figure 7.3 Rapier loom. Courtesy of Atema.

Figure 7.4 Creel frame. Courtesy of ITEAMA.

Figure 7.5 Warp beam being made. Courtesy of Glen Raven, Inc.

Figure 7.6 Weaving shed. Courtesy of Glen Raven, Inc.

each end is threaded through a drop wire, an eye in a heddle, and a dent in the reed, and tied onto the cloth beam.

Whether a simple or a complex interlacing pattern is being woven, the weaving sequence includes four steps. Harnesses are lifted creating a V-shaped **shed** that the weft yarn passes through. Next, one or more filling yarns travel through the shed.

After the weft thread is inserted, the warp yarns are lowered and the reed moves forward, pushing or beating the filling yarn in place so that it aligns parallel to the other filling yarns. This procedure helps to ensure uniform spacing of the yarns. Woven fabric is then **taken up** on the cloth beam, and more warp yarn length is **let off** from the yarn beam.

Basic Interlacing Patterns

The basic interlacing patterns include the plain, twill, and satin weaves. Each of these weaves has one or more variations. The variations can be produced by slightly altering the shed patterns used, by varying the number of picks inserted in each shed, and by using warp and filling yarns of different sizes.

Plain and Plain Weave Variations

The **plain weave** is also known as the **tabby**. The notation used to describe the interlacing pattern is 1×1, which indicates that one warp yarn and one filling yarn alternately pass over one another (Figure 7.1). Plain weave can be woven on a two harness loom. Two variations of plain weave, basket weave and rib weave, are described next.

Basket Weave

In the **basket weave**, two or more warp yarns are grouped together. When two warp yarns alternately pass over and under one filling yarn, the pattern is described as a 2×1 basket weave (Figure 7.7a). Interlacing two warp yarns with two filling yarns is a 2×2 basket weave (Figure 7.7b).

Rib Weave

Rib weaves can also be called ottoman weaves or file, and they have a distinctive rib effect. They can be created in the warp and weft direction. The warp rib weave creates a rib effect lengthwise in the fabric, because there are more yarns in the warp direction or by incorporating larger yarns in the lengthwise direction. Crosswise three-dimensional ribs or ridges distinguish filling rib weave fabrics. The ribs are produced by using a higher number of filling yarns than warp yarns per inch or by incorporating larger yarns in the weft direction.

Twill and Twill Weave Variations

Just like plain weave, there are many variations of **twill weave**. Notations used with twill weaves describe the interlacing pattern of each warp yarn. The 2/1 notation

(a)

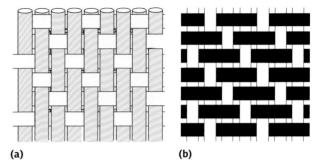

(a)   **(b)**

Figure 7.8 2/1 twill weave interlacings: (a) warp-faced twill weave, (b) filling-faced twill weave. Illustrations by Andrea Lau/ Fairchild Books.

(b)

Figure 7.7 Basket weave interlacings: (a) 2 × 1 interlacing, (b) 2 × 2 interlacing. Courtesy of Amy Willbanks, www.textilefabric.com.

Figure 7.9 Twill weave. Courtesy of Amy Willbanks, www. textilefabric.com.

shown in Figure 7.8a, for example, indicates that each warp yarn passes or **floats** over two filling yarns, under one filling yarn, over two filling yarns, and so on. In the 2/1 interlacing depicted in Figure 7.8b, each filling yarn passes over two warp yarns and under one filling yarn, over two warp yarns, and so on. The weave steps either to the right or to the left, creating an obvious diagonal pattern in the fabric (Figure 7.9). In general, twill weave is more flexible and therefore more drapable than plain weave.

Twills can be either warp face, weft face, or even. When the warp yarns float over a greater number of filling yarns than they pass behind, the fabric is described as a warp-faced twill. When the filling yarns float over a

greater number of warp yarns than they pass behind, the fabric is described as a weft-faced twill. When an interlacing pattern has equal amounts of warp and filling yarns covering the fabric surface, the fabric is described as an even-sided twill.

Twill Weave Variations

Herringbone is a twill weave variation created by changing the direction of the diagonal, as shown in Figure 14.6, p. 186. This process creates a striped chevron pattern that can vary in size. A **houndstooth** is a twill pattern created by using a unique color arrangement. As you can see in Figure 14.5, p. 186, groups of four light

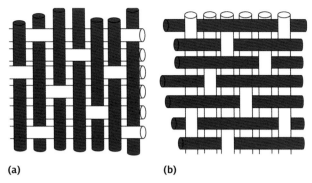

(a)   (b)

Figure 7.10 Satin interlacing patterns. (a) Warp-faced satin weave, (b) filling-faced satin weave. Illustration by Andrea Lau/ Fairchild Books.

and four dark threads are grouped together in the warp and weft direction.

Satin and Sateen Weaves

Like warp-faced twill fabrics, **satin** fabrics have floating warp yarns. Satin weaves have a smooth surface designed to hide the weave or interlacings. They require more harnesses than basic twill patterns. To produce a satin weave at least five harnesses are needed. This pattern is described as five-shaft construction, indicating that each warp yarn is floating over four picks and under the fifth.

Satin-weaves are characterized by high luster and sheen, produced by light reflection from the uninterrupted warp floats. Figures 7.10a and 7.11a show a draft and a sample of a warp faced satin. **Sateen** is a weft-faced satin where the filling yarns float over the warp yarns, as shown in Figures 7.10b and 7.11b.

(a)

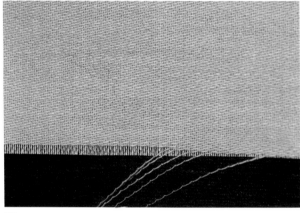

(b)

Figure 7.11 Satin and sateen weaves. (a) Satin: warp-faced satin weave, (b) sateen: filling-faced satin weave. Courtesy of Amy Willbanks, www.textilefabric.com.

Decorative Interlacing Patterns

The relative simplicity of the basic weaves and their variations can readily be appreciated when they are compared to the more complex weave structures that use a combination of simple weaves and often multiple sets of warp and weft yarns to create complex patterns.

Dobby Weave

Dobby weaves are simple, small-scale patterns (Figure 7.12) produced on dobby looms. These fabrics can also be embellished with an **e**xtra yarn added to produce

raised figures while the base fabric is being woven. When not being used on the face of the fabric, these extra weft yarns floated on the back of the fabric. The floating yarns on the back can be left in place or clipped depending in the fabric and the end-use. The floating yarns are clipped if the ground is opaque and the yarns will show through. For upholstery fabrics the back yarns are clipped because the bulkiness might cause a rippling effect. Simple designs can be produced on dobby looms with multiple harnesses; however, the dobby weaving has limited design possibilities compared to Jacquard weaving.

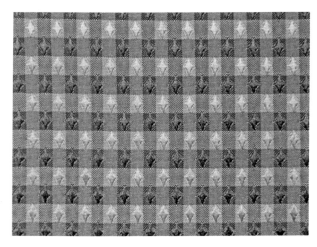

Figure 7.12 Dobby weave. Courtesy of Amy Willbanks, www. textilefabric.com.

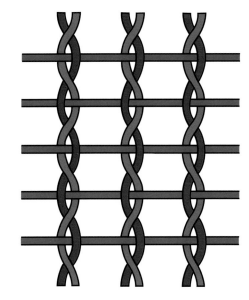

Figure 7.13 Leno weave. Illustration by Andrea Lau/Fairchild Books.

Leno Weave

Leno is woven with a special attachment that allows the warp yarns to twist around one another (Figure 7.13). Although the individual warp yarns are not parallel, the paired groups are, and the structure is essentially biaxial. This type of weaving adds dimensional stability to lightweight, sheer fabrics.

Marquisette, a transparent, leno-weave window covering, is pictured in Figure 17.18, p. 231.

Jacquard Fabrics

Jacquard fabrics often have extremely complex interlacing patterns combining two or more simple weaves, multiple sets of yarns, and strategically placed colors. Typically, the pattern repeats are large and composed of various motifs, each having finely detailed curved and swirled shapes. Jacquard fabrics are woven on Jacquard looms (Figure 7.14) that have the capacity to form an almost unlimited variety of multi-colored fabrics with intricate patterns.

The Jacquard loom eliminates the need for a harness. Instead, it has a system of cords and hooks. Each warp yarn is threaded through a cord heddle that is linked to a needle by a rod and hook apparatus. In effect, each cord heddle functions as a miniature harness that can be raised and lowered, allowing each warp thread to function independent of the next. Each design has a unique set of

Figure 7.14 Jacquard loom. Courtesy of ITEMA Weaving, www. itemagroup.com.

cards that dictate how the warp threads are raised and lowered.

Today, Jacquard fabrics are designed with computer software that sends the pattern information directly from the design station to the loom, eliminating the need for Jacquard cards. Jacquard woven upholstery fabrics are

Figure 7.18 **Velvet woven on a wire loom.** From *Swatch Reference Guide for Interior Design Fabrics* by Deborah E. Young, published by Fairchild Books.

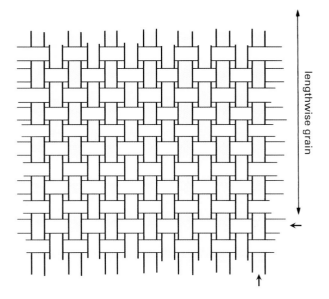

lengthwise grain

Figure 7.20 **Components and features of a grain-straight biaxially woven fabric.** Illustration by Andrea Lau/Fairchild Books.

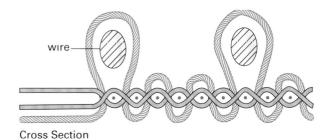

wire

Cross Section

Figure 7.19 **The over-the-wire construction technique.** Fairchild Books.

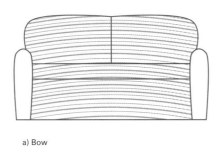

a) Bow

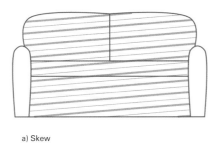

a) Skew

Figure 7.21 **Effects of filling bow and skew in the appearance of upholstered furniture items.** Fairchild Books.

Grain

A quality woven fabric is **grain-straight**: all the warp yarns are perpendicular to all the filling yarns (Figure 7.20). If the yarns do not interlace at 90 degrees, the fabric is **off-grain**. Off-grain fabrics will result in bowing or skewing (Figure 7.21). Fabrics with a bowed yarn alignment tend to sag, and fabrics with a skewed yarn alignment tend to produce a lopsided or crooked appearance, as shown in Figure 7.20. Fabrics are strongest in the warp direction and least strong on the diagonal or bias.

Selvage

Selvages (or selvedges) are the narrow lengthwise edges of a woven fabric. The main purpose of selvages is to ensure the edges of the fabric will not tear during the weaving and finishing processes. They are also designed to prevent or minimize raveling. Selvages can vary in design depending on what type of loom the fabric is woven on.

Thread Count

Thread count denotes how closely the yarns are aligned and is determined by adding up the number of warp and weft yarns in one square inch of fabric. Sometimes the number of warp and weft threads per inch are given separately, with warp yarns listed first (e.g., 90 × 84). With bed sheets typically one number (threads per square inch) is given. Fabrics can have a **balanced construction**, that is, an equal number of warp and filling yarns (Figure 7.20) or an unbalanced construction usually with the warp out numbering the weft. The thread count used in weaving helps to determine the appearance, serviceability, cost, drapability, and hand of a fabric.

shuttleless loom	velvet
slack tension technique	velveteen
slashing	W pattern
tabby	wales
taking up and letting off	warp pile fabrics
thread count	warp yarn
twill weave	weft yarn
V pattern	yarn beam

Key Terms

balanced construction	heddles
basket weave	herringbone
beater	houndstooth
bobbin	interlacing
cloth beam	Jacquard
corduroy	leno
creel frame	loom
dents	marquisette
dents per inch	nap
dobby weave	off-grain
double cloth construction	pick
drop wire	plain weave
end	reed
filling pile fabrics	rib weave
filling yarns	sateen
float	satin
frieze	selvage
grain-straight	shed
grospoint	shuttle
harnesses	shuttle loom

Review Questions

1. Identify the features of a grain-straight fabric.
2. Name the parts of a simple loom and explain the function of each part of the loom in the basic weaving process.
3. Why are complex yarns rarely, if ever, used as warp yarns?
4. In what direction is a fabric the strongest?
5. Explain the four steps of the basic weaving operation.
6. Differentiate between the three basic weaves.
7. What is the difference in warp yarns and filling yarns?
8. How do dobby and Jacquard looms differ?
9. How is terry toweling produced?
10. When should the floats be clipped in dot or spot weaving? When should they be left unclipped?
11. State three reasons why fabrics with the same weave can have totally different appearances.
12. How is corduroy produced?
13. Define the terms float and interlacing. How do these affect durability?
14. Why it is important for a designer to understand nap?
15. What is frieze or grospoint?

8

Other Fabrications

Several techniques other than weaving or interlace yarns can be used to combine yarns into fibrous structures suitable for interior applications. Yarns can be interlooped, inserted or embedded into substrates, braided, knotted, and twisted. Producers can combine fibers directly into fabrics, skipping yarn making altogether. Producers can convert polymer solutions directly into film fabrics.

Films and Coated Fabrics

Coated fabrics hold a substantial place in both upholstery and wallcovering fabrics. Their smooth, washable surface, reasonable price, and durability make them highly functional and popular. By extruding solution through a spinneret that has a narrow slit rather than minute holes, polymers can be converted directly into **polymer film sheeting** fabrics, or **films**. As the polymer ribbon emerges, it is stretched into a thin film or sheet. Controlling the extrusion pressure and varying the amount of stretching determines the thickness of the film.

Film sheetings may be used on their own, for example as shower curtains, but for most furnishing applications a fabric substrate is coated with the compound, or the film is laminated to a substrate. Impermeable to moisture and easy to clean, **coated fabrics** are popular for seating applications in healthcare and food service areas where germ growth is of increasing concern. Coated fabrics can simulate leather, or simply make a design statement of their own. Versions are also used for drapery linings, shower curtains, outdoor tablecloths, and wallcovering.

The most popular compounds used for film materials in interiors are **vinyl** (polyvinyl chloride, or PVC), **polyurethane** (PU), and **silicone**, or combinations thereof. Polypropylene is also used as a film/coated fabric for wallcovering. Each of the compounds have different attributes.

PVC

What we call *vinyl* is PVC, or polyvinyl chloride, which is a flexible plastic made of resins, plasticizers, and various fillers. Fossil fuel is processed into ethylene, and salt is processed in order to produce chlorine. The ethylene and chlorine are then combined into ethylene dichloride, which is then further processed into vinyl chloride monomer, a gas. The chloride configuration is a very strong chemical bond, which is partly responsible for the tough, hard surface of the resulting material.

The gas molecules are then converted through polymerization into a fine, white powder, which is vinyl resin. In the final process of compounding, the vinyl resin is blended with additives such as plasticizers (which add flexibility), stabilizers (which add durability), and sometimes with pigments to add color. The result is the chemical compound called PVC, or polyvinyl chloride. PVC has long been the material of choice for many building, automotive, and medical products, because it is the best-performing material available at low cost that we have so far developed for these purposes. Vinyl is a durable, versatile fabric that is popular for hospitality, residential, marine, and other highly demanding sites.

In order to produce a seating fabric, PVC is used to coat one side of a knit or woven substrate. Sometimes a foam layer is sandwiched in between. The material can be printed, embossed, or produced in solid colors. Although it is naturally flame resistant, treatments are often added in order to pass specific flammability tests.

Figure 8.1 "Loophole," vinyl face with polyester backing.
Photo courtesy of CF Stinson, LLC. All rights reserved. Copyright 2017.

In spite of vinyl's ubiquitous presence in products from food storage containers to children's toys to building materials, its environmental attributes make its use controversial. When ingested, the plasticizers (called phthalates) that are added to turn PVC from a hard plastic into a flexible material have been linked to health risks (organ damage and hormonal abnormalities) in some rodent studies. (Phthalates are also used in shampoo, soap, makeup, nail polish, adhesives, paint, and many other materials that we encounter every day.)

PVC is not only found in surface materials, but is also the most common chlorine-containing product in household items such as toys, furniture parts, window blinds, packaging materials, pipes, and exterior materials. Many of these objects end up in waste sites. PVC is likewise prominent in industrial waste, and in cars that are ultimately scrapped. Therefore, it is present in vast amounts in waste sites, many of which are incinerated.

When PVC is burned, dioxin is released, just as it is from burning wood in home barbeques or wood-heating stoves, and in especially large proportions in automotive exhaust. The EPA has classified dioxin as a persistent organic pollutant because it is a very stable chemical that does not break down in the environment readily, and has also classified the most potent of the dioxins as a human carcinogen. Dioxin can be minimized when appropriate waste management practices are exercised. Vinyl manufacturers state that the material can be properly incinerated so that dioxin is not produced, by heating it very slowly, under controlled conditions. Some vinyl manufacturers delaminate and otherwise re-manufacture seconds and other unusable PVC product into recycled, first quality wallcovering vinyl material that also can provide LEED credit points.

PVC is recyclable. Almost all post-industrial PVC byproduct created in plants and not laminated, such as edge material that is pre-trimmed, is not wasted, but is returned to the manufacturing cycle and is recycled within the plant. Post-consumer recycling programs for PVC are limited, in part because vinyl's chlorine bonding is difficult to break down. If it is broken, the same chemicals that can be negative in other aspects of its life-cycle (chloride gas and dioxins) can be released. Furthermore, for interior surface materials it is most often laminated to substrates, which must be separated after its useful life is over in order to recycle the PVC. Also, the reclamation processes themselves are limited with most interior furnishings, and those that exist have met with limited success.

Since both burning the material and recycling it are problematic, much PVC wallcovering ends up in landfills. It is not biodegradable, and its additives are not bound to the plastic and can, potentially, leach out into groundwater. These environmental issues notwithstanding, in many of the applications where vinyl is specified, another alternative would not last as long or serve as well, and would therefore end up in the waste stream sooner. When making product selections, the positive and negative attributes of any material need to be considered.

Polyurethane

Polyurethane is softer, more rubbery, and more malleable than PVC, and therefore features an appealing, less "plastic" hand, but it is also more vulnerable to scratching and marring because of its softness. Because of its suppleness, PU simulates leather more realistically than vinyl does, in part because it looks soft when gathered and tufted. It also costs quite a bit more than comparable PVC. It is less dense than PVC, and therefore is more breathable. Like vinyl films, polyurethane is layered over a fabric backing for use in upholstery, and can be colored and embossed. PU is in naturally flame resistant, but flame retardants are sometimes added during manufacturing.

Polyurethane is considered environmentally more favorable than PVC because neither phthalates nor chlorine are part of its make-up. It will eventually degrade. Over time, polyurethane becomes brittle and flakes. It also degrades in high humidity and hot environments; in these conditions the material will puddle and the surface layers will delaminate.

Polypropylene

In addition to its popular and broad applications in woven fabrics and in floorcovering, polypropylene is also produced as a film for wallcovering application.

Figure 8.2 "Effervescence," polyurethane with polyester backing. Photo courtesy of CF Stinson, LLC. All rights reserved. Copyright 2017.

Figure 8.3 "Groove, Cycle, Acoustic, and Hive," polyurethane. Momentum Textiles.

Silicone

Silicone has been developed in films/coated fabrics as a more sustainable alternative to vinyl. This chemically inert polymer material, made primarily of silicon and oxygen, is used in many products, including sealants, adhesives, cooking utensils, and medical devices. It is heat resistant and rubbery in texture.

Silicone's thermal stability, low chemical reactivity and toxicity, resistance to UV light, and water repellence make it an attractive covering material. When burned, silicone forms a white powder and emits gases, and it is biodegradable. Unfortunately, it is considerably more expensive than PVC or PU.

Figure 8.4 "Silica Friz Eco," 100 percent silicone. Momentum Textiles.

Knits

Whereas weaving interlaces two sets of yarns, **knitting** is the interlooping of yarns. Knitting operations are separated into two major categories: warp knitting and weft knitting, according to the manner in which the yarns are interlooped. Although different stitches are used in these operations, all knitted fabrics have some common features.

Rows of yarn loops running lengthwise in a knitted fabric are known as **wales**, and those running crosswise are known as **courses**. The wales and courses should be at right angles to one another, in much the same way as warp yarns are perpendicular to filling yarns in woven fabrics. Unlike woven fabrics, in which the true bias offers the greatest elasticity, knitted fabrics are generally most stretchable in the crosswise direction, since the rounded loops expand and contract laterally.

The **gauge** is the number of loops per inch or per bar inch ($1^1/_2$ inches) and is controlled by the size of the knitting needles. Along with the size of the yarns used, gauge helps to determine the transparency, porosity, and weight of the fabric and determines the compactness of construction of knitted fabrics.

Warp Knitting

In **warp knitting**, fabrics are produced by the simultaneous interlooping of adjacent yarns in a vertical direction.

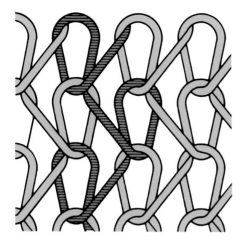

Figure 8.5 Interlooping of adjacent yarns in warp knitting.
Illustration by Andrea Lau/Fairchild Books.

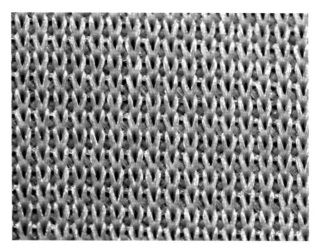

(a)

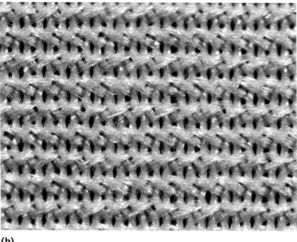

(b)

Figure 8.6 Tricot: (a) front, (b) back. Courtesy of Amy Willbanks, www.textilefabric.com.

As shown in Figure 8.5, a portion of each yarn has a diagonal orientation but the wales are essentially parallel.

Warp knitting is an extremely fast operation, with large machines producing more than four million loops per minute. Warp knitting machines can construct fabrics up to 168 inches in width, but only in flat, rectangular shapes.

Stitches

Two warp knitting stitches, the **tricot stitch** and the **raschel stitch**, are commonly used for interior fabrics—for sheer window coverings, laces, and as ergonomic seating material, especially those with mesh chair backs. **Tricot** fabrics are distinguished by the presence of herringbone-like wales on the face of the fabric (Figure 8.6a) and by a crosswise rib-like effect on the back of the fabric (Figure 8.6b). The tricot stitch is produced using spring needles, illustrated in Figure 8.7a, and one or two guide bars, attachments that guide or shift yarns around the hooked or curved portion of the needles prior to interlooping. Tricot-stitched fabrics have comparatively low stretchability. When these fabrics are made of thermoplastic fibers, heat setting can be used to improve their dimensional stability. Tricot fabrics are used for automobile interiors, upholstered furniture coverings, and wallcoverings.

The raschel stitch is executed on a machine that may be equipped with up to 30 guide bars, which select and position the various yarns in preparation for interlooping. Increasing the number of guide bars is equivalent to increasing the number of harnesses on looms; thus, raschel machines are extremely versatile. As shown in Figure 8.7b, the needles used have a latch that opens and closes to secure the yarn, enabling the manufacturer to use virtually any fiber and any style of yarn.

Weft Insertion

Warp knitting and weaving are combined in a fabrication technique known as **weft insertion** (Figure 8.8). In this operation, weft or filling yarns are inserted or "woven" through the loops being formed in a tricot-stitching operation. Because laid-in yarns are not knitted in, but

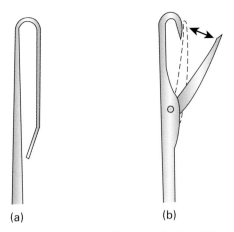

Figure 8.7 Heads of needles used in tricot stitching: (a) head of spring needle, (b) head of latch needle. Courtesy of Celanese Corporation.

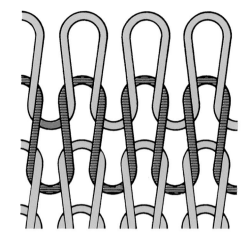

Figure 8.9 Continuous interlooping of one yarn in filling or weft knitting. Illustration by Andrea Lau/Fairchild Books.

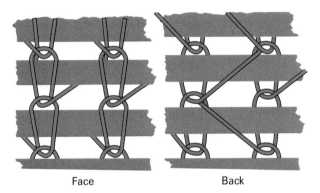

Face   Back

Figure 8.8 Fabric produced by weft insertion. Illustration by Andrea Lau/Fairchild Books.

are caught in the knit stitches, novelty yarns that might not have the consistency of denier or the needed strength to be used as a knitting yarn can be featured. Heavy yarns used as laid-in yarns increase stability and provide covering power and better insulation properties.

Weft Knitting

Weft knitting (Figure 8.9) produces fabrics by continuously interlooping one or more yarns from side to side, creating one course after another. Weft knitting is slower than warp knitting. Whereas warp-knitting machines can produce only flat, straight-sided fabrics, weft-knitting machines can produce rectangular fabrics, fabrics with a circular or tubular form (Figure 8.10), and fabrics with a preplanned, angular shape. Knitting flat-to-shape, a procedure used extensively in the production of

Figure 8.10 Circular knitting machine.

apparel items, is rarely used in the production of interior textile items, but some manufacturers of ergonomic seating do produce pieces knit to shape for specific chair frames.

Stitches

Jersey stitch and interlock stitch are among the filling knitting stitches used to manufacture interior fabrics. **Jersey stitch** is used in some bedsheets. It creates herringbone-like wales on the face of the fabric and crescent-shaped loops on the back of the fabric (see Figure 8.6). **Knitted pile fabrics**, used to make

Figure 8.11 An interlock-stitched fabric. Illustration by Andrea Lau/ Fairchild Books.

simulated-fur bedspreads, incorporate additional yarns or fibers into a jersey base fabric.

The **interlock stitch** is formed by continuously interlooping two yarns. The completed **double-knit fabric** appears to be two interknitted fabrics, as shown schematically in Figure 8.11. Interlock-stitched fabrics are resistant to running and snagging and have high dimensional stability when heat set. Although double-knit fabrics offer favorable attributes for interior furnishings, they have not found favor in the marketplace.

Stitch-Knitting

Stitch-knitting, also known as *knit-sewing* and by the patented name of Malimo, layers and chain-stitches together webs of yarns, essentially reinforcing a nonwoven material. The chain-stitching is, in effect, sewing with knitting stitches, and the rate of fabric production is high. As no abrasive mechanisms (such as drop wires, heddles, or reeds) are used, highly decorative, complex yarns can be incorporated in either fabric direction. Although manufacturers can use supplementary yarns to vary visual and textural features, the technique has been used primarily to make very inexpensive drapery or industrial fabrics—a nonwoven with a bit of extra reinforcement.

Stitch-Bonding

Along the same principle as stitch-knitting, **stich-bonding** is executed by chain-stitching across a fibrous batt, converting the layered webs of fibers into a more stable structure.

Pile Fabrics

Separate from woven pile fabrics covered in the previous chapter, tufting and fusion bonding operations are used to introduce pile yarns to already-formed fabrics. Both techniques are fast and efficient.

Tufting

In **tufting** operations, pile yarns are threaded through needles that are mounted across the tufting machine and suspended vertically above a base fabric. As shown in Figure 8.12, the needles punch through the back of the base fabric and loopers engage the yarns. As each needle is withdrawn, a pile loop is formed. Loopers are equipped with oscillating knives in order to achieve cut-pile textures.

At this stage, the tufted pile yarns could easily be pulled out as they are only mechanically held in the base fabric. To provide better stability, a thin coating of an adhesive compound is normally applied to the fabric back. Tufted upholstery fabrics are rare, but more than 96 percent of all carpet and rugs produced are tufted. Tufting is discussed further in later chapters.

Bonding

In **fusion bonding** operations, pile yarns are inserted, or, more precisely, embedded, into an adhesive coating that has been applied to a base fabric. The composite is then heated to a melting point, so that the materials meld. This technique is used occasionally in some wallcoverings and soft floorcoverings.

Knotted and Twisted Fabrics and Braided Yarns

Knotting or twisting intersecting yarn techniques are used to make some decorative lace fabrics. Braiding techniques are similar to, and thought to be precursors of, weaving and twisting operations. As in weaving, the yarn

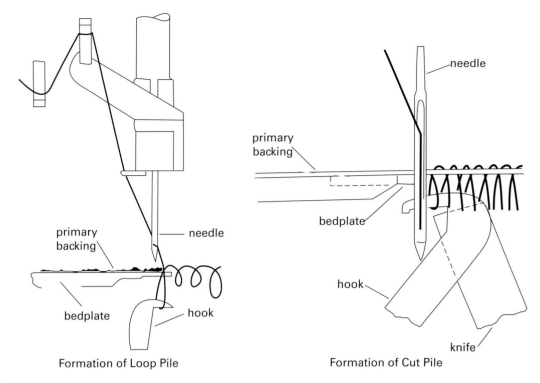

Formation of Loop Pile   Formation of Cut Pile

Figure 8.12 Tufting operations. Illustration by Andrea Lau/Fairchild Books.

strands in braiding are interlaced, and as in twisting, the yarns are all parallel, but the yarns' directions or orientations are continually interchanged as production progresses.

Lace Making

Various techniques produce a variety of lace effects. The yarns in lace fabrics are not parallel and perpendicular; they are instead oriented in various directions. Machine-made lace is used in window coverings, bed coverings, and tabletop accents. Hand-made lace, produced using small bobbins, is used as trimming for bedding products and draperies. Complex machinery is used to twist relatively fine yarns around one another in the manufacture of some lace fabrics.

Creating Bobbin Lace

Multiple pairs of **bobbins** (spools) are used to twist and cross yarns in the production of **bobbin lace**. The small wooden bobbins are wound with a length of yarn and hung below the work area to keep the yarns under slight tension.

With practice, skill, and patience, artisans manipulate the several bobbins in twisting and crossing motions. These motions are combined to execute various stitches. Bobbin lace is designed and constructed for many apparel and decorative uses, including open casements in window treatments and for decorative pillows.

Braided Yarns

To produce **flat braids**, which are used as trims or converted into rugs, three yarns or yarn-like structures are interlaced (Figure 22.14, p. 303). To produce the **circular braids** used as accent tie-backs for draperies, several strands are interlaced around a textile cord or other round structure.

Combined Fiber Fabrications

Textile machinery engineers and producers have devised new ways to produce nonwovens, which are fabric structures that bypass the yarn stage. Techniques such as spunbonding and spunlacing have joined the age-old technique of felting and the efficient method of needle punching as ways to combine fibers directly into fabrics.

Bonding Fibrous Batts

In one fabrication, **fibrous batts** are bonded into essentially flat structures with a paper-like quality. (These nonwoven structures are different from the three-dimensional fibrous batts produced for use as fillings and paddings; see Chapter 13). Webs of fibers are first layered to form a relatively thin batt. The webs may be layered parallel to each other, at right angles, or randomly (Figure 8.13a). An adhesive must be sprayed over the batt to cause non-thermoplastic fibers to adhere to one another. Heat can be used to soften thermoplastic fibers and cause them to stick together.

Bonded-web or **nonwoven fabrics** are used as interfacing in upholstery skirts (to add body and weight) and in curtain and drapery headings (to support pleats, scallops, and similar treatments).

Felting Fibrous Batts

In the production of **felt**, wool (or other animal fleece) fibers are cleaned and carded into thin webs, which are then layered at right angles to form a batt. The batt is exposed to controlled heat, agitation, moisture, and pressure. These conditions cause the overlapping scales of the fibers to intermesh and entangle, compacting and shrinking the batt into felt.

Felt is widely used to prevent artifacts from scratching hard-surfaced tabletops. Thick felt is an effective insulation material, and in some parts of the world, tents (called yurts) take advantage of felt's excellent moisture resistance and ability to retain warmth to make it a popular material for housing. Felt is also used to make hats, unstructured garments, and as an art medium to create two- or three-dimensional sculptural pieces. To reduce its cost, felt can be produced from a blend of wool and rayon fibers. A blended felt fabric must be at least 80 percent wool to achieve the interlocking of the scales.

Needle Punching Fibrous Batts

The technique of using barbed needles to create a mechanical chain stitch within a fibrous batt has long been employed in the production of some carpet and blankets.

(a)

Figure 8.13 Fabric structures that bypass the yarn stage: (a) bonded fibrous batt. Courtesy of Amy Willbanks, www.textilefabric.com.

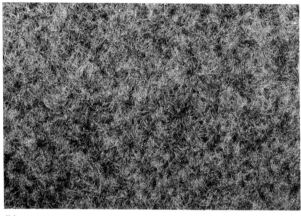

(b)

Figure 8.13 Fabric structures that bypass the yarn stage: (b) needle-punched carpeting. Courtesy of Lisa Klakulak, www.strongfelt.com, image by Mary Vogel.

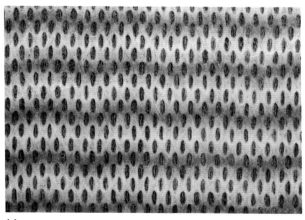

(c)

Figure 8.13 Fabric structures that bypass the yarn stage: (c) spunlaced disposable wipe. Courtesy of Amy Willbanks, www.textilefabric.com.

More recently, **needle punching** has been refined and used in the production of carpet, wallcoverings, and blankets. Figure 8.13b shows a needle-punched carpet. For added stability, a loosely woven fabric, called a **scrim**, or an adhesive may be enclosed within the batt prior to needle punching.

Spunbonding Webs of Filaments

Spunbonding converts thermoplastic filaments directly into fabric structures. After the filaments are arranged into a thin web, they are stabilized with heat or chemical binders. For added strength, stability, weight, or reduced transparency, additional compounds can be sprayed over the fine web. Spunbonded fabrics are used as tablecloths, as coverings for bedding products, and as backings for wallcoverings and carpet.

Spunlacing Fibers

Textile fabrics produced by mechanically entangling fibers are referred to as **spunlaced fabrics**. Whereas an adhesive or other type of binder is generally used with spunbonded and bonded-web fabrics, the fibers in spunlaced fabrics are stabilized solely by fiber-to-fiber friction. Today, spunlaced fabrics are used to back textile wallcoverings, simulated leather upholstery fabrics, mattress pads, and comforters, and they are also made into pillow coverings. Disposable towels and wipes are also produced by this method (Figure 8.13c). Figure 8.14 shows a spunlaced fabric used to make inexpensive draperies.

Figure 8.14 Spun-laced curtain fabric. Courtesy of Amy Willbanks, www.textilefabric.com.

Review Questions

1. Explain how these terms compare between woven and knitted fabrics:
   a. filling and warp
   b. course and wale
2. What is the difference between warp and weft knitting?
3. How can one distinguish between tricot and jersey fabrics?
4. Both warp knitting and filling knitting are extremely fast production techniques. How does this translate into savings for the consumer? How does it limit customers' choices?
5. Why is stitch-knitting sometimes referred to as knit-sewing?
6. Differentiate between tufting and fusion bonding.
7. Why are bonded-web fabrics known as nonwoven fabrics?
8. Distinguish between spunbonded and spunlaced fabrics.
9. Describe the uses of spunlaced fabrics.
10. Differentiate between needle punching and felting.
11. What are differences in woven versus knit fabrics?

9

Dyes and Colorants

Colored textiles enhance interior environments. Color choices can be tricky, however, because colors seem different when viewed under varying conditions, such as under different lighting conditions. Understanding factors that alter the apparent characteristics of fiber color helps designers make more confident color choices.

Textile products can be colored by three basic methods: dyeing, printing, and combinations of the two. Usually, a producer specializes in one, or maybe two, coloring processes. Wholesalers and distributors assemble a product line that features products colored by a variety of methods, and interior designers choose those that they, and their clients, prefer. Although most natural fibers have an inherent color, most textiles' color appearances are due to added color-producing substances.

Colorants and Color Perception

We do not perceive color until incident light waves are reflected to the eye and transmit optical sensations to the brain for interpretation. What the viewer sees as color is a concentration of light waves of certain lengths. Because light waves play a critical role in color stimulus and sensation, a brief review of the nature of light will augment our discussion of textile colorants and color perceptions.

Nature of Light

Light is visible electromagnetic energy, which accounts for a relatively small portion of the **electromagnetic spectrum**. This spectrum, schematized in Figure 9.1, includes waves of vastly different lengths, but all are very short. At one end are cosmic and gamma rays, which are quite short; at the opposite end are radio and electrical power waves, which are relatively long in comparison with cosmic waves. The actual length of most waves—the distance from the crest of one wave to the crest of the next—is measured and reported in minuscule units called **nanometers** (nm). One nanometer is equal to one billionth of a meter or to 0.000000039 inch.

In the central portion of the electromagnetic spectrum is an area known as the **visible spectrum**. The lengths of waves in this region range from some 400 nm to about 700 nm. When reflected to the eye, these radiations stimulate the eye to send messages to the brain, allowing us to interpret the sensation and see color. While the human eye is not sensitive to wavelengths outside of the visible spectrum, we are aware that some of the so-called invisible rays, for instance, ultraviolet and infrared rays, can have negative effects on colored textiles, altering

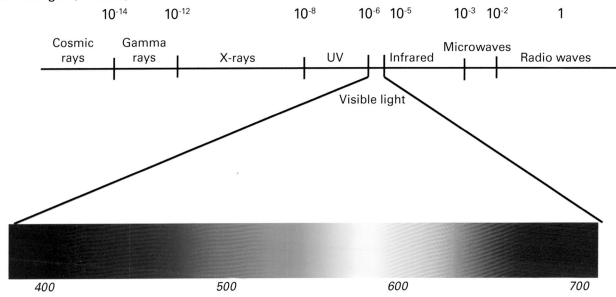

Figure 9.1 The electromagnetic spectrum. Michael J. Gregory/Fairchild Books.

the reflective characteristics of colorants and degrading the fibers.

Natural and artificial light sources emit all wavelengths within the boundaries of the visible spectrum. They do not, however, have equal mixtures of the various lengths; some have predominantly longer waves, others predominantly shorter waves. Colorants differ in their capacities to reflect the various wavelengths. The length of the waves emitted by the light source together with the length of the waves reflected by the colorant determine the particular color or hue perceived and affect other color characteristics as well.

Color Characteristics

Three color characteristics are determined by the emission, reflection, and interpretation of light waves. These are hue, value, and intensity.

Hue

Depending on the light source, larger quantities of certain wavelengths will be emitted, and, depending on the colorant, larger quantities of certain lengths will be reflected. The length of the waves that predominate in both emission and reflection will determine the particular **hue**, or color perceived. When blue is perceived, for example, the illuminant is emitting a high concentration of waves around 465 nm in length and the colorant is reflecting a high concentration of these waves and absorbing other lengths. When green is perceived, a high concentration of waves around 520 nm is being emitted and reflected; when red is perceived, waves around 650 nm are being emitted and reflected; and so on.

Value

Value refers to the relative lightness or darkness of a color. When a compound known to reflect all wavelengths, creating white, is used with colorants, a **tint** is produced and value is increased. The coloration produced would be perceived as a lighter value of a hue such as pale blue. When a compound known to absorb all wavelengths, creating black, is used with colorants, a **shade** is produced and value is decreased. The coloration produced would be perceived as a darker value of a hue such as navy.

Intensity

Intensity, or **chroma**, describes the purity or strength of a color. A blue hue, for example, may appear strong, bright, and clear, or weak, grayed, and dull. Changes in intensity generally produce concomitant changes in value. The effects of various fiber- and fabric-related variables— such as inherent fiber characteristics, the presence or absence of delusterants, fiber cross-sectional shapes, and the fabric structure—on the luster and brightness of colored textiles were discussed in Chapters 4 and 5. The effects of certain finishing agents and processes on color dimensions are described in Chapter 10.

A thorough understanding of colorants and their reaction with and attraction for different fibers requires formal study in the fields of dye chemistry and textile chemistry. This high level of knowledge is mandatory for the dye chemist, but not for the interior designer, architect, or consumer. Chemists work cooperatively with fiber, yarn, fabric producers, and converters to select colorants and mixtures of colorants and additives in order to create desired hue, value, and intensity and the necessary lightfastness properties.

Color not only provides visual appeal, but the mixture of colors in a surface material also effectively camouflage soil that accumulates in use, and general wear and tear. Patterned or variegated materials show less wear than do solid-color materials.

Textile Colorants

Textile colorants may be dyes or pigments. **Dyes**, or **dyestuffs**, are color-producing compounds that are normally soluble in water. **Pigments** are also color-producing agents, but they are insoluble in water. The chemical structure of either type of colorant enables it selectively to absorb and reflect certain wavelengths. Pigments are held to the fabric surface with a binding agent that works like an adhesive. Dyes penetrate the fabric surface and chemically bond with the fiber. Because of this difference, dyes are usually more durable than pigments. Pigments are only used to color textiles in the fabric stage, while dyestuffs are used to color textiles in the solution, fiber, yarn, fabric, or finished textile stage.

Dyes are classified by their chemical composition. Because dyes involve a chemical reaction with the fiber, the dyestuff must be chemically compatible with the fiber. This is referred to as having an **affinity** to the fiber. If not compatible, the fabric will not accept the dye. No one dyestuff is colorfast to all fiber contents and color range varies within each dye classification. Each dyestuff is carefully chosen based on the chemical composition, fiber content, range of colors, and desired performance characteristics.

Because pigments are held to the surface by a binding or adhesive agent, any color can be used on any fiber content. Pigments, which resemble paint lying on the surface of the fabric, can lead to fabric problems such as stiffening and cracking (think logo-printed T-shirts). Pigment printing is very fast and inexpensive, but it also can achieve certain effects that dye would not accomplish. Colors are easier to match because of the surface treatment.

Colorants contain groups called auxochromes and groups called chromophores. **Auxochromes** are responsible for the selective absorption and reflection of light waves; these groups determine the hue. **Chromophores** control the quantity of waves reflected, influencing the value of the hue. The intensity is controlled by the mixture of colorants and the amount of dyestuff accepted by the fibers. Some highly amorphous fibers, such as wool, readily accept high amounts of dye; other fibers, especially those with highly crystallized interiors, do not readily accept dyestuffs, and high pressure and temperature or dye-carriers may be required during the dyeing operation. In some cases, the affinity between the fiber and the dyestuff can be improved by the use of special agents known as **mordants**.

The dye chemist is responsible for the correct match of fiber and colorant; dyers and printers determine the precise application of the dyestuff or pigment. The planned intensity and acceptable level of color retention require adequate penetration of the colorant. In printing, accurate placement or registration of all colors makes for better clarity and definition of pattern areas.

Dyeing Fabrics and Fabric Components

Dye operations can be carried out at the fiber, yarn, or fabric stage. Most dyeing operations require immersion of the fiber material into **dye liquor**, an aqueous solution of dyestuff.

Dyeing in the Fiber Stage

Color-producing agents can be added in the fiber stage by one of two methods: solution dyeing, and fiber or stock dyeing. Solution dyeing can be used only with manufactured fibers, but fiber dyeing may be used with both natural and manufactured fibers.

Solution Dyeing

Solution dyeing and **dope dyeing** are synonyms for an operation in which dye pigments are added to the polymer solution by the manufacturer prior to extrusion from the spinneret. Coloring agents are locked inside solution-dyed manufactured fiber. Solution dyeing is used where permanence of color over a long period of time is required, and some fibers can only be dyed in the solution state.

With the color-producing dyes incorporated as an integral part of the fiber, solution-dyed fibers have comparatively high color retention and stability. This supports the use of solution dyeing to color fibers that will be used for installation outdoors. These fibers also have little or no capacity to absorb moisture, which is the reason they cannot absorb sufficient quantities of aqueous dye liquor. Note that when acetate fabrics are solution dyed, the problem of fume fading (color change caused by exposure to certain VOCs) is eliminated.

Fiber or Stock Dyeing

Immersing natural or manufactured fibers into dye liquor (before being spun into yarn) is known as **fiber** or **stock dyeing**. While it is argued that dyestuff can be absorbed more readily and thoroughly into loose masses of fiber than into yarns or fabrics are (fiber packing and twisting may physically restrict the level of dyeing; in fabrics, yarn crossings and structural compactness are physical barriers), properly dyed fabrics do not reveal undyed portions. However, stock dyeing offers blending possibilities for heather and tweed yarns that are not possible through other dyeing methods.

Fiber dyeing is frequently used with manufactured staple fibers to produce yarns that simulate the soft, mellow patina of wool. The wool-like appearance is further enhanced when the colored fibers are spun on the

Figure 9.2 Heather yarns in a plain weave fabric. Courtesy © Judy Juracek.

woolen system. Two or more colors of fibers that are mixed together and then spun into yarn create a distinctive, multicolor blend effect called **heather** (Figure 9.2). Similarly, throwing different colors of synthetic filaments also produces a heather appearance.

The term **marled** identifies the coloration produced by combining two differently colored rovings together in spinning. Although the resulting structure is a single yarn, its visual spiral resembles that produced by plying two differently colored yarns. A marled yarn is pictured in Figure 9.3.

Ombré, French for **shade**, describes color styling in which there is a gradual change in the value of a single hue, for instance, from pink to red to maroon. Carefully controlling the introduction the appropriate shade and tints during yarn spinning can produce this delicate color

Figure 9.3 A marled yarn. Courtesy © Judy Juracek

style. The location of a change is barely noticeable if the process is well executed.

Dyeing in the Yarn Stage

Adding colorants to yarn structures before fabric formation is known as **yarn dyeing**. While space dyeing can be used to produce multicolored yarns (and is described later in this chapter) most yarn-dyeing operations produce single-colored yarns, which cannot be distinguished from those constructed of one color of fiber.

Package Dyeing

The equipment used in **package dyeing** is shown in Figure 9.4. Yarns are first wound on perforated cylinders, or **packages**, of yarn. Because carpet and rug yarns have relatively large diameters, smaller amounts of the strands are wound on the packages. Several packages are then mounted on posts and lowered into a pressure cooker-like vessel known as a **dye beck**. Dye liquor is then forcibly circulated throughout each package of yarn. To ensure adequate penetration of the dye, high levels of pressure and temperatures may be used in the operation; this may be necessary when manufactured fibers with low moisture regain values, such as when polyester, nylon, and acrylic are being dyed.

Beam Dyeing

Beam dyeing is a second way of dyeing yarns a single color. In preparation for the operation, warp yarns are wound on a perforated beam barrel. The beam is then loaded into a beam dyeing machine and the dye liquor is circulated through the yarns, from the outside to the inside and from the inside to the outside, via the perforations. The beams of dyed warp yarns, when rinsed and dried, are ready to be placed on a loom, bypassing the unwinding and rewinding operations required after package dyeing. Beam dyeing may also be used for greige goods.

Skein Dyeing

Immersing long skeins of yarn into troughs filled with dye liquor is known as **skein dyeing**. This procedure may

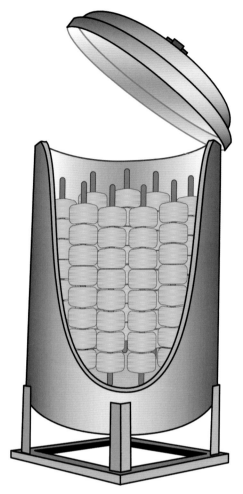

Figure 9.4 Dyeing packages of yarn in a dye beck. Lauren Rudd/ Fairchild Books.

be employed when the winding and compacting of yarns on cylinders or beam barrels could alter their textural features, or when a relatively small quantity of custom-colored yarn is required. The procedure is rarely used for dyeing large quantities of yarns, however, because it is a relatively slow and therefore costly operation.

Space Dyeing

Space dyeing produces multicolored yarns. Unlike heather yarns, in which the colors are uniformly distributed throughout the yarns, and unlike ombré yarns, in which various values of one color are repeated, space-dyed yarns have differently colored segments along their lengths. The various hues may be related or contrasting; the segments may be equal or unequal in length; and the junctures between colors may be sharp or muted.

Space-dyed yarns, also known as **variegated yarns**, are popular in both hand and machine knit apparel and in upholstery fabrics and pile carpet (Figure 9.5). Various techniques can produce this color styling. Although some of these techniques are printing rather than dyeing operations, they fall in the category of space dyeing because they create the characteristic coloration. When well-defined, sharp color junctures are planned, sheets of yarns will be printed. When muted junctures of the selected colors are desired, segments of the yarns will be dipped into dye liquor or **jet spraying** may be used. In the latter technique, pressurized dye jets spray dye liquor onto skeins of yarns. Another method uses dye-loaded needles, called **astrojets**, to give packages of yarn repeated, programmed injections. This **package-injection technique** requires minimal handling of the yarns.

Yarn texturing and color application are combined in **knit-de-knit space dyeing**. Pile yarns, undyed or pre-colored, are rapidly knitted into a long, jersey-stitched tube. One or more colors are then printed onto the tubing with dye jets before heat setting. Finally, the tube is de-knit or unraveled, producing variegated, crinkled pile yarns.

Dyeing Greige Goods

Fabrics that are intended to be dyed or printed but have not yet been are called **greige goods**. Unless colored fibers or yarns were used in fabrication, greige goods bear little resemblance to those offered to residential and commercial consumers. Except for any textural and visual interest contributed by complex yarns or decorative

Figure 9.5 Space-dyed weft yarn. Courtesy © Judy Juracek

weaves, such fabrics have virtually no aesthetic appeal to an end-user. Not only do greige materials lack color, but they are usually stiff, and may contain sizings and other additives (used to improve the weaving process) that leave an unpleasant hand. Cloth in the greige state is similar to a half-baked loaf of bread.

Dyeing operations usually produce only solid-colored surfaces, and printing techniques only patterned surfaces, but multicolored designs can be achieved through both ancient and innovative immersion processes. Additionally, printing techniques are sometimes used for the production of solid-colored surfaces.

Piece Dyeing

In **piece dyeing**, greige goods are immersed in a dye solution, which is called *dye liquor*. A "piece" of upholstery or multipurpose fabric is normally 50 to 60 yards (meters) of fabric, which is a maximum length that can be handled, given the weight of bolts. (Bolts of fine fabrics, like sheer drapery cloth, may hold longer yardage since they are not as heavy; bolts of carpet will be much shorter.) Piece dyeing produces single-colored fabrics with identical color characteristics on both sides.

When tufted greige goods are piece dyed, the primary backing may be thinly coated with an adhesive to stabilize the pile tufts; secondary backings are added after the goods are dyed. Any secondary backing would add bulk and weight, making handling of the long lengths cumbersome. A secondary backing of jute would absorb a large amount of dye liquor, increasing the cost of the dyestuffs, as well as the time and expense of drying the floorcovering. (A secondary backing may be applied prior to printing some fabrics in order to add dimensional stability and ensure good registration of the colors in the motifs.)

Greige goods may be dyed in a discontinuous or a continuous dyeing operation. Discontinuous operations are so named because the coloring process is interrupted when the wet material must be removed from the dyeing machine and dried elsewhere.

Discontinuous Dyeing

Because relatively small quantities, or batches, of cloth can be dyed in **discontinuous-dyeing** operations, they are often known as **batch-dyeing** operations. They are carried out in various vessels, or becks, which may include a jet beck, a horizontal beam-dyeing machine, or a carpet winch.

Batch-dyeing operations are economical for dyeing smaller quantities of greige goods compared with some other piece dye methods, and also consume less water and energy than continuous-dyeing methods require. Specifically, the becks are designed to use comparatively low **liquor ratios** (pounds of liquor to pounds of greige goods). Because water is the principal component in most dye liquors, this results in substantial savings in water cost and drying expenses.

Carpet Winch

Low-priced carpet is often batch dyed utilizing a **carpet winch**. In preparation, the ends of a batch of greige goods weighing approximately 2,000 pounds are sewn together and loaded into the beck. This weight roughly corresponds to 330 linear yards of goods. The full width of carpet is plaited or folded as it is fed into the dye liquor. If the plaiting operation is controlled so that it will produce folds from 8 to 16 inches deep and never creases the carpet in the same place twice, the development of crosswise surface markings will be minimized; avoiding these markings is especially important for velour and plush textures. The carpet is cycled through the dye liquor, which is continually filtered, for an average of 2 to 4 hours, and it is then rinsed, unloaded, and dried.

Jet Dyeing

In preparation for dyeing in a **jet beck**, a batch of cloth in rope form is loaded into a long vessel (Figure 9.6). The unit is nearly 40 feet long, and can accommodate some 2,800 pounds of goods. Jets introduce the dye, and the material is cycled through the liquor. Temperature and pressure can be elevated for effective dyeing of polyester.

Beck Dyeing

Beck-dyeing operations begin with the winding of an open width of greige goods on a perforated beam. The batch is loaded into a horizontal dyeing machine and the dye liquor is forcibly circulated through the rolled goods.

Figure 9.6 Beck dyeing.

Beck dyeing is inappropriate for carpets other than those of low pile because the carpet would become severely deformed by the twisting and handling that the material must endure during the process. However, beam dyeing, a variation of beck dyeing in which the greige goods are rolled flat onto the perforated beams rather than being wound, is popular for low-pile, loop-surface carpet texture. (Because the carpet is rolled flat onto the beams, soft, deep-pile textures would be severely deformed by the process.) Since the goods are not folded in beam dyeing, no crossmarks can develop in the carpet, which is a distinct advantage.

Jig Dyeing

In a **jig-dyeing** machine (Figure 9.7), fabric is passed through a stationary dye bath (not immersed); then the fabric reverses and is passed through the dye bath again. For large quantities, jig dyeing is more economical than jet dyeing because runs of several thousand yards are possible, but it is impractical for many typical interior furnishings fabric styles, since uniqueness is at a premium for most end-users.

Pad Dyeing

Pad dyeing is produced with a machine called a dye pad (Figure 9.8). Fabric passes through the dye bath, then through the rollers, where the dye solution is squeezed into the fabric. Large quantities of fabric can be run through the dye pad.

Continuous Dyeing

Continuous-dyeing operations are used when large quantities of greige goods are to be dyed one color. Because several lengths of greige goods or undyed carpet are sewn together, their construction and composition must be identical or quite similar in order to produce uniform color characteristics. The dyeing machinery,

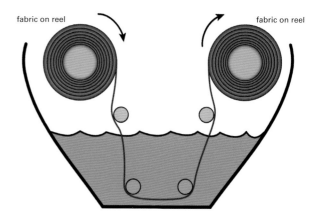

Figure 9.7 Jig dyeing machine. Illustration by Lauren Rudd/Fairchild Books

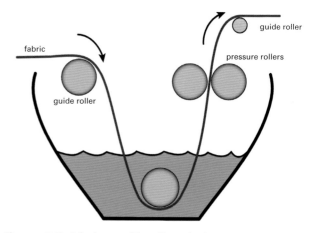

Figure 9.8 Pad dyeing machine. Illustration by Lauren Rudd/ Fairchild Books.

known as **dyeing ranges**, comprise units for wetting the material, applying the dyestuff, steaming, washing, drying, and rolling up the dyed and dried goods. These units are aligned so the fabric goes directly from one step to the next. Such operations do not require unloading of the greige goods and transporting them to other units for final processing, so they are said to be *continuous*.

When cloth is introduced into a continuous-dyeing range, it is wetted to increase dye absorption. In some systems, a squeegee-like blade transfers the dye liquor from a roller to the wet surface. Steaming helps increase the movement or **migration** of the liquor through the cloth, promoting uniform application of the dye. (In carpet, this helps avoid the problem of **tippiness**, which is the concentration of color on the tips of the pile yarns.)

In some cases, the dye is applied as a spray, that is, a mixture of air and dye; in other cases, the dye is carried on the surface of bubbles. One method involves depositing dye on the carpet as foamed dye liquor. The foam is an unstable froth that collapses on the fiber and dyes it.

The spray, bubbles, or foam can be delivered through tubes, jets, or spray nozzles oriented toward the pile layer. They may also be delivered by blades and rollers, blowers, and rotary screens. If the quantity warrants the setup for and running of these methods, reduction in water usage can result in marked processing costs savings. As the cloth continues through the system, it is washed, dried, and rolled.

Special Dyeing Techniques

Cross Dyeing

Cross dyeing (sometimes called **differential dyeing**), is a color application process based on chemical variables. The process produces a multicolored fabric from a single immersion in one (or sometimes two) dye bath formulation. Two or more fibers that are chemically different—classified in different generic groups or variants of the same fiber—are strategically placed in yarns or in greige goods. Carpet and rug producers generally use a blend of nylon variants, rather than generically dissimilar fibers, in this coloring operation. For a heather appearance, different fibers are uniformly distributed in the yarns; for plaids or stripes, warp or filling yarns with different fiber contents are used in bands; and for multicolored design motifs, yarns of different fibers are selectively incorporated during fabrication.

The dye chemist, with the aid of a computer, selects specific dyestuffs, each of which will be accepted by one fiber and rejected by all other fibers, or use one dyestuff that will be absorbed in different amounts by related fiber variants. In the former case, each type of fiber or variant has a different hue, and, in the latter case, each variant has a different level of intensity of the same hue. A second major advantage of any method of piece dyeing, including cross dyeing, is that orders for specific colors can be filled quickly. Whatever the color mixture ordered, the stored greige goods are ready for immediate dyeing, finishing, and shipping, which is an economic and marketing advantage.

Although dye houses that are willing to cross dye are fewer than those that dye solid colors, cross dyeing is a useful technique. (In the United States, piece dyers in general are quite limited in number.) Without cross-dyeing technology, yarns would have to be dyed in two or three colors in separate lots; the colored yarns packaged or wound on beams, fill yarn would need to be prepared on cones, then the order would be woven. Cross dyeing offers specific aesthetic possibilities, but it offers a buffer against an inventory of unpopular color for producers who would need to stock yarns or finished goods projected against the market's direction.

Union Dyeing

Like cross dyeing, **union dyeing** is based on chemical variables. Unlike cross dyeing, however, union dyeing is chosen when two or more different fibers are used in a fabric that is to become a single, uniform color. Again, a single dye bath is formulated but each fiber becomes the same color.

Tone-on-Tone Dyeing

Tone-on-tone effects are also possible by using one dye bath. These effects are light and dark shades of the same color on a fabric containing two different types of one generic fiber. The different types of fibers combine with the dye, but one fiber has a stronger affinity for the dye, so it becomes darker. The other fiber remains a lighter shade of the same color. The tone-on-tone effect is widely used in the floorcoverings industry for producing tweed-effect designs on carpeting.

Printing Greige Goods

In prints, only certain areas of the fabric's surface are colored in order to create a surface pattern. Most printing techniques were—and still are in some instances— executed by hand. But high-speed mechanized operations are generally used to print greige goods for commercial purposes. Printing requires thicker dyestuffs from those used in dyeing operations. Whereas migration or movement of the dye is required to achieve a uniform level of color in dyed textile structures, such migration in printed goods would result in poor definition of the shapes and details of the motifs. Therefore, the dyestuff used in most printing operations is a **dye paste** rather than a highly aqueous dye liquor. After application of the dye paste, the textile is exposed to steam, heat, or chemicals to fix the dye in or on the fibers. Pigments may also be used to print greige goods.

Whereas dyes chemically bond with fibers to change color permanently, in **pigment printing**, water-insoluble pigments are mixed with an adhesive compound or resin binders and applied to textiles surfaces. Because the pigments are not absorbed by the fibers, the printed designs stand in slight relief. Frequently, white or metallic-colored pigments are printed on a previously dyed surface and may be referred to as **overprinting**. Overprinting also describes printing over Jacquard fabrics, so that one pattern comes from the weave and one from the print.

Direct Printing

In **direct printing**, color is applied directly to specific areas of the face of a fabric or yarns. Application can be done by hand or machine.

Block Printing

In preparation for **block printing**, artisans hand carve all shapes of the planned design that will be the same color so that those areas stand in relief on the face of a block of wood. A separate block is prepared for each color to be printed. Probably the oldest method of fabric printing, block printing is time- and labor-intensive. These distinctive prints are, as would be expected, quite expensive. The blocks are generally made by artisans in developing countries where labor costs are relatively low, which raises issues of sustainable practices.

During printing, the artisan dips the face of the carved design into the dye paste and then presses it onto the fabric surface. Since the printer may pick up different quantities of dye paste each time and exert different levels of pressure with each printing action, various levels of intensity may be seen for the same hue, although expert hand-block printers execute their craft at a nearly perfect level.

Hand-blocked prints represent only a tiny percentage of the market; nonetheless, the block-printing aesthetic, and traditional motifs developed through this print

Figure 9.9 Block print. Courtesy of Lee Jofa.

method, are popular inspiration in other methods of printing and have significantly influences our American vision of surface pattern.

Roller Printing

Lightweight, flat fabrics lend themselves as a vehicle for printing with engraved metal rollers. The shapes of those portions of the repeat that are to be the same color are etched into the surface of one roller. The number of colors planned dictates the number of rollers prepared, thus the name **roller print**. As schematized in Figure 9.10, small cylinders revolve through the dye paste and transfer the paste to the engraved rollers. A metal, squeegee-like blade, called a **doctor blade**, then removes the excess dye paste from the smooth, non-engraved surface areas. As the rollers revolve against the fabric surface, the dye paste is transferred and the pattern repeat is completed.

Accurate registration is critical with any printing method. With roller printing, the rollers and the fabric must be properly aligned to ensure that patterns, especially those having linear motifs, are printed on grain. If the rollers are improperly aligned, the result will be an **out-of-register** print (Figure 9.11).

Roller printing is an extremely fast operation, but it requires large quantities to warrant setup per colorway. Because of the increased value placed on broad product lines and varied choices, and because of the growing sophistication of both screen and digital printing, its use has diminished. Additionally, the cost of both the copper used to cover the rollers and the cost of the labor needed to prepare the rollers have increased. Roller printing is, however, excellent for very detailed patterns that feature fine lines, such as paisleys or toiles (Figure 9.12).

Figure 9.11 Out-of-register print. Courtesy of Amy Willbanks, www.textilefabric.com.

Figure 9.12 Roller print. Courtesy of Amy Willbanks, www.textilefabric.com.

Warp Printing

In **warp printing**, patterns are applied on the warp yarns by engraved rollers, flat-bed screens, or rotary screens prior to weaving. Fabrics printed by this method have a muted, hazy appearance because the warp yarns shift slightly from their position during printing to when they are woven. Warp printing is a time-consuming and expensive process, but the effects are often simulated in direct printing. A warp printed fabric is shown in Figure 9.13.

A similar, though more random effect is achieved through warp resist dyeing, in which warp yarns are bound before being dyed, so that the bound areas are masked. Again, when placed on the loom, the yarns shift slightly, so hazy edges are the end effect. Similar printing

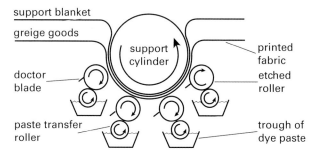

Figure 9.10 Roller printing. Fairchild Books.

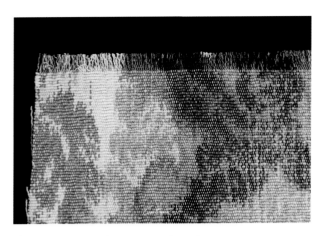

Figure 9.13 Warp print. Courtesy of Max Concra.

and resist dyeing of fill yarns is possible, though rare, other than in antique ethnic fabrics.

Resist Printing

Various techniques that prevent absorption or flow of the dyestuff block color absorption in **resist printing**. When the fabrics are subsequently piece dyed or printed, the dye is absorbed only in the areas that are free of the resist. Artisans use several different hand-resist printing operations to create distinctive interior fabrics. Batik, tie-dye, and ikat are examples of hand methods; screen and gum printing are industrial or mechanical resist-printing operations.

Although consumers may prefer an authentic batik, tie-dye, or ikat fabric, many are unable to find the yardage or they find these handmade fabrics cost prohibitive. Recognizing this dilemma, manufacturers often simulate the hand-printed patterns with high-speed, commercial printing techniques. Professionals and consumers can readily distinguish authentic prints from most simulated ones by examining the back of the fabric. All authentic batik, tie-dye, and ikat fabrics have the same depth of color on both sides of the fabric.

Batik

Beeswax is the resist agent in traditional **batik** fabrics. It is melted and applied with a **tjanting** tool to all areas of the fabric that are to resist penetration of the dye liquor. The tjanting has a small copper cup and a tiny spout. In use, the tool functions somewhat like a fountain pen,

and skilled artisans can apply fine lines of wax to create intricate details within the motifs.

After the wax hardens, the fabric is immersed into a dye bath; only the nonwaxed areas absorb the dye. The wax is then removed from the fabric by boiling. The artisan again applies melted wax, this time to all areas—including those that are to remain the first color—that are to resist the second dye liquor. If a crackle effect characterized by linear striations is planned, the artist randomly cracks the hardened wax at this time. Piece dyeing then results in absorption of the second color in all unwaxed areas, as well as in those areas below any cracks (Figure 9.14a). This sequence of wax removal, wax application, and immersion is repeated until all planned colors have been applied. Fabrics are sometimes printed to simulate true batiks (Figure 9.14b) as a less expensive alternative.

(a)

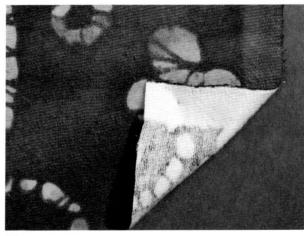

(b)

Figure 9.14 Batik and roller print comparison. (a) Authentic batik print with crackle effects, (b) batik effect simulated by direct printing. Courtesy of Amy Willbanks, www.textilefabric.com

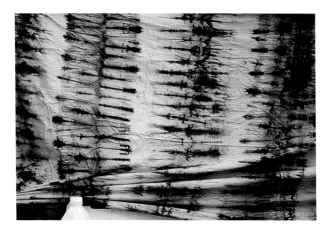

Figure 9.15 Tie-dyed fabric. Courtesy © Judy Juracek

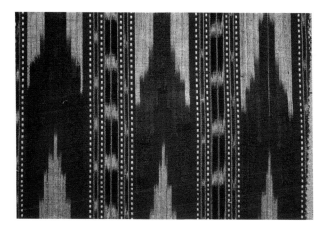

Figure 9.16 Ikat fabric. Courtesy of Amy Willbanks, www. textilefabric.com.

Tie-Dye

In **tie-dyeing**, folds, gathers, and knots, which are introduced in the fabric and secured with waxed thread, function as the resist medium. These are selected and positioned according to the motifs and pattern scale planned. When the fabric is immersed into the dye bath, the tied-off areas resist penetration of the dye liquor. The fabric is then opened flat and again tied off and immersed in a second dye bath. The processes will be repeated in sequence until all planned colors and designs have been introduced. A tie-dyed fabric is pictured in Figure 9.15.

Ikat

In **ikat** (*e-cot*) fabrics, specific portions of bundles of warp and filling yarns, not fabric, are wrapped to resist dye penetration. The wrapping is carefully positioned to create the planned motifs. Subsequent dyeing results in absorption of the dye liquor by the unwrapped yarn portions only. Portions of the wrapping may be removed and additional colors applied. Because the aqueous dye liquor migrates through the yarns and varied levels of relaxation shrinkage may occur after weaving, ikat motifs have a striated appearance (Figure 9.16).

Screen Printing

Screen printing, developed in the mid-twentieth century, is widely used in both flat-bed screen and rotary screen iterations. Both methods can deliver large concentrations of dyestuff, and both can facilitate the printing of

large-scale motifs and repeats. Because most upholstery fabrics are relatively heavy and require large quantities of dye, and because sheetings and curtain and drapery fabrics are often designed with large-scale motifs and pattern repeats, these interior fabrics are very frequently screen printed (Figure 9.17). Rotary screen printing has long been the most popular printing method for interior fabrics, however, digital printing is likely to take over in short order.

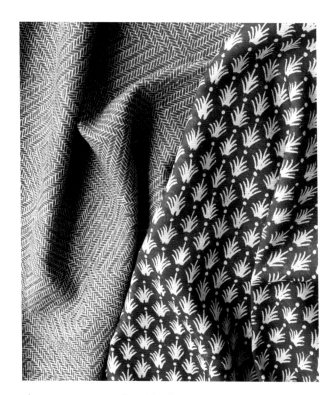

Figure 9.17 Screen-printed fabrics, "Reeds" and "Rattan." Courtesy of Clay McLaurin Studio, LLC.

The apparatus and procedures used in flat-bed and rotary screen printing operations differ. Both techniques, however, are based on the principle of a stencil: portions of the printing equipment are blocked to resist the flow of dye.

Flat-Bed Screen Printing

In preparation for **flat-bed screen printing**, large rectangular frames are covered with a fine, strong fabric. The compactness of the fabric determines the amount of dye paste allowed to flow through the fabric interstices. Today, nylon and polyester filaments have replaced silk filaments in these fabrics, mostly as a result of the higher cost of the natural fiber. The frames are as wide as the greige goods, generally 45 or 60 inches, and up to 80 inches in length (wallpaper may be narrower).

Each screen will be used to print one color, so the number of planned colors determines the number of screens that must be prepared. Some areas of each screen are treated with a compound that can prevent or block the flow of the dye paste; other areas are left untreated to allow the paste to pass through the fabric. The untreated areas on each screen are in the shapes of the designs in the repeat that are to be the same color.

For printing, the screens are aligned and mounted horizontally above the fabric, as shown in Figure 9.18. The dye paste is spread over the screen surface from one side to the other, flowing through the untreated areas and printing the fabric below. The fabric is then advanced and the procedure is repeated. Because each screen adds one color, the fabric must advance under all the screens for the coloration of the repeat to be completed. It is evident that the width of the pattern repeat and the width of the fabric govern the number of repeats that can be printed side by side; the length of the repeat and the height of the screen limit the number of repeats that can be simultaneously printed end to end.

Because large quantities of dyestuff can be passed through the screens, a good level of saturation can be obtained in screen printing heavier flat fabrics and pile structures. When working with pile structures, printers must carefully position the screens to avoid distortion of the pile yarns, and the dye paste must be drawn into the pile layer or the colored design will be carried only by the yarn tips.

Figure 9.18 Flatbed screen printing. Courtesy of Zimmer Austria.

Rotary Screen Printing

Developed in the early 1960s, **rotary screen printing** has become the predominant method of printing fabric and wallpaper, although digital printing is gaining popularity. The technique is used to print both flat and pile fabrics. It is also used to print sheets of warp yarns with motifs and with randomized, space-dyed effects. In addition, it is frequently used to print the paper used in transfer-printing operations, which are discussed in the following section.

Rotary screen printing is so widely used because several of its features make it economical. It is generally faster and more accurate than other printing techniques, and it produces a more uniform level of coloration when large quantities of goods are being run (Figure 9.19).

The cylindrical rollers used in rotary screen printing have microscopic openings in their nickel-coated surfaces. While earlier screens had some 120 holes per inch, newer screens have up to 215 holes per inch. The holes in the newer screens are more regular and well defined, and the surface is smoother. These improvements have facilitated more precise control of shaded effects and better definition of design details.

The planned pattern motifs are transferred to the surfaces of the cylinders. The holes in the areas to be printed are left open and those in the adjacent areas are blocked with water-insoluble lacquer. During printing, the dye paste is continually forced from the interior of the cylindrical screen through the minute openings. One color of the repeat is applied by each rotating screen.

Figure 9.19 Rotary screen printing. Courtesy of Zimmer Austria.

After the fabric has passed under all screens, all colors and designs will have been added. Some rotary screen printing machines can accept up to 20 screens, so they can print up to 20 colors.

Rotary screen printing is used infrequently to print soft floorcoverings. In most cases, rotary screens have not been designed to supply the large amount of paste required for dyeing heavier pile layers. The recent introduction of a system that uses foam instead of paste, however, may increase the popularity of this high-speed printing technique.

Gum Printing

In **gum printing**, a gum compound known to resist dye absorption is applied to the tips of the pile yarns prior to dyeing. The gum will prevent dye absorption and migration, causing the upper portion of the pile layer to have a frosted appearance. **Frostiness** describes the absence of dye on the yarn tips. It is a planned color style, unlike *tippiness*, the unplanned and unwanted concentration of dye on the yarn tips that occurs when dye migration is not sufficient to produce uniform intensity. Gum printing for frostiness has the drawback of consuming additional utilities in removing the gum.

Fabric immersion can be used in combination with a printing procedure to produce interior fabrics that have colored backgrounds and non-colored design motifs. Discharge printing and resist printing are examples of such combinations.

Discharge Printing

Discharge printing is an efficient way to color large areas of the ground and create a pattern. The fabric is first piece dyed, producing the same depth of color on both sides. It is then printed with a discharge paste, similar to bleach, that removes the color wherever the design motifs are planned. Recent developments in discharge-printing equipment turn discharging and immediate color printing into one sequential operation.

Discharge prints can be identified by examining the fabric on both sides. The background will be the same color on both the face and back of the fabric. The design on the back of the fabric may show parts of the background color where the dye was not completely removed. Also, a halo effect around motifs is typical (see Figure 9.20).

Inkjet Printing

Inkjet printing is among the more recent and innovative developments for coloring soft floorcoverings. In most cases, the same dye applicator units used to produce solid-colored surfaces in continuous-dyeing operations, including tubes, nozzles, blowers, and jets, are used in these operations. In inkjet printing, however, the delivery of the dye is precisely controlled to create detailed designs and pattern repeats.

Some inkjet-printing systems have applicator components placed only 1.10 inch apart. This helps to ensure full coverage of the surface. To produce sharp, well-defined designs, carpet greige goods are generally sheared and vacuumed prior to being printed. Because no equipment is in contact with the floorcovering during the printing, the potential problem of pile distortion is avoided.

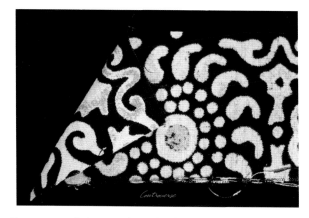

Figure 9.20 Discharge-printed fabric. Courtesy of Max Concra.

Inkjet printing is a comparatively inexpensive operation—because of its high rate of production, it utilizes relatively little water, dye, and energy. Although the capital investment initially required to purchase and install certain units can be substantial, other digital printers are relatively inexpensive and are becoming increasingly popular.

The engineering is sophisticated in jet printing systems. The intricate color placement and elaborate patterning capabilities can be used to simulate authentic Oriental rugs, for example. The printing is electronically controlled by a computer, which triggers the jets to shoot the surface with dye liquor in a programmed sequence.

Some jet-printing systems have applicator components placed only 0.10 inches apart. This helps to ensure full coverage of the surface. To ensure the production of sharp, well-defined designs, carpet greige goods are generally sheared and vacuumed prior to being printed. Because no equipment is in contact with the floorcovering during printing, the potential problem of pile distortion is avoided.

Jet printing is a comparatively inexpensive operation because of its high rate of production and because it utilizes relatively little water, dye, and energy. Although the capital investment initially required to purchase and install certain units can be substantial, other digital printers are relatively inexpensive and are becoming increasingly popular.

Heat Transfer Printing

Heat transfer printing, also known as **sublistatic printing**, involves the use of heat to transfer dyestuff from paper to fabric. The difference between transfer printing and other methods of printing described in this chapter is that the surface of the fabric is not directly printed. Instead the pattern is first created on paper and is then transferred from the paper to the fabric (Figure 9.21). The technique has long been used to print the outlines of motifs in preparation for hand embroidering, and, more recently, colored motifs have been available as tear-out pages in popular magazines. The technique was adapted for the industrial-scale printing of textile fabric in the early 1970s.

In preparation for this operation, transfer paper is printed by one of four techniques—gravure, flexo, rotary screen printing (Figure 9.22), and computerized digital

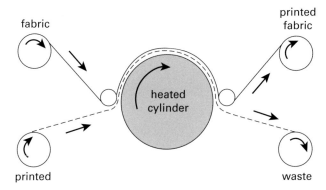

Figure 9.21 Heat transfer printing. Courtesy of Celanese International Corporation.

printing. *Gravure* identifies roller printing with engraved copper-covered rollers, *flexo* identifies roller printing with engraved rubber-covered rollers, and *rotary screen* identifies rotary screen transfer printing.

The recent introduction of computerized heat transfer printing allows for greater customization in textile printing. Computerization also allows access to a wide variety of colors and gradient patterns at a more economical price. Customized bedding and team sportswear apparel are just a few of the many textiles that are increasing in popularity with this type of printing method. Although the computerized printing equipment and inks are still slightly more expensive and slower to produce than more traditional methods, customers are willing to pay for the uniqueness of the customization gained through computerized heat transfer printing. As printing and ink technology advances, the printing speed will increase as well as the cost effectiveness of the process.

For printing, the colored paper is placed face down on the face of the greige goods. The dyestuffs used have a higher affinity for the fibers than for the paper; when they are exposed to heat they **sublime**, changing from a solid on the paper, to a gas, to a solid on the fabric. The procedure is fast and energy-efficient, and the fabric requires no afterwash because no excess dye-stuff remains.

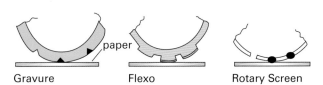

Figure 9.22 Techniques used for printing transfer paper. Fairchild Books

The use of transfer printing as an industrial technique was initially encouraged by widespread consumer acceptance of polyester knits in the 1970s. The inherent elasticity of the fiber and the knitted structure resulted in relatively high relaxation shrinkage following release of the tension used in roller and screen printing operations. The shrinkage caused distortion of the printed patterns. In order to avoid this problem, manufacturers used transfer printing, which requires minimal fabric tensioning.

Transfer printing is relatively uncommon in interior furnishings because the quantities required to print the paper are large and lot-to-lot consistency is not ideal. Furthermore, digital printing, which requires very small minimums and low startup investment, is much more convenient.

New classes of dyes have been produced that allow heat transfer printing on nylon fabrics in addition to polyester. The majority of fabrics printed with the heat transfer method contain polyester, nylon, or blends with a high polyester content.

Digital Printing

Digital printing is essentially the same as printing on paper from a computer. A digital image file in the computer directs the digital printer, which accommodates fabric rather than paper. The fabric is fed in and printed across the entire width of the goods.

Digital printing is increasingly pervasive. The cost of digital printers is relatively small, and the operation can be cost effective in small lots, so custom projects are easy to accommodate. The printing works best on smooth, relatively lightweight fabrics, but nearly any fiber is printable.

Acid Printing

Acid printing produces a color style known as a **burnt-out** or **etched-out print**. In this styling, the motifs and the ground have different levels of transparency. Because this technique is a chemically dependent process and one in which no colorants are added, some textile authorities prefer to classify the procedure as a finishing operation.

Fabrics used in an acid-printing operation must be composed of an acid-resistant fiber and an acid-degradable fiber; a blend of nylon and rayon is typically used. During printing, weak sulfuric acid is printed on selected areas of the fabric, destroying or burning away the acid-degradable

rayon. This chemical reaction changes the composition of these areas to 100 percent nylon, creating a higher level of transparency than is seen in the untreated areas. A burnt-out print is pictured in Figure 17.10, p. 229.

Fusion Printing

Fusion printing is a type of pigment printing used to secure colorants to the surface of fabrics composed of glass fiber. Colored acrylic resins are first printed on the surface of the fabric. Heat is then used to soften the thermoplastic compound and fuse it to the nonabsorbent glass. Like other pigment-printed designs, fusion-printed designs stand in slight relief.

Factors Affecting Apparent Color

Several factors have no direct effect on colorants but may alter perception of the original color of a product. Some of these factors, including changes in texture and soiling, relate to end-use activities; others, such as the source and quantity of light, are aspects of the interior environment. These variables alter the apparent color characteristics of interior textiles; the actual color characteristics are unchanged.

Following virtually every method of color application, the textile structures must be washed, rinsed, and dried. Dyed goods may be **tentered** (pulled out on a frame to hold a consistent width) and some may be heat set. A secondary backing will be applied to some clothes, including tufted structures, after dyeing. To restore distorted pile yarns to their upright position, an angled blade is passed against and lifts the pile yarns. Cut pile textures and wool fabrics may be sheared to create a uniform pile height and vacuumed to remove lint. A final inspection is made prior to shipment.

A colorant may be scientifically selected and precisely applied, but the immediate and long-term appearance of the color will be affected by substances and conditions such as cleaning agents and atmospheric contaminants that produce changes in actual color characteristics. These variables, and test methods to measure their effects, are described in later units. The potential effects of various factors on apparent color characteristics are discussed in the following sections.

Light Source

Color may be the most important aesthetic variable in the selection of an interior textile product. Unfortunately, color choices are often made in a setting other than the one in which the product will be used. Inevitably, the lighting in the showroom or retail display area differs from that in the residential or commercial interior. Viewing a colored item in the separate locations, an observer may perceive marked differences in hue and value. Products to be used in an interior space should be color matched under lighting conditions that mimic those of the actual space to avoid the potential for mismatched colors once they are installed.

As mentioned earlier in this chapter, artificial light sources differ from each other and from natural light in the mixture of visible wavelengths they emit. Whereas natural light emits almost equal quantities of all wavelengths, artificial sources emit unequal quantities. Incandescent lamps contain more of the warmer colors or longer wavelengths of red, orange, and yellow. Fluorescent lamps are available in a wide variety of colors and should be selected to enhance the colors of the space. Lamps are rated in two ways that will facilitate selection of the appropriate light to give the best appearance to a space. The first rating is the **apparent color temperature**, which describes the visual appearance of the light source and is expressed in degrees kelvin (K). The lower the K value, the warmer the light will appear. Higher K values indicate a cooler or bluer appearance of the light. This measure does not indicate how accurately the light source will show color.

The second rating is the **color rendering index (CRI)**, which measures how well the lamp renders color. The CRI is expressed on a scale of 0 to 100, with 100 being the best color rendering. Incandescent lights have a CRI of 100, whereas fluorescents typically range from the 60s to the 90s. A CRI of 85 or higher is considered acceptable for fluorescent lamps in spaces where true colors are desirable. When comparing fluorescent light sources for color rendering, accurate comparisons can only be made when sources have the same color temperature. Both the apparent color temperature and the color rendering index should be provided by the manufacturer lamp specifications.

Fluorescent bulbs raise environmental concerns because they contain mercury, and therefore are on the decline. LED bulbs and fixtures, which omit an altogether different kind of light, are on the increase.

Quantity of Light

The quantity of light incident on a textile directly affects its color characteristics, especially its value—increases in the level of light produce apparent increases in the lightness of the surface. The amount of light emitted from artificial light sources can be controlled by dimmers and the wattages of lamps. The amount of natural light can be regulated by the compactness of the window coverings and the use of exterior awnings. Of course, the size of windows and skylights and their orientation to the seasonal angles of the sun are also very important.

In interior settings, the quantity of light is not limited to that radiating through the windows and emanating from artificial sources. A significant amount can be **indirect light** or reused light reflected from walls, ceilings, doors, and furnishings.

Natural light can appear cooler in the early part of the day and shift to a much warmer appearance as the day progresses; thus, colors may appear to change as the natural light illuminating the changes. This is especially apparent in the late afternoon. Light can vary greatly from one geographic region to another. When coupled with the color variations available in artificial lighting, even minimal changes in the quantity of light affect the perception of an object's color value or intensity. Darker values may appear almost black in very low light levels, and much muted color intensity may appear gray. It is important to keep in mind that without light, there is no color; therefore, quantity of light can dramatically alter the perceived hue, value, and intensity.

Changes in Texture

The abrasive and crushing forces that textile structures may encounter during use produce changes in their original textural features. Such changes affect the apparent lightness and darkness of colored surfaces. As people shift their seated positions and move their arms over upholstery fabrics, they can compress yarn surfaces and alter decorative effects. Such physical changes have no effect on the colorants, but the abraded areas appear darker because the pattern of light reflection is altered.

For example, when fibers and yarns used in soft floorcoverings are abraded by shoe soles, furniture casters, and the like, their surfaces may be roughened as dirt and sharp-edged grit particles grind severely against the fibers. Deterioration of the smoothness of the fibers and yarns results in deflection of incident light waves and a decrease in apparent value. A decrease in lightness is also apparent when abrasive forces rupture the loops of pile floorcoverings and other pile fabrics, because the quantity of light reflected from the fiber ends is less than that reflected from the sides of the yarns in the intact loops.

Textural changes caused by crushing, especially of pile surfaces, may be less readily noticed or less objectionable if the compression is spread uniformly over the surface. However, people tend to sit in the central portion of upholstered cushions, to repeatedly lean against the same region of back cushions, and to walk in established traffic patterns. These practices result in localized compression, which may gradually result in a non-uniform pile depth across the textile surface. This creates variations in the apparent value of the surface, with flattened areas appearing lighter and distorted areas appearing darker than undisturbed pile areas. Consumers and professionals can minimize the development of this unsightly effect by selecting pile fabrics made of resilient fibers and having high pile construction densities when a high level of use is expected.

Soil Accumulation

Regular cleaning is the most step in retaining the original appearance and color of a material. Residential and commercial consumers may be convinced that the original color of their textile product has changed when in fact it is merely masked by soil. As soil accumulates, especially on bright, solid-colored surfaces, the coloration appears duller. As is true for changes in texture, soiling is often localized, with heavier buildup occurring on the arms and seat cushions of furniture and in traffic lanes and entrance areas. If soil accumulation is expected to be rapid, a multi-colored surface that can mask the appearance of soil should be considered. Protective items, such as removable arm covers and walk-off mats, are also available.

Composition and Structural Variables

Different fibers have different color characteristics even when dyed the same color. This difference is the result of the chemical structures of the fibers and dyes used and the affinity the fibers have for the colorants. Increasing or decreasing yarn size causes accompanying changes in the intensity of the chosen hue. Similar effects appear with changes in pile construction density. Contract designers and architects must consider the potential impact on apparent color of specifying composition or construction features that differ from those characterizing the color samples.

Consumers and professionals must be aware that even yarns and fabrics intended to look identical generally have differences in color intensity when dyed or printed in different operations. To avoid this problem, the initial order should include sufficient yardage for the planned project.

Textile chemists, colorists, and engineers constantly strive to refine and improve methods of applying color to textile structures. The urgent need to conserve energy and reduce production costs encourages this effort. Moreover, the rapid shifting of consumer style preferences requires that colorists be capable of an equally speedy response to remain competitive.

Key Terms

acid print	direct printing
affinity	discharge printing
apparent color	discontinuous dyeing
temperature	doctor blade
astrojets	dope dyeing
auxochromes	dye beck
batch dyeing	dye liquor
batik	dye paste
beam dyeing	dyeing ranges
beck dyeing	dyes
block print	dyestuffs
burnt-out print	electromagnetic spectrum
carpet winch	etched-out print
chroma	fiber dyeing
chromophores	flat-bed screen printing
color rendering index	frostiness
(CRI)	fusion printing
continuous dyeing	greige goods
cross dyeing	gum printing
differential dyeing	heather
digital printing	heat transfer printing

hue	pigments
ikat	resist printing
indirect light	roller printing
inkjet printing	rotary screen printing
intensity	screen printing
jet beck	shade
jet spraying	skein dyeing
jig dyeing	solution dyeing
knit-de-knit space dyeing	space dyeing
liquor ratio	stock dyeing
marl	sublime
migration	sublistatic printing
mordant	tentered
nanometer	tie-dyeing
ombré	tint
out-of-register	tippiness
overprinting	tjanting
package dyeing	tone-on-tone effect
package-injection technique	union dyeing
	value
packages	variegated yarns
pad dyeing	visible spectrum
piece dyeing	warp printing
pigment printing	yarn dyeing

Review Questions

1. Discuss the impact that increased energy costs and heightened concern for water conservation have had on the dyeing and printing industries.
2. Explain the difference between the electromagnetic spectrum and the visible spectrum.
3. What is meant by the term *wavelength*?
4. Explain how the combination of incident light waves and colorant present determine the hue we see.
5. Distinguish between tints and shades.
6. What is the role of a mordant?
7. Explain the difference in a discharge print and a resist print.
8. What is a distinct advantage of solution dyeing? Why is it not routinely used?
9. What is apparent color temperature? How is it expressed?
10. Differentiate among the following color styling terms: heather, marl, and ombré.
11. Why is the use of skein dyeing generally limited to smaller quantities of yarn?
12. Which operation is more efficient, discontinuous dyeing or continuous dyeing?
13. Explain the acid printing operation. What are two other names for acid printing?
14. Distinguish between tippiness and frostiness.
15. Explain the advantages of cross dyeing. What has led to the growth of both cross dyeing and union dyeing?
16. What are the resist media used in batik, tie-dye, and ikat fabrics?
17. Why can't large motifs and large pattern repeats be printed with rollers?
18. Discuss the advantages of rotary screen printing.
19. Why has digital printing become more popular?
21. Could a blue fabric with white polka dots be made with either discharge printing or resist printing?
22. Explain the critical need to examine colored textiles in the setting in which they will be used or installed.
23. Cite examples where changes in texture occur and have concomitant changes in the apparent luster of a colored textile surface.
24. If different fibers and various sizes of yarns are dyed the same color, will they all look the same?
25. Explain the differences between pigments and dyestuffs.

10

Finishes

The metamorphosis of greige to finished goods is called *conversion*. Dyed, printed, and finished fabrics are more appealing than **greige goods** (unfinished goods). In fact, greige goods may bear little resemblance to the finished product and lack the aesthetic characteristics preferred by consumers. The fabrics may also lack structural stability and may not exhibit the service-related performance features sought by consumers or those required by an agency with jurisdiction over their selection and installation. The finish may be added at the mill where the fabric is produced or it may be done in a different facility by a converter. **Converters** perform finishing operations for mills by converting greige goods to finished goods following exact specifications from the mill. Converters may also buy fabric directly from mills and perform finishing operations. They then sell the finished fabric, typically under their trade name.

In many cases, the converter's design team specifies the pattern and finishes to be produced. Sometimes a contract designer or architect may specify the converter's product because they desire an interior fabric with a unique appearance characteristic or require a specific level of performance in end-use. Diverse finishes greatly expand the variety of fabrics available to end-product producers and consumers.

Transforming Surface Appearance

Various agents and processes can transform the surface appearance of greige goods. When necessary they can remove or neutralize inherent color, and when specified they can control the level of surface luster, alter the fabric form, and embellish the fabric face.

Removing Inherent Color

The **inherent colors** of natural fibers are determined by nature. Bleaching neutralizes or removes the natural color, which allows a consistent whiteness in fibers, yarns, or fabrics in order to achieve true and consistent colors in the dyeing process. Not all **bleaching agents** are suitable for all fibers; therefore, bleaches are selected for use according to the fiber content. Most fibers also change color with age—for example, animal fibers become more yellow. Bleached fabrics may yellow with age.

Controlling Surface Luster

Luster describes the way light is reflected from the surface of a material. Manufactured-fiber producers can manipulate the luster of their fibers, decreasing it by incorporating delusterant particles in the polymer solution, and finishing processes such as brushing and pressing impact the final fabric's luster levels. Natural fibers have distinctive, inherent luster levels, which is likewise variable due to how the yarn made, which weaves are used, and how the fabric is finished. Finishing processes virtually always increase, rather than decrease, the quantity of light reflected from the fabric surface, thereby increasing luster, which is also called **sheen**. (*Shine* is not considered a positive word when used to refer to a fabric's luster.)

Friction Calendering

With the help of high levels of pressure and heat and a fast rate of revolution, highly polished metal cylinders, known as calendering rollers, can be used to flatten the cross section of the yarns. Just like in ironing at home, this pressing increases the amount of yarn surface area available to reflect light. This change in the physical configuration of the yarns is illustrated in Figure 10.1. Friction **calendering** is frequently used to increase the luster and improve the hand of bed sheets, satin-weave cotton (known as **sateen**) and cotton damask fabrics.

Beetling

Beetling increases the surface luster of fabrics composed of flax. In the operation, heavy wooden planks hammer the fabric and flatten the cross section of the yarns. This process is often used on **damask** fabrics. The yarns in the contrasting weaves reflect incident light in different directions and in different quantities; beetling augments the reflections and adds richness to the surface. More light reflected from the floating yarns increases the visual distinction between the motifs and the ground, as shown in Figure 10.2.

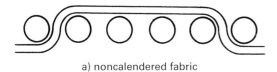

a) noncalendered fabric

b) calendered fabric

Figure 10.1 Effect of friction calendering on the cross section of yarns. Fairchild Books.

Figure 10.2 Damask tablecloth. Courtesy of Amy Willbanks, www.textilefabric.com.

Glazing

In **glazing** operations, the surface of greige goods is impregnated with resin, shellac, or wax. The fabric is then run through high-speed calendering rollers, which buffs and polishes the fabric surface. Glazing produces a smooth surface texture and a high level of surface luster. **Chintz** fabrics produced for use as upholstered furniture coverings and curtain fabrics are frequently glazed.

Schreinering

The **schreinering** process creates fine hills and valleys on the surface of the fabric. In preparation for this mechanical treatment, calendering rollers are etched with fine, parallel lines that approximate the angle of yarn twist. The number of etched lines may range from 250 to 350 per inch. After schreinering, the modified surface develops a soft luster as light is reflected in different directions from the fine peaks and flattened valleys. The effect is not permanent unless heat or resin treatments are also performed. Schreiner finishes are rarely produced.

Moiré

Moiré is a special effect achieved by calendering **faille** weaves (filling-rib-woven fabric, usually plain weave with a fine warp and heavy fill yarn). Two fabrics are laid face to face and passed between paired calendering rollers. The pressure causes the mirrored ribs to impact on each other, slightly altering their form and changing the pattern of light reflection. Moiré fabrics are described as having a wood-grain appearance or a water-marked effect (Figure 10.3).

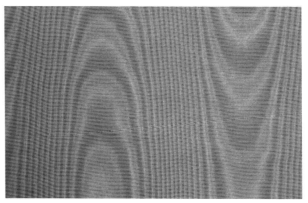

(a)

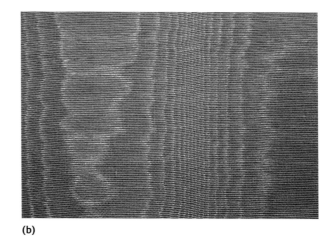

(b)

Figure 10.3 Moiré calendering: (a) moiré taffeta, (b) moiré faille. Courtesy of Amy Willbanks, www.textilefabric.com.

Introducing Three-Dimensional Designs

Embossing, like schreiner and moiré finishing, involves the use of calender rollers that alter the form of the greige goods. Embossing creates highly visible three-dimensional surface effects. Whether the changes are slight or marked, their preservation depends on the application of heat or resins.

Embossing

Embossing converts flat, essentially two-dimensional fabrics into three-dimensional structures with convex and concave design forms. The planned designs are first etched into the surface of one calender roller (or plate, in some cases; Figure 10.4), which is then paired with a soft-surfaced roller (or plate). As the fabric passes between the two intermeshing rollers, it conforms to the etched forms, as shown in Figure 10.5. Greige goods are often embossed for use as decorative curtain fabrics. Almost all film/coated fabrics for interiors are embossed.

With heated calender rollers fabrics composed of thermoplastic fibers can be embossed and heat set in one operation. The heat loosens the strained lateral bonds of the distorted fibers, and the new lateral bonds that form as the fibers cool preserve the imposed configuration.

When fabrics composed of non-thermoplastic fibers, such as cotton and rayon, are processed, chemical cross-linking resins must be applied to preserve the imposed changes. The resins form lateral bonds, linking adjacent polymer chains and stabilizing the distorted configurations of the fibers. This treatment, also used to improve resiliency, is schematized in Figure 10.6.

Changing the Orientation of Pile Yarns

Mechanical treatments are used to alter the upright positions of the pile yarns in virtually all pile fabrics. The realignment affects the reflective characteristics and tactile features of the pile layer.

Brushing, Smoothing, and Shearing

Brushing, smoothing, and shearing operations are used to align, smooth, and level the pile yarns in such fabrics as corduroy, velveteen, and velvet. In **brushing**, cylinders

Figure 10.4 Engraved embossing plates.

Figure 10.5 Embossed velour. Courtesy of Amy Willbanks, www.textilefabric.com.

covered with straight wires revolve against the matted cut-pile surface, raising the pile yarns and aligning them parallel to one another. Brushing is followed by **smoothing**, laying the pile yarns in one direction. The results of these processes are essentially the same as those produced by combing and brushing hair. Because the angle at which the pile yarns are oriented to the base fabric is reduced, a surface feature known as **pile sweep**,

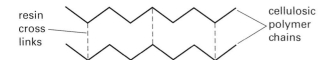

resin cross links → | cellulosic polymer chains

Figure 10.6 Resin cross-links introduced into cellulosic fibers to improve their resiliency. Courtesy of Amy Willbanks, www. textilefabric.com.

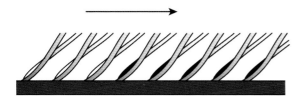

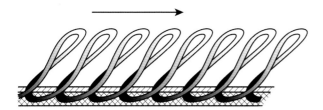

Figure 10.7 Directional pile lay, pile sweep, or fabric nap. Illustration by Lauren Rudd/Fairchild Books.

directional pile lay, or **fabric nap** is introduced (Figure 10.7).

After the pile yarns have been brushed and smoothed, they undergo **shearing** to produce an even pile height. This is accomplished by passing the fabric against a rotating cylinder with a spiral blade. The shearing cylinder is similar to that in rotary lawn mowers.

Obviously, the tactile characteristics of a pile surface will be altered by these operations. The fabric will feel smooth when stroked in the direction of lay and rough when stroked in the opposite direction. And because the quantity of light waves reflected by the sides of the yarns will be significantly greater than that reflected by the cut tips, the level of luster observed will depend on the position of the viewer. The tactile and visual qualities of nap make it imperative that all fabric pieces cut for an item and all adjoining carpet lengths have the same direction of pile lay. The positioning of pile lay in carpet is discussed in Chapter 26. For upholstered furniture, pile yarns are oriented downward on the vertical pieces and "out" on the horizontal seat pieces ("down and out").

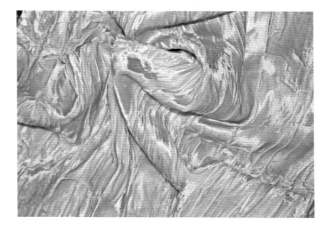

Figure 10.8 Crushed velvet. Courtesy of Amy Willbanks, www. textilefabric.com.

In this way, the pile maintains its original appearance after the person exit's the seat.

Crushing

A mechanical finishing operation known as **crushing** is used on some velvet fabrics. In this operation, the pile yarns in some areas are crushed or flattened, while the pile yarns in the adjacent areas are oriented in various directions. Because each area reflects incident light waves in different quantities and in different directions, the surface has various levels of luster. A crushed velvet upholstery fabric is pictured in Figure 10.8.

Embellishment

The appearance of greige goods, especially those to be used as curtain fabrics and tabletop accessories, is often embellished by the addition of fibers, yarns, beads, or other fabrics to their surfaces. Embroidery adds yarns, beans, and baubles; flocking adds fibers; appliqué adds layers of fabric.

Skilled artisans use textile yarns or fabrics to create such items as needlepoint pictures, crewel pillow coverings, quilts, doilies, throws, laces, and soft sculptures. They may hold onto completed projects for personal use or sell them in wholesale or retail markets. In some cases, an artist is commissioned to design and produce fiber artwork for interiors, from corporate offices to airport lounges or residences.

Hand Needlework

Fiber artists use various techniques to embellish fabric surfaces for use as accents in interiors. Among the most common are embroidery and appliqué.

Hand Embroidery

Hand embroidery is the stitching of colored yarns in decorative patterns on a portion of a base fabric, leaving the other portion unadorned to serve as the ground and accentuate the slightly raised motifs. Embroidered fabrics are used as the outercoverings of decorative pillows and as cases for bed pillows. They are also framed and hung as wall accents, and cut and finished for use as tabletop accessories. Figure 10.9 pictures a hand-embroidered wallhanging.

Appliqué

In most **appliqué**, shaped pieces of coordinating or contrasting fabric are placed over the face of a second fabric. The raw edges are turned under and blind stitches or embroidery stitches are used to secure the applique. Appliquéd fabrics are constructed into decorative pillow coverings, bedspreads, tablecloths, wallhangings, and are used as the face fabric in quilts.

An intricate technique called **reverse appliqué** is employed by needlework artisans in South America to produce *mola* cloth, as shown in Figure 10.10. **Mola** has multiple layers of fabric and is typically characterized by highly stylized animal motifs. Various colors of fabrics are layered, and a large, shaped area is cut from the top fabric. The raw edges are turned under, and the folded edge is stitched to the second fabric. A slightly smaller shape is then cut from the second fabric and the raw edges are turned and stitched to the third fabric; this reverse appliqué sequence is repeated until the base fabric is reached. *Mola* cloths are prized as framed wall accents and decorative pillow coverings.

Machine Embroidery

Machine embroidery offers a more economic alternative to hand embroidery, which is a labor- and time-intensive process. Fiber artists use machine embroidery as a way to manipulate the base fabric for a three-dimensional effect (Figure 10.11). Many machine-embroidered curtain and drapery fabrics are stitched on Schiffli machines. Each of these machines is equipped with more than a thousand needles that operate at right angles to the base fabric. For multicolored motifs, each needle is threaded with

Figure 10.9 Hand embroidery. Courtesy © Judy Juracek.

Figure 10.10 *Mola*, **a textile accent produced by a reverse appliqué technique.** Courtesy © Judy Juracek.

Figure 10.11 **Machine embroidery in progress.** Courtesy of Dedar.

Figure 10.12 **Vellux® blanket.** Courtesy of Amy Willbanks, www. textilefabric.com.

a specific color of yarn; control mechanisms similar to those used on the dobby loom are programmed with the planned design shapes and shift the position of the fabric during the embroidering operation.

Flocking

Extremely short fibers, known as **flock**, are embedded in an adhesive or resin compound to produce an effect known as **flocking**. In curtain, drapery, and upholstery fabrics, the flock is generally used to create raised motifs and patterns (Figure 10.12). In simulated suede upholstery fabrics and some blankets and floor mats, the flock is applied to the entire fabric surface. Lightweight, warm blankets can be produced by flocking nylon over the surfaces of a thin slab of polyurethane foam, which restricts air flow, thereby minimizing heat transfer.

In preparation for flocking, an adhesive or resin is printed on all areas of the fabric that is to be flocked. In **mechanical flocking** processes, the flock is then sifted through a screen to the coated surface. Beater bars encourage the short fibers to orient themselves perpendicularly to the base fabric. In **electrostatic flocking** operations, an electrostatic field induces the flock to embed itself into the coating.

Quilting

Quilting joins three separate layers: a face fabric, a fibrous batting, and a backing fabric (Figure 10.13a), and imparts a surface pattern as well. **Commercial quilting** may be done by sewing or by melding. Machine stitching and pinsonic melding are used in commercial quilting operations. The equipment used in machine stitching operates in the same manner as a conventional sewing machine, except that many needles stitch at the same time (Figure 10.13b). In **pinsonic melding**, a wide cylinder with raised designs is rolled over the multilayer structure while heat and sound waves meld the layers at the contact points. The meld points simulate the appearance of sewn quilting stitches (Figure 10.14).

With hand **quilting**, artisans join the three layers of fabric by hand stitching. The face fabric may be an appliquéd fabric, a solid-colored or printed fabric, or constructed of small pieces of coordinated fabrics. In **high-frequency welding**, an electrical charge connects the top and bottom layers, following the form of a mold or embossed plate.

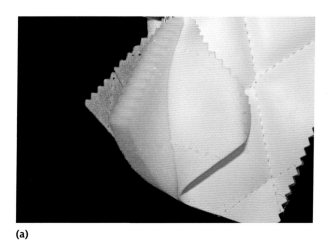

(a)

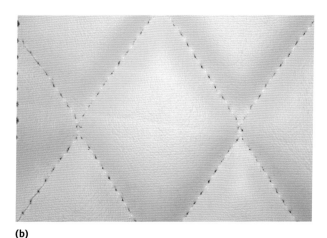

(b)

Figure 10.13 Quilted vinyl and layers of a machine-quilted fabric. (a) Layers of a quilted fabric, (b) stitched, quilted. Courtesy of Amy Willbanks, www.textilefabric.com.

Figure 10.14 Pinsonic quilted. Courtesy of Amy Willbanks, www. textilefabric.com.

Functional Finishes

Some finishing procedures improve the quality and potential serviceability of the structural features of fabric. They can, for example, use a mechanical process to improve the alignment of yarns in woven fabrics; a heat setting operation to stabilize the shape and form of fabrics composed of thermoplastic fibers; and small flames to minimize the formation of pills on fabrics composed of cellulosic fibers.

Correcting Fabric Grain

When all the warp yarns are not perpendicular to all the filling yarns in a woven fabric, the fabric is said to be **off-grain**. Off-grain fabrics have a negative effect on appearance when used in the construction of such end products as upholstered furniture, curtains, draperies, and tabletop accessories. The negative effects of off-grain upholstery fabrics are illustrated in Figure 19.2, p. 249. A drapery fabric with a **bowed** yarn produces treatments that appear to sag, and, an undulating or waving effect can develop if several widths are used. Fabrics with excessive **skew** produce a lopsided appearance, as shown in Figure 19.2b, p. 249, and attempts to align crosswise pattern repeats when seaming fabric widths only compound the problem.

Tentering

To minimize **yarn distortion** resulting from bow and skew, or to set a fabric at a consistent width during dry or backcoating, finishers use a mechanical finishing process known as **tentering**. In this operation, the fabric is mounted full-width on a tenter frame (Figure 10.15). Tension is applied to properly align the warp and filling yarns, and the fabric is then steamed, passed through a heated oven, and dried. Computer-assisted mechanisms often monitor and control the alignment of the yarns during the operation. Small holes are visible in the selvage areas of tentered fabrics, indicating where the fabric was secured by pins or metal clips. Tentering precedes printing processes so that the greige goods are set in place. Patterns would be distorted if tentered.

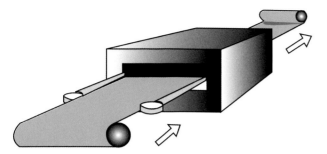

Figure 10.15 Tenter frame. Fairchild Books.

Latex Backing

Many fabrics benefit from the addition of an adhesive compound, such as polyurethane or latex, to the fabric back. The coating helps to prevent distortion from yarn slippage and raveling. Fabrics to be directly glued as wallcoverings or applied in many ergonomic seating applications need backing so that adhesive does not bleed through the fabric face (known as *strike-through*, Figure 10.16). For ease in handling by the furniture manufacturer, most upholstery fabrics are synthetically backed. Backing minimizes raveling and seam slippage, and also makes fabrics easier to handle, as they hold a more rigid and consistent shape.

Raveling occurs when yarns fall from cut edges of fabrics. This becomes a problem in upholstery when seam allowances have been closely trimmed to reduce bulk and the fabric has been pulled to fit smoothly over the frame and filling. The stress exerted on the seams with use may force the yarns in the narrow seam allowances to

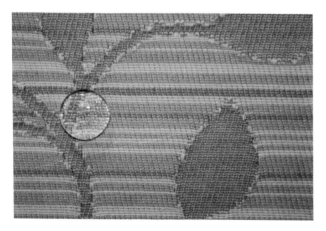

Figure 10.16 Strike-through of latex backing bleeds through fabric face. Courtesy of Amy Willbanks, www.textilefabric.com.

slide off the cut edge, weakening the seam and causing the stitching to rupture. For upholstery, a 0.5 inch seam allowance with 7 stitches per inch in sewn seams is standard, although more stitches may be required for some fabrics. Skimpy seam allowances and stitching will increase raveling and seam slippage.

Stabilizing Fabric Shape

A textile structure that maintains its original size and shape after use and care is said to have **dimensional stability**. Dimensionally stable fabrics do not exhibit growth, bagging, or sagging from unrecovered stretch— nor do they exhibit shrinkage.

With most interior textile fabrics, there is great concern for the potential problems caused by relaxation shrinkage, and to a lesser extent for those caused by residual shrinkage. **Residual shrinkage** is shrinkage of the fibers; it generally occurs over time in frequently laundered items like towels and table linens. **Relaxation shrinkage** occurs when strained components relax after the stress forces involved in various manufacturing processes are released.

Several processes subject fibers and yarns to stress, deforming and straining them. Extruding and drawing strain the polymer chains in manufactured filaments, while drawing out and spinning can strain or distort spun yarns. During weaving, tension introduces strain to the warp yarns, and bobbin tensioning devices may impart strain to the filling yarns. The pulling and forcing of yarns and fabrics through dyeing or printing and finishing operations can add various amounts of strain.

The behavior of strained fabric components is similar to that of elastic bands that have been stretched, but there is a marked difference between the rates at which the two materials recover from imposed deformations. When the stretching force is released from an elastic band, it will generally exhibit immediate and complete relaxation shrinkage, returning to its original length. By contrast, when manufacturing stress forces are released, textile components relax only gradually and incompletely. Unless the imposed strain has been released or the fabric components have been intentionally stabilized prior to shipment to the end-product producer or fabric retailer, full recovery may not occur until sometime during end-use, destroying the appearance or fit of the fabric. Heat setting, fulling, and compressive shrinkage processes encourage relaxation of strained components. The fiber composition of the goods determines the appropriate technique used.

Heat Setting

Many fabrics composed of thermoplastic fibers are scoured (washed) and then stabilized by **heat setting** before they reach the market, especially non-upholstery fabrics. Unless textured yarns have been used, this procedure is normally carried out during tentering of the greige goods to ensure that the strains introduced during fabrication are released. When heat setting is combined with tentering, converters must correctly align the warp and filling yarns in woven structures. Fabrics that have been heat set off-grain cannot be straightened.

Fulling

Fabrics composed of wool fibers are encouraged to relax by a finishing process known as **fulling**. The goods are exposed to controlled conditions of moisture, heat, and pressure, which cause the yarns to relax and shrink, resulting in a fuller, more compact fabric. Although this procedure reduces the potential for relaxation shrinkage of the fabrics in end-use, it does not reduce the possibility of felting shrinkage.

Compressive Shrinkage Treatments

The dimensional stability of fabrics composed of cotton can be improved during tentering or with a **compressive shrinkage treatment**. In compressive shrinkage procedures, the greige goods are laid over a supporting fabric, moistened, and mechanically shifted to encourage relaxation of the yarns. Labeling practices that distinguish fabrics stabilized by such treatments are discussed in Chapter 11.

During tentering, cotton yard goods can be compressed lengthwise by feeding them onto the metal pins at a faster rate than the pins are moving forward. This technique encourages the warp yarns to relax; in some cases, a 10-yard length of fabric can shrink to 8 yards. Reducing the distance between the parallel rows of tenter pins encourages crosswise relaxation.

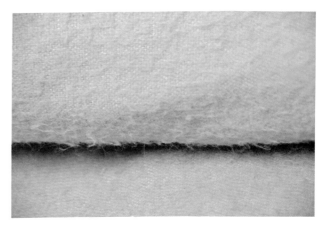

Figure 10.17 Pilling on an electric blanket. Courtesy of Amy Willbanks, www.textilefabric.com.

Heat-setting helps minimize bagging and sagging of fabrics composed of thermoplastic fibers; fulling and compressive shrinkage treatments have little or no effect on this performance feature. Wool fibers are highly elastic and fabrics composed of them recover well after being stressed. However, cellulosic fibers, including cotton, flax, and rayon, have comparatively low elasticity and may exhibit excessive growth.

Reducing Pilling

As discussed in Chapter 4, **pilling** occurs when abrasive forces cause free fibers and fiber ends to roll up into minute balls that tend to cling to the surface of the fabric (Figure 10.17). Singeing can reduce pilling. In **singeing**, small gas flames are used to burn away loose fibers, bits of lint, and fiber ends from fabrics composed of cotton, flax, rayon, or hemp. Fabrics made of thermoplastic fibers cannot be singed with flames because the intense heat would melt the base fabric; instead, hot, smooth, metal plates are used to soften and carefully shrink the protruding fibers so that they can be sheared from the surface. Fabrics composed of wool or silk are not singed because these fibers decompose and form a crusty residue when exposed to flames.

Engineering Service-Related Features

Numerous finishing agents and treatments impart specific service-related features to fabric that are not characteristic of the inherent material and cannot be achieved by changing the structural features of the goods. For example, finishes can retard the rate and level of soil accumulation, minimize the need to be ironed, and repel moisture. Such properties are not only service-related, but are frequently important to consumer selection.

These finishes often require a trade-off. They often change the hand or appearance of the fabric, for example. Many are considered to have deleterious environmental effects, and the addition of a chemical to a fabric may eliminate the possibility that it could be recycled.

Decreasing Antistatic Propensity

Antistatic finishes are chemical substances that are applied to the fabric or added to the spinning solution of manufactured fibers for the purpose of reducing or eliminating static. The chemicals work by absorbing small amounts of moisture from the atmosphere, reducing the dryness of the fabric, hence, reducing the static electricity. In carpeting, another method used for static control is to incorporate metallic yarns in the face.

Increasing Apparent Brightness

Optical brighteners are used to overcome the dulling effects produced by the accumulation of soil. Brighteners are fluorescent compounds. Whether they are incorporated as an integral part of manufactured fibers or absorbed onto exterior surfaces, they increase reflectance by the same mechanism. Incident ultraviolet rays react with brightener molecules, causing them to reflect more light waves. In effect, brighteners convert invisible wavelengths to visible wavelengths, increasing the apparent, not the actual, whiteness or brightness of fibers and fabrics. The effectiveness of most brighteners depends on the quantity of ultraviolet rays reflecting on the textile surface.

Reducing Fiber Flammability

Flame resistance is engineered in natural cellulosic fibers by adding **flame retardants** to the greige goods. These compounds inhibit or halt the combustion process at some stage in the cycle. Flame resistance is engineered in manufactured fibers by incorporating a compound-based chlorine or bromine in the polymer solution prior to extrusion.

Insulative Value

Napping increases the insulative value of fabrics, as does adding a cellular coating to the face or back of a fabric.

Napping

In **napping**, rotating bristle brushes raise the ends of many fibers to the surface. Fabrics napped on both sides are called **flannel**, and those napped on one side are called **flannelette**. In use, the raised fibers entrap air and provide thermal insulation, while also providing a soft hand and pleasing appearance, hence their use in blankets. Flannel sheeting is also popular.

Applying Coatings

Drapery fabrics and linings with foamed acrylic backing offer increased insulative value (Figure 17.23, p. 234) but the fabrics can be stiff and lack drapability.

Reducing Microbial Spread

Antimicrobial finishes, also known as antibacterial finishes, involve adding chemical agents that inhibit the growth of bacteria and odor causing germs. The growing healthcare market appreciates these developments in order to help minimize bacterial infection spread in hospitals and nursing homes, where infectious diseases can be transmitted from surface to textile products such as furniture, privacy curtains, and bedding.

Increasing Moisture Absorption

Mercerization improves the ability of cellulosic fibers, especially cotton, to absorb moisture and increases the luster of the fibers and their ability to withstand stress loads and abrasive forces.

Mercerizing

In **mercerization**, threads, yarns, or fabrics are exposed to sodium hydroxide (NaOH) or liquid ammonia while they are held under tension to prevent excessive shrinkage. This treatment alters various internal and external structural features of the fibers, producing changes in their properties. The degree of orientation is increased, boosting the strength or tenacity of the fibers, and the level of crystallinity is reduced, increasing the moisture absorption. Mercerized cotton's more rounded cross-sectional shape and fewer longitudinal twists contrasts with the flat shape and highly twisted configuration of cotton that has not been mercerized. Although flat cross sections typically reflect higher amounts of incident light than do round cross sections, removal of the twist results in increased luster.

Because mercerization improves the absorption as well as the luster and strength of cotton, the finish is routinely used on yarns and fabric for almost every end-use application, from upholstery fabric and drapery to greige towelings and sheetings. Colorants are generally applied after mercerization, using the increased absorbency to develop deep, rich color characteristics.

Increasing Insect Repellency

Insects, most notably moth and carpet beetle larvae, thrive on wool fibers. Moths and beetles prefer to live and breed in dark places, where the larvae will be undisturbed and can sustain themselves on the nutrients obtained from the wool fibers. In unprotected wool carpet the damage is more likely to be seen under rarely moved furniture, and in wool blankets and wool upholstery the attack generally occurs during storage. Today, all domestic wool floorcoverings are treated to repel these insects, but residential and commercial consumers must examine the labels of imported products to confirm the use of such treatments.

Converters render wool fiber moth resistant by adding a chemical finish that simply makes the wool indigestible. Because mothproofing treatments are generally combined with dyeing or finishing operations to control processing costs, the protective agents become integral parts of the fibers.

Soil and Stain Resistance

Many textile authorities differentiate soil and stain on the basis of how tenaciously the soil or dirt clings to the textile structure. When dirt or other foreign matter is mechanically held and comparatively easy to remove, it is known as **soil**; when the dirt becomes chemically bonded to the fiber surfaces and is comparatively difficult to remove, it is called a **stain**. Producers use compounds that enable the fibers to repel or resist soil by increasing surface tension or by blocking sites where selected foreign matter could chemically bond.

Fluorocarbon compounds are used extensively to help textile fibers and fabrics repel or resist soil accumulation. These agents make the textile component more **oleophobic**, or oil-repellant, as well as more **hydrophobic**, or water-repellant. Rather than spreading over the fabric surface, wetting it, and penetrating into the fibers and yarns, spilled water and oily compounds bead up, maintaining their **surface tension**. As schematized in Figure 10.18, **high surface tension** means that the molecules in the foreign matter have a higher affinity for one another than for the fibers. Similar action can be observed when raindrops bead up on a waxed car surface.

Even with stain-repellent finishes, protection is temporary. The rate of absorption is slowed, not halted, so spilled liquids should still be absorbed immediately from the surface. As the surface tension gradually lowers, the droplets will spread, as shown in Figure 10.18, wetting and potentially staining the fabric.

Trade names identifying fluorocarbon finishing compounds include Scotchgard®, produced by the 3M Company, and Teflon®, produced by Chemours, though many finishers supply non-branded versions. Various federal agencies, scientific associations, chemical suppliers,

Figure 10.18 Water beads on certain fluorocarbon finishes.

environmental groups, and product manufacturers hold that the use of fluorocarbon compounds creates health and environmental hazards.

Colorless acid dyes are used to help carpet fibers resist staining. Here, the carpet is saturated with a dyestuff that attaches itself to acid-receptive sites on the fibers. As these compounds occupy sites to which foreign matter, especially such foods as acid-colored fruit drinks, could attach, staining is prevented. Trade names identifying carpet protected in this manner include StainMaster®, owned by Invista, and Wear Dated®, owned by Mohawk.

Soil Release

Soil release compounds may be used to help fibers release stains. These compounds are designed to function in unison with detergent molecules in the laundry solution. The detergent molecules will reduce the surface tension of the water; in effect, this makes the water "wetter" by causing it to spread rather than bead. At the same time, the fluorocarbon-based finishing agent will increase the surface energy of the fibers, making them more hydrophilic, so the water can more readily carry the detergent molecules into the fiber crevices and emulsify and remove the soil and stain material.

Retaining Smoothness

Stress forces such as bending, folding, twisting, and crushing in use and after care strain and deform a fabric's surface. Some fabrics exhibit a high level of recovery and are resilient; in effect, they "remember" their original configuration. Heat setting and durable press finishing operations that contain resins can increase **resiliency** and "memory" in some fabrics.

Heat Setting

The application of heat to stabilize the dimensions of fabrics composed of thermoplastic fibers was discussed earlier in this chapter. Heat setting also can be used to help flat fabrics remain smooth and wrinkle-free, minimizing the need for ironing. Most polyester drapery and privacy curtain fabrics are scoured and then heat set after they come off the loom.

Durable Press Finishing

Smooth fabrics composed of cotton, flax, or rayon exhibit extremely poor recovery when crushed, folded, or wrinkled, and remain crumpled. **Durable press finishing** treatments compensate for this poor resiliency. These fabrics are impregnated with a **resin or reactant compound**, which has generally been a formaldehyde-based substance. Heat is then used to cure the compound, causing it to form strong cross-links between the polymer chains within the cellulosic fibers. These bonds function in the same manner as those found in wool and thermoplastic fibers. They stabilize the positions of the chains and introduce to the fibers the so-called memory for whatever shape and form they were in when heat-cured.

Relatively high amounts of resin must be applied to ensure no-iron performance. While the resin significantly improves the resiliency, it also decreases absorption and increases soil retention. There may be a temporary fishy odor that remains until any unreacted resin is washed away. The resin weakens the fibers, lowering their abrasion resistance and shortening their use-life. The loss in abrasion resistance also can result in an effect known as **frosting**. This unsightly problem occurs when abrasive forces remove some of the resin-weakened cellulosic fibers: as the color carried by the fibers is also removed, the abraded area appears faded and lighter than the adjacent areas. Although frosting is a color-related problem, it is the result of fiber failure, not of colorant failure.

To compensate for the decreased strength and abrasion resistance suffered by the cellulosic fibers, manufacturers often blend them with polyester fiber. The polyester extends the wear-life of the fabric. It does not strengthen the cellulosic components. Together with the potential for loss of the cellulosic fiber, development of a frosted appearance remains a possibility in blends.

Currently, various federal agencies, scientific associations, chemical suppliers, environmental groups, and product manufacturers hold that the use of formaldehyde compounds and their subsequent release from durable press fabrics create health and environmental hazards. Some consumers report an allergic reaction to such resins. Members of the textile industry are now supporting research activities focused on the development and perfection of new durable press finishing agents and procedures.

Waterproof and Water-Resistant Finishes

A **waterproof fabric** will not become wet regardless of the amount of time it is exposed to water or the force with which the water strikes the fabric. High-yarn-count fabrics have less space between the yarns so it is harder for the liquid to penetrate the fabric, and a waterproof finish, usually a fluorocarbon, fills in the spaces between the fibers and yarns.

Finishes of **silicone compounds** reduce the rate at which fabrics absorb water. Because these compounds offer little or no protection from oily soiling and staining, their use is diminishing in favor of fluorocarbon compounds, which provide both water and soil resistance.

Although waterproof and water-resistant finishes tend to impart a hard hand and make the surfaces very flat, several branded finishes for upholstery fabric are popular for healthcare, restaurant, and even residential interiors because they are both stain- and water-resistant. Some are also bacteria-resistant.

Nanofinishes

Nanotechnology, the science and technology of manipulating structures at the molecular level, is bringing forward many variations to fibers and improved finishes. Because fiber molecules themselves are manipulated, the hand, texture, luster, and drape of the material does not change with addition of coatings applied in nanolayers, which can provide multiple attributes to the fabric. For example, bedding might have a waterproof finish in addition to being coated with a layer of enzymes, which destroy toxins.

Microencapsulation

Microencapsulation technology is being used in the bedding and toweling industry. A substance is contained in nano-sized capsules, which are stored in the fiber structure. As the fabric moves against the skin, the capsules break and release the contents. The contents could be a moisturizing agent used to hydrate the skin, an antibacterial agent that eliminates odor, a fragrance agent, a medication to soothe arthritic pain, or an insect repellent.[1]

Inspection

Trained personnel carefully examine finished fabrics for flaws and defects, rejecting those that contain an unacceptable number of irreparable defects, before they leave any factory. Together, quality-control tests and visual examinations help to ensure acceptance of the fabrics by end-product producers and residential and commercial consumers. These evaluations also help suppliers and producers maintain their companies' reputations for quality product.

Key Terms

antimicrobial finishes	fluorocarbon compounds
antistatic finishes	frosting
appliqué	fulling
beetling	glazing
bleaching agents	greige goods
bowed yarn alignment	hand embroidery
brushing	heat setting
calendering	high-frequency welding
chintz	high surface tension
commercial quilting	hydrophobic
compressive shrinkage	inherent colors
treatment	luster
converters	machine embroidery
crushing	mechanical flocking
damask	mercerization
dimensional stability	microencapsulation
directional pile lay	moiré
durable press finishing	*mola*
electrostatic flocking	nanotechnology
embossing	napping
embroidering	off-grain
fabric nap	oleophobic
faille	optical brighteners
flame resistance	pile sweep
flame retardant	pilling
flannel	pinsonic melding
flannelette	quilting
flock	raveling
flocking	relaxation shrinkage

residual shrinkage	singeing
resiliency	skew
resin or reactant compound	smoothing
	soil
reverse appliqué	soil release
sateen	stain
schreinering	surface tension
shearing	tentering
sheen	waterproof fabric
silicone compounds	yarn distortion

Review Questions

1. Explain the physical changes to fibers and yarns imposed by friction calendering, beetling, schreinering, and moiréing. Are these changes permanent?

2. Virtually all moiré fabric is one color. How is it possible, then, to see a water-marked or wood-grain pattern on the fabric surface?

3. Discuss the effect of pile sweep, pile lay, or fabric nap on the luster of a fabric. Why is it critical to carefully position adjoining fabric pieces or carpet lengths having directional pile lay?

4. Cite examples or commercial locations of textile works created by artisans that you have seen.

5. Explain what is meant by reverse appliqué.

6. Differentiate between mechanical flocking processes and electrostatic flocking operations.

7. Sketch some applications of interior textile products, such as a window treatment or a piece of upholstered furniture. Then, add a bowed and a skewed fabric to each and note the appearance. Does this help you to appreciate the critical need for grain-straight fabrics, especially those having strong motifs, stripes, or plaids?

8. Why are production costs lowered when converters combine tentering and heat setting?

9. Define microencapsulation and discuss end products that use this technology.

10. How are the finishing agents and the finish processes determined?

11. Discuss how optical brighteners work. What is meant by apparent color?

12. Why is singeing useful in reducing pilling? Does it reduce the number of pills or does it simply make them easier to remove?

13. Are the approaches for reducing the flammability of natural and manufactured fibers different?

14. In what end-use applications is it highly advisable to reduce microbial action?

15. How does mercerization increase the absorption and dyeability of cellulosic fibers? How does it extend the wear-life of the fibers? What effect does it have on the luster of cotton fibers?

16. How is moth resistance achieved?

17. Explain the type of protection offered by silicone compounds and by fluorocarbon compounds.

18. What role does surface tension play in water and soil repellency?

19. How do colorless acid dyes reduce staining? How would a consumer know whether this stain resistant method had been used?

20. Explain how memory is introduced to fabrics composed of thermoplastic fibers and to fabrics composed of cellulosic fibers.

21. Differentiate among tippiness, frostiness, and frosting.

22. How is frosting caused by failure of the fiber rather than the colorant?

Note

1. Allen C. Cohen and Ingrid Johnson. (2012). *Fabric Science*, 10th edition. New York: Fairchild Books, p. 215.

11

Interior Textile Product Labeling

To add to competitive advantage, some corporations develop distinctive methods of product labeling. Trade associations have also undertaken similar efforts on behalf of their member firms. Often, a name or symbol is added to the label to increase product recognition. The label signifies quality, care, reliability, or special performance features. Such information assists the consumer and design professional to choose textile products that meet their private needs or specification requirements. The immediate goal of this voluntary, optional labeling is to secure the initial purchase of a firm's products; the long-term goal is to encourage repeated selection of products bearing the firm's label.

Use of voluntary product labeling and brand identification is optional, but compliance with certain prescribed commercial practices is not. Labeling rules and guidelines, as well as antitrust regulations established by the U.S. Congress and the Federal Trade Commission help ensure that consumers and members of the industry are protected from abusive practices by companies in many industries, including textiles.

Federal Trade Commission

Responsibilities and Powers

The **Federal Trade Commission (FTC)** is empowered and directed to prevent unfair methods of competition in commerce unfair or deceptive acts or practices. For example, failure to disclose that a product or material is not what it appears to be, such as a faux-leather fabric masquerading as leather, would be an infraction of FTC regulations. The agency has the responsibility to investigate commercial trade practices, to encourage voluntary corrective action and compliance, and to commence legal proceedings when necessary. The Commission also has the power to stipulate policy related to unfair or deceptive commercial acts and policies, which has led the FTC to issue various rules and guidelines to be followed in labeling textile products.

The FTC has enforcement and administrative responsibilities for several practices pertaining to the marketing of interior textiles. Within the FTC, the Bureau of Consumer Protection has several major program divisions that gather and provide information, investigate practices reported to be deceptive, monitor marketplace activities, and enforce federal statutes assigned to them. The Energy and Product Information Division, for example, focuses its work principally on energy policy and conservation, enforcing such rules as the one governing the disclosure of the insulative value (R-value) of home insulation, much of which is glass fiber batting.

The Product Reliability Division is of particular interest to consumers and producers alike because it is responsible for enforcement of the **Magnuson-Moss Warranty Act**, which sets forth the procedures to be followed when written warranties are offered. This act and the growing use of warranties for interior textiles are described later in this chapter. Also of critical interest is the work of the Regional Offices Division. The offices in this unit are located in major cities nationwide and have exclusive responsibility for enforcing the mandatory fiber product labeling acts passed by Congress, as well as the trade regulation rules prescribed and promulgated by the FTC.

What some call "regulations" can likewise be referred to as "protections." Producers often feel that governmental agencies impose onerous requirements, and that proof of compliance adds cost to products. Nonetheless, these measures are established, first and foremost, to protect purchasers.

As noted in Chapters 1 and 3, the current administration of the U.S. government is actively minimizing the role of regulatory agencies, and eliminating laws, including those designed as consumer protection measures. Therefore, makeup of these agencies and their activities are shifting rapidly.

Investigative and Rulemaking Procedures

The FTC is not authorized to handle individual consumer complaints, but acts when it sees a pattern of marketplace abuse. Complaints from individual consumers may serve to provide both the pattern and the evidence necessary to begin an investigation.

Investigations can begin in many different ways. Complaint letters, scholarly articles on consumer or economic subjects, or congressional requests may trigger both *public* and *nonpublic* investigations. Generally, public announcements will be made of investigations of the practices of an entire industry. An investigation of an individual company is usually nonpublic in order to protect that company's privacy until the agency is ready to make a formal allegation.

After an investigation, the staff may find reason to believe that a business has violated the law. If the case is not settled voluntarily by some official corrective action by the company (a *consent order*), the Commission could issue a *complaint*. After that, and if no settlement is reached, a formal hearing is held before an administrative law judge. Members of the public can participate at this point if they have evidence relating to the case. The administrative law judge issues a decision. There may be an appeal to the FTC commissioners. The commissioners' decision may be appealed to the U.S. Court of Appeals and ultimately to the U.S. Supreme Court.

After an investigation, the FTC staff may find what it believes to be unfair or deceptive practices in an entire industry. The staff then could make a recommendation to the commissioners to begin rulemaking. If the recommendation is accepted, a presiding officer is appointed, and a notice is published in the *Federal Register*, setting out the proposed rule and what the commissioners believe are the central issues to be discussed. Members of the public can, at this point, comment or testify on the rule or suggest issues to be examined.

The presiding officer conducts public hearings, which include cross-examination on certain issues. After the hearings, the staff prepares a report on the issues. This is followed by the presiding officer's report. Then members of the public have another opportunity to comment on the entire rulemaking record.

The matter then goes before the commissioners, who deliberate on the record (which includes the presiding officer's report, the FTC staff report, and the public comments) to decide whether to issue the rule. They can make changes in the provisions of the rule and issue a revised version as they judge appropriate. This procedure has been followed to establish labeling and marketing rules that apply to various segments of the interior textile industry. Some of these rules are mandatory; others are advisory.

Regulatory and Advisory Labeling Practices

While product labeling is not generally required with some regulations, such as flammability standards, labeling rules and guidelines are intended to afford consumers protection, not from any hazardous product, but from things such as misrepresentation of the composition of textile products. However, mandatory labeling also protects industry members by stipulating acceptable and legal practices.

Fiber Product Labeling Acts

The U.S. Congress has passed three acts specifically designed to protect consumers and producers from misrepresentation and false advertising of the fiber content of textile fiber products. The provisions of these acts are especially important today as fibers can be engineered successfully to simulate the appearance of other fibers: acrylic can resemble wool; rayon can imitate flax; and acetate, nylon, and polyester can look like silk. (One of the acts, the Fur Products Labeling Act, is not included because fur is rarely used in interior applications.)

Failure to accurately disclose fiber content is an unfair and deceptive commercial act or practice. Illegal misbranding can be avoided by strict adherence to each act's provisions and its accompanying set of rules and regulations. The latter are established and issued by the FTC to help producers, distributors, and consumers interpret the mandates of each act.

Wool Products Labeling Act (WPLA)

The **Wool Products Labeling Act (WPLA)** focuses on the labeling requirements for products containing any percentage of wool fiber. Interior textile products subject to the provisions of the WPLA include conventional blankets and underblankets that are composed in whole or in part of wool. Interior textile products that have been specifically exempted include carpets, rugs, mats, and upholstery.

Products included within the scope of the WPLA must conspicuously display a label or hangtag disclosing the following information:

1. The percentages of all fibers present in amounts of 5 percent or more. Constituent fibers are identified by the following terms:
   - Wool means the fiber from the fleece of the sheep or lamb or hair of any of the specialty wool that has never been reclaimed from any woven or felted wool product.
   - **Recycled wool** means the fibers obtained by reducing (shredding) a previously manufactured product to its original fibrous state and then again subjecting the fibers to the product manufacturing sequence.
   - **Virgin wool**, **new wool**, and *wool* are synonymous terms. The use of these terms means the constituent fibers have undergone manufacturing only once; they have not been reclaimed.
2. The identifying name or registered number of the manufacturer of the product must be included.
3. The country of origin must be included. The FTC and the U.S. Customs Service have issued country-of-origin regulations. Under the FTC rules, all products entirely manufactured and made of materials manufactured in the United States must bear the label "Made in the U.S.A." For products substantially manufactured in the United States using materials from another country, the label must read "Sewn in the U.S.A. of Imported Components," or words of equivalent meaning.

On October 31, 1984, new country-of-origin regulations established by the U.S. Customs Service, a unit of the Department of Treasury, went into effect and are used in determining the country of origin of imported goods for the purpose of product labeling. These rules apply to products fully processed in one or more foreign countries and subsequently imported into the United States under trade quotas. For quota purposes, the Customs Service designates the country in which there has been a substantial transformation (generally cutting and sewing) of the product as the country of origin; the product is then counted in that country's import quota. (The Customs Service believes these regulations also will curb the practice of exporting products to the United States via countries having an unfilled quota or no quota limitation.)

Textile Fiber Products Identification Act (TFPIA)

Before World War II, consumers, distributors, and producers had few types of fibers from which to choose in comparison to the number available today. There were the widely used natural fibers, including wool, silk, linen, and cotton, and the less widely used natural fibers, such as jute, hemp, sisal, and camel. Rayon and acetate were also available. Consumers were familiar with the appearance, general performance properties, and care requirements of most of those fibers.

As each new fiber was developed and manufactured by various companies, many of which assigned a different name to the fiber (called a *brand name*), the market became filled with what appeared to be many distinct and unrelated fibers. Consumers, distributors, and producers had no way of knowing the composition of the new fibers, what performance to expect, and what care might be appropriate. Ultimately, the **Textile Fiber Products Identification Act (TFPIA)** was adopted to minimize this confusion and to prevent unfair and deceptive marketing practices (intentional or not). Provisions of the TFPIA apply to many textile fiber products, including articles of wearing apparel, bedding, curtains, casements, draperies, tablecloths, floorcoverings, towels, furniture slipcovers, afghans and throws, and all fibers, yarns, and fabrics. Specifically exempted are such products as upholstery stuffing (unless it was previously used); outercoverings of furniture, mattresses, and box springs; and backings of, and paddings or cushions to be used under, floorcoverings. Thus, although carpets, rugs, and mats are specifically exempted from the WPLA, the face or pile layers of these floor products are subject to the provisions of the TFPIA. Also, while upholstery fabrics are exempted from the WPLA, they come under the TFPIA when they are marketed in fabric form; that is, when not permanently attached to the furniture frame.

Products included within the scope of the TFPIA must bear a conspicuous label or hangtag displaying the following information:

- The constituent fiber or combination of fibers in the textile fiber product, designating with equal prominence each natural or manufactured fiber in the textile fiber product by its generic name and percentage in the order of predominance by weight, if the weight of such fiber is 5 percent or more of the total fiber weight of the product. Fibers present to the extent of less than 5 percent of the total fiber weight of the product are designated as "other fiber" or "other fibers," except when a definite functional significance has clearly been established. In the latter case, the percentage by weight, the generic name, and the functional significance of the fiber should be set out, for example, "3 percent spandex for elasticity."
- Nondeceptive and truthful terms are permitted with the generic name, for example, combed cotton, solution-dyed acetate, and antistatic nylon.
- The identifying name or registered number of the manufacturer of the product.
- The first time a trademark appears in the required information, it must appear in immediate conjunction with the generic name in equally sized type. Unlike the generic name, trademarks are not required information.
- The country of origin, according to the rules established by the FTC and the U.S. Customs Service. These regulations were described in the discussion of the WPLA.

Content labeling helps consumers recognize the familiar features generally characteristic of each generic class of chemically related fibers. However, fiber content is only a small part of the overall performance make-up of a fabric. The form of the fiber, the yarn quality and type, the color application method, the structure of the fabric, and its finish are all critically important. Most important of all is that a fabric is fabricated and used appropriately, in accordance with its targeted end-use application.

Care instructions are not required under the WPLA, the FPLA, or the TFPIA. The disclosure of safe care procedures for finished fabrics and apparel items is governed by a trade regulation rule.

Trade Regulation Rules Regarding Labeling

Trade regulation rules set out provisions for mandatory and acceptable practices considered to be in the public interest. Producers following the rules will avoid illegal and unacceptable marketing practices as defined in the FTC pertinent act.

Some of the rules apply to a specific interior textile market segment. One example is the Trade Regulations Rule Relating to the Deceptive Advertising and Labeling as to Size of Tablecloths and Related Products; another is the Trade Regulation Rule Relating to Failure to Disclose That Skin Irritation May Result from Washing or Handling Glass Fiber Curtains and Draperies and Glass Fiber Curtain and Drapery Fabrics.

The Trade Regulation Rule Related to the Care Labeling of Textile Wearing Apparel and Certain Piece Goods covers some, but not all, interior fabric types. The rule includes a glossary of relevant standard terms. (These are based on ASTM D3136 Terminology Relating to Care Labeling for Apparel, Textile, and Leather Products Other Than Textile Floor Coverings and Upholstery.)

As import/export trade impacts nearly every country's fabric businesses, it important that all labeling, including care instructions, be readily available in multiple languages. With adoption of the North American Free Trade Agreement (NAFTA), members of the United States textile industry worked through ASTM International to develop a guide that provides a uniform system of care symbols.

Although textile floorcoverings and textile-upholstered furniture are not included in the Care Labeling rule, consumers still need care instructions for carpet, rugs, and upholstery. In response, industry members continue to evolve care instructions as new materials emerge. ASTM D5253 Standard Terminology Related to Floor Coverings and Textile Upholstered Furniture provides a uniform language for the writing of care instructions to be supplied with carpets, rugs, and upholstered furniture, excluding leather. Sellers who voluntarily provide care information to their consumers typically use language from the standard. Additionally, ACT (Association for Contract Textiles) actively polls member companies for current best practices, and its committees continually develop guidelines for many issues. Cleaning is currently a hot topic.

Trade Practice Rules and Guides Regarding Labeling

As generally set forth in the introduction of each **trade practice rule and guide**, the provisions are interpretive of laws administered by the FTC Commission, and thus are advisory in nature. These rules are designed to foster and promote the maintenance of fair competitive conditions for both the industry and the public.

The major difference between trade practice rules and guides lies in who initiated the proceedings. In the case of trade practice rules, a single industry segment has requested assistance from the FTC in an effort to clarify what trade practices are acceptable. Conferences are then held to provide a forum for all industry members; thereafter, proposed rules are published, responses considered, and final advisory rules published. Guides are the result of proceedings initiated by the Commission, and they supersede several trade practice rules.

Trade practice rules and guides, like trade regulation rules, have a specific and limited scope. There are, for example, guides for the household furniture industry and guides for the feather and down products industry. Some of these guides are discussed in Chapters 11, 12, and 28.

Voluntary Labeling Programs

Textile firms must label their products in accordance with all applicable acts, rules, and guides. In order to gain a competitive edge in the marketplace, they may also choose to label their products with a distinctive name or logo, or to offer a warranty pertaining to in-use performance. The use of such labeling is strictly voluntary.

Voluntary labeling programs are used extensively in the marketing of interior textile products. These programs are primarily intended to increase sales by providing product information and name recognition through the supply chain of the labeled product. Labeling relating to nondescriptive fiber names, certification marks, licensing programs, warranty programs, and trademarks may provide helpful information to contract designers, architects, and consumers.

Use of TM and ®

Trademarks are distinctive names, words, phrases, and stylized logos (letters or symbols) that aim to capture the attention of professionals and consumers. The ownership and use of trademarks is carefully guarded. Producers and trade associations allocate significant amounts of money, time, and talent to coining names, designing graphic symbols, and writing eye-catching phrases that will be effective trademarks.

After this effort is completed, the chosen name, phrase, or logo appears on product labels and in promotional materials accompanied by the letters TM, which exhibits ownership of the trademark, assuming the person or firm was the first to use the trademark in commerce. Frequently, the user elects to apply for registered ownership of the trademark with the U.S. Patent and Trademark Office. Following approval of the application, the symbol ® is used in lieu of TM to indicate registered ownership.

Cotton Incorporated grants permission to qualifying retailers, manufacturers, and mills to use its registered trademark on packaging, hangtags, or in advertisements. The trademark is a stylized design, the Seal of Cotton Trademark, illustrated in Figure 11.1.

Figure 11.1 The Seal of Cotton Trademark. Registered trademark of Cotton Incorporated.

Trademarks are widely promoted to ensure recognition of the mark by the consumer. At the same time, the use of the mark is carefully controlled. Trademark owners take every effort to protect the reputation of the mark, and to ensure that the legal owner is the only one benefiting from the increased recognition and selection of products labeled with the mark. (Rights to use several trademarks could not be obtained for this textbook, for example.) Unauthorized adoption of a trademark is illegal: in recent years, such piracy has resulted in several multimillion-dollar lawsuits and confiscation of illegally branded goods.

Fiber Trade Names

Fiber suppliers and producers use **trade names** and logos to distinguish their products from those of their competitors. Manufactured fiber producers use trade names extensively, and apparently their promotional efforts have been successful. Many consumers are more familiar with fiber trade names than with their generic names. A trademarked fiber may be considered unique when in fact several other chemically related fibers produced by other companies are also available. Appendix A lists generic fiber names.

Informed consumers and trained professionals can make valuable use of fiber trade names, especially those that designate a special property. They may, for example, know that solution dyeing has been used or that a fiber is self-extinguishing (i.e., stops burning when the source of ignition is removed) when special trade names are used.

Some companies license or certify the use of their fiber trade names on end products. In this marketing, the fiber company tests fabrics or end products for quality and performance. Fiber trademark licensing should not be confused with other licensing and certification programs applying to textile products.

Certification Marks

Certification marks are coined names and stylized logos that may be used alone or in conjunction with other types of voluntary labeling. They may be used on the labels of end products that conform with fiber content specifications or performance specifications established by the owner of the mark.

Some fiber trade associations control or certify the use of their registered trademark logos. The Woolmark Company, for example, owns and controls the use of the Woolmark, the Woolmark Blend, and the Wool Blend trademarks (Figure 11.2). End products carrying these symbols have been quality tested by an independent laboratory for compliance with the Woolmark Company's performance and fiber content specifications. The Woolmark and Woolmark Blend trademarks are certification trademarks in many countries.

Members of the contract (or commercial) fabrics industry formed the **Association for Contract Textiles (ACT)** in order to address issues concerning contract fabrics, such as performance standards and industry education. Members of the association established guidelines related to various physical and performance characteristics of fabric. The ACT Voluntary Guidelines certify to appropriate ASTM, NFPA, and AATCC standards. Fabrics that meet the guidelines can be labeled with corresponding icons, each of which is shown in Figure 11.3. For more information on ACT Voluntary Guidelines, refer to Chapter 2. ACT's Fact® certification signifies that a fabric complies with NSF/ANSI 336 Fabric Sustainability Standard and is certified by an authorized third-party certifier. For more information on ACT's Facts® certification, refer to Chapter 3.

PURE NEW WOOL

WOOL RICH BLEND

WOOL BLEND PERFORMANCE

Figure 11.2 Registered trademark logos used by the Woolmark Company. Logos courtesy of the Woolmark Company.

Association for Contract Textiles

Icon	Function
🔥	Flammability
✳	Colorfastness to Light
🫘	Wet & Dry Crocking
✶	Physical Properties
a	Abrasion Low Traffic / Private Spaces
A	Abrasion High Traffic / Public Spaces
◎ facts	Facts NSF/ANSI 336 – 2011: Sustainability Assessment for Commercial Furnishings Fabric

Figure 11.3 The marks are Registered Certification Marks at the U.S. Patent and Trademark Office and are owned by the Association for Contract Textiles, Inc. Courtesy of the Association for Contract Textiles, Inc.

Licensing Programs

Licensing companies sell the right to use their company-owned processes, designs, or logos to producers and converters; they do not process any components or manufacture any end products. Licensing companies do, however, certify the use of their coined names in the labeling and marketing of products. Up until the 1930s, shrinkage of cotton fabrics was a problem—in men's work shirts, for example. The now-defunct Sanforized Company registered trademarks for its compressive shrinkage and durable press processes and licensed producers that used its techniques to label and promote their end products with names like Sanforized, Sanfor®, and Sanforizota®.

The presence of a certified or licensed name or logo on a label may confirm a specific fiber content, the use of a particular process, or that the product has met standard performance specifications, but it does not guarantee any features.

Warranty Programs

Today, **warranty** or guarantee **programs** are used more frequently than ever in textile marketing as competition increases and designers, architects, and consumers seek protection from defective or faulty merchandise and the expense of premature replacement. Fiber companies may, for example, voluntarily offer to stand behind products composed of their fiber. This is an especially frequent practice with soft floorcoverings.

There are important differences among the various types of warranties. A review of the important differences between the major types of warranties—spoken, implied, and written—can help to identify and clarify these differences.

Spoken Warranties

Spoken warranties are merely verbal promises, virtually impossible to enforce.

Implied Warranties

Implied warranties are not written, and they are not voluntary; they are rights provided to consumers by state law. These rights include things such as the *warranty of merchantability*, for instance, that an electric blanket will heat, and the *warranty of fitness for a particular purpose*, for instance, that a carpet produced for installation around a swimming pool will not dissolve in water. In states having such laws, implied warranties are not voluntary; they come automatically with every sale unless the product is sold *as is*.

Written Warranties

A **written warranty** constitutes a legally binding promise that the warrantor is insuring quality and performance and is willing to stand behind the warranted product, assuming it is neither misused nor abused by the warrantee. While written warranties are strictly voluntary, when they are offered they are subject to a federal law (the Magnuson-Moss Warranty Act), which is under the jurisdiction of the FTC. (For detailed information on the act, see https://www.ftc.gov/enforcement/statutes/magnuson-moss-warranty-federal-trade-commission-improvements-act.)

Under written warranties, and by exercising their respective rights under the act, consumers can protect themselves from defective products and producers' responsibilities are clear. In essence, the act requires that a written warranty must spell out in simple language the terms and conditions of the warranty.

Written warranties are required to be labeled as full warranties or limited warranties. **Full warranty**, as the name implies, indicates that the item is completely covered for replacement in the case of product failure. **Limited warranty** provides less coverage. The specifics of a limited warranty must be stated in writing.

Sample Labeling

Sample labeling, which is the use of style, color, and design names on product samples, is another form of voluntary labeling used by producers. In most cases, these names are primarily to attract and hold prospective purchasers' attention. For example, "blue-green" may identify a color accurately, but "sea foam" may sound more enticing; the terms "level, cutpile" may describe a carpet texture informatively, but "plateau" may seem more interesting; "polka dot" may be readily understandable, but "micro dot" may add contemporary flair; and so on.

Using a well-known designer's name on product labels similarly adds marketing appeal. After confirming that a specific name will add marketing appeal, producers purchase the right to use the name under agreed conditions.

Key Terms

Association for Contract Textiles (ACT)	Textile Fiber Products Identification Act (TFPIA)
certification marks	trademark
Federal Trade Commission (FTC)	trade name
full warranty	trade practice rule and guide
implied warranties	
licensing programs	trade regulation rules
limited warranty	virgin wool
Magnuson-Moss Warranty Act	warranty programs
new wool	wool
recycled wool	Wool Products Labeling Act (WPLA)
sample labeling	written warranties
spoken warranties	

Review Questions

1. Explain what is meant by "unfair or deceptive acts or practices" in commerce.
2. Describe the investigative and rulemaking procedures followed by the FTC.
3. What are the purposes of the fiber product labeling acts?
4. Differentiate between virgin wool and recycled wool as they apply to wool product labeling.
5. When a product is labeled "virgin wool," are there connotations of quality?
6. How is the country of origin determined for imported textile products? How are these regulations used in controlling textile imports to the United States?
7. Distinguish between the provisions of trade regulation rules and labeling acts and between the provisions of trade regulation rules and trade practice rules. Differentiate between trade practice rules and guidelines.
8. Why are care instructions required for textile upholstered furniture, carpet, and rugs?
9. How have members of the industry responded to the desire and need for care instructions for these products?
10. Explain the use of TM and ®.
11. Discuss the importance of trademarks in textile marketing.
12. When an informed consumer or design professional sees an ACT certification symbol on contract upholstery, what is understood?
13. Are written warranties mandatory? When are warranties subject to the provisions of the Magnuson-Moss Warranty Act?
14. Identify some differences between full and limited warranties.
15. Cite various types of sample labeling. What is the purpose of such labeling?

12

Interior Textile Products and Fire

Courtesy of Amy Willbanks, www.textilefabric.com.

Although there is no federal fire code for buildings, in accordance with provisions of the Flammable Fabrics Act, a congressional act administered by the Consumer Product Safety Commission (CPSC), specific interior products must meet mandatory local, state, and federal flammability standards before they can be marketed. The standards often relate to specific end-uses, types of installations, and contents.

Since fabrics and other materials must be clearly labeled as to these required flammability codes, interior design professionals and consumers can easily and safely select appropriate materials. This chapter describes some of the codes and types of testing that fabric suppliers must conduct. See Chapter 2 for review of definitions for standards, guidelines, codes, regulations, ratings, and certifications. General descriptions of federal regulatory agencies are also discussed in Chapter 2. As noted in that chapter, the current U.S. administration is working to minimize consumer protections and the agencies that monitor and manage them. Much is in flux.

Consumer Product Safety Commission

The **Consumer Product Safety Commission (CPSC)**, an independent federal agency, administers and enforces certain safety-focused acts, including the **Flammable Fabrics Act (FFA)**. The CPSC analyzes information and statistics regarding the frequency and severity of injury associated with consumer products. When products are found to pose an unreasonable risk to consumers, the Commission has the power to initiate the necessary proceedings that may lead to developing a new or revised safety standard. When regulating interior textile products, the CPSC adheres to FFA procedures.

Flammable Fabrics Act

The U.S. Congress passed the FFA in the 1950s in order to eliminate highly flammable clothing. Congress amended the act in 1967, expanding its scope to include interior furnishings and permitting the establishment of additional textile product-related standards.

The 1967 Amendment

In addition to expanding the scope of the FFA, the 1967 amendment directed the Secretary of Commerce and the Secretary of Health, Education, and Welfare (now Health and Human Services) to study and investigate all manner of damages, both economic and personal, from accidental burning of fabrics and related products. Much of the statistical information pertaining to fabric-related burning accidents is provided by the **National Electronic Injury Surveillance System (NEISS)**. The NEISS records personal injury data from scores of hospital emergency rooms throughout the United States and forwards it to the CPSC for analysis.

The 1967 amendment also authorized the Secretary of Commerce to:

1. Conduct research into the flammability of products, fabrics, and materials.
2. Conduct feasibility studies on reduction of flammability of products, fabrics, and materials.
3. Develop flammability test methods and testing devices.
4. Offer appropriate training on the use of flammability test methods and testing devices.

The federally funded **National Institute of Standards and Technology (NIST)** carries out much of the investigative work involved in the laboratories of its Center for Fire Research. NIST does not promulgate standards; it provides information to the CPSC and other federal agencies.

When statistical injury data and laboratory test results support the possibility that a new or revised safety standard is needed, it is the responsibility of the CPSC to initiate and carry out the following procedures:

1. Publish the notice of a possible need and the proposed standard in the *Federal Register*.
2. Invite and consider response from affected and interested persons.
3. Publish the final version of the standard in the *Federal Register*.
4. Allow one year for firms affected by the standard to manufacture products meeting specified performance criteria. (The CPSC may set an earlier or later effective date if it finds good cause.)

5. Prohibit noncomplying products manufactured after the effective date from being introduced into commerce. (The CPSC may allow exceptions.)

Flammability Standards

Various standards have been promulgated and proposed as a result of the 1967 amendment. The standards are published with their **Code of Federal Regulations (CFR)** notation and include:

16 CFR 1630

Large Carpets and Rugs

16 CFR 1631

Small Carpets and Rugs

16 CFR 1632

Mattresses and Mattress Pads—Smoldering Resistance

16 CFR 1633

Mattresses and Mattress Pads—Open Flame Resistance

UFAC Voluntary Action Program

Officially launched in 1979, the **Upholstered Furniture Action Council (UFAC)** Voluntary Action Program was designed to encourage development of residential upholstered furniture that resists catching fire from a burning cigarette, which is the most common source of furniture ignition. Fortunately, smoking is no longer allowed in most public buildings, including offices, restaurants, healthcare facilities, and college dormitories, or in airplanes. Since it is allowed in some hotel rooms and in homes, these are the most likely fire-safety risk areas.

The UFAC program includes four aspects: fabric classification, which is determined by a prescribed test method; construction criteria, which are paired with test methods; a labeling plan; and a compliance procedure. The test methods used in the program are described later in this chapter. By combining the ability of the outercovering to resist catching fire from a burning cigarette with construction method, the industry's goal was to produce upholstered furniture that is as safe as possible, but also to offer a broad selection of appealing upholstery fabrics.

The UFAC hangtag (Figure 12.1a and b) identifies furniture meeting UFAC criteria and is designed to be easy to read in English, French, and Spanish. It adds a precaution about small open flames (matches, candles, lighters, etc.). UFAC provides the tags at a nominal cost to manufacturers, and revenues from tag sales are used to finance the UFAC Voluntary Action Program, including compliance verification, to fund additional research, and to promote the program to the industry and consumers.

UFAC encourages furniture component suppliers and end-product manufacturers to participate and provides technical assistance to promote compliance. Independent laboratories verify that materials meet the UFAC performance criteria.

Periodically, the results of verification tests and the level of industry participation in the program are reported to the CPSC. Through this reporting, UFAC and members of the industry demonstrate that upholstered furniture is built to be safe, and also aim to eliminate the need for a federal flammability mandate. Currently there are no national flammability standards or codes.

Combustion Processes and Byproducts

Combustion is a chemical process in which oxidation, the combination of oxygen with elements or compounds, produces heat energy. In some combustion reactions, light and other byproducts (such as molten polymer compounds, smoke, and toxic gases) are also produced.

Combustion Processes

Pyrolysis initiates **flaming combustion**, in which heat causes organic compounds to decompose, producing combustible materials. A burning match, a lit cigarette, glowing embers, or an electrical spark may supply heat. As previously mentioned, the most common source of ignition heat for interior textile products is a burning cigarette. (A lit match reaches a temperature of approximately 1000°F). When the **kindling or ignition temperature** is reached, the combustible materials combine with oxygen, ignite, and produce heat and light in the

(a)

⚠ WARNING: FLAMMABLE	**⚠ AVERTISSEMENT** INFLAMMABLE	**⚠ CUIDADO** INFLAMABLE
• Keep upholstery away from flames or lit cigarettes. • Upholstery may burn rapidly, with toxic gas & thick smoke. • Keep children away from matches and lighters. • Fires from candles, lighters, matches, or other smoking materials are still possible. • Be careful when smoking. • Smoke detectors properly installed and maintained save lives.	• Gardez vos produits rembourrés à l'écart du feu ou des cigarettes allumées. • Les produits rembourrés peuvent prendre en feu rapidement; dégager des gas toxiques ou produire de la fumée épaisse. • Ne laissez pas des allumettes ou des briquets à la portée des enfants. • La proximité de chandelles, allumettes, briquets ou tout autre objet émettant des flammes augmente les risques de feux. • Nous vous recommandons d'être vigilants lorsque vous fumez. • Les détecteurs de fumée sauvent des vies; il suffit de bien les installer et de les entretenir régulièrement.	• Mantenga la tapiceria alejada de fuego, flamas o cigarillos encendidos. • La tapiceria puede encenderse rapidamente y emite gases toxicos y humo denso. • Mantenga los niños alejados de fósforos y de encendedores. • Existe la posibilidad de que un incendio sea producido por velas encendidas, encendedores, fósforos o articulos de fumar. • Tenga cuidado cuando fume. • Los detectores de humo bien instalados y revisados pueden salvar vidas.
The manufacturer certifies this furniture is made in accordance with UFAC$_{SM}$ methods designed to reduce the likelihood of upholstery fires from cigarettes.	Le fabricant certifie que ce meuble rembourré est fabriqué en respectant les normes de UFAC$_{SM}$ en vue de réduire les risques ante tapiceria d'incendies dues aux cigarettes.	Los fabricantes certifican que los muebles están manufacturados de acuerdo a las regulaciones de la UFAC$_{SM}$. con métodos diseñados para reducir la posibilidad de incendios producidos por cigarrillos encendidos.
CLEANING INFORMATION: Never remove cushion covers even if they have zippers. **Woven and Knit Fabrics:** Vacuum or brush with soft bristle brush weekly. Use a professional furniture cleaning service for overall soiled conditions. **Vinyl:** Sponge with warm, mild soapy water. Remove solutions with clean, damp, soft cloth. **Leather:** Follow Manufacturer's instructions. ⓢ 01/08	**ENTRETIEN:** N'enlevez jamais une housse même celle avec fermeture èclair. **Pour les lainages ou tricots:** nettoyez une fois par semaine en passant l'aspirateur avec une brosse souple. Pour un nettoyage plus en profondeur, faites nettoyer professionnellement. **Pour le vinyle:** nettoyez à l'aide d'une éponge et d'une eau savonneuse tiède. Asséchez en utilisant un chiffon propre et humide. **Pour le cuir:** suivez les instructions du fabricant.	**INFORMACION DE LIMPIEZA:** Nunca remueva las coverturas de los cojines aunque tengan cremalleras. **Téjidos Y Telas De Punto:** Aspire o cepille semanalmente con capillo de cerda suave. Use un servicio profesional de limpieza de muebles para condiciónes totalmente monohadas. **Vinyl:** Esponjé con agua tibia jabón suave. Remuèva la solucion con tela suave, limpie y humeda. **Piel:** siga las instrucciones del fabricante.

(b)

Figure 12.1 Upholstered Furniture Action Council hangtag: (a) front, (b) back. Courtesy of the Upholstered Furniture Action Council.

form of flames. The heat generated can promote further decomposition of a nearby material, causing the cycle to continue until the entire fuel source is consumed.

Spontaneous combustion occurs when a material is heated to its kindling temperature without a flaming ignition source. Although this is not common with fibers, it is a potential hazard with latex foam compounds, especially when they are being tumbled in a heated dryer. Because cellular latex is a good heat insulator, heat builds up, the relatively low ignition temperature of the material is quickly reached, and it bursts into flame.

In addition to flaming combustion, **flameless combustion** can also occur. One type of flameless combustion, **glowing**, is characteristic of cellulosic fibers: after a small area of flame has been extinguished, the fiber continues to be consumed without flames rising. **Smoldering** is another type of flameless combustion, which may occur with fibrous fillings and battings. This suppressed combustion often produces large volumes of dense smoke filled with deadly toxic materials.

Byproducts of Combustion

Besides the heat energy and light produced during most combustion reactions, burning materials generate various other products. Among these, toxic gases pose the greatest threat to life.

Molten Polymer Compounds

When thermoplastic fibers are heated to their melting points, the molten polymer compounds produced can play conflicting roles in interior fires. When window coverings and wallcoverings contain thermoplastic polymer fibers, for example, the molten material may drip and carry the flames downward. This is a good thing if the burning fabric **self-extinguishes** and the flaming droplets fall on noncombustible flooring material. It is a negative if the flaming droplets spread the fire to a flammable floorcovering.

Smoke

Smoke generated by items undergoing flaming combustion or smoldering have a major effect on safe exit procedures because smoke reduces visibility and obscures illuminated exit markers. A test method to evaluate **smoke density** is discussed and illustrated later in this chapter, on page 157. Smoke, rather than heat or flame, is the primary cause of all fire deaths. Smoke is deadly because of the toxicants it contains. While limiting smoke development is required under aviation regulations, currently there are no specific codes or ordinances that focus on smoke emitted from fires in interiors.

Toxic Gases

Toxicity studies have shown that varied quantities of specific gases can be detected after the isolated combustion of commonly used fibers. The most toxic of these gases, carbon monoxide (CO), which is present in all fires, causes death by preventing red blood cells from absorbing oxygen.

Currently, no textile flammability regulations include specific requirements related to **toxic gases**, although it may be reasonable to expect such mandates in the future. ASTM International has developed two standards to assist fire safety researchers in measuring amounts of toxic gasses during fires: ASTM E800 Standard Guide for Measurement of Gases Present or Generated During Fires, and ASTM E1678 Standard Test Method for Measuring Smoke Toxicity for Use in Fire Hazard Analysis.

Stages of an Interior Fire

The principal concern of fire-safety professionals is for human health and safety. Burned furnishings can be repaired or replaced! Reducing probability of ignition, installing appropriate sprinkler systems, and planning and marking efficient paths of **egress** from a burning area or structure can save lives in the unlikely event of a fire.

The three distinct stages of an interior fire's progress illustrate that safe building egress and the value of early warning systems and automatic sprinkling systems save lives. (Obviously, furnishing materials do not dictate either of these factors.)

Stage 1

In a **Stage 1 fire** (Figure 12.2) only the ignited item is burning. If an interior fire starts, the primary goal is that it remain localized. If a burning cigarette is carelessly dropped onto an item (a carpet or an upholstered chair, for example), the item should be designed to resist ignition. It is more challenging to extinguish a fire and more difficult to exit safely if an ignited item spreads the flame throughout the room. When a fire is small and isolated, smoke detectors or other alarm systems alert residents. The early warning may enable occupants to contain the fire, preventing its growth to Stage 2.

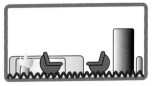 

Side Elevation (Room)   Floor Plan (Room)

Figure 12.2 Stage 1 of an interior fire.
I.A. Benjamin and S. Davis, Flammability Testing for Carpet, NBSIR 78-1436, Center for Fire Research, Institute for Applied Technology, National Bureau of Standards, Washington, DC, April 1978.

Stage 2

A **Stage 2 fire** is illustrated in Figure 12.3. Here, the fire has spread from the area of origin, igniting other items in its path. As the fire spreads and grows, more heat is generated and the air in the room becomes hotter and hotter. When sufficient heat has built up, all combustible items in the room burst into flames, which produces a situation known as **flashover**.

Side Elevation (Room)   Floor Plan (Room)

Figure 12.3 Stage 2 of an interior fire.
I.A. Benjamin and S. Davis, Flammability Testing for Carpet, NBSIR 78-1436, Center for Fire Research, Institute for Applied Technology, National Bureau of Standards, Washington, DC, April 1978.

Automatic sprinkling systems, which are usually heat activated, can halt **flame spread** (or **flame propagation**), which minimizes heat buildup and prevents flashover. Using smoke detectors and automatic sprinkling systems in all buildings and residences greatly reduces overall injuries, loss of life, and property damage.

Stage 3

In a **Stage 3 fire**, shown schematically in Figure 12.4, the flames spread beyond the burning room into the corridor or passageway. In addition to the flames, a significant amount of heat may be radiating into the corridor as the fire spills out. If the fire spreads down the corridor, all exits may be blocked.

Side Elevation (Corridor)   Floor Plan (Building)

Figure 12.4 Stage 3 of an interior fire.
I.A. Benjamin and S. Davis, Flammability Testing for Carpet, NBSIR 78-1436, Center for Fire Research, Institute for Applied Technology, National Bureau of Standards, Washington, DC, April 1978.

Fire researchers consider the three stages of fire growth when they design flammability test methods. Members of the CPSC and other regulatory agencies consider them when they establish flammability standards for selected interior textile products.

Flammability Testing

Various types of testing are used to measure the fire-related behavior of interior textile products and components. Currently, small-scale, large-scale, and full-scale procedures are used in this work.

Small-Scale Test Methods

Small-scale test methods are used in the laboratory to measure specific flammability characteristics. Like other standard test methods, these are designed to simulate the conditions associated with real-life situations; in some test methods, for example, a lit cigarette is the source of heat for ignition (Figures 12.5 through 12.7). Small-scale tests enable the producer to make reasonably accurate predictions concerning the behavior of the item being tested in a Stage 1 fire.

Methenamine Tablet (Pill) Test Method

The **methenamine tablet test**, designated ASTM D2859 Standard Test Method for Ignition Characteristics of Finished Textile Floor Covering Materials, is designed to simulate a situation in which a textile floorcovering is exposed to a small source of ignition, such as a burning

Figure 12.5 Interior fire at 0 seconds. Courtesy of the National Institute of Standards and Technology.

Figure 12.6 Interior fire at 90 seconds. Courtesy of the National Institute of Standards and Technology.

Figure 12.7 Interior fire at 180 seconds. Courtesy of the National Institute of Standards and Technology.

match, an ignited cigarette, or a glowing ember. Structures that resist ignition and do not propagate the flame could reasonably be expected to contain a fire in Stage 1.

Test Specimens and Procedures

Eight specimens, each one 9 inches square, are dried in an oven so that they will be free of moisture. Then, one at a time, the specimens are placed in a draft-protected burn chamber and covered by a steel flattening frame with an opening 8 inches in diameter. As shown in Figure 12.8, a methenamine tablet, which is formulated to burn for two minutes, is placed in the center of the specimen and ignited. Testing is complete when burning of the tablet or the carpet specimen ceases, whichever occurs last.

Analysis of Results

A **char length** measurement is taken on each of the eight specimens. Measurements are made of the shortest

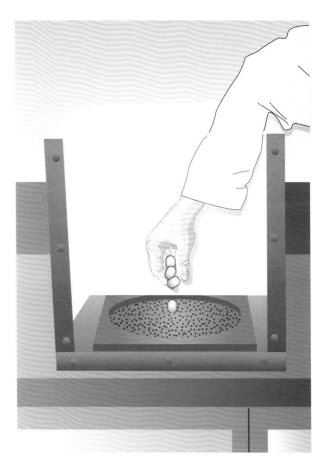

Figure 12.8 Methenamine tablet test. Illustration by Andrea Lau/Fairchild Books.

distance between the edge of the hole in the ring and the charred area. Smoke and toxic gases are not considered.

Performance Requirements

A specimen meets either standard when the char area does not extend to within 1 inch of the hole in the ring. Seven out of the eight specimens must pass for the floorcovering to pass. The provisions of 16 CFR 1631 permit rugs that fail the test to be marketed as long as they carry a label warning: "flammable (fails U.S. CPSC Standard 16 CFR 1631: should not be used near source of fire)."

Adoption of the Method

This test has been adopted as the method to be used in 16 CFR 1630 and 16 CFR 1631. The scope of 16 CFR 1630 is limited to large carpets and rugs, those having an area greater than 24 square feet and one dimension greater than 6 feet. Carpet modules, because they are installed to cover large areas, are also subject to the provisions of 16 CFR 1630. The scope of 16 CFR 1631 includes floorcoverings that are not large enough to fall within the scope of 16 CFR 1630. Such structures include scatter rugs, bathroom rugs, and smaller area rugs. These standards became effective in 1971, and virtually all imported and domestic soft floorcoverings offered for sale in the United States must conform to the provisions of the applicable standard.

45-Degree Angle Test Method

Although ASTM D1230 Standard Test Method for Flammability of Apparel Textiles was originally designed for use with apparel textiles, it may be selected to evaluate the flammability of towelings. This small-scale test is also known as the 45-degree angle test.

Test Specimens and Procedure

In accordance with ASTM D1230, exploratory testing is used to determine the direction in which the most rapid rate of flame spread occurs. With pile fabrics, flame spread is most rapid when progressing against the lay of the pile, so the long dimension of the specimens should parallel the lay of the pile. Five specimens are then cut 2 inches by 6 inches, oven dried, and placed in a specimen holder. One at a time, each specimen is placed in the flammability tester at a 45-degree angle. Automated mechanisms are then activated to apply a flame to the lower edge of the specimen for 1 second; timing begins upon application of the flame and ends when burning releases a stop cord.

Analysis of Results

The arithmetic mean flame-spread time of the preliminary specimen and the five test specimens is calculated.

Performance Guidelines

Materials that achieve a Class 1 rating on this test do not have a raised fiber surface but have an average time of flame spread in the test of 3.5 seconds or more, or they have a **raised fiber surface**, including the pile loops of terry, and an average time of **flame spread** in the test of more than 7 seconds or burn with a surface flash (time of flame spread less than 7 seconds), provided the intensity of the flame is insufficient to ignite, char, or melt the base fabric. Class 2 textiles have a raised fiber surface and had an average time of flame spread in the test of 4 to 7 seconds, inclusive, and the base fabric was ignited, charred, or melted. Class 3 textiles have a raised fiber surface and had an average time of flame spread in the test of less than 4 seconds, and the base fabric was ignited, charred, or melted.

Adoption of the Method

If purchaser and supplier agree to have the flammability of toweling evaluated, they may use this test.

Flooring Radiant Panel Test Method

The NIST maintains corridor-like testing facilities. Using these facilities, fire researchers have confirmed that the amount of heat radiating onto a floorcovering directly affects the distance flames spread in a Stage 3 fire. Because such spreading may restrict or prevent safe egress, a small-scale test method including **radiant heat** as a condition is increasingly used to measure the flame spread of floorcoverings intended for installation in corridors.

This test method has been designated as ASTM E648 Standard Test Method for Critical Radiant Flux of Floor Covering Systems Using a Radiant Heat Energy Source and NFPA 253 Standard Method of Test for Critical Radiant Flux of Floor Covering Systems Using a Radiant Heat Energy Source. It accurately simulates real-life floorcovering installation practices and the conditions characteristic of a Stage 3 interior fire. This test does assess the critical relationship between heat energy radiating from the ceiling and flame spread along a corridor floorcovering. Because it has thus overcome the major shortcoming of the tunnel test, which is described in the section "Large-Scale Test Methods," the radiant panel test method is increasingly used by authorities who have jurisdiction over the selection of interior floor finishes for commercial interiors.

The radiant panel test apparatus is much smaller than the other tunnel-shaped furnace devices but, like them, it has a corridor-like design. An inclined panel radiates heat energy to the surface of the specimen. Because the level of heat radiating onto a corridor carpet would be highest at the point of **spillover**, the panel is positioned at an angle of 30 degrees to the carpet specimen. The amount of heat energy radiating along the carpet during testing ranges from a maximum of 1.0 watts per square centimeter immediately below the panel to a minimum of 0.10 watt per square centimeter at the opposite end of the specimen.

Test Specimens and Procedures

A carpet specimen, with or without a separate or attached cushion, is cut 42 inches long and 10 inches wide and placed pile side up on the floor of the chamber. A gas flame is impinged on the surface of the specimen immediately below the preheated panel for five minutes. Air is allowed to flow through the chamber bottom and exit via a chimney-like opening. The test continues until the floorcovering ceases to burn. Three replicate tests are normally required.

Analysis of Results

A numerical value, the **critical radiant flux (CRF)**, is determined by converting the distance of flame spread into watts per square centimeter. The CRF indicates the minimum heat energy that is necessary, or critical, to sustain burning of the floorcovering and support flame propagation. According to Figure 12.9, a test sample that stops burning at a distance just short of 20 inches

(50 centimeters) down its length would have a CRF of 0.34 watt per square centimeter, whereas a carpet that burned the entire distance would have a CRF of 0.10 watt per square centimeter. Higher CRF values thus indicate safer systems. The CRF value reported is the average of the three replicate tests. No analysis is made of smoke generation. The ASTM E648 standard classifies flooring as having either a Class I (0.45 watts/cm^2) or Class II (0.22 watts/cm^2) rating.

Performance Requirements

The levels of fire performance of soft floorcoverings mandated by municipal, state, and federal agencies are frequently based on recommendations set forth in the **NFPA 101**® Life Safety Code®. Table 12.1 summarizes recommendations pertaining to interior finishes, such as carpet installed on walls, and to interior floor finishes. The materials used for interior finishes are classified in accordance with the tunnel test, and those used for interior floor finishes are classified in accordance with the radiant panel test. Because all large floorcoverings must conform with 16 CFR 1630 (FF 1–70), the NFPA does not recommend additional testing for floorcoverings other than those installed in exit ways and corridors in certain occupancies.

Adoption of the Method

Several local, state, and federal regulatory agencies have adopted the radiant panel test in lieu of the tunnel test. Some also have established standards pertaining to smoke development. When these agencies have jurisdiction over an installation, smoke development must be measured in a separate test.

Smoke Chamber Test Method

This test method is assigned the designation ASTM E662 Standard Test Method for Specific Optical Density of Smoke Generated by Solid Materials and measures the **smoke generation** of solid materials under flaming and nonflaming (smoldering) conditions. The purpose of such testing is to identify materials that would generate large volumes of dense smoke, which would hinder quick and efficient egress by obscuring exit markers and would also hamper breathing.

TABLE 12.1

NFPA 101® LIFE SAFETY CODE® INTERIOR FINISH AND INTERIOR FLOOR FINISH RECOMMENDATIONS

The following is a compilation of the interior finish requirements of the occupancy chapters of the Code.

Occupancy	Exits	Access to Exits	Other Spaces
Places of Assembly—new*			
> 300 occupant load	A	A or B	A or B
	I or II	I or II	NA
< 300 occupant load	A	A or B	A, B, or C
	I or II	I or II	NA
Places of Assembly—existing*			
> 300 occupant load	A	A or B	A or B
< 300 occupant load	A	A or B	A, B, or C
Educational–new	A	A or B	A, B, or C On low partitions
	I or II	I or II	NA
Educational—existing	A	A or B	A, B, or C
Child Daycare Centers—new	A	A	A or B
	I or II	I or II	NA
Child Daycare Centers—existing	A or B	A or B	A or B
	I or II	I or II	
Daycare homes—new	A or B	A or B	A, B, or C
	I or II	NA	NA
Daycare homes—existing	A or B	A, B, or C	A, B, or C
Healthcare—new	A	A, B allowed on lower portion of corridor wall	A, B allowed in small individual rooms
	I or II	I or II	NA
Healthcare—existing	A or B	A or B	A or B
Detention & Correctional—new (sprinklers mandatory)	A	A	A, B, or C
	I or II	I or II	NA
Detention & Correctional—existing	A or B	A or B	A, B, or C
	I or II	I or II	NA
One- & Two-Family Dwellings & Lodging or Rooming Houses	A, B, or C	A, B, or C	A, B, or C
Hotels & Dormitories—new	A	A or B	A, B, or C
	I or II	I or II	NA
Hotels & Dormitories—existing	A or B	A or B	A, B, or C
	I or II	I or II	NA
Apartment Buildings—new	A	A or B	A, B, or C
	I or II	I or II	NA
Apartment Buildings—existing	A or B	A or B	A, B, or C
	I or II	I or II	NA
Residential Board & Care, see NFPA 101, chapters 32 & 33			
Mercantile—new*	A or B	A or B	A or B
	I or II	I or II	NA

Occupancy	Exits	Access to Exits	Other Spaces
Mercantile—±existing Class A or B* stores	A or B	A or B	Ceilings: A or B Walls: A, B, or C
Mercantile—existing Class C* stores	A, B, or C	A, B, or C	A, B, or C
Business & Ambulatory HealthCare—new	A or B	A or B	A, B, or C
	I or II	NA	NA
Business & Ambulatory Health Care—existing	A or B	A or B	A, B, or C
Industrial	A or B	A, B, or C	A, B, or C
	I or II	I or II	NA
Storage	A or B	A, B, or C	A, B, or C
	I or II	I or II	NA

*Exposed portions of structural members complying with the requirements for heavy timber construction may be permitted.

Notes:

Walls & Ceilings:

Class A Interior Finish—flame spread 0–25, smoke developed 0–450

Class B Interior Finish—flame spread 26–75, smoke developed 0–450

Class C Interior Finish—flame spread 76–200, smoke developed 0–450

Flooring:

Class I Interior Floor Finish—minimum 0.45 watt per sq. cm

Class II Interior Floor Finish—minimum 0.22 watt per sq. cm

Automatic Sprinklers—Where a complete standard system of automatic sprinklers is installed, interior finish with spread rating not over Class C may be used in any location where Class B is normally specified and with rating of Class B in any location where Class A is normally specified; similarly, Class II interior floor finish may be used in any location where Class I is normally specified and no critical radiant flux rating is required where Class II is normally specified.

Reprinted with permission from NFPA 101–2012, Life Safety Code, Handbook, Copyright 2011, National Fire Protection Association, Quincy, MA. This reprinted material is not the complete and official position of the NFPA on the referenced subject, which is represented only by the standard in its entirety.

Test Specimens and Procedures

A specimen, 3 inches square and up to 1 inch thick, is suspended vertically in an enclosed test chamber. Three replicate tests are conducted by exposing the specimen surface to an irradiance level of 2.5 watts per square centimeter; the individual tests are conducted by impinging six flamelets (small flames) across the lower edge of the specimen in combination with the radiant heat. A light beam is passed vertically through the smoke chamber. The test is completed when a minimum **light transmittance value** is reached or 20 minutes have elapsed, whichever occurs first.

Analysis of Results

A photometric system measures the continuous decrease in light transmission as smoke accumulates. These measurements are converted into specific **optical density values**.

Performance Requirements

Required values vary from a low of 50 to a maximum of 450. In some cases, an agency may specify an average of the flaming and nonflaming tests; in other cases, only the results of the flaming tests may be involved.

Adoption of the Method

Various city, state, and federal agencies have adopted this test method for materials installed in facilities they oversee. The General Services Administration (GSA), for example, has combined CRF and smoke development limits to establish two classifications, and defined a third through 16 CFR 1630. The three classes (A, B, and C) and the various GSA spaces to which they apply are listed here. These classes must not be confused with the A, B, and C classes that categorize the results of tunnel testing, described in the section "Large-Scale Test Methods."

- Class A: a CRF of 0.50 watt per square centimeter or greater and a maximum specific optical density not over 450 flaming. Class A carpet is not needed in office buildings.
- Class B: a CRF of 0.25 watt per square centimeter or greater and a maximum specific optical density not over 450 flaming. Class B carpet is required in unsprinklered corridors exposed to office space having a controlled equivalent fuel load of 6 pounds per square foot or less.
- Class C: the face and back of the carpet and separate cushion pass 16 CFR 1630. Class C carpet may be installed in all office areas and in corridors protected with automatic sprinklers.

FAA Paragraph 25.853 (b)

The Federal Aviation Administration (FAA) flammability regulation for textile items used in compartments occupied by the crew or passengers in airplanes is designated as **Paragraph 25.853 (b)**. Other paragraphs in the standard, which was issued on February 15, 1972, concern items such as landing gear systems, escape routes, exit markers, and nontextile interior finishing materials. The general focus of the standard is to improve the crashworthiness and emergency evacuation equipment of airliners.

Test Specimens and Procedures

The specimens are cut 2¾ by 12½ inches, with the most critical flammability conditions corresponding to the long dimension. The specimens are conditioned for 24 hours at a temperature of 70°F and a relative humidity of 50 percent; they are then clamped in a U-shaped frame. The secured specimen is vertically suspended in a draft-free test chamber, shown in Figure 12.9. A flame is impinged on the lower edge of the specimen for 12 seconds and then removed.

Analysis of Results

Three results are determined for each specimen:

1. The **after flame time** is the time the specimen continues to flame after the burner flame is removed.
2. The **afterglow** time is the time the specimen continues to glow after it stops flaming.

Figure 12.9 Vertical flammability tester. Courtesy of SDL Atlas, LLC.

3. The **char length** is measured by inserting the correct weight (determined by the weight of the fabric being tested) on one side of the charred area and gently raising the opposite side of the specimen. The length of the tear is measured and recorded.

Performance Requirements

Materials used in compartment interiors must be self-extinguishing. The average char length may not exceed 8 inches and the average after flame time may not exceed 15 seconds.

Adoption of the Method

The provisions of Paragraph 25.853 (b) apply to upholstery, draperies, floorcoverings, seat cushions, padding, decorative and nondecorative coated fabrics, leather, trays, and galley furnishings. They also apply to such items as acoustical insulation.

NFPA 701 Test Method 1 and 2

NFPA 701 Standard Methods of Fire Tests for Flame Propagation of Textiles and Films may be used to evaluate the effectiveness of polymer additives and finishing compounds in reducing the flammability of textile window coverings. Test Method 1 can be used to evaluate the flame resistance of single-layer and multilayer fabrics with a total weight of 21 oz/yd or less that do not have a vinyl coated blackout lining. Test Method 2 may be used for single-layer and multilayer fabrics, vinyl coated black out lining, films, plastic blinds, awnings, tents, banners, and similar items that have a total weight over 21 oz/yd.

Test Specimens and Procedures—Method 1

Ten specimens of the covering are cut 5.9 inches by 15.8 inches, with the length parallel to the lengthwise direction of the material. The specimens are then conditioned in an oven at a temperature of 220°F for 30 minutes or, if they would melt or distort in the oven, they are conditioned at 68°F for a minimum of 24 hours. Each specimen is then placed in an open-ended specimen holder and suspended in a 26.6 inches wide by 27.5 inches high by 19.7 inches deep vertical flammability tester. The flame from a burner is then applied to the lower edge for 45 seconds.

Flame Resistance Requirements—Method 1

In order for the material to pass, the specimens must meet the following three requirements:

1. Fragments or residues of specimens that fall to the floor of the test chamber shall not continue to burn for more than an average of 2 seconds per specimen for the sample of 10 specimens.
2. The average weight loss of the 10 specimens in a sample shall be 40 percent or less.
3. No individual specimen's percent mass loss shall deviate more than three standard deviations from the mean for the 10 specimens.

Test Specimens and Procedures— Test Method 2

Specimens of the covering material may be tested in single, flat sheets or they may be hung with folds. For flat testing, 10 specimens, 4.9 inches by 47.25 inches, are cut. For testing with folds, four lengths of the covering, each cut 24 inches by 47.25 inches, are folded longitudinally to form four folds, each approximately 5 inches wide. In either case, half the specimens have their long dimension in the direction of the warp and half have their long dimension in the direction of the filling. The specimens are conditioned as described for Test Method 1.

The specimens, flat or folded, are suspended in the tester, which is a sheet-iron stacked 12 inches square and 7 feet high similar to the apparatus in Figure 12.11. The lower edge of the specimen is 4 inches above the burner tip and an 11-inch flame is held under the specimen for two minutes.

Flame Resistance Requirements— Test Method 2

For the covering material to pass Test Method 2, the specimens must meet the following four requirements:

1. No specimen shall continue flaming for more than 2 seconds after the test flame is removed from contact with the specimen.
2. The vertical spread of burning on the material in single sheets shall not exceed 10 inches above the tip of the test flame. This vertical spread shall be measured as the distance from the tip of the test flame to a horizontal line above which all material is sound and in original condition, except for possible smoke deposits.
3. The vertical spread of burning on the folded specimens shall not exceed 35 inches above the tip of the test flame, but the afterglow may spread in the folds.
4. At no time during or after the application of the test flame shall portions or residues of textiles or films that break or drip from any test specimen continue to flame after they reach the floor of the tester.

Adoption of the Method

NFPA 701 is intended for use with textiles and films treated with flame-retardant agents or composed of flame-resistant manufactured fibers, and may be used to measure the ignition propensity of fabrics to be installed indoors or outdoors. Fabrics expected to retain their flame-resistant qualities through dry-cleaning, laundering, weathering, or other exposures to water are subjected to accelerated exposure procedures prior to testing. Treated awning fabrics, for example, would be exposed to simulated weathering conditions and then tested.

In the event of fire, fabrics meeting the flame resistance requirements included in Test Method 1 and Test Method 2 would not be likely to propagate the flames to the floor, wall, and ceiling. This reduces the threat of a Stage 1 fire growing into a Stage 2 fire.

UFAC Fabric Classification Test Method

The **UFAC Voluntary Action Program**, discussed in the section on the Flammable Fabrics Act, is designed to improve the ability of upholstered furniture to resist catching fire from a burning cigarette, the most common source of furniture ignition. At the outset, upholstery fabrics are divided into two categories of ignition propensity, based on their ability to resist ignition when exposed to a burning cigarette. The procedures used are outlined in the UFAC Fabric Classification Test Method—1990.

This test is similar to NFPA 260, Standard Methods of Tests and Classification System for Cigarette Ignition Resistance of Components of Upholstered Furniture, and ASTM E1353, Standard Test Methods for Cigarette Ignition Resistance of Components of Upholstered Furniture.

Test Specimens and Procedures

In this test method, vertical and horizontal panels are upholstered using the cover fabrics to be tested and 2-inch-thick polyurethane foam filling materials. As schematized in Figure 12.10, the panels are placed in the test assembly, and a lighted nonfilter cigarette is placed in the crevice of the assembly and covered with a piece of cotton bedsheeting fabric. The cigarette is allowed to burn its entire length unless an obvious ignition occurs. Three replicate tests are required for each fabric.

Test Criteria

If ignition occurs on any one of the three specimens, the fabric is Class II. If no ignition occurs, the vertical char length is measured from the crevice to the highest part of the destroyed or degraded cover fabric. If the char length is less than 1¾ inches, the fabric is Class I; if the char length is equal to or greater than 1¾ inches, the fabric is Class II. This classification determines which construction methods must be employed with the cover fabric to comply with UFAC construction criteria.

Adoption of the Method

In accordance with the UFAC Voluntary Action Program, Class I fabrics may be used directly over conventional polyurethane in the horizontal seating surfaces of upholstered furniture bearing the UFAC hangtag. Class

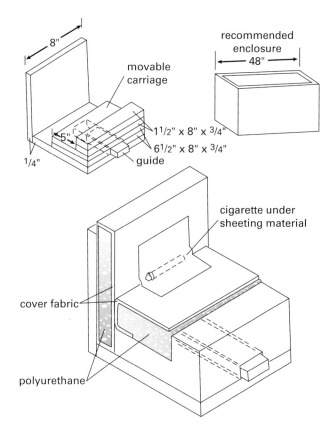

Figure 12.10 The assembly used in the UFAC Fabric Classification Test. Courtesy of the Upholstered Furniture Action Council, Inc.

II fabrics require an approved barrier between the cover fabric and conventional polyurethane foam in the horizontal seating surfaces.

UFAC Welt Cord Test Method

This test method is employed to identify welt cording that is suitable for use in seats, backs, and pillows in UFAC-approved constructions. The welt cords must meet the requirement of the UFAC Welt Cord Test Method—1990.

Test Specimens and Procedures

In this test, welt cording is placed in the center of a piece of UFAC Standard Type II cover fabric that is folded to make an unsewn welt. This cover fabric, a 100 percent bright, regular rayon in basket weave construction, is also used to cover the vertical and horizontal panels. The welt is placed in the crevice formed by the abutment of the horizontal and vertical panels in the test assembly, which is similar to that shown in Figure 12.10. As shown

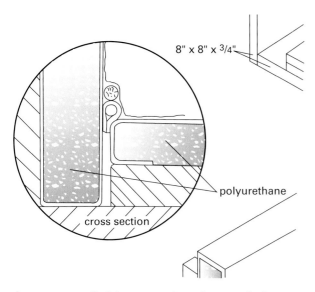

Figure 12.11 Detail of the UFAC Welt Cord Test Method. Courtesy of the Upholstered Furniture Action Council, Inc.

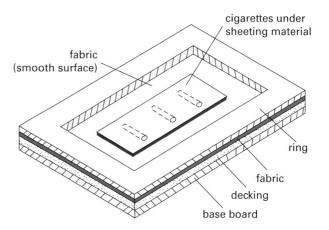

Figure 12.12 The assembly used in the UFAC Decking Materials Test Method. Courtesy of the Upholstered Furniture Action Council, Inc.

in Figure 12.11, a lighted cigarette is placed on the welt and covered with a piece of cotton bedsheeting. Three replicate tests are run.

Test Criteria

The welt cording is acceptable if no ignition occurs, or if the maximum height of the vertical char on each of the vertical panels does not equal or exceed 1½ inches. If one specimen has a vertical char equal to or greater than 1½ inches, three additional specimens are tested. If one or more additional specimens have a vertical char equal to or greater than 1½ inches, the test material fails.

Adoption of the Method

In accordance with the UFAC Voluntary Action Program, welt cording used with furniture carrying the UFAC hangtag must meet the requirements of this test.

UFAC Decking Materials Test Method

As part of the UFAC Voluntary Action Program, deck padding materials used under loose cushions should resist ignition from smoldering cigarettes. The resistance of polyurethane foam, bonded fiber pads, treated cotton batting, and other padding materials intended for use in decking under loose cushions can be assessed by subjecting them to the UFAC Decking Materials Test Method—1990.

Test Specimens and Procedures

In preparation for this test, decking material is cut to size and placed on a plywood assembly base, shown schematically in Figure 12.12. The decking material is covered with UFAC Standard Type II fabric and the layered fabrics are held in place by a wooden retainer ring. Three lighted cigarettes are placed on the decking cover fabric and covered with 100 percent cotton sheeting. The cigarettes are allowed to burn their full lengths, and the maximum char lengths measured from the cigarettes are recorded.

Test Criteria

The decking material is acceptable if it meets the same criteria listed for the Welt Cord Test Method.

Adoption of the Method

In accordance with the UFAC Voluntary Action Program, decking material used with furniture carrying the UFAC hangtag must meet the requirements of this test.

UFAC Filling/Padding Component Test Method

UFAC Filling/Padding Component Test Method, Parts A and B—1990, determines which filling or padding components intended for use in upholstered furniture exhibit sufficient resistance to smoldering cigarette ignition to merit use in items bearing the UFAC hangtag. Part A of this test method is used with slab or garnetted filling/padding components that include, but are not limited to, battings of natural and man-made (manufactured) fibers, foamed or cellular fillings or cushioning materials, and resilient pads of natural or man-made (manufactured) fibers. Part B of this test method is used with fibrous or particulate materials that include, but are not limited to, staple of natural and man-made (manufactured) fibers, shredded foamed or cellular filling materials, and composites of any of these, together with any protective interliners that may be necessary to meet the requirements of the test method.

Test Specimens and Procedures

The filling material to be tested is used in the vertical and horizontal panels of the test assembly shown in Figure 12.10, in place of the polyurethane. It is covered with UFAC Standard Type I mattress ticking, which is composed of 100 percent cotton and has been laundered and tumble-dried once in accordance with prescribed UFAC procedures. One at a time, three ignited cigarettes are placed in the crevice and covered with sheeting fabric.

Test Criteria

In Part A, the filling/padding material is acceptable if no ignition occurs, or if no vertical char equals or exceeds $1^1/2$ inches. If one specimen has a vertical char equal to or greater than $1^1/2$ inches, three additional specimens are tested. If one or more additional specimens have a vertical char equal to or greater than $1^1/2$ inches, the test material fails. Part B has an additional criterion: no specimen can have evolvement of smoke or heat.

Adoption of the Method

In accordance with the UFAC Voluntary Action Program, filling/padding material used with furniture carrying the UFAC hangtag must meet the requirements of this test.

UFAC Interior Fabric Test Method

For upholstered furniture items to bear the UFAC hangtag, interior fabrics used in intimate contact with the outer fabrics must exhibit an acceptable level of performance with respect to cigarette ignition resistance. UFAC Interior Fabric Test Method—1990 can be used to assess this performance.

Test Specimens and Procedures

The assembly used in the required three replicate tests is like that illustrated in Figure 12.10, except that an interior fabric test specimen is placed between the outercovering and the foam filling of the horizontal panels. For this test, the vertical and horizontal panels are covered with UFAC Standard Type I mattress ticking. The three lighted cigarettes are again placed one at a time in the crevice and covered.

Test Criteria

The test criteria for this test are identical to those for the Welt Cord Test Method.

Adoption of the Method

In accordance with the UFAC Voluntary Action Program, interior fabrics used with furniture carrying the UFAC hangtag must meet the requirements of this test.

UFAC Barrier Test Method

UFAC Barrier Test Method—1990 is intended to define the minimum performance level for barrier materials to be placed between Class II fabrics and conventional polyurethane foam in horizontal seating surfaces. This will minimize the likelihood of ignition of the foam in the event a Class II fabric is generating considerable heat as it undergoes decomposition and combustion.

Test Specimens and Procedures

Three tests are run using the assembly illustrated in Figure 12.13. UFAC Standard Type II cover fabric is used as the covering. The barrier material to be tested is placed between the cover fabric and the polyurethane substrate in both vertical and horizontal panels. A lighted cigarette is placed in the crevice and covered with a piece of sheeting material.

Test Criteria

The test criteria for this test are identical to those for the Welt Cord Test Method.

Adoption of the Method

In accordance with the UFAC Voluntary Action Program, barrier materials used with furniture covered with Class

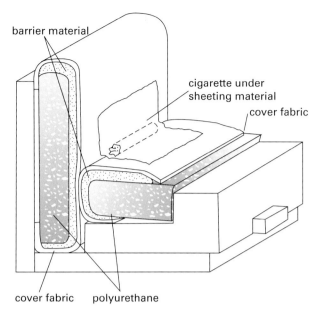

barrier material

cigarette under sheeting material

cover fabric

cover fabric   polyurethane

Figure 12.13 The assembly used in the UFAC Barrier Test Method. Courtesy of the Upholstered Furniture Action Council, Inc.

II fabric and filled with polyurethane foam must meet the requirements of this test if the item is to bear the UFAC hangtag. Actual fires spread quickly, with flashover occurring within two and a half minutes after ignition when a chair with no flame-resistant barrier is used. It is evident in tests that the presence of UFAC protective barriers in chairs prevent ignition of the foam substrate. The charred area may be substantial, but ignition is prevented.

UFAC Decorative Trim Test Method

In a continuing effort to make upholstered furniture safer when exposed to an ignition source, members of the UFAC developed the UFAC Standard Test Methods for Decorative Trims, Edging, and Brush Fringes—1993.

Test Specimens and Procedures

The test apparatus used in this test is similar to that used in the Welt Cord Test Method shown in Figure 12.11. Again, Type II cover fabric, polyurethane foam, and cotton sheeting are used. A lighted cigarette is placed on top of the trim, edging, or brush fringe being tested and covered with sheeting.

Test Criteria

If all test specimens have no ignition, or if the vertical char of each is less than $1\frac{1}{2}$ inches upward from the crevice, the test material passes. If one test specimen has a vertical char equal to or greater than $1\frac{1}{2}$ inches, three additional specimens are tested. If all three additional specimens have a vertical char of less than $1\frac{1}{2}$ inches, the test material passes. If one additional specimen has a vertical char equal to or greater than $1\frac{1}{2}$ inches, the material fails. If two or more original test specimens have a vertical char of $\frac{1}{2}$ inches or more, the material fails.

Adoption of the Method

Trims meeting the above criteria will be classified as UFAC Type I decorative trim, edging, or brush fringe; providing the remainder of the upholstered furniture meets UFAC requirements, the UFAC hangtag may be used when Type I trim is present.

In the event the trim fails to conform to the above criteria, it should be retested, using a polyester fiber barrier and UFAC Standard Type II covering. If the trim then meets the above requirements, it is labeled UFAC Type II trimming. The furniture would then be eligible to bear the UFAC hangtag, as long as a garnetted polyester fiber barrier is used.

If the decorative trim, edging, or brush fringe fails with both the Type II fabric alone and the Type II fabric and polyester fiber barrier, the trimming is classified as Type III. UFAC hangtags are not permitted with upholstered furniture using Type III decorative trim, edging, or brush fringe.

California Technical Bulletins

California is one of only a few states that regulate seating products through mandatory testing. These requirements, known as **California Technical Bulletins**, are developed by the State of California Department of Consumer Affairs Bureau of Home Furnishings and Thermal Insulation. California Bulletins are laws that must be complied with by all who provide products sold in California, which is a large market for most manufacturers. Therefore, if manufacturers must sell in California, they usually design their products so that they comply with California regulations.

California Bulletin 117 Flammability Test Procedure for Seating Furniture for Use in Public Occupancies (CAL 117) is a small-scale upholstery fabric flammability test developed by the California Bureau of Home Furnishings and Thermal Insulation. The test is similar to the UFAC test, and has a pass/fail rating system. California Bulletin 133 Requirements, Test Procedure and Apparatus for Testing the Flame Retardance of Resilient Filling Materials Used in Upholstered Furniture (CAL 133) is a full-scale upholstered seating flammability test used to evaluate seating for occupancies such as prisons, hospitals, nursing homes, and other high-risk public spaces. This test also utilizes a pass/fail rating system. A furniture manufacturer undertakes CA 133 testing with all the materials that will be used in a specific style of furniture. Neither a fabric nor filling materials alone can be tested for CA 133.

Similarly, electrified furniture, such as moveable office panels, must be tested by UL (Underwriters Laboratories) as a composite. Furniture manufacturers are responsible for obtaining "UL Listing" for their products. A fabric cannot be UL listed, although UL is a certified tester for certain standards that apply to fabric.

Large-Scale Test Methods

Large-scale test methods are also laboratory procedures, but they use larger test specimens than do small-scale tests. A large-scale test method is used with textile wallcoverings, window coverings, soft floorcoverings, and mattresses.

Tunnel Test Method

This test method, also known as the **Steiner Tunnel Test Method**, measures the surface burning characteristics of building materials. It has been designated as ASTM E84, and UL 723 Standard Test Method for Surface Burning Characteristics of Building Materials. The testing apparatus is structured to simulate a corridor, and the testing procedures and results are used to assess flame spread and smoke generation. The method is thus intended to evaluate the potential hazard of a textile floorcovering in a Stage 3 fire.

Test Specimens and Procedures

A specimen, 25 feet by 1 foot 8 inches, is mounted on the ceiling of the tunnel chamber. The sample may be adhered to a gypsum or cement-based board, or it may be "unadhered," in which case the fabric is draped over a chicken-wire mesh. The sample is then subjected to gas jet flames and heat for ten minutes. Temperatures range from 1600 to 1800°F. Testing is complete when ten minutes have elapsed or the specimen has burned completely, whichever occurs first.

Analysis of Results

Time and flame spread distance values are plotted graphically and compared with those recorded for asbestos-cement board (assigned a flame spread rating of 0) and select-grade red oak flooring (assigned a flame spread rating of 100) to arrive at a flame spread classification. Class A includes flame spread ratings from 0 to 25, Class B from 26 to 75, and Class C from 76 to 200. Smoke density values are determined separately.

Performance Requirements

Flammability requirements for selected interior finishes, such as textile wallcoverings, are classified according to the tunnel test. The NFPA 101 Life Safety Code includes recommendations that may be mandated by an agency having jurisdiction over an occupancy and the materials to be installed within the facility (see Table 12.1).

Adoption of the Method for Wall Application

Since the fabric can be handled by different methods for this test, discussion surrounds the appropriate specimen preparation for a meaningful result. Generally speaking, the material should be tested according to the way it will be installed. ACT Voluntary Performance Guidelines are based on an unadhered test for fabric for upholstered walls or panels. Fabric to be direct glued to a wall is usually applied to a gypsum board for testing.

Adoption of the Method for Carpet

In recent years, the use of the tunnel test as a method for evaluating the potential fire hazard of textile structures to be installed as floorcoverings has been diminishing. Although the long, tunnel-shaped testing apparatus does indeed resemble a corridor, the method has two major shortcomings when correlated to end-use. First, because the specimen is mounted on the ceiling, the test does not realistically portray real-life installations. Second, the method fails to incorporate the critical variable of the heat energy that will be radiating into a corridor in the event an interior fire progresses from Stage 2 to Stage 3. Nonetheless, testing by this method continues to be required for some installations, and is often recommended or required for carpet to be used as an interior finish on walls and ceilings (see Table 12.1).

Mattress and Mattress Pad Test Method

The Standard for the Flammability of Mattresses, 16 CFR Part 1632, was established in 1974 to protect the public against unreasonable risk of mattress fires. The most common mode of bedding ignition, a burning cigarette, is used as the source of ignition in the test.

Test Specimens and Procedures

In testing, the bare sleeping surface of mattresses, including smooth, tape edge, and quilted or tufted locations, is exposed to as least nine ignited cigarettes that are 85 millimeters long and have no filter tips. These locations are also tested by placing nine additional burning cigarettes between two bed sheets that cover the mattress (Figure 12.14). The muslin or percale sheets used must be 100 percent cotton, have no durable press resins or flame-retardant agents, and be laundered one time prior to testing.

Mattress pads are tested in the same manner before they are laundered or dry-cleaned and again after they have been cleaned in accordance with prescribed procedures. Pads treated with a flame-retardant agent must be labeled with precautionary care instructions to help prevent the use of agents or procedures that could impair the effectiveness of the finishing compound.

Analysis of Results

The char length of each test location is measured and reported in inches.

Performance Requirements

Individual cigarette test locations pass the test if the char length of the mattress or mattress pad surface is not more

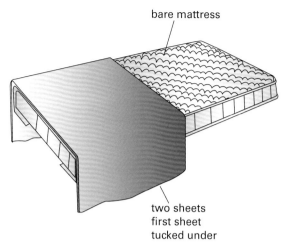

a) mattress preparation

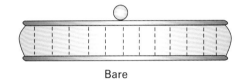

Bare

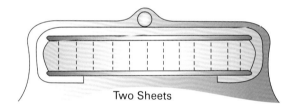

Two Sheets

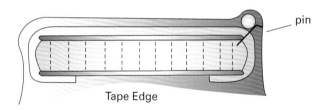

Tape Edge

b) cigarette location

Figure 12.14 Mattress preparation and cigarette locations used in 16 CFR 1632. Fairchild Books.

than 2 inches in any direction from the nearest point of the cigarette. All 18 cigarette locations must pass the test in order for the mattress or pad to be marketed.

Adoption of the Method

The provisions of 16 CFR 1632 apply to domestic and imported mattresses. Included in the definition of mattresses are mattress pads; adult, youth, crib, and portable crib mattresses; bunk bed mattresses; corner group and daybed mattresses; rollaway and convertible sofa bed mattresses; high risers; trundle bed mattresses; and **futons**. Items specifically excluded from 16 CFR 1632 are sleeping bags, pillows, mattress foundations such as box springs, water bed and air mattresses, and other items such as chaise lounges and sofa beds, which are distinct from convertible sofa beds. A **convertible sofa bed** is an upholstered sofa with a mattress concealed under the cushions; a **sofa bed** is an upholstered sofa with a hinged back that swings down flat with the seating cushions to form the sleeping surface.

16 CFR Part 1633

In 1996 the Sleep Product Safety Council (SPSC) and CPSC studied residential mattress fires set by open flames. Based on this research, the mattress industry began discussing a federal regulation for mattresses and resistance to open flame sources, such as candles, matches, and cigarette lighters. In 2001 the CPSC proposed a new federal regulation to address mattress flammability to open flame sources. The CPSC approved 16 CFR Part 1633, the Federal Standard for the Flammability (Open-Flame) of Mattress Sets, in 2006. The standard is the first new federal flammability regulation for mattresses in 35 years and became effective July 1, 2007.

The CPSC issued the flammability regulation to reduce deaths and injuries related to mattress fires, particularly those initially ignited by open flame sources. 16 CFR Part 1633 was developed with the active support of many members of the U.S. mattress industry, barrier suppliers, and the polyurethane foam industry and applies to residential mattresses and mattress sets manufactured in the United States.

The standard addresses stringent manufacturing, testing, and document retention requirements. The mattresses that comply with the requirements will generate a smaller-size fire with a slower growth rate, thus reducing the possibility of **flashover** occurring. Flashover is the point at which the entire contents of a room are ignited simultaneously by radiant heat, making conditions in the room untenable and safe exit from the room impossible. About two-thirds of all mattress fatalities are attributed to mattress fires that lead to flashover.

The law was based on California's TB603, a mattress flammability standard adopted in 2005. California has since withdrawn TB603 and now uses 16 CFR Part 1633. The standard was based, in part, on research performed by the NIST. A key advantage of the new mattress standard is its flexibility. It requires composite performance and leaves it up to the manufacturer to find the best way to comply. Compliance is not optional, and the standard preempts individual states from setting different mattress flammability rules.

Test Specimens and Procedures

16 CFR Part 1633 is a full-scale test necessary to evaluate the fire performance of a mattress. The specimen, a mattress and foundation or mattress alone, is exposed to a pair of T-shaped propane gas burners. The specimen is to be no smaller than twin size, unless the largest size mattress or set produced of that type is smaller than twin size, in which case the largest size must be tested. The burners impose a specified heat simultaneously to the top and side of the mattress set for a specified period of time. The mattress is allowed to burn freely for 30 minutes. Measurements are taken of the heat release rate from the specimen and the energy generated from the fire.

Test Criteria

The standard established two test criteria, both of which the mattress set must meet in order to comply with the standard: (1) the peak rate of heat release for the mattress set must not exceed 200 kilowatts at any time during the 30-minute test; and (2) the total heat release must not exceed 15 megajoules for the first ten minutes of the test. Mattresses that meet the standard's criteria will make only a limited contribution to a fire, especially in the early stages of a fire. This will allow occupants to discover the fire and escape.

Adoption of the Method

Each mattress set must bear a permanent label stating (1) the name of the manufacturer; (2) the complete physical address of the manufacturer; (3) the month and year of manufacture; (4) the model identification; (5) prototype identification; and (6) a certification that the mattress complies with the standard. Specifically excluded from the definition of mattress are mattress pads, pillows, and other items used on top of a mattress, upholstered furniture that does not contain a mattress, and other product pads.

Most mattress manufacturers have initially complied with the new flammability standard by adding an ignition-resistant barrier material between the outside covering and the interior component material. Using this approach, manufacturers use better quality foam cushioning materials, which offer all the comfort, support, and lasting physical performance required of a good mattress product. These improved mattresses have resulted in significant reductions in deaths and injuries associated with the risk of mattress fires.

Full-Scale Test Methods

Full-scale testing facilities may be constructed to replicate a room or a corridor. Room-size facilities make possible observation of the progressive growth of an interior fire, and they are particularly useful in assessing the involvement of each of several items. Corridor-like facilities can be used to determine the effects various conditions have on a Stage 3 fire; results obtained with them underscore the importance of preserving a safe means of egress (Figure 12.15).

Flame Retardant Chemicals and Treatments

Many fibers and fabrics will only pass current flammability standards if they are treated with specific flame-resistant chemicals. Depending on the fabric and code, these treatments may be applied in the fiber (solution) stage, as an aftertreatment, or as a flame-retardant backing. Simultaneously, tremendous resistance to added chemicals is increasing. Numerous municipalities prohibit the sale of these chemicals; California's **Proposition 65** requires that manufacturers post warnings on their products if they contain any of the approximately 900 chemicals on the current schedule. Manufacturers make best efforts to obtain assurance from their suppliers up the supply chain. The pressure to eliminate chemicals from the environment will surely continue to increase.

Figure 12.15 Mock-up room comparing the flammability of a Trevira CS fabric on the left with poly/cotton fabric on the right. Courtesy of Trevia GmbH/Silent Gliss International, LTD.

Key Terms

after flame time

afterglow

California Technical
Bulletins

char length

Code of Federal
Regulations (CFR)

combustion

Consumer Product Safety
Commission (CPSC)

convertible sofa bed

critical radiant flux (CRF)

egress

flameless combustion

flame propagation

flame spread

flaming combustion

Flammable Fabrics Act
(FFA)

flashover

full-scale testing

futon

glowing

ignition temperature

kindling temperature

large-scale test methods

light transmittance value

methenamine tablet test

National Electronic Injury
Surveillance System
(NEISS)

National Institute of
Standards and
Technology (NIST)

NFPA 101® Life Safety
Code®

NFPA 701

optical density values

Paragraph 25.853 (b)

Proposition 65

pyrolysis

radiant heat

raised fiber surface

self-extinguish

small-scale test methods

smoke density

smoke generation

smoldering

sofa bed

spillover

spontaneous combustion

Stage 1 fire

Stage 2 fire

Stage 3 fire

Steiner Tunnel Test
Method

toxic gases

UFAC Voluntary Action
Program

Upholstered Furniture
Action Council (UFAC)

Review Questions

1. Discuss the responsibilities of the CPSC in fire safety work.

2. What prompts the CPSC to propose a new flammability standard?

3. Cite some of the developments in fire safety that followed the 1967 amendment.

4. Why is a one-year grace period allowed before a new flammability standard goes into effect?

5. Discuss the UFAC Voluntary Action Program. What is the purpose of fabric classification? How are construction methods incorporated into the program?

6. To which test would a "flame spread of 26 to 75" refer, and what is the class indicated by this flame spread rating?

7. When can upholstered furniture bear the UFAC hangtag?

8. Explain the cyclic combustion process.

9. Distinguish among combustion, spontaneous combustion, glowing, and smoldering.

10. Why do toxic gases pose the greatest threat to life in interior fires?

11. Discuss the influence of smoke density on egress.

12. In the event of fire, why is it critical to preserve the means for quick and efficient egress?

13. Differentiate among a Stage 1, a Stage 2, and a Stage 3 fire. Then, discuss the value of early warning systems and automatic sprinklers in each stage.

14. What are the unique values of small-scale test methods, large-scale test methods, and full-scale test methods to fire researchers?

15. How does the methenamine tablet test simulate real-life situations?
16. At which stage of an interior fire is radiant heat an important variable?
17. Cite two significant reasons the flooring radiant panel test method is replacing the tunnel test method in the evaluation of the flammability hazards of soft floorcoverings.
18. Which carpet would be safer in the event of fire: one having a CRF of 0.14 watt per square centimeter or one having a CRF of 0.30 watt per square centimeter?
19. Are the standards set forth in the NFPA 101 Life Safety Code recommended or mandatory?
20. When would the large-scale test method, rather than the small-scale test method, be used for evaluating the flame resistance of textiles and films?
21. Why are full-scale fire testing facilities especially useful in studying the phenomenon of flashover?
22. When is NFPA 701 usually required? When is ASTM E84 usually required?
23. What is CA 133 and who is responsible for initiating and completing CA 133 testing?
24. For what products is UL testing required, and who is responsible for initiating and completing UL testing?

13

Construction Features
of Upholstered Furniture

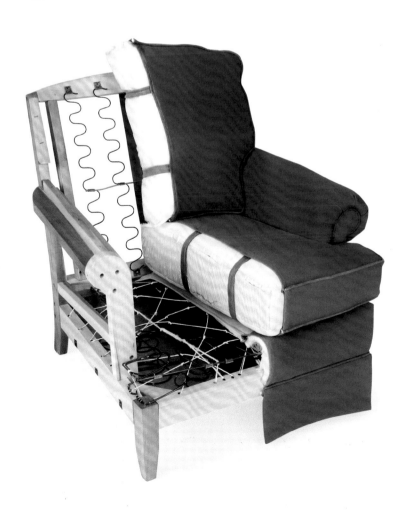

R esidential and commercial consumers have a vast variety of upholstered furniture styles from which to choose. All these forms and decorative stylings have some components in common. By definition, an upholstered item has an outercovering that surrounds and conceals a filling or stuffing, and such other structural components as springs, fabric linings, and framework. The various construction techniques for applying outercoverings expand the range of styling features available to consumers. Filling materials in upholstered furniture serve structural as well as functional purposes. In fact, it may be the most important component of a given piece of furniture.

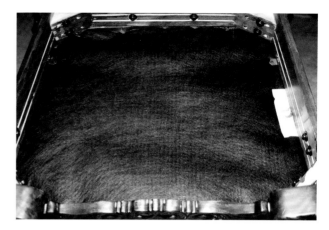

Figure 13.1 An example of spunbonded polypropylene olefin for bottom fabric applications. Courtesy of Amy Willbanks, www.textilefabric.com.

Construction Features

In addition to the upholstery fabric used to cover the cushions, backs, arms, and sides of furniture items, other fabrics are used to cover the deck and bottom areas. Bottom fabrics are rarely seen, but deck fabrics may be exposed if the furniture has loose cushions. Other construction features, including the styling of the skirt and any surface embellishments, also affect the appearance of an upholstered item.

Deck Fabrics and Bottom Fabrics

The **deck** of an upholstered item comprises the platform, springs, and filling structures that support the seat cushions. To conceal these units and to prevent dust and objects from falling into the deck, a fabric covers the uppermost filling layer. When the fabric is the same as the exposed outercovering, it is referred to as a **self-deck treatment**. If the outercovering is heavy or highly textured, a smoother, lighter-weight, less-expensive deck fabric in a color that coordinates with that of the outercovering will be used. With outercoverings that have low porosity, such as simulated leather fabrics, a porous deck fabric must be used to allow air movement when the seat cushions are compressed.

Bottom fabric (usually an inexpensive spunbonded olefin fabric, also called *black bottom*) is only visible if the furniture is turned upside down (Figure 13.1). The original purpose of the bottom fabric was to catch the dust

particles from the jute and cotton materials that were used in the deck so that a dust layer did not accumulate under the furniture. Today, bottom fabric it is mainly decorative, in that it covers springs, webbing, and polyester side that are used in the seat. (Polyester batting does not shed like the old natural materials did.)

Bottom fabric must be dimensionally stable to prevent sagging and it must resist moisture and mildew. The synthetic nonwovens popularly used do not ravel like older woven materials did and are more dimensionally stable.

Patterned Fabric Applications

Unless the fabric has an overall design of no particular orientation precise fabric cutting and motif positioning are required for upholstery fabrics with either woven-in or printed patterns. First, a fabric should be cut either **up-the-bolt** or **railroaded**, depending upon the orientation of motifs. (See the schematic illustration in Figure 13.2.) As an example, assuming the linear path of the leaf motifs in the fabric covering the chair in Figure 13.3 paralleled the selvages, the leaves would have appeared to grow sideways if the fabric had been railroaded.

When a fabric has a main motif, the motif must be centered on the back pillows, as well as on the seat cushions. For maximum aesthetic appeal, distinct patterns can also be cut and applied in a process known as **4-way match**. A matched pattern flows uninterrupted down the back pillows, the seat cushions, the seat boxing, and the

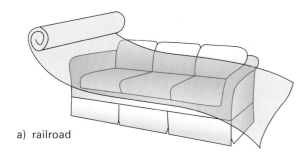

a) railroad

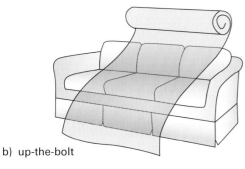

b) up-the-bolt

Figure 13.2 Illustrations of terms describing the directional cutting and placement of patterned upholstery fabric: (a) railroad, (b) up-the-bolt. Fairchild Books.

Figure 13.3 If this pattern had been cut railroaded, the leaves would appear to grow horizontally. Courtesy of C.R. Laine Furniture, www.crlaine.com.

Figure 13.4 Sofa with large motif that aligns with the back and seat cushions. Courtesy of Burton James, www.burtonjames.com.

seat front. See Figure 13.4, in which the diamond motifs in the fabric are centered and matched.

Cushion and Pillow Treatments

Three constructions of upholstery cushions and pillows are illustrated in Figures 13.5 through 13.7. The use of a plain seam to join the fabric pieces is called a **knife-edge treatment** (see Figure 13.5). Inserting a fabric-covered cord into the seam is known as **welting**. Welts may be of the same **body cloth** that covers the furniture—called **self-welt**—or may contrast (see the **contrast-welt** in Figure 13.6). When welts are planned for items covered with highly textured, bulky fabrics, a smooth fabric is often used to cover the cords. Wrapping a strip of fabric around the front and sides of cushions is known as **boxing** (Figure 13.7).

Most high-quality upholstered products have zippers on seat cushions, back pillows, and throw pillows so that manufacturers can insert the filling materials easily and end-users can have covers cleaned more easily. At lower price points, the cushions have zippers but back and throw pillows are usually machine-sewn closed.

Upholstered (seat) cushions and (back) pillows are treated two different ways in the construction of end products. In **tight-pillow styles**, also called *attached-pillow styles*, the pillows are securely attached to the framework and cannot be shifted or removed. In **loose-pillow styles** (Figure 13.7), the pillows are not secured. Unless a different fabric has been used to cover the backs of the pillows, they can be frequently reversed to equalize wear patterns and soiling levels.

Figure 13.5 Knife-edge seams. Courtesy of C.R. Laine Furniture, www.crlaine.com.

Figure 13.6 Contrast-welt seams. Courtesy of C.R. Laine Furniture, www.crlaine.com.

Figure 13.7 Slipcovers used to protect the permanent covering and to change the seasonal appearance of the furniture (boxed cushion). Courtesy of C.R. Laine Furniture, www.crlaine.com.

Skirt Options

Several options are available for the treatment of upholstered furniture **skirts**. Some typical construction styles are illustrated in Figure 13.8. The skirt may be flat with single or double kick pleats; it may be shirred; it may have box pleats; or it may be shirred only at the corners in a princess style. Buttons may be added as decorative accents.

Kick-pleat skirts are designed to hang straight and flat, so a bonded-web interfacing (such as Pellon®), which comes in several thicknesses, is used to provide support. Dressmaker skirts are lined with a thin layer of bonded polyester fiber in most cases, although some don't have a liner. Crinoline, similar to what is used in men's neck ties, is the best liner material, but it is considered too expensive for most manufacturers.

Slipcovers

Many consumers use **slipcovers** out of aesthetic preference, as a change from one season to another, or to protect the attached covering from excessive wear and soiling (Figure 13.7). Slipcovers are cut, seamed, and fitted over furniture. Some manufacturers offer upholstered furniture **in-the-muslin**—the items are covered in muslin, an undyed, plain-woven fabric composed of carded cotton yarns. Consumers can then order one or more sets of decorative slipcovers.

Arm Covers and Head Rests

Arm covers, also called **arm caps** and **armettes**, protect the arms of upholstered furniture from excessive abrasion and soiling. Frequently, these covers are offered optionally. **Head rests** or **head covers** protect the upholstery fabric from neck and hair oils and hair coloring. They may be cut from the outercoverings, be cut from a highly decorative lace or be richly embroidered, or as is the case in commercial airliners, buses, and trains, they may be cut from disposable fabric. Exposed wood arms can have padded arm rests or arm boards (Figure 13.9).

Surface Embellishments

Furniture manufacturers can use various treatments to embellish the surface of upholstery fabrics and finished

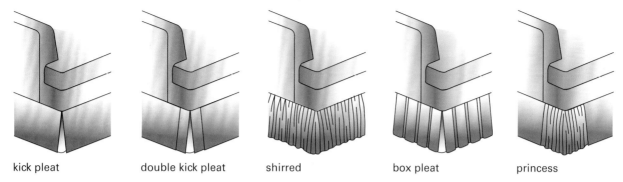

| kick pleat | double kick pleat | shirred | box pleat | princess |

Figure 13.8 Optional skirt treatments. Fairchild Books.

products. These treatments are distinct from others, such as coloring and finishing, which also enrich the surface appearance but are performed on fabric prior to end-product construction.

Quilting is generally offered as an optional fabric treatment. The stitching may be done in parallel rows or on curved and angled lines to create slightly raised design motifs. On pattern fabrics, it may follow the outline of the

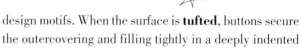

design motifs. When the surface is **tufted**, buttons secure the outercovering and filling tightly in a deeply indented three-dimensional pattern (Figure 13.10). Extensive buttoning should not be used on delicate fabrics with low levels of tear strength. **Channel back tufting** can run horizontally or vertically (Figure 13.11).

Figure 13.10 Sofa with button tufted back. Courtesy of Burton James, www.burtonjames.com.

Figure 13.9 Wrapped arm board. Courtesy of C.R. Laine Furniture, www.crlaine.com.

Figure 13.11 Channel back tufting on headboard. Courtesy of Burton James, www.burtonjames.com.

Figure 13.12 Sofa embellished with nailhead trimming. Courtesy of Burton James, www.burtonjames.com.

Nailhead trimming may be used to secure heavier coverings, such as genuine leather, to the framework (Figure 13.12) or as a decorative accent for many styles. The nails are generally aligned to emphasize the lines of the upholstered item, although they may be arranged in any pattern that the manufacturer is willing to execute. Nailheads are available in many colors, sizes, and finishes.

Quality construction features and interior components (some of which are fabrics) are critical to the appearance and timeframe for a useful life of residential and contract upholstered furniture.

Interior Textile Components

Several textile components, including fabric linings, filling structures, and cords, are present inside most upholstered furniture. **Textile cords** are used to hand-tie or hand-knot spring units together; the network of cords helps to stabilize the configuration of each spring and to minimize lateral shifting. A fabric lining, such as burlap or spunbonded olefin, is generally laid over the springs to prevent them from penetrating the filling materials. Two layers of filling, one for softness and one for firm support, may be used over the fabric linings. In most cases, the inside vertical walls and the extended portions of the frame will be padded with one or more layers of filling.

The framing material used in upholstered furniture may be hardwood, wood veneer, metal, or molded polymer. The soundness and stability of the frame, determined by the quality of the framing material and the sturdiness of framing joints, is especially important in evaluation of a piece of upholstery. Frame stability, along with the composition and structural features of the filling materials, which consumers and interior designers can often specify, are important to the comfort level and support of the cushions and pillows.

Fillings Used in Upholstered Furniture

The type of filling or stuffing material will depend on how the upholstered furniture is to be used, the desired comfort level, the style, and whether the piece is used in a residential or commercial setting. Fibrous battings, foam cushions, and loose particulate materials are the three main types of filling materials used to stuff or cushion upholstered furniture components and pillows. These structures differ in compressibility, loftiness, resiliency, and flammability. The Federal Trade Commission advises manufacturers to disclose the presence of such filling materials as goose down and feathers and requires disclosure of the presence of previously used filling materials.

Service-Related Properties

Upholstered furniture must pass flammability tests (see Chapter 12) in order to be saleable. Furthermore, the use of flame-retardant chemicals in upholstery materials sold in California is highly problematic under Senate Bill 1019 (https://leginfo.legislature.ca.gov/faces/billNavClient.xhtml?bill_id=201320140SB1019). Therefore, manufacturers have eliminated offending materials, and are required to attest to this point. In order to pass required certifications without flame-retardant chemicals, specific furniture fabrication methods are called for. (Not only is California a huge market, but other jurisdictions generally follow suit with California's safety initiatives.)

Along with their fire-related attributes, the physical properties of filling materials influence the serviceability of upholstered furniture items. For example, filling materials that fail to recover after compression show deep indentation in the cushions, which destroys the original design of the item and the smooth appearance of the outer fabric.

Compressibility

The ease with which a textile structure can be crushed or reduced in thickness is the measure of its **compressibility**. All filling structures must be somewhat compressible for comfort. An overstuffed chair is specifically designed to be easily compressed under the weight of the seated person; unless they are nursing back problems, people generally prefer these chairs over straight-backed, non-compressible wooden ones.

The degree of resistance a filling structure offers to being crushed or compressed can be measured in the laboratory. Structures that require a heavier load, in pounds per square inch, to produce a given deflection or reduction in thickness provide firmer support than those that reach this deflection with a lighter load.

Loftiness

Loftiness is bulk without heaviness. This feature is especially desirable for fillings used in residential furniture cushions and pillows. If identical cushion or pillow forms are filled—one with down and one with polyurethane foam—they would have equal thickness and volume. The foam pillow, however, would be heavier. Down and feather filling materials are prized for their inherent loftiness. Even extremely large upholstered cushions filled with these natural materials are light in weight. To increase the loftiness of fiberfill without increasing the weight, fiber chemists have engineered polyester fibers with hollow interiors.

Compressional Resiliency

Compressional resiliency and **compressional loft** are synonyms that describe the ability of a textile structure to recover from compression deformations. Filling structures must be compressible, but their serviceability depends on their ability to spring back to their original thickness. Without compressional loft or resiliency, fillings would not recover from the force exerted by body weight, and the cushions would develop permanent depressions.

Flammability

Some popular filling materials—notably polyurethane foam—are highly flammable. The flammability characteristics of filling materials become very important variables when upholstered furniture catches fire. Therefore, guidelines and standards developed for both residential and contract installations focus on barrier materials to protect the interior materials from igniting even if an ignition source, such as a cigarette, falls onto a chair or sofa. Fortunately, with the decrease in the popularity of smoking, such incidents have become less frequent, but have not been eliminated. These fire-related variables are discussed in Chapter 12.

Fibrous Battings

Battings are three-dimensional nonwovens (structures formed directly from either natural or man-made fibers, bypassing the yarn stage). They are used to provide a smooth, slip resistant, soft surface over cushions and frame edges. The thickness of upholstery batting can range from 1/8 inch up to 2 inches thick.

Bonded Polyester Batting

Batting of staple-length polyester fibers that are produced by breaking or cutting the crimped filaments in a tow bundle is the ubiquitous batting material used in furniture. Batting for upholstered furniture must provide comfort, superior resiliency, and firm support.

To engineer these features, manufacturers frequently combine two distinctly different layers of polyester fibers into one batt. The upper layer contains fine, low denier fibers that are easily flexed and soft, making for comfort; the lower layer contains coarser, stiffer fibers that provide firm support as they resist flexing and compression. For increased stability and greater resiliency, resin is sprayed throughout such dual-denier batts, bonding the fibers into position. Polyester is also mildew resistant, so it is also suitable filler for outdoor furniture, patio cushions, and boat cushions.

Natural Fiber Batting

Half a century ago, before synthetics had taken hold, thin webs of **cotton batting**, jute, kapok, wool fibers, and even hairs (such as **horsehair**, **hoghair**, and **cattlehair**) were formed into batts and used in upholstery. They have become obsolete because they are flammable (they do not pass UFAC and CA 117 tests), have low resiliency, rot over time, cause odors if damp, and are expensive.

Foam Cushions

Three-dimensional polyurethane foam structures, frequently referred to as **slab cushions**, usually fill upholstered furniture items to preserve their shape and form. (Latex foam is rarely used today because of its expense.) Because of the carcinogenic nature of flame-resistant chemicals, combustion-modified (CM) foam, which was previously used extensively in commercial furniture to meet flammability requirements, is being eliminated in favor of barrier upholstery fabrics (sandwiched between inner foam and outer fabric). Manufacturers of furniture are required by law in California and some other states and jurisdictions to provide detailed information on the types of foams, barriers, and other stuffing materials used in their products. (See above references to California Senate Bill 1019.)

New technology has enhanced both natural and synthetic foams, creating high-quality **viscoelastic** (memory) foam. It is temperature sensitive and helps to relieve pressure points. Viscoelastic foam is a slow-recovery foam used for mattresses, pillows, seat cushions, wheelchair pads, and other healthcare-related applications.[1]

Most foam cushions may be in slab form or molded for office seating (desk, guest, and conference chairs). Not only does molded foam allow for the complex shapes and curves with thinner profiles that are popular in ergonomic seating, but the chemical formulations used to make molded foam produce a stronger cell structure with improved physical properties. Molded foam also has a higher density than slab foam does, making it more durable over time and more comfortable.[2]

Foam Structures

Latex foam may be produced from natural rubber or from synthesized rubber compounds in furniture applications, but is rarely used today. **Polyurethane foam** compounds do not disintegrate with age as latex does, and they are resistant to both microbes and moisture. Polyurethane is also much less expensive than latex.

During manufacturing, the urethane compound is expanded by heating, increasing the apparent volume and decreasing the density. Structures are produced

Figure 13.13 Foam cushion fillings. Courtesy of Taylor King, www.taylorking.com.

with lower densities when softness and comfort are the performance features of principal importance, and with higher densities when greater support and resistance to crushing and compression are sought.

A polyurethane (or latex) foam structure may be used alone to fill and impart form to a furniture cushion, but in quality furniture cushions the foam usually forms a core unit surrounded by polyester batting. Springs may be embedded in the foam to provide resiliency. In either a spring/foam or a foam cushion, the polyester batting wrap adds softness and also helps the outercovering maintain its dimensional stability and smoothness. An additional layer of feather material may be added. Figure 13.13 is an example of foam covered with batting and feathers.

Foam Density, Firmness, and Resiliency

As noted, polyurethane foam is the major component in most upholstered seat cushions. Foam is measured by density, firmness, and resiliency. ASTM D3574 Standard Test Methods for Flexible Cellular Materials—Slab, Bonded, and Molded Urethane Foams is used to test these characteristics.

Density identifies the weight of one cubic foot of foam. Generally, as density increases, so does the quality of the cushion; the higher the foam density, the heavier and better quality the cushion. The best density levels for sofa and lounge chair seat cushions range between 1.8 and 3.2. Good-quality seat cushions have a density of 2.5 pounds per cubic foot. If foam is used for backs or arms, look for a density of 1.2 to 1.5.[3]

Firmness is evaluated using a compression test. Compression is a measure of how much weight is required to depress the foam a given percentage. The Indentation

Force Deflection (IFD) test is used to measure foam firmness. This test uses a standard round disc, which is placed onto a piece of 4-inch (10.16 cm) foam. The foam is then compressed to 75 percent of its original height and the pounds of pressure required to reach this point is recorded.[4] Firmness is key to engineering a comfortable cushion and will vary from 20 to 35 pounds for a seat cushion and 10 to 20 pounds for a back cushion.[5]

Resiliency is the ability of the foam to spring back to its original shape after compressed. Resilience is typically measured by the ball rebound test included in ASTM D3574. A steel ball is dropped onto the foam cushion and measurements record how high the ball rebounds, how quickly the foam returns to its original shape, and percent of decrease in foam height. The higher the resiliency, the higher the quality and the longer lasting the seat cushion. High resilience (HR) foam is engineered to outperform conventional foam. The basic difference between conventional foam and HR foam is the chemicals used to make the foam. HR foam uses higher-quality chemicals, which give it more resiliency and longer life.[6]

Loose Particulate Materials

Masses of loose particles are used to fill some upholstered furniture structures. Today, these particles include shredded or flaked latex or urethane foam, feathers, down, and fiberfill. (The use of such materials as straw, sawdust, and newspapers has been discontinued because of cleaning and flammability problems.) Shredded foam particles are less expensive than slab foam cushions, but they may clump with use. **Down**, the soft undercoat feathers retrieved from waterfowl, is soft, easily compressed, and lightweight, but the labor costs incurred in retrieving the necessary volume of the tiny feathers make the material comparatively expensive. To decrease cost, residential upholstered foam cushions can be wrapped in down or polyester/down blend and encased in down-proof ticking. The feathers of waterfowl are lofty because they have curved shafts, while other **feathers** (e.g., from chickens) are straight shafted and have no loft value, which is why there is no "chicken down."

Because feather and down filling materials are used more extensively in bedding products than in upholstered furniture, selection guides are reviewed in later chapters. **Fiberfill**, usually composed of crimped polyester fibers, is lofty and resilient. Polyester offers a cost advantage over down, and unlike down and feathers, manufactured fibers are not allergens.

Loose filling materials are frequently enclosed in an inner fabric structure (ticking) before being inserted into the sewn outercoverings. Today, the inner fabric is often a spunbonded polypropylene fabric.

Labeling Upholstery Fillings

The Textile Fiber Products Identification Act (TFPIA) and state labeling laws are in place to assure consumers that manufacturers do not engage in unfair or deceptive commercial practices. These provisions pertain to upholstery filling products that are sold domestically and imported from other countries. For additional information regarding both upholstered furniture and casegoods, refer to the Guide to United States Furniture Compliance Requirements, developed by the National Institute of Standards and Technology for the U.S. Department of Commerce.

Textile Fiber Products Identification Act

Although the provisions of the TFPIA do not specifically apply to new upholstery stuffings and fillings, the act does concern itself with used components. When the stuffing or filling has been used previously, the product must carry a label or hangtag clearly stating the presence of reused materials; if not labeled appropriately, it is considered to be misbranded or unfairly and deceptively marketed. The terminology requirements under TFPIA section 16 CFR 303, Rules and Regulations, include reused stuffing, secondhand stuffing, previously used stuffing, or used stuffing.

Uniform Law Label

The International Association of Bedding and Furniture Law Officials (IABFLO) is an association comprised of state officials responsible for the enforcement of bedding and furniture laws within their respective states. In the early 1990s, IABFLO established a uniform law labeling system to create consistency in how manufacturers label contents of furniture and bedding items. The purpose of the **law label** is to inform consumers of the hidden contents or filling materials inside these products. Law labels must describe the filling materials of the article as a percentage of those filling materials by weight.

Thirty-one states require law labels. The products requiring law labels in each state vary, as do the labeling requirements, but in today's market, most manufacturers produce a label that satisfies all states, since it is very difficult to predict where furniture will ultimately be sold. Most states require that the law label display a Uniform Registry Number, which identifies the manufacturing facility that produced the product. This applies to any company in the world whose products are sold in the United States.[7]

Key Terms

4-way match	horsehair
arm caps	in-the-muslin
arm covers	knife-edge treatment
armettes	latex foam
battings	law labels
body cloth	loftiness
bottom fabrics	loose-pillow styles
boxing	nailhead trimming
cattlehair	polyurethane foam
channel back tufting	quilting
compressibility	railroad
compressional loft	self-deck treatment
compressional resiliency	self-welt
contrast-welt	skirt
cotton batting	slab cushions
deck	slipcovers
density	textile cords
down	tight-pillow styles
feathers	tufted
fiberfill	up-the-bolt
head covers	viscoelastic
head rests	welting
hoghair	

Review Questions

1. Discuss the selection and functions of deck fabric.
2. What advantages are offered by spunbonded fabrics when used as bottom fabric?
3. Distinguish between "up-the-bolt" and "railroad" applications. When is it critical to use the correct positioning of upholstery fabric on the furniture frame?
4. Sketch an example of "4-way match" as it relates to upholstery fabric application.
5. What is the purpose of zippers in boxed cushions?
6. Do slipcovers have both a functional and a decorative purpose?
7. Why is the use of hair batting diminishing?
8. When two distinctly different layers of polyester fibers are combined into one batt, the structure is referred to as a "dual-denier batt." Why is this an appropriate descriptive name, and what advantages are offered by the fibers used?
9. What advantages does polyurethane foam offer over latex foam?
10. Distinguish between compressibility and compressional resiliency.
11. What is the TFPIA? What are its requirements pertaining to the labeling of upholstery fabric and furniture fillings?
12. What is a law label? Are law labels advisory or mandatory?

Notes

1. The International Association of Bedding and Furniture Law Officials. (2013). "Classification of Filling Materials," Section 10: Wool, http://abflo.info.
2. Polyurethane Foam Association. (1994). "Joint Industry Foam Standards and Guidelines." http://www.pfa.org.
3. Bryn Hill Industries. (2013). "Product Data Sheet: Flexible Molded Urethane Foam."
4. Barbara Raskauskas. (2013). "How to Choose the Right Upholstery Foam." http://www.ehow.com/how_6170667_choose-right-upholstery-foam.
5. Polyurethane Foam Association. "Joint Industry Foam Standards and Guidelines."
6. Barbara Raskauskas. "How to Choose the Right Upholstery Foam."
7. Polyurethane Foam Association. "Joint Industry Foam Standards and Guidelines."
8. American Law Label, Inc. (2013). http://www.americanlawlabel.com.

14

Upholstery Coverings

The variety of fabrics available for use on furniture is extensive. In addition to a wide array of woven and knitted fabrics, animal hide leathers and coated fabrics composed of polymer films with woven or knitted backings represent a substantial portion of the market. Fabric patterns, yarns, and contents range in complexity, from small, geometric figures to large and elaborately detailed motifs, from simple yarns to complex novelties, from synthetics to natural fibers.

Upholstery Fibers and Yarns

Although virtually every natural and manufactured fiber is used in textile upholstery fabric, cotton, rayon, and manufactured synthetic fibers currently hold significant portions of the market, which includes attached upholstery and slipcovers. According to the provisions of the Textile Fiber Products Identification Act (TFPIA), which is also known as the Textile Labeling Rule, textile products must be labeled with generic fiber names and percentages of contents, name of the producer, and country of origin.

The scope of the TFPIA also includes **slipcovers** (furniture coverings that are cut, seamed, and fitted over the permanently attached coverings), swatches, and samples. The required labeling information may be listed on the end of a bolt of fabric and on a label or hangtag attached to a slipcover. With swatches smaller than two square inches in size, the information may appear in accompanying promotional matter. Other swatches and samples may be labeled with the required information or keyed to a catalog, so that prospective purchasers can obtain it.

Nearly every fiber, from spandex to alpaca, has a place in the upholstery market. At present, polyester, cotton, and rayon are the most popular fibers for both residential and contract fabrics. Wool fabrics hold a special place, especially in contract applications, because the fiber is so durable and resilient, but its price limits its market share, and current trends run to a cleaner, sleeker surface and hand rather than the soft, fibrous appearance and feel of wool.

Fabric performance depends on many factors. Fiber content is only one of them. How the yarn is made, how the fabric is constructed, and how it is finished all contribute to a fabric's features. Additionally, fabrics are used everywhere from the White House dining room to bus terminal waiting areas. There is no ideal fabric for every upholstery use.

Backcoating

Fabrics are backcoated for many reasons—sometimes because they are flimsy, and need a backing to make them stable. However, many furniture manufacturers require backcoating in order to minimize raveling during cutting of the fabric, or to prevent strikethrough (seepage through to the face) of adhesive used in some upholstery making. Backings can also impart particular performance features, such as flame retardancy, and may be required or requested in order to meet code requirements.

Sometimes **backcoating** can be visible on the face of the fabric. This problem generally occurs only when the coating has been used to compensate for low-quality fabric construction. Coating can, however, be color coordinated with the face yarns to make it as inconspicuous as possible.

Flat-Weave Upholstery Fabrics

Greige-good producers, dyers, printers, designers, converters, and wholesalers work together to market an expansive variety of fabrics. Some are identified by specific fabric names that may be based on fiber content or on structural and appearance features.

In the current market, few fabrics are identified by weave. Due to innovation and creative development, and a general trend away from strict "rules" and categories, fabrics are most commonly called by their appearance or intended end-use. Nonetheless, this section describes and illustrates flat, or non-pile, upholstery fabrics.

Several relatively simple upholstery fabrics are produced with basic weaves or variations of them, and a few are produced with a simple knitting operation. Others are produced with decorative dobby, surface-figure, or Jacquard-woven effects. These structures are discussed and illustrated in detail in Chapter 7.

Plain Weaves

Some traditional plain-woven upholstery fabrics (Figure 14.1) and their names are no longer used outside of hand-weaving circles ("homespun" and "hopsacking" are examples). Nonetheless, plain weave and other basic weaves are popular upholstery fabrics in many fibers (Figure 14.2).

Chintz is a plain weave cotton fabric, produced in heavy weight for upholstery and lighter weight for window treatments. Chintz is printed or piece dyed in solid colors and is usually glazed (a heavy press with heat; see Chapter 10). The term "chintz print" usually connotes a traditional floral or geometric pattern printed in bright colors, although the cloth and finish can be printed with any pattern. Popularity for the high surface luster, glazed finish of chintz ebbs and flows, and is not currently at the forefront.

Taffeta may be the most predominant plain weave in upholstery and drapery use. The most beautiful taffeta is of silk, but fine polyester taffetas are popular, especially when flame retardancy or special finishes are desired. Taffeta is a plain weave of very fine, smooth yarns, has a crisp hand, and makes a rustling sound. Many other fabric patterns, such as plaids and checks, are typically woven in plain weave, though other weaves can be used.

Figure 14.2 Wool upholstery fabrics in plain weave and plain weave variations. Courtesy of Maharam Fabrics.

Figure 14.1 Plain weave, plaid, wool fabric. Courtesy of Maharam Fabrics.

Basket Weaves

Basket weave is a variation on plain weave. To make the cloth heavier, multiple yarns are used "as one" in both warp and filling direction. For example, 4 × 4 basket pattern (using 4 warp yarns and 4 filling yarns together at each interlacing) is often used to weave heavy sisal or other jute into rug material. Basket-woven upholstery fabrics of contrasting warp and filling yarns colors are popular in Scandinavian wool fabrics. **Duck** is a basket-woven fabric often used in slipcovers for furniture, outdoor furniture, and boat covers. Cotton duck, of a specific construction, is also the specified abradant material for the test used for ACT abrasion guidelines.

Filling-Rib Weaves

Upholstery fabrics produced with a filling-rib weave including repp, **faille**, ottoman, and Bengaline. **Repp,**

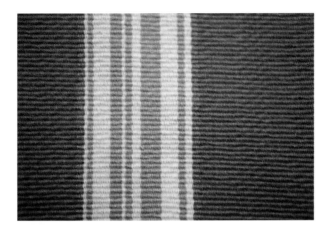

Figure 14.3 Repp weave. Photo courtesy of Max Concra.

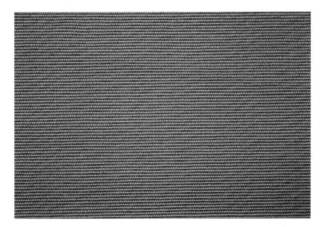

Figure 14.4 Ottoman weave. Courtesy of Amy Willbanks, www. textilefabric.com.

Figure 14.5 Houndstooth fabric. From *Swatch Reference Guide for Interior Design Fabrics* by Deborah E. Young, published by Fairchild Books.

Figure 14.6 Herringbone weave. From *Swatch Reference Guide for Interior Design Fabrics* by Deborah E. Young, published by Fairchild Books.

commonly used in men's striped neckties, shown in Figure 14.3, has fine ribs, while **ottoman** ribs are thicker and heavier (Figure 14.4).

Twills

Different colors or sizes of warp and filling yarns are often used to accentuate the visual diagonal of twill-woven upholstery fabrics. The twill interlacings and colored yarns in **houndstooth** vary to create broken checks or a unique star pattern (Figure 14.5). Houndstooth patterns, like plaids, are popular both for casual residential interiors and for office furnishings.

The reversed diagonals of **herringbone** make for a visual interest that may be enhanced by using different colors or sizes of warp and filling yarns (Figure 14.6). Because twill yarn interlacings occur less frequently than those in plain weaves, higher fabric counts must be used to properly construct a suitable twill fabric. Twills are widely used in high-use residential and commercial applications, including transportation installations. Many Jacquard fabrics are based on combinations of twill weaves.

Satins and Sateens

In a **satin** the face of the fabric is almost only warp yarns, which makes it inherently more fragile than other weaves. Depending on the fiber, yarn type, and finish, satin-woven fabrics—for example, silk satins and other fine-filament warp cloths—may be limited to areas of light use and abrasion. However, worsted wool, linen, and cotton satins are all popular and sturdy cloths. Damask, described in the section "Jacquards," is made up of satin and reverse satin (sateen) and is ubiquitous.

Sateen, a filling-faced satin weave, is the exact opposite of a satin weave. In a satin-woven fabric, warp yarns dominate. The back side of a satin fabric is a sateen, in which filling yarns dominate. **Warp sateen** is an oxymoron, but it is a term-of-art that describes a common upholstery or drapery fabric that is a warp-faced satin weave composed of spun yarns. Warp sateen is frequently used to produce drapery lining fabrics and sheeting, and is typically made of cotton.

Crepes

Crepe weave has a random, or irregular, interlacing pattern. The floats appear to be of unequal length in no distinct pattern. A crinkly, pebbly, or rough surface characterizes **crepe** fabrics. True crepe fabrics, made with high-twist yarns in a crepe weave, are popular in clothing but not in interiors because the yarn effect is not permanent.

Furniture manufacturers like working with crepes because they give and stretch slightly, but not as much as do fabrics that contain elastomers. Crepe-woven fabrics also hold their shape and are one of the most wrinkle resistant of all the weaves, and their texture disguises day-to-day wear well. For these reasons, solid-color and two-tone crepe fabrics are ubiquitous seating and vertical surface covers, especially in contract applications. The irregular interlacing pattern is shown in Figure 14.7.

Dobbies

Dobby-woven upholstery fabrics are simple weaves other than plain, twill, satin, or crepe, or they are small geometric effects made up of combinations of various simple weaves in blocks (Figure 14.8). Dobby repeat

Figure 14.7 Crepe fabric made from recycled polyester. Courtesy of Amy Willbanks, www.textilefabric.com.

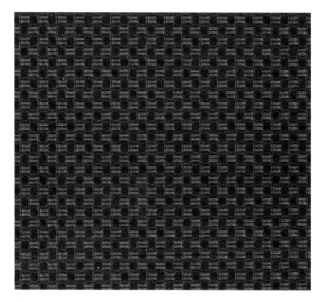

Figure 14.8 Dobby effect. Courtesy of Momentum Group.

sizes are generally very small. Few upholstery fabrics are actually woven on dobby looms today. Instead, dobby effects are achieved on Jacquard looms, and the term "dobby" most often refers to the appearance of small-scale geometric woven patterns, rather than strictly to fabrics that are woven on dobby looms.

Jacquards

Most fabrics that are not plain, texture, or pile fabrics are simply referred to as Jacquards, and these distinctive fabrics are some of the most popular furniture coverings

Figure 14.9 Jacquard fabrics. Courtesy of Chella Fabrics.

Figure 14.10 Damask. Courtesy of F. Schumacher & Co.

(Figure 14.9). Fabric is, essentially, woven in layers. To create effects, some yarns are hidden and some are brought to the surface. In many structures yarns are broken into sets, in which, for example, one set of warp yarns has a specific job, and the other has a different job. For example, the warp may be one set, and the fill may have two different jobs, or vice versa. In any case, Jacquard weaving allows great versatility in patterning, so that relatively elaborate motifs and multiple interlacing patterns are possible. Following are some of the most basic, traditional structures that are woven on Jacquard looms.

Damask is woven from one set of warp yarns and one set of filling yarns using only two weaves, which are exact inverses of each other (Figure 14.10). Traditionally, they feature a satin-weave ground and a sateen-weave motif so that on the reverse side a damask is exactly the opposite of the face, in that the satin areas become sateen and vice versa. (Warp- and fill-faced twills are also used as opposites.)

Traditional damask fabrics generally incorporate one color in the warp, and the same or a different color in the fill. When the fill color matches the warp, the design motifs are highlighted because the weaves in the figure and ground pick up different light and texture levels. The motif areas may be further accentuated by the use

of yarns differing in brightness, level of twist, and degree of complexity from the yarns in the ground. In the market today, basic damasks might have other weaves added in for interest. These are still generally called "damasks" in commercial parlance.

Traditional damask patterns are framed, symmetrical layouts that feature vases, flowers, and vines, though damask structures need not be. Often, patterns of this traditional format are referred to as "damasks," although they are not actually a damask structure. A damask structure could be a simple geometric made of satin and sateen weaves, and a damask pattern could be designed with many weaves, or even be a print.

Brocade, developed in the late sixteenth century as a less-expensive alternative to embroidery, is woven from one set of warp yarns, with two or more sets of filling or weft yarns; the number of sets is governed by the number of colors that are to appear in the motifs. The extra yarns (called *supplementary weft*) are generally woven in a filling-faced twill or sateen weave, giving the design motifs a slightly raised effect. The ground is compactly constructed in a plain, twill, satin, or filling-rib weave.

Simple geometric patterns can also be brocade-woven. Dots or other small motifs are often floated on a plain ground, and in simple designs these are referred to as *tissue patterns* (because the extra filling used to achieve the pattern is called a *tissue pick*). Also, they are sometimes called **dot or spot weave**s.

If the floats of yarn on the back of the brocade, or tissue pattern, are long, they may be cut out. Whether cut or not, the brocade weave creates a raised surface on the face of the fabric, which is a feature of the structure, not a flaw. (When cut, the effect yarn is called *discontinuous weft*; when uncut, it is a *continuous weft*; Figure 14.11a and b).

A traditional technique and pattern type that is mostly passé at present, **liseré** was developed as a less expensive version of brocade. These fabrics are woven from two sets of warp yarns and one set of filling yarns. In liseré, one set of warp yarns is generally identical in color to the filling yarns; together, these form the ground. The second set of warp yarns is composed of a variety of single-colored yarns, which are wound in bands of various widths on a separate loom beam. During weaving, the Jacquard mechanism raises these yarns and controls their interlacing to produce detailed motifs in lengthwise bands. In many liseré fabrics, the patterned bands are interspersed with satin-woven stripes.

Today, the term liseré is synonymous with the pattern styles traditionally woven with this technique. Ironically, in current production brocade is more economical to produce than is liseré because special warp set ups are far more inefficient than the complex filling patterning that is needed for brocade weaving.

Brocatelle (Figure 14.12) has a raised pattern with a distinctive, puffy appearance. These fabrics are made with two sets of warp yarns (one is usually fine and the other heavy) and two sets of filling yarns. One of the filling yarns shows on the face, creating the color. The other is a **stuffer yarn** that is buried on the back, but creates the raised motifs.

Jacquard-woven tapestry should not be confused with hand-woven tapestry. The two differ not only in their modes of production, but also in the manner in which the filling or weft yarns are handled. Hand-woven tapestry is a fill-faced, plain-woven fabric, in which the warp is completely buried. Each filling color is woven within the perimeter of its designated motif area and then cut, leaving

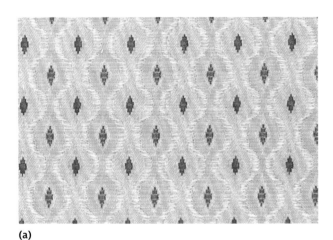

(a)

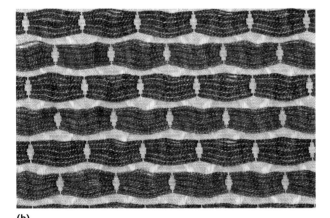

(b)

Figure 14.11 Brocade with unclipped (continuous) supplementary filling yarns floating on the back of the fabric: (a) front, (b) back. Courtesy of Amy Willbanks, www.textilefabric.com.

Figure 14.12 Brocatelle. Courtesy of Mary Paul Yates, photo by Judy Juracek.

Figure 14.13 Jacquard-woven tapestry fabric. Courtesy of Mary Paul Yates, photo by Judy Juracek.

Figure 14.14 Double weave pocket cloth. Courtesy of Amy Willbanks, www.textilefabric.com.

a short length of yarn hanging fringe-like on the back. (This is called discontinuous weft because individual fillings do not traverse the entire width of the fabric.)

In machine-woven **tapestry** (Figure 14.13), the multicolor effect comes primarily from the warp. Various colors, laid out in the warp color arrangement, are introduced in lengthwise bands. When the colors in a band are not used in the face designs, they are interlaced in the back, creating stripes on the backside of the fabric. Fill yarns are carried from one selvage to the other, interlacing into the face when needed. In both hand-woven and Jacquard-woven tapestries, floral and picture-like motifs are typical, but geometrics and abstract designs are also popular in tapestry for upholstery.

In **doublecloth** two distinct fabric structures face each other, with areas where there is no interlacing between. As shown in Figure 14.14, the face of the pocket is composed of one set of warp yarns and one set of filling yarns, and the back of a second set of warp yarns and a second set of filling yarns. These pockets may show up in the motifs or in the ground; closure occurs where the positions of the face yarns and the back yarns are shifted at the juncture of the motifs and the ground. Sometimes, the weave tacks the two layers together, which adds some durability to the fabric. If there are no tie-downs between the layers, these fabrics are commonly referred to as **pocket cloth**.

In **matelassé**, a pocket structure is used to form motifs, and the interlacing points are used to produce the appearance of quilting stitches. A third set of filling yarns is floated in the pockets so that the designs stand

out in relief, puffing the fabric and enhancing the quilt-like appearance (Figure 14.15).

Cloqué is essentially a matelassé without the stuffing; the pockets are not padded. Both matelassé and cloqué are usually offered in solid colors, most often piece dyed. The piece dyeing process enhances the puffy appearance of the fabric.

Lampas is a version of double cloth that was developed hundreds of years ago to simulate brocade. In lampas, one of the layers generally weaves a balanced plain, twill, or satin, and the other layer runs a heavier filling that is used as an effect yarn. The layers are tacked together so that no pockets appear, but the effect yarn is hidden when

Figure 14.15 Matelassé. Courtesy of Mary Paul Yates, photo by Judy Juracek.

Figure 14.16 Lampas. Courtesy of Amy Willbanks, www.textilefabric.com.

not needed on the surface. Although a large percentage of Jacquard wovens currently produced are actually lampas structures, the term lampas is generally used only to label traditional lampas patterns (Figure 14.16).

Knits

Most knitted upholstered furniture coverings are flat structures produced by interlooping simple yarns with an interlock stitch. This stitch helps ensure that the fabrics will be serviceable during use because, unlike other weft knitting stitches, the interlock stitch is resistant to running and snagging. These fabrics cannot be varied by incorporating complex yarns or by altering structural features, but designers provide variety by specifying the use of two colors of yarns, Jacquard patterns, printed patterns, heather colorations, or cross-dyed effects. Upholstery knits are generally composed of polyester or nylon fibers, which can be heat-set to impart dimensional stability and resiliency.

Some manufacturers (primarily inexpensive residential specialists) appreciate the elasticity and flexibility of knitted fabrics, which make them particularly suitable for use as coverings on curved furniture frames. Others, especially commercial-furniture makers, prefer the consistency of woven fabrics. Nonetheless, knits are also popular as the mesh backs of many popular ergonomic chairs, many of which are engineered to produce the individual pieces that cover a specific chair, much as socks or sweaters are produced.

Pile Upholstery Fabrics

In some pile fabrics, pile yarns are uniformly distributed over the fabric surface. In others, pile yarns are strategically placed to create a patterned layer. The techniques used to produce woven pile fabrics were described and illustrated in Chapter 7, and those used to produce knitted pile and tufted fabrics were discussed in Chapter 8.

Pile-Weave Fabrics

Two filling-pile fabrics, corduroy and velveteen, are used as furniture coverings. Both have a cut-pile surface texture and are normally composed of cotton or cotton/polyester blends. The surface of **corduroy** fabric is uniformly covered with densely constructed wales. **Velveteen** has a uniform pile surface and is created by interlacing an extra set of filling yarns with a single set of warp yarns.

Velvet, velour, frieze (frieze is from England, commonly called *frisé* from French), and grospoint are warp-pile upholstery fabrics. All except grospoint and some frisé fabrics have cut-pile textures. **Velvet** is normally woven to have a uniform pile surface. The pile is created by an extra set of warp yarns that interlace with filling yarns. Omitting selected pile yarns and thus exposing some portions of the base fabric produces a variation in velvet upholstery called **voided velvet** (Figure 14.17).

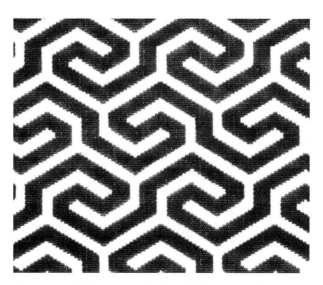

Figure 14.17 Voided velvet. Courtesy of F. Schumacher & Co.

Velour, which is generally produced by the over-the-wire construction technique, has a slightly deeper pile and a more pronounced nap than velvet. Most velour is composed of cotton fibers, which give the fabric a soft, warm hand. Wool pile and mohair pile fabrics are generally referred to as **plush**, which is equivalent to velour.

Frisé (**frieze**) upholstery fabrics normally have a level, uncut-pile surface (Figure 14.18). *Epinglé* generally refers to fabrics that feature areas of both cut and uncut pile to create interesting patterns, especially when combined with variation in color areas (Figure 14.19).

Grospoint, pictured in Figure 14.20, has a level surface with pronounced loops larger than those characteristic of frisé. Worsted wool or multifilament nylon yarns are often used in the loops to augment their durability.

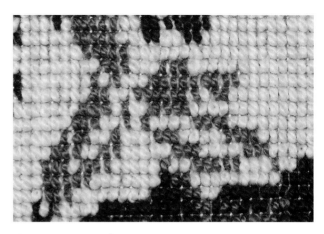

Figure 14.20 Grospoint. Courtesy of Amy Willbanks, www.textilefabric.com.

Figure 14.18 Frisé. Courtesy of Mary Paul Yates, photo by Judy Juracek.

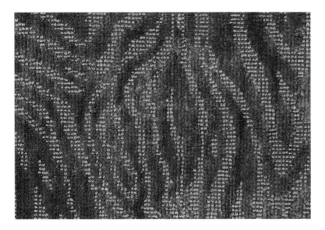

Figure 14.19 Epinglé. Courtesy of Amy Willbanks, www.textilefabric.com.

Surface patterns may also be introduced by exposing areas of the base fabric and by combining two or more colors of pile yarns. Grospoint fabrics are frequently used for covering office chairs and the bottom and back cushions installed in transportation vehicles.

Tufting machines can produce the pile construction density desired in **tufted upholstery fabrics**. High density is necessary to prevent exposure of the base fabric, especially on curved areas of furniture. Today, some machines can insert up to 400 pile yarns per square inch of base fabric. Together with the high rate of production characteristic of tufting, these developments result in use of this technique for budget upholstery fabric.

Leather

Animals' skin and hides are processed into leather, in assorted sizes, shapes, and thicknesses. **Skins**, retrieved from small animals such as lambs, goats, and calves, are thinner than hides and have an average size that does not normally exceed (approximately) 9 square feet. **Hides**, retrieved from large animals such as deer, horses, and cattle, on average reach a maximum size of about 25 square feet. Hides are usually selected and processed whole because heavier and larger pieces of leather are required for upholstery applications.

In spite of the relatively high cost of skins and hides and the lengthy and expensive processing required to convert them into finished coverings, leather upholstery

Figure 14.21 Face and back of leather. Courtesy of Amy Willbanks, www.textilefabric.com.

remains popular. Many grades are available, but, as with most materials, quality does have a higher price.

Composition and Structure of Raw Hides

Raw hide has three distinct sections: the epidermis, the corium, and the flesh layer. The indentations in the top layer, the epidermis, are the hair follicles or pores. After the hair is removed, the exposed pores are seen as the **grain markings**, a surface feature found naturally only in coverings produced from the topmost layer of the hide. The central portion of the hide, the corium, is a network of interlaced bundles of tiny fibers composed of a protein called collagen. Gelatinous matter surrounds the fibrous bundles. The bottommost portion of the hide is flesh tissue (Figure 14.21).

The processing of raw skins and hides is an involved procedure that may be divided into four major operations: curing and cleaning, tanning, coloring, and finishing. A single firm in a vertical manufacturing operation usually carries out these operations.

Curing and Cleaning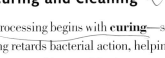

Processing begins with **curing**—salting the raw hides. Curing retards bacterial action, helping prevent putrefaction or decomposition, and it also removes the gelatinous matter from the corium. The hides must be thoroughly cleaned, defleshed, and dehaired before further processing. If the hides are thick enough to be split into multiple layers, the splitting will also be done at this stage, prior to tanning.

Tanning

In earlier times, **tanning** solutions were often made from tannins extracted from sources such as tree bark. Because these vegetable tanning agents are slow-acting, they are rarely used in commercial tanning operations. Today, tanning solutions are composed of mineral substances, such as chromium-based salts and oils. The cured and cleaned hides are immersed in the solution, where the tanning agents react with the collagen, rendering the fibers insoluble. The agents and oils fill the spaces that were formerly filled by the gelatinous materials. The hides are now soft, water- and mildew-resistant, pliable leathers.

Coloring

Coloring helps camouflage an uneven natural color or introduces currently popular fashion colors. The color may be applied by piece dyeing or surface dyeing. In piece dyeing, referred to in the leather industry as **drum dyeing**, the tanned leather is rotated in large vessels filled with dye liquor. In **surface dyeing**, pigments are mixed with binding agents and spread or brushed over the surface of the leather; this technique is actually a type of staining and colors the surface portion only.

Finishing

Finishing operations may involve the application of lubricants and softening agents to increase the suppleness of the leather. Imperfect areas of grain may be corrected by gently abrading the surface or by shaving a thin film off the surface. If the natural grain is very imperfect, mechanical embossing operations may be employed to impart attractive markings. Resins, waxes, and lacquer-based compounds may be applied and polished for a **glazed finish** (Figure 14.22). Compounds used in glazing also increase the moisture resistance of the leather.

Finished leather fabrics are labeled with such terms as full-grain leather, top-grain leather, and split leather. The natural grain markings in **full-grain leather** have not been corrected or altered in any way. **Top-grain** **leather** has undergone minor corrections to its natural grain markings.

Split leather is produced from a central portion of the hide; because the top layer of the hide is not present in

Figure 14.22 Glazed leather. Courtesy C.R. Laine Furniture.

split leather coverings, no natural grain markings appear. Split leather may not be as durable as full- and top-grain leathers. **Suede**—leather fabric produced with the flesh side of the hide exposed—is rarely used in upholstery because of its habit of crocking or rubbing off color. Laboratory procedures to evaluate crocking are reviewed in Chapter 19.

Coated Fabrics

Coated fabrics, discussed in Chapter 8, were initially developed to simulate leather and suede at a lower price, but have captured a market section all their own due to performance and appearance features.

Simulated Suede

Many upholstery coverings that appear to be genuine suede are actually simulated structures, most often made of polyester. Two operations, **flocking** and sueding, are used to produce these fabrics.

Flocking and Sueding

An **electrostatic flocking** operation is generally used to produce **simulated suede**. In **sueding** or **emerizing** operations, sandpaper-covered disks revolve against the flocked surface. Brushing and smoothing finishes raise

and orient pile yarns in one direction; napping finishes raise fiber ends. Sueding, however, roughens the surface and generally orients the flock in all directions, though the flock may be given directional lay or nap.

The durability of a flocked and sueded surface is determined by the cohesiveness of the substrate, resin, and flock. The surface must resist abrasive forces and the resin must be stable to cleaning agents. Simulated leather and suede fabrics are used extensively to cover dining chairs and the seats, backs, and armrests in automobiles. Apart from any damage caused by cutting or puncturing, heavier **vinyl** and urethane fabrics can withstand the high levels of use in mass transit vehicles.

Extruded Film Sheeting

The compounds used most often to create **coated fabrics** and **simulated leather** fabrics include polyvinyl chloride, polyurethane, and **silicone**. Solutions of these compounds are extruded as film sheeting using the process described in Chapter 8. To provide the dimensional stability required for upholstery applications, the sheeting is bonded to a supporting fabric, generally a conventional knitted, woven, bonded-web, or spunlaced fabric.

The grain markings that distinguish full- and top-grain leathers are introduced to simulated leathers by **embossing**. This is accomplished by pressing a metal-coated die that has been prepared with the desired markings into the surface of the film. Many popular embossing patterns have nothing to do with leather grain inspiration, however.

Incorporating air into the compounds expands polymer solutions. As with whipping cream or egg whites, the apparent, but not the actual, volume is increased. The **expanded polymer solution** is then applied to a base fabric as a coating (Figure 14.23). This process increases the comfort characteristics. Polymer films and coatings have little or no porosity. Because of this lack of breathability, many people find these fabrics uncomfortable, especially in hot weather, but they have many popular performance features, especially for restaurants, health-care facilities, and hotels. Polyurethane coated fabrics, for example, are widely used in hotels as headboards because it is a hostile material to bedbugs!

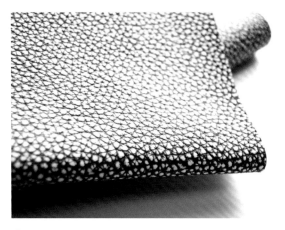

Figure 14.23 "Expanded" vinyl. Courtesy of Joseph Noble Inc.

Key Terms

backcoating	Jacquard-woven tapestry
brocade	lampas
brocatelle	liseré
chintz	matelassé
cloqué	ottoman
coated fabrics	plush
corduroy	pocket cloth
crepe	repp
curing	sateen
damask	satin
dobby	silicone
dot or spot weave	simulated leather
doublecloth	simulated suede
drum dyeing	skins
duck	slipcover
electrostatic flocking	split leather
embossing	suede
emerizing	sueding
expanded polymer	surface dyeing
solution	taffeta
faille	tanning
flocking	tapestry
frieze	top-grain leather
full-grain leather	tufted upholstery fabric
glazed finish	velour
grain markings	velvet
grospoint	velveteen
herringbone	vinyl
hides	voided velvet
houndstooth	warp sateen

Review Questions

1. Why are both natural and synthetic fibers popular for upholstery fabrics?
2. Is fiber the most important attribute to consider in selecting an upholstery fabric? Is weave most important?
3. Identify pros and cons of backcoated upholstery fabric.
4. Distinguish between hand-woven and machine-woven tapestry.
5. Knitted fabrics have specific uses in upholstered furniture covering. Where are they used, and why?
6. Grospoint fabrics have frequently been used for commercial upholstery applications. Why?
7. Differentiate among full-grain leather, top-grain leather, and split leather.
8. How are natural grain markings simulated?
9. When are coated fabrics most often used, and why?

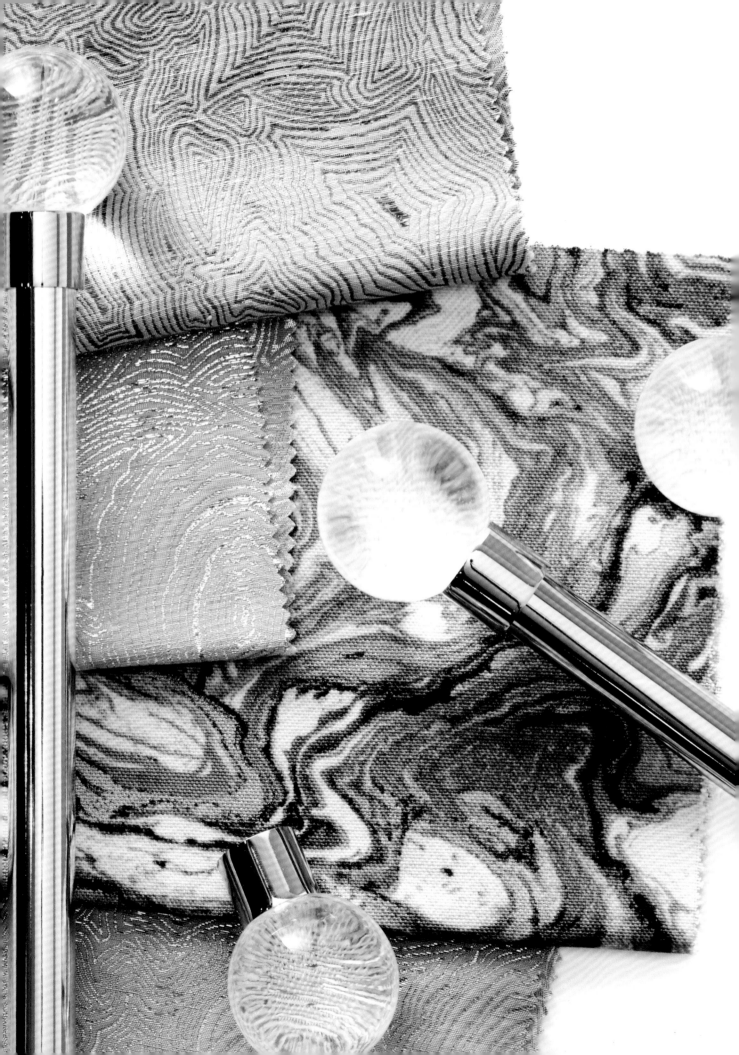

UNIT THREE
WINDOW TREATMENTS AND WALLCOVERINGS

15

Window Treatment Selection

Many factors are important to designers and consumers in window covering selection, whether fiber-based or nontextile products are being considered. As for all product choices, aesthetics are probably the primary factor, but for a successful end result many other attributes come into play.

At the outset, the **fenestration**—the design, arrangement, and proportion of the windows and doors—may limit the range of styles that can be considered. Designers need to consider what the window treatment will look like from the outside, window by window, and in relationship to the entire façade. Structural defects needing to be camouflaged impose additional limitations, and so do desires for such functional properties as privacy enhancement and noise or glare reduction. Sources and quantity of light and the presence of atmospheric contaminants narrow the range of colored covering choices. Legal standards or codes apply to the covering choices for certain commercial interiors. Costs of multiple fabric components, hardware fixtures, and trimming must stay within budget. The long-term costs (such as for cleaning or repair) or savings (for energy-cost reduction) of selected products are important considerations.

Appearance

Visual and textural features of the material, along with effects of various factors on color, are some of the most critical considerations for any window covering.

Aesthetics

At least initially, consumers limit the window treatment styles and coverings they will consider based on personal preferences. Interior designers typically use design elements and principles to create a treatment that dominates the interior setting or one that attracts little attention and serves as a backdrop for other furnishings. Treatments may be symmetrical or asymmetrical, formal or informal. Whatever the design, it should offer the most appropriate solution for the client's need.

As with upholstery fabrics discussed in earlier chapters, a wide variety of fibers, yarn types, and weaves have a

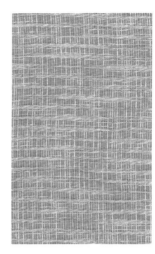

Figure 15.1 Complex yarns add visual and textural interest to curtain and drapery fabrics. Courtesy of Fabricut, Inc.

place in window covering fabrics (Figure 15.1). There are silk or polyester taffeta, rough-hewn linen, glazed chintz, open-mesh leno, and other casement effects; smooth yarns, novelty yarns, and many color effects are popular.

All window coverings intended to be used as free-hanging panels must be drapable, but those fabrics intended for such overhead and side treatments as swags, jabots, and cascades must be exceptionally so. Satin weave, for example produces excellent drapability, whereas plain weave makes a stiffer cloth, all other factors being equal.

Fabrics produced for gathered and ruffled curtain styles are usually made from fabrics with a crisp hand (made from fine, high-twist yarns) in order to support the gathers and ruffles. Fine, soft yarns are selected for fabrics intended to be used in sash curtains and Austrian shades; such cloths produce soft, rounded folds that enhance the shirred effect while preserving the preferred level of transparency. Fabrics intended for awnings or other exterior treatments are often composed of relatively large-gauge, high-twist yarns strong enough to resist rupturing when the fabric is stretched over a framework and when it is repeatedly stressed by wind gusts, and of course they must also have superlative lightfastness properties.

Woven-wood blinds may be constructed with simple ply or cord yarns contrasting with or matching the color of the wooden slats. In these coverings, the yarns are often incorporated in lengthwise bands to create stripes that enhance the visual and textural interest of the shade.

Structure

Within an interior space, the fenestration may suggest that two windows be covered with a single treatment, that treatments on neighboring windows be mounted to equalize differences in height, or that the coverings draw one way or not at all. A small, isolated window may require a large-scale treatment with fabric identical to that used for other windows in the interior to make it appear larger and integrated. Certain types of windows preclude the use of certain treatment styles. Bow windows, for example, cannot be covered with Roman shades or with accordion-pleated shades. Windows that open inward cannot be covered with stationary panels unless the panels and rods are attached to the window sashes.

The large expanses of glass typical of contemporary homes and office buildings may require coverings to control light and heat transmission during the day and to provide privacy and avoid a black wall effect at night. (Increasingly, the glass itself in these windows may take on some of these tasks, such as high UV light filtering, so that fabrics requirements are less restrictive.) Walls in need of repair and windows in need of replacement can be camouflaged by covering them with stationary treatments.

Color Variables

By taking into account both the apparent color of textile materials (discussed in Chapter 9) and factors that affect actual color, ultimate selections should appear the same over a reasonable period of time as they did when initially installed. Careful planning helps ensure that the coordination between the window treatments, other interior furnishings, and wallcoverings is successful.

Factors Affecting Apparent Color

It is critically important to evaluate color changes based on the specific lighting conditions in an interior prior to final selection. Professionals and consumers are advised to hang sample lengths of their possible choices at their windows, along with any planned shades or linings, and evaluate them at different times of day. Color appears different before sunset, when more of the light comes from outside, than it does after dusk, when the room's lighting highlights the furnishings. Multiple layers may be needed or color selections may need to be adjusted in order to achieve the desired effect.

Window coverings are normally not subject to the surface abrasion that is inflicted on upholstery fabrics and soft floorcoverings. Therefore, fabrics with heavy texture or featuring prominent relief effects, like those provided by complex yarns, that would not hold up well in upholstery use may be appropriate for window treatments.

Although all fabrics need to be cleaned regularly, soiling accumulates more slowly on vertical surfaces than on upholstery, flooring, and other horizontal surfaces. However, areas of window covering that are repeatedly handled may rapidly accumulate soil. In stationary treatments especially, airborne dust, smoke, and oily cooking fumes may settle on the fabrics and gradually alter the apparent colors.

Factors Affecting Actual Color

Window coverings are continually subjected to solar rays. Sun-related alterations in the structure of dyes produce concomitant changes in the structure of the fibers. To help minimize the degradation of the colorants and the fibers used in decorative panels, the use of permanently attached or separately hung lining materials, and possibly exterior awnings, is advisable.

Lightfastness, gasfastness, and fastness to cleaning agents are all concerns for indoor window covering appearance retention. When coverings are to be installed outdoors, the stability of the colorants to weather elements and changing ambient temperature are critical.

Function

Consumers, interior designers, and architects may choose window treatments that provide specific functional benefits, such as light control, privacy, insulation, and noise reduction. Some knit and woven fabrics, called **casements**, feature open areas—which may vary from nearly closed to mostly open—between the yarns and across the area of the fabric (see Figure 15.2). Casements often feature loop or curl yarns to add aesthetic interest and engineer the degree of **fabric openness**. The airy projections of complex yarns effectively cover the surface area and increase the opacity (Figure 15.3).

(a)

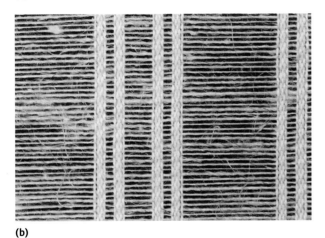

(b)

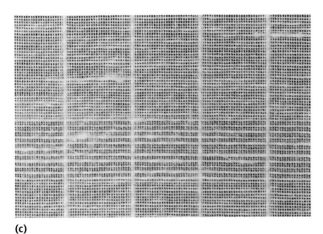

(c)

Figure 15.2 Levels of fabric openness: (a) open, (b) semi-open, (c) semi-closed. Courtesy of Amy Willbanks, www.textilefabric.com.

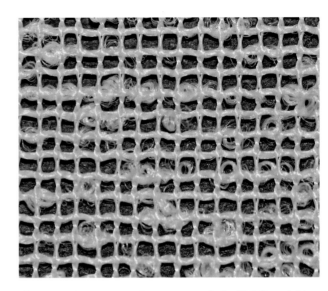

Figure 15.3 Loop yarns reduce openness but add little weight to this leno casement. Courtesy of Amy Willbanks, www.textilefabric. com.

Numerous factors other than openness affect light transmission into interior environments. A portion of the light waves striking any object are reflected, another portion absorbed, and the remaining portion transmitted. Light-colored fibers permit more light waves to be transmitted to the room interior. Increasing the fullness of the panels reduces this transmission, since more fibers reflect and absorb more waves.

In addition to casements, window coverings range from **sheers** (Figure 15.4), which offer various levels of

Figure 15.4 Sheer drapery fabrics. Courtesy of Momentum Group.

transparency and translucence, to opaque cloths, and even to cloths that completely black out light. Consumers' preferences and desires for these different styles and the functional properties they offer shift over time, as do all trends.

Reduction of Glare

The glare, or brightness, control provided by fabric window treatments themselves is influenced not only by the inherent characteristics of the fiber used, but by color characteristics of the coverings, the number of layers used, the fullness of the panels, the addition of fiber delusterants and fabric coatings, and the fabric's openness.

The degree of glare control that window coverings should provide depends on the solar exposure conditions, the type of glass in the window, and the preferences and needs of the people who use the interior space. Tinted or reflective-coated vision glass in lieu of clear glass may reduce the level of light transmission adequately.

Window treatments are often designed to provide varied levels of light and glare control throughout the day, ranging from full light transmission to total blackout. Multiple layers of window coverings widen the range of brightness control options needed as the quantity of direct and reflected light varies throughout the day. For maximum flexibility, various combinations of shades, curtains, draperies, and awnings may be used. Shades or fabrics with opaque coatings may be installed for total blackout in interiors such as motel rooms. (Blackout fabrics are discussed further in Chapter 17.)

Controlling the level of glare and brightness in an interior can be critical for residents or other occupants who have impaired vision. As the human eye ages, it becomes more sensitive to excessive glare. Uncontrolled levels of brightness can contribute to discomfort or safety issues, such as falls, and may be visually uncomfortable for employees stationed near windows. Computer monitors and other screens must be considered when determining the need for window treatments, since electronic devices are particularly susceptible to glare from bright windows, which create veiling reflections that obscure the image on the screen.

Restriction of Inward Vision

A basic function of window coverings is to provide privacy for occupants. Most coverings will reduce the view inward during daylight hours, but a lining or separate curtains may be needed to ensure privacy at night when artificial illuminants brighten the interior. Moreover, when a window faces a private outdoor area, coverings may be specified so that the occupants do not feel that they are open to observation. Full, stationary curtains may be selected for windows placed for inward vision to be continually restricted.

Modification of Outward Vision

A window covering may also be used to modify or completely block an unsightly view by, for example combining relatively heavy, closed fabrics with opaque linings in stationary mountings.

Reduction of Interior Noise

Three types of sounds may be heard within interiors. **Airborne sounds** radiate directly into the air from people talking and typing, photocopiers and printers producing copies, telephones ringing, video machines, radios, and the like. **Surface sounds** are produced as people traverse across the floor or push and pull items along it. **Impact or structurally borne sounds** result from impacts on a structural surface that cause it to vibrate, for instance, walking, jumping, dancing, bouncing balls, knocking on doors, and hammering nails. Activities such as walking and vacuuming create more than one type of sound. Also, most sounds can be transmitted to areas well beyond their origin. Sounds from lawn mowers, cars, trucks, buses, airplanes, and the neighbor's dog all come from the exterior environment but impact the interior.

Sounds that we want to hear can be entertaining and enlightening; unwanted sounds become noise, which can be annoying and disruptive. Thus, residential and commercial consumers often seek ways to control sounds and prevent them from becoming unwanted noise.

Figure 15.5a illustrates how interior sound can be prolonged and magnified as it is reflected from the floor to the ceiling and from a bare wall to a bare window. Figure 15.5b illustrates how ceiling materials and soft floorcoverings will absorb sound that is traveling vertically; window and wallcoverings can be installed to absorb sound that is traveling horizontally. (The sound absorption qualities of wallcoverings are discussed in Chapter 18.)

Hard Surface Classroom

Black arrows represent direct sound, with a clear path from teacher to student. Red arrows represent reflected sound. Note the many red arrows which indicate the longer, more indirect path taken to reach the student.

Accoustically Treated Classroom

high NRC acoustical coiling

acoustical wall treatment

The addition of sound absorbing materials reduces late arriving reflected sound, lowers reverberation time, and improves speech intelligibility.

Figure 15.5 Interior sound travel (a) without sound absorbing materials and (b) with sound absorbing materials. The addition of sound-absorbing materials reduces late-arriving reflected sound, lowers reverberation time, and improves speech intelligibility. Black arrows represent direct sound, with a clear path from teacher to student. Red arrows represent reflected sound. Note the many red arrows which indicate the longer, more indirect path taken to reach the student. Illustrations by Ron Carboni.

The sound absorption quality of draperies varies with the density of the weave and whether the drapery panel construction consists of a single layer or multiple layers of fabric. The degree to which materials such as ceiling tiles, carpeting, wallcoverings, and window treatments will absorb noise is indicated in terms of its **noise reduction coefficient (NRC)**. The higher the NRC, the more noise is absorbed.

Free-hanging fabric partitions (called **privacy curtains**, or **cubicle curtains**) are hung primarily to provide privacy in multibed healthcare facilities; in large, open interiors they may be used principally for decoration and to divide space. However, these interior partitions also lessen horizontally reflected sound if they are of closed, compactly constructed fabrics.

Conservation of Energy

Concern for the depletion of energy sources and the pressures of rising heating and cooling costs have impelled consumers and manufacturers to search for ways to reduce energy consumption. Substantial improvements in the design of windows have reduced the role of window treatments as the primary control of the amount of light and glare coming in and the amount of heat gain or loss through windows. Appropriate window treatments can, however, contribute to the maintenance of efficient interior temperatures. Since 2005, windows have been consistently evaluated and labeled to indicate ratings for several characteristics. The National Fenestration Rating

Figure 15.6 Example of an NFRC label. Courtesy of NFRC.

Council (NFRC) energy performance label is shown in Figure 15.6.

The thermal performance criteria for window treatments change as the seasons change. In winter, insulation helps reduce heat loss, and in summer, rejection of radiant energy reduces heat gain. Convection, conduction, and radiation are the main mechanisms by which heat is lost and gained through windows.

Convection is the tendency of hotter, less dense material to rise, while colder, denser material tends to sink. These movements, which include wind and forced circulation, result in heat transfer. As wind circulates against exterior surfaces, it will convect heat away; the loss will be more pronounced with higher air speeds and greater differences between inside and outside temperatures. In an interior, warm air may be drawn between the window coverings and the window glass, where it is cooled, becomes heavier, and flows under the lower edges of free-hanging coverings and back into the room. Air movement is also responsible for the infiltration of cold air through structural openings such as cracks between window and wall frames and wall joints, called drafts.

Conduction is the movement of thermal energy through solids, liquids, and gases when a difference of temperature exists. Insulation resists thermal transfer and stems conduction. In residential and commercial structures, heat energy will be conducted through the walls, doors, floors, and roof areas as well as the windows. Conditions vary dramatically from one structure to another, but in many buildings the largest percentage of heat loss is through the windows.

The extent to which windows and window treatments retard heat loss in the winter and heat gain in the summer can be measured and the results reported numerically in terms of U-values. **U-values** indicate how much heat actually does pass outward in winter and inward in summer. To become familiar with U-values, we can examine the values for various types of windows; these values are approximate and vary with construction, thickness of the glass, and the presence of tints or coatings. Single-pane window glass has a U-value of 1.13, double panes with $\frac{3}{16}$ inch of insulating air space between them have a U-value of 0.41, and triple panes with a total of $\frac{5}{8}$ inch of insulating air space have a U-value of 0.35. A U-value of 1.13 BTU/ft²-hr-°F means that 1.13 British thermal units of heat pass through each square foot of window configuration every hour for each Fahrenheit degree of difference between inside and outside temperatures.

Because air is a poor heat conductor and a good heat insulator, window coverings that can contribute to the reduction of energy loss in winter require a tight enclosure that will entrap dead air between the fabric and the glass, similar to the enclosure between the panes in double- and triple-pane windows. The dead air will

retard conduction, and the sealed covering also helps to prevent warm air from being drawn against the window. The installation of a free-hanging, traversing drapery treatment has been found to be minimally effective. The use of tight-fitting, closed draperies may reduce heat loss significantly. To reduce air flow between drapery panels and the glass, the top of the window treatment should go all the way to the ceiling or be topped with a cornice. The sides of the panels should be sealed along the wall or facing, and the panels should overlap where they meet in the center. The bottom hem should be long enough to allow fabric to stack on the floor, preventing cool air from escaping into the room along the floor. Similarly, the use of a tight-fitting lining, sealed around the perimeter of the window, has been found to be more effective than a free-hanging lining.

Multilayered roller shades can be used for their insulative value. Dead air is trapped between the layers; again, thermal efficiency improves when the edges of the shade are sealed to restrict air flow. With Roman shades constructed of woven wood, an increase in the quantity of complex yarns relative to wood increases the insulative quality. Cellular shades incorporate dead air spaces within their construction to provide more insulation.

Conventional Venetian blinds and vertical blinds, especially those made of metal, are comparatively ineffective in reducing winter heat loss, because of the small gaps remaining between the closed louvers and the high conductivity of the metal components. On the other hand, their louvers can easily be angled to let in sunlight and increase heat gain during daylight hours in winter. Interior shutters without louvers that fit tightly and are used consistently can contribute significantly to energy conservation. Like blinds, louvered shutters provide little value in preventing heat loss in winter. They can, however, be effective in blocking intense summer sunlight.

Radiation is the transfer of heat in the form of waves or rays. Waves radiating against the exterior surfaces of windows include those emanating directly from the sun, as well as those reflected from the sky and other surfaces such as the facades of neighboring buildings, paved parking areas, streets, and sidewalks. As schematized in Figure 15.7, some of the incident waves are rejected, some absorbed, and some transmitted. Of the rays transmitted through the outdoor glass, various portions

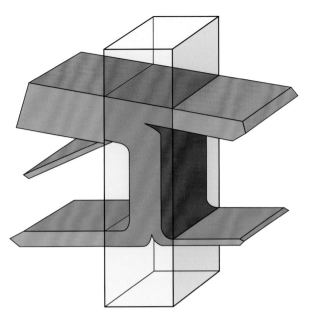

Figure 15.7 Glass transmission properties. Illustration by Ron Carboni.

will be rejected, absorbed, and transmitted by the indoor glass in double pane windows. Finally, various portions of the rays transmitted through the indoor glass will be rejected, absorbed, and transmitted by the draperies.

Clearly, window treatments that can be opened and closed provide the flexibility needed to control seasonal solar heat gain. On sunny winter days, the coverings can be opened to increase the level of heat transmission; on sunny summer days, they can be closed to increase the level of heat rejection. Solar heat gain in the summer, of course, warms the interior and increases the air conditioning load.

The effectiveness of windows and window coverings in reducing the level of radiant energy transmitted into the interior can be measured and the results reported numerically in terms of the **shading coefficient (S/C)**. To calculate the S/C, the total amount of heat transmitted by a window glass and covering combination is divided by the total amount of heat transmitted by a single pane of clear ⅛-inch-thick glass. S/C values (ranging from 0 to 1) indicate how well a window and covering reduce heat gain, with lower values indicating more effective control. The actual amount of heat gain is reported in terms of the U-value.

Although drapery treatments produce insignificant reductions in the S/C value of insulated reflective glass,

they produce significant decreases in the values of clear and tinted vision glass. Closed, light-colored draperies produce the most significant reductions in these cases.

Conventional Venetian blinds and vertical blinds are relatively ineffective in retarding winter heat loss, but they are quite effective in reducing summer heat gain. Various types and colors of roller shades are also highly effective in reducing heat gain. The color of both blinds and shades will affect the amount of light reflected and the light energy absorbed. White and light colors will reflect higher amounts of light, whereas black and dark colors will reflect less light, absorbing the heat energy of the light not reflected. In turn, this absorbed heat will be transferred into the room, a negative effect in the summer but a positive effect in the winter.

Exterior shutters and awnings can be highly effective in reducing solar heat gain. Light colors should be used for both types of coverings for high reflection and low absorption of radiant energy. Heat absorbed by these coverings can be transferred through the windows to the interior. For maximum effectiveness, awnings must be correctly angled over the windows to reflect all direct rays and vented to avoid trapping heat. During summer, correctly sized and placed awnings on south-facing windows can reduce solar heat gain significantly, especially for sun-drenched, west-facing windows.

Protection of Other Interior Furnishings

The radiant energy of the sun warms and brightens interior spaces, but also weakens textile fibers and changes their apparent and actual color characteristics. Drawn window coverings, however, minimize light transmission, which protects other furnishings. This will, of course, subject the window coverings themselves to higher levels of sun exposure. The replacement cost of the window treatments, however, is normally less than that of other furnishings, and relatively inexpensive curtains and linings can be used to protect more expensive overdraperies.

Microbe Resistance

Window treatments, like all furnishings, become soiled over time, and should be vacuumed regularly. They may occupy a significant amount of wall area and are subject to handling by many users. Hard surface treatments such as blinds can be washed down to reduce the presence of bacteria, but cleaning fabrics is more time-consuming and expensive.

In some instances, window coverings benefit from antimicrobial finishes and treatments, especially in healthcare or senior care facilities (where occupants are weak or vulnerable) or where large numbers of users may be present, such as in educational and daycare facilities. Fibers and aftertreatments with antimicrobial characteristics are available in certain drapery fabrics and blinds.

Budgets

Various cost-related factors must be considered prior to final selection of any material, including window treatments. Together with the initial costs of the materials, labor, and accessories required, residential and commercial consumers should consider financial variables related to replacement and maintenance.

Initial Costs

Whether consumers choose readymade coverings, elect to have a custom-designed treatment, or plan to construct the treatment themselves, the initial cost of a window treatment includes the cost of all outercoverings, linings, curtains, shades, shutters, hardware to be used, and removal of old window coverings. The choice of expensive material, elaborate styling, fuller panels, or trims will escalate the materials cost. The cost is higher still when treatments such as flame-resistant finishes and reflective coatings are specified. Custom projects can involve separate charges for consultations with the designer, workroom, and fabricator and for measuring, cutting, sewing, trimming, and installing.

Some window covering treatments that are considered effective insulators have traditionally qualified endusers for energy tax credits. Tax regulations change; these incentives have time limits and may be extended or allowed to expire. Although materials that boost energy efficiency may cost more upfront, their cost may balance against the energy savings that will be realized during the use-life of the treatment. Regardless of potential savings, however, the total cost and terms of payment—whether due in full on delivery or made in installments with interest charges—must coincide with the ability of the purchaser to pay. Financial institutions may permit the cost of some window treatment projects to be included in long-term mortgage obligations.

Replacement Costs

As with any substantial purchase, when selecting window treatment styles and coverings, consumers should consider the initial cost in relationship to the expected use-life. Fiber and fabric variables, styling features, exposure conditions, and care affect the use-life of textile coverings, which is generally considered to be from about three to five years.

Maintenance Costs

For any material, the first line of maintenance protocol for any furnishing material, including window covering, is regular vacuuming. Several variables related to fabric composition, such as the type of fiber used, the dimensional stability of the fabric, the use of durable press resins or other finishes, the stability of the colorants, and the structural characteristics of the coverings are the main determinants of whether laundering or dry-cleaning is required as a next step.

Elaborate styling and multiple components, such as shades, curtains, draperies, and swags, will increase maintenance cost, because charges are incurred for the commercial laundering or dry-cleaning of each covering and component. Wide, long panels are also more expensive to clean than are narrow, short panels. Separate charges may be assessed for removing and transporting the coverings to the cleaning plant, for ironing and reforming the folds, and for returning and rehanging the treatment. Of course, the anticipated frequency of cleaning—determined to a large extent by the specific environment, the regular cleaning protocol, and the owner's standards—must be considered when estimating longterm maintenance costs.

Key Terms

airborne sounds

casement

conduction

convection

cubicle curtains

fabric openness

fenestration

impact or structurally
   borne sounds

noise reduction coefficient
   (NRC)

privacy curtains

radiation

shading coefficient (S/C)

sheers

surface sounds

U-values

Review Questions

1. Identify complex yarns that give maximum visual and textural interest to window coverings. Why can some of these yarns be used in window coverings but not in upholstery fabric?

2. Cite examples of how a window treatment can be effectively used in meeting challenges presented by the fenestration in an interior.

3. Identify window styles that severely limit treatment choices.

4. Differentiate between apparent and actual color.

5. Why is it critically important to examine colored textiles in the end-use setting?

6. Discuss the factors that affect the level of light transmission.

7. Explain the roles of yarn size and compactness of construction in determining fabric openness.

8. Discuss factors affecting the apparent color and those that affect the actual color.

9. Explain how window treatments can support energy conservation efforts.

10. Identify all variables affecting the cost of window treatments.

16

Window Treatment Styles

indow treatments, which include curtains, draperies, shades, blinds, shutters, and awnings, used alone or in combinations, may be decorated with rods, cornices, hold-backs, tie-backs, and valances. Treatments may require soft or stiff, heavy or lightweight fabric in order to achieve the desired effect.

Window treatment styles have remained consistent over time, but their popularity and the availability of specific materials continues to evolve. For example, café curtains, illustrated in Figure 16.1f, are always distinguished by scalloped headings and hung by rings over a loop rod, but are not fashionable at all times, or in all markets. As the variety of contemporary fabrics, colors, motifs, and components changes constantly, age-old styles continue to be realized in dramatically different iterations.

Curtain and Drapery Treatments

In general, **curtains** are relatively sheer, lightweight coverings that are hung without linings, while **draperies** are heavy, often opaque coverings that are usually hung with linings. The term **casement** may be assigned to fabrics of medium weight and some degree of openness. Casement fabrics may be hung as unlined curtains or as lined draperies. Sheers are hung without linings, and are of lightweight, translucent fabric. Curtains and draperies are normally wovens or knits, but some novel treatments involve such components as strands of glass and polymer film fabrics.

The coverings in some curtain and drapery treatments are hung as stationary, **nontraversing panels**. Other coverings are hung as **traversing panels** that can be opened and closed as desired. Additional styling features may be added with the judicious use of decorative headings and side treatments, trimmings, and hardware fixtures.

Curtains

Figure 16.1 shows some typical styles of curtain treatments. **Stationary casement panels** (Figure 16.1a) are approximately 2 $^{1}/_{2}$ times wider than the window. The panels are supported by a conventional, nontraversing curtain rod inserted through a **casing** sewn into the upper edge of the fabric. The casing may be plain or constructed with a heading to form a ruffle.

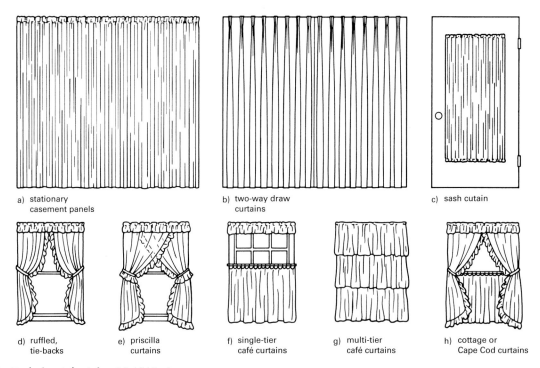

a) stationary casement panels

b) two-way draw curtains

c) sash cutain

d) ruffled, tie-backs

e) priscilla curtains

f) single-tier café curtains

g) multi-tier café curtains

h) cottage or Cape Cod curtains

Figure 16.1 Typical curtain styles. Fairchild Books.

A traditional panel treatment involves the use of tambour-embroidered curtain panels. The rich embroidery on such transparent fabrics as organdy and voile is shown best by having limited fullness. A heading, such as pinched pleats, and a traversing rod convert stationary panels into **draw curtains** (Figure 16.1b). Panels anchored at their upper and lower edges are known as **sash curtains**, and are typically used on French doors (Figure 16.1c). As the width of the fabric is increased with respect to the width of the window, the shirred effect becomes more pronounced, increasing privacy and reducing the degree of light transmission.

Whereas the panels in ruffled, **tie-back curtains** (Figure 16.1d) do not cross at their upper edges, the panels in **priscilla curtains** overlap; priscilla treatments always involve ruffled tie-backs as well (Figure 16.1e). The use of such crisp, transparent fabrics as organdy, voile, and dotted Swiss (described in Chapter 17) can help to minimize the visual weight of these treatments, as well as provide the body required for attractive ruffles.

Café curtains (Figure 16.1f and g) may be used alone or in combination with draperies. They are frequently constructed with scalloped headings and hung by rings looped over a rod. Multi-tier café curtains, with each tier normally overlapping the lower tier by about three inches, may be hung by rings or by rods run through fabric casings. When single-tier café curtains are combined with ruffled, tied-back panels, the treatment is labeled a **cottage or Cape Cod curtain** style (Figure 16.1h).

Some contemporary treatments have fabric panels with limited fullness to accentuate the window and highlight the rod. Frequently, the panel headings have tabs that are formed into two- or three-inch-long loops (Figure 16.2), knots, or bows for visual interest. The top may have deep scallops, resulting in a dramatic drooping effect, or it may have large buttonholes for a more tailored look. While the rods are nontraversing, a yard-long wooden rod, known as a **curtain tender**, may be used to open and close the panels.

Draperies

Typical drapery treatments are illustrated in Figure 16.3. **One-way draw draperies** (Figure 16.3a) are drawn in one direction, stacking on one side of the window; **two-way draw draperies** (Figure 16.3b) are drawn to stack on both sides.

Cords, chains, medallions, hooks, and the like secure the panels in **held-back** and **tied-back** styles (Figure 16.3c and d), but the panels can be easily released when preferred. **Pinned-up** styles are held by two-piece, stylized magnets or by decorative pins that function like large tie-tacks. These allow the designer or consumer to be more creative with such things as asymmetrical draping as the pins or magnets are not anchored to the wall or window frame. **Pouf or bishop's sleeve treatments** (Figure 16.3e) have tiers of bouffant or billowed-out areas created by periodically gathering the fabric panels.

When draperies are combined with sheer curtains, they are called **overdraperies**, and the curtains are called **sheers**. Combining draperies and curtains increases the cost of a window treatment, but it may also improve interior insulation, light control, and acoustics.

Headings

Headings, which appear at the top of curtain and drapery panels, finish the upper edge and distribute fullness evenly across the finished width. Figure 16.4 illustrates various styles of headings. Headings may be hand measured and sewn or produced with commercial tape. Pleats produced with tape are slightly rounded instead of sharply creased, but the hooks can be removed for cleaning.

Sewn headings, in contrast to those formed with tape, should be interfaced with a fabric such as buckram or crinoline. These plain-woven fabrics are stiffened with

Figure 16.2 Tab-top curtain. Courtesy of Calico Corners, www.calicocorners.com.

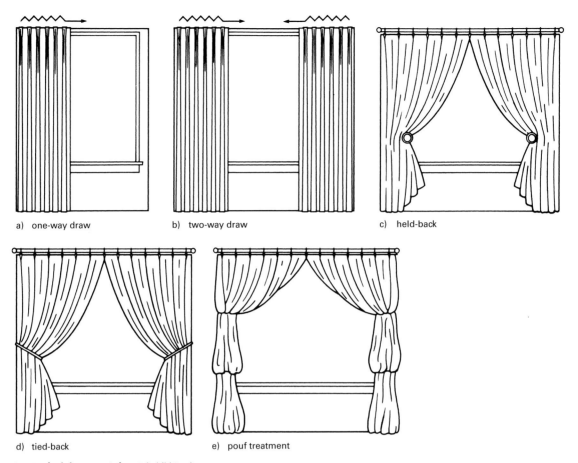

a) one-way draw   b) two-way draw   c) held-back

d) tied-back   e) pouf treatment

Figure 16.3 Typical drapery styles. Fairchild Books.

sizing, starch, or resin and can provide support for the heading treatment. The stability of the stiffening agent to cleaning agents should be determined prior to use.

Trimmings

Curtain and drapery treatments may be enriched by the use of ornamental **trimmings**, such as cord, tasseled or looped fringe, gimp, piping, rickrack, lace, beading, galloons (narrow lengths of braid, embroidered fabric, or lace), or ribbon (Figure 16.5). Some trimmings may be sewn directly to the covering fabric, whereas others may be used as tie-backs.

Overhead and Side Treatments

Overhead treatments cover and conceal panel headings and hardware and enrich window treatments. Valances and swags are overhead treatments executed in fabric and are generally used in combination with such side treatments as cascades and jabots; other overhead treatments employ wood or metal.

In effect, **valances** are short draperies and may have various heading styles. Relatively simple valances may have lower edges that are pointed, curved, or crescent shaped, or finished with trimming or a simple, straight hem, and may be pleated, gathered, or flat. Figure 16.6a has a scalloped, pleated effect; Figure 16.6b illustrates a soft valance with pleated corners. Sheer fabric valances may have a **French tuck hem**, which is double-folded so that no raw edge is apparent. More elaborate valance treatments include Austrian, tapered, puffed, balloon, or festoon styling.

Unlike the structured styling of valances, **swags** are softly draping lengths of fabric (Figure 16.6c). Swags may be paired with cascade or jabot side panels. **Jabots** are pleated, and the lower edges may be level, or they may be angled as in Figure 16.6d. The side treatments can

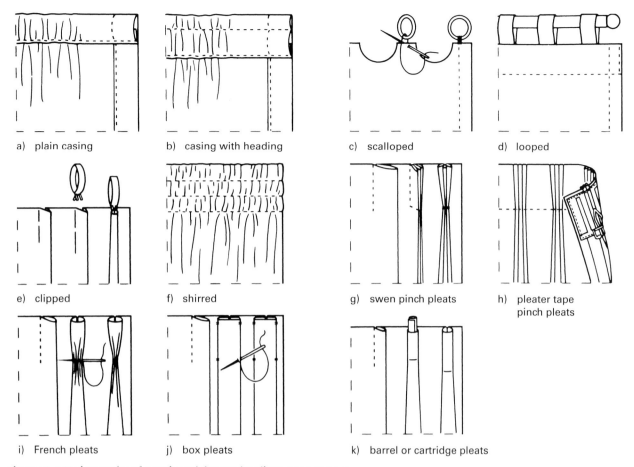

a) plain casing b) casing with heading c) scalloped d) looped

e) clipped f) shirred g) swen pinch pleats h) pleater tape pinch pleats

i) French pleats j) box pleats k) barrel or cartridge pleats

Figure 16.4 Various styles of curtain and drapery headings. Fairchild Books.

be short or long. **Cascades** are side treatments that are gathered rather than pleated, and are designed to fall in folds of graduated length; they are used with or without a valance.

Cornices, cantonnières, and lambrequins are rigid overhead treatments constructed of wood or metal. They can be covered with fabric to match or coordinate with the main drapery fabric, or they may be painted, stained, or left as natural wood. A **cornice** (Figure 16.7 and Figure 16.14) is mounted to cover the drapery heading and hardware. Typically, cornices project 4 to 6 inches from the wall. Adding straight sides and shaped front panels to a cornice board converts it into a **lambrequin**. A **cantonnière** fits flush to the wall and has a shaped overhead panel and sides that extend to the floor. Although the cantonnière is frequently fabric covered, it can also be stenciled directly to the wall surface, coordinating with the fabric panels, blinds, or shades used.

Figure 16.5 Various styles of trimmings are used on these draperies to add visual interest: (a) scalloped, pleated valance, (b) draped valance with pleated corners, (c) swag valance, (d) swag valance with jabot. Les Marquises Collection is courtesy of www.houles.com.

(a)

(b)

(c)

(d)

Figure 16.6 Overhead and side treatments. 16.6a Soft valance with pleated effect and scalloped edge. 16.6b Soft valance with pleated corners. 16.6c Swag valance with fixed drapery panels. 16.6d Swag valance with pleated jabot. Courtesy of Calico Corners, www.calicocorners.com.

Figure 16.7 Hard cornice. Courtesy of Calico Corners, www. calicocorners.com.

Figure 16.8 Soft treatment. Swag over pleated jabot. Courtesy of Calico Corners, www.calicocorners.com.

Hardware

The assortment of hardware used with curtains and draperies includes rods, mounting screws and bolts, batons, curtain tenders, and fabric weights. **Batons** and curtain tenders are used manually to open and close the panels; **fabric weights**, placed in the lower hem area, improve the draping quality of the fabric. The assortment also includes such decorative accessories as café rings and clips, chains, medallions, pin-ups, and two-piece magnets. Medallions are permanently attached to the window frame for use as hold-backs, whereas pin-ups and magnets are used selectively to hold the panels in distinctive folds or configurations.

Conventional Rods

A variety of conventional, nondecorative curtain and drapery rods is available. Conventional rods are comparatively inexpensive, but may be unsightly when not covered by the headings. A note of safety: Conventional traversing rods are usually equipped with a system of cords to control opening and closing. Numerous cases of young children being seriously injured by closed cord systems have been reported, and the U.S. Consumer Product Safety Commission has restricted the use of some loose cords. Local codes also may require closed cord or cordless. Cords wrapped on a cord cleat attached to the wall to keep them out of the reach of children or pets may not be a sufficient safety precaution. This is a simple, but serious problem. For window treatments that require a closed cord system to function, a tie down device can be mounted on the wall or floor to keep the cord pulled tight.

The **continental rod** is a conventional and inexpensive rod style that is threaded through a "pocket," or **casing**, at the top of the curtain so that the curtain completely covers the rod. The continental rod is used for relatively lightweight fabrics, and usually extends either 2¹/₂ inches or 4¹/₂ inches from the window. A shallower rod is often used to carry a sheer while a deeper, paired rod carries an overcurtain.

Decorative Rods

Decorative curtain and drapery rods are made of wood, metal, or plastic resembling, for example, brass, pewter,

Figure 16.9 Various types of decorative rods. Courtesy of Calico Corners, www.calicocorners.com.

gold, or natural wood (Figure 16.9). Coordinating rings can secure the panels. In many cases, matching tieback chains, hold-back medallions, and various styles of **finials** (the decorative pieces attached to the ends of rods) are available (Figure 16.9). Decorative traversing rods may be controlled electrically, by a system of cords, or by batons. Grommets inserted in the drapery heading eliminate the need for rings to attach panels to the rod (Figure 16.10).

Nontraversing decorative rods are especially useful for supporting stationary panels. These panels are hung from wooden or metallic rings or fabric tabs looped over the rod. If the panels are to be opened and closed, they should be shifted by a baton or curtain tender and not by pulling on the side hems, which could deform the fabric edge and add excessive soiling and wear.

Figure 16.10 Drapery panels with built-in grommets. Courtesy of Calico Corners, www.calicocorners.com.

Calculating Yardage Required

The measurements taken when determining the amount of fabric required for a project are critical. If the quantity of fabric initially ordered is insufficient to complete the treatment, a second order may very well be from a different dyelot, with slightly differing color characteristics. Two drapery panels with even slight color differences may prove to be unacceptable.

Product manufacturers, interior furnishings retailers, trade publications, and the internet offer guidelines for yardage requirements for specific styles and various overhead treatments. The following sections summarize the variables for curtains and drapery measurements.

Rod Length and Placement

A yardstick or steel tape should be used for taking all measurements, beginning with those needed to determine the rod length and placement, which depends upon where the drapery panels are to lie when the panels are open. If the window is to be kept as clear as possible, the panels should stack back on the wall, to the sides of the window glass. The values listed in Table 16.1 will help to determine the length of the rod needed when full clearance of the glass is preferred. The distances can be adjusted when the panels must camouflage a structural defect and when a portion of the glass is to be used for **stackback space**.

Rods should be mounted so that the drapery headings will not be visible from outside. Headings are normally 4 inches in height; thus, the rod should normally be located 4 inches above the top edge of the window glass. Again, if structural defects, such as unequal frame heights, must be camouflaged, the location of the rod can be adjusted. The rod should be installed prior to taking the measurements needed for determining the yardage required.

Panel Length

Lengthwise measurements are taken from the top of conventional rods and from the bottom of the rings on decorative rods. The panels may extend to the windowsill, to the apron (the horizontal board below the sill), or to the floor. One inch should be subtracted from the measurement taken to the floor to allow for clearance, especially

TABLE 16.1
CONSIDERATIONS FOR ESTABLISHING ROD LENGTHS

For window width of (including glass, moldings and casings)	Typical* stackback for two-way** draw	Typical rod length and drapery coverage, not including ■ overlaps and returns ■ size/length of rod support hardware or finials
38″	26″	64″
44″	28″	72″
50″	30″	80″
56″	32″	88″
62″	34″	96″
68″	36″	104″
75″	37″	112″
81″	39″	120″
87″	41″	128″
94″	42″	136″
100″	44″	144″
106″	46″	152″
112″	48″	160″
119″	49″	168″
125″	51″	176″
131″	53″	184″
137″	55″	192″
144″	56″	200″
150″	58″	208″
156″	60″	216″
162″	62″	224″
169″	63″	232″
175″	65″	240″
181″	67″	248″
187″	69″	256″

Note: Perpendicular walls near a window may dictate rod length or finial size choices.

* "Typical" figures are for light- to medium-weight fabric. Bulky fabrics require extra space for stackback.

**For one-way draws, deduct 7″ from stackback.

Data Courtesy of Stevens Enterprises.

when soft floorcoverings are in place. For distinctive styling and reduced air infiltration, consumers and designers may elect to have the panels stack or mound on the floor, in which case extra yardage is needed. For the purpose of this discussion, assume the finished panel will be 85 inches in length.

If patterned fabrics are chosen, extra yardage must be added for matching repeats. The lengthwise measurement must be evenly divisible by the length of the repeat. Thus, assuming the length of the repeat is 18 inches, 5 inches must be added to the measured 85 inches so that it will be divisible by 18. Normally, a full repeat is placed at the lower hem of sill- and apron-length panels, and at the top hem of floor-length panels.

Yardage must now be added for the hem allowances. For unlined panels, a doubled, 4-inch top hem is planned, and for lined panels, 0.5 inch is allowed for top turnover. The lower hem allowance is generally 4 inches, but as a precaution against potential relaxation and residual shrinkage, this figure should be doubled. In the event that in-use shrinkage shortens the panels, the fabric needed for lengthening is readily available. The hem allowance must always be doubled when such fabrics as taffeta, faille, and bengaline are to be used. The numerous fibers in the crosswise ribs of these fabrics, especially if they are cotton or rayon, may swell during cleaning; this increase in the diameter of the ribs would draw up the warp yarns, causing lengthwise shrinkage. Whatever its fiber content, any fabric may exhibit from 1 to 3 percent residual shrinkage, even if it was preshrunk to encourage relaxation shrinkage.

The total cut length of the panel fabric may now be calculated as follows:

Finished length of panel	85	inches
+ Allowance for pattern matching	5	inches
+ Allowance for top hem	0.5	inch
+ Allowance for bottom hem	8	inches
= Total cut length of panel	98.5	inches

For the lining fabric, no yardage is needed for pattern matching; the bottom hem is generally single and 2 inches deep, and the lower edge is 1 inch above the lower edge of the drapery panel. Again, an allowance may be made for potential in-use shrinkage. The total cut length of the lining fabric may now be calculated as follows:

Finished length of panel	85	inches
Lining shorter than panel	1	inch
+ Allowance for top hem	0.5	inch
+ Allowance for bottom hem	2	inches
= Total cut length of lining	88.5	inches

Panel Width

Fabric panel is not synonymous with fabric width. A fabric panel is formed by seaming a number of fabric widths and, if necessary, a partial width together. *Pleated panel coverage*, *pleat coverage*, and *coverage* are synonyms that refer to the horizontal distance covered by the pleated area of the panel. Coverage does not include the portion of the panel that covers the overlap at the center, or the portion that covers the return, the bracket extending perpendicularly from the wall at each end of the rod.

For the purposes of discussion, we will assume that the length of the installed rod is 56 inches. For a one-way draw treatment, the panel coverage would be 56 inches, with no allowance required for overlap. For a two-way draw treatment, the coverage for each panel would be 28 inches, and the allowance for overlap is normally 3.5 inches. Yardage must now be added for **fullness**, a requirement that generally doubles the yardage but may triple it when sheer fabrics are used. The allowance for the return is equal to the bracket projection distance, typically 3.5 inches. Each of the two side hems requires an allowance of 2 inches. Of this, 0.5 inch will be used as an allowance when seaming the lining, and 1.5 inches will be turned to show at the side of the lining. The total width of one flat, unhemmed panel for a two-way draw treatment may now be calculated as follows:

Coverage	28	inches
+ Allowance for fullness	28	inches
+ Allowance for overlap	3.5	inches
+ Allowance for return	3.5	inches
+ Allowance for side hems	6	inches
= Total width of one flat panel	69	inches

The values listed in Table 16.2 were calculated in this manner and can be used after coverage is determined. The table also contains guidelines for spacing pleats to control the fullness.

One inch must be allowed for seaming the sides of the lining to the drapery panel. The flat, unhemmed lining is thus cut 3 inches narrower than the flat, unhemmed drapery panel that will be turned 1.5 inches inward on each side.

Total Yardage

If, for example, the width of the covering fabric is 45 inches, one full fabric width and one partial width would be seamed to produce the 67-inch-wide panel. Because a second panel is needed for the two-way draw treatment, we may at first assume four fabric widths are required. In this particular case, half the divided fabric width could be used for each of the two panels and thus, only three fabric widths are required. Such an economical use of fabric is not always possible, especially when allowances must be made for matching crosswise repeats and for seam allowances, but we should be alert to the possibility. For some projects, especially those involving expensive fabric, it may even be desirable to slightly reduce the width of the fabric included in each pleat. Multiplying the total length of the unhemmed panel by the number of fabric widths needed yields the total required quantity of fabric. The required quantity of lining fabric can be calculated in the same manner.

Blinds and Shades

In contrast to curtains and draperies, which are drawn horizontally, almost all blinds and shades are drawn vertically. Some styles of blinds and shades are executed with fabric, others with metal or wood, and still others combine textile and nontextile components. Blinds and shades may be operated by hand, or they can be motorized. They can provide blackout and solar conservation features.

Blinds

Venetian blinds, slatted blinds, and vertical blinds are the most basic **blind** styles.

Venetian Blinds

Venetian blinds are made up of horizontal slats, or louvers, laced together with textile cords (Figure 16.11).

TABLE 16.2
DRAPERY PANEL WIDTHS AND PLEATING GUIDELINES

Desired width of finished panel	Width of flat fabric before hemming (allowance for standard 3" hem on each edge)	Width of hemmed fabric before pleating	Number of 4" Flat spaces between pleats	Number of pleats	Width of fabric in each pleat (for standard pinch pleats)
16"	45"	39"	4	5	$3^1/_8$"
20"	53"	47"	5	6	$3^1/_4$"
24"	61"	55"	6	7	$3^3/_8$"
28"	69"	63"	7	8	$3^1/_2$"
32"	77"	71"	8	9	$3^1/_2$"
36"	85"	79"	9	10	$3^9/_{16}$"
40"	93"	87"	10	11	$3^5/_8$"
44"	101"	95"	11	12	$3^5/_8$"
48"	109"	103"	12	13	$3^5/_8$"
52"	117"	111"	13	14	$3^5/_8$"
56"	125"	119"	14	15	$3^3/_4$"
60"	133"	127"	15	16	$3^3/_4$"
64"	141"	135"	16	17	$3^3/_4$"
68"	149"	143"	17	18	$3^3/_4$"
72"	157"	151"	18	19	$3^3/_4$"
76"	165"	159"	19	20	$3^3/_4$"
80"	173"	167"	20	21	$3^3/_4$"
84"	181"	175"	21	22	$3^3/_4$"
88"	189"	183"	22	23	$3^3/_4$"
92"	197"	191"	23	24	$3^3/_4$"
96"	205"	199"	24	25	$3^3/_4$"
100"	213"	207"	25	26	$3^3/_4$"
104"	221"	215"	26	27	$3^3/_4$"
108"	229"	223"	27	28	$3^3/_4$"
112"	237"	231"	28	29	$3^3/_4$"
116"	245"	239"	29	30	$3^3/_4$"
120"	253"	247"	30	31	$3^7/_8$"
124"	261"	254"	31	32	$3^7/_8$"
128"	269"	263"	32	33	$3^7/_8$"

Data Courtesy of Stevens Enterprises.

Slats are typically made of enamel-coated aluminum, painted or stained wood, wood composite, or vinyl (PVC). Off-gassing of PVC materials and the danger of inhaling PVC dust when sizing vinyl blinds is of concern to environmentally conscious consumers. Louvers vary in width from ⅝ inch (micro) to 1 inch (mini) to 2 inches. The wider variety is available with decorative cloth tapes for a more decorative look or with only the textile cords that minimize interference with views when blinds are open. Cords and wands allow blinds to be raised and lowered or tilted to the desired level of privacy or openness.

Figure 16.11 Parkland® Venetian blinds on doors. Parkland® is a registered trademark of Hunter Douglas Inc.

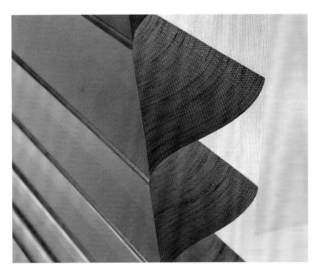

Figure 16.12 Silhouette® window shades. Silhouette® is a registered trademark of Hunter Douglas Inc.

Softer variations of the hard-surfaced louvers use fabric vanes (Figure 16.12) rather than wood or aluminum slats. Sheer fabric front and back panels on some models add to the softness and light-filtering capabilities. Both the traditional Venetian blinds and the newer fabric blinds can be stacked at the upper portion of the window.

Vertical Blinds

In vertical blinds, which may also be referred to as vertical Venetian blinds, the louvers or vanes are suspended

Figure 16.13 Luminette® vertical blinds. Luminette® is a registered trademark of Hunter Douglas Inc.

vertically from traversing or nontraversing rods (Figure 16.13). They may be rotated 180 degrees to balance privacy and inward light transmission. Traversing styles may have a one- or two-way draw.

The louvers or vanes used in vertical blinds may be as narrow as 2 inches or as wide as 6 inches. They may be constructed of vinyl, stable fabric, metal, or wood. Fabric vanes may be inserted into ivory or white vinyl backings to give greater light blockage and present a uniform streetside appearance. New variations of the traditional vertical blinds include soft-vane vertical systems and wide panels that operate on a wheel track system. The wider panels are especially good for large expanses of glass or as room dividers.

Shades

There are several types of **shades** including Austrian shades, balloon shades, accordion-pleated shades, honeycomb shades, roller shades, blackout shades, and solar shades.

Balloon Shades

Balloon shades (Figure 16.14) are composed of fabric and are vertically drawn. Their name derives from the balloon-like puffs they form when raised. The fullness of the panels may be distributed by shirring the top casing over a rod or by using inverted pleats. In inverted-pleat

Figure 16.14 Balloon shade shown with hard cornice. Courtesy of Calico Corners, www.calicocorners.com.

styling, the panels are essentially flat until raised, a feature that makes possible full visual appreciation of the fabric.

Austrian Shades

Austrian shades are similar in construction to balloon shades; the difference is that when they are not raised, balloon shades appear flat while Austrian shades feature vertically shirred lengthwise bands of horizontally draping folds. In both types of shades, the level of transparency is determined by the compactness of construction of the fabric and the amount of fabric taken up in the gathering.

Accordion-Pleated Shades

Accordion-pleated shades are commercially produced of woven or knitted fabric that has been stiffened and set in a three-dimensional, folded configuration. As the shades are raised and lowered, the folds open and close, the same way the folds in an accordion's bellows open and close when the instrument is played. A 24-inch-long shade of a thin material takes up only $2^{1}/_{4}$ inches stackup space when raised, measuring from the top of the headrail to the bottom of the bottom rail; a 96-inch-long shade takes up as little as $3^{3}/_{4}$ inches.

The textural characteristics of these shades vary readily with the style of yarn used; the compactness of construction and the selective application of backcoatings

control their transparency. Metallic coatings may be used for insulation, and also for static reduction, which reduces the attraction for dust. These window coverings are frequently used in commercial interiors, generally in combination with drapery panels.

Honeycomb or Cellular Shades

Another type of accordion-pleated shade is the **honeycomb or cellular shade** (Figure 16.15). In these commercially manufactured products, spunbonded polyester fabrics are permanently pleated and paired to create a single or double-cell structure with an insulating layer of air that significantly reduces heat transfer. The fabric facing outward is always white to provide high heat reflection and present a uniform exterior appearance. Because the pleats are smaller than those in conventional accordion-pleated shades, a 24-inch-long honeycomb shade requires only 2 inches of stackup space; a 96-inch-long shade requires only $3^{1}/_{2}$ inches. With appropriate hardware, these shades can be lowered from the top, raised from the bottom, or positioned anywhere within the window opening.

Roman Shades

Roman shades hang flat at the window until raised; when raised, horizontal pleats form. The pleats may be supported by wooden or other hard material inserts

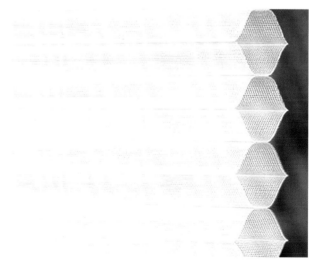

Figure 16.15 Duette® honeycomb shade. Duette® is a registered trademark of Hunter Douglas Inc.

(a)

to keep the pleats crisp (Figure 16.16a) or they may be made exclusively of fabric, which creates a soft, relaxed appearance (Figure 16.16b).

Roman shades can be, and are, constructed of nearly any material. For example, wood slats can be used as filling against a warp of yarns that vary in color, luster, size, and complexity. Fabric linings or coatings may be used to increase privacy with these blinds.

Some Roman shades are hand woven from grasses, cane, or wheat straws crosswise and textile yarns lengthwise. These shades are relatively transparent, but they nonetheless diminish the view into the interior and provide a natural look heightened by the irregularity of the materials and the hand weaving.

Commercially produced Roman shades are made of a wide variety of stiffened fabrics—from sheer to opaque—to achieve a crisp, architectural effect (Figure 16.17). A variation of the conventional Roman shade styling is the use of two shades, normally constructed of fabric. In these coverings, known as **athey shades**, one shade is lowered and one shade is raised for full closure.

Roller Shades

A **roller shade** may be plain or patterned, constructed of a fabric or a sheet of polymer film. It may mount at the bottom of the window and unroll upward or mount at the top of the window and unroll downward (Figure 16.18). Decorative hems and pulls, including rings, carved wood, molded plastic, and tassels, augment the visual interest of contemporary shades.

Figure 16.17 Vignette® shades. Vignette® is a registered trademark of Hunter Douglas Inc.

(b)

Figure 16.16 (a) Roman shade, (b) relaxed Roman shade.
Courtesy of Calico Corners, www.calicocorners.com

Figure 16.18 Roller shades. Courtesy of Amy Willbanks, www. textilefabric.com.

Figure 16.19 Solar shades made of 100 percent Ingeo Revolution fabric developed by M+N Projecten, in Delfgauw, the Netherlands. Image courtesy of NatureWorks LLC.

Blackout Shades

Because opening in vertical and horizontal blinds and shutters can produce a glare, **blackout shades** are available in materials that can create a totally dark room. Shade systems that track the sun are integrated with building management systems so that the shades open and close depending on the location of the sun. This allows for centralized control of window treatments and facilitates the integration of electrical light sources and dimming controls.[1]

Solar Shades

Solar shades, or **screen shades**, are shades of synthetic mesh fabric that filter light while allowing a view out (Figure 16.19). The degree of openness of the mesh determines the percentage of light filtration. They provide attractive sustainable features by protecting against the heat of the sun and also against unwanted brightness and glare. The benefits of lighting and a view of the outdoors can be enjoyed without the ill effects of harsh sunlight.

Solar shade manufacturers provide information on UV transmission, solar and visible transmittance, and shading coefficient. Manufacturers express these as percentages. **Solar transmittance** and **visible transmittance** are the amount of solar energy and visible light, respectively, that passes through a solar shade. Lower visible transmittance percentages indicate that the material is better for glare control. Higher percentages designate that the material will emit more natural light.[2]

Ultraviolet transmittance refers to the quantity of UV rays that penetrate a material. The UV transmittance is associated with a material's *openness factor*, or the percentage of material area that is open.[3] When a sheer fabric has an openness factor of 10 percent, the UV blockage is 90 percent. **Shading coefficient (SC)** indicates the amount of heat gain generated by the sun that passes through the glass and window treatments. The lower the SC rating of a solar shade, the less the heat gain in that particular space.

The various characteristics of materials that provides the optimum light and thermal condition are important for each space. A north-facing window treatment might include a solar shade with a high-visible transmittance. West-facing rooms might require a window treatment with a low-visible transmittance.[4]

Awnings and Shutters

Both interior and exterior awnings and shutters are constructed from either rigid materials or from a combination of rigid materials and drapable fabrics.

Awnings

Awnings are either rigid structures composed of metal or molded polymer sheeting, or are of fabric stretched and held over a rigid frame (Figure 16.20). Awnings are

Figure 16.20 Retractable Sunbrella® awning. Sunbrella® photo provided by Glen Raven, Inc.

and interior heat loss in the winter. This current application of shutters is a revival of the practice in colonial homes of using folding shutters for protection from the elements.

Shutters are usually constructed of pine or oak, which is stained or painted the desired color. Stiles are shifted vertically to open and close the crosswise louvers in each rectangular section, and hinges permit the units to be folded and unfolded to control inward and outward vision, the level of light transmission, and heat gain and loss. Textile fabrics are sometimes used to soften the appearance of wooden shutters. Shirred fabric may be inserted in some sections, or used in lieu of the wooden louvers.

occasionally used for novel interior applications, but are usually exterior window treatments. Awnings on the exteriors of windows both reduce solar heat transmission and provide protection from weather elements.

Textile awning fabric may be used in outdoor applications other than window treatments. For example, privacy screens, windbreaks, and canopies over patios, gazebos, and carports are popular. Coated vinyl fabrics and woven fabrics of solution-dyed acrylic and olefin fibers are the most popular cloths for outdoor applications because of their resistance to sunlight, mildew, insects, water, wind, and atmospheric contaminants.

Shutters

Decorative, stationary **shutters** have long framed windows on the exteriors and interiors of buildings. Today, folding shutters are increasingly being mounted to unfold over the glass, reducing solar heat gain in the summer

Key Terms

accordion-pleated shade	nontraversing panel
athey shade	one-way draw draperies
Austrian shade	overdraperies
awning	overhead treatment
balloon shade	pinned-up panel
batons	pouf or bishop's sleeve
blackout shade	treatment
blinds	priscilla curtain
café curtain	roller shade
cantonnière	Roman shade
cascades	sash curtains
casement	screen shade
casing	shades
cellular shade	shading coefficient (SC)
continental rod	sheers
cornice	shutters
cottage or Cape Cod curtain	solar shade
curtain tender	solar transmittance
curtains	stackback space
draperies	stationary casement panel
draw curtains	swags
fabric panel	tie-back curtain
fabric weights	traversing panel
finials	trimmings
fullness	two-way draw draperies
headings	ultraviolet transmittance
held-back panel	(UV)
honeycomb shade	valance
jabots	Venetian blind
lambrequin	visible transmittance

Review Questions

1. What is the purpose of an athey shade?
2. What are important considerations for fabric selection when choosing ruffled curtain styles or using fabrics such as velvet in overdraperies?
3. Describe how overhead and side treatments can be used alone or in combinations.
4. Design a window treatment having multiple layers (e.g., overdraperies with separate lining and sheers, decorative rods and tie-backs, valance, and so on). Calculate the yardage required and its cost, together with the cost of the hardware. You may want to vary the styling features and fabrics used in two or three treatments and calculate the total cost of each.

5. What advantages are offered by honeycomb or cellular shades?
6. Discuss the purpose of solar shades.
7. What is the purpose of overhead treatments?

Notes

1. Susan M. Winchip. (2011). *Sustainability and the Built Environment*, 2nd edition. Fairchild Books. New York. p. 138.
2. *Ibid.*, p. 138.
3. *Ibid.*, p. 138.
4. *Ibid.*, p. 138.

17

Window Coverings and Linings

Although fabric materials have long held the lion's share of window coverings, the variety of options available to today's residential and commercial consumers is almost limitless. The range of fibers, yarn types, weaves, and finishes varies greatly, as is the case in the upholstery market. Natural and synthetic fibers, in fine, simple, heavy, and coarse yarns—in both spun and filament forms—are all utilized. Almost every type of weave, pattern, and fabrication that has been discussed in earlier chapters is used for window covering—sometimes in lighter-weight versions than their upholstery counterparts. Additionally, since openness and transparency can be a desirable trait for curtains, some fabrics that would not be appropriate for upholstery are produced especially for window coverings.

Curtains, which are usually unlined, are often made of sheer, lightweight, or crisp fabrics. **Draperies** are usually of heavier fabrics and are typically lined. Because draperies are used for blocking out light, noise, cold, and heat, and also for privacy, linings are available in many types, including those that are permanently attached to the outer material. Both attached and unattached linings also help to protect the decorative drapery panels from sunlight and degradation.

Window Covering Fibers and Yarns

Fiber composition is no longer the distinguishing characteristic for particular furnishing fabrics—a taffeta was traditionally a silk fabric, but today taffeta may be woven of silk, polyester, or another fine synthetic, for example. Nonetheless, knowing the fiber content and considering care instructions, both of which are readily available in consumer labeling, can help users select appropriate solutions for their interior and exterior window treatments.

Both synthetics and natural fibers hold large market shares in curtain and drapery fabrics. For example, the majority of outer drapery and drapery linings in the decorative market are cotton. Most window covering fabrics in commercial interiors are composed of polyester in order to meet flammability codes. Polyester is also popular in mass-market residential window coverings, alone or in blends, because it is less expensive than cotton, and it is considered easy to care for. It can be machine-washed at home in many cases.

Solution-dyed acrylic and olefin are used for applications that require high sunlight and moisture resistance, just as they are in comparable upholstery settings. Acetate lacks aesthetic appeal, but it is an excellent fine warp yarn in drapery fabrics in which the warp is largely hidden and a fancy filling yarn is showcased.

Rayon is generally inappropriate for warp yarn in drapery (and other vertical) fabrics because it stretches dramatically, and yet rayon is attractive as a novelty filling-yarn fiber. High-quality rayon slub or other fancy filling effects can look almost like silk.

Wool's market share in curtain and drapery fabrics is small, but in spite of its high cost, wool challis is beloved for upscale residential and commercial applications, as are wool casements, due to wool's soft hand and luxurious drapability. The inherent flame resistance of the fiber will usually pass drapery flame codes for private offices without additional treatment.

In recent years, linen has captured a large share of both high-end and mass-market residential window coverings because rougher, casual surfaces are popular. Linen's poor recovery and stiffness mean that it wrinkles, but this is not a negative attribute to all users (Figure 17.1).

Glass fiber was once ubiquitous in commercial curtains and draperies in spite of its stiffness and poor drapability because it is noncombustible. However, its negatives are serious—when the material is cut or washed, fine glass fibers come into contact with fabricators and end-users, which causes sometimes extreme skin irritation. Polyester began to overtake the glass fiber curtain market many decades ago, and has made glass fiber obsolete in curtains.

Figure 17.1 Linen. Photo courtesy of Max Concra.

The yarn types used in curtains, draperies, and other window coverings are as varied as the fiber choices. Generally speaking, natural fibers (and rayon) for this market are processed into spun yarns, while synthetics are most often plied, texturized, filament yarns. Some spun synthetics are also utilized.

Window shades and blinds are made from wood, metal, and polymers, and also from many natural fibers, including some that are not strong or flexible enough to be appropriate for yard goods. Reeds, jute, hemp, flax, and grasses produce a soft, natural look that is popular for contemporary or traditional spaces.

Figure 17.2 Sheers. Courtesy of Chella Textiles.

Woven Window Covering Fabrics

Decorative Fabrics

Any fabric that has been discussed in this book can be used as drapery fabric. Printed fabric, velvet, and woven fabrics of all sorts, from dobby to brocade, tapestry, brocatelle, matelassé, and lampas, have all been used as window coverings for centuries. This chapter focuses on fabrics that are specifically developed for, or are primarily used for, window coverings.

As with upholstery fabrics, the direction that window covering fabric is cut is critical. All panels must be used in the same direction, and pile fabrics and satin weaves must be used in the direction as they come off the bolt, and not railroaded, even for small sections such as valances. Pile should run down. Extra-strong rods and additional brackets may be required to support the panels constructed when using heavy fabrics.

General window covering categories are **sheers** (Figure 17.2), diaphanous fabrics of fine yarns that are used alone or under the drapery; **casements**, which feature a degree of openness and may be woven or knit; and opaque or semi-opaque fabrics that are simply called *drapery fabrics*, or the outer fabric.

Plains and Sheers

Taffeta, traditionally woven of fine, high-twist silk in a balanced plain weave, has a crisp, stiff, rustling hand and is opaque. Synthetic taffetas that simulate silk are

popular, especially in commercial projects where fire codes must be met.

Shantung and **dupioni** (Figure 17.3) are plain weave, crisp silk fabrics, produced by using a fine warp yarn and uneven filling reeled from two or more entangled cocoons in the weft. The fabric appears to have an uneven ribbed surface in the crosswise direction, although it is a plain weave. Dupioni usually refers to a finer cloth, while shantung is heavier.

Batiste, voile, and organdy are very similar. All are plain-weave, translucent or semi-translucent fabrics that are usually marketed in solid colors. They may be printed or offered in yarn-dyed effects. They are most often simply referred to as sheers.

Batiste (Figure 17.4) was traditionally composed of fine, combed cotton yarns to yield a soft hand, which was perfect for handkerchiefs and lingerie. It is also used for drapery linings. **Challis** is very similar to batiste, but has a different hand and bounce since it is made of wool.

Voile is woven of highly twisted yarns composed of cotton or a blend of cotton and polyester fibers (Figure 17.5). Its crisp hand lends it to use in ruffled curtains and other styles that require body. Voile is a popular base fabric for **flocked dotted Swiss**. A parchment-like hand characterizes **organdy**; originally produced as an all-cotton fabric that had undergone a multi-step chemical process to create its finish, today it is usually made of nylon or polyester monofilament.

In **dimity**, a warp-rib woven, sheer fabric used for curtains, a lengthwise rib effect may be produced by

Figure 17.3 Dupioni. Photo courtesy of Max Concra.

Figure 17.4 Batiste. Courtesy of Amy Willbanks, www.textilefabric. com.

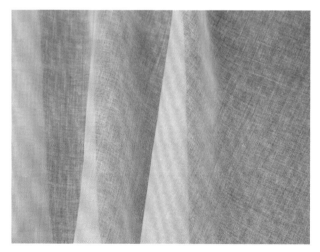

Figure 17.5 Voile. Courtesy of Amy Willbanks, www.textilefabric.com.

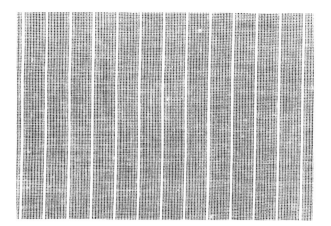

Figure 17.6 Dimity. Courtesy of Amy Willbanks, www.textilefabric. com.

periodically placing one large warp among fine yarns, or, as shown in Figure 17.6, by periodically placing a group of warp yarns among fine yarns. Fine, combed cotton yarns produce a smooth surface; they are generally mercerized to increase luster and fiber strength. The degree of fabric openness is similar to that of organdy and voile.

Sheer Variations

Brocade weaving effects add surface figures to sheers, frequently voile. As explained in Chapter 7, in these fabrics, extra yarns are woven into the base fabric to create decorative motifs, figures, or dots. Between the motifs, the extra yarns are floated on the back of the fabric.

When brocade base fabric is sheer, supplementary filling yarns that float between motifs are obvious from the face, so they are normally clipped between motifs. The result is a **clipped-dot** or **-spot** fabric. (The technique is called *discontinuous brocade*.) The floating yarns may be left **unclipped** in opaque fabrics (which is called *continuous brocade*). Either side of a clipped-dot or -spot fabric can be used as the face side (Figure 17.7).

Dotted Swiss (Figure 17.8) is a spot-woven curtain fabric, although **flocking** is often used to simulate the effect, which is popular with sheer fabrics. In flocking, a fine powder of loose fiber is attached to the base cloth with adhesive or by mechanical processes to create motifs (Figure 17.9). Any pattern can be created; the opaque, flocked motifs form an interesting contrast with the unflocked sheer areas.

Figure 17.7 Brocade sheer. Courtesy of Judy Juracek.

Figure 17.9 Flock-printed sheer. Courtesy of Amy Willbanks, www. textilefabric.com.

Flocking, **burn-out** techniques, and **pigment print** on sheer grounds all feature different levels of transparency in the same fabric to produce sheer-opaque, positive-negative patterns for drapery and curtains. In burn out, acid is used to burn away the acid-degradable fibers (frequently, rayon). Only the acid-resistant fiber (often polyester) remains in the highly transparent areas of the fabric (Figure 17.10).

Opaque Fabrics

Chintz (Figure 17.11) is a dense, opaque, plain-weave cotton fabric popular for upholstery and, in a slightly lighter weight, for window coverings. Chintz's glazed finish adds body and high surface luster. Most chintz fabrics feature medium- to large-scaled, colorful, printed designs, but some are solid colored.

Figure 17.8 Clipped dotted Swiss. Swatch 78 from *Swatch Reference Guide for Interior Design Fabrics* by Deborah E. Young, published by Fairchild Books.

Figure 17.10 Burn-out. Swatch 132 from *Swatch Reference Guide for Interior Design Fabrics* by Deborah E. Young, published by Fairchild Books.

Figure 17.11 Chintz. Courtesy of Amy Willbanks, www.textilefabric. com.

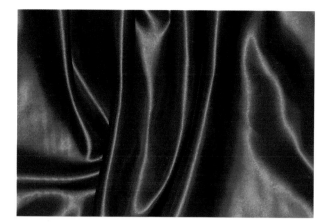

Figure 17.12 Satin. Courtesy of Amy Willbanks, www.textilefabric.com.

Figure 17.13 Antique satin. Courtesy of Fabricut Inc.

Satin weaves produce opaque, highly drapable, lustrous drapery fabrics (Figure 17.12) that are ideal for swags, jabots, and cascades (see Figure 16.6). Both satin- and sateen-woven fabrics are also often used in drapery lining fabric. (Note that fabrics of cotton warp in a satin weave are, as a term-of-art in the drapery market, referred to as **warp sateen**.)

Antique satin (Figure 17.13) has simple warp yarns and novelty or slub filling yarns. The slub yarns float over the face of the fabric in a sateen weave. The warp is often of polyester (or, in years gone by, acetate) and hardly shows on the fabric's surface. The filling-effect yarns may be cotton, rayon, or almost any fiber.

Faille, repp, ottoman, and other warp-faced rib fabrics are popular for window coverings, but of note, **faille**'s smooth warp yarns and rib texture lend itself to a moiré finish, which at times is a popular effect for drapery. Traditionally a silk-warp fabric, simply rolling two faille fabrics together, face-to-face, produces the distinctive **moiré** wood-grain or water-marked patterning (Figure 17.14). True moiré is not a permanent finish, and therefore not appropriate for upholstery. Embossing and heat setting a synthetic base fabric with a moiré pattern simulates the effect, however, and is permanent.

Duck (also known as **canvas**) and osnaburg are fabrics of a heavier, rougher appearance than those discussed above. Duck is often made from strong, two-ply yarns,

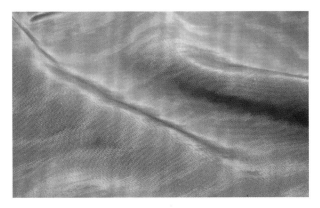

Figure 17.14 **Moiré.** Photo courtesy of Max Concra.

Figure 17.15 **Osnaburg.** Courtesy of Amy Willbanks, www.textilefabric.com.

Figure 17.16 **Privacy (cubicle) curtains.** Courtesy of Momentum Group.

is used for exterior awning treatments, and is usually fabricated of solution-dyed acrylic or olefin fibers for high UV and moisture resistance.

Osnaburg is composed of coarse, unbleached cotton yarns in which bits of dark-colored fibers have not been removed. Similar to muslin or burlap, Osnaburg was originally produced as sacks for grain and cement. Some say it was the fabric used for covered wagons in settling western North America; still in use for casual curtains, its unrefined look is apparent in Figure 17.15. This cloth is used as backing for most Type II vinyl wallcoverings.

Privacy Curtains

Privacy curtains, also called **cubicle curtains**, are a unique category of window covering, and are most commonly used to create visual privacy between individual patient areas in multi-bed healthcare facilities. Most are Jacquard-woven of flame-resistant polyester, and are sturdy fabrics that receive much abuse. Not only do hospitals wash these curtains to 160°F (in order to kill staph germs), but when installed, the curtains are vigorously pulled and tugged by patients and medical personnel alike. They are usually woven 72 inches wide—a throwback—because they were originally railroaded so that no seams were needed. Currently, few are railroaded, but the 72-inch width remains. Privacy curtains are suspended from the ceiling in track systems, with a knit mesh topper attached to the curtain so that, in case of fire, water from sprinklers can reach the entire room and not be blocked by the curtains (Figure 17.16).

Open Weaves, Knits, Knotted Fabrics, and Nonwovens

Gauze has a slightly higher fabric count than cheesecloth; stiffening agents are used to impart body. The semi-transparent fabric may be dyed and used for traversing curtain panels in residential and commercial interiors. **Monk's cloth** (Figure 17.17) is usually produced in a 4 × 4 or a 2 × 2 basket weave of yarns that simulate those traditionally used for monk's robes. The fabric is generally bleached and occasionally dyed and is characterized by a heavy but slightly open weave.

Because the crossed warp yarns of **leno**-woven fabrics effectively lock the filling yarns into position and minimize yarn slippage, leno weave is particularly

Figure 17.17 Monk's cloth. Swatch 46 from *Swatch Reference Guide for Interior Design Fabrics* by Deborah E. Young, published by Fairchild Books.

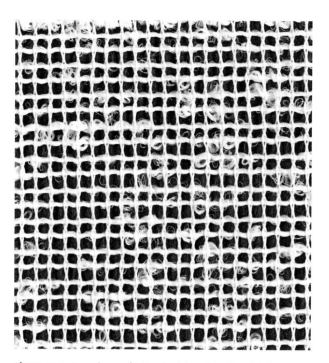

Figure 17.18 Leno/marquisette. Swatch 90 from *Swatch Reference Guide for Interior Design Fabrics* by Deborah E. Young, published by Fairchild Books.

useful for creating open-weave, stable window covering fabrics such as **marquisette. Mosquito netting** is also transparent but compactly constructed; it is used as a curtain-like bed canopy in tropical climates, forming a barrier against mosquitoes. Novelty yarns, such as the seed yarn in Figure 17.18 and contrasting monofilaments and plied yarns, add visual interest to leno casements.

Knitting is ideal for producing stable fabrics with specific levels of openness. It is a relatively fast and economical method of production, but the design flexibility can be limited. All of the knitting processes described in Chapter 8 are used to produce window covering fabrics; for example, **raschel** machines produce fabrics ranging from delicate, lacy curtain structures to heavy, elaborately interlooped casements with high-dimensional stability, non-run performance, and design flexibility (Figure 17.19). Weft insertion and **stitch-knitting** are also used to fabricate inexpensive window coverings that allow control of the transparency and covering power.

Knotting and twisting operations produce lace and **net fabric** window coverings. Unless they are made of thermoplastic fibers that are properly heat set, panels of airy, delicate, and highly ornamental **lace fabric** are likely to sag (Figure 17.20).

Figure 17.19 Raschel knit. Swatch 109 from *Swatch Reference Guide for Interior Design Fabrics* by Deborah E. Young, published by Fairchild Books.

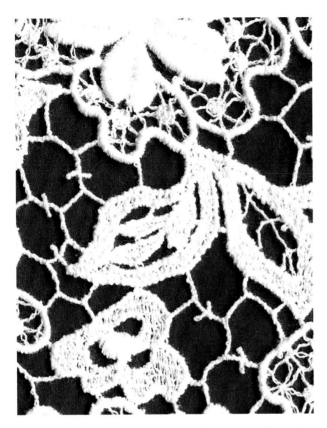

Figure 17.20 Lace. Swatch 118 from *Swatch Reference Guide for Interior Design Fabrics* by Deborah E. Young, published by Fairchild Books.

Figure 17.21 Embroidery. Courtesy of Threads at GP&J Baker.

The stitch-bonding and **spunlacing** techniques described in Chapter 8 enable manufacturers to produce fabrics inexpensively, directly from fibers. Spunlaced fabrics, for example, produce open, airy constructions for such a low price that they are routinely treated as disposable in facilities where maintenance expenses are critical.

Surface Embellishments

As discussed in Chapter 10, embellishments such as embroidery (Figure 17.21), appliqué, and even quilting are used in window coverings. Embroidered fabrics for curtains feature a range of stitches, including chain-stitched, lace-like designs. Frequently, mirror-image panels with finished edges are produced from such fabrics as batiste and organdy, although heavy cottons, linens, and even Jacquards are embellished with embroidery.

Eyelet (Figure 17.22) is produced with an embroidery machine used to stitch around holes created in the greige

Figure 17.22 Eyelet. Swatch 116 from *Swatch Reference Guide for Interior Design Fabrics* by Deborah E. Young, published by Fairchild Books.

goods. Formerly, destroying cotton fibers with sulfuric acid produced these holes; today, knives are used. Scalloped edges with eyelet-stitched details are often a decorative feature for single-tier curtain treatments.

Hard Window Covering Materials

Nontextile (hard material) window coverings include wood, metal, and solid synthetic polymer options. The slats of Roman shades, traditional Venetian and vertical blinds, and shutters are usually made of pine or oak. The wood is first kiln dried to minimize the potential for cracking and splitting; it is then sanded and stained or painted. Venetian blinds with slats of enamel-coated aluminum or molded polymer compounds became popular in the mid-twentieth century, and are available in a blinding array of fashion colors.

Metal, glass, and plastic beads are occasionally strung into chains and hung vertically as panel-like treatments. Metals, generally aluminum, are also frequently used for exterior shutters, awnings, and canopies. Polymer compounds, such as polyvinyl chloride (PVC), are extruded as film sheeting for use in manufacturing conventional roller shades.

Drapery Lining Materials

Lining Fabrics

Lining fabrics may be sewn into draperies or hung as separate panels. Virtually all of these fabrics have a plain, satin, or sateen weave, but a variety of surface appearance features and functional properties vary.

Plain-Woven Lining Fabrics

A great deal of lining fabric is produced from simple plain-weave fabrics. The greige goods are then finished in various operations, the first of which is bleaching. Silicone compounds may be applied for water-repellent performance. The silicone slows the rate of moisture absorption, minimizing the wetting of the fabric from moisture condensed on panes and frames and from rain that blows in when windows are inadvertently left open.

Silicone may also help to minimize the staining and streaking that can occur when moisture combines with smoke and oily cooking residues that have settled on the fabric; more effective protection against soiling and staining can be provided, however, by fluorocarbon compounds. Treatments may be added to encourage relaxation

shrinkage; chemical cross-linking resins may be used to improve appearance retention. Greige lining fabrics finished with some or all of these conversion processes are often marketed with a registered trade name.

Sateen-Woven and Satin-Woven Lining Fabric

Sateen weave drapery linings are popular because the fabric has an appropriate weight and drape for most face materials. Sateen linings are composed of fine, combed cotton yarns, bleached to whiteness or piece dyed, and calendered to enhance the cloth's soft luster.

Interlining

Interlining is sandwiched between two fabrics of the window treatment, either between the face fabric and the lining or between two layers of face fabric. Cotton flannel interlining provides additional thermal and acoustical properties as well as fullness to the treatment, for example.

Permanently Attached Lining Materials

Coatings and film sheetings may be permanently attached to the back of drapery fabrics. These self-lined drapery fabrics display specific functional attributes. The application of foamed acrylic compounds to the back of drapery fabric to increase its **insulative value** was introduced in Chapter 10. The air-filled cells of these coatings retard heat loss by convection as the compound restricts the flow of air through the yarn and fabric interstices. The insulative value of window treatments using these fabrics largely depends, however, on how tightly the panels are mounted (see Chapter 16). Acrylic polymers, which have high resistance to sunlight, provide the added benefit of slowing the fabric's rate of fiber and color degradation from sunlight.

The quantity of light transmitted through a window covering fabric is inversely related to its **opacity** or **level of openness**—obviously, increasing the opacity of the structure decreases the **level of light transmission**. In certain interiors, such as hospitals and similar facilities, coverings may need to be nearly opaque to block as many incident rays as possible and provide **partial blackout**. In other interiors, such as rooms used for viewing films,

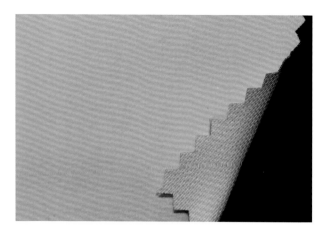

Figure 17.23 Blackout drapery lining. Courtesy of Amy Willbanks, www.textilefabric.com.

the coverings must be fully closed or fully opaque, blocking all incident rays and providing **total blackout** (Figure 17.23).

Coatings and film sheetings can increase the opacity of greige drapery fabrics. For total blackout, layers of acrylic foam coating may be spread over the surface or vinyl film sheeting may be bonded to a base fabric. The vinyl component is frequently colored for aesthetic appeal. In many motel and hotel rooms, especially those operated by national chains, these multicomponent structures are the only window covering, functioning as both covering and lining and providing the necessary privacy and blackout.

Key Terms

antique satin	dotted Swiss
batiste	draperies
burn-out	duck or canvas
casement	dupioni
challis	eyelet
chintz	faille
clipped-dot or -spot fabric	flocking
cubicle curtain	flocked dotted Swiss
curtains	gauze
dimity	insulative value

interlining	pigment print
knitting	privacy curtains
lace fabric	raschel stitching
leno	satin
level of light transmission	shantung
level of openness	sheers
marquisette	spunlacing
moiré	stitch-knitting
monk's cloth	taffeta
mosquito netting	total blackout
net fabric	twisting
opacity	unclipped-dot or -spot
organdy	fabric
osnaburg	voile
partial blackout	warp sateen

Review Questions

1. What properties support the growing dominance of polyester and other synthetic fibers in the curtain and drapery markets?
2. What are examples of knitted window covering fabrics?
3. What is interlining and why is it used?
4. Name some nontextile materials used in window coverings.
5. When should the floats be cut in dot or spot fabrics? When should they be left uncut?
6. Name two ways to manufacture dotted Swiss. Which one is the least expensive technique? Which one is the most expensive? Which one is considered a true dotted Swiss?
7. What advantages does raschel stitching offer?
8. Explain the role of the filling or weft yarns in fabrics produced with weft insertion.
9. Identify the advantages of foamed acrylic compounds applied to the back of drapery fabric.
10. Differentiate between total blackout and partial blackout and describe when either might be used.
11. Identify finishes commonly used with textile linings.

18

Wallcovering and Panel Fabric

Interior walls provide a large canvas that designers can use to create visual and tactile interest. Fabrics are often chosen to cover walls, panels, and partitions not only because they add aesthetic interest, but also because they absorb sound and define work (and living) areas. Almost every fiber and a large variety of fabrications are used in vertical applications. The wide assortment of wallcoverings, which differ in color styling, textural features, tactile characteristics, construction, and weight, offer designers and consumers multiple choices with which to achieve any desired aesthetic.

Figure 18.1 Sound-absorbing vertical panels. Courtesy of DFB Sales.

Functional Attributes

Noise Reduction

Soft surfaces lower the noise level in an interior, which increases both comfort and productivity for the inhabitants. Current popular interior design trends favor hard surfaces, which have minimized sound-absorbing materials. Ceilings exposed to the rafters, hardwood floors, metal chairs with little or no cushioning, and painted walls all reflect sound waves and prolong duration of noise. This popular aesthetic combines with the desire for ease of cleanability, for example, in restaurants and healthcare facilities, so that hard surfaces currently prevail. The convergence of these two trends has lead to an interest in alternative approaches that will add sound-softening features to rooms where hard surfaces prevail.

Textile-covered interior panels or partitions correctly placed throughout open areas may be wall mounted or suspended to baffle sound and interrupt the horizontal travel of sound waves (Figure 18.1); some of the sound generated within a room or area can be contained this way. Textile coverings on permanent walls can help reduce both the volume of waves reflected back into the interior and the volume transferred through the walls to adjoining rooms.

Although the acoustical benefits of wallcoverings can be analyzed through laboratory testing, the results are meaningless unless the specimen tested represents the exact fabric (backing, finish, etc.) and simulates the construction of the wall or partition, as well as the installation technique. Testing each combination may well be impractical. Additionally, acoustical materials will achieve different results depending on where they are placed within the interior.

Nonetheless, common sense and logic can prevail when precise test data is not available. Fabric mounted on concrete will reflect back more sound than the same fabric mounted on fiberfill-foam-padded drywall, for example. Likewise, a porous fabric will allow more sound waves to pass through to whatever is behind it than will a denser fabric with heavy backing.

In laboratory testing, the effectiveness of the coverings in reducing noise is numerically reported in terms of a **noise reduction coefficient (NRC)**; higher values indicate greater sound absorption. It is important to note that sometimes a fabric that reflects sound waves is the solution to creating a pleasing environment, while in other situations the users prefer that sound pass through the area. Generally speaking, if the goal is to add features to an interior that will absorb sound, additional soft furnishings—furniture, acoustical panels, or curtains—that are covered in fibrous, porous materials with cushioned backing are the first line of defense.

Wall Protection

Painted walls show marks, fingerprints, and marring at the slightest touch. Especially in busy, high-traffic commercial interiors, painted walls requires continuous maintenance to keep a facility looking sharp; frequent painting becomes both disruptive to the workings of the operations and expensive.

Any sort of fibrous covering absorbs some abuse, but Type II and Type III vinyls are especially popular because they are easy to clean, even with aggressive methods and cleansers (Figure 18.2). High-performance wovens are

Figure 18.2 Embossed vinyl wallcovering. Courtesy of Maharam.

preferred over vinyl because they are not easily gouged or marred. Like vinyl, they can also be aggressively cleaned, but retain more soiling than do coated fabrics, due to the inherent texture of woven fabrics. These fabrics are most often made from polypropylene, polyester, or a blend, and can be plain fabrics, dobby effects (as shown in Figure 18.3) or Jacquard-woven. Figure 18.4 illustrates a high-performance Jacquard-woven fabric installed and in detail.

(a)

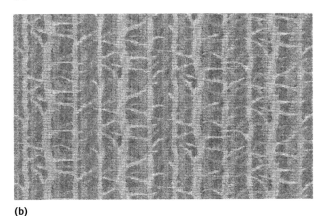

(b)

Figure 18.4 High-performance Jacquard-woven wallcovering: (a) installed, (b) detail. Courtesy of DFB Sales.

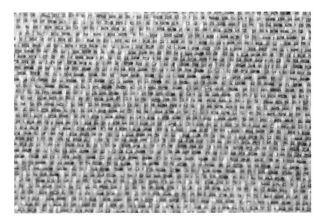

Figure 18.3 High-performance dobby wallcovering. Courtesy of Amy Willbanks, www.textilefabric.com.

Very durable fabrics with rough textures, especially those of bristly fibers, discourage occupants from touching the surface, and take abuse. For example heavy, rug-like jute or sisal fabrics are often used below wainscoting in elevators, cabs, and dorm rooms (Figure 18.5a and b).

(a)

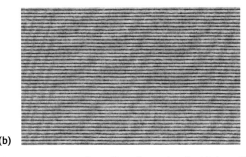

(b)

Figure 18.5 Heavy jute rib wallcovering for high-traffic areas such as elevators and dorm rooms: (a) installed, (b) detail.
(a) Courtesy of DFB Sales; (b) Courtesy of Tri-Kes.

Wallcovering Installation Methods

Wallcovering installation types are broadly broken into three categories: materials that are directly glued to a substrate, applications in which the fabric is upholstered on the wall, and fabrics that are applied to moveable systems that are commonly called panel, or office furniture, systems. These three types of application have many features in common, and several distinct differences.

Direct-Glue Installation

Since, as the name implies, **direct-glue** wallcoverings are attached directly to a wall or other substrate with an adhesive, the fabrics are usually either bonded to a heavy paper or other nonwoven (Figures 18.6 and 18.7), bonded to a lightweight woven or knit fabric, or they receive a heavy latex backing so that the adhesive does not come through to the front of the material (which is called **strikethrough**). Nearly every fiber has a presence in direct-glue wallcoverings, which are available in woven, knit, nonwoven, and coated fabric versions.

Fabric structures with a paper, acrylic, or foam backing may be handled in essentially the same manner that wallpaper is handled in the hanging procedure. With paper-backed textile structures, the adhesive is generally applied

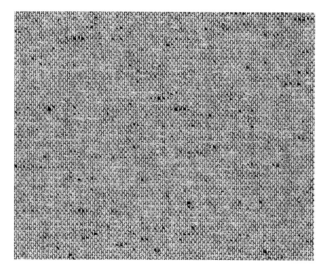

Figure 18.7 Paperbacked multi-fiber tweed. Courtesy of Lori Weitzner.

to the paper; with acrylic and foam-backed structures, the adhesive is generally applied to the wall. With vinyl wallcoverings, the adhesive is generally applied to the vinyl prior to installation. Some lightweight vinyl wallcoverings are prepasted, in which case the material is soaked in water for a few minutes to activate the adhesive.

Upholstered Walls

Unbacked or lightly backed fabric can be applied to walls to achieve a plush, padded appearance. If the wall surface is the edges of fabric may be stapled directly to the wall surface. More typically, lath strips are first nailed to the top, bottom, and sides of the wall and next to the framework of the doors and windows. The fabric is then stapled to the laths. Because the lath strips that support the fabric are a small distance from the wall surface, surface irregularities are concealed. In either of these installations, double welting, decorative tape, or braid is typically glued over the exposed edges to conceal the staples (Figure 18.8).

Polyester padding is typically installed between the fabric and the wall surface in **upholstered walls**. This helps to mitigate irregularities in the wall and also adds to the luxurious surface effect. (Use of traditional cotton padding is discouraged because it is highly flammable.) Upholstered walls are primarily used residentially. The craftsmanship and labor involved, along with commercial fire codes, make them contraindicated for most contract interiors.

Figure 18.6 Polyester fabric over paper ground with metal studs. Courtesy of Lori Weitzner.

Figure 18.8 Tape used as edging on an upholstered wall.
Courtesy Samuel & Sons, Inc.

Upholstered Wall Systems

For commercial installations, specialized **wall systems** use tension and support to create an upholstered-wall-like appearance (Figures 18.9 and 18.10). The fabric may be held in wall-mounted channels by locking clips or loop-and-hook fasteners. A polyester batting is placed within the mounting frame to increase acoustical features. It is possible to cover the entire wall surface in this manner; a variety of edge styles are available with clip-edge styles, and the fabric can be removed and replaced without removing the wall-mounted channels.

In the loop-and-hook style of installation, the wallcovering is backed with a soft fabric covered with tiny loops, while the mounting strips have tiny hooks on their surfaces. Contact between the loops and hooks secures the fabric to the wall, and the raw edges are tucked into channels in the strips. Sewn seams are avoided by tucking the fabric edges into parallel panels built into double strips. Individual fabric-wrapped acoustical panels can be attached to the wall or ceiling surfaces using glue or metal cleats. The edges are fabric-wrapped because they are visible. Again, various edge styles are available.

As with traditional upholstered walls, fabric for wall systems may be unbacked or lightly back, depending on the fabric and the system manufacturer's requirements. Since these systems are primarily specified in commercial interiors, fire codes apply.

Panel Fabrics

Moveable walls in office environments are called *panels*, or *office systems furniture* (Figure 18.11). Fabric coverings for these furniture items are a special category. **Panel fabrics** are usually unbacked, and in addition to passing fire and building codes, must meet requirements established by the specific furniture manufacturer, which needs to predetermine that the material can be smoothly handled in its specific upholstering process.

Because many panel systems are electrified, the fabrics may need to be tested for flammability as a composite of the system itself, which the furniture manufacturer must initiate and handle. Panel fabrics are almost all 100 percent polyester because it usually passes the required flammability tests and is dimensionally stable in the weight and density required. Panel fabrics are commonly woven at a 66-inch width because, when originally

Figure 18.9 Fabric panels mounted on entire hall. Courtesy of DFB Sales.

Figure 18.10 Fabric panels of contrasting colors create a striking pattern in an upholstered-wall system application. Courtesy of DFB Sales.

Figure 18.11 Office system workstation with fabric-covered panels. Courtesy of Cube Solutions®, www.cubesolutions.com.

marketed, nearly all panels were 5 feet high, so the fabric could easily be railroaded for minimal waste. Currently, panels can be nearly any size, and the fabrics are often upholstered "as woven" (rather than railroaded) but most are still woven at 66-inch widths.

Note that although workers may consider their work space a "cubicle," panel fabrics are not referred to as "cubicle fabrics." Cubicle fabrics (or privacy curtains) are the fabrics used to create privacy between patients in multibed healthcare facilities.

Component Materials and Constructions

Because residential and light commercial textile wallcoverings are primarily expected to provide visual and tactile interest, and are subjected to few stresses in use, they are fabricated with a wide variety of components and construction techniques. Furthermore, inherent properties of fibers are relatively unimportant for many direct-glue wallcoverings because virtually all of these fabrics are backed for dimensional stability and easy installation. Nonetheless, in some contract interiors, specific performance features as well as flammability and cleanability attributes are required.

Fibers and Yarns

Eye-catching reflections appear in wallcoverings that incorporate a mix of juxtaposed fibers—bright manufactured fibers, silk, metal filaments, and metallic yarns. In some coverings, spiral yarns containing metallic strands are plied with simple yarns that are strategically positioned to create reflective highlights as viewers pass the wall.

Natural fibers, including wool, silk, flax, jute, sisal, hemp, cotton, and even thin strips of paper are extensively and effectively used in wallcovering fabrics. The inherent surface irregularities of natural fibers produce distinctive warm and rich textural characteristics. Nonetheless, synthetic wovens (such as polypropylene and polyester) can closely approximate the appearance of natural fibers and offer additional performance features that are required in many environments.

Polyester is the preferred fiber for panel fabrics. Rayon is a popular fiber for direct-glue wallcovering fabrics, especially in blends. Its lustrous character is appealing, and the backings used for direct-glue wallcoverings stabilize the material. Unbacked fabrics of rayon are generally not appropriate for unadhered vertical applications such as upholstered walls, panel fabric, and drapery because of rayon's poor dimensional stability and because it is highly flammable.

Fabrications

Because wallcoverings and panel fabrics are not subjected to significant levels of abrasion or repeated flexing, a great variety of structures, materials, and constructions are appropriate. The assortment of coverings offered to contemporary consumers includes a number of distinctively constructed fabrics (Figures 18.12 and 18.13), as well as fabrics produced by conventional fabric-making procedures (Figure 18.14) and fabrication techniques unique to wallcovering application.

Fabric wallcoverings for contract interiors are constructed to provide the surface durability and serviceability that are essential in high-use areas. Commercial products must also meet sustainability, indoor air quality, antimicrobial, and flammability guidelines and codes.

Wovens

Flat-woven wallcovering fabrics range from simple interlacing patterns to decorative dobby and Jacquard weaves (Figure 18.15). Woven pile fabrics such as corduroy and velvet are also used on vertical surfaces. Dense, flat weaves with heavy, horizontal ribs can be extremely

Figure 18.12 Woven maps. Courtesy of Lori Weitzner.

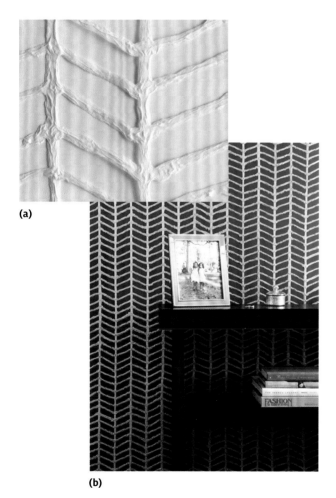

(a)

(b)

Figure 18.13 (a) Lines are drawn with natural pulp to create an open herringbone design. (b) Product installed on a painted wall. Courtesy of DBF Sales.

Figure 18.14 Simulated suede wallcovering (coated fabric). Courtesy of Maharam and Kvadrat.

Figure 18.15 Woven grasscloth. Courtesy of F. Schumacher and Co.

durable and appear almost as if they were pile fabrics (Figure 18.5). Conversely, some woven coverings intentionally feature a low compactness of construction so that the backings are visible. Such fabrics are often laminated to a contrasting-colored paper or nonwoven.

Grasscloth, a plain weave fabric with a fine, sparse warp utilizes filling yarn of native grasses (typically sea grass, arrowroot, jute, or hemp) and is then laminated onto a paper backing. Figure 18.16 shows a printed grasscloth. It is traditional and popular for low-traffic, residential interiors, although it is simulated in more durable synthetic versions. Grasscloth cannot be sidematched; its strong horizontal effect creates obvious seams, so that the overall effect is of vertical panels, which is part of the character of grasscloth installations.

High-performance woven fabrics are an important direct-glue category and are sometimes used in unadhered applications. These fabrics are made of polypropylene and other polymers, and are heat set to form a hard surface so that they are highly durable to marring and other surface wear. High-performance wovens are also washable, even with harsh cleansers.

Warp Laminates

Many other products are marketed as paper-backed wallcoverings—strings, or **warp laminate**s, are simply yarns lined up vertically, parallel, next to each other and laminated to a backing that is usually colored, or even printed (Figure 18.17). The appearance is that of a warp without filling. In these warp laminates, which are colloquially called *strings*, the parallel yarns may be closely or widely spaced, and the yarns may be fine or coarse, the same color or a stripe.

Coated Fabrics

The vast majority of direct-glue wallcoverings are vinyl. Lightweight **Type I vinyl** is used in residential or

Figure 18.16 Printed grasscloth. Courtesy of F. Schumacher and Co.

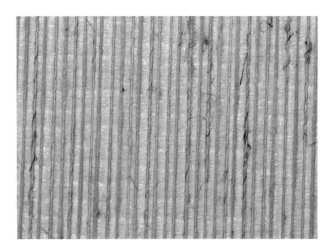

Figure 18.17 Warp laminate. Courtesy of Amy Willbanks, www.textilefabric.com.

light-commercial areas, while **Type II vinyl** (medium- to heavy-duty) is appropriate for high-traffic and public areas in commercial interiors. **Type III vinyl** is typically used in very high abuse areas, such as in healthcare corridors where carts are constantly bumping into the walls, or in back-of-the-house areas in hotels and restaurants.

Although it is considerably more expensive, polyurethane is a popular alternative to vinyl because of its softer look and hand. In many cases, coated fabrics are subsequently embossed to simulate the textural effects of woven fabrics.

Wallpaper

The design is printed directly onto a paper substrate to create *wallpaper*, which is popular and appropriate for residential use (Figure 18.18). A very lightweight vinyl is often used instead of paper so that the material can be more easily cleaned.

Acoustical Coverings

Tufted and needle-punched materials made of polyester and polypropylene resemble a low-pile carpet, but are lightweight and designed for vertical installation so as to reduce noise levels and handle heavy abuse within an interior. These fabrics are typically acrylic backed for direct-glue application. Figures 18.19a illustrates a typical vertical rib style installed; Figure 18.19b is a detail of the same fabric.

Figure 18.18 Wallpaper. Courtesy of Winfield Thybony.

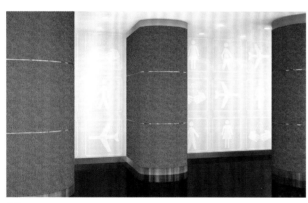

(a)

(b)

Figure 18.19 Acoustical needle-punched wallcovering: (a) installed, (b) detail. Courtesy of DBF Sales.

(a)

(b)

Figure 18.20 Acoustical needle-punched and embossed wallcovering: (a) installed, (b) detail. Courtesy of DBF Sales.

Figures 18.20a (installed in an elevator) and 18.20b (detail) show an acoustical fabric that has been embossed over the needle-punched vertical rib. Woven fabrics of various fiber contents, such as sisal and jute, function similarly, as described in Chapter 5.

Printing and Novelty Effects

Wood veneer and **cork veneer** are thin slices of natural materials that are laminated to paper or nonwoven backing. The possibilities offered by printing wallcoverings are almost limitless, from straightforward digital printing to novelty effects such as **flocking**, to application of fine glass beads or countless other materials. Both paper- and acrylic-backed fabrics are often embroidered (Figure 18.21).

Backings and Finishes

Various backings and finishing agents are used with wall and panel fabrics. Some of these serve both functional and aesthetic purposes.

Figure 18.21 Embroidered grasscloth. Courtesy of F. Schumacher and Co.

Backings

Acrylic foam, vinyl spray, paper, gypsum, or a spunlaced or spunbonded fabric must be applied to the back of most textile fabric coverings to prevent the application adhesive from soaking through and producing a stained appearance (**strikethrough**) and to provide dimensional stability. Spunbonded backings, normally composed of polypropylene fibers, are designed to be strippable, an attractive feature for end-users, since furnishings are inevitably replaced.

Vinyl and polyurethane wallcoverings require backing for dimensional stability. The three backings used with vinyl wallcoverings are scrim, osnaburg, and drill. Lightweight **scrim** backing is used for Type I wallcoverings. **Osnaburg**, a medium-weight woven, usually made of polyester and cotton, is used to back most Type II wallcoverings. **Drill**, a heavy-duty, tightly woven fabric backing, is suitable for Type III vinyl backing in high-traffic areas.

Unbacked vinyl prelaminated to 4 × 8 sheets of drywall (with cut vinyl edges that are usually wrapped under) are commonly used in the manufactured housing business and other lower-priced construction applications. These pre-fab sheets are adhered to studs as a finished product.

One of many specialized products on the market, **gypsum**, is a high-density, uncrystallized plaster, which is used to coat the back of open-weave burlap wallcovering. When applied, the compound is soft, permitting the coverings to be rolled for shipment. After contact with the special adhesive that secures the fabric to the wall, the coating crystallizes and sets into a hard backing. The compound, available in numerous colors, fills fabric interstices and hides any surface defects for a budget price.

Functional Finishes

To meet fire codes in commercial buildings, wallcovering and panel fabrics are sometimes treated with flame-retardant compounds during the manufacturing phase. It is also possible to have finished fabrics treated to increase flame retardancy. The design professional is advised that these treatments may change physical properties of the fabric such as colorfastness, strength, dimensional stability, and hand. Additionally, the fabric may give off noxious fumes.

As with upholstery fabrics, fluorocarbon compounds applied to fabric wallcoverings add soil repellency by reducing the fabric's affinity for staining and by increasing the ease of surface cleaning. As discussed in Chapter 10, the market is exerting growing pressure to eliminate added chemical treatments. Some cities and states have prohibited such chemicals from being sold in their jurisdictions.

Flammability Requirements

City, state, and federal agencies require that materials used inside certain occupancies conform to the requirements of the NFPA 101® Life Safety Code®. Material installed as a vertical interior finish must usually exhibit a Class A rating in accordance with the procedures outlined in ASTM E84. (Depending upon the type of occupancy and area of installation, a B or C rating is sometimes sufficient.) The test requirements for ASTM E84, also called the Steiner Tunnel Test, are described in Chapter 12. The material should be tested on the same substrate that will be used for its installation.

If a fabric is part of a fixture that is permanently attached to a wall or furniture, a "room corner" burn test may be required. (Acoustical panels that cannot be easily removed are an example.) This is a **large-scale test method** that is used for surface materials that, for some reason, cannot be tested on a small scale.

Energy Conservation

Heat transfer and air infiltration can be improved by installing fiber-based wallcoverings. As is true for acoustical evaluations and flammability testing, in order to accurately assess a material's attributes, evaluations must be conducted using the actual material in a mock-up that simulates the specific construction features of the substrate, structural walls, and techniques that will be used for the actual installation.

Facility managers and owners may require certain noise-reduction and insulation criteria. Specifiers must benchmark any testing against the client's requirements, just as local fire marshals are the final determinants as to whether all materials meet flammability regulations.

Key Terms

cork veneer
direct-glue
drill
flocking
grasscloth
gypsum
noise reduction coefficient
    (NRC)
osnaburg
panel fabric

scrim
strikethrough
Type I vinyl
Type II vinyl
Type III vinyl
upholstered wall
wall system
warp laminate
wood veneer

Review Questions

1. What are some positive attributes of fabric wallcoverings? Name at least two functional characteristics and two aesthetic features.
2. List the advantages of natural fibers for use in wallcoverings, and explain when they may present a problem.
3. What is the purpose of backings for fabrics to be used as wallcoverings? What are the main types of backings?
4. What are the three types of vinyl wallcoverings and when is each preferred?
5. What are the disadvantages of applying a flame-retardant finish to fabrics?
6. Discuss the three backings used on vinyl wallcoverings.
7. List three methods of installing textile wallcoverings.
8. What are high-performance wallcoverings?
9. Describe typical attributes of panel fabrics.
10. What pretesting is required for panel fabric application?

19

Evaluation and Maintenance of Furnishing Fabrics

The characteristics and quality of the components and the quality of the manufacturing processes used determine the appearance and serviceability of fabrics. Although quality finishing can sometimes improve the performance and enhance a fabric's visual features, it cannot compensate for inferior fibers and yarns, unstable structures or colorants, poor pattern registration, or shoddy fabrication. Since producing quality end products requires attention to detail at each step of manufacturing, fabric producers are highly interdependent.

Chapter 2 describes various protocols used to evaluate, test, and certify materials for the interior. Representatives from all segments of the industry cooperate in establishing and maintaining standards and guidelines for fabrics' performance. The **Association for Contract Textiles (ACT)** Performance Guidelines; ASTM D3597, Standard Performance Specification for Woven Upholstery Fabrics—Plain, Tufted or Flocked; ASTM D4771, Standard Performance Specification for Knitted Upholstery Fabrics for Indoor Furniture; and the Joint Industry Guidelines, developed by residential furniture and fabric manufacturers, are examples of such umbrella guidelines. Although ASTM D3691, Standard Performance Specification for Woven, Lace, and Knit Household Curtain and Drapery Fabrics, was withdrawn in 2018 because it had not been updated in accordance with ASTM requirements, it is a comparable composite protocol for window-covering fabrics and may still be used by some producers.

All of these composite standards address physical and colorfastness characteristics of fabric, and relate only to indoor furniture use. The ACT Guidelines are geared toward contract fabrics, while the others were developed for residential fabrics. All refer to ASTM International and American Association of Textile Chemists and Colorists (AATCC) fabric test procedures and expected results. Although each refers to different individual standards as a part of its total package, the objectives of each are very similar, much overlap exists, and all have influenced one another. However, for flammability performance, National Fire Protection Association (NFPA) standards, governmental regulations, and local building codes prevail.

Standards help assure both suppliers and end-users of clear expectations for and features of finished products.

Residential and commercial product and upholstered furniture manufacturers, interior designers, purchasing agents, and end-users (purchasers) communicate their specific fabric performance requirements to the fabric manufacturers and wholesalers, and so on, up the chain to finishers, dyers, and spinners.

Other than for flammability requirements, use of industry standards and guidelines is strictly voluntary; levels of performance are recommended, not required. However, manufacturers want customers to be happy, and do not want to have complaints about performance of their products or claims due to field failures. These standards identify properties that are usually considered when fabrics are developed and marketed, and they provide a basis for manufacturers to evaluate quality and predict end-use serviceability. Also, specifiers and purchasers within specific markets expect that fabrics suitable for their use will be marked as passing certain performance tests. (Code requirements pertaining to fabric flammability are discussed in Chapter 12. Note that appropriate fire code requirements must always be confirmed with the code compliance officials on a project.)

Members of the ACT established voluntary performance guidelines for fabric intended for contract applications, and the ACT Guidelines are the best known and most commonly used composite standards for interior furnishing fabrics. While the ASTM composite standards address specific and narrowly defined end-uses, ACT Guidelines address drapery, wallcovering, panel fabric, and both woven and coated-fabric upholstery. The **ACT symbols** (Chapter 11 and Appendix B) placed on fabrics make a designer or end-user's job easier by providing assurance that the fabrics have performed to the standards set by the industry. If a fabric carries the ACT icons, and comes from a reputable supplier, a specifier or purchaser can rest assured that the material is appropriate for its intended end-use, unless the intended end-use is out of the ordinary. Quality fabric from reliable suppliers in appropriate application, with quality fabricators, and cared for properly generally performs well. Suppliers can help with recommendations for any unusual end-uses, and are a wealth of information related to their products.

Understanding how each fabric performance test is run and how its results are measured is out of the purview of specifiers and end-users. Moreover, residential designers and end-users are not typically interested in the detailed technical data, since the suppliers vet material prior to its being marketed. Nonetheless, this chapter outlines some of these test procedures and objectives.

A weakness with comprehensive standards is that while individual standards are updated or withdrawn relatively often, the comprehensive standards are frequently routinely reapproved without updating the changes to the referenced standards, so that some of the test methods that are part of the standards may be out-of-date or no longer in use. The ACT Guidelines are the exception; the organization keeps the guidelines current and expands and reduces the qualifiers as the market shifts. For this reason among others, the ACT Guidelines are the most meaningful for the specifier or consumer marketplace; therefore, this chapter focuses on its component requirements. Figure 19.1 illustrates the ACT

Voluntary Performance Guidelines in their entirety, with disclaimers, restrictions for use, and qualifiers. Note that flammability standards, including the ACT flammability guidelines, are discussed in Chapter 12, and not in this chapter. The ACT website is the best source for current guidelines because it incorporates any recent updates (www.contracttextiles.org).

Evaluations of Physical Performance Properties

Structural Qualities

Two standards concern the structural qualities of finished fabric. One pertains to **yarn alignment** (bow and skew) and the other to **yarn distortion**. These flaws are usually evident with visual inspection or with instruments that identify defects. Computer-aided fabric evaluation (CAFE) systems increase the accuracy of the inspection and speed up the process of inspection.

Yarn Alignment

Figure 19.2 illustrates problems caused by the use of **off-grain fabrics** on furniture. The sofa pictured appears to be sagging when covered with a **bowed** fabric and crooked when covered with a **skewed** fabric. Bow and skew are most noticeable in linear patterns of yarns of contrasting colors (such as stripes and plaids). Fabrics with bow or skew flaws are equally disconcerting in drapery and wallcovering application.

In accordance with ASTM D3882 Standard Test Method for Bow and Skew in Woven and Knitted Fabrics, measurements of bow are taken at the maximum point of distortion in three widely spaced places along the length of fabric. The measurements of maximum distortion produced by skew are taken parallel to and along a selvedge. ASTM International performance specifications recommend that the average of the three bow measurements not exceed 0.5 inch, and the average of the three skew measurements not exceed 1.0 inch. This is the customary accepted tolerance in the interior fabrics market, although ACT is developing bow and skew guidelines, which may differ from the ASTM tolerances.

Figure 19.1 ACT Voluntary Performance Guidelines. Courtesy of the Association for Contract Textiles.

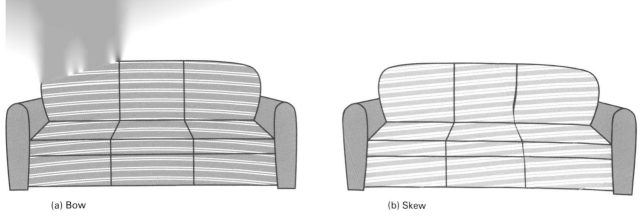

(a) Bow   (b) Skew

Figure 19.2 Effects of filling bow and skew on the appearance of upholstered furniture items. Fairchild Books.

Yarn Distortion and Seam Slippage

ASTM D1336, Standard Test Method for Distortion of Yarn in Woven Fabrics, is used as an indicator of the tendency of yarns to slip or distort, causing an unsightly appearance in woven fabrics (Figure 19.3) ASTM D1336 covers the measurement of yarn distortion in woven cloth following the application of surface friction. According to the performance specifications included in ASTM D3691, conventional weight woven upholstery coverings and draperies should exhibit a maximum distortion of 0.1 inch under a two-pound load. This test method is especially applicable to low yarn count upholstery and window-covering fabrics and satin-woven fabrics made of smooth filament yarns.

Since contract upholstery fabrics are densely constructed, ACT does not include a yarn distortion threshold in its voluntary guidelines, but includes ASTM D4034 (D434 for drapery), which measures seam slippage. **Seam slippage** is the movement of yarns in a fabric that occurs when it is pulled apart at a seam. Although

field failures are rare, seam slippage is one of the most common field failures, however, it is not usually the fault of the fabric itself. Rather, it is most often caused by a too-skimpy seam allowance or by seams with too few stitches per inch (Figure 19.4).

ASTM D4034 has been withdrawn by ASTM, pending additional evaluation; nonetheless, the ACT Guidelines rely upon it, and require a result measured as 25 pounds minimum in both warp and weft directions for upholstery fabrics and drapery fabrics that weigh over 6 ounces per square yard. The standards require 7 stitches per inch for upholstery and 14 per inch for drapery. Seam allowance should be 0.5 inch. The standards do not account for seam raveling, which varies from fabric to fabric. The standard is not appropriate for knits.

Pattern Distortion

As part of quality-control work, printers and weavers examine the uniformity in vertical repeat size variation. Upholstery fabrics exhibiting inconsistent color or pattern

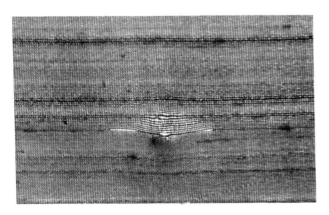

Figure 19.3 Yarn distortion. Courtesy of Amy Willbanks, www. textilefabrics.com.

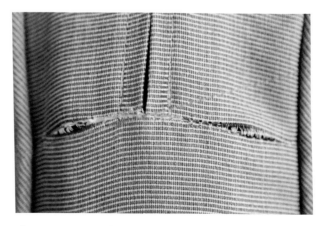

Figure 19.4 Seam slippage. Courtesy of Max Concra.

placements are unacceptable as first quality goods. If printing process speed or weaving picks-per-inch vary throughout a production run, or if a fabric is stretched in finishing, the vertical repeat size may vary along the length of the goods. In fact, some variation almost always occurs, but it should be within acceptable limits.

To evaluate the variation, the **pattern repeat** size is measured from the center point to center point of contiguous repeats, or from a dominant line or edge of motif to the same point in the next repeat. A minimum of four measurements should be taken in a continuous length of 50 yards. Current practice is that when pattern repeats are 13 inches or more in length, the variation should not exceed 0.5 inch; when pattern repeats are less than 13 inches in length, the variation should not exceed 0.25 inch. (ACT is working on recommendations for this variability, which may diverge from these.)

Tear Strength

Tear strength is the measurement of stress exerted to rip a fabric when it is under tension. The test results aim to predict the likelihood that a small cut or puncture would become a large tear with continued use of the specific fabric. With regard to coated fabrics, ACT Guidelines recommend ASTM D2261 Standard Test Method for Tearing Strength of Fabrics by the Tongue (Single Rip) Procedure (Constant-Rate-of-Extension Tensile Testing Machine) and ASTM D5733-99 Standard Test Method for Tearing Strength of Nonwoven Fabrics by the Trapezoid Procedure (although this standard was withdrawn in 2008).

Breaking Strength and Elongation

The **elongation** and **breaking strength** of upholstery fabrics can be determined in one testing procedure, ASTM D5034 Standard Test Method for Breaking Strength and Elongation of Textile Fabrics (Grab Test). Breaking strength is the measurement of stress exerted to pull a fabric apart under tension. While the comprehensive ASTM guidelines for elongation differ for different categories of fabrics, it specifies a minimum breaking force of 50 pounds for all fabrics, regardless of construction and weight. Most fabrics perform well under the standards.

ACT guidelines for contract upho... a minimum of 50 pounds of **breaking force** ... although for panel and upholstered wall fabrics 35 pounds is required. Breaking strength is not relevant for drapery or direct-glue wallcovering fabrics and is not recommended for knit fabrics because of their high stretch.

Bursting Strength

Because knit fabrics stretch, **bursting strength** rather than breaking strength is often a more relevant property. This may be measured using ASTM D6797 Standard Test Method for Bursting Strength of Fabrics Constant-Rate-of-Extension (CRE) Ball Burst Test.

Dimensional Stability

Fabrics must maintain their original dimensions after use, within reasonable limitations. With both permanently attached and removable furniture coverings, there should be no prolonged bagging and sagging of the fabric after a person rises from the seat. Neither should window-covering or panel fabric exhibit excessive **growth** in use. Cleaning a fabric should not cause shrinkage or stretching. Excessive **shrinkage** of fabric in use or cleaning causes distortion of the three-dimensional form of the cushions (because the fabric becomes smaller than the filling) and also places stress on the fabric seams and zipper closures, causing them to ripple, split, or develop seam slippage.

Upholstery Fabrics

ACT has chosen not to establish minimum requirements for the ability of a fabric to return to its original state because furniture construction (including foam density), fabrication quality, and environmental factors significantly impact the recovery performance of fabrics. The SAE J855 test can be used to evaluate "stretch and set" for coated fabrics. Furthermore, ISO 1419 Tropical Test Method is routinely run to evaluate polyurethane coated fabrics' hydrolysis resistance (ability to withstand exposure to extended periods of humidity). Humidity can cause polyurethane coated fabrics to delaminate, crack, peel, or puddle.

Window-Covering Fabrics

Dimensional stability is a critical performance property for window-covering fabrics. For example, in swag valances, priscilla curtains, and Austrian shades, sagging would destroy the balance of the laterally draping folds. In straight, free-hanging panels, sagging could cause the lower part of the fabric to stack on the floor. Sagging is more likely to occur in fabrics of loose construction or those made of low-twist yarns, and in fabrics composed of certain fibers (especially rayon, which is not recommended as a warp fiber for fabrics that are unadhered and installed vertically).

Shrinkage of the overdraperies in multiple-layer treatments exposes the lower edge of the curtains to the interior, and shrinkage of the lining panels exposes a portion of the overdraperies to the exterior. If the panels shrink, fabric transparency is reduced and the tight closure that maintains an insulating layer of dead air between the covering and the glass may be destroyed.

Finishers can use compressive shrinkage processes and heat-setting operations to stabilize curtain and drapery fabrics. Laboratory tests can be used to evaluate the effectiveness of these treatments. Specimens of the stabilized fabric are prepared. The specimens are laundered in accordance with AATCC 135 Dimensional Changes of Fabrics After Home Laundering, and then dry-cleaned in accordance with ASTM D2724 Test Methods for Bonded, Fused, and Laminated Apparel Fabrics.

Abrasion Resistance

Multiple factors affect fabric durability and appearance retention, including end-user application and proper maintenance, but, unfortunately, interior designers and architects have come to rely on a quantitative test result that theoretically predicts the level of **abrasion** to which the covering will be subjected in specific laboratory tests, which report relative yarn breakage as the penultimate predictor of an upholstery fabric's useful life. As has been discussed, this approach is badly misguided for several important reasons. (Fabrics for uses other than upholstery are not usually evaluated for abrasion resistance.)

First, surface abrasion, as measured in yarn breakage, is rarely a problem during the useful life of an upholstery fabric. ACT recently polled its members (all the major suppliers

to the contract market) and found that field failures due to poor abrasion were essentially nonexistent. In fact, the top several reasons for field failure had nothing to do with the inherent properties of the fabric, but were caused by external factors such as improper or lack of cleaning.

Second, the method most commonly used to theoretically measure abrasion is a highly unreliable test. Third, abrasion is only one of many types of wear that a fabric needs to endure. The goal of most users and suppliers alike is for the fabric to maintain its appearance for as long as possible. For example, if no thread breaks, but the fabric is very dirty, it will look like it is "worn out."

Although ACT guidelines certify to ASTM D4157 Standard Test Method for Abrasion Resistance of Textile Fabrics (Oscillatory Cylinder Method, referred to as the **Wyzenbeek Test Method**), the organization and most of its members equivocate the use of this method. Note ACT's disclaimer regarding Wyzenbeek test results in Figure 19.1. The Oscillatory Cylinder Abrasive Machine (Figure 19.5) used is described in the following section.

Test Specimens and Procedures

Test specimens are cut 2⅞ inches by 9⅝ inches. The long dimensions are cut parallel to the warp yarns to test warp-wise abrasion resistance and parallel to the filling yarns to test filling-wise abrasion resistance. The specimens are secured in the clamps of the apparatus after conditioning. The specimen supports are then lowered over the curved cylinder, which is covered with #10 cotton duck

Figure 19.5 Wyzenbeek machine used to evaluate abrasion resistance. Courtesy of Schap Specialty Machine, Inc.

as the abradant. (A specific quality of cotton duck, by an approved supplier, must be used.) The cylinder oscillates at the rate of 90 cycles (double rubs) per minute, effecting unidirectional rubbing action on the specimens.

Analysis of Results

At the end of 3,000 cycles (double rubs), the specimens are examined for loose threads and wear; slight discoloration from the abradant on light-colored fabrics is disregarded. If no noticeable change is apparent, the test is continued for another 5,000 cycles and the specimens are again examined. If no noticeable change is apparent, the test is continued for another 5,000 cycles or until the fabric ruptures.

Performance Guidelines

As noted in Figure 19.1, the ACT Guidelines recommend different levels of abrasion resistance for different end-uses. The ACT Guidelines, geared for the contract market, suggest that upholstery fabric that shows no noticeable wear at 15,000 is appropriate for low traffic and private spaces. No noticeable wear at 30,000 cycles is considered appropriate for typical contract interiors, that is, public spaces with high traffic. Other testing might be required to evaluate appropriateness of fabric for applications that receive an unusual amount of abuse, such as college dorms, 24-hour call centers, and law enforcement offices. Suppliers rarely offer abrasion-testing data for residential fabrics, but lower results than those for contract fabrics are common in fabrics that perform well for home use.

The ACT Guidelines also include abrasion resistance standards for fabric tested by ASTM D4966 Standard Test Method for Abrasion Resistance of Textile Fabrics (**Martindale Abrasion Test Method**). In this method, the fabric is mounted flat and abraded in a figure-eight fashion by a worsted wool fabric. (A Martindale tester is shown in Figure 19.6.) The ACT Guidelines recommend that general contract upholstery should withstand 20,000 rubs and heavy-duty upholstery should withstand 40,000 rubs before showing an objectionable change in appearance. Martindale testing is more widely used by European manufacturers than by American counterparts. Note: Martindale and Wyzenbeek results do *not* correlate. They represent different methodologies.

Figure 19.6 Martindale machine. Courtesy of SDL Atlas.

An important note: Wyzenbeek test results do not correlate to actual field performance, and are considered to be highly unreliable predictors of fabric life-span. Results do not offer valid comparisons between dissimilar fabrics. Repeatable results are often difficult to achieve. (ACT studies indicate that results of multiple abrasion tests performed on some woven fabric, even from the same bolt of cloth, may vary significantly—as much as 60 percent or more.) At times, the test method has come close to being removed from ASTM standards because it had not been updated per ASTM requirements. Furthermore, abrasion field failures are nearly nonexistent. When considered as a single attribute, abrasion resistance is not a meaningful barometer of a fabric's useful life, and abrasion testing methods do not correlate well with the variables encountered in actual use by the end-user.

Rather than abide by customary industry practice of meeting the ACT Guidelines, which are developed to assure customers that the fabric is suitable for contract use, some suppliers go for higher results, under the ill-conceived notion that the higher the Wyzenbeek number, the longer the fabric will last. This is unfortunate, as it confuses the end-users and discourages the development and marketing of many fabrics that are perfectly suitable. To mitigate some of the confusion, ACT requires licensees who use their performance certification marks and publish test results in excess of 100,000 double rubs to provide the following statement in their sampling, marketing materials, and on their company website: "Wyzenbeek results above 100,000 double rubs have not been shown to be a reliable indicator of increased fabric lifespan."

Resistance to Pilling

Small balls or pills on the surface of fabrics are unsightly, especially when fibers of contrasting colors are present. To assess the extent of **pilling**, ACT recommends that contract fabrics be subjected to the procedures in ASTM D3511, Standard Test Method for Pilling Resistance and Other Related Surface Changes of Textile Fabrics: Brush Pilling Tester, or ASTM D4970, Standard Test Method for Pilling Resistance and Other Related Surface Changes of Textile Fabrics: Martindale Tester. (A different test for pilling resistance is used for fabrics that will be machine-washed and dried.)

In both methods, the fabric specimens are rubbed according to the test procedures and then compared with visual standards, which may be actual fabrics or photographs of fabrics, that show a range of pilling resistance. The fabric is evaluated and categorized into classes according to the visual standards. The test apparatus for ASTM D3511 is shown in Figure 19.7. The ACT Guidelines suggest that upholstery fabric be rated a minimum of Class 3 for either test. (On a scale of 5 to 1, in which 5 is no pilling and 1 is very severe pilling.)

Spun synthetic fibers and soft natural fibers like cotton and cashmere are most likely to pill. Synthetics hold the pills, while natural materials tend to release them. These yarns and fibers, especially in heavy gauge or loose weaves, are best avoided in very high abuse areas or for users who find pilling particularly unsightly.

The rating system for the brush pilling test is very subjective. While both poor-performing fabrics and fabrics that perform excellently are easily identified, identifying the in-between fabrics is up to the discretion of the testers, which leads to inadequate differentiation.

ACT Symbols

Contract upholstery fabrics that meet or exceed the recommended performance levels in all the physical property categories of pilling resistance, breaking strength, and yarn distortion may be marketed with the ACT symbol that resembles a star. Depending upon the fabric's test results for abrasion testing it may be marketed with the ACT capital or small "A" (Figure 19.1). ACT's website explains specific requirements for use of the symbols.

Appearance Retention for Window Coverings

Textile window coverings are repeatedly folded and bent as panels are opened and closed. They also are folded, bent, twisted, and crushed during cleaning. To help curtain and drapery fabrics composed of cotton, linen, or rayon to recover from such treatment, finishers apply **durable press resins** to minimize the need for ironing.

AATCC has established recommended levels of performance for knit, lace, foam back, stitch bonded, and conventional-weight woven curtain and drapery fabrics with a durable-press finish. After specimens of the fabric have been laundered five times as directed in AATCC 124 Appearance of Fabrics After Repeated Home Laundering, their appearance is compared with that of AATCC Smoothness Appearance Replicas. Smoothness progressively increases from the first to the fifth replica; each specimen is assigned the number of the replica it most closely resembles. Backcoatings for window-covering fabrics should exhibit no evidence of cracking or peeling when the fabric is subjected to prescribed laundering and dry-cleaning tests.

Examination of Color Consistency and Retention

Color Consistency

Although manufacturers strive to produce exactly the same product with each lot, fabric is produced a few hundred

Figure 19.7 Brush pill tester Courtesy of SDL Atlas.

yards at a time, and some inconsistencies naturally occurs. A customer can order a cutting for approval (CFA) from the supplier in order to see the actual fabric that is in stock at the time. In that instance, the designer calls the supplier, puts on hold the yardage quantity to be ordered, and requests the CFA. The goal is for the CFA, or current stock, to work within the desired application even though it may not be exactly the same as the sample originally provided. If it is acceptable it is called a *commercial match*.

Color Retention

Colorfastness refers to the ability of colorants to retain their original properties when they are exposed to various environmental conditions, cleaning agents, and end-uses. Manufacturers specify to their dyers the standards that need to be met, test the yarns or dyestuffs before they weave or print with them, and discontinue the use of any that fail to exhibit acceptable levels of fastness. Residential consumers, contract designers, and architects should avoid sources that are likely to harm colorants. Sophisticated **electronic color meters** can be used to detect differences in the color characteristics of fabrics. Colors of a fabric should not vary within any single piece or roll, and streaks are unacceptable.

Pile fabrics must be packaged, stored, and handled to avoid distortion of the original pile yarn orientation so as to protect the texture of pile fabrics. Changes in the apparent brightness or color of these fabrics occur if pile is distorted. Care during processing and shipping can minimize the development of apparent shading problems, which can be difficult to rectify. Changes in color characteristics may be described as barely perceptible, quite noticeable, and so on; the degree of change can be measured and rated in numerical terms by using standard test methods.

Colorfastness to Crocking

Rubbing may cause unstable colorants to crock. **Crocking** is the transfer of color from one surface to another, such as if an upholstery fabric's color rubs off onto a person's clothing who is sitting in the chair. The loss or transfer can occur differently under dry or wet conditions, and therefore tests are run for both.

The term *reverse crocking* has been adopted to describe color from a fabric in the environment rubbing off onto a furnishing fabric. Reverse crocking has become a pervasive problem in commercial settings because dark-colored and over-dyed jeans have become popular office apparel. Some companies have established dress codes to eliminate jeans in the office because of ruined furniture. Clothing rubbing onto furniture is a flaw with the apparel, and not with the upholstery.

Although crocking is a more serious problem in upholstery fabrics, certain situations may lead to crocking (and reverse crocking) problems in colored window-covering and wallcovering fabrics. Color transfer may occur when fabrics rub together or are handled during shipping, sewing, hanging, and when users rub against them.

The **Crockmeter**, shown in Figure 19.6, is the instrument used in AAATC 8 Colorfastness to Crocking (Rubbing): AATCC Crockmeter Method. During testing, the test fabric is cyclically rubbed by a rod covered with white fabric. Transfer of color from the upholstery surface to the white fabric is evidence of crocking (Figure 19.8).

After the test is completed, the test sample is evaluated using the **AATCC Chromatic Transference Scale** (Figure 19.9) to quantify the amount of color transferred. The scale is a card with six colors (neutral gray, red, yellow, green, blue, and purple) mounted in each of four horizontal rows. In each of six vertical rows,

Figure 19.8 The Crockmeter testing apparatus. Courtesy of SDL Atlas.

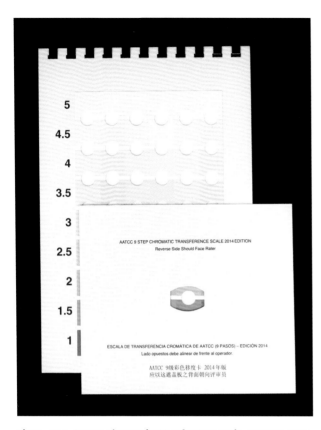

Figure 19.9 AATCC Chromatic Transference Scale. Courtesy of the American Association of Textile Chemists and Colorists.

Figure 19.10 AATCC Gray Scale for Color Change. Courtesy of the American Association of Textile Chemists and Colorists.

the chroma or intensity of each hue is varied, beginning with an extremely light tint and ending with a moderately deep shade. The vertically aligned chips are separated by holes in the card.

If no color is transferred from the upholstery fabric surface to the white test fabric, a rating of 5 is recorded. If transfer occurs, the degree of contrast observed between the unstained and stained areas on the test fabric are compared with that observed between the paired chips on the scale, and the appropriate number is then assigned. The higher the reported value, the more stable the colorant and the better the resistance to crocking.

Alternatively, the **AATCC Gray Scale for Color Change** can be used for this evaluation. As shown in Figure 19.9, the reference chip is a saturated gray color that is successively paired with lighter gray chips. The ACT Guidelines require a Class 4 minimum for dry crocking, and a Class 3 minimum for wet crocking. Contract fabrics meeting or exceeding these minimums may be marked with the ACT symbol, an artist's palette (Figure 19.1), to denote compliance.

Colorfastness to Light

Colorfastness to light testing measures the amount of light exposure needed to produce a noticeable color change. While several tests measure this characteristic, the correlation between machine testing and actual use depends on the conditions of actual use. How near to the windows is the fabric? What kind of glass is used for the windows? Which direction do the windows face? Is the facility located in Arizona, or Maine? What artificial light sources is the fabric exposed to?

In 2012, AATCC 16 Colorfastness to Light was withdrawn and then rewritten into three separate test methods to make it more user-friendly in evaluating the **lightfastness** of colored fabrics by breaking down procedures for accelerated laboratory testing and for extended outdoor exposure testing. Various light sources and testing conditions are specified in each test procedure.

- AATCC 16.1 provides the general principles and procedures for determining the colorfastness to light of textile materials outdoors behind glass (Figure 19.11).
- AATCC 16.2 provides the general principles and procedures for determining the colorfastness to light of textile materials using carbon-arc lamps, which are rarely used today.
- AATCC 16.3 provides the general principles and procedures for determining the colorfastness to light of textile materials using xenon-arc lamps (Figure 19.12a and b).

Figure 19.11 Outdoor colorfastness to light testing. Courtesy of SDL Atlas.

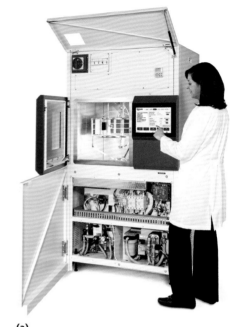

(a)

After completion of the selected lightfastness testing procedure, producers visually evaluate and rate the level of color retention in essentially the same manner as crocking evaluations are made. In this case, however, the AATCC Gray Scale for Color Change is used.

Numerical ratings are determined by comparing the difference observed between an original and an exposed fabric specimen with that observed between the members of a pair of chips on the scale. Again, the higher the reported value, the more stable the colorant. A rating of Class 4 or higher after 40 hours of exposure to light is required to meet the ACT Guidelines and the ASTM standard. Class 5 indicates no fading, while Class 1 indicates a high degree of fading.

Colorfastness to Burnt Gas Fumes

Atmospheric contaminant fading, ozone or O-fading, fume fading, and **gas fading** are terms that describe the destructive effects of various gases on colored textiles. Gases that commonly cause problems include oxides of sulfur, oxides of nitrogen, and ozone. Exposing colored textiles to various concentrations of these gases may weaken or fade the original color or change its hue.

Greater numbers of fume fading incidents occur in industrial centers, areas where coal and fuel oil are major heating sources, and densely populated areas with heavy traffic. (Automobile exhaust can contain as much as 50,000 times more nitric oxide than a normal

Xenotest® 220+

Ci3000 Weather-Ometer®

Atlas Material Testing Technology LLC

(b)

Figure 19.12 Laboratory colorfastness to light testing apparatus (Weather-Ometer®): (a) open, (b) closed. Courtesy of SDL Atlas.

atmosphere.) Whereas emission control devices on automobiles and clean air standards are reducing the concentrations of some atmospheric pollutants, the increasing use of fireplaces and wood-burning stoves for home heating is generating greater concentrations for others.

Figure 19.13 Gas fume chamber. Courtesy of SDL Atlas.

Fume fading occurs in acetate fibers (which are not currently popular) that are dyed with disperse dyestuffs. After prolonged exposure to oxides of nitrogen or sulfur, certain colors gradually and permanently change hue. Blues turn pink, greens turn brownish yellow, and browns turn red. Solution-dyed acetate does not have this propensity.

ACT does not offer guidelines for colorfastness to gas, but AATCC 23 Colorfastness to Burnt Gas Fumes, which is generally used to determine the effects of nitrogen dioxide, can be used for analyzing the negative effects of various gases. The test is conducted in an enclosed chamber, such as the one in Figure 19.13, with controlled concentrations of the gas. After completion of two cycles of testing, the level of color change is determined in the same manner as lightfastness ratings are determined, using the Gray Scale for Color Change. AATCC 129 Colorfastness to Ozone in the Atmosphere Under High Humidities is used to measure the deleterious effects of ozone on colored textiles.

Colorfastness to Cleaning Agents

The fastness of the dyes used determines the cleanability of upholstery fabrics when they are exposed to water and to solvents, the agents that are typically used to clean fabric. In addition to fading, manufacturers are specifically concerned with the potential for color bleeding and migration (movement of the dyestuff through the fabric components). **Bleeding**, either to the interior of the covering or onto cleaning cloths, would weaken the surface color. **Migration** would create various levels of intensity over the surface and could transfer color from one area to another area of a different color.

Common test methods used to evaluate colorfastness properties with regard to cleaning give reliable information related to water and to solvent only and do not take into account the typical rubbing or blotting action as part of the cleaning processes. Therefore, fastness to water or solvent does not necessarily guarantee a satisfactory outcome to actual cleaning. Most reliable Internet cleaning instruction describe methods that work reasonably well. Most important: All fabrics should be cleaned regularly, including vacuuming for most, and washing or dry-cleaning for some. Stains should be dealt with as quickly as possible. These protocols are the best assurance that the material will maintain its appearance for a reasonable period of time.

Colorfastness to Water

AATCC 107 Colorfastness to Water is used to evaluate upholstery fabrics. In preparation for testing, a multifiber woven fabric that has narrow bands of six different fibers backs the fabric specimen. The paired fabrics are immersed in distilled water, removed, pressed between glass plates, and heated according to the test specs. After air-drying, the fabric specimen is visually evaluated and rated for color change using the AATCC Gray Scale for Color Change (Figure 19.10). The multifiber fabric backing is visually evaluated for staining using the **AATCC Gray Scale for Staining** (Figure 19.14).

Accelerated testing for colorfastness to laundry and dry-cleaning agents can be conducted according to AATCC 61 Colorfastness to Laundering: Accelerated with a **Launder-Ometer**® (Figure 19.15), which contains stainless steel jars that hold the specimens, control fabrics, and contain the specified cleaning solution. During testing, the jars are rotated to simulate agitation. Washfastness valuations as to both colorfastness and staining of the control fabric are made at the end of the test procedures.

Figure 19.14 AATCC Gray Scale for Staining. Courtesy of the American Association of Textile Chemists and Colorists.

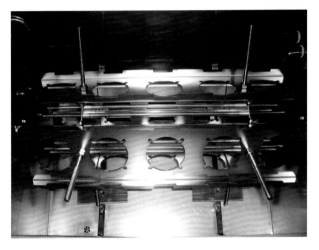

Figure 19.15 Interior view of the Launder-Ometer®. Courtesy of SDL Atlas.

Colorfastness to Solvents

AATCC 107 is also used to evaluate the fastness of colored fabrics to solvents. In this procedure, however, the paired fabrics are immersed in a solvent, perchloroethylene, instead of in water. The exposed fabrics are again evaluated for color change and staining.

Colorfastness to Ozone

AATCC 129 Colorfast to Ozone in the Atmosphere Under High Humidities is recommended for evaluation of upholstery. As in other colorfastness tests, a multifiber test fabric backs the test specimens. They are simultaneously exposed to ozone in a testing chamber until the control

sample shows a color change. After drying, a fabric specimen is rated for color change using the Gray Scale for Color Change (Figure 19.10). The multifiber backing is rated for staining using the Gray Scale for Staining (Figure 19.14).

Maintenance of Upholstery Fabrics

Preventive Maintenance

Residential and commercial consumers should not expect an upholstery fabric to retain its new, fresh, clean appearance forever. On the other hand, they do not anticipate that an elaborate maintenance program will be required. Consumers also expect stain removal will not be an impossible challenge. Care needed varies by fabric and by installation, however, and choosing a suitable fabric for an appropriate use includes not only considering its users, but its cleaners. Cleaning instructions are only useful if someone is keeping up with the maintenance.

Soiling is not only unsightly—dust and dirt weaken fibers. Residential and commercial consumers can assist in the long-term appearance retention of upholstery fabrics by following protocols for routine care and by immediately addressing stains. With appropriate maintenance the need for an overall or restorative cleaning procedure is postponed, or can even become unnecessary.

Routine Care

Upholstered furniture products should be frequently and thoroughly vacuumed to remove airborne dust and lint. If possible, loose cushions should be turned and rotated to equalize wear and soiling levels. Protective arm covers and headrests should be cleaned to minimize any differences between these items and the other exposed areas.

Coated fabrics of PVC (polyvinyl chloride) or PU (polyurethane) may be washed with warm water and a mild soap (not a detergent), and then rinsed with a dampened cloth and dried. Some harsh cleansers, such as those required in healthcare facilities, can cause damage to polyurethane, so following suppliers' maintenance instructions is imperative. Rinsing can be critical as these cleansers can destroy the surface of coated fabrics.

Genuine leather coverings may be cleaned with cheesecloth soaked in a solution of warm water and any mild soap. The surface should then be wiped with a slightly damp cloth and dried with a soft cloth. Waxes, oils, and furniture polishes must not be applied to genuine leather coverings because they may damage the finish.

Cleaning Codes

Frequently, upholstery manufacturers voluntarily label their products with a **cleaning code**. The code to be used is determined by measuring the level of color migration and bleeding caused by water and by solvent, using the standard test methods described in the previous section. Industry representatives recommend that all upholstered furniture be identified as to its cleanability code, using the letter codes defined as follows:

- W—Use water-based upholstery cleaner only.
- S—Use solvent-based upholstery cleaner only.
- WS—Can use water-based or solvent-based cleaners.
- X—Do not clean with water-based or solvent-based cleaners; use vacuuming or light brushing only.

Water-based cleaning agents are commonly labeled upholstery shampoo. These agents are commercially available as foams, concentrated liquids, and dry compounds.

It should be emphasized that these cleaning codes apply to the outercovering fabric only; it is imperative that overwetting of the fabric be avoided to prevent contact with the filling materials. It must also be noted that zippered covers should not be removed for cleaning because excessive shrinkage may occur and the backing compound may be damaged. Zippers are used to facilitate filling the cushions, not to facilitate cleaning.

Emergency Action

A spill requires prompt attention! Fluids must be immediately absorbed from the surface to limit (or prevent) its penetration into the fibers and fabric backing. Solid materials, such as candle wax and crayon, should be broken up, scraped, and vacuumed to remove as much of the substance as possible before stain removal agents are used.

Stain removal agents should first be tested, as directed, on an inconspicuous area of the material. To avoid spreading the stain and overwetting the fabric, stain removal compounds should be applied in small amounts from the outside edges toward the center of the stain. To avoid distortion of the surface texture, the agent should be blotted on, not rubbed into, the foreign matter and fabric. Rinsing the fabric and blotting it dry to remove cleaning agent residue is critical.

Waterborne stains can be removed from most fabrics with a mild detergent diluted with warm water, using one teaspoon of detergent per cup of water. Oil-borne stains can be removed with a solvent-based dry-cleaning fluid.

Procedures used to remove stains will also remove accumulated soil. This may result in a localized clean area that can readily be distinguished from adjacent soiled areas. When such differences are apparent, or when large areas are soiled, the entire surface should be cleaned.

If a stain or damage seems significant, a professional cleaner is a good idea. Professional cleaning fees are small in comparison with the cost of a piece of furniture that can be ruined with inappropriate cleaning, which is a major reason for field failures in upholstered furniture.

Salvage Maintenance

When an upholstered furniture covering no longer has an acceptable appearance, even after overall cleaning, consumers may elect to have the item reupholstered. The material costs, skilled labor charges, and transportation expenses involved make reupholstery relatively expensive. For this reason, reupholstering is often restricted to well-constructed items and antique pieces. Unfortunately, most upholstered furniture is not recyclable, but many charities offer options for reuse.

Maintenance of Window Covering Structures

Preventive Maintenance Measures

Preventive maintenance techniques preserve the original appearance of window coverings and reduce the weakening that occurs to soiled fibers. Curtains and draperies are especially vulnerable to environmental threats. Rainwater can blow in on linings and other fabric layers; panels can hang in contact with framework on which water condenses. Water, including vapor-phase moisture, may combine with soil present on the fibers and cause staining of the fabric. Water may also combine with pollutants and oily cooking fumes to soil and weaken the fibers.

Routine Care Practices

Drapery panels, especially those that are stationary or laterally draped, should be regularly vacuumed. Washable curtains should be laundered regularly. When practical, window coverings of hydrophobic fibers, whose tendency to build up electrical charges increases the fibers' attraction for airborne should be tumbled in an automatic dryer, using low heat or none at all, to remove airborne soil. The louvers and vanes in blinds and shutters and the surfaces of roller shades should be routinely vacuumed to remove accumulated dust.

Restorative Maintenance Procedures

Curtains and draperies are not included in the scope of the Federal Trade Commission (FTC) trade regulation rule related to care labeling, but many producers elect to provide a cleaning code. Usually, the cleaning code letters for upholstery fabrics are used for curtains and draperies as well. These code letters and their meanings were given in the section "Cleaning Codes."

Curtains of glass fiber are not generally marketed today. These fabrics should never be washed or dry-cleaned because agitation promotes the breaking of glass fibers, which are dangerous to handle or inhale. Fabrics with a durable press finish may be laundered in an automatic washer. Strong oxidizing bleaches, such as chlorine compounds, should not be used. In high concentrations, these agents may be retained by the fibers, turning the fabric yellow and further weakening the cellulosic components. (Chlorine is also deleterious to water systems and to human health, if ingested.) The laundered panels should be tumbled with low heat in an automatic dryer until dry, followed by a cool-down cycle and prompt removal.

Excessively high heat should not be used on any fiber. Unfortunately, consumers often find that iron dials are divided by fiber type or by finish, not by specific temperatures. Moreover, the same setting on different irons may produce quite different temperatures. Consumers and professional cleaners should strive to use the lowest effective temperature for dryer heat or ironing, and be alert for signs of fiber and fabric damage. For fabrics composed of thermoplastic fibers, the slightest amount of fabric shrinkage and the slightest resistance of the soleplate to gliding are indications that the ironing temperature is too high.

A professional cleaner can best handle long, heavy panels with multiple folds, which require large cleaning tanks and special pressing equipment. Frequently, laundry and dry-cleaning firms offer removal and rehanging as optional services. Consumers can evaluate the cost-to-benefit value of professional cleaning compared with replacement expenses.

Maintenance of Wallcovering Fabrics

Care of wallcovering and panel fabrics is simple and straightforward. Other than routine vacuuming for heavy-use areas, spot cleaning is usually all that is required. The exceptions are healthcare facilities, food service businesses, or similar areas. Users require washable wallcoverings for such installations. Suppliers of washable wallcoverings offer specific recommendations for suitable cleaning agents.

Key Terms

AATCC Chromatic Transference Scale	bleeding
	bow
AATCC Gray Scale for Color Change	breaking force (load)
	breaking strength
AATCC Gray Scale for Staining	bursting strength
	cleaning code
abrasion	colorfastness
ACT symbols	crocking
Association for Contract Textiles (ACT)	Crockmeter
	dimensional stability
atmospheric contaminant	durable press resins
fading	electronic color meter

elongation	ozone or O-fading
fume fading	pattern repeats
gas fading	pilling
growth	seam slippage
Launder-Ometer®	shrinkage
lightfastness	skew
Martindale Abrasion Test Method	tear strength
	Wyzenbeek Test Method
migration	yarn alignment
off-grain fabrics	yarn distortion

Review Questions

1. Are the recommended levels of flaws and defects in upholstery fabrics reasonable?

2. Distinguish between filling bow and filling skew. What causes these yarn alignment problems, and how do they affect the appearance of things such as upholstered furniture and window coverings?

3. Discuss how waterborne and oilborne stains are removed.

4. How would fabric shrinkage affect the appearance of upholstered furniture? Would fabric growth present problems with an upholstered item?

5. Describe the problems caused with yarn distortion.

6. Why would colorfastness to crocking be an important test for upholstered furnishings?

7. Why is frequency of use a reasonable measure to use in defining in-use applications terms for upholstered furniture (i.e., light-duty, medium-duty, and heavy-duty)?

8. Explain the membership and work of ACT. What symbols are used by this group, and what connotations are associated with each symbol?

9. Differentiate between brightness and apparent brightness. What causes changes in the apparent brightness of fabrics, especially pile fabrics?

10. Explain how the AATCC Gray Scales and the AATCC Chromatic Transference Scale are used in fabric evaluations.

11. Identify the problems that atmospheric contaminants cause with colored textiles.

12. Identify the cleanability codes voluntarily used with upholstery fabric. What does each indicate? How do manufacturers determine which code to include on a label?

20

Soft Floorcovering Selection

loorcoverings, like all interior finishes, are usually selected based on the owner's preference, taking professional recommendations and anticipated in-use conditions and activities into account. Features prescribed by regulatory agencies and functional and safety characteristics of floorcoverings are also important. Interior floor finishes must add to, and not hinder, mobility of occupants. Environmental attributes of carpet are especially important because it generally represents the largest quantity of surface material in an interior. When selecting floorcovering, use-cost analyses, which reflect not only material cost but include installation, maintenance, and expected useful life, often indicate that carpet and cushion assemblies are more economical than other flooring materials.

The **Carpet and Rug Institute (CRI)** is the national trade association that represents the carpet and rug industry. Carpet manufacturers and suppliers of raw materials and services to the industry are members, and the organization's website offers excellent resources for general information on subjects such as:

- Aesthetic, functional, and financial benefits of carpet
- Carpet or rug selection process
- Installation guidelines
- Characteristics of fibers
- Carpet construction
- Carpet's role in indoor air quality and the environment
- Daily maintenance and long-term care
- Technical information
- Health-related carpet issues
- Sustainability issues

Carpet and rug producers use billions of pounds of fibers each year, approximately 80 percent of which is incorporated into face or pile yarns, and the balance in backings. The fiber composition of face yarns and backing structures is markedly different. Whereas tufting has become the dominant construction method today, weaving, knitting, and other techniques such as fusion bonding and needle punching remain important.

Fibers Used in Carpet and Rugs

As extensively discussed in Unit 1, many features determine the performance of every fabric, but carpet is strongly influenced by fiber characteristics and yarn features.. Table 20.1 outlines the various fibers used in carpet production, along with their characteristics and attributes as carpet materials.

Face Yarn Fibers

The development of fuzz on the surface of pile floorcoverings, for example, depends on the ability of the yarns to maintain their original level of twist. Yarn properties have a strong effect on floorcovering serviceability.

BCF Nylon and BCF Olefin

Bulk continuous filament (BCF) nylon dominates the assortment of fibers used in **face yarns**. Polypropylene and polyester are also widely used, and polyester is increasing in popularity, especially because advancements in fiber development improve new versions. Fiber engineering continues to ensure and improve the serviceability of these manufactured fibers in soft floorcoverings, while designers develop new aesthetics for the yarns and coloration possibilities.

Rugs are increasingly popular in outdoor environments, and are most often made of solution-dyed olefin (polypropylene) or acrylic; some are of polyester. Most are flat woven, although some are pile rugs (Figure 20.1).

Wool

Long considered to be the finest and most luxurious of the face fibers, wool dominated the floorcoverings market for centuries. In recent decades, however, wool carpeting has slowly declined in large part because of rising costs of carpet wool combined with improvements in synthetic fibers and yarns. (All wool fiber used in carpet and rugs is imported because domestic wool is too fine for these products.)

TABLE 20.1

FIBER/YARN TYPES AND CHARACTERISTICS

Fiber	Definition and Characteristics	Characteristics in Carpet
Nylon	• Fiber-forming substance of any long-chain synthetic polyamide having recurring amide groups as an integral part of the polymer chain; available as Nylon 6 or Nylon 6,6 • Offered as bulk continuous filament (BCF) or staple, both used for residential and commercial applications • Can be a solution-dyed fiber or yarn • Extensively used for commercial carpet and accounts for 60% of all carpet face fibers	• Durable, resilient • Abrasion-resistant • Versatile in coloration possibilities • Wet-cleaning friendly • Excellent colorfastness • Excellent color clarity
Olefin (Polypropylene)	• Fiber-forming substance of any long-chain, synthetic polymer composed of at least 85% by weight of ethylene, propylene, or other olefin units • Offered as BCF (or staple for needle punch carpet) • Solution-dyed fiber or yarn • Can be engineered for outdoor applications • Accounts for 33% of all carpet face fibers	• Resists fading • Generates low levels of static electricity • Chemical, moisture, and stain-resistant • Favorably priced
Acrylic	• Fiber-forming substance of any long-chain, synthetic polymer composed of at least 85% by weight of acrylonitrile units • One of the first synthetic fibers used in carpet • Used in bath mats, rugs • Sometimes used in blends with other fibers in carpet • Always used in staple yarn form	• Wool-like characteristics • Excellent bulk and cover • Seldom used in commercial carpet
Polyester	• Made from terephthalic acid and ethylene glycol • Offered in BCF, but mainly in staple form • Used in residential and some low-traffic commercial applications	• Excellent color clarity • Excellent colorfastness • Resistant to water-soluble stains • Noted for luxurious hand
Wool	• Natural fiber from sheep • Inherent resilient property	• Luxurious hand • Durable • Scaly character of fiber scatters light and reduces visible soil • Largely self-extinguishing when burned; will char rather than melt or drip
Cotton	• Natural fiber from cotton plant • Used in various area rugs, such as bath mats	• Soft hand • Seldom used in broadloom

Figure 20.1 Flat-woven outdoor rug. Courtesy of Mohawk Home.

If cost is no consideration, many people believe that the beauty, durability, inherent soil and flame resistance, and excellent resiliency of wool support its choice. Wool carpet captures a significant share of luxury residential, hospitality, and corporate installations.

Backing Fibers

Most of the fiber produced for carpet and rug backing structures is used to back tufted goods. A smaller amount of fiber is used for the yarns in the backing layers of other constructions. Polypropylene (olefin) is the dominant fiber used for backing, but minor amounts of nylon and polyester are also used. Some cotton yarn appears in the back of woven constructions and in fabrics used to back small, tufted rugs and mats, but none is used for tufted rollgoods.

Other backing materials include foam rubber, fiberglass, vinyl, latex, and jute. Fabrics of jute are dimensionally stable unless they are overwetted during cleaning or flooding. Because they retain moisture and may rot and mildew, they should not be used with floorcoverings installed below-grade where ground moisture can move through the floor to the carpet back. Because jute is imported from tropical areas, supply and delivery problems have often plagued producers using jute. Jute is no longer used as a backing for commercial tufted carpet. Table 20.2 describes the various types of carpet backings.

Fiber Composition Labeling

The fiber composition of the pile layer of soft floorcovering must be disclosed in accordance with the provisions of the Textile Fiber Products Identification Act. Backing fibers and yarns are exempt (see Chapter 11).

Fiber Properties Affecting Floor Performance

The selection of carpet and rug fibers should be based on an evaluation of both engineered and inherent properties. Virtually every inherent property can be engineered or altered for improved performance. Unless a particular feature is required by law, residential and commercial consumers may weigh appearance and performance benefits against any added cost. Features such as abrasion resistance, optical characteristics, static propensity, and soil-related properties are discussed in Chapters 4 and 26.

Yarn Features and Serviceability

The appearance and floor performance of carpet and rugs relate to several yarn features, including some structural characteristics and the stability of the yarn twist. Often, spinners and throwsters can produce the desired appearance and expected service-related properties by manipulating these features.

Structural Characteristics

Virtually all carpet and rug yarns, of whatever content, are constructed as simple, relatively coarse structures.

Design Features

Complex yarns, except for speck yarns, are not used in floorcoverings because loops, curls, and other irregular textural effects would readily be abraded and snagged. Decorative appeal, however, can be introduced by other variables, including color styling, pile height, and yarn twist.

TABLE 20.2
CARPET BACKING SYSTEMS

Construction Method	Typical Backing Fabrics and/or Backing Components	Typical Backcoating Chemical Compounds
Tufted	Primary: • woven polypropylene slit film • non-woven, polypropylene or polyester Secondary: • woven leno weave polypropylene • non-woven polypropylene, or polyester woven jute, fiberglass reinforcement (seldom used)	• synthetic SBR latex • polyurethane • polyvinyl acetate • ethylene vinyl acetate • polyvinyl chloride • amorphous resins or thermoplastic polyolefin
Woven	Construction yarns may in-clude: • cotton • jute • polypropylene • polyester • viscose rayon • blends or combinations	• Similar materials as tufted, but usually thinner coatings
Bonded	Fiberglass matting	• polyvinyl chloride
Needle punched	(None typically used)	• SBR latex • acrylics • ethylene vinyl acetate • SBR latex foam

SBR = styrene-butadiene rubber.
Source: Courtesy of the Carpet and Rug Institute.

Form

For good floor performance, two- or three-ply spun yarns are produced from staple fibers 4, 6, or 8 inches long. Longer lengths help to reduce the number of protruding fiber ends and to increase yarn strength, and thus to minimize the problems of shedding, fuzzing, and pilling induced by abrasion during use.

Most multifilament carpet yarns are textured, using the false-twist coiling or knit-de-knit crinkling techniques. Again, as noted earlier, there has been shifting from spun to BCF yarns. Because most of the filament ends are buried in the yarn bundle, BCF yarns, like longer staple spun yarns, exhibit less pill formation. In combination with heather color styling, BCF yarns often have a wool-like appearance (Figure 20.2).

Figure 20.2 Level-loop pile made of BCF yarn. Courtesy of Amy Willbanks, www.textilefabric.com.

Size and Weight

Size and Weight

The fineness of manufactured fibers is described as **denier**. Although the average denier of filament nylon yarns has been decreasing, some carpet yarns and some carpet fibers are being manufactured with extra high denier counts. These extra large yarns, which have denier counts as high as 7,000, are used in floorcoverings intended for installation in commercial interiors that undergo heavy traffic. Most commercial carpet will have an average pile yarn density between 4,500 and 6,000.

Pile Yarn Integrity

Pile yarn integrity refers to the ability of the face yarns to maintain their stability and resist the effects of abrasion. Loop-pile yarns should not rupture, and cut-pile yarns should not splay or untwist. Such abrasion-induced changes would result in changes in apparent luster, which wrongly suggest colorant failure. The original texture would also change from smooth to fuzzy.

When cut-pile yarns fail to maintain their original level of twist, they are said to **yarn splay**, flare, or blossom, as shown in Figure 20.3. Because incident light waves are reflected from the small tips of the multiple, disoriented fibers, areas of splayed yarns appear duller than surrounding areas. Surface luster will also vary when fibers that are part of loop-pile yarns are snagged and ruptured. Pile yarn integrity can be improved with the use of abrasion-resistant fibers, BCF yarns, and more highly twisted and heat-stabilized yarns. Higher pile construction densities also increase the integrity of yarns in a carpet.

Constructions Used in Soft Floorcoverings

Dominance of Tufting

Tufting accounts for more than 90 percent of the floor-coverings market. This is largely the result of the economic advantages offered by high-speed, wide-width tufting machines, and by the use of nylon instead of nonresilient cotton and expensive wool fibers. It has also resulted from improvements made in the quality of tufted carpet that have enabled designers and architects

Figure 20.3 Yarn splaying. Fairchild Books.

increasingly to specify tufted floorcoverings for commercial interiors, including areas of heavy traffic. Together with woven constructions and hand techniques, tufting is discussed in detail in Chapter 21. Table 20.3 outlines carpet construction types.

Appearance Features

Not only do residential and commercial consumers have widely varying and constantly changing tastes, but conditions such as end-use lighting and traffic patterns within the room impact a floorcovering's likely appeal and appearance retention. A carpet that is appealing for a bedroom is probably different from one that is appropriate for a general office area, and practical requirements for the two purposes are very different.

Sizes and Shapes

Rollgoods and carpet tiles are designed to cover all of the floor space within an interior. Rugs are generally designed to define a limited area, such as an entrance foyer or the space under a furniture grouping. The floorcovering style chosen determines the method of installation. A securely fastened or anchored floorcovering is typically referred to as **carpet**, and a loosely laid structure is called a **rug**. (Rug dealers also refer to very large, antique rugs as carpets.) The term **broadloom** is frequently used to identify rollgoods that are more than 54 inches wide. These terms do not describe the method of construction, and carry no implication about quality.

Wall-to-Wall Carpet

Wall-to-Wall Carpet

Wall-to-wall carpet covers the entire floor space, baseboard to baseboard (Figure 20.4). As is true for other

TABLE 20.3
CARPET CONSTRUCTION

Type/Description	Special Characteristic
Tufting	
600–2,000 rows of pile yarn simultaneously stitched through carrier fabric (primary backing)	• Most prevalent method for carpet fabric production (over 90 percent) • Textural flexibility achieved with varying colors, surface textures, using various types of yarns, etc.
Cut pile carpet Pile surface with all of the yarn tufts of the same height	• Custom tufting available for specially designed carpet orders • Patterned effects created in the cut pile constructions by using different colors of yarns • Geometric designs created with a pattern attachment called a shifting needle bar
Loop pile Level loop Multilevel loop	• All loops same height from row to row • A patterning attachment is used to achieve different pile heights in a pattern repeat
Cut and loop A combination of cut and loop pile	• Varying levels of pile height and pile textures create surface interest
Weaving	
Colored pile yarns and backing yarns woven simultaneously into finished product	• Primarily used in commercial installations • Heavy, firm hand; high strength • Often used in hospitality settings
Velvet carpet Carpet made on velvet loom; cut or loop, level or multilevel pile	• Simplest loom of the three • Dominated by solid colors, but multicolor and multi-texture effects are becoming more widespread • Service quality is achieved with pile density (high pile density is achieved by specifying high pitch or a heavy yarn weight)
Wilton carpet Carpet made on a Wilton loom; can have various pile heights (level or multilevel) and can have loop or cut pile	• Capable of intricate patterning, styling, and coloration versatility • Withstands heavy traffic; used mostly in commercial applications and area rugs • Weaving process contributes to durability, strength, firmness, and flexibility (bends all ways)
Axminster carpet Carpet made on an Axminster loom; cut pile only; most are single-level cut pile, but can be multilevel as well	• Offers wide range of patterns and colors • Withstands heavy traffic; used mostly in commercial applications and area rugs • Weaving process contributes to durability, strength, firmness, and flexibility (bends only horizontally)
Knitting	
Warp-knitted yarn fabricated on face and back simultaneously; pile, backing and stitching yarns are looped together by three sets of needles	• Similar to woven carpet, but less stiff; bends horizontally only • Most is solid colored or tweed • Quality depends on the amount of pile yarn and strength of attachment of the face, chain, and backing yarns; quantity of yarn depends on the gauge and stitches per inch warpwise, which are related to the yarn size
Needle Punching	
Web of fibers moves through machine; barbed felting needles penetrate and entangle fibers into durable felt-like fabrics	• Usually made with a solution-dyed polypropylene • Diverse range of designs—ribs, sculptured designs, and patterns • Only used in glue-down installations
Bonding	
Yarns are implanted into vinyl or thermoplastic coated backing	• Often die-cut for modules (tiles) • Cut pile produced by slitting two parallel sheets of face-to-face carpet

Source: Carpet and Rug Institute.

Figure 20.4 Wall-to-wall installation of rollgoods. Courtesy of Moooi Carpets.

consumer purchases, certain compromises are inevitable when one style of floorcovering is selected over another.

A wall-to-wall installation has some negative features:

- Costs are incurred for installation.
- It must be cleaned in place.
- Repair of large damaged areas is difficult.
- It cannot be shifted to equalize traffic patterns and soiling.
- Extra yardage may be required for matching patterns.
- It is difficult to remove for relocation.

On the other hand, a wall-to-wall installation has these positive features:

- It is securely anchored to prevent shifting.
- There are no loose edges to cause tripping.
- There is no "curb" effect for wheelchairs if low level pile is used.
- Potential for energy conservation is maximized.
- Rooms generally appear to be larger with a consistent floorcovering than when broken into sections with rugs.
- Carpet can camouflage slightly worn or uneven floors.
- No special preparation of the floor is usually required. In fact, carpet can (and often is) installed directly over a sub-floor, which saves the cost of finished flooring.

In addition to standard 12-foot widths, some broadloom carpets are also available in 6-, 9-, and 12-foot widths.

(15-foot wide carpet is sometimes available but is not a standard offering.) Broadloom can be cut to any size, and the raw edges can finished by serging (machine overcasting), fringing, binding with twill-woven tape, or with a seam-sealing cement so that the end product resembles an area rug.

If a room is narrower than the width of the rollgoods, the rug can also be cut to nearly fill the room. This is appealing to some residential customers who rent or anticipate frequent relocation, because these floorcoverings can be rolled up for moving and recut to a smaller size later, whereas wall-to-wall carpet remains installed the residence. Unsecured edges may cause tripping. A "curb" effect may be presented to wheelchair drivers.

For large orders, such as for hotels and convention centers, carpet producers offer broadloom rollgoods with rug-like designs strategically placed. Although these goods are installed wall-to-wall, the engineered focal point is surrounded by a plain-textured ground, which yields the appearance that the central design point is a loose-laid rug (Figure 20.5). This approach is advantageous for high-traffic areas in commercial interiors where an area rug can create tripping hazards, and perhaps not meet codes for accessibility. Carpet for hospitality application is often designed in this way to differentiate separate areas within large spaces.

Carpet Tiles

Carpet tiles are generally 18, 24, or 36 inches square, although other specialty sizes, and even non-rectilinear shapes, are offered. Tiles are the predominant soft

Figure 20.5 Inset carpet. Hero Images/Getty Images.

Figure 20.6 Carpet tile installation. Gary Ombler/Dorling Kindersley/Getty Images.

floorcovering in offices and commercial interiors, and are gaining in the hospitality segment. Most tiles are glued directly to the floor with a permanent or a releasable adhesive, although a few manufacturers produce extra-heavy, stiff tiles designed to be free-laid that rely on gravity to hold them in place. When correctly installed, the surface has many of the same features as wall-to-wall carpet because the squares are laid across the entire floor space (Figure 20.6).

Carpet tiles have some limiting characteristics:

- Initial materials costs are high.
- Edge curl can occur with low-quality tiles.
- Butted joints can separate with improper installation.

They also offer some distinct advantages, especially when releasable or no adhesive is used:

- Loss of materials during installation is minimal.
- Tiles are easily rotated to equalize traffic and soiling patterns.
- They may be replaced if damaged.
- They may be lifted for access to under-floor service trenches.
- Tiles offer design customization with stock components.

Runners

A **runner** is a long, narrow rug or carpet used primarily for use in hallways and on stairs. Runners can be

wall-to-wall, or broadloom can be cut to a variety of widths and can be cut to any length. Machine-made runners may be serged, and fringe may be added on the cut ends. Selvedges usually make up the long edges of handmade rugs, including runners, and rugs usually have warp-yarn fringe on the short ends. On stairs, runners can be held in place with metal or wooden rods that are securely anchored at the back of the treads.

A special form of runner is the **walk-off mat** used in entrance areas subjected to high traffic levels. These mats are intended to capture tracked-in dirt and grit so that they protect the carpet from abrasion and apparent changes in color caused by such materials. Walk-off mats must be heavy and stiff enough to prevent edge curl that causes users to trip.

Area Rugs

A wide range of **area rugs** is available to fit any room or area (Figure 20.7). Square, round, oval, rectangular, octagonal, and free-form shapes; handmade or machine made; in any fiber—area rugs come in a wide variety and may or may not have fringe. Coupled with the wide variety of constructions, fiber contents, textures, and colorations, area rugs offer endless design appeal. Some consumers and designers lay area rugs directly on smooth floors, especially on fine hardwood; others lay them over wall-to-wall carpet to define a furniture grouping or accentuate a living area; and still others hang them as decorative wall accents.

Figure 20.7 Area rug used to define a furniture grouping. Courtesy of Mohawk Home.

The selection of an area rug involves considering their drawbacks:

- They can be hazardous to persons having limited vision or mobility, and are prohibited by building codes in some commercial installations unless the rug has a curbed edge.
- They may shift or slide on smooth floors.
- They tend to "walk" off thick padding and move on carpet.

However, area rugs are attractive because:

- They come in an extensive variety of sizes, shapes, designs, and textures.
- No installation is required.
- They are easily moved.

Scatter Rugs

Scatter rugs are small rugs, often 2 feet by 3 feet or smaller. They are used in the home where traffic and soiling are concentrated, such as inside the entrance area and in front of sinks. Novelty scatter rugs are also decorative accents, and are available in imaginative designs and shapes ranging from simulations of traditional styles to a dog's paw or a favorite team logo. They may be machine washable, although rubber backings should not be machine dried. These rugs are relatively inexpensive, but they are easily tripped over, and they slide on smooth surfaces, so they are not practical in many interiors.

Surface Texture

Besides their length and width, most textile floorcoverings have a noticeable third dimension, that of depth, which is produced by a pile layer. Variations in the visual and tactile characteristics of pile layers depend on differences in pile height, **pile thickness**, construction, density, and yarn twist, as well as whether the pile tufts have been cut.

Pile Direction and Nap

Most pile fabrics, including pile carpets and rugs, appear to be different colors or shades when viewed from different directions. Generally, due to the slant of the pile yarns, looking into the pile direction, the fabrics seems

darker, and appears to be lighter from the vantage looking with the pile. Therefore, most pile floorcoverings must be installed so that the nap goes in the same direction for all of the material (see Chapter 26).

In use, napped textures also exhibit shading effects when the orientation of the pile yarns is physically changed. When foot traffic or vacuum cleaning alters the direction of the pile yarns, the effect is normally temporary; the yarns gradually recover their original positions. When pile is crushed against the grain, a darker area may appear. This appearance problem is variously described as **pile reversal**, **watermarking**, **shading**, or **pooling**.

Pile Height

Pile height is the length of the pile tufts above the backing; the length of the pile yarn that is incorporated in the backing is excluded. Pile height is normally reported in decimal form, and is routinely supplied to contract designers, architects, and others who specify floorcovering.

Pile Density

Pile density is determined by the closeness of the pile tufts in the wear layer. A dense construction has closely spaced tufts; a sparse construction has widely spaced tufts (Figure 20.8). Density has a major influence on the surface appearance, texture retention, and wear-life of pile structures.

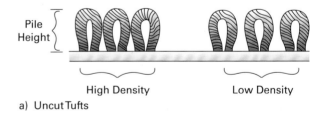

a) Uncut Tufts

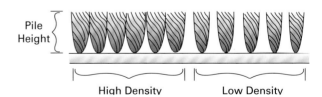

Figure 20.8 High- and low-pile construction densities: (a) uncut tufts, (b) cut tufts. Andrea Lau/Fairchild Books.

Consumers and professionals can make an "eyeball" evaluation of construction density by flexing a carpet or rug and judging how much backing is exposed; that is, how much the structure **grins**, or smiles (Figure 20.9). Lower densities produce broader grins. Pile construction density and exposure of the backing are especially critical factors to examine when selecting carpet for installation on stairs.

(a)

(b)

(c)

Figure 20.9 Eyeball evaluation of pile construction: (a) 20-ounce carpet, (b) 30-ounce carpet, (c) 51-ounce carpet. Courtesy of Amy Willbanks, www.textilefabric.com.

Cut and Uncut Pile

The yarn loops in some soft floorcoverings are cut, producing independent tufts. In other coverings, the loops are left uncut (Figure 20.8).

Yarn Twist

The level of twist used in pile yarns has a major influence on the appearance of soft floorcoverings. Higher levels create well-defined yarn ends, and lower levels create flared tips (Figure 20.10). Differences in twist level are largely responsible for the appearance differences observed among one-level cut-pile surface textures (Figure 20.11). Heat setting processes, which essentially melt the cut ends of the pile yarn, are also used to manipulate the yarn-tip effect. Some of the wide variety of textures available in pile floorcoverings are illustrated in Figure 20.11.

One-Level Cut-Pile Styles

Several cut-pile styles have a uniform level across their surfaces. These styles differ among themselves in pile height, pile density, and yarn construction, however. **Velour** surfaces are fine, short, dense cut-pile carpet constructions (Figure 20.11a) that are not heat set, and therefore have no yarn-tip definition.

Plush, also called **velvet** and **velvet plush** (Figure 20.11b) is a general term for cut-pile carpet in which the pile yarns have relatively low levels of twist that yields a luxurious, velvet-like look and feel. A typical cut plush pile called **Saxony** (Figure 20.11c) usually uses yarns that are heat set to reduce the amount of flaring at the tips of the cut yarns. Rather than blending together in a continuous surface, each yarn tip (or yarn end) is well defined, and the set twist minimizes splaying and improves thickness retention. Saxony can encompass a range of many pile heights, densities, and textures.

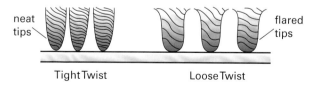

Figure 20.10 Effect of twist level on the appearance of pile yarns. Andrea Lau/Fairchild Books.

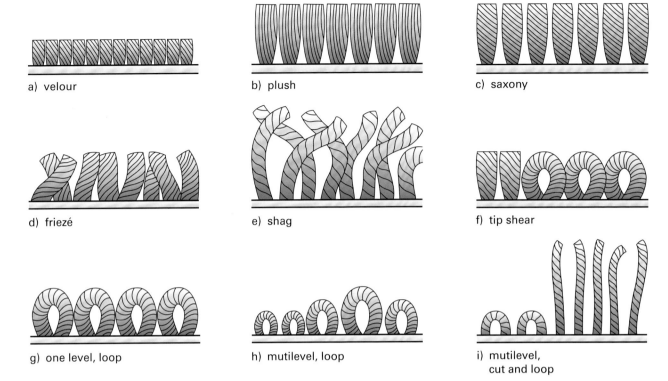

a) velour   b) plush   c) saxony

d) friezé   e) shag   f) tip shear

g) one level, loop   h) mutilevel, loop   i) mutilevel,
                                                cut and loop

Figure 20.11 Surface textures of contemporary pile floorcoverings: (a) velour, (b) plush, (c) Saxony, (d) frieze, (e) shag, (f) tip shear, (g) one level, loop, (h) multilevel, loop, (i) multilevel, cut and loop. Andrea Lau/Fairchild Books.

Frieze textures, also known as twist textures, are constructed of yarns having maximum twist for high stability and wear-life. Each yarn is clearly visible, because the high twist defines each yarn and encourages it to seek its own direction of orientation in the lower density pile (Figure 20.11d).

Shag-pile yarns are long, often with a high twist (Figure 20.11e). The pile density is lower than that in other textures; the longer pile yarns are responsible for covering the backing. **Tip shear** surfaces are produced by selectively shearing the uppermost portion of some yarn loops (Figure 20.11f). Subtle differences in luster appear because more light is reflected from the smooth loops than from the sheared fibers. Frequently, low-pile, densely constructed floorcoverings are sheared to camouflage future soil accumulation.

One-Level Loop-Pile Styles

In the past, carpet with a short, level loop pile (Figure 20.11g) was normally seen only in commercial settings

such as restaurants, airport terminals, and hospitals. Many professionals and consumers thought this surface had an "institutional" appearance. Today, durable, wear-resistant loop-pile carpets are popular for residential installations (Figure 20.12).

Multilevel Loop-Pile Styles

Multilevel loop-pile styles show noticeable differences in the height of their pile yarns (Figure 20.11h). The variations can be used to create an all-over, seemingly random texture, or they may be designed to create a pattern. These surfaces are quite durable if density is reasonably high (Figure 20.13).

Multilevel Cut- and Loop-Pile Styles

Combining cut loops, uncut loops, and multiple pile heights (Figure 20.11i) produces broad possibilities for design variations and patterning. (Figure 20.14). Sculptured pile, high-low effects, and random shear textures are just three of the possibilities.

Figure 20.12 Level loop pile. Courtesy of Amy Willbanks, www.textilefabric.com.

Figure 20.13 Multilevel loop pile. Courtesy of Amy Willbanks, www.textilefabric.com.

Figure 20.14 Cut and uncut pile. Courtesy of Martin Patrick Evan, Ltd.

Figure 20.15 Sculptured pile. Courtesy of Martin Patrick Evan, Ltd.

Sculptured pile surfaces (Figure 20.15) have a definite three-dimensional appearance. In most cases, the higher loops are all cut and the lower loops all uncut for an embossed effect. Normally, the cut-pile areas are dominant, and the visual impact is strong and formal.

The exquisite texture of some custom floorcoverings is produced by hand or machine carving dense, cut-pile surfaces. Shears that cut, or *carve*, the pile on a bevel produce variations in the carpet pile height, which creates the patterns. Inlaid carved designs utilize two or more pieces of carpet, textures, and sizes, into a desired pattern (Figure 20.16).

Bas-relief connotes carving in which entire areas of fiber are removed or lowered from the carpet face to produce designs that exhibit dramatic shadows.

Figure 20.16 Carved pile. Courtesy of Martin Patrick Evan, Ltd.

High-low is the name given to some multilevel cut and loop styles with an informal appearance. Sometimes, the higher tufts have the appearance of shag textures. **Random shear** textures differ from tip-shear textures because they contain multiple levels of pile yarns instead of a single level. They differ from sculptured surfaces in that the uppermost portions of some of the higher yarn tufts are sheared, while in sculptured coverings all are sheared.

Surface Coloration

Soft floorcoverings often dominate the aesthetics of an interior, at least by surface area. A carpet or rug may have a subdued, solid-colored surface and serve as a backdrop for other, more distinctive furnishings, or it may have detailed designs or bold graphic colorations whose strong visual impact attracts attention. In choosing floorcovering or any other interior material, a consumer or designer certainly seeks a pleasing color, but also considers end-use limitations such as light exposure, traffic, and types of use for the space.

Color Styling

Consumer tastes in carpet and rugs fluctuate in the same cycles that hold for other fashion merchandise, such as apparel and cars. Manufacturers offer a vast range of color styling, from solid-colored surfaces in dark, deep hues to finely detailed designs in light, intense hues, along with patterns of all sorts.

Solid-colored surfaces can be produced in any number of color combinations. Distinctive multicolored stylings are produced with heather, Berber, space-dyed, and moresque yarns. Authentic **Berber yarns**, a type of hand-spun speck yarn produced in northern Africa, contain the deep, rich browns and grays of the wool retrieved from the sheep. Dyed, staple-length acrylic, olefin, and nylon fibers are blended to simulate Berber yarns (Figure 20.17). The varied colorations of space-dyed and moresque pile yarns not only add visual interest, but, like other multicolor effects, effectively mask the appearance of soil and stains (Figure 20.18).

Patterned floorcoverings may have designs created with colored fibers and yarns during construction or printed on the greige rollgoods. A large segment of multicolored, patterned effects are produced with digital jet printing, which is similar to ink-jet printing on paper. The almost infinite variety of patterns and colors available in stock lines can be expanded by custom design and color work. Large commercial installations, especially for hospitality, are often custom projects, and the top-end producers offer custom area rugs for residential interiors.

Factors Affecting Apparent Color

As discussed in Chapter 9, soiling, light exposure from the exterior and interior light sources, and other furnishing materials are a few variables that impact apparent color. Generally speaking, multicolor materials with textural variety mask the appearance of soil better than do solid-colored materials, and all-over textures and

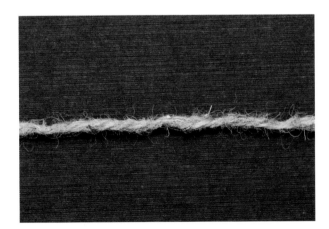

Figure 20.17 Simulated Berber yarn. Courtesy of Amy Willbanks, www.textilefabric.com.

Figure 20.18 Level loop pile with space-dyed color styling. Courtesy of Amy Willbanks, www.textilefabric.com.

patterns hide soiling better than geometric patterns do. In some locations, it may even be advisable to coordinate the carpet color with the color of the soil in the area.

Quality materials that withstand wear and hold their shape and color are the best bet in areas that must withstand heavy traffic. Additionally, regular, appropriate cleaning is critical to color maintenance and to durability. It is important to select floorcoverings—and all materials—that the available maintenance team can properly care for.

Serviceability

Service-related considerations influence the selection of all materials, including soft floorcoverings.

Functional Properties

Soft floorcoverings can help camouflage a room's structural defects, reduce noise, and conserve energy. They may offer safety features, and may improve—or lessen—mobility for people with visual or physical limitations.

Camouflage Worn and Uneven Floors

Older buildings may be structurally sound, but still have worn or uneven floors. In addition to aesthetic attributes, carpet and cushion assemblies can help to fill uneven spaces and hide damaged floor areas. A multilevel, loop-surface texture can be particularly effective in this regard.

Add Comfort and Reduce Fatigue

In contrast to the lack-of-give characteristic of smooth, hard, non-resilient surfaces like slate and quarry tiles, the tactile pleasure of stepping onto a deep pile, cushioned surface is clear. Textile floorcoverings absorb and cushion the impact forces of walking because they are compressible. For people who spend the major portion of the working day on their feet—from homemakers to nurses to food-service workers and bank tellers—the cushioning effect of carpet can be critically important. It may lessen orthopedic problems, reduce fatigue, and increase productivity.

Increase Safety

The compressibility of soft floorcoverings contributes to comfort; it also is responsible for increasing the margin of safety. When falls are cushioned, the severity of injury may be reduced. This criterion is especially important to the selection of carpet and rugs for use in interiors where older people work or reside.

Some soft floorcoverings may also create conditions that help occupants avoid tripping and falling. They provide a slip-resistant surface for better footing, and they do not have the slippery-when-wet problem characteristic of some hard floorings. A Veterans Benefits Administration report, for example, made recommendations for the design of residences for use by veterans with physical disabilities: "Low pile, high density carpet may be installed in any appropriate location. In addition to its aesthetic qualities, carpet greatly reduces sound transmission and serves to cushion accidental falls."[1]

Improve Interiors for People with Disabilities

Although the warm, soft texture of carpet is pleasing to many people, it can also improve safety for occupants. Soft floorcoverings can provide a slip-resistant surface for persons using canes and crutches, which is especially critical for swing-through movement, when body weight is transferred to the crutches. Whereas hard flooring can be difficult for wheelchairs, appropriate carpet allows wheelchairs to move smoothly without skidding or slipping.

On the other hand, a poor carpet choice, or poor installation, can present a hazard for impaired occupants. Floorcoverings suitable for wheelchair users must have low pile height that is dense and minimally compressible, which allows for easy movement of a chair over the surface. Shaggy, loose pile yarns can entrap the wheels. **Shearing**, which occurs if the carpet and cushion move in opposite directions, can occur when a chair is driven over the surface. Directly gluing carpet to the floor can minimize shearing, warping, and rippling.

All carpet and rug edges that are not securely attached to the floor create tripping hazards and allow the movement of the carpet surface under the impact of footsteps and wheelchairs. An added curb, or beveled edge, must be used on rugs to allow a smooth transition from a lower-level surface.

Low carpet pile height is also important in environments where people who have difficulty walking, including elderly people, may tend to shuffle their feet, which makes them more susceptible to falls. Thick, plush carpeting installed over thick padding creates a sensation similar to that of walking in wet sand and can intensify balance difficulties.

The Americans with Disabilities Act (ADA) federally mandates most of the requirements discussed above for commercial buildings and for public transportation. For example, the ADA stipulates maximum combined thickness of pile, cushion, and backing pile heights for carpet or carpet tile used on any accessible ground or floor surface. Rugs or mats must have a curbed edge for a transition between the hard and soft surfaces. ADA recommendations are useful for interiors frequented by elderly people and certain municipalities require compliance for various applications, even for non-public buildings. The ADA is discussed further at the end of this chapter.

People who are visually impaired or are unable to see at all become keenly aware of their environment. For them, carpet and rug features can provide cues for orientation and location within an environment and allow them to travel through the space with ease. Patterns of variance in the texture underfoot may aid in orientation, helping the person to feel where he or she is within the interior. The surfaces must have marked textural differences if they are to be detected, such as carpet alternated with smooth flooring. Different surfaces can also provide auditory cues. The edges of carpet and rugs not only need to follow ADA requirements, but additionally can serve as a physical guide for the visually impaired.

Although patterned carpeting may be disorienting to the visually impaired, carpet and rug surfaces have no troublesome glare or bright reflections that highly polished smooth surfaces sometimes have. Carpet, along with direct lighting, can help clarify areas such as stairways, where limited depth perception is problematic. Coordinating carpet patterns can be spliced together to delineate areas within a room, while maintaining a level surface (Figure 20.5). All users and occupants of a space, but especially those of limited sight, offer significant insights into space design and furnishings, which is a great help and timesaver for the designer or specifier.

Reduce Noise

Noise abatement is often one of the more important functions of soft floorcoverings. This is especially useful in, for example, classrooms, conference rooms, music recording studios, open offices, and healthcare facilities. Along with the tests used to measure the acoustical values of carpet, alone and in combination with padding, various factors influencing this property are identified in Chapter 25.

Conserve Energy

Extensive research has shown that certain structural features of carpet and padding increase thermal resistance. Research has also shown that certain appearance features can increase light reflectance, decreasing the quantity of artificial light needed. Studies have also shown than people may "feel" warmer in a carpeted room so that less supplemental heating is needed to create comfortable conditions.

Use-Life Characteristics and TARR Ratings

Most consumers' and professionals' main interest is in selecting a floorcovering that will look good for a reasonable period of time. Several variables impact the retention of the material's original color and texture.

Fiber properties, yarn characteristics, the construction features of the floorcovering, and end-use conditions are all factors that contribute to carpet's anticipated use-life and appearance retention. Traffic conditions, for example, vary for different interior locations. High levels of traffic are normally expected in corridors and lobbies, and low levels in such spaces as executive offices and rooms within apartments.

Through a consensus process involving industry experts and government specifiers, the Carpet and Rug Institute (CRI) developed the Texture Appearance Retention Rating (TARR) for specific areas of use. This system provides a quantitative guide for carpet intended for moderate, heavy, severe, or extreme use (Table 20.4).

In most cases, a soft covering intended for use in areas of little traffic would not be serviceable where traffic is

TABLE 20.4

TRAFFIC RATINGS FOR SELECTED INTERIOR SPACES

Area (by Major Category)	Traffic Rating	Area (by Major Category)	Traffic Rating
Educational		**Commercial**	
Schools and colleges		*Banks*	
private/open office	L-M	executive	L-M
classroom	H	lobby	H
dormitory	H	teller windows	H
corridor	S*	corridors	H*
cafeteria	H	*Retail establishments*	
libraries	L-M	aisle	H*
auditorium	H	dressing rooms	L-M
vending	H	outside entrance	S
common area/lobby	S	inside entrance	H
Museums and art galleries		check-out	H
display room	H	sales counter	H
private/open offices	L-M	smaller boutiques, etc.	H
common area/lobby	H	window and display area	L-M
Medical		*Office buildings*	
Health care		private/open offices	L-M
private/open offices	L-M	clerical/reception	H
patient's room	H	corridor/lobby	S*
lounge	H	cafeteria	H
nurses station	H	conference	M
corridor	S*	*Supermarkets*	H
common area/lobby	S	*Food services*	H
emergency room lobby	S	**Recreational**	
dining	H	*Recreational areas*	
examination rooms	M	fitness center	S
Multiresidential		private/open offices	L-M
Apartments		clubhouse	H
lobby/public areas	H*	locker room	H
corridors	H	swimming pool	H
rooms	L-M	recreational vehicles	H
Religious		boats	H
Churches/temples		*Theaters and stadiums*	H
worship	L-M	*(indoors)*	H
meeting room	H	*Convention Centers*	
lobby	H	auditorium	H
		corridor	S*
		lobby	S
		Hospitality	
		lobby	H-S
		front desk	H-S
		dining	H
		meeting rooms	M
		guest room (outside entry)	M
		guest room (inside entry)	L
		private/open offices	L-M

Traffic levels: L = Light; M = Moderate ($\geq$ 2.5 TARR); H = Heavy ($\geq$ 3.0 TARR); S = Severe ($\geq$ 3.5 TARR).

*If objects are to be rolled over an area of carpet, the carpet should be of maximum density to provide minimum resistance to rollers. For safety, select only level loop or low, level dense cut pile.

Note: Some areas may require higher ratings, e.g., public transportation terminals, elevators, and stairs.

heavy. Early replacement, accompanied by annoying dislocation, interruption of normal activities, and a second outlay of money and time, would be necessary. Conversely, selecting a carpet engineered for use in a commercial corridor for installation in a residential interior may entail a higher initial investment than necessary. It may also require postponement of the inevitable redecorating desired when tastes and styling preferences change. Quality control and performance evaluations, a routine part of the production efforts of industry firms, provide assistance in making suitability decisions. Testing enables producers to label their products with specific performance data and recommendations pertaining to installations, for instance, whether the products are suitable for low-traffic, residential interiors, or for high traffic, commercial interiors (see Chapter 25).

Cost Factors

Three basic elements of cost impact soft floorcovering assemblies: the initial purchase price, installation charges (including floor preparation and removal of any existing carpet), and maintenance expenses. For the purpose of comparing various types of carpet, padding, and hard-surfaced floorings, the life-cycle cost of each should be amortized according to its life expectancy. In this way, the important impact of maintenance expenses and the length of the product's use-life are taken into account.

Initial Purchase Price

The purchase price of carpet and cushion materials is normally given in dollars per square yard, although square foot prices are sometimes quoted for more expensive product. Quoted prices may be for the carpet only, the cushion only, or for the assembly. Labor costs must also be considered. Of course, the dollar figure must be multiplied by the number of square yards required, including any extra yardage that may be needed for matching pattern repeats and for fitting and trimming (see Chapter 26).

Installation Charges

A number of cost variables are involved in site preparation and installation. There may be per square-yard charges assessed for removing the existing floorcovering, for

filling cracks and smoothing rough areas, and for reducing the amount of moisture and alkaline concentration, if necessary. Charges for installing the new carpet may be separate from those for installing the new cushion.

Maintenance Expenses

The cost of maintaining a flooring material at an attractive level of appearance is a critical factor in any installation. In commercial settings, the major cleaning expense is generally the cost of labor. Other maintenance expenses include the purchase and repair of equipment and the continual replacement costs of expendable cleaning supplies.

The results of an investigative project sponsored by the Carpet and Rug Institute showed that the annual amortized cost (initial cost per square foot of the material divided by years of life expectancy) of purchasing and installing reinforced vinyl tile is significantly less than that of carpet, sheet vinyl, and terrazzo. When maintenance expenses were considered, however, the annual amortized life cycle or use-cost of carpet was significantly less than that of other flooring materials.

Life-Cycle Costing

Several producers of commercial carpet have established **life-cycle costing** which compile material, installation, and maintenance costs. Figures are prepared for each flooring material being considered by the designer or architect, and then form the basis for making use-cost comparisons.

In certain new constructions, the cost of soft floorcoverings can become part of the mortgage obligation, in which case the tax savings from the portion of interest attributable to the carpets also impacts the cost analysis. Depreciation and capital investment credits may be additional factors in costing of a project. Similar tax-related assessments can be made when replacement installations involve interest charges.

Specifying Environmentally Preferable Carpet

Today, most consumers and end-users are highly concerned about the environmental impact of items they select. In this regard, the carpet industry is a leader; its major players have been pioneers and trailblazers in environmental initiatives for over 30 years. Ray Anderson, a leader in environmental awareness and in manufacturing responsibility, was the founder of Interface Inc., a large carpet manufacturer.

Carpet is perhaps *the* interior product for which specifiers and consumers have truly excellent options in environmentally preferable selections. Some readily available options are:

1. Many carpet and backing materials are made with recycled content. Nylon, polyester, and polypropylene (olefin) are the most common fibers that are recycled.

2. Every major carpet manufacturer has one, or several, recycling platforms within their product offerings. Many have take-back programs for their used carpet, and offer programs to help designers and end-users manage carpet reclamation for recycling. (These programs are often administered through third-party recyclers.) New products made from recycled carpet range from fibers for new carpet and carpet backings to landscape wall systems, automotive parts, outdoor decking, and plastic products. Commercial specifiers and users often request recycling; virtually no residential consumer does so. Like most textile manufacturers, in addition to post-consumer recycling, carpet and fiber manufacturers have systems in place to recycle or reuse post-industrial (PI, or post-production) wastes.

3. Extending carpet life through regular and appropriate cleaning and maintenance procedures is the best way to keep material out of a landfill.

4. Professional cleaning or stain removal can often restore a carpet so that it does not need to be discarded.

5. In some cases, carpet tiles are a good alternative to broadloom. Although tiles are initially a more expensive choice, individual sections, rather than the entire floorcovering, can be easily replaced when tiles are damaged. Tiles are common for commercial use, and rare for residential interiors.

6. Carpet with low pile height and high density lasts longer than those with high pile height and low density.

7. A high-quality carpet pad reduces carpet wear and extends carpet life.

8. Refurbished carpet may meet project requirements.

Carpet America Recovery Effort (CARE)

In the late 1990s, members of the carpet industry, government representatives, and industry-related organizations began to discuss possible ways to encourage recycling of fiber and carpet. The group began the **Carpet America Recovery Effort (CARE)**, and its participants signed a **Memorandum of Understanding (MOU) for Carpet Stewardship** that established industry-wide goals to increase recycling and reuse of post-consumer carpet and to reduce the amount of waste carpet going into landfills. The MOU had a 10-year life, and efforts to renew the agreement failed. There is currently no active MOU for Carpet Stewardship. However, CARE continues to operate the national program and serve as the carpet stewardship organization for the state of California, the only state with extended producer responsibility (EPR) legislation mandating the recycle of post-consumer carpet (PCC).

CARE encourages using recycled materials in carpet manufacture, recycling of post-consumer carpet, and designing for recyclability. CARE participants represent fiber and carpet manufacturers, retailers, installers, trade organizations, design professionals, recycling/waste management firms, utility/energy service companies, international organizations, and individuals. Since its inception in 2002, CARE members are the largest users of recycled polyethylene terephthalate (PET) from plastic water bottles, and have recycled over 5 billion pounds of post-consumer carpet in the United States.

Most major manufacturers can facilitate recycling and collecting of used carpet, which is handled by regional providers that are often small, entrepreneurial companies. Recycling is not, however, free of charge; fees may apply to this undertaking. Table 20.5 shows comparisons from 2015 through 2017 of how many pounds of fiber carpet producers have taken out of the waste stream.

Of carpet face fiber that is being recycled, roughly equal quantities are polyester and nylon, with a slightly percentage of nylon in the total, and with polyester on the rise (Figure 20.19). Polypropylene that is recycled represents only about a quarter of the amount of either nylon or polyester. Although wool is, theoretically,

TABLE 20.5
POST-CONSUMER CARPET RECYCLING AND
DIVERSION STATISTICS, 2015–2017

Weight, in millions of pounds			
Year	2015	2016	2017
Total Discards*	3427	3756	3371
Diversion			
Reuse	13	3	2
Recycled Output**	170	167	178
Int'l Recycle Yield (45%)	7	4	5
Total Recycled	177	171	183
Total Reuse and Recycle	190	174	185
Waste-to-Energy	68	55	46
CAAF or Cement Kiln	120	89	44
Int'l Ship (Gross-Yield)	6	4	5
Other Internal Use	0	0	0
Sent Back to Landfill	191	174	107
Total Diverted	555	489	458
Net Diversion***	364	315	351
Recycling	6%	5%	5%
Gross Diversion	16	13%	14%

*Total discards calculation includes deselection (DS)

**Includes a 45% yield on international pounds

***Net diversion is gross diversion subtracted by pounds sent to landfill

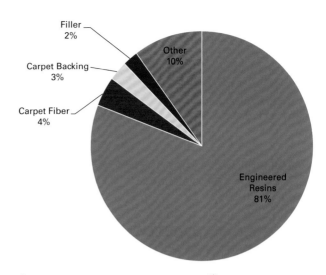

Figure 20.19 2017 post-consumer carpet fiber type. Note: N66 = nylon 6,6; N6 = nylon 6; PP = polypropylene; PET = polyethylene terephthalate. *Percentage decrease versus 2016. Courtesy of Carpet America Recovery Effort.

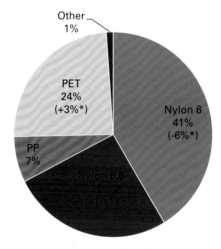

Figure 20.20 2017 end-product markets for post-consumer carpet. Courtesy of Carpet America Recovery Effort.

biodegradable, and can sometimes be reclaimed, wool recycling is not currently possible. (Less than 1 percent of carpet sold in the United States is wool.)

Most carpet backing cannot be recycled, but, along with other waste carpet that cannot be recycled, can be used to produce energy. Clean, waste-to-energy (WTE) processes produce heat and electricity by breaking materials down chemically, mechanically, and with heat. Mills that produce carpet tile often take their products back and process it into backing. Some companies offer carpet that is 100 percent recyclable because the carpet and backing are of homogenous fiber; both the face and back of these products are 100 percent polyester, polypropylene, or PVC, as only a pure, single fiber can be recycled. This initiative, along with continually improving life-cycle processing, represent major breakthroughs in sustainable initiatives (Figure 20.20).

ANSI/NSF 140 Sustainable Carpet Assessment Standard

Many industries have formed consensus-based standards for sustainability in conjunction with the American National Standards Institute (ANSI), an organization that oversees the development of standards, and NSF International, which assists organizations in developing standards (see Chapters 2 and 3). In 2007, ANSI approved NSF/ANSI 140, Sustainable Carpet Assessment Standard for Environmentally Preferable Building Materials.

This standard provides criteria for recycled content, reclamation, and end-of-life management. The standard is discussed in Chapter 3.

Design and Performance Regulations

Carpet and rugs must comply with specific mandated regulations for accessibility by persons with disabilities. Various local, state, and federal regulatory agencies have established these regulations (see Chapter 2). Laws pertain to structural characteristics such as pile height and pile construction density and functional properties such as noise reduction, as well as to flammability. (Expectations for carpet flammability testing is discussed in Chapter 25.)

Americans with Disabilities Act (ADA)

Although carpet is pleasing to occupants, and carpet can improve safety for occupants, the wrong soft floorcovering can become a barrier. The 1990 Americans with Disabilities Act (ADA) mandates accessible design and stipulates guidelines for new and existing construction in public buildings, among other applications. The statute also takes the guesswork out of preferable options—it allows carpet, but stipulates specific requirements for pile height and handling of transitional areas where flooring shifts in all public buildings. (The ADA is issued by the Department of Justice; the current version is 2010 ADA Standards for Accessible Design, and can be found online at https://www.ada.gov/2010ADAstandards_index.htm.)

The ADA is an outgrowth of earlier legislation. The Architectural Barriers Act, enacted in 1968, required certain federally owned, leased, or funded buildings and facilities to be accessible to people of limited mobility. Congress established the Architectural and Transportation Barriers Compliance Board (ATBCB) in 1973 to develop design criteria for accessibility, and to function as a coordinating body between federal agencies.[2] Several iterations later, the ADA expanded standards to all public buildings (and such venues as public transportation), but the references first established by various government agencies provide valuable input to the ADA.

The ADA stipulates maximum combined thickness of pile, cushion, and backing pile heights for carpet or carpet tile used on an accessible ground or floor surface. Rugs or mats must have a curbed edge for a transition between the hard and soft surfaces. Rationale for and advantages of these conditions were discussed in the section on how floorcoverings can improve interiors for people with disabilities.

Key Terms

area rugs	pile thickness
Berber yarns	pile yarn integrity
broadloom	plush
carpet	pooling
Carpet America Recovery	random shear
Effort (CARE)	rug
Carpet and Rug Institute	runner
(CRI)	Saxony
carpet tiles	scatter rugs
denier	sculptured
face yarns	shading
frieze	shag
grin	shearing
high-low	tip shear
life-cycle costing	tufting
Memorandum of	velour
Understanding (MOU)	velvet
for Carpet Stewardship	velvet plush
pile density	walk-off mat
pile height	watermarking
pile reversal	yarn splay

Review Questions

1. Identify two fibers that dominate the soft floorcoverings face yarn market. What accounts for their prominence?
2. Review the usage of wool in soft floorcoverings. What variables have influenced the significant shift in the consumption of this natural fiber for textile floorcoverings? In what type of floorcoverings does wool usage remain strong?
3. Identify the dominant fiber in the carpet and rug backings market. Why has the usage of jute declined?

4. Discuss the relative importance of spun yarns and BCF yarns in the face or wear layer of soft floorcoverings. What advantages are offered by BCF yarns?

5. Explain the shift in the average denier of nylon carpet filament in the past two decades. How has this shift influenced surface texture design?

6. When did tufting begin to enjoy widespread usage as a construction technique? What advantages does it offer over weaving techniques?

7. Identify some advantages that carpet tiles offer over wall-to-wall installations.

8. Consider some of the aesthetic values offered by area rugs.

9. Why is pile height likely to be greater than pile thickness?

10. Identify ways in which the carpet industry is promoting environmental sustainability.

11. What causes watermarking to occur with soft floorcoverings?

12. Identify surface textures and colorations that help to camouflage soil.

13. Describe the color styling seen with Berber yarns.

14. Identify factors to be considered when selecting and installing soft floorcoverings in an interior used by a person with mobility limitations. Which of these variables are positive?

15. How can soft floorcoverings be chosen to help blind and partially sighted persons?

16. What is the purpose of life-cycle costing?

Notes

1. Department of Veterans Affairs, Veterans Benefits Administration, *Handbook for Design: Specially Adapted Housing, VA Pamphlet 26–13*, Washington, D.C., March 20, 2008.

2. The full text of the ATBCB Minimum Guidelines for Accessible Design may be reviewed in the *Federal Register*, Vol. 47, Wednesday, August 4, 1982, 33873–33875.

21

Construction of Floorcoverings: Tufting

Textile floorcoverings may be divided into two broad categories: pile and nonpile structures. Nonpile structures are produced by methods such as braiding, weaving, and needle punching. Weaving can also be used to produce pile structures. Other pile structures are produced by methods such as tufting, knitting, and fusion bonding; in some cases, identical textures can be produced by any of several techniques. Understanding tufted floorcoverings' structural qualities makes data supplied by producers more meaningful, which helps specifiers and consumers make informed decisions about product choices.

Figure 21.2 Illustration of construction layers in tufted carpet. Courtesy of Brintons.

Basic Components of Tufted Floorcoverings

Whether a carpet or rug is machine tufted or hand tufted, the principal components are the same. Tufted constructions include **pile or face yarns**, a **primary backing**, a layer of adhesive, and a **secondary backing** (Figures 21.1 and 21.2).

Pile or Face Yarns

The composition and structural characteristics of face yarns used in pile floorcoverings were discussed in Chapter 20, p. 268. Bulked continuous filament (BCF) yarns of nylon and olefin fibers dominate.

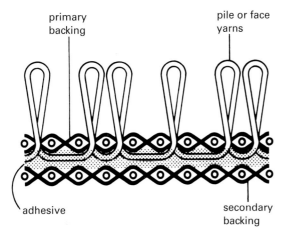

Figure 21.1 Components in tufted constructions. Fairchild Books.

Primary Backing Fabrics

Typical primary backing fabrics are shown in Figure 21.3. Although jute (Figure 21.3a) formerly dominated the market, it has largely been replaced by olefin, except for certain specific carpet types. Plain-woven fabrics of yarn-like tapes or ribbons of olefin (Figure 21.3b) have high stability, unless heated above 338°F. These fabrics are impervious to moisture; they resist mildew and the development of odors. To minimize raveling, a thin butyl coating is frequently applied to bond the warp and filling strands. When low pile construction densities are planned, producers can use a plain-woven olefin backing with a "nylon cap," produced by needle punching a thin nylon batt into the backing. Because nylon fibers accept dye more readily than olefin fibers, the needle-punched fibers can be colored to coordinate with the face yarns. In the event the backing is exposed in use, any difference in color between the face fibers and the backing is masked.

Spunbonded olefin fabric (Figure 21.3c) exhibits no fraying or raveling and is not susceptible to problems from moisture. During tufting, the filaments are pushed aside; thus, the needle is only minimally deflected, which helps ensure uniform pile height and tuft placement.

Secondary Backing Fabrics

Secondary backing fabrics, also referred to as **scrims**, must adhere well and provide high dimensional stability. Fabrics

(a)

(b)

(c)

Figure 21.3 Typical primary backing fabrics: (a) plain-woven jute, (b) plain-woven olefin, (c) spunbonded olefin. Courtesy of Amy Willbanks, www.textilefabric.com.

composed of jute are naturally rough and adhere well; spunbonded fabrics are smooth and have poor adhesion. Some manufacturers use a glass fiber scrim to reinforce a vinyl secondary backing. This combination has high dimensional stability and virtually no moisture-related problems.

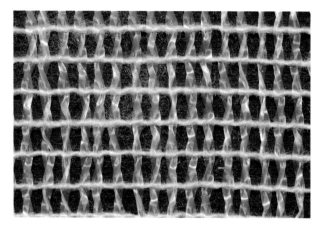

Figure 21.4 A leno-woven olefin secondary backing uses spun filling yarns for improved adhesion. Courtesy of Amy Willbanks, www.textilefabric.com.

A leno-woven fabric composed of olefin fibers is specifically manufactured for use as a secondary backing. The leno interlacing minimizes yarn raveling at the fabric edges, and the spun filling yarns provide the necessary roughness for adhesion of the fabric (Figure 21.4).

Permanently attached foam rubber or polyurethane cushions may be used as secondary backings, eliminating the need for a separate cushion. Secondary backings may or may not be used with commercially produced, hand-tufted carpet and rugs. Hard-backed polyvinyl chloride (PVC) is used as a backing for modular carpet tiles. Unitary backings are used primarily with tufted loop pile carpet and consist of either rubber or latex used without an additional secondary backing. They are suitable only for direct glue-down installations.

Adhesives

The most frequently used adhesive is synthetic latex; approximately 12 ounces per square yard should be applied to most tufted floorcoverings. Some carpet producers are replacing latex adhesives with molten thermoplastic compounds.

To control electrical charge buildup, tufted carpet producers may incorporate a conductive compound into the adhesive used to secure the secondary backing, or they may sandwich an antistatic coating between the primary backing and the adhesive. Some carpet producers combine a conductive compound in the adhesive or backing fabric with an antistatic component in the pile layer. Tufted carpet producers may also incorporate a flame-retardant compound into the adhesive. To be effective, the coating must penetrate the primary backing.

Tufting Operations

Unlike most weaving operations, tufting is a relatively simple, uncomplicated process. Pile yarns are inserted into an already-formed primary backing fabric, and surface textures and construction densities can easily be varied.

Forming the Pile Layer

Pile yarns are supplied in one of two ways: either from cones mounted on a creel frame, or from large spools called *beams*, erected in back of the tufting machine. So that they will not tangle, the yarns are fed through thin plastic tubes, visible in the upper portion of the photograph in Figure 21.5, to tension-control devices and the tufting needles. The tension controls determine the quantity of yarn supplied to the needles, helping to ensure the production of the planned pile height. Figure 21.6 shows a close up of tufting needles picking up individual pile yarns.

Many needles are aligned crosswise on the machine. The number of needles required depends on the width and the planned crosswise density, or gauge. **Gauge** is the fractional distance between adjacent needles; it can be converted to a **needle count**, which is the number of needles per crosswise inch on the machine. A gauge of ⅛ inch is equivalent to a needle count of eight; a gauge of

Figure 21.5 Commercial tufting machine. Courtesy of CTS Group Pty Ltd.

Figure 21.6 Close up of tufting needles. Courtesy of Martin Patrick Evan, Ltd.

Figure 21.7 Highly skilled artisans hand tufting a circular rug. Courtesy of Martin Patrick Evan, Ltd.

$1/10$ inch is equivalent to a needle count of ten. To prepare a tufting machine to produce carpet 12 feet wide, with a gauge of $1/10$ inch, 1,440 needles must be aligned and threaded with pile yarns (12 feet × 12 inches = 144 inches; 144 inches × 10 needles = 1,440 needles).

The sequence used to form loop pile floorcoverings is schematized in Figure 8.12 (p. 102). Threaded with pile yarns, the needles descend through the back of the primary fabric. Working in a timed relationship with the descending needles, loop pile hooks rock forward, catching and holding the yarn loops while the needles ascend. The pile layer is then formed on the face of the primary fabric. One crosswise row of tufts is produced in each tufting cycle.

When a cut pile surface is planned, a knife blade is attached to the pile hook, which cuts the loops, forming one U-shaped tuft from each loop (Figure 8.12, p. 102). For either loop or cut pile coverings, the descend-and-ascend tufting cycle is followed by the advancement of the primary backing a predetermined distance and the repetition of the cycle.

The number of tufts or stitches per inch determines the distance the primary backing is advanced after each tufting cycle, and thus governs the lengthwise density. Typically, the number of stitches per inch ranges from 4 to 11. If, for example, a stitch of 8 is selected, the crosswise bank of needles would punch into the fabric 8 times in each lengthwise inch, and there would be $1/8$ inch between each crosswise row of tufts.

Modern tufting machines are capable of completing more than 500 tufting cycles per minute. Depending upon width, density, and surface texture, this capability can translate into the production of more than 1,000 square yards of cut pile carpet per day, and about twice that amount of loop pile carpet.

In comparison to machine tufting, hand tufting is an extremely slow and expensive process. It is used only for custom orders requiring a relatively small amount of yardage. Hand tufting is done with a hand-held, electrically powered tufting gun (Figure 21.7).

Creating Multilevel Surface Textures

Various attachments are available for tufting multilevel surfaces in random and patterned shapes. Differences in pile height are achieved by controlling the quantity of yarn supplied to the needles prior to their descent. The needles and loop hooks continue to operate in the conventional manner. Most manufacturers utilize computerized programming to control pile height variations.

When tufting of the pile yarns is completed, several operations are required to convert the greige carpet into finished carpet. Among these, tip shearing, random shearing, and hand carving create even more variety in surface texture.

Applying an Adhesive and Scrim

Unless the tufted pile yarns are permanently anchored in the primary backing, they could easily be pulled out when snagged. In cut pile styles, this would show up as an empty space the size of the space once occupied by the removed tufts. In loop pile styles, pulling the continuous length of yarn would expose a lengthwise line of backing void of tufts, as illustrated in Figure 21.8.

In preparation for application of the adhesive, the back of the primary fabric is beaten to drive the pile yarn segments tightly against the fabric base. The coating is then applied uniformly across the back, securely binding the yarns into their positions. The secondary backing is then rolled onto the adhesive coating.

Most tufted broadloom carpet is manufactured in 12-foot widths. Some manufacturers also offer 6-foot and 15-foot widths to meet special needs. The yardage may be **rollgoods**, or may be cut into small rugs and mats. The products are converted and then subjected to quality testing.

Structural Qualities of Tufted Constructions

As part of their quality-control programs, tufted carpet producers evaluate the strength of the bond between the primary and secondary backings and the pile construction density. Some measure various weight-related characteristics for use in selection guidelines that coordinate minimum weight values with anticipated traffic levels.

Bundle Penetration

Visual examination enables carpet producers to estimate how thoroughly the adhesive penetrates the pile yarn bundle. A high degree of **bundle penetration** helps to prevent individual staple or filament fibers from being pulled out of the yarns and rubbed into fuzz and pills on the carpet surface.

Delamination Strength

A strong bond between the adhesive coating and secondary backing is important in order to prevent **delamination** or separation of the backings when they are subjected to heavy stress forces. The movement of heavy equipment or the flow of much traffic across a carpet surface can have a "snowplow" effect, crushing and pushing the structure, which in turn can cause shearing, the movement of the

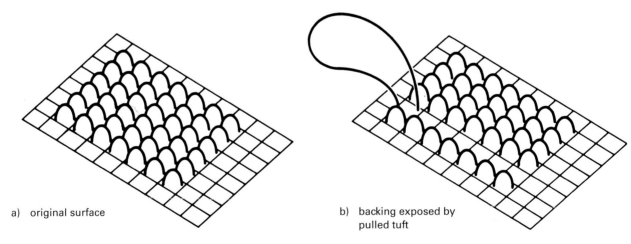

a) original surface

b) backing exposed by pulled tuft

Figure 21.8 Potential problem with poorly anchored pile yarns. Fairchild Books.

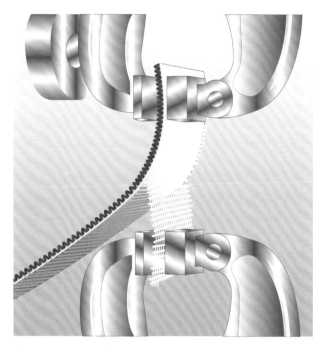

Figure 21.9 Measuring secondary backing adhesion strength.
Fairchild Books.

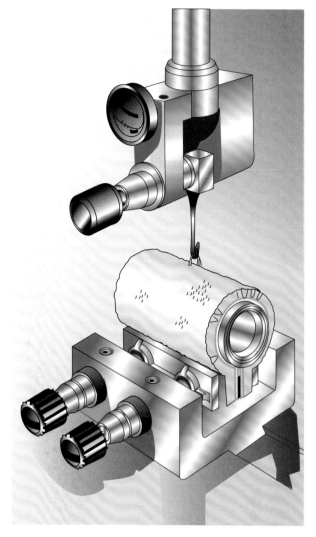

Figure 21.10 Measuring tuft bind strength. Fairchild Books.

primary and secondary backings in opposite directions. Unless the bond between the two fabrics is strong, shearing can cause delamination, which could result in bubbling, rippling, and straining at the seams.

ASTM D3936 Standard Test Method for Delamination Strength of Secondary Backing of Pile Floorcoverings outlines procedures to measure the strength of the bond between the backings. In Figure 21.9, stress is exerted on the specimen clamped in the jaws of the test apparatus. The force required to separate the components is measured for each of three specimens; the average is then reported in pounds per inch of specimen width. Values frequently range from 2.5 to 8.33 pounds per inch.

Tuft Bind

ASTM D1335 Standard Test Method for Tuft Bind of Pile Floorcoverings outlines procedures for measuring **tuft bind**. The force required to pull one loop of pile tuft from a floorcovering is measured by first anchoring the structure in clamps, as shown in Figure 21.10. A hook is inserted into the test loop, and the loops on either side of the test loop are cut. Raising the hook then exerts force.

Three tufts on each of five, 6-inch by 8-inch samples are tested. The average force required to remove the tufts is reported in pound-force. Values typically range from 4.5 to 20 pounds. For loop pile carpet, the recommended minimum value is 10 pounds of force per loop. This procedure can also be used on cut pile structures, where a tweezer-like device is clamped onto one side or leg of a cut loop.

Tufts per Square Inch

Although the eyeball method illustrated in Figure 20.9 can be used to roughly evaluate pile construction density, a more precise technique is to determine the actual number of **tufts per square inch**. ASTM D5793 Test Method for Binding Sites per Unit Length or Width of Pile Yarn Floorcoverings provides instructions on how to count binding sites per unit length and width. Producers measure and report the necessary lengthwise and crosswise values separately on data and specification sheets.

Gauge, needle count, and number of tufts or stitches per inch were explained earlier in this chapter. The number of tufts per square inch may be calculated by multiplying the needle count by the number of stitches per inch. If other construction features are equal, carpet and rugs with higher construction density values should exhibit better durability and texture retention.

The important influence of construction density on thickness retention can be appreciated by reviewing a simple principle of physics. When a stress load is distributed over a large, rather than a small, number of supports, the force or load each must bear is minimized. The same idea is behind the magic we see when a performer lies on a bed of nails without injury to the skin: each one of many nails supports an extremely small portion of the body weight, so the skin is not punctured. To pursue the analogy, each tuft in a pile floorcovering may be considered equivalent to one nail; as the number of tufts is increased, the load each must support is reduced. Denser construction also helps to reduce yarn flexing within the pile because adjacent tufts support one another.

Pile construction density values are important, but they should not be used alone to predict thickness retention. For example, each square in Figure 21.11 has the same number of pile tufts, but the size and thus the weight of the yarns in each is significantly different. Therefore, weight is also a factor in predicting serviceability.

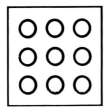 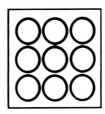

Figure 21.11 Equal pile construction densities having different sizes of yarns. Fairchild Books.

Weight-Related Factors

In general, as the weight of a textile floorcovering increases, so does its quality, its potential texture retention, and its wear-life. For this reason, producers of tufted carpet and other soft floorcoverings generally report various weight-related measurements. These include pile yarn weight, effective face weight, total weight, density factor, weight density, and the density required by the Federal Housing Administration (FHA; see Chapter 2). The challenge is to understand the differences among these measurements. Minimum weight values are often part of design standards established for certain commercial interiors.

Pile Yarn Weight

Pile yarn weight is the weight of the yarns used in the wear layer and those portions of the pile yarn that extend into the backing layer. Pile yarn weight values are expressed in ounces per square yard or in grams per square meter. Several construction variables are reflected in pile weight values, including fiber density, yarn weight, pile height, and pile construction density. Pile yarn weight values are among the better references for judging the potential serviceability of similarly constructed floorcoverings. Distribution of the pile yarns between the wear layer and the backing layer shows proportional differences in constructions.

Effective Face Yarn Weight

The **effective face yarn weight** is a way to express the weight of the pile yarns in the wear layer, excluding those in the backing. Because fusion-bonded structures (discussed in Chapter 22) contain a relatively small amount of pile yarns in the backing layer, producers of these carpets often report the effective face yarn weight.

Total Weight

The **total weight** of a floorcovering includes the weight of the pile yarns as well as the weight of the backing yarns, backing fabrics, and backcoatings. Weight measurements and other construction variables should be coordinated with traffic conditions for good performance. (Traffic classifications for various areas are listed in Table 20.4.) Because the weight values listed are minimums, increasing them should provide increased floor performance, but material quality and other factors play into performance.

Density Factor

The **density factor** or **density index** is a calculation that reflects both pile construction density and yarn size (denier). Increasing the density factor will increase floor performance, up to a point. The following formula is used to calculate this factor:

$$\text{Density factor} = \text{yarn size} \times \text{needle count} \times$$
$$\text{stitches per inch}$$

The usefulness of pile yarn weight, effective face yarn weight, and total weight measurements is limited in that they do not reflect the true pile density (mass or amount of matter per unit of volume). Consider, for example, two carpets that have the same pile yarn and identical pile construction densities, but different pile heights. The carpet with the higher pile would weigh more, but would have lower true density (Figure 21.12). On the other hand, if two carpets differed only in their yarn size, the carpet containing the heavier yarns would not only weigh more but would also have a higher true density. The density factor also does not reflect true density because it does not consider pile height. It would seem that structures with equal construction densities and yarn sizes, but different pile heights, will have identical density factors, but increasing the pile height will in fact reduce the true density. Therefore, measurements that reflect the true density are often reported.

Average Density and Weight Density

Average density and **weight density** measurements take pile height (finished thickness) into consideration and thus can indicate the true density of floorcovering structures. Minimum density values may be recommended or required in some settings. For example, HUD/FHA Use of Materials Bulletin 44d (see Chapter 2) sets out

Figure 21.12 Carpet with higher pile height may weigh more, but will also have a lower true density than a comparable carpet with lower pile of heavier yarn. Courtesy of Aronson's Floor Covering.

required minimum values required for use in interiors under the agency's purview. (Further requirements are that certification must be carried out by an independent laboratory administrator approved by the FHA. The bulletin offers formulas for calculating average density and weight density.)

Weight-related features affect texture retention and functional values such as noise control and insulation. Test methods for evaluating these and other service-related properties are discussed in Chapter 25.

Key Terms

average density	pile yarn weight
bundle penetration	primary backing
delamination	rollgoods
density factor	scrims
density index	secondary backing
effective face yarn weight	total weight
gauge	tuft bind
needle count	tufts per square inch
pile or face yarns	weight density

Review Questions

1. Draw and label a cross-sectional illustration of a tufted floorcovering.
2. Identify the advantages and limitations of the three types of primary backings.
3. How is a "nylon cap" produced, and what positive features does it offer in use?
4. Distinguish between gauge and needle count.
5. Discuss the problems that could occur when pile yarn is not securely anchored in the primary backing.
6. Explain the importance of having the adhesive penetrate the pile yarn bundles.
7. Explain the meaning of "snowplow" effect and shearing.
8. Differentiate between pile yarn weight and effective face yarn weight.

22

Construction of Floorcoverings: Weaving and Other Machine Techniques

Commercial weaving of textile floorcoverings began in the United States in the late 1700s. The principal product was a flat-woven, yarn-dyed, reversible structure called *ingrain*. Gradually, braided and hand-woven rugs made in the home replaced ingrain. Pile carpet was imported until the mid-1800s, when domestic power looms were adapted for production of a patterned, loop pile carpet known as Brussels. Over the years, other techniques and looms augmented the production capabilities of domestic manufacturers. In addition to ingrain and Brussels carpet, cut-pile constructions, such as Wilton, Axminster, velvet, and chenille, also became available. Together, woven floorcoverings dominated markets until the mid-1950s, when large-scale tufting operations were widely adopted.

In addition to tufting and weaving operations, other machine techniques are currently used to produce carpet and rugs. Although machine techniques other than tufting produce only a small portion of today's residential and commercial floorcoverings, even small percentages translate into millions of rugs, carpets, and revenue dollars.

Woven Pile Floorcoverings

Several methods of weaving are used to produce pile floorcoverings. Among these, the yarns used, the structure and operation of the looms, the nature of the surface patterns formed, and the degree of interlacing complexity involved differ quite a bit.

Basic Components

Most woven pile floorcoverings contain warp yarns, stuffer yarns, filling shots (yarns), and pile yarns. These yarns are illustrated schematically in Figure 22.1.

Filling or weft shots (yarns) are crosswise yarns used to anchor the **pile warp yarns**. The shots are generally of polypropylene olefin, jute, or cotton, and the pile yarns may be spun or multifilament yarns of any fiber. For added body and weight, extra warp yarns, called **stuffer yarns**, serve as a back-layer plane in between the **chain warp yarns**, which pass over and under the shots, securing all components of the structure tightly together. The zigzag configuration of these yarns in most woven floorcoverings makes them easy to recognize. Chains are generally composed of polyester.

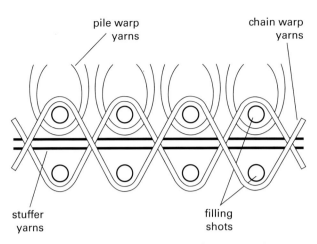

Figure 22.1 Basic components of woven pile carpet and rugs. Fairchild Books.

Unlike tufting, in which the pile layer is added to an already-formed base fabric, weaving forms the pile and backing layers simultaneously. Some methods, such as velvet weaving, are relatively simple procedures that have only limited design capabilities; others, including Axminster and Wilton, are quite complicated and virtually unlimited in the range of designs they can produce. Weaving operations are comparatively slow and labor-intensive, however, so they are used less frequently than tufting by domestic producers.

Axminster Carpet

Axminster carpet, named for the British town where the technique was developed, is the top-of-the-line cut pile carpet. The technique allows elaborate patterning and many colors, but it requires a lot of preparation and is slow to weave.

Two illustrations of Axminster carpet are shown in Figures 22.2 and 22.3. A distinctive feature is the use of paired filling shots, with either two pairs used per tuft row, as shown in the sketch on the left in Figure 22.2, or three pairs per tuft row, as shown in the sketch on the right in Figure 22.2. This makes the crosswise direction of the carpet somewhat rigid and inflexible, a distinguishing characteristic of Axminster floorcoverings.

Preparation for Axminster weaving is lengthy and involved; the more intricate and complex the design and pattern repeat to be woven, the more complicated preparation becomes. First, a colored **print design** displaying the full length and width of one pattern repeat

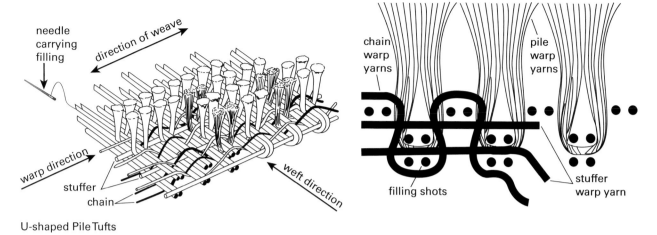

needle carrying filling

direction of weave

warp direction

stuffer

chain

weft direction

U-shaped Pile Tufts

chain warp yarns

pile warp yarns

filling shots

stuffer warp yarn

Figure 22.2 Cross-sectional sketches of Axminster carpet with paired filling shots. Courtesy of Mohawk Carpet.

(a)

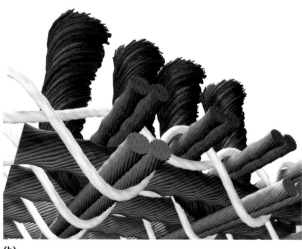

(b)

Figure 22.3 Illustrations of Axminster weaving pattern: (a) side view, (b) back view. Courtesy of Brintons.

is prepared. A portion of the design prepared for weaving an intricate pattern is shown in Figure 22.4a and b. Each small block represents one pile tuft. Clearly, the colored tufts must be woven precisely in their planned positions, as shown in Figure 22.5a, or the motifs will be irregular and flawed.

When the print design is ready, skilled technicians assemble cones of yarns colored according to its specifications. They then wind the various colors of yarns onto 3-foot-long **spools**, following the sequence printed on one crosswise row of the point design. For a repeat 18 inches in width, the sequence would be used twice on each spool. Spools are linked end-to-end to form a **bracket**. If the carpet is to be woven 12 feet wide, four spools are used, and the sequence would be repeated eight times across the bracket.

The pitch determines the number of yarns wound on each spool. **Pitch** is the number of pile units (loops or cut, U-shaped tufts) per 27 inches of width; it commonly ranges from 162 to 216. The pitch method of reporting crosswise density in woven carpet has persisted from earlier times when looms were narrower: carpet was woven in 27-inch widths and seamed as often as necessary. If a carpet is to be 12 feet wide and have a pitch of 189, a total of 1,008 tufts will form each crosswise row. This is calculated as follows: 12 feet × 12 inches = 144 inches; 144 inches divided by 27 inches = 5.33; that is, there are five and a third of the 27-inch segments in the carpet width; and $5\frac{1}{3}$ × 189 tufts = 1,008 total tufts. Each bracket thus carries

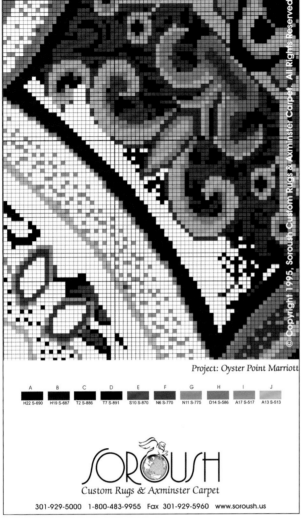

Project: Oyster Point Marriott

A	B	C	D	E	F	G	H	I	J
H22 S-690	H19 S-687	T2 S-886	T7 S-891	S10 S-870	N6 S-770	N11 S-775	D14 S-586	A17 S-517	A13 S-513

SOROUSH
Custom Rugs & Axminster Carpet
301-929-5000 1-800-483-9955 Fax 301-929-5960 www.soroush.us

(a)

(b)

Figure 22.4 Axminster pattern: (a) print design for a portion of Axminster pattern, (b) Axminster pattern made from design.
Courtesy of Soroush Custom Rugs & Axminster Carpet, www.soroush.us.

(a)

(b)

Figure 22.5 Axminster weaving: (a) weaving the design on an Axminster loom, (b) Axminster carpet. Courtesy of Soroush Custom Rugs & Axminster Carpet, www.soroush.us.

1,008 yarns, and each 3-foot-long spool carries one-third of the total, or 336 yarns.

After the first bracket is completed, spools are wound with yarns according to the sequence shown in the second row of squares on the print design. The process continues until one bracket has been prepared for each crosswise row in the pattern repeat. The length of the repeat and the planned lengthwise density governs the number of brackets required.

The number of **rows per inch**—the number of crosswise rows of tufts per lengthwise inch—in an Axminster carpet is commonly within the range of seven to ten. If, for example, a count of eight rows per inch is selected, eight brackets would be prepared for weaving one lengthwise inch of carpet. A repeat 25 inches long would then require 200 brackets.

In preparation for weaving, the multiple brackets are positioned in proper order on the loom (refer to Figure 22.5a). Yarn from the first bracket is rolled off and lowered into position, and the stuffers, chain warp yarns, and pairs of weft shots are integrated with the pile yarns, locking them into the structure. The amount of yarn reeled off is determined by the planned pile height. The pile yarn is cut, the bracket is moved away, and the second bracket is lowered. A complete cycle of all the brackets would produce the length of one repeat; a second cycle would produce another length, and so on.

Wilton Carpet

Unlike Axminster, which is always a cut pile, both loop- and cut-pile effects can be achieved with Wilton weaving. Formerly, loop-pile carpet woven on a Jacquard loom was called **Brussels**, and cut pile carpet was called **Wilton**, which is the British town where Wilton carpet was developed (Figure 22.6). Today, most pile floorcoverings woven on a Jacquard loom are called Wilton, although a few less-common Jacquard techniques are produced.

The number of colors of pile yarns in one warp line used in the pattern is denoted by the number of **frames**; for instance, a three-frame Wilton has three colors that alternate in the same vertical line, a six-frame Wilton has six colors, and so on. When the variously colored yarns are not required to form part of the surface design, they are carried in a plane in the backing layer. Figure 22.7 shows a diagram of a cross-section. The presence

Figure 22.6 Wilton carpet. Courtesy of Kravet Inc.

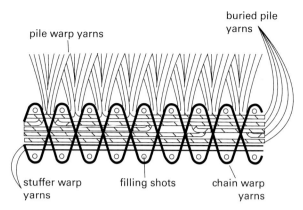

Figure 22.7 Cross-sectional sketch of a Wilton carpet. Courtesy of Mohawk Carpet.

of such buried yarns distinguishes Wilton constructions. (Producers use vernacular such as high, low, and floating, or **dead-and-buried** to refer to these yarns.) Although the hidden lengths contribute weight, cushioning, and resiliency, they also add to the material's cost.

Warp colors can be arranged in a striped warp in many pile constructions, which is a different concept. In a simple striped warp, each warp pile color stays in its defined vertical line position for the entire length of the cloth. In Wilton, or any multi-frame pile fabric, colors in different frames can be switched off in the same vertical line through the length of the fabric.

Color arrangements in Wilton carpets rotate a number of colors in both the warp and pile colors. To further expand design possibilities, a system of **planting** colored pile yarns may be employed, that is, an added color of yarn is periodically substituted ("planted") for one of the basic pile colors. Planting can cause a three-frame Wilton carpet to appear to be a four-frame structure; an investigation of the backing, however, would uncover only two buried pile yarns behind each tuft (Figure 22.8a and b).

Jacquard carpet weaving is similar to other Jacquard weaving operations (see Chapter 7). In carpet weaving, however, the Jacquard attachment controls the pile yarns, not the base yarns; additional harnesses are used to control the chain warp yarns; and additional loom beams are used to hold the chain and stuffer yarns. As shown schematically in Figure 22.9, wires are inserted into the shed formed by the pile yarns, and weft shots are inserted into the separate shed formed by the chain warp yarns. The reed moves forward, pushing the wire and shot

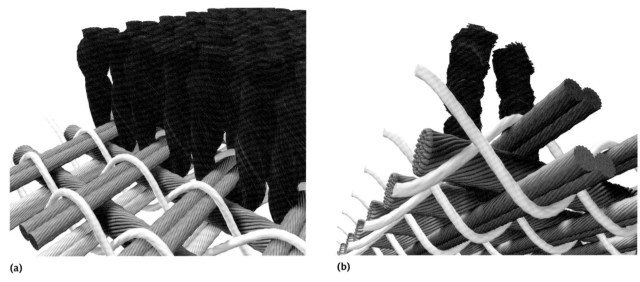

(a)

(b)

Figure 22.8 Illustrations of Wilton carpet: (a) side view, (b) back view. Courtesy of Brintons.

against the already-woven carpet. The heddle-like cords holding the raised pile yarns then descend, lowering the pile yarn over the wires. A weft shot is carried across the carpet, above the pile yarns and below the chain warp yarns. Then, a new pile yarn shed is formed, the harnesses reverse their positions, and the sequence is repeated.

The pile loops are formed over wires whose height determines the pile height. If a cut pile is planned, the

wires are equipped with knives on one end; as the wires are withdrawn, they cut the loops. If a looped pile texture is planned, the wires will have rounded ends.

Since one wire is used for each crosswise row of pile tufts, the lengthwise density of Wilton carpet is reported as the number of **wires per inch**. Typically, this number is within the range of seven to ten. The crosswise density commonly ranges from a pitch of 189 to 252, but it may be as high as 270 or 346.

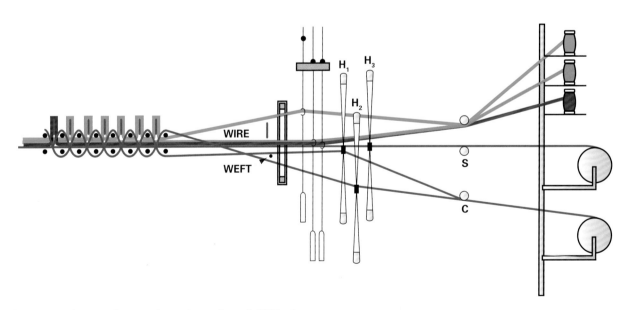

Figure 22.9 Diagram of Jacquard carpet weaving. Fairchild Books.

Velvet Carpet

Velvet carpet weaving is an over-the-wire construction technique used to produce velvet carpet. This use of "velvet" must not be confused with its use to name a surface texture, nor with its use as a name for an upholstery fabric.

Velvet weaving is one of the least complicated methods of producing pile carpet. As in Wilton construction, the wire height determines the pile height. Again, the wires may or may not have knives on their ends. Unlike Wilton weaving, however, no Jacquard attachment is used, so intricate details and elaborate patterns are not possible. Appearance variations may be created by combining cut and loop textures, by incorporating different colors of pile yarns in bands of various widths, or by employing pile yarns with distinctive color styling.

The cross sections in Figure 22.10 show two structural forms of velvet carpet. In Figure 22.10a, the pile yarns are anchored by the upper filling shots only. In Figure 22.10b, they are held by both the upper and lower filling shots: The carpet constructed this way would be described as a **woven-through-the-back** velvet. If other construction variables are the same, a woven-through-the-back velvet is more serviceable because the pile tufts are more securely bound and the total weight is greater. The carpet back in either type of velvet weave may be coated with latex or a thermoplastic compound for greater stability. The pitch of velvet carpet ranges from 165 to 270. The number of wires per inch ranges from a low of seven to a high of ten.

Chenille Carpet

True **chenille carpet** is made from authentic chenille yarns that are created by the leno-weaving and fabric-cutting processes described in Chapter 7. The chenille strips are folded for use as pile yarns; the leno-entwined warp yarns form a base and the extended **filling yarns** form a V shape. True chenille yarn is rare today; the yarns are simulated with a twisting process in which loose fibers are inserted as the yarn is produced.

Chenille carpet is also rare today. It is comparatively expensive due to material costs and the labor intensiveness required, and it is not domestically produced. Figure 22.11 diagrams chenille carpet construction.

Pile Construction Density

The number of tufts per square inch in woven floorcoverings can easily be calculated by first dividing the pitch value by 27. The resulting figure, the number of pile units per crosswise inch, is equivalent to the needle count with tufted constructions. Tufted constructions in tufts per inch directly correlates with the product that results after multiplying the number of rows or wires per inch times the converted pitch calculated with the formula from the paragraph above.

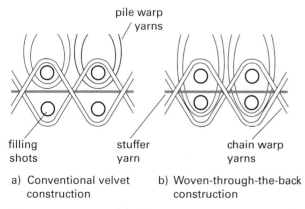

Figure 22.10 Cross-sectional sketches of velvet carpets: (a) pile yarns anchored by the upper filling shots, (b) pile yarns held by both the upper and lower filling shots. Fairchild Books.

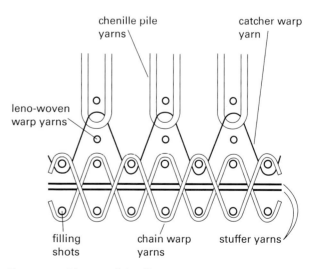

Figure 22.11 Diagram of chenille carpet structure. Fairchild Books.

Other Machine Operations

Machine operations other than tufting and weaving are also used to produce soft floorcoverings. Among these are fusion bonding, braiding, and needle punching.

Fusion Bonding

Fusion-bonding techniques offer potential for innovation in both rollgoods and for carpet tiles.

Basic Components

Fusion-bonded structures have a minimum of three components: pile yarns, adhesive, and a primary backing (Figure 22.12). The adhesive, which is generally a vinyl compound such as polyvinyl chloride (PVC), is placed on the face of the backing, which may be woven jute or a nonwoven glass fiber fabric. The pile yarns are embedded or implanted into the vinyl; they are not woven or tufted through the primary backing.

Fusion-bonded carpet has approximately 5 to 8 percent of the total pile yarn weight embedded in the adhesive; tufted structures may have 15 to 30 percent of the pile yarn weight enclosed in the primary backing; and woven constructions may have 20 to 50 percent of the total pile yarn weight interlaced in the backing layers. Thus, fusion-bonded carpet and modules can have more of the yarn available to the wearing face. Together with denser gauge fusing capabilities, this feature helps producers to engineer fusion-bonded floorcoverings, even those having fine velour textures, to withstand the high levels of traffic encountered in commercial installations. The processing is slower than tufting, however, and the vinyl compound is more expensive than tufting substrates.

A special use of fusion bonding is the production of entrance mats made of coir fibers. Figure 22.13 provides a close-up cross-sectional view of the implantation of the ends of the fibers in PVC. The superior stiffness of these fibers helps them function like hundreds of miniature brushes, efficiently cleaning shoe soles and protecting the interior carpet from excessive amounts of tracked-in dirt. Coir mats generally range in total thickness from 0.68 to 1.2 inches. Some producers offer coir rollgoods and carpet modules, as well as mats.

Braiding

Braiding is believed to be one of the oldest fabric structures. Braided rugs are not braided, themselves, but are made by coiling braids into a desired shape and then using machine zigzag stitching to link adjacent braids. Braided rugs were originally handmade, and were a staple in colonial America as an excellent way to repurpose household cloth or clothing that was past its prime.

The braids in the rug in Figure 22.14 were formed by interlacing groups of filament yarns. Core yarns composed of waste fibers were incorporated for weight, body, and cushioning. Yarn-like strands of sponge rubber can also be used as "core yarns" for this purpose.

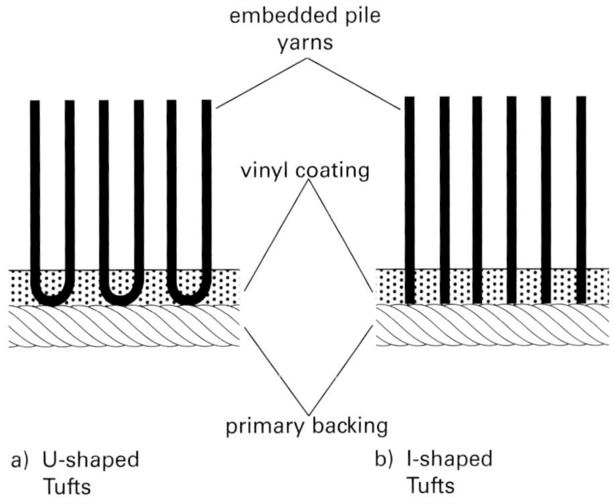

Figure 22.12 Diagram of fusion-bonded floorcovering structure. Fairchild Books.

a) U-shaped Tufts   b) I-shaped Tufts

embedded pile yarns — vinyl coating — primary backing

Figure 22.13 Cross-sectional view of rug containing implanted coir yarns. Courtesy of Amy Willbanks, www.textilefabric.com.

Figure 22.14 Braided rug. Courtesy of Amy Willbanks, www. textilefabric.com.

Needle Punching

Needle-punched floorcoverings are often referred to colloquially as "indoor-outdoor carpet." To manufacture these structures, various colors of 3- to 4-inch fibers are blended to achieve uniform distribution of the colors. Long webs, as wide as the needle loom and weighing approximately 0.5 to 1.0 ounce per square yard, are formed by laying the fibers flat. Layering the webs at 45- or 90-degree angles to one another forms a thick batt of the desired weight, which typically ranges from 16 to 32 ounces per square yard. For strength and dimensional stability, an adhesive-coated jute or nylon scrim may be centered in the batt or placed behind it. The batt is then tacked or prepunched to reduce its thickness and fed into a needle loom. Here, hundreds of barbed needles punch into the batt some 800 to 1,200 times per square inch, creating a mechanical chain-stitch among the fibers and locking them into the scrim and adhesive.

The barbed needles used in the punching operation produce flat carpet with a felt-like appearance (Figure 22.15a). If needles with crescent-shaped points are used for the final punches, the carpet will feature loop-like protrusions (Figure 22.15b).

When needle-punched structures are to be installed outdoors, on patios and golf greens and around pools, their composition must withstand the ravages of sunlight, rain, and insects. They are permeable, so they can be hosed to flush away dirt. If these structures are installed indoors, their permeability presents obvious problems when liquids are spilled on them.

(a)

(b)

Figure 22.15 Needle-punched floorcoverings: (a) nonpile texture, (b) simulated loop pile textures. Courtesy of Amy Willbanks, www.textilefabric.com.

Key Terms

bracket	pile warp yarns
braiding	pitch
Brussels	planting
chain warp yarns	print design
chenille carpet	rows per inch
dead-and-buried yarns	spools
filling or weft shots	stuffer yarns
filling yarns	velvet carpet weaving
frames	Wilton
fusion bonding	wires per inch
needle punch	woven-through-the-back

Review Questions

1. Draw and label a cross-sectional sketch of a woven carpet.
2. What is the purpose of stuffer yarns?
3. How can one identify chain warps?
4. What construction feature tends to make the crosswise direction of Axminster floorcoverings inflexible?
5. Explain the use of pattern designs, spools, and brackets in the preparation of Axminster weaving.
6. Identify the positive and negative features of having "dead-and-buried" pile yarns in Wilton carpet.
7. How does the Jacquard loom used for weaving floorcoverings differ from that used for weaving fabric?
8. Why is the lengthwise density of Wilton carpet reported as wires per inch?
9. Why is chenille carpet construction comparatively expensive?
10. How does one use pitch and needle count to compare the crosswise densities of a woven carpet and a tufted carpet?
11. Fusion-bonded floorcoverings are said to have more effective face weight; that is, they have more of the yarn available to the wearing face. How does this help such floorcoverings to withstand high levels of traffic?
12. What is actually braided in braided floorcoverings?

23

Construction of Floorcoverings: Hand Techniques

Hand operations produce rugs rather than rollgoods. Commercial organizations, such as authentic Middle Eastern and Native American rug producers, carefully control the quality of their products and produce sophisticated marketing strategies to promote them.

The distinctive styling of many hand-constructed rugs leads many people to use them as ornamental wall accents. Most of these rugs are woven, but some are constructed in braiding, hooking, and felting operations. Hand weaving and hand knotting are generally combined to produce pile structures, and plain- or tapestry-interlacing patterns are used to produce many flat structures.

Hand-Woven Pile Rugs

The pile in Oriental rugs and rya rugs are hand-knotted. In the flokati rug, the pile may be laid-in as it is woven, or the pile may be pulled through the hand-woven ground.

Oriental Rugs

So-called **Oriental rugs** are hand-knotted carpets from Asia. Iran, Russia, Afghanistan, Turkey, Pakistan, India, Tibet, China, Nepal, and Russia are some of the countries that produce and export these rugs, which feature intricate motifs of many colors in elaborate patterns. Geometric shapes, stylized animals, rosettes, medallions, trees, flowers, vines, and many styles of borders are typical. Historically, weavers executed only their own ancestral designs or those first produced in their geographic regions; the designs reflected the cultural heritage and life of the weavers. The origin of these rugs could be identified by their pattern, and were known by the names of their region and culture, for example, Persian, Turkoman, and Caucasian. Today, weavers throughout the world have adapted most of the traditional patterns, and it is no longer possible to accurately identify the origin of a rug by its design.

The distinguishing feature of all authentic Oriental rugs is that each pile tuft is hand-knotted. The **Sehna (Senna) knot** or **Persian knot** (Figure 23.2a) or the **Ghiordes knot** or **Turkish knot** (Figure 23.2b) is used. The Sehna knot can be tied to slant to the left or right,

Figure 23.1 Oriental knotted-pile rug (late nineteenth century, possibly Turkish/central Asian). Courtesy Judy Juracek.

but must be tied the same way throughout a project. The Sehna knot completely encircles one warp yarn and passes under the adjacent warp yarn; as a result, one pile tuft projects from every space between the warp yarns. When the Ghiordes knot is tied, both ends of the pile yarn extend from the same space; no pile tufts fill the alternate spaces. If other construction features are identical, a Sehna-knotted rug is finer than a Ghiordes-knotted rug, and the pattern is more sharply defined. A specific knot tends to be commonly used in particular geographic regions.

During the hand-weaving operation, several weavers may work simultaneously on the same project, knotting the pile yarns in horizontal rows. Normally, one or two filling (weft) yarns in plain weave are woven between each crosswise row of pile knots. Increasing the number of filling yarns decreases the pile construction density.

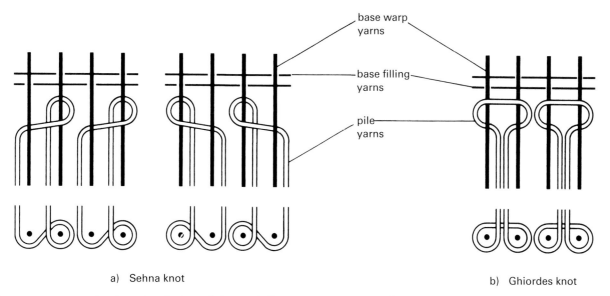

base warp yarns

base filling yarns

pile yarns

a) Sehna knot

b) Ghiordes knot

Figure 23.2 Knots used to form the pile layers in knotted-pile rugs: (a) Sehna, or Persian, knot, (b) Ghiordes, or Turkish, knot. Fairchild Books.

The quality of Oriental rugs depends on many factors, including the number of knots per square inch. Whereas the number of warp yarns per inch and the frequency of knot placement determine the crosswise density, the skill of the weavers, the size of the pile yarns, and the number of filling yarns per tuft row determine the lengthwise density. **Antique rugs**, those produced prior to the mid-1800s, often had as many as 500 knots per square inch. Old or **semi-antique rugs**, those woven during the latter part of the nineteenth century, and **modern rugs**, those produced during this century, generally have 100 to 225 knots per square inch, but some have as many as 323 knots per square inch.

Other important quality-related factors are pile height, fiber content, and level of luster. The use of natural dyestuffs for antique Oriental rugs resulted in a subdued, mellow luster. Synthetic dyestuffs developed in the mid-1850s simplified dyeing operations and were adopted by weavers. Because these colorants produce brighter colors than the natural dyestuffs, many of today's Oriental rugs are treated with chlorine or acetic acid and glycerin to simulate the prized sheen and soft luster of the older rugs—this processing is variously described as **chemical washing, culturing**, and **luster washing**. This treatment may weaken the fibers, but many producers and consumers consider the treatment to be worth the trade-off. Today, most Oriental rugs have pile yarns of wool and base yarns of cotton. Due to its high price, silk is rarely used today, but many older rugs feature silk pile yarns.

The labor-intensive, tedious, and slow production of hand-knotted Oriental rugs makes them relatively expensive, beyond the reach of many consumers. To lower the cost, manufacturers have increasingly produced rugs with traditional Oriental patterns on power looms, principally on Axminster looms. Machine-woven **Oriental design rugs** generally have a sewn-on fringe, which may differ from the base warp yarns; in hand-knotted rugs, the base warp yarns extending from the ends of the rug form the fringe. Traditional designs are also replicated through tufting and through computerized printing systems, which have increased the availability and affordability of these prized designs.

European Rugs

The French **Savonnerie** rug factory was the earliest prestigious European knotted-pile rug maker, originating in the mid-seventeenth century. Its name comes from the original factory, which was situated in an old soap factory. (*Savon* is the French word for soap.) Typical Savonnerie designs feature finely detailed, classical imagery and soft pastel colors. A Savonnerie rug woven in India is pictured in Figure 23.3.

Figure 23.3 Savonnerie rug. Courtesy of Nazmiyal, Inc., www. nazmiyalantiquerugs.com.

French **Aubusson** rugs take their name from the town and factory where these rugs were originally produced, which was first known for its production of wall tapestries. The factory began to produce rugs in the eighteenth century, first in the same plain-weave tapestry technique as the wall tapestries, and later of fine loop pile. Aubusson rugs are typically similar to Savonnerie styles, but are somewhat simplified, and feature more plant forms.

Rug weavers in many other countries have liberally copied Aubusson and Savonnerie designs in subsequent centuries. The design of Aubusson and Savonnerie rugs is often emphasized by hand carving.

Rya Rugs

Rya rugs originated in Scandinavian countries where weavers hand-knotted long pile yarns. Today, authentic rya rugs are still hand-knotted, but machine-made rya rugs are also available; both are prized worldwide for their decorative value. As illustrated in Figure 23.4a and b, yarns in the pile layer of rya rugs are generally related colors and the designs are gently flowing and curved.

In rya rug construction, the pile yarns are knotted with the Ghiordes knot, as in Oriental rugs. Rya rugs differ from Oriental rugs, however, in two principal ways. The

pile height in rya rugs is considerably longer, ranging from 1 to 3 inches (Figure 23.4b). As the pile height increases, the spacing between the pile rows can also increase, since the longer pile yarns will readily cover the base fabric. Therefore, wider bands of plain-woven filling are used between each crosswise row of knotted pile yarns in rya constructions. Pile yarns in authentic rya rugs are normally composed of wool.

So that the pile loops will be uniform in height, the yarn is continuously looped over a **rya stick** or **flossa stick**. The depth of the stick determines the pile height in the same way the wire height determines the pile height in Wilton and velvet carpet constructions. The stick is grooved to facilitate cutting the loops after a row has been knotted on it. Producing these rugs is labor intensive and requires large quantities of yarn; they are, therefore, relatively expensive.

Flokati Rugs

Flokati (flocati) rugs feature long piles of natural wool, and are woven in Greece. (Rugs produced in similar techniques are common in other rug-weaving areas around the world.) The weaver pulls a wooden rod inserted under the yarns to control the pile yarn length. The loops are then cut by hand. After weaving, every authentic flokati rug is immersed in a deep vat in a pool beyond a natural waterfall. The swirling water causes the wool fibers to felt, converting the yarns into pointed strands. Like authentic rya rugs, these rugs use large amounts of wool and labor-intensive processing, making them comparatively expensive. Flokati rugs are often undyed, which maintains the natural wool color, but they are sometimes piece dyed in solid colors. The pile yarns in flokati rugs are laid into the ground, but are not knotted into the warp, so they can be pulled out easily. Consequently, these rugs require a bit of care in use.

Contemporary Rugs

Tibet, Indian, and Pakistan are current centers of hand-woven rugs of both traditional styles and contemporary designs of subtle colorations (Figures 23.5 and 23.6). Chemical washes are sometimes applied to the rugs to add a worn, aged patina.

(a)

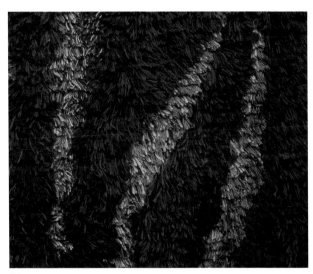

(b)

Figure 23.4 (a) Shaped rya rug, (b) detail of rya rug. Courtesy of Nazmiyal, Inc., www.nazmiyalantiquerugs.com.

Figure 23.5 Contemporary Tibetan knotted-pile wool rug with high and low pile. Courtesy of Spart Design LLC.

Figure 23.6 Contemporary Tibetan knotted-pile wool rug, uniform pile height. Courtesy of Spart Design LLC.

Hand-Constructed Flat Rugs

Most hand-constructed flat rugs are woven in a plain or tapestry-based interlacing pattern. The motifs of these floorcoverings, like those of Oriental rugs, often reflect the cultural heritage of the weavers.

Khilim Rugs

Khilim (kelim, kilim) rugs are woven in Eastern European countries. These colorful floorcoverings have graceful, stylized designs depicting flowers, animals, and other natural things (Figure 23.7).

The construction of khilim rugs is similar to tapestry weaving. The filling yarns are woven in plain weave, in sections according to color. Unlike those in tapestry structures, however, the ends of all filling yarns in khilim rugs are woven in, so the structure is reversible. In some cases, the weaving may produce slits or openings where the colors change in the design motif. These openings are finished and will not ravel (Figure 23.8). The slits may be retained as part of the design or they may be sewn together by hand.

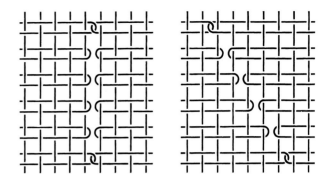

Figure 23.8 Slits found in khilim rugs. Fairchild Books.

Rugs Woven by Native Americans

Rugs produced by Native Americans, primarily the Diné (often referred to as Navajo, a name they do not use), Cheyenne, and Hopi peoples, are hand woven with a tapestry-related interlacing. Because the end of each filling yarn is woven in at the juncture of color changes, these rugs, like khilim, are reversible. In contrast to the khilim rug technique, however, the filling yarns are woven to avoid slits, with a dovetailing or interlocking technique (Figure 23.9).

The designs used in these rugs are bold graphic symbols (Figure 23.10) or detailed patterns representing tribal life and culture. Weavers throughout the world frequently adapt them. Today, these rugs are often chosen to act as wall accents.

According to the rules and regulations issued by the FTC pursuant to the Textile Fiber Products Identification

Figure 23.7 Khilim rug. De Agostini Picture Library/Getty Images.

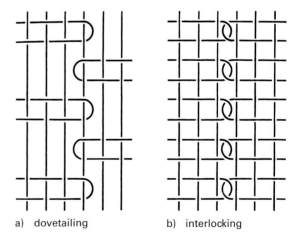

a) dovetailing   b) interlocking

Figure 23.9 Techniques used to avoid the formation of slits in tapestry. Fairchild Books.

Figure 23.10 Diné (Navajo) rug. Courtesy of www.indianterritory.com.

Figure 23.11 Dhurrie rug. scotto72/iStock.com

Act (TFPIA), all hand-woven rugs made by Diné people ("Navajo Indians" that carry the "Certificate of Genuineness" supplied by the Indian Arts and Crafts Board of the U.S. Department of the Interior) are exempt from the provisions of the TFPIA. Here, the term "Navajo Indian" means any Native American listed on the register of the Navajo Indian tribe or eligible for listing thereon.

Dhurrie Rugs

Dhurrie (durrie, durry) rugs are flat, hand-woven rugs made in India. They have a plain, twill, or tapestry interlacing. These rugs may display crosswise striations, produced by interspersing various colors of heavy, hand-spun cotton filling yarns, or stylized designs executed with wool filling yarns (Figures 23.11 and 23.12).

Figure 23.12 Dhurrie rug production. hadynyah/iStock.com.

Other Flat-Woven Rugs and Mats

Floor mats composed of nearly any fiber—various grasses, coir, sisal, linen, hemp, jute, wool (Figure 23.13), or synthetic polymer fibers—are available in an extensive variety of sizes, shapes, and weaves. Various weaves are used to create diamond, herringbone, and other geometric patterns over the surface. For larger floorcoverings, several small mats can be sewn together. Rugs used outdoors are usually flat-woven of solution-dyed polypropylene or acrylic, or of polyester, as discussed in Chapter 20.

Rag rugs are hand woven in plain weave. Rolled and twisted strips of new or previously used fabric forms yarn-like structures that are used as the filling component. Small rugs and mats can be braided or felted. Some felted rugs are embellished with surface embroidery.

Braided rugs, a staple of early, colonial American culture, are made of a long cloth braid wound around itself and sewn together to form a mat. Both rag rugs and braided rugs were first made to use scraps of clothing while providing warmth for the family home, but are commercially produced today.

Figure 23.13 Hand-woven flat-weave wool rug. Courtesy of Aronson's Floor Covering.

Review Questions

1. Why is it difficult today to identify the origin of Oriental rugs by their motifs?
2. Identify the distinguishing feature and key quality that indicates an Oriental rug is authentic.
3. Identify differences between the Sehna and Ghiordes knots.
4. Differentiate among the following: antique Oriental rugs, old or semi-antique Oriental rugs, and modern Oriental rugs.
5. Identify differences in the construction of the pile portion of Oriental and rya rugs.
6. How is the pile height controlled in rya rugs and flokati rugs?
7. Discuss similarities and differences between khilim rugs and rugs woven by Native Americans.

24

Carpet and Rug Cushions and Pads

Many names—cushion, pad, padding, lining, foundation, underlayment—identify the structure placed between a carpet or rug and the floor. Today, members of the industry most commonly use the terms *cushion* and *pad*, and may use each to refer to different types of material. For example, some carpet tiles come with a *cushion* back, which is never called a pad, while the felt-like materials used under rugs or carpet is generally called *padding*.

Carpet cushions vary in chemical composition, thickness, weight, density, compressibility, resiliency, resistance to moisture, resistance to microbes, and cost. They also differ in acoustical value, insulative benefit, and the contributions they make toward extending the wear-life of the soft floorcovering. The choice of a cushion involves an assessment of these features, as well as an analysis of the traffic levels and activities anticipated in the interior area to be carpeted. Some cushions can only be used separately; others can be separate or permanently attached to the carpet back.

Cushion-related variables should be considered in light of the carpet or rug selected, the kind of feel preferred underfoot, the environmental and traffic conditions anticipated in end-use, and the floorcovering budget. Moisture barrier backing systems usually combine cushioning with a barrier to prevent spills from penetrating the backing and soaking into the subfloor. The backing is typically made of PVC or other hard material and can be applied on either broadloom or modular carpet tiles.

Professionals must understand the evaluation of carpet cushions, so that they can interpret the data provided by producers and understand the end-user's or code requirements. Professionals must be able to supply accurate data for custom projects. The information required depends on the type of cushion selected. The cushions available in today's market fall into three major categories: fibrous cushions, cellular rubber cushions, and polyurethane foam cushions.

Fibrous Cushions

Fibrous cushions are the oldest form of carpet padding, and are produced by needle punching new or recycled fibers into felt-like structures. Recycled textile fibers are impregnated with resins for stability. Hair and jute are

Figure 24.1 Fibrous cushions made of hair. Courtesy of Amy Willbanks, www.textilefabric.com.

the common natural fibers used for this purpose. All-hair structures are normally made of cleaned, stiff cattle hair (Figure 24.1). Like all-jute cushions, all-hair cushions are relatively inexpensive, but both types tend to shift, bunch, and clump under heavy traffic conditions. For added stability, a loosely woven jute scrim may be centered in the batt prior to needle punching. Anti-microbial agents are recommended to retard the growth of mildew and fungi and the odor and deterioration they cause.

These cushions tend to exhibit aging; they can crumble and disintegrate after prolonged use. Because these fibers are subject to moisture damage, the use of latex sheets as protective barriers is recommended when below-grade installation is planned. Synthetic fibers (nylon, polyester, polypropylene, acrylic), both virgin and recycled, are more commonly used because they are more dimensionally stable, stand up to heavy traffic, and are more moisture resistant.

For skid resistance, as well as to compensate for the somewhat low compressibility and resiliency, the surfaces of the fibrous batts and latex sheets are generally embossed. Fibrous cushions are available in rolls up to 12 feet wide. Their weights range from 32 to 86 ounces per square yard.

Rubber and Latex Cushions

Latex is a dispersion of rubber in a liquid (usually water) that is subsequently solidified to form latex rubber. (Latex is also a common misnomer used to indicate foam rubber in items such as pillows and mattresses.) Elastomeric fibers are, by definition, flexible and capable of recovering their size and shape after deformation. They can be produced from natural rubber coming from rubber trees or from synthetic polymer substitutes.

Many people are highly allergic to latex rubber, so synthetic substitutes are increasingly common for many products, such as for latex gloves. For this reason, and because the raw materials are of limited supply, rubber cushions represent only a small part of the market.

Rubber Cushions

Cellular rubber cushions are often referred to as foam rubber, sponge rubber, expanded rubber, or latex rubber cushions. The **Carpet Cushion Council** classifies these as *sponge rubber* cushions and reserves use of the word *foam* for cushions made from polyurethane. They identify two specific types of sponge rubber carpet cushions: waffled sponge rubber cushions (which have a bubbled or rippled surface) and flat sponge rubber cushions (which have a smooth or flat surface).

Waffled sponge offers a soft feel; flat sponge is firmer. Grades are measured by weight in ounces per square yard. Manufacturing processes can produce different levels of density and firmness. Both types can be made from natural or synthetic rubber or latex compounds. A polyolefin film is normally laminated to the top of sponge rubber cushions. The fabric facilitates installation and minimizes moisture passage between the subfloor and the carpet.

Waffled Rubber Cushions

Waffled rubber cushions frequently contain chemicals, oils, and fillers that are added to the rubber compound for weight. The mixture is pulverized and heated. During the curing process, the mixture expands and a three-dimensional pattern is formed. A typical profile is shown in Figure 24.2.

Waffled sponge rubber has larger cells and thicker cell walls than flat sponge rubber; its structures are, therefore, more porous and less likely to retain odors. The cellular qualities also contribute buoyancy and softness. These cushions are highly compressible and produce the plushness often sought in residential interiors and executive

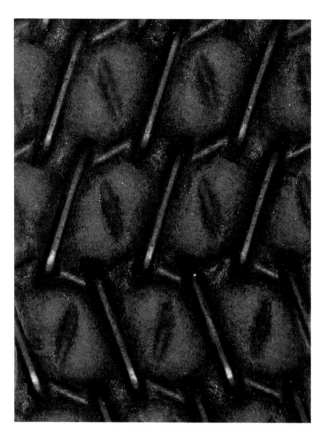

Figure 24.2 Bubble sponge rubber cushion. Courtesy of Amy Willbanks, www.textilefabric.com.

offices. Under heavy commercial traffic, however, the waffle forms do not provide uniform support. Moreover, in lesser-quality cushions, the clay or ash fillers may grind against other components, which may cause crumbling. Flat sponge rubber cushions can provide more uniform support for carpet used in areas of medium and heavy traffic, and better skid resistance for area rugs.

Waffled sponge rubber cushions are available in rolls up to 12 feet wide. Their weights range from 41 to 120 ounces per square yard, with uniform thicknesses that range from 0.124 to 0.624 inch. Generally, $^7/_{16}$-inch thickness is preferred because it works best with the tack strip height.

Flat Rubber Structures

Flat rubber cushions are manufactured by converting liquid latex and fillers into flat, continuous sheets (Figure 24.3). The sheets may be as thin as $^1/_8$ inch to $^1/_3$ inch. Because flat sponge rubber has smaller cells than rippled sponge rubber, flat cushions provide firmer, more uniform

Figure 24.3 Bonded foam cushion. Courtesy of Amy Willbanks, www.textilefabric.com.

TABLE 24.1

RECOMMENDED MINIMUM SPECIFICATIONS FOR ATTACHED LATEX FOAM CUSHIONS

Weight	38 oz/sq yd
Thickness	⅛ in
Density	17 lb/cu ft
Compression loss	Maximum of 15% loss
Compression deflection	Not less than 5 psi
Delamination strength	2 lb/in
Accelerated aging	(a) Heat aging: 24 hrs at 275°F; after flexing, should remain flexible and serviceable. (b) Fade-Ometer aging: 20 hrs exposure; sample should show only slight crazing.
Ash content	Maximum of 50%

Compiled from Carpet Cushion Council recommendations.

support, but they may exhibit more odor retention. Flat sponge rubber cushions are available in rolls up to 12 feet wide, and in weights ranging from 28 to 65 ounces per square yard.

In thinner forms, foam rubber cushions can be permanently bonded to the back of carpet structures. The assembly can then be laid on the floor without installing a separate cushion; for maximum stability, it can be glued to the floor. Some installations, such as installing the cushion between a hard surface (e.g. concrete) and a heavy commercial carpet, require glue between each layer, or *double glue down*. Textured flat sponge rubber cushions are produced with a fine textured appearance on the bottom and non-woven or paper backing on the top. **Reinforced rubber carpet cushions** are manufactured with an open cellular structure and are made from ground tire scrap rubber granules bonded with latex.

Minimum standards for consistent quality in attached flat sponge rubber cushions are listed in Table 24.1. In this table, **density** refers to the amount of rubber per unit of volume; increasing the density would increase the weight of the cushion and the level of support provided. **Compression loss**, also called **compression set**, is the extent to which the structure fails to recover its original thickness after being compressed 50 percent under a static load. **Compression deflection** is the extent (reported as psi, or pounds per square inch) to which the structure resists compression force. **Delamination strength** is the force per inch of width required to separate the cushion from the carpet; it is measured as described in Chapter 21. Procedures for measuring other properties are discussed later in this chapter.

Several of the recommended specifications for attached foam cushions have been adopted as required standards by a number of federal agencies, including the Department of Housing and Urban Development, the General Services Administration, and the Department of Veterans Affairs. These authorities have also set forth additional requirements pertaining to fire performance. The test methods used to evaluate flammability are explained in Chapter 12.

Polyurethane Foam Cushions

Three types of polyurethane foam cushions are available for residential and commercial use: prime (in grafted and densified forms), mechanically frothed, and bonded. The chemical composition of these cushions is basically the same, but different manufacturing processes produce them, and their cellular structures differ. Polyurethane is highly flammable, but because carpet cushioning represents minimal quantity compared with carpet, no stringent flammability codes apply to it as a standalone material.

All these types of polyurethane foam cushions are manufactured in several thicknesses, generally ranging from $1/4$ to $3/4$ inch, and all usually have a spunbonded facing to facilitate installation. In their thinner forms, these cushions can provide skid resistance to area rugs and runners. Like other types of cushions used for this purpose, the thin form minimizes the problem known as *rug walking* or *rug crawling*, which is the tendency for rugs to shift or move off cushions under the stress of traffic. Cushions with higher densities have higher compression deflection values and provide firmer support underfoot.

Prime Polyurethane Foam Structures

Prime polyurethane foam cushions, exactly like cushioning used in upholstered furniture, are manufactured by foaming individual polyurethane polymer units into a continuous sheet, generally 6 feet wide. For carpet cushions it is sliced into thin sheets. There are two types of prime polyurethane carpet cushions: grafted prime and densified prime.

Grafted prime polyurethane cushions are manufactured by a chemical mixing reaction process. They are flexible cushions formulated with additives that provide reinforcement for increased load bearing. With **densified prime polyurethane cushions**, the foam's chemical structure is modified during the manufacturing process to produce a product with specific performance characteristics. As the name implies, densified prime polyurethane foam has a higher density than grafted prime foam. The higher density is produced from a finer, elongated cellular structure and somewhat horizontal struts. No fillers are used. These cushions are said to be odorless, resilient, mildew-resistant, and resistant to bottoming out.

Frothed Polyurethane Structures

Mechanically frothed polyurethane cushions combine polyurethane chemicals and reinforcing fillers that are frothed with air while in a liquid state. The result is a denser, firmer type of foam that can be attached directly to the carpet or used as a separate cushion. Frothed foam cushions are among the best on the market because they

are extremely durable and provide excellent support. Unlike other foam cushions, they contain no volatile organic compounds (VOCs), so off-gassing after installation is not a problem. They can be used with all carpets, and they resist indentation from furniture, which decreases carpet wear.

Bonded Polyurethane Foam

Bonding and compressing chopped pieces of recycled prime and polyurethane foam create **bonded polyurethane foam** (sometimes called rebond). The Carpet Cushion Council estimates that bonded foam carpet cushion represents in excess of 80 percent of U.S. annual sales of carpet cushion (of all categories/types). The strength of these structures largely depends on the strength of the prime polyurethane foam material used in the chopped pieces. To reinforce the cushion and aid in ease of placement, it is covered on one side with scrim netting. Bonded foam grades are measured by density. The bonded foam cushion in Figure 24.4 has been reinforced with a woven scrim.

A major recycling achievement, bonded foam cushions are made of 100 percent recycled foam from post-industrial and post-consumer scrap from used foam cushions, furniture, mattresses, and automotive parts. Additionally, bonded foam is itself recyclable. The Carpet Cushion Council reports that these efforts divert over 1 billion pounds a year from landfills.

Historically, foam was treated with chemicals for flame resistance that the EPA determined are bioaccumulative

Figure 24.4 Bonded polyurethane foam cushion. Courtesy of Amy Willbanks, www.textilefabric.com.

and toxic to both humans and the environment. One of the polybrominated diphenyl ethers (PBDEs) in particular, **pentabromodiphenyl (PentaBDF)**, was used extensively in foams prior to 2005, so reusing foam that contained these chemicals was concerning. Since over a decade has passed since the phasing out of PentaBDF, contamination of materials bound for recycling in the United States is minimal, and as a result, bonded carpet cushion produced in this country complies with U.S. law in terms of PentaBDF content. Recovered foam from overseas may not comply with the recommended content levels. Neither PentaBDF nor other fire-retardant additives are used in the finished bonded carpet cushion itself.

Listing Specification Data for Carpet Cushions

Carpet cushion producers, like with all other interior products, provide data on results of laboratory testing of their products with product samples, or on their websites. Specification requirements for cushions are less extensive than those prepared for carpet and rugs (see Chapter 25). Nonetheless, specifiers need to evaluate certain levels of performance and meet standards established for the specific installation.

The recommended minimum specifications for attached foam cushions are listed in Table 24.1 on p. 316; Table 24.2 exemplifies the various features that may be listed in a specification for densified prime polyurethane foam cushions. The first item in Table 24.2 states the composition of the cushion; the second item states that a spunbonded fabric is to be applied to the top side of the structure; the next two items describe structural characteristics; and the remaining items detail performance features and levels. The values used are for illustrative purposes only. Table 24.3 provides minimum recommendations for commercial applications.

Evaluating the Performance of Cushions

Some performance features, including compression loss and compression set, are important to all cushion

TABLE 24.2
SAMPLE CUSHION SPECIFICATION/DATA LIST

Cushion compound: densified prime, unfilled polyurethane foam; clean and free of defects
Coating: spunbonded polypropylene olefin
Density: 5.0 lb/cu ft
Thickness: 0.265 in
Compressive load deflection:
25% deflection   1.5 psi minimum
65% deflection   6.5 psi minimum
75% deflection   11.0 psi minimum
Compression set: maximum of 15% at 50% deflection
Tensile strength: 25 psi minimum
Elongation: 50% minimum
Flammability:
(a) CFR 1630 (FF 1-70/tablet test): passes
(b) Flooring radiant panel test: greater than   0.25 watt/sq cm

materials. One performance variable, aging, is important only in cellular rubber cushions, and, as noted earlier in this chapter, delamination strength is a concern only with permanently attached cushions. Refer to Chapter 25 for information on cushions regarding sound absorption, thermal insulation, and indoor air quality (IAQ).

Accelerated Aging

In prolonged use, rubber and latex cushion compounds may be affected by heat and exhibit aging in the form of cracking, crumbling, and sticking. To assure that the cushion will not show **accelerated aging**, the structure can be evaluated in accelerated laboratory testing. In one procedure, latex cushion material may be exposed for 24 hours to a temperature of 275°F in a circulating air oven prior to evaluation. In a second accelerated procedure, a specimen may be placed in a Fade-Ometer® (or Weather-Ometer®, shown in Figure 19.12) for 20 hours in accordance with AATCC 16-3 Colorfastness to Light: Xenon-Arc. As stated in Table 24.1, foam latex samples should withstand these exposures with no more than slight discoloration or surface degradation. Upon flexing, a slight cracking or crazing is acceptable.

TABLE 24.3

MINIMUM CARPET CUSHION RECOMMENDATIONS FOR COMMERCIAL APPLICATIONS

Types of Cushion	Class I Moderate Traffic	Class II Heavy Traffic	Class III Extra Heavy Traffic
Commercial Application A	**Office Buildings:** Executive or private offices, conference rooms	**Office Buildings:** Clerical areas, corridors (moderate traffic)	**Office Buildings:** Corridors (heavy traffic), cafeterias
	Health Care: Executive, administration	**Health Care:** Patients' rooms, lounges	**Health Care:** Lobbies, corridors, nurses' stations
	Airports: Administration	**Schools:** Dormitories and classrooms	**Schools:** Corridors, cafeterias
	Retail: Windows and display areas	**Retail:** Minor aisles, boutiques, specialty	**Airports:** Corridors, public areas, ticketing areas
	Banks: Executive areas	**Banks:** Lobbies, corridors (moderate traffic)	**Retail:** Major aisles, checkouts, supermarkets
	Hotels/Motels: Sleeping rooms	**Hotels/Motels:** Corridors Libraries/Museums: Public areas, moderate traffic Convention Centers: Auditoriums	**Banks:** Corridors (heavy traffic), teller windows
	Libraries/Museums: Administration		**Hotels/Motels:** Lobbies and public areas
			Libraries/Museums: Public areas Country Clubs: Locker rooms, pro shops, dining areas
			Convention Centers: Corridors and lobbies
			Restaurants: Dining area and lobbies
Fiber, oz/sq yd			
Synthetic Fiber	Wt: 22 Th: .25" D: 7.3	Wt: 28 Th: .3125" D: 7.3	Wt: 36 Th: .35" D: 8.0
Resinated Recycled Textile	Wt: 24 Th: .25" D: 7.3	Wt: 20 Th: .30" D: 7.3	Wt: 38 Th: .375" D: 8.0
Rubber, oz/sq yd			
Flat	Wt: 62 Th: .15" D: 21 CFD@20 psi	Wt: 62 Th: .15" D: 21 CFD@20 psi	Wt. 62 Th: .15" D: 26 CFD@30 psi
Ripple	Wt: 56 Th: .27" D: 15 CFD@2 psi	not recommended	not recommended
Textured Flat	Wt: 56 Th: .22" D: 18 CFD@3 psi	Wt: 64 Th: .235" D: 22 CFD@5 psi	Wt. 80 Th: .25" D: 26 CFD@6 psi
Reinforced	Wt: 64 Th: .235" D: 22 CFD@40 psi	Wt. 64 Th: .235" D: 22 CFD@40 psi	Wt. 54 Th: .20" D: 22 CFD@50 psi
Polyurethane foam, lbs/cu ft (pcf)			
Grafted Prime*	Th: .25" D: 2.7 CFD@2.5 psi	Th: .25" D: 3.2 CFD@3.5 psi	Th: .025" D: 4.0 CFD@5 psi
Densified Prime*	Th: .25" D: 2.7 CFD@2.4 psi	Th: .25" D: 3.5 CFD@3.3 psi	Th: .025" D: 4.5 CFD@4.8 psi
Bonded**	Th: .375" D: 5.0 CFD@5.0 psi	Th: .25" D: 6.5 CFD@6.0 psi	Th: .025" D: 8.0 CFD@8 psi
Mechanically Frothed***	Th: .30" D: 13.0 CFD@20.0 psi	Th: .223" D: 15.0 CFD@30.0 psi	Th: .183" D: 19.0 CFD@30.5 psi

All thicknesses, weights, and densities allow a 5% manufacturing tolerance.

Densities are listed in lb/cu ft.

Maximum thickness for any product is 3/8".

CFD = Compression Force Deflection as measured by ASTM D3574 Test C. Indicates pounds per square inch (psi) required to compress the foam to 65% of its original size.

* = Polymer densities

** = Particle size not to exceed 1/2"

*** = Ash content is 50% max

Compiled from Carpet Cushion Council recommendations.

Compressibility

Compressibility evaluations measure the degree of resistance a cushion offers to being crushed or deflected under a static load. The measurements are made by following the procedures outlined in ASTM D3574 Standard Test Methods for Flexible Cellular Materials—Slab, Bonded, and Molded Urethane (Polyurethane) Foams. In preparation for evaluating this performance quality, cushion specimens are cut into small squares (often 2 inches square) and layered to a thickness of 1 inch. The plied structure is then placed on the platform of a testing unit (Figure 24.5). The support platform has perforations to allow for rapid escape of air during the test. A flat, circular foot is used to indent or deflect the layered specimens.

The force required to deflect or compress the specimen assembly to a given percentage of its original thickness is measured for each of two replicate tests. Together with the percentage of deflection used, the average number of

Figure 24.5 Compression deflection testing apparatus. Courtesy of SDL Atlas.

pounds per square inch required to compress the cushion material is reported to the nearest pound. Several federal agencies have mandated specific levels of **compression force deflection (CFD)**; these vary with the type of cushion and the interior facility.

The compressibility of a cushion correlates with the degree of softness felt underfoot. Cushions having low CLD values are soft and easily compressed; cushions having high values are firmer, less compressible structures. Firmer cushions should be selected for interior floor space subjected to rolling equipment or wheelchairs.

Compression Set

Compression set is synonymous with **compression loss**. It describes the extent to which a structure fails to recover its original thickness after static compression. In most evaluation procedures, cushion specimens are layered to a thickness of 1 inch and deflected 50 percent. The compressed structure is then placed in an oven at 158°F for 22 hours. At the end of this period, the load is removed and the thickness is measured after a 30-minute recovery period. The compression set is calculated with the following formula, and the average of two replicate tests is reported:

$$\text{compression set} = [(\text{original thickness} - \text{thickness after compression})/\text{original thickness}] \times 100.$$

A high recovery of cushion thickness is desirable, and a minimum recovery level of 85 percent (maximum loss of 15 percent) is frequently recommended or mandated. As a cushion recovers from compression, it exerts an upward pressure that encourages the carpet also to recover. The actual level of recovery depends upon the particular combination of carpet and cushion.

Tensile Strength

The **tensile strength** of cushion structures is measured in the laboratory according to prescribed test methods, such as FTMS 191A, Method 5100.1. The value reported is the average of five replicate tests and is the force per unit of cross-sectional area necessary to cause rupture. Required minimum tensile strength values may range from 8 to 20 psi.

Elongation

Elongation values describe how far a cushion structure extends before rupturing. The performance is evaluated as part of the procedure for evaluating tensile strength. The value reported is the average of five readings, each calculated by the following formula:

$$\% \text{ elongation at break} = (\text{length stretched/original length}) \times 100.$$

Because cushions are always used in combination with a carpet or rug, some performance evaluations are more meaningful when they are made on the floorcovering assembly. This is especially true when such functional values as noise reduction and insulation benefits are being considered. In some cases the functional benefits of an assembly will be more strongly influenced by the cushion than by the carpet; in many cases, carpet and cushion both contribute to a functional value. Evaluations of floorcovering assemblies are described in the next chapter.

Review Questions

1. Identify the types of fibrous cushions produced and cite the positive and negative features of each.
2. Distinguish between rippled sponge rubber and flat sponge rubber cushions.
3. Why is one form of polyurethane foam cushion less susceptible to "bottoming out"?
4. How can the consumer minimize rug walking or rug crawling?
5. What is the purpose of using a spunbonded facing fabric with sponge rubber and polyurethane cushions?
6. What are the advantages of having minimum compression loss?

Key Terms

accelerated aging

bonded polyurethane foam

Carpet Cushion Council

cellular rubber cushions

compressibility

compression deflection

compression force deflection (CFD)

compression loss

compression set

delamination strength

densified prime polyurethane cushions

density

elongation

fibrous cushions

flat rubber cushions

grafted prime polyurethane cushions

mechanically frothed polyurethane cushions

pentabromodiphenyl (PentaBDF)

polybrominated diphenyl ethers (PBDEs)

reinforced rubber carpet cushions

tensile strength

waffled rubber cushions

25

Evaluations and Specifications
for Soft Floorcoverings

For suppliers, producers, colorists, and converters of textile floorcoverings and components, standard test methods and performance specifications are an important part of manufacturing and marketing efforts. Data gathered from this quality-control work help industry members identify the need for changes in the composition, manufacturing, or conversion of their products. The data also provide the basis for claims about performance made in promotional materials, whether targeted at the trade or at the consumer (Table 25.1).

Interior designers, architects, commercial specifiers, and retailers must understand the test methods used to measure structural and performance qualities of carpet and cushions and the implications of the reported data. Such an understanding makes it possible for professionals to interpret data supplied by producers and determine the suitability of a carpet or an assembly for relevant traffic and other end-use conditions. The informed professional also can prepare specification listings that cover specific features and levels of performance required by end-use conditions or a regulatory agency.

Listing Specification Data for Carpet

Because tufting is the dominant floorcovering construction technique, the sample **specification listing** presented in Table 25.2 is written for a tufted structure. Several of the items would, however, also be listed for woven and fusion-bonded carpet. Virtually all test methods listed in the table and discussed in this chapter apply to all textile floorcoverings, regardless of their construction. The specific values listed in the table are for illustrative purposes only.

The first several items listed in Table 25.2 describe the appearance, composition, and construction features of the carpet. The functional benefits and performance properties of a carpet are also enumerated. Test methods for determining the values reported for these characteristics may be identified in specification lists. In addition to the tests and specifications listed in Table 25.1, numerous other standard test methods, guides, and practices may be used to determine the data reported for

these features. The Carpet and Rug Institute (CRI) website is an excellent resource for the current performance standards.

As discussed in Chapters 5 and 11, trade names frequently distinguish fibers, especially those engineered to exhibit special properties. When a trade name is used to advertise a carpet, the fiber composition of the pile layer must be disclosed in accordance with the provisions of the Textile Fiber Products Identification Act (TFPIA).

Pile construction density, pile height, weight-related factors, and structural variables are specified to ensure that a floorcovering will withstand the traffic conditions in the end-use location, and will conform to design codes if applicable. These construction features were reviewed in Chapter 20.

Evaluating Functional Features

Carpet and cushion assemblies may be designed and selected to provide such functional benefits as noise control and insulation. Carpet may also be selected to reduce energy consumption by contributing to the efficient management of interior light and by helping to lower the rate of heat exchange.

Acoustical Ratings

One of the more important functional benefits of floorcovering assemblies is their **acoustical value**, that is, the extent to which they prevent sound from becoming unwanted noise. (For more information see the CRI Technical Bulletin *Acoustical Characteristics of Carpet*, available on the CRI website at www.carpet-rug.org.)

Sound Absorption

Residential interiors are often filled with many electrical appliances and pieces of entertainment equipment, each one of which generates sound. Contemporary office designs frequently call for large open areas that will permit maximum flexibility in space utilization. Such areas can contain numerous people, telephones, computers, and printers, all of which, again, generate sound. Commercial structures are often built to serve several firms

TABLE 25.1
COMMON TEST METHODS USED FOR FINISHED COMMERCIAL CARPET

Characteristic	Test Method/Explanation	Suggested Requirement
Average Pile Yarn Weight (Ounces/ Square Yard)	ASTM* D5848 Method of Testing Mass per Unit Area: Chemically dissolves parts of the finished carpet sample to determine the pile mass or weight. Pile mass or weight includes the pile yarn, both above the primary backing and the amount hidden or buried below the backing.	As specified
Pile Thickness/Tuft Height	For level-loop carpet: ASTM D6859 Method of Testing Pile Yarn Floor Covering Construction. For cut pile carpet: ASTM D5823. For multilevel loop carpet: ASTM D7241 Standard Test Method for Pile Thickness of Finished Multilevel Pile Yarn Floor Coverings.	As specified. Accurate laboratory determination of height is important for the average pile yarn density determinations.
Average Pile Yarn Density	Calculation: Measures the amount of pile fiber by weight in a given area of carpet space. Typically calculated in ounces per cubic yard. Important element in equating quality of carpet to wearability, resilience, and appearance retention.	As specified
Tuft Bind	ASTM D1335 Test Method for Tuft Bind of Pile Floor Coverings: The amount of force required to pull a single carpet from its primary backing. Determines the ability of the tufted carpet to withstand zippering and snags.	Loop pile: GSA requires 10.0 lbs of force for loop pile only (minimum average value) VA, FHA, HUD require 6.25 lbs Cut pile: HUD requirement 3.0 lbs
Delamination Strength of Secondary Backing	ASTM D3936 Test Method for Delamination Strength of Secondary Backing of Pile Floor Coverings: Measures the amount of force required to strip the secondary backing from the primary carpet structure. Measured in pounds of force per inch width. Its importance is to predict secondary delaminating due to flexing caused by traffic or heavy rolling objects.	2.5 lbs of force per inch is the minimum average value
Colorfastness to Crocking	AATCC Method 165 Colorfastness to Crocking: Textile Floor Coverings—Crockmeter Method: Transfer of colorant from the surface of a carpet to another surface by rubbing. The transference of color is graded against a standardized scale ranging from 5 (no color transference) to 1 (severe transference).	Rating of 4 minimum, wet and dry, evaluated on AATCC Color Transference Scale, or Gray Scale for Staining (the latter takes precedence over color transference if there is a dispute between labs)
Colorfastness to Light	AATCC Method 16 Option 3 Colorfastness to Light: Water–Cooled Xenon–Arc Lamp, Continuous Light: Accelerated fading test using a xenon light source. After specified exposure, the specimen is graded for color loss using a 5 (no color change) to 1 (severe change) scale.	Rating of 4 minimum after 40 AATCC fading units using AATCC Gray Scale for Color Change (GSA and HUD minimum is 4)

TABLE 25.1

COMMON TEST METHODS USED FOR FINISHED COMMERCIAL CARPET (*continued*)

Characteristic	Test Method/Explanation	Suggested Requirement
Electrostatic Propensity	AATCC 134 Electrostatic Propensity of Carpets: Assesses the static-generating propensity of carpets developed when a person walks across them by laboratory simulation of conditions that may be met in practice. Static generation is dependent upon humidity conditions; therefore, testing is performed at 20% relative humidity. Results are expressed as kilovolts (kV). The threshold of human sensitivity is 3.5 kV, but sensitive areas may require that a lower kV product be specified.	Less than 3.5 kV for general commercial areas
Flammability		
Surface Flammability	16 CFR 1630 and also ASTM D2859: This small-scale ignition test is required of all carpet for sale in the United States. Methenamine tablet is used as an ignition source.	All carpet must meet this standard, per federal regulation
Critical Radiant Flux	ASTM E648, Critical Radiant Flux of Floor Covering Systems Using a Radiant Heat Energy Source: Depending upon occupancy use and local, state, or other building or fire codes, carpets for commercial use may require flooring radiant panel test classification (Class I or II). Class I is considered to be a minimum rating of 0.45 watts per sq cm or greater. Most codes require flooring radiant panel testing only for carpet to be installed in corridors and exit-way areas.	Applicable local, state, and federal requirements
Additional Requirements for Modular Carpet		
Tile Size and Thickness	Physical measurement	Typical tolerances are in the range of five thousandths of an inch (5 mils, 0.0005 inch), within 1/32 inch of stated dimensional specifications
Dimensional Stability	ISO 2551 Machine-Made Textile Floor Coverings—Determination of Dimensional Changes in Varying Moisture Conditions (also called the Aachen Test; currently out of publication); ASTM standard is ASTM D7570	GSA requires +/– 0.15% maximum; no maximum set within standard
Requirement for Indoor Air Quality (IAQ)		
CRI IAQ Testing Program Labels	CRI IAQ Testing Program Labels: Assesses emission rates of carpet product types to meet program criteria. When using carpet cushion or adhesive, include CRI IAQ label.	Total volatile organic compounds criteria not to exceed 0.5 mg/m2*hr

*ASTM standard test methods are available from ASTM International, 100 Bar Harbor Drive, West Conshohocken, PA 19428 Telephone: 877-909-2786, www.astm.org.

TABLE 25.2
SAMPLE CARPET SPECIFICATION/DATA LIST

Style: Kamiakin

Surface texture: one level loop

Coloration: jet printed

Face fiber: 99% Super® XYZ nylon; 1% Stat-Redux® stainless steel for static control

Face fiber size: 20 dpf

Yarn size: 2.00/2cc (equivalent denier 5315)

Body construction: tufted

    gauge: 1/10

    stitches per inch: 8

    primary and secondary backing: 100% woven polypropylene olefin

Pile height: 0.250 in

Pile yarn weight: 40.0 oz/sq yd

Total weight: 65 oz/sq yd

Average density: 4383

Weight density: 122,713 (optional)

Structural stability:

    bundle penetration: 80%

    delamination strength: 2.5 lbs/in

    tuft bind: 6.25 lbs (for HUD—6.25 lbs for loop pile, 3.0 for cut) (for general commercial use—10.0 for loop, 3.0 for cut)

Acoustical ratings:

    NRC .45 over 40 oz hair pad; IIC 73 over 40 oz hair pad (INR +22)

Insulative value: R-2 over concrete slab

Colorfastness

    crocking: 4.0 (AATCC 165)

    gas fade: 4.0 (AATCC 23)

    ozone fade: 3.0 (AATCC 129): 4.0 (AATCC 109)

    shampoo: 4.0 (AATCC 138)

    lightfastness: Class 4 (AATCC 16E, option 3)

Flammability

    tablet test (ASTM D2859, 16CFR 1630): passes

    tunnel test (ASTM E84): Class A

    flooring radiant panel test (ASTM E648): CRF greater than 0.25 watts/sq cm

Static generation: 3.5 static kilovolts at 70°F and 20% RH (AATCC 134)

Wear resistance

    ASTM D5252 Hexapod—manufacturer's discretion as to light, medium, or heavy durability ratings

and many employees and executives; places where people assemble, such as theaters, often house thousands; schools accommodate hundreds of students. In these interiors, the constant movement of equipment and people, continual verbal exchange, and the like create sound. These routine activities create **surface noise radiation**. Lowering the level of airborne and surface sounds in these environments is highly desirable; in some cases it is mandatory.

Results of controlled testing for the sound absorption of carpets are reported numerically as the **noise reduction coefficient (NRC)**. Higher NRC values indicate greater sound absorption. Cut pile textures are somewhat more efficient in absorbing sound than loop pile textures. Increasing the weight of the pile layer or the height of the pile yarns in cut pile structures will increase the sound absorption capabilities. In loop textures, pile height apparently has a greater positive influence than does pile weight. CRI has reported that such structural variations produce similar effects when the carpet is glued directly to the floor. Regardless of the method of installation, the fiber content of the pile yarns has virtually no effect on sound absorption.

Permeable structures absorb sound more efficiently than do less permeable materials. For example, hair and hair-jute cushions are more effective acoustically than less-permeable sponge rubber cushions of similar weight. Attached cushions reduce **permeability** and thus the level of sound absorption. Carpet absorbs sound better than do hard and resilient flooring materials, which have very low permeability.

Sound Transmission

Controlling **impact and structurally borne sounds** is especially important in multilevel structures, where impact sounds can be transmitted as noise to the interior spaces below. Evaluations of the acoustical role of carpet and cushions in such a situation are made in a chamber with 100 square feet of either concrete or wood joist flooring. The ISO R 140 Tapping Machine is used to impact the surface. In this test, a microphone picks up the noise transmitted to the room-like chamber below. A diagram of the machine is illustrated in CRI Technical Bulletin *Acoustical Characteristics of Carpet*, which is updated periodically. (The current version can be found on the CRI website at www.carpet-rug.org.) The ability of a floor, carpet, or cushion to minimize **noise transmission** is evaluated and reported numerically as an **impact noise rating (INR)** or as an **impact insulation class (IIC)**. Higher values indicate greater noise control, that is, a reduced level of transmission. As an estimate, IIC values are roughly equal to the INR value plus 51.

CRI Technical Bulletin *Acoustical Characteristics of Carpet* includes a comparison of noise transmission reduction between various carpet and cushion features. In this test, carpet was laid directly on concrete because concrete floors are common in commercial structures. They are less effective in controlling impact sounds than are the wood joist floors commonly used in residential construction. When tested without floorcoverings, a concrete slab had an INR of 17 and a wood joist floor had an INR of 19.

The test results indicate that increases in the weight of the pile layers of the test carpets improved their performance. All of the carpet and cushion assemblies tested were more effective than any of the test carpets alone. The rubber cushion specimens were more effective when used separately under the carpet than when permanently attached. While increased permeability increases sound absorption, it has a negative influence when the goal is to minimize transmitted sound.

Insulative Value

Heat conductivity and **heat resistivity** are reciprocal terms referring to the rate at which a material conducts or transfers heat. The rate of heat transmittance is given numerically as the **K-value or K-factor**. Materials such as copper conduct heat rapidly and have relatively high K-values. Materials, including textile fibers, that have low K-values are poor heat conductors and can contribute insulative value.

R-values or R-factors numerically describe how effectively structures resist heat flow; that is, how effectively they insulate and prevent heat exchange. The following formula determines R-value:

$$R\text{-value} = \text{thickness}/K\text{-value}$$

From the formula, it is apparent that resistance to heat flow is determined not only by the rate of conduction, the K-value, but also by the thickness of the structure. Increasing the thickness of a material does not increase its K-value, but does increase its R-factor, making it a more effective insulator. When various carpets and carpet assemblies are tested, the thickness of components, rather than the fiber or yarn type, contributes most directly to the total R-value of the assembly. Furthermore, R-values tend to vary in direct proportion to thickness and pile density.[1]

Indoor Air Quality

As discussed in Chapter 3, with improvements in the quality of building materials and construction methods over the years, newer residential and commercial structures have become almost airtight. Although this helps conserve energy used for heating and cooling, it limits the amount of fresh air available to the occupants. In particular, commercial buildings have few operable windows that allow fresh airflow. In both residential and commercial buildings, fresh air is pumped into the interior environment through the heating, ventilation, and air conditioning (HVAC) system. Indoor air is filtered, mixed with a small amount of outdoor air, and recirculated throughout interior spaces.

The ability of HVAC systems to adequately clean the air varies, depending on equipment size, quality of filters, and the amount of indoor and outdoor air pollution. Health problems related to poor air quality continue to rise. Sensitivities to airborne bacteria, fungi, and chemicals can cause problems ranging from eye, sinus, and lung irritation to severe allergic reactions and infections. Many airborne chemicals have the potential to cause cancer and other disabling diseases. Considering that we spend the majority of our time indoors, **indoor air quality (IAQ)** is an important health consideration.

The CRI, in collaboration with the Environmental Protection Agency (EPA) and ASTM International, developed the Green Label and Green Label Plus programs to identify carpet, cushions, and adhesives that produce very low emissions of volatile organic compounds (VOCs). When installed according to CRI-recommended standards, the low-level VOC emissions from new carpet typically dissipate within 48 to 72 hours after installation. Manufacturers are permitted to display the CRI green-and-white logo on products that meet the low-VOC standards. This certification tests according to ASTM D5116 Guide for Small-Scale Environmental Chamber Determinations of Organic Emissions from Indoor Materials/Products, which identifies maximum allowable levels of VOCs for carpet, cushions, and adhesives.[2] (For more information see the CRI Technical Bulletin *Indoor Air Quality*, available on the CRI website at www.carpet-rug.org.)

Evaluating Performance Properties

Besides the functional properties discussed in the preceding section, other properties, including colorfastness, flammability, static generation, and wear resistance, also help to determine the in-use performance of textile floorcoverings. Such properties should be evaluated prior to selection; again, professionals may be required to specify or select floorcoverings exhibiting a mandated level of performance.

Colorfastness

Standard laboratory test methods are available to evaluate the stability of the colorants in most colored floorcoverings. Generally, fastness to crocking, atmospheric gases, light, and cleaning agents are measured.

Fastness to Crocking, Gases, and Light

The standard test methods used to measure colorfastness and lightfastness were discussed in Chapter 19. The designations of these test methods may be listed with the appropriate fastness ratings, as in Table 25.2.

Fastness to Shampoo and Water

Textile floorcoverings are frequently tested for their fastness to water and to shampoo using the methods in AATCC 107 Colorfastness to Water and AATCC 138 Cleaning: Washing of Textile Floorcoverings. Either test method allows for analysis of the test results in terms of bleeding and staining, as well as in terms of color change. Test specimens are compared with the AATCC Gray Scale for Color Change or Gray Scale for Staining (Figures 19.10 and 19.14, pp. 255 and 258), and the numerical values recorded.

Microbe Resistance

Protecting soft floorcoverings from the deterioration, discoloration, and odor development caused by

microorganisms is an area of ongoing research in the floorcoverings industry. For floorcoverings installed in damp areas, the growth of odor-causing fungi and bacteria should be inhibited; for carpet and rugs exposed to pets, the retention of odors in the structure should be prevented. Carpet installed in hospitals, nursing homes, and similar facilities should be resistant to a variety of bacteria and fungi, so that the structures will remain odor free and will not harbor microbes that could spread disease and slow patient recovery. Simply by walking across a floor, carpet, or other flooring material, microbes can become airborne. At this point they are identified as bioaerosols. Some bioaerosols are harmless; some can cause noninfectious airway diseases, such as allergies and asthma; and others are associated with serious infections.

Several studies support findings that indoor environments can promote the growth of microbes. Contaminants are first introduced via human occupants, activities, animals, machines, furnishings, building materials, and infiltration of outdoor microbes. Often, indoor conditions provide enough moisture, warmth, and nutrients to support the growth and proliferation of these microbiotic contaminants. The moisture content of elements within the building, the relative humidity and temperature, outdoor microbe concentrations, HVAC air exchange rates, and the number of people in the space dramatically affect contamination levels.[3] According to the U.S. Department of Labor, Occupational Safety and Health Administration (OSHA), indoor air should be treated to remove air contaminants as well as control room temperature and humidity.

OSHA recommendations for air treatment include:[4]

- The use of filtration, electronic cleaners, and chemical treatment with activated charcoal or other sorbents
- Humidity control in the range of 20 percent to 60 percent
- Temperature control in the range of 68–76°F
- Appropriate HVAC air exchange rates based on occupancy and equipment

There are no uniform international standards for the collection and analysis of bioaerosols, levels of acceptable maximum bioaerosol loads, or for guidelines on human tolerance levels.[5] In the United States, there are some states that have published recommended bio-aerosol levels based on specific microbes and environments (hospitals, nursing homes, correction facilities). There are also national standards that may be utilized when collecting and testing microbes for antimicrobial efficiency pertaining to fabric and carpet. These tests do not provide a pass/fail rating system on microbe levels. Two tests often used for testing the effects of antimicrobial carpet treatments are ASTM E2471 Standard Test Method for Using Seeded-Agar for the Screening Assessment of Antimicrobial Activity in Carpets and AATCC Test Method 174 Antimicrobial Activity Assessment of New Carpets.

ASTM E2471 is used to assess the durability of antimicrobial treatments on new carpets, and on those repeatedly shampooed or exposed to in-use conditions. The test provides guidelines on methods used to evaluate both antibacterial and antifungal activity both at the fiber layer and at the primary backing layer of carpet. AATCC 174 is designed to determine the antimicrobial activity of new carpet materials and consists of three procedures: a qualitative antibacterial assessment, a quantitative antibacterial assessment, and qualitative antifungal assessment. It may also be used to evaluate the effect of a cleaning process on the antimicrobial resistance of carpets.

OSHA also provides air contamination indicators; however, levels in excess of the recommended limit do not necessarily imply that the conditions are unsafe or hazardous. The type and concentrations of the airborne microorganisms will determine the hazard to occupants.[6]

Biological resistance has been engineered into some fibers by incorporating **antimicrobial agents** into the polymer solution or by adding them early in the production sequence. The intended purpose of these treatments is to provide protection, primarily against mold, when the soiled carpet is exposed to high humidity conditions. While such treatments and additives are popular with some users, other specifiers eschew finishes, treatments, and added chemicals in the products that they choose. Typical antimicrobials for carpets include zinc compounds, such as zinc pyrithione, phosphated amines, common metals (silver, copper), and phenol-based compounds.[7]

Antimicrobial treatments are not a substitute for proper and regular cleaning and maintenance of the carpet. Synthetic fiber does not in itself provide the moisture or nutrients that microorganisms need for survival. However, if not kept clean, any material can become a host for unwanted pests.

All antimicrobials marketed in the United States must:[8]

- Be registered with the U.S. Environmental Protection Agency (EPA) in order to curb over-zealous marketing claims. A product cannot be labeled with human-health claims unless the finished product is EPA registered (i.e., the carpet would have to be registered, not only the treatment).
- Be low in toxicity to humans, animals, and the environment (during manufacture and under conditions of use).
- Be easy to apply.
- Be compatible with other additives.
- Have no negative impact on properties, appearance, or useful life of the carpet.

For more information see the CRI Technical Bulletin *Antimicrobial Carpet Treatments*, available on the CRI website at www.carpet-rug.org.

Flammability

Flammability regulations and testing methods were discussed earlier, in Chapters 2 and 12. As is true of other laboratory testing procedures, test methods that assess the potential flammability of soft floorcoverings have been designed to simulate real-life conditions. Prior to marketing most carpet and large rugs, producers must subject them to the methenamine tablet test to confirm that they conform to the performance standards outlined in the Flammable Fabrics Act, which is administered by the Consumer Product Safety Commission (CPSC). For use in commercial interiors, carpet and rugs are required to conform to additional flammability codes. In such cases, the floorcoverings are often tested in accordance with the procedures outlined in the flooring radiant panel test.

All domestic and imported carpets and rugs sold in the United States must pass the methenamine tablet test. There are two Code of Federal Regulations standards that pertain to this test: 16 CFR 1630 (carpet) and 16 CFR

1631 (small rugs); the rating system is either pass or fail. Carpet for use in commercial spaces must meet certain flame spread and smoke development requirements based on building code occupancies, also known as *use groups*. The flame spread test for commercial carpet is the radiant panel test. The test method is accepted by ASTM International and the National Fire Protection Association (NFPA), and is identified as ASTM E648 and NFPA 253.

The rating system is divided into two categories: Class I, with a minimum critical radiant flux of 0.45 watts per square centimeter, and Class II, with a minimum critical radiant flux of 0.22 watts per square centimeter. Carpeting with a Class I rating is more fire resistant than that with a Class II rating. These and other flammability tests are described and illustrated in Chapter 12, and fire performance recommendations are presented in Table 12.1 (p. 158). (For more information see the CRI Technical Bulletin *Flammability and Carpet Safety*, available on the CRI website at www.carpet-rug.org.)

Static Generation

The test method generally accepted in the industry for evaluating the static propensity of floorcovering assemblies is AATCC 134 Electrostatic Propensity of Carpets. The test procedure, designed to closely simulate actual end-use conditions, is conducted in an atmosphere having 20 percent relative humidity and a temperature of 70°F. During the testing, a person wearing clean, neolite-soled shoes walks across a carpet while linked to an electrometer. This device measures the voltage building up on the body, and the recorded level is then reported in static volts. Generally, acceptable maximum voltage ratings are 5.0 kilovolts for residential carpet and 3.5 kilovolts for commercial carpet. For environments with sensitive electronic equipment, 2.0 kilovolts is an acceptable upper limit. In highly critical areas, such as the handling of semiconductors, the typical antistatic carpet may not provide sufficient static protection.[9]

Regulations and/or specifications may state that the control of static generation must be durable. In such cases, the agency having jurisdiction may require that floorcoverings be cleaned in accordance with the procedures outlined in AATCC 138 Cleaning: Washing of Textile Floorcoverings prior to testing with AATCC 134. (For more information see the CRI Technical Bulletin *Static Control*, available on the CRI website at www.carpet-rug.org.)

Wear Resistance

Several factors influence a carpet or rug's satisfactory appearance retention and durability. The abrasion resistance of the floorcovering will affect the extent to which fuzzing, pilling, and fiber loss occur. The resiliency of the structure will affect the degree to which the original thickness and luster are retained when the assembly is subjected to the static pressure of furniture legs, repeated loads of foot traffic, and the rolling stresses of moving equipment. If the original texture is lost, the consumer may regard the structure as worn out, even though fiber loss may be negligible. Therefore, service performance analyses related to wear cannot be limited to abrasion-related performance; they must also include evaluations of textural changes.

Textural Changes

ASTM D6119 Standard Practice for Creating Surface Appearance Changes in Pile Yarn Floor Covering from Foot Traffic may be used in evaluations of textural changes. The practice is directed to appearance changes, such as matting, flattening, or the loss of tuft definition, that do not necessarily involve fiber loss by abrasion or the development of a threadbare appearance. It does not simulate surface appearance changes resulting from soiling, pivoting, or rolling traffic.

Carpet specimens are securely placed in a floor layout having an odd number of traffic lanes that require walkers to automatically reverse their direction with each pass through the course. Counting devices accurately count **foot traffic units**, the number of passes by human walkers (not the number of times each specimen is stepped on). A traffic level high enough to cause noticeable change is used. The cumulative change in surface appearance is analyzed by comparing unexposed and exposed specimens. Purchasers and suppliers may mutually agree on the minimum number of foot traffic units a floorcovering should withstand before the textural change is unacceptable.

ASTM D5251 Standard Practice for the Operation of the Tetrapod Walker Drum Tester may be used to produce changes in texture on the surface of pile floorcovering caused by mechanical action. Test carpet is installed as the lining of a rotatable cylindrical chamber with the pile surface exposed. During testing, the plastic-tipped feet of the tetrapod walker tumble against the carpet surface as the drum revolves, simulating foot traffic. The change in texture may be assessed visually, by measuring the change in pile thickness, and measuring the pile weight.

Abrasion Resistance

ASTM D3884 Standard Test Method for Abrasion Resistance of Textile Fabrics (Rotary Platform, Double Head Method) is used in the carpet and rug industry for the accelerated laboratory testing of the abrasion resistance of floorcoverings. The apparatus used in the test has two flat platforms, or turntables, each supporting and rotating one specimen under two abradant wheels (Figure 25.1). The pressure of the wheels on the specimens can be controlled during the testing operation, and a vacuum unit may be employed to remove abraded particles continually.

During testing, the abradant wheels rotate in opposite directions (Figure 25.2). This results in abrasion

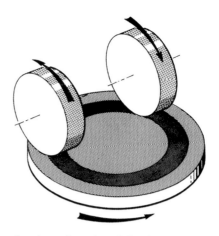

Figure 25.2 Directions of rotation of the abradant wheels and support platform during abrasion resistance testing. Courtesy of Taber Industries.

marks that form a pattern of crossed, slightly curved, herringbone-like arcs over an area of approximately 4.5 inches. Some producers evaluate the results in terms of the number of cycles (revolutions of the turntable carrying the specimen) required to cause exposure of the backing. Other producers measure the percent of pile weight loss or the percent loss of breaking load. The value reported is the average of five replicate tests.

As noted in Chapter 19, manufacturers of tufted carpet seek to reduce the number of loose, individual fibers that travel to the surface and form pills through the proper application of adhesive coatings. Part of their quality-control effort involves ascertaining how thoroughly the adhesive has penetrated the pile yarn bundle, to lock the fibers side by side.

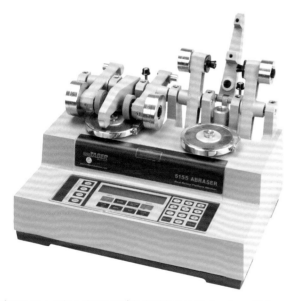

Figure 25.1 Taber abraser with double heads. Courtesy of Taber Industries.

Key Terms

acoustical value	indoor air quality (IAQ)
antimicrobial agents	K-values or K-factors
foot traffic units	permeability
heat conductivity	noise reduction coefficient
heat resistivity	(NRC)
impact and structurally	noise transmission
borne sounds	R-values or R-factors
impact insulation class	specification listing
(IIC)	surface noise radiation
impact noise rating (INR)	

Review Questions

1. Discuss the value standard test methods and performance specifications have for members of the industry.
2. Explain the usefulness of product performance data for the design professional.
3. Discuss the influence pile construction density, pile height, and pile weight have on the end-use of carpet and rugs.
4. Identify the textural characteristics and weight factors of soft floorcoverings that aid in sound absorption.
5. Does any fiber have significantly greater value in absorbing sound?
6. Explain how permeability relates to noise reduction within an interior by carpet and cushions. How does this principle relate to noise transmission?
7. Are textile fibers relatively good heat conductors or relatively good heat insulators?
8. If one wants to improve the insulative value of a carpet and cushion assembly, is the R-value or the K-value changed?
9. When specifying products and materials for a carpet installation, what factors should be considered that pertain to indoor air quality?
10. Does a soft floorcovering have to have measurable fiber loss to be perceived as worn out?

Notes

1. *The Carpet Primer*, Dalton, GA: Carpet and Rug Institute, 2017, p. 25.
2. Carpet and Rug Institute, "Technical Bulletin: Carpet and Indoor Air Quality," 2018.
3. Jyotshna Mandal and Helmut Brandl. (2011). "Bioaerosols in Indoor Environment—A Review with Special Reference to Residential and Occupational Locations," page 83.
4. OSHA Indoor Air Quality Standard, 1999, OSHA Technical Manual Section III: Chapter 2.
5. Ibid.
6. Ibid.
7. Jyotshna Mandal and Helmut Brandl. (2011). "Bioaerosols in Indoor Environment—A Review with Special Reference to Residential and Occupational Locations," page 83.
8. Robert Brentin. "Protecting Carpets with Antimicrobials," *SpecialChem*, March 20, 2012. http://www.specialchem4polymers.com.
9. Carpet and Rug Institute, "Technical Bulletin: Static Control," 2018.

26

Installation and Maintenance of Floorcovering Assemblies

nstallation and maintenance factors are critical to long-term serviceability of textile floorcoverings and cushions. The most beautiful carpet with the highest-rated performance variables can end up with ripples, bubbles, prominent seams, and mismatched patterns if not properly installed. An unsecured installation could be hazardous, and also create extra wear on the material itself.

All materials need to be properly cleaned on a regular basis. Some require more care than others. It is important that appropriate floorcoverings match up with available regular maintenance programs. If no one is available to actually perform the maintenance, the material will not be cleaned, and will show "wear" quickly. (What appears to be worn material is often simply unsightly soiling; soiling also causes deterioration of fibers.) Routine cleaning and stain removal procedures should neither cause marked changes in texture nor alter the original color of a product. Recommended installation and maintenance are critical factors to consider when floorcovering selections are made.

Installing Soft Floorcoverings and Cushions

It is the specifier's or end-user's responsibility to stipulate seam placement and to choose the method of installation for floorcoverings. Pile lay, pattern repeat sizes and configurations, and floor space measurements all figure into the carpet layout design for a room. The required yardage and material and labor costs depend upon the layout.

Proper installation procedures are also critical to carpet performance and can help protect the quality of the indoor air. The installer must follow the manufacturer's installation guidelines and the minimum guidelines in the CRI 104/105 Carpet Installation Standard, which is available on the Carpet and Rug Institute (CRI) website. General installation parameters are outlined in Table 26.2.

Wall-to-Wall Installation Methods

Stretch-in, glue-down, and free-lay techniques are the typical methods for **wall-to-wall installation**, but before any installation begins, skilled workers must prepare the site.

Site Preparation

Obviously, removing any old, previously installed carpet is the first step in a new installation. If old carpet is left in place, the new cushion cannot slide smoothly into place during installation, preventing proper stretching of the new carpet, which can become distorted and bumpy. Additionally, for glue-down installations, sheet vinyl and linoleum must be removed for the new structure to adhere well.

Although the subfloor should be dry for any installation, dryness is especially critical for glue-down installations. New concrete floors, which may require up to four months to dry, should be checked carefully for dryness; so should subfloors that are close to or in contact with the ground, either on-grade (ground level) or below-grade. Ground moisture may be transported upward through the slab, facilitating the migration of alkaline compounds at the same time. The moisture can prevent good adhesion of the floorcovering and foster microbe-related problems. The alkaline substance may react with the adhesive compounds that stabilize the carpet and with those that secure it to the floor, causing degradation and loosening of the carpet. In order to avoid such problems, the moisture condition must be resolved and the alkaline must be neutralized prior to installation.

The interior floor space to be covered should be smooth and free of cracks, crevices, and holes, for a more pleasing appearance and uniform support for the assembly. Rough areas should be sanded, and openings should be filled. Finally, the floor should be free of dust, lint, and grit.

Stretch-In Installations

Stretch-in installations involve stretching rollgoods and fastening them over pin-holding strips that have been secured to the perimeter of the floor space. These plywood or metal strips, also known as **tackless strips**, are approximately 1.5 inches wide, and have rows of rust-resistant metal pins protruding upward at an angle of 60 degrees (Figure 26.1). The strips are up to 0.375 inch thick; the thickness of the strip is coordinated with the thickness of the cushion to be installed. When carpet lengths greater than 30 feet are being installed or when heavy traffic loads are anticipated, three rows of pins should be

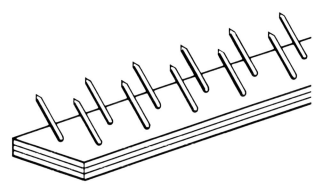

Figure 26.1 Pin-holding strip used in stretch-in tackless installation projects. Fairchild Books.

(a)

(b)

Figure 26.2 Tools used to install rollgoods in stretch-in tackless projects: (a) telescoping power stretcher, (b) knee kicker. Courtesy of Kraft Tool Co.

used; for residential installations and small commercial installations, two rows of pins should be sufficient.

The strips are nailed or glued to the floor, with the pins angled toward the wall. A gully or space slightly narrower than the thickness of the carpet is left between the wall and the strip. If a separate cushion is used, it is laid within the perimeter of the strips and stapled or glued to the floor.

When seams and pattern matching are required, the parallel edges of the floorcovering must be carefully aligned and trimmed to fit tightly. Butting of factory edges is not recommended because they may be slightly irregular; there may be a slight excess of pattern repeat provided for trimming to an accurate match. After the rollgoods are cut, a thin bead of an adhesive should be applied to prevent edge raveling and fraying during subsequent handling, seaming, and use.

Seams may be formed by hand sewing or by applying various types of tape. Crosswise seams are often sewn. Hot melt tape is often used for lengthwise seams. This tape has a thermoplastic coating that becomes tacky when heated with a special iron. The carpet edges are sealed together by the adhesive when it cools. In lieu of hot melt tape, a strip of pressure-sensitive or adhesive tape may be placed behind the parallel carpet edges and a latex bead applied along the seam line to secure the join.

After the seaming is completed, the carpet is stretched, generally 1 to 1.5 percent in length and width, and anchored over the pins in the wooden strips. A **power stretcher** is used to place uniform stretch over the surface of the carpet, and a **knee kicker** is used to grip and anchor the edges over the pins (Figure 26.2a and b).

The procedures recommended for stretching tufted carpet are shown in Figure 26.3. The power stretcher is anchored at the base of the walls and telescoped as needed. Stairway carpet may be installed with a stretch-in technique, using pin-holding strips and a knee kicker. It may also be glued down.

Glue-Down Installations

Glue-down installations involve securing floorcovering structures to the floor with an adhesive. When no cushion is used, the procedure may be referred to as direct glue-down; when an attached cushion is involved, the procedure is called double glue-down. The same procedures are used in both operations, except that structures without a cushion are rolled onto the adhesive and structures with a cushion are pressed into the adhesive.

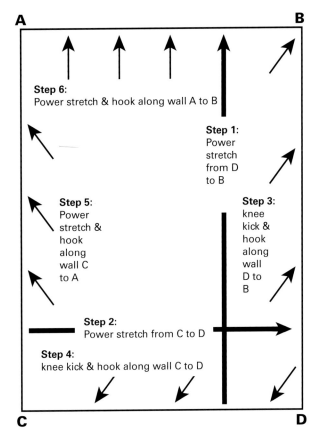

Figure 26.3 Stretching tufted structures. Yelena Safronova/ Fairchild Books.

Step 6:
Power stretch & hook along wall A to B

Step 1:
Power stretch from D to B

Step 5:
Power stretch & hook along wall C to A

Step 3:
knee kick & hook along wall D to B

Step 2:
Power stretch from C to D

Step 4:
knee kick & hook along wall C to D

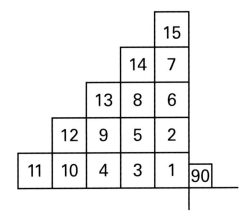

Figure 26.4 Pyramid technique recommended for positioning carpet modules. Yelena Safronova/Fairchild Books.

When installing rollgoods, the layout and seam placement must be carefully planned, and the floor measurements must be exact. If the carpet is too large for the space, buckles and ripples may develop; if the carpet is too small, separation of the seams may occur. The cut edges of the carpet must be precisely marked, trimmed, and secured with a bead of latex. The selected adhesive is then spread over the floor with a notched trowel and the carpet is bonded to the adhesive.

When working with carpet modules, the installer should locate a starting point that will maximize the cut size of the perimeter modules. From this point, a grid is established and the selected adhesive is spread over the area. Each module is then slid into position, taking care to avoid catching any pile tufts in the joint. Successive tiles should be laid in a pyramid or stairstep manner (Figure 26.4). Perimeter modules can be precisely cut to fit the floor space.

The adhesive used to bond rollgoods and modules may be a nonreleasable (permanent) or a releasable type. Releasable adhesives may permit the floorcovering

structure to be repeatedly lifted and rebonded into position. This permits some degree of access to underfloor service trenches or to flatwire cable systems installed directly on the floor. It may also permit the rotation or removal of carpet modules.

Free-Lay Installations

Free-lay installations may be considered for carpet modules when consumers wish to maximize the flexibility of the carpet tile, as long as heavy rolling traffic is not expected. Rolling casters on office chairs would have an insignificant effect, but heavy items such as hospital gurneys wheeled down corridors and automobiles driven into showrooms could have a snowplow effect, raising the edges of the modules.

Modules must have superior dimensional stability for free-lay use. This feature is often achieved with the application of a heavy secondary backing. Some free-lay tiles alternate layers of heavy-gauge vinyl and glass fiber scrims for the necessary stability (Figure 26.5).

In preparation for installation, a control grid is again planned to maximize the cut size of the perimeter modules. Within this grid, specific crosswise and lengthwise rows of modules should be secured to the floor with adhesive or double-face tape to minimize shifting. Selective glue-down leaves approximately 80 to 90 percent of the modules in the free-lay mode; tape, which is removed after installation, leaves all of the tiles held by gravity.

Like installations with releasable adhesives, free-lay installations permit easy access to floor and underfloor

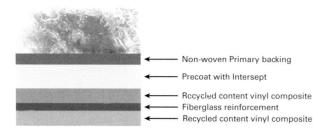

← Non-woven Primary backing
← Precoat with Intersept
← Recycled content vinyl composite
← Fiberglass reinforcement
← Recycled content vinyl composite

**Figure 26.5 Fusion-bonded, free-lay tile with GlasBac®
secondary backing.** Yelena Safronova/Fairchild Books.

utility systems. Free-lay also offers maximum convenience in shifting modules.

Loose-Laid Rug Installations

Cut edges of rugs and runners must be bound by sewing twill-woven tape over the raw edges or by serging (machine overcasting). Cushions used with loose-laid rugs and runners should be thin and about 1 or 2 inches narrower and shorter than the floorcoverings. This allows the rug or runner to lie close to the floor and minimizes the tendency for the soft floorcovering to advance off the cushion. On stairs, runners may be securely installed with brass rods (see the chapter opener figure).

Factors Affecting Choice of Installation Method

Besides the site-related considerations identified in the previous section, other factors may limit the type of installation chosen for soft floorcoverings. These include traffic conditions, planned space utilization, and concern for noise reduction and energy conservation.

Traffic Conditions

The traffic conditions in the area to be carpeted include a number of variables, such as an estimate of anticipated number of persons who will walk over the floorcovering (see Table 20.1). At low and medium levels, 500 to 1,000 traffic counts per day, the carpet may be stretched-in over most types of cushions; at higher levels, the carpet may be stretched-in over a thin, high-density cushion, over no cushion, or it may be glued down.

Also, the usual type of traffic is important. For example, if people with canes, crutches, or limited vision will use the interior, area and room-size rugs and runners should be avoided or their edges should be beveled to create a smooth transition between levels, and they should be securely attached to the floor. When rolling traffic, such as wheelchairs and equipment, will impact the floorcovering, strong consideration should be given to gluing the carpet structure directly to the subfloor. This installation technique will help to minimize shearing and seam separation. The Americans with Disabilities Act (ADA) mandates these safety features in public and commercial buildings. To meet ADA specifications, carpet can also be set into another flooring material—wood, stone, or the like (Figure 26.6).

The amount and type of dirt and grit likely to be tracked in is another important traffic-related factor. If a rapid rate of accumulation is expected, the specifier may elect to install carpet modules with a releasable adhesive or in a free-lay mode. The modules could then be rotated to minimize apparent and actual differences in appearance and texture throughout the interior. Soiled modules could be removed for off-site cleaning, and damaged modules lifted out and replaced.

Planned Space Utilization

Frequently, modern commercial offices have an open design; movable wall partitions, called **panels** in the industry (see Chapter 18), define work-stations in an

Figure 26.6 Carpet set into a stone tile floor to create a level surface for easy transition between materials. Courtesy of Martin Patrick Evan, Ltd.

open-office plan. As a facility grows and changes, the panels can be moved to define new spaces consistent with current needs. If rollgoods are used for such interiors, they are installed before the furniture is in place, since, if they were installed to the base of each movable wall, a bare strip of subfloor (that would have to be patched with carpet) would show when the panels were rearranged. Additionally, rearranging panels over rollgood carpet may eventually reveal unsightly lines, which would then require a large amount of replacement carpet. For these reasons, carpet tiles may offer a better solution for open-office installations, since these problems may be avoided with carpet modules.

As shown in Figure 26.7a, a common grid can be planned for the placement of the modules. When a square falls on a wall, it can be cut to fit on either side of the wall (Figure 26.7b). Later, when the wall panels are shifted, the cut modules can be lifted and a row of full-size modules laid in place (Figure 26.7c).

Acoustical and Insulative Control

The need for noise control and insulation may call for the installation of a carpet and cushion assembly, rather than a carpet glued to the floor. As noted in Chapter 25, a separate cushion increases the level of sound absorption, and any combination of a carpet and cushion provides greater reduction of impact noise transmission than does carpet alone. Chapter 25 also discussed the finding that the insulative values of a carpet and cushion are additive, and are higher when the two structures are used separately. If traffic conditions dictate the selection of a direct glue-down installation, less effective control over noise and energy consumption may be partially offset by increasing the pile yarn weight and pile height of the carpet.

Cost-Related Factors

As discussed in Chapter 20, costs for carpet installation include charges (based on the size of the area) for site preparation, installation of the new cushion, and installation of the new carpet. Because acoustical benefits and energy savings may add value that outweighs the additional installation costs, cushions are generally recommended. Furthermore, appropriate pads and

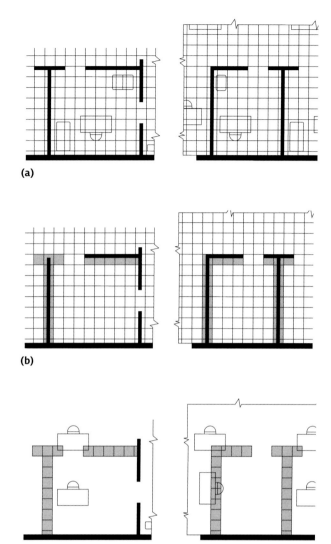

(a)

(b)

(c)

Figure 26.7 Use of carpet modules in interior space with movable walls: (a) common grid for module placement, (b) modules cut to fit base of wall panels, (c) full-size replacement modules. Yelena Safronova/Fairchild Books.

cushions normally extend the useful life of rugs and carpet. Of course, it is advisable to compare life-cycle costs of appropriate floorcovering options.

Determining Yardage Required

Ordering sufficient quantity of carpet in the initial order is critical. As with materials discussed earlier such as draperies and wallcoverings, if the original order is insufficient, slightly different color characteristics and finishes vary from lot to lot, and in material that covers a large expanse the differences can seem quite pronounced.

The original order should include not only the amount needed based on the size of the project, but also a reasonable overage that can be used to repair damaged areas in emergencies. Of course, ordering too much excessive yardage is a waste of budget. Careful planning and correct measuring must take pile direction, the placement of seams, and the size and nature of pattern repeats so that the yardage order is accurate.

Measuring Floor Space

These are the important rules to observe when measuring floor space for carpet:

1. Between opposite walls, each of which is uninterrupted, measure the distance from baseboard to baseboard and record the information on a sketch of the floor plan.
2. Between opposite walls, one of which is interrupted by an opening (e.g., a door or window), measure from the baseboard to the mid-point of an archway or to a point halfway under the bottom edge of the closed door (Figure 26.8). Record the measurement on the floor plan sketch.
3. Measure stairs as illustrated in Figure 26.9. Landings are treated as if they were large steps. From 2 to 4 inches must be added to each of the recorded lengthwise and crosswise measurements. This will provide the yardage required for fitting and trimming.

Positioning the Pile Lay

The directional lay of pile yarns (Figure 10.7) must be uniform for all adjoining pieces of carpet. The layout

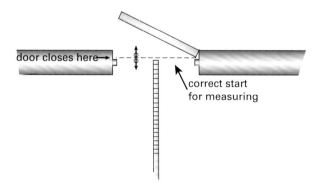

Figure 26.8 Measuring for carpet at a door jamb. Fairchild Books.

door closes here →

correct start for measuring

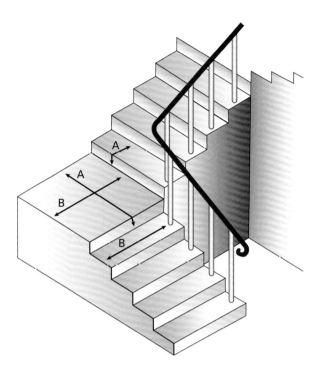

Figure 26.9 Measuring stairs and landings for carpet.
Fairchild Books.

should be planned so that the lay parallels the longest dimension of the largest room to be carpeted, as shown in Figure 26.10a. Unless pattern orientation or a similar feature must be considered, the pile lay direction should be away from the strongest source of light and toward entrance areas.

Figure 26.10b illustrates an incorrect layout. One length has been reversed, and one length has been given a quarter turn. Because the quantity of light reflected by each section would be different, there would be marked differences in their apparent color. The carpet would appear darkest when the viewer is looking at the tips of the pile tufts and lightest when the viewer is looking at the sides of the yarns. Therefore, after the correct positioning of the pile lay direction has been established, all adjoining lengths of carpet of the same color and quality must be laid with their pile lay in the same direction, as show in Figure 26.10a.

With carpet tiles or modules, designers may purposely vary the pile direction of adjoining units in order to create marked differences in their apparent brightness. Examples of possible patterns for the placement of carpet modules are shown in Figure 26.11a through d. In each

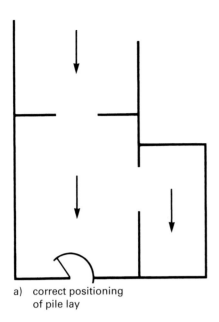

a) correct positioning
   of pile lay

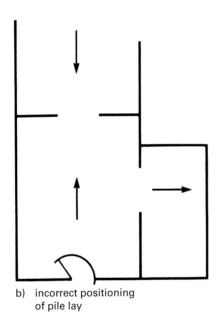

b) incorrect positioning
   of pile lay

Figure 26.10 Planning pile lay direction: (a) correct layout, (b) incorrect layout. Fairchild Books.

of these four patterns, shading variations would alter the aesthetic characteristics of the installation.

When pile carpet is installed on stairs, the width of the carpet must parallel the width of the stairs so that carpet **grin** (the exposure of the backing on the nose edges; see Figure 20.9) will be minimized. With angled stairways, this will necessitate installation of the carpet with quarter turns of the pile lay (Figure 26.12). In such cases, the critical

importance of avoiding grinning (exposure of the backing through the pile) overrides concern for shade variations.

Planning Seam Placement

Several principles should govern the placement of seams. Whenever possible, seams should run lengthwise, parallel with the pile lay, not crosswise. Crosswise seams interrupt the pile sweep and are therefore more visible. Seams should not run perpendicular to a doorway, although they may run across the opening (Figure 26.13a). Parallel seams on either side of a doorway, which is called a **saddle** (Figure 26.13b), create tripping hazards. The carpet can be shifted so that the seams are placed in safer and less conspicuous locations (26.13a.) **Seams** in traffic pivot areas and on stair treads create stability challenges and safety hazards.

Allowing Yardage for Matching Patterns

Patterned floorcoverings have either a set-match (or side-by-side) or drop-match pattern repeat. The type of match and the lengthwise and crosswise dimensions of the repeat affect the yardage required.

Set-match (or side-by-side) **patterns** repeat themselves across the width of the carpet. Depending on the width of the repeat and the width of the carpet, the crosswise repeats may be fully completed or partially completed (Figure 26.14). In the latter case, the pattern is generally scaled so that the complement of the incomplete repeat unit is at the opposite edge.

Set-match patterned carpet needs to be cut at the next highest multiple of the pattern repeat length beyond the amount actually required. Thus, if the repeat is 12 inches long and 17 feet 6 inches are required, the carpet would be cut 18 feet long (18 is the next highest multiple of the 1-foot length); if the repeat is 36 inches long and 21 feet 6 inches are required, the carpet would be cut 24 feet long (24 is the next highest multiple of the 3-foot dimension). This cutting plan provides the additional yardage needed for side matching. The installer shifts the long edges of the parallel carpet lengths, matching the pattern. The waste is cut away, but not necessarily from one end of each length (Figure 26.15).

In **drop-match patterns**, the repeat unit is shifted up or down by one-half or one-quarter unit, so that the

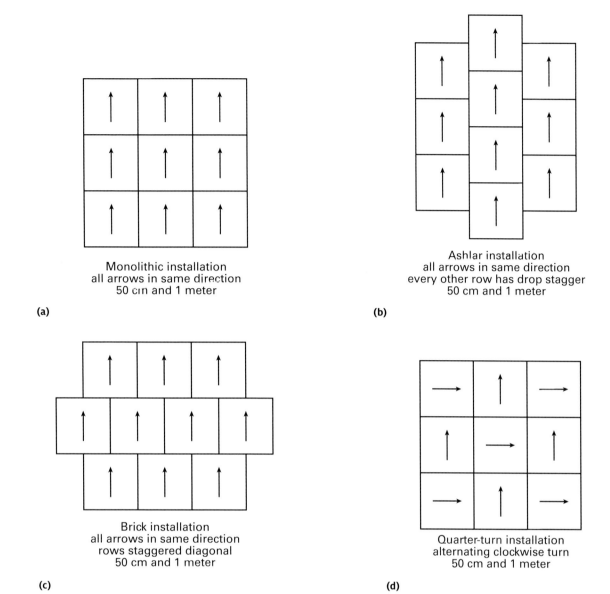

Figure 26.11 Four patterns for installing carpet modules: (a) monolithic—corner to corner, (b) monolithic—ashlar, (c) brick, (d) quarter turn. Yelena Safronova/Fairchild Books.

pattern appears to repeat diagonally across the width of the carpet. In **half-drop-match patterns**, the complementing portion of a design is located at a point up or down one-half the length of the repeat, as shown in the draft in Figure 26.16a and b.

Two methods may be used to cut carpet having half-drop-match patterns. The first method is to cut on multiples of the repeat. If three 9-foot widths of carpet that has a 36-inch-long repeat are being installed in a room that measures 20 feet 6 inches in length, the first and third cuts would be cut on seven multiples or 21 feet. The second strip would then be cut 22 feet 6 inches, minimizing waste.

The second method is to cut on multiples of the repeat plus half a repeat. This method utilizes a half repeat to advantage. For example, a 12-inch pattern can be cut in lengths of 1 foot 6 inches, 2 feet 6 inches, 3 feet 6 inches, and so on. If three widths of carpet with a 36-inch repeat are being installed in a room that measures 22 feet 6 inches in length, all lengths can be cut seven-and-a-half repeats, or 22 feet 6 inches long.

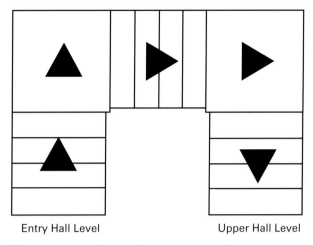

Entry Hall Level   Upper Hall Level

Figure 26.12 Direction of pile lay on angled stairs. Fairchild Books.

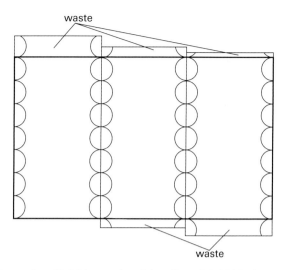

Figure 26.15 Matching a set-match pattern. Fairchild Books.

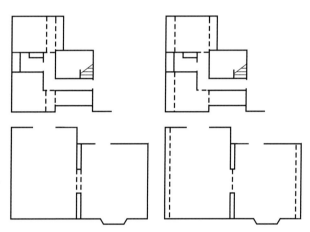

a) incorrect seam placement b) correct seam placement

Figure 26.13 Planning carpet seam placement: (a) correct seam placement, (b) incorrect seam placement. Fairchild Books.

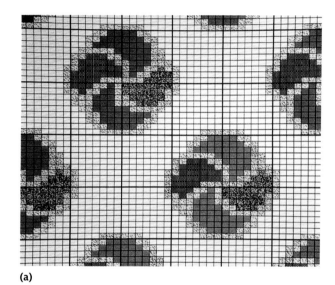

(a)

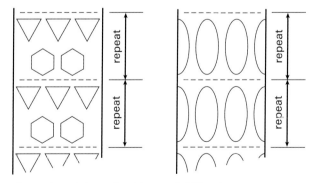

Figure 26.14 Set-match patterns. Fairchild Books.

(b)

Figure 26.16 Half-drop-match pattern: (a) draft of half-drop-match pattern, (b) example of installed half-drop-match pattern. (a) Courtesy of Mohawk Carpet, (b) courtesy of Tesri, www.tesri.fr.

The **quarter-drop-match pattern** is a second type of drop-match pattern. This type of repeat is frequently seen in colonial patterns; it has four blocks to a repeat. So that figures match one-quarter of the repeat on the opposite edge (Figure 26.17), successive pieces of carpet are shifted and aligned to preserve the diagonal pattern. According to the length required and the length of the repeat, quarter-drop patterns can be cut in multiples of the repeat plus one, two, or three blocks. Side matching can then be achieved by dropping one, two, or three blocks.

A layout sketch of the carpet lengths on graph paper is essential for all planned installations. The sketch should specify the direction of pile lay, the placement of seams, and the orientation of patterns. The floor measurement and the calculations of the extra yardage needed for pattern matching should be rechecked. This plan will help ensure that the tally of the total quantity of carpet required is accurate; later it will serve as the cutting guide (Figure 26.18).

Linear measurements must be converted into square yards for ordering. Because most carpet is produced 12 feet wide, the conversions presented in Table 26.1 are

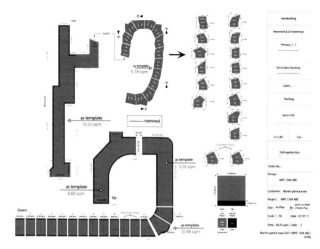

Figure 26.18 Schematic plan for carpet installation. Courtesy Martin Patrick Evan, Ltd.

based on this width. This conversion also facilitates an estimate of materials costs, since these charges are normally quoted on a per-square-yard basis. To convert square yardage to square feet, divide the square yardage by 9.

Upon receipt, floorcovering must be inspected for flaws, color variations, and to confirm that the quantity ordered was delivered. Most manufacturers will not assume responsibility for defects after carpet has been cut.

Maintaining Textile Floorcoverings

Without proper care, a carpet that has been carefully selected, correctly specified, and skillfully installed may **ugly out** (show wearing, soiling, matting, loss of color) long before it is "worn out." End-users and consumers frequently mistake soiling or improper cleaning for "wear" of the material.

To ensure that the carpet (or carpet and cushion assembly) retains a high level of appearance, a planned maintenance program is critical. In contrast to sporadic maintenance, in which cleaning is undertaken as a last resort after excessive soil has already accumulated and visibly altered the look of the surface, scheduled maintenance increases a carpet's appearance retention. Regular

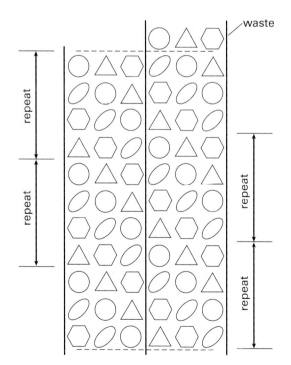

Figure 26.17 Matching a quarter-drop-match pattern. Fairchild Books.

TABLE 26.1
CONVERSION OF FEET AND INCHES TO SQUARE YARDS OF 12-FOOT-WIDE CARPET

				Example								
				74'5" of 12' width								
				74' = 98.67 sq. yds.								
				5" = .55 sq. yd.								
				Total = 99.22 sq. yds.								
Inches					**Feet**							
Linear in.	Sq. yds.	Linear ft.	Sq. yds.	Linear ft.	Sq. yds.	Linear ft.	Sq. yds.	Linear ft.	Sq. yds.	Linear ft.	Sq. yds.
1	11	7	9.33	26	34.67	45	60.00	64	85.33	83	110.67
2	22	8	10.67	27	36.00	46	61.33	65	86.67	84	112.00
3	33	9	12.00	28	37.33	47	62.67	66	88.00	85	113.33
4	44	10	13.33	29	38.67	48	64.00	67	89.33	86	114.67
5	55	11	14.67	30	40.00	49	65.33	68	90.67	87	116.00
6	67	12	16.00	31	41.33	50	66.67	69	92.00	88	117.33
7	78	13	17.33	32	42.67	51	68.00	70	93.33	89	118.67
8	89	14	18.67	33	44.00	52	69.33	71	94.67	90	120.00
9	1.00	15	20.00	34	45.33	53	70.67	72	96.00	91	121.33
10	1.11	16	21.33	35	46.67	54	72.00	73	97.33	92	122.67
11	1.22	17	22.67	36	48.00	55	73.00	74	98.67	93	124.00
Feet		18	24.00	37	49.33	56	74.67	75	100.00	94	125.33
Linear ft.	Sq. yds.	19	25.33	38	50.67	57	76.00	76	101.33	95	126.67
1	1.33	20	26.67	39	52.00	58	77.33	77	102.67	96	128.00
2	2.67	21	28.00	40	53.33	59	78.67	78	104.00	97	129.33
3	4.00	22	29.33	41	54.67	60	80.00	79	105.33	98	130.67
4	5.33	23	30.67	42	56.00	61	81.33	80	106.67	99	132.00
5	6.67	24	32.00	43	57.33	62	82.67	81	108.00	100	133.33
6	8.00	25	33.33	44	58.67	63	84.00	82	109.33		

Courtesy of Milliken & Company.

maintenance minimizes soil from being spread throughout the carpet and grit from embedding in the surface yarns. Regular, frequent vacuuming and cleaning and prompt stain removal for spills and mishaps are protocol.

In addition to preserving carpet appearance, prolonging carpet life through proper maintenance will improve indoor air quality by reducing the accumulation of allergens, provide cost savings attributed to premature replacement, and reduce the amount of carpet going to landfills and recycling centers. Commercial cleaning programs are available, but professionals and consumers may design appropriate plans themselves. A planned maintenance program delays or prevents the development of apparent changes in color caused by excessive soil accumulation; it also reduces changes in texture and luster caused when traffic grinds gritty soil against fiber surfaces.

The CRI offers detailed information on caring for carpets in commercial spaces. Refer to Carpet Maintenance Guidelines For Commercial Applications, which are available on the CRI website, http://www.carpet-rug.org/.

Initial Care

Inspection of a newly installed carpet may reveal shedding, sprouting, missing tufts, and small dots of latex grinning through to the face. Simple measures can correct these irregularities.

TABLE 26.2

INSTALLATION CHECKLIST—PROPER PROCEDURES TO ENSURE GOOD INDOOR AIR QUALITY (IAQ)

Pre-Installation

- Choose a carpet with the CRI IAQ Testing Program logo.*
- Store carpet at room temperature (between 65°F and 95°F) for at least 48 hours prior to installation in order for it to relax. Ideally, it should be unrolled, to allow it to condition to the ambient temperatures. Protect carpet from soil, dust, moisture, and other contaminants.
- If replacement carpet, vacuum the old carpet prior to removal, and vacuum the subfloor to minimize the amount of airborne dust.
- Carefully plan the carpet installation, using manufacturer's guidelines and/or the CRI Carpet Installation Standard.
- Confirm that the substrate is clean, dry, and smooth.

During Installation

- For glue-down installations, use low-emitting (non-solvent) adhesives identified by the CRI Adhesive Green Label Plus Program.*
- Use low-emitting carpet cushion (for installations in which cushion is specified).*
- Use low-emitting accessories.*
- Maintain fresh-air ventilation and circulation for 48 to 72 hours. For acceptable indoor air quality, fresh air ventilation in commercial spaces is recommended to conform to current guidelines specified in ASHRAE Standard 62 published by the American Society of Heating, Refrigerating and Air Conditioning Engineers.
- Open windows and doors, use exhaust fans, or both.
- Operate ventilation systems at full capacity.
- If possible, segregate the air circulation of the renovation area from the remainder of the building.

Post-Installation

- Vacuum new carpet to remove excess fibers loosened during installation.
- Continue fresh air ventilation for 72 hours at normal room temperatures to help dissipate any possible odors.
- Implement efficient carpet maintenance program to protect your investment.

Refer to CRI Technical Bulletin: Carpet and Indoor Air Quality and the CRI 104/105 Carpet Installation Standard.

*Look for and purchase carpet, carpet cushion, and floorcovering installation adhesive products that display the CRI Indoor Air Quality label (http://www.carpet-rug.org/green-label-plus.html). These three indoor air-quality testing programs identify the products that have been tested to meet stringent indoor air quality requirements for low emissions. For further information on these programs, plus the CRI vacuum cleaner testing program, visit the CRI website at www.carpet-rug.org.

Shedding occurs when short lengths of fibers that have accumulated during manufacturing work to the surface. It is characteristic of cut pile textures, especially wool fiber, and will soon be corrected by regular vacuuming. The fiber loss will not be significant. **Sprouting** refers to the protrusion of a tuft above the surface of the wear layer. This may result from the release of a small fold of pile yarn that was caught during manufacturing. The extended tuft should simply be clipped to the proper pile height; it must never be pulled. The floorcovering dealer, in a procedure known as **burling**, can replace a missing tuft.

During manufacturing, a small dot of latex is frequently used to join or splice ends of pile yarns. Normally, the factory inspector removes visible bits of latex. If, however, some were hidden and appear in the new carpet, the installer or consumer can simply cut them out, removing any residue with a small amount of dry-cleaning fluid. Casters placed under wheeled desk chairs protect carpet pile from excessive abrasion, shearing, and crushing, which prolongs the wear-life and helps retain the original texture of the carpet.

Preventive Maintenance

Preventive maintenance removes soil and grit so that it is not spread throughout a facility, which can significantly minimize spotting and staining and reduce wear and tear.

Using Protective Mats

Because over 80 percent of carpet soil is tracked in, preventive maintenance begins with walk-off mats or runners placed outside and inside of entrance areas. Walk-off mats should also be placed where foot traffic may transfer wax and dust from hard-surfaced floors to carpet surfaces. In areas where commercial traffic is concentrated or channeled, such as lobbies, elevators, in front of vending machines and file cabinets, down corridors, and at doorways, protective mats should be strategically located to capture soil.

Walk-off mats and runners must also be cleaned regularly so that they do not become sources of soil and grit themselves. Removable rugs or carpet modules in elevators make off-site cleaning and rotation convenient. As previously discussed, in all commercial environments, carpets and mats should meet the ADA Design Guidelines for construction and installation methods.

Vacuuming

In most planned maintenance programs, a thorough vacuuming (five to seven passes of the sweeper over the surface) every day or two with an upright, rather than a canister, vacuum is recommended for areas that withstand heavy traffic. For areas subjected to lower levels of traffic, vacuuming may be light (three passes of the sweeper) and as infrequent as every seven to ten days. Such light maintenance is reasonable for many areas: approximately 70 to 80 percent of all interior floor space is rarely walked on.

An example of a planned maintenance schedule for a commercial interior is presented in Figure 26.19. Vacuuming, stain removal, and interim cleaning activities are listed. Heavy traffic and heavily soiled areas are scheduled for dry-cleaning once every twenty days; stain

Recommended Cleaning Schedule				
Monday	Tuesday	Wednesday	Thursday	Friday
1	2	3	4	5
HT vacuum	HT vacuum	HT vacuum	HT vacuum	HT vacuum
MT vacuum	Spot cleaning	MT vacuum	MT vacuum	MT vacuum
Rotate mats			Spot cleaning	
8	9	10	11	12
HT vacuum	HT vacuum	HT vacuum	HT vacuum	HT vacuum
MT vacuum	Spot cleaning	MT vacuum	MT vacuum	MT vacuum
Rotate mats			Spot cleaning	
15	16	17	18	19
HT vacuum	HT vacuum	HT vacuum	HT vacuum	HT vacuum
MT vacuum	Spot cleaning	MT vacuum	MT vacuum	MT vacuum
Rotate mats			Spot cleaning	
22	23	24	25	26
HT vacuum	HT vacuum	HT vacuum	HT vacuum	HT vacuum
MT vacuum	Spot cleaning	MT vacuum	MT vacuum	MT vacuum
Rotate mats			Spot cleaning	
29	30	31	1	2
HT vacuum	HT vacuum	HT vacuum	HT vacuum	HT vacuum
MT vacuum	Spot cleaning	MT vacuum	MT vacuum	MT vacuum
Rotate mats			Spot cleaning	LT cleaning

HT = high traffic areas, MT = medium traffic areas, LT = low traffic areas: vacuum as needed. TF = traffic lane cleaning: overall cleaning performed periodically; increase during inclement weather. Schedule assumes no maintenance operations on Saturday or Sunday.

Figure 26.19 Commercial carpet cleaning frequency chart.
Courtesy of Ascend Performance Materials.

removal and dry-cleaning procedures are discussed later in this chapter.

The CRI launched the Green Label Vacuum Testing Program in 2000 to assist consumers in identifying the best vacuum cleaners for use on carpeting. CRI-approved vacuums are part of its Seal of Approval (SOA) program. End-users can identify these machines, which have not only outstanding cleaning qualities but reduced amounts of dust put back into the air, by the CRI Seal of Approval "Green Label" on approved machines and packaging.

Pretesting Cleaning Products

Pretesting stain removal and carpet cleaning products is an important preventive activity, because it minimizes the chance that products will damage the fibers, cause color transfer, produce color changes, or leave sticky residues. The CRI recommends the use of two types of pretests. In one test, approximately one teaspoon of the prepared product is worked into the fibers in an inconspicuous area of the floorcovering. The fibers are then pressed between a clean, white tissue for about ten seconds. The tissue is examined for evidence of bleeding, and the fibers are examined for evidence of damage. The procedure should be repeated until a safe agent is identified.

In the second test, a half-cup of the prepared product is poured into a clear glass dish. After the liquid portion of the product has evaporated, the residue is examined. If a dry, powdery residue is found, it would be reasonable to expect that vacuuming could remove such deposits from the carpet. If a sticky or waxy residue is found, it is evident that such deposits would remain in the carpet after cleaning, causing the fibers to adhere to one another and promoting rapid resoiling.

The CRI introduced the Seal of Approval (SOA) Carpet Cleaning Products Testing Program in 2007. This program evaluates carpet-cleaning products for cleaning effectiveness without damage to carpet fibers and backings. An important aspect of cleaning products is that they not strip the carpet of its stain-resistant properties, thus allowing dirt to adhere easily to the carpet in the future. Products tested include pre-spray and in-tank cleaning detergents and extraction equipment.

Minimizing and Removing Stains

Promptly and efficiently removing solid and liquid spills and deposits is critical to preventing lasting carpet stains. A few basic rules for stain removal include:

1. Act promptly. Foreign substances are more difficult to remove after they have aged.
2. Vacuum dry substances, scoop up excess thick substances, and absorb as much spilled liquid as possible before proceeding with additional removal procedures. To avoid diluting and spreading spilled liquids, do not wet at this time. Immediately place absorbent towels over the spill and apply pressure with the hands or heels to promote transfer of the moisture from the carpet to the towels. Use a blotting action—rubbing could cause distortion of the pile. Continue blotting until no more of the spot shows on the towels. Next, cover the area with a half-inch thick layer of absorbent tissues topped by a sheet of foil, and place a heavy object (for example, a stack of large books) on the foil-covered towels. Wait patiently overnight while the liquid wicks into the towels. If some of the spill remains, proceed with the appropriate removal technique listed in Table 26.4, or consult a reputable supplier for specific advice. The CRI's website (www.carpet-rug.org) offers numerous bulletins on the subject of maintenance and cleaning.
3. Be prepared. Have a kit of cleaning agents and materials assembled for immediate use. A list of common stain removal supplies is provided in Table 26.3. It does not include carbon tetrachloride, gasoline, or lighter fluid, which are flammable and hazardous to human health. Label the containers and store them in a locked cabinet out of the reach of children.
4. Pretest before using any cleaning agent.

Common stains and the procedures recommended for removing them from nylon fibers are listed in Table 26.4. Retailers, fiber and carpet producers, and trade associations can provide additional stain removal guides and care instructions.

When small bits of carpet fibers have been melted or singed, they can be carefully clipped and removed. If the

TABLE 26.3
SPOT AND STAIN REMOVAL SUPPLIES

Absorbent dry powders—examples include HOST and Capture®

Abundant supply of absorbent white tissues and towels for blotting

Acetic acid or white vinegar solution (⅓ cup of vinegar to 1 cup of water)

Acetone or fingernail polish remover, non-oily type

Aerosol cleaners—commercial type available from floorcovering dealers and in grocery stores

Alcohol, denatured or rubbing type

Ammonia solution (1 tablespoon to ¾ cup of water)

Detergent (use 1 teaspoon of mild hand dishwashing type without oily conditioners to 1 cup of warm water or 1 tablespoon of dry powdered laundry type to 1 cup of water)

Dry-cleaning fluid—examples include Carbona®, Renuzit®, and Energine®

POGR (paint, oil, and grease remover)—examples include Pyratex® and Buckeye®

Pre-soak laundry product (enzyme digester)

Squeeze bottles, medicine droppers, wooden scrapers

TABLE 26.4
REMOVAL OF SPOTS AND STAINS FROM NYLON FIBERS

Stain/Procedure		Stain/Procedure		Procedure A	Procedure D	Procedure H
Asphalt	A	Lard	A	Apply solvent	Detergent	Apply solvent
Beer	E	Linseed Oil	A	*POGR	Blot	Wait several minutes
Berries	E	Machine Oil	A	Blot	Acetic acid	Blot
Blood	B	Mascara	A	Apply solvent	Blot	Detergent
Butter	A	Mayonnaise	B	Detergent	Rust remover	Blot
Candle Wax	G	Mercurochrome	E	Blot	Blot	Water
Candy (Sugar)	D	Merthiolate	E	Ammonia	Detergent	Blot
Carbon Black	A	Milk	B	Blot	Blot	
Catsup	B	Mimeo Correction Fluid	C	Detergent	Water	Procedure I
Charcoal	A	Mixed Drinks	E	Blot	Blot	Denatured alcohol
Cheese	B	Model Cement	L	Water		Blot
Chewing Gum	G	Mustard	E	Blot	Procedure E	Repeat, if necessary
Chocolate	B	Nail Polish	L		Detergent	Note: pretest as for other solutions
Coffee	E	Paint—Latex	A	Procedure B	Blot	
Cooking Oil	A	Paint—Oil	A	Detergent	Ammonia	
Crayon	A	Rubber Cement	A	Enzyme digestor	Blot	Procedure J
Créme de Menthe	F	Rust	D	Soak	Acetic acid	Detergent
Dye—Blue, Black, Green	F	Shellac	I	Ammonia	Blot	Blot
Dye—Red	E	Shoe Polish	A	Blot	Detergent	Vinegar

TABLE 26.4

REMOVAL OF SPOTS AND STAINS FROM NYLON FIBERS (*continued*)

Stain/Procedure		Stain/Procedure		Procedure A	Procedure D	Procedure H
Earth	B	Shortening	A	Detergent	Blot	Blot
Egg	B	Soft Drinks	E	Blot	Water	Ammonia
Excrement	B	Soy Sauce	B	Water	Blot	Blot
Fish Slime	B	Starch	B	Blot		Detergent
Foundation Makeup	A	Tar	A		Procedure F	Blot
Fruit Juice	E	Tea	E	Procedure C	Detergent	Water
Furniture Polish	A	Tooth Paste	B	Apply solvent	Blot	Blot
Furniture Polish with Stain	H	Typewriter Ribbon	A	*POGR	Acetic acid	
Gravy	A	Urine—Dry	J	Blot	Blot	Procedure K
Hair Oil	A	Urine—Fresh	K	Apply solvent	Ammonia	Blot
Hair Spray	A	Varnish	C	Blot	Blot	Water
Hand Lotion	A	Vaseline	A	Detergent	Water	Blot
Ice Cream	B	Wax—Paste	A	Blot	Blot	Ammonia
Ink—Ballpoint	A	White Glue	B	Water		Blot
Ink—Fountain Pen	F	Wine	E	Blot	Procedure G	Detergent
Ink—India	A				Freeze with ice cube	Blot
Ink—Marking Pen	A				Shatter w/blunt object	Water
Ink—Mimeo	A				Vacuum out chips	Blot
Lacquer	C				Apply solvent Wait several minutes Blot Repeat, if necessary	Procedure L Polish remover (non-oily) Blot Repeat

*Paint, oil, and grease remover.

See the CRI website (*www.carpet-rug.org*) for a wide range of information on cleaning and maintenance of rugs and carpet.

Courtesy of Shaw Industries.

damaged area is large, it can be cut out and replaced with a piece of the carpet from the original order that was reserved at the time of installation.

Interim Maintenance

Interim maintenance is designed primarily to assure a high level of appearance retention for an extended time period and to delay the need for restorative procedures. Interim maintenance is, specifically, the use of a restorative cleaning procedures in areas that withstand heavy traffic every 20 or 31 days. A planned schedule will prevent soil accumulation in areas of heavy traffic from developing an appearance noticeably different from that of adjacent areas.

Both dry and wet cleaning systems are used in interim cleaning. Frequently, dry-cleaning is recommended so that no drying time is required and the area being cleaned can extend beyond the soiled area to prevent marked differences in appearance between the cleaned site and the adjacent areas. Retailers offer dry-cleaning compounds from various suppliers; many contain fluorochemical stain repellents and other chemical compounds that are objectionable to some users, and are thought to present deleterious environmental effects.

Pills, fuzz, and snags should also be removed as needed. When abraded, fibers in loop pile textures tend to rupture, which causes fuzziness, leaving one end in the base of the yarn and one end protruding; the yarn stands out from all others because it is no longer a loop. The protruding length should be clipped away and definitely should not be pulled, which could pull out more loops. Unsightly pills should be clipped away, although this is a tedious job. Snagged tufts are treated in the same manner as sprouting tufts. If evident rippling or seam separation occurs, the installer can restretch or reglue the structure and secure it to the seams. Area and room-size rugs and runners should be reversed and modules rotated to even the level of wear and soiling. Furniture may be shifted a few inches to allow crushed areas to recover; steaming the areas with an iron held approximately 4 inches above the surface aids recovery. Occasionally raking pile tufts in shag floorcoverings can help keep them erect.

Restorative Maintenance

Overall or wall-to-wall cleaning (**restorative maintenance**) should ideally be scheduled regularly, usually every year or two, depending upon the rate of soil accumulation and the effectiveness of regular maintenance. Of course, the owner's opinion about the acceptability of the surface appearance, along with budgetary concerns, is usually decisive. Four major restorative maintenance procedures are most commonly used: dry extraction, dry foam, wet shampoo, and hot water extraction.

Dry Extraction

Dry extraction cleaning is also referred to as absorbent powder or absorbent compound cleaning. The soil-extracting particles are generally composed of water-based cleaning fluids or detergents and a small amount of solvent. Their minute size results in an extremely high surface area-to-volume ratio that increases their capacity for absorption.

The particles are sprinkled over the carpet structure and vigorously brushed by hand or machine into the pile layer. There, the solvent releases the soil and the porous particles act like tiny sponges, absorbing the soil. Subsequent vacuuming removes the soil-holding particles.

The advantage of dry extraction cleaning is that the fibers are not wetted. This avoids not only the need for drying, but also the problem of over-wetting the structure, which could lead to shrinkage and microbe-related problems. For carpet or rugs with jute backing, over-wetting can also cause **browning**, which is a staining of the pile as the water wicks from the backing upward. The particles must be cautiously brushed into the pile layer to avoid distortion of cut pile yarns.

Dry Foam

Dry foam cleaning is also called aerosol cleaning. The cleaning agent is usually a water-based shampoo that has been converted into foam. The foam is sprayed onto the carpet surface and worked into the pile layer with a hand-held sponge or with mechanically operated brushes. The surface must be thoroughly vacuumed or rinsed with a damp sponge to remove the soil-foam residue after the compound dries. Some electrically powered units apply the foam and vacuum the carpet in a one-step operation.

Other methods are more thorough than dry foam cleaning, which may not be the ideal choice when a large amount of soil is deeply embedded in the pile layer. The risk of over-wetting the carpet is minimal.

Wet Shampooing

The **wet shampoo method** of carpet restoration is commonly referred to as the rotary brush method. The properly diluted detergent solution or foam is driven into the pile with one or two rotating brushes. A thorough vacuuming, preferably with a wet vacuum, must follow. Wet vacuums, unlike conventional vacuums, are engineered to safely and efficiently suction both fluids and dry matter from surfaces.

While the mechanical action of the rotating brushes works the detergent solution into the carpet, it may also cause pile distortion, especially of cut surfaces.

The solution or foam must be carefully applied to avoid over-wetting the structure. Vacuuming of the soil-shampoo compound must be thorough, since any residue will accelerate resoiling.

Hot Water Extraction

Hot water extraction cleaning is commonly called steam extraction, although extremely hot water is used, not steam. The properly diluted shampoo is driven into the pile as a spray by high-pressure jets; it is then immediately extracted by the vacuum component of the machine.

Because no mechanical brushing is used in this extraction method, pile yarns are minimally distorted. Spots and stains must be removed before the cleaning operation is begun so that the hot water will not set them. As in wet shampooing, the detergent must be thoroughly removed to retard rapid resoiling.

Salvage Maintenance

Salvage maintenance is used to clean extremely soiled carpet or for removing built-up residue. A combination of wet shampooing and hot water extraction with mechanical rotary brushes will help to loosen the soil, and the extraction will make for better removal.

Recycling

Many recycling options are available for carpet at the end of its useful life. Carpet suppliers and manufacturers, the CRI, and CARE (Carpet America Recycling Effort) are all excellent resources. For further information, see Chapter 3 and Chapter 20.

Key Terms

browning	free-lay installation
drop-match patterns	glue-down installation
dry extraction cleaning	grin
dry foam cleaning	half-drop-match patterns

hot water extraction cleaning	salvage maintenance
	seams
interim maintenance	set-match patterns
knee kicker	shedding
panels	sprouting
power stretcher	stretch-in installation
preventive maintenance	tackless strips
quarter-drop-match patterns	ugly out
	wall-to-wall installation
restorative maintenance	wet shampoo cleaning
saddle	

Review Questions

1. Identify several tasks that may have to be completed on site before a new floorcovering assembly is installed.
2. Explain the techniques used in stretch-in installations. How is the stretching accomplished? How is the carpet secured?
3. Distinguish between double glue-down and direct glue-down installations. What advantages are offered by these modes of installation when rolling traffic is anticipated?
4. Identify some advantages of using releasable adhesives with carpet modules.
5. What factors limit the use of free-lay installations with carpet modules? What advantages are offered by this mode of installation?
6. Illustrate and discuss the important influence that the directional lay of pile yarns has on the quantity of light reflected from the carpet surface.
7. Differentiate among set-match, drop-match, half-drop-match, and quarter-drop-match patterns.
8. Cite the objectives of planned maintenance programs.
9. Confirm the importance of pretesting cleaning products.
10. What are the advantages and disadvantages of each of the restorative cleaning procedures?

UNIT FIVE
HOUSEHOLD AND
INSTITUTIONAL TEXTILES

27

Textile Products for the Bath

Fabric designers' extensive output of innovative decorative towels, rugs, mats, and shower curtains are spread across the retail market. Whereas the primary function of towels is to absorb water, the colors, patterns, and textures of bath products contribute significantly to a home's aesthetics; they are often as ornamental as they are functional. Manufacturers have expanded the size range of towels, increased the types of materials used in shower curtains, and varied the shapes and constructions of small bath rugs and mats. Bath furnishings are frequently offered in coordinated ensembles, and are sometimes part of elaborate collections that include bedding and other household products.

Retailers, distributors, and manufacturers us standard performance specifications, such as those published by ASTM International, to establish required structural features and performance levels of toweling products, especially for those intended for institutional use.

Towels and Toweling

Various fabrication techniques including weaving and bonding webs of fibers are used to produce toweling. In contrast to many other interior products, which are composed primarily of manufactured fibers, cotton dominates the market for towels and toweling. Cotton is highly absorbent and soft, features that make it attractive and efficient for toweling. Flax, which has slightly higher moisture absorption and produces less lint than cotton, is also used, but in small amounts. The harsh hand and low abrasion resistance of flax preclude its use in bath towels, and the comparatively high cost of the fiber limits its use in dish towels.

Manufacturers sometimes blend cotton and polyester to save on costs. However, this decreases the towel's softness, comfort, and absorbency. Industrial toweling is generally made of cotton/polyester blends. Manufactured cellulosic fibers, including rayon made from bamboo and lyocell, are also used for bath products. Rayon is soft and absorbent but is less durable than cotton, and has negative environmental impacts. (Manufactured cellulosic fibers are discussed in Chapter 4.) Although synthetic fibers can be spun into yarns that simulate the appearance and hand of yarns composed of cotton, their hydrophobic characteristics make them unappealing for toweling.

Fiber Composition

With the exception of nontextile shower curtains, bath products are subject to the provisions of the Textile Fiber Products Identification Act (TFPIA; see Chapter 11). Small rugs and bath mats are also subject to a federal flammability standard, 16 CFR 1631.

Manufacturing Toweling

Manufacturers use a variety of fabrication techniques to produce flat or nonpile toweling. A warp pile weaving operation produces pile toweling.

Constructing Pile Toweling

Pile or **terry toweling** is also known as **Turkish toweling**. The components of this toweling are illustrated in Figure 27.1. One set of filling or weft yarns is interlaced with one set of base or ground warp yarns and two sets of pile warp yarns. If loops are planned for only one side of the fabric, only one set of pile warp yarns is used. Fabrics with loops on both sides have more fiber surface area for absorbing moisture, but they are also more expensive if the construction density is not reduced. For visual interest, the pile yarns appearing on each side can be of different colors.

Terry toweling is manufactured by the slack tension technique (see Chapter 7). For economical production, terry looms are generally threaded for full-width weaving.

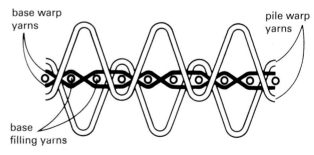

Figure 27.1 Cross-sectional sketch of terry toweling that has three filling picks per crosswise row of pile loops. Fairchild Books.

When hemmed edges and ends are planned, the dimensions of individual towels are demarcated by the omission of pile yarns in narrow lengthwise and crosswise bands; when fringed ends are planned, the crosswise bands are also void of filling picks. A dobby mechanism may be used to produce woven border designs.

For increased efficiency and economy in both weaving and finishing, textile machinery engineers have developed extra-wide looms capable of simultaneously weaving multiple widths of toweling. Looms of the type shown in Figures 27.2a and b can weave several widths of toweling during one operation. The several widths of toweling have tucked-in selvedges. Typical terry toweling is shown in Figure 27.3. The Jacquard terry toweling in Figure 27.4 has been woven in a visually appealing geometric pattern.

(a)

(b)

Figure 27.2 (a) Loom engineered to weave multiple widths of terry toweling. (b) Terry toweling on loom. (a) Courtesy of Picanol. (b) Courtesy of Itema Weaving, www.sultex.com.

Figure 27.3 Typical terry toweling. malerapaso/iStock.com.

Figure 27.4 Jacquard terry toweling. heinteh/iStock.com.

Figure 27.5 Terry velour toweling. Courtesy of Amy Willbanks, www.textilefabric.com.

Figure 27.6 Crash. Courtesy of Amy Willbanks, www.textilefabric.com.

Terry velour toweling (Figure 27.5) has a conventional looped pile surface on one side, and a dense, cut pile surface on the other side. The sheared velour surface has a thick and luxurious appearance and hand, but the level of moisture absorption is relatively low since only the small tips of the yarns are exposed.

Fabricating Flat Toweling

Flat or non-terry toweling is generally produced by weaving yarns in a basic or dobby-weave pattern or by bonding webs of fibers. **Crash**, shown in Figure 27.6, is a plain-woven fabric composed of coarse, irregular yarns spun from flax. The fabric is constructed into dish towels intended for the lint-free drying of glassware. Twill-woven toweling, often referred to as **institutional toweling**, is generally produced with brightly colored stripes on each long side and constructed into towels used in restaurants. **Huck toweling (huckaback)** is woven on a dobby loom and has small filling floats. These slightly raised floats, visible in the close-up photograph in Figure 27.7, improve the drying efficiency of the towel.

Bonding webs of fibers with heat or an adhesive is used to produce **disposable toweling**, some of which are intended to be used once, while others are intended for repeated use (Figure 27.8). For increased strength, a scrim of fine yarns may be anchored between the layered webs.

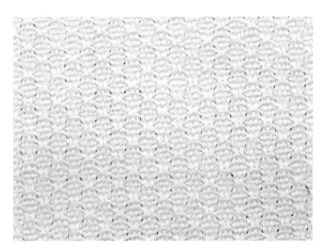

Figure 27.7 Huck toweling. Courtesy of Amy Willbanks, www. textilefabric.com.

Range of Towel Offerings

Towels come in a variety of sizes and with a variety of edge finishes. Trim and embroidery embellish their surfaces.

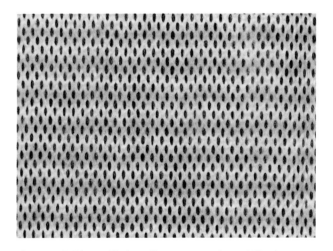

Figure 27.8 Disposable toweling. Courtesy of Amy Willbanks, www. textilefabric.com.

TABLE 27.1

TRADITIONAL TYPES AND SIZES OF TOWELS (MANY VARIATIONS ARE AVAILABLE)

Type	Inches (Width × Length)
Dish towel	12 × 24 to 16 × 30
Fingertip/guest	9 × 14 to 11 × 20
Washcloth	12 × 12 to 14 × 14
Face/hand towel	15 × 25 to 20 × 36
Bath towel	20 × 40 to 27 × 50
Bath sheet	35 × 66 to 45 × 75

Types and Sizes

Several types of towels are included in today's market assortment. The approximate size ranges of the various types are listed in Table 27.1. If the toweling is not preshrunk, the towels may be oversized to compensate for relaxation shrinkage in laundering.

Edge Finishes and Decorative Treatments

Terry toweling is cut along the flat lengthwise and crosswise bands spaced throughout the pile greige goods. Cutting produces unfinished towels of various sizes. The sides may be finished with a small, machine-stitched hem or with machine serging. The ends may be hemmed or left with a yarn fringe. Squares of pile fabric are cut for washcloths, and the four raw edges are serged. For decorative interest, bands of embroidered fabric or trim may be sewn across towels and washcloths, or the surface may be embellished with an embroidered monogram or motif (Figure 27.9).

Coordinated Items

Yarn-dyed, solid-colored, and printed toweling are used not only for dish towels, but also for oven mitts, pot holders, small appliance covers, and aprons. The color styling and decorative treatment of bath towels may be replicated in bedding products; the bath and bedding products are then offered and promoted as a coordinated ensemble.

Evaluating Physical Performance Properties

To assure satisfactory performance in use, manufacturers may elect to evaluate the properties of their towels

Figure 27.9 Embroidered toweling at VillaHotel Contenta, Miami Beach. normallens/iStock.com.

in conjunction with recommendations set forth in ASTM D5433, Standard Performance Specification for Towel Products for Institutional and Household Use. Specifications for woven terry items, including kitchen towels, dishcloths, bath and hand towels, washcloths, and bath sheets, are listed in Table 27.2; those for non-terry fabrics, including dishcloths, huck toweling, and crash, are shown in Table 27.3.

Breaking Force (Load)

The breaking force (load) of woven terry and non-terry towelings may be measured in accordance with the grab test procedure of ASTM D5034, Standard Test Method for Breaking Strength and Elongation of Textile Fabrics (Grab Test). This procedure was discussed in Chapter 19, and as shown in Tables 27.2 and 27.3, the minimum force for towelings ranges from 30 to 50 pounds, depending on the fabric construction and the product.

TABLE 27.2

STANDARD PERFORMANCE SPECIFICATION FOR WOVEN OR KNITTED TOWEL PRODUCTS FOR INSTITUTIONAL AND HOUSEHOLD USE

Characteristic	Test Method Number	Requirement		
				Bath, Hand, Washcloths,
		Kitchen Towels	Dishcloths	Bath Sheets
Breaking force (load)	ASTM D5034			
Length		178 N (40 lbf) min	220 N (50 lbf) min	178 N (40 lbf) min
Width		133 N (30 lbf) min	178 N (40 lbf) min	133 N (30 lbf) min
Bursting force (knits only)	ASTM D3786			
Diaphragm		222 N (50 lbf) min	222 N (50 lbf) min	222 N (50 lbf) min
Dimensional change	AATCC 96 or AATCC 135			
Length		10% max	10% max	10% max
Width		5% max	5% max	4% max
Skew	AATCC 179, Option 1	5% max	5% max	5% max
Colorfastness[a]				
Laundering	AATCC 61			
Shade change		Class 4[b] min	Class 4[b] min	Class 4[b] min
Staining		Class 3[c] min	Class 3[c] min	Class 3[c] min
Crocking	AATCC 8 for solids or AATCC 116 for prints			
Dry		Class 4[d] min	Class 4[d] min	Class 4[d] min
Wet		Class 3[d] min	Class 3[d] min	Class 3[d] min
Light (20 AATCC fading units), xenon	AATCC 16.3	Class 4[b] min	Class 4[b] min	Class 4[b] min
Absorbency	ASTM D4772	Pass	Pass	Pass
Laundered appearance	ASTM D5433, 7.2	Acceptable	Acceptable	Acceptable

[a] Class in the colorfastness requirements is based on a numerical scale from 5 for no color change or color transfer to 1 for severe color change or color transfer.

[b] AATCC Gray Scale for Color Change.

[c] AATCC Gray Scale for Staining.

[d] AATCC Chromatic Transference Scale.

Adapted, with permission from D5433 (2012) Standard Performance Specification for Towel Products for Institutional and Household Use, copyright ASTM International, 100 Barr Harbor Drive, West Conshohocken, PA 19428, www.astm.org. A copy of the complete standard may be obtained from ASTM International.

Dimensional Change

Because towelings are used primarily to absorb liquids, and they are frequently laundered, it is critical that they exhibit relatively high dimensional stability. The fabrics may be tested after five launderings following prescribed care instructions, or in accordance with directions in AATCC Method 135, Dimensional Changes of Fabrics After Home Laundering, or AATCC Method 96, Dimensional Changes in Commercial Laundering of Woven and Knitted Fabrics Except Wool. As shown in Tables 27.2 and 27.3, recommendations range from a maximum of 4 percent shrinkage for bath and hand

TABLE 27.3

STANDARD PERFORMANCE SPECIFICATION FOR NON-TERRY TOWEL PRODUCTS FOR INSTITUTIONAL AND HOUSEHOLD USE

Characteristic	Test Method Number	Requirement	
		Huck and Crash Towels	**Dishcloths**
Breaking force (load)	ASTM D5034		
Length		178 N (40 lbf) min	220 N (50 lbf) min
Width		133 N (30 lbf) min	178 N (40 lbf) min
Bursting force (knits only)	ASTM D3786		
Diaphragm		222 N (50 lbf) min	222 N (50 lbf) min
Dimensional change	AATCC 96 or AATCC 135		
Length		10% max	10% max
Width		5% max	5% max
Skew	AATCC 179, Option 1	5% Acceptable	5% Acceptable
Colorfastness[a]			
Laundering	AATCC 61		
Shade change		Class 4[b] min	Class 4[b] min
Staining		Class 3[c] min	Class 3[c] min
Crocking	AATCC 8 for solids or AATCC 116 for prints		
Dry		Class 4[d] min	Class 4[d] min
Wet		Class 3[d] min	Class 3[d] min
Light (20 AATCC fading units), xenon	AATCC 16.3	Class 4[b] min	Class 4[b] min
Absorbency	ASTM D4772	Pass	Pass
Flammability	ASTM D1230	Class I	Class I
Laundered appearance	ASTM D5433, 7.2	Acceptable	Acceptable

[a] Class in the colorfastness requirements is based on a numerical scale from 5 for no color change or color transfer to 1 for severe color change or color transfer.
[b] AATCC Gray Scale for Color Change.
[c] AATCC Gray Scale for Staining.
[d] AATCC Chromatic Transference Scale.
Adapted, with permission from D5433 (2012) Standard Performance Specification for Towel Products for Institutional and Household Use, copyright ASTM International, 100 Barr Harbor Drive, West Conshohocken, PA 19428, www.astm.org. A copy of the complete standard may be obtained from ASTM International.

towels in the crosswise direction to a maximum of 10 or 15 percent shrinkage for the lengthwise direction for both terry and non-terry towelings.

Bow and Skew

The yarn alignment of towelings may be assessed in accordance with the procedures set forth in AATCC Test Method 179, Skewness Change in Fabric and Garment Twist Resulting from Automatic Home Laundering. This test method determines the skewness in woven and knitted fabrics or twist in knits when subjected to repeated laundering. Woven and flat knit test specimens are marked with a benchmark 10-inch square and laundered according to directions. Tubular knitted fabrics are to be tested in the tubular state. Although the recommended level of bow and skew is 5 percent, purchaser and supplier may agree upon acceptable performance levels.

Appearance

The appearance of the construction features of towelings (e.g., selvages, hems, seams, dobby borders, and hem failures) may be evaluated before and after laundering. Purchasers and suppliers should reach mutual appearance requirements.

Evaluating Colorfastness

ASTM D5433, Performance Specification for Towel Products for Institutional and Household Use, includes recommendations for the acceptable levels of colorfastness of towelings. These recommendations focus on fastness to laundering, crocking (rubbing), and light.

Colorfastness to Laundering

The colorfastness of towelings to laundering is critical for both household and institutional uses. Because towels are frequently part of coordinated ensembles, marked fading or shade changes would be unacceptable. Bleeding could lead to staining of the body, dishes, swimwear, and so on.

The colorfastness of toweling to laundering may be evaluated in accordance with procedures set forth in AATCC Method 61, Colorfastness to Laundering: Accelerated. The general nature of this method is described and the apparatus used, the Launder-Ometer®, is shown in Chapter 19. Shade changes are evaluated using the AATCC Gray Scale for Color Change; staining is evaluated using the AATCC Gray Scale for Staining. The recommended class ratings are presented in Tables 27.2 and 27.3. The minimum recommended change in the level of staining is Class 3, while the minimum recommended level of shade change is Class 4.

Colorfastness to Crocking

It is readily apparent that towels exhibiting color transfer when rubbed against the body or other fabrics would be unacceptable. The crocking of solid-colored towelings may be assessed by following procedures set forth in AATCC Method 8, Colorfastness to Crocking: AATCC Crockmeter Method; this method is discussed and the apparatus used to rub the specimens is presented in Chapter 19. For printed toweling fabrics, the procedures

in AATCC Method 116, Colorfastness to Crocking: Rotary Vertical Crockmeter Method, should be followed. Evaluations are done with the AATCC Chromatic Transference Scale. Dry tests should yield a minimum rating of Class 4, wet tests a minimum of Class 3.

Colorfastness to Light

With the exception of beach towels, towels and dishcloths are not normally subjected to extended exposure to light. Nonetheless, their lightfastness may be assessed with AATCC Method 16.3, Colorfastness to Light: Xenon-Arc. The apparatus used in these tests, the **Fade-Ometer**®, is presented in Chapter 19. Both terry and non-terry toweling should exhibit a Class 4 rating on the AATCC Gray Scale for Color Change after 20 hours of AATCC fading units of exposure.

Evaluating Absorbency

How efficiently toweling can absorb liquid water from such surfaces as human skin and dishware is a critical concern for both household and institutional applications. By following the procedures outlined in ASTM D4772 Standard Test Method for Surface Water Absorption of Terry Fabrics (Water Flow), manufacturers can numerically assess the absorbency of terry toweling.

Test Specimens and Procedures

As directed in ASTM D4772, three face and three back specimens are secured, one at a time, in an embroidery hoop. The hoop/specimen assembly is then mounted at a 60-degree angle to a table surface and a pan is placed below the hoop assembly. Fifty milliliters of distilled water are then allowed to flow onto the surface of the specimen, some being absorbed and some flowing as runoff water into the pan.

Analysis of Results

The difference between the original 50 milliliters of water and the number of milliliters of water in the runoff pan gives the quantity of water absorbed. An average is determined for the three face specimens and for the three back specimens to determine the surface water absorption of the fabric.

Performance Guidelines

The purchaser and the supplier shall agree on an acceptable level of absorbency.

Evaluating Flammability

The purchaser and the supplier shall agree on the flammability requirements of towelings. If flammability is to be tested, ASTM D1230 Standard Test Method for Flammability of Apparel Textiles may be used. As shown in Table 27.3, a Class 1 rating is recommended for terry fabrics and non-terry fabrics.

Evaluating Microbe Resistance

The humid conditions present in bathrooms are an inviting breeding ground for unwanted **microbes**, such as bacteria and fungi. Manufacturers are responding to the growing concern of professionals in the healthcare, hospitality, and educational fields, as well as homeowners, regarding microbes and the problems associated with them—illness, odors, mold, and mildew. Toweling, bath rugs, and shower curtains are now available with microbe-resistant properties and are labeled with various trade names.

Antimicrobial testing for textiles is similar to other manufacturing processes in which the antimicrobial agent is added onto or into the fiber or finished fabric. Different laboratory tests are appropriate depending on the antimicrobial and how it is applied to the finished textile.

AATCC offers number test methods used for testing antimicrobial performance. Several related ISO standards are also used in the testing of textile resistance to bacterial and fungal growth. Determining which microbial test method is appropriate is resolved by considering the use, environment, antimicrobial type, and application method.

Caring for Towels

Although care labeling is voluntary, virtually all towels carry instructions for machine washing using warm water and machine drying. Towels with decorative borders and trims may carry extra cautionary care instructions, such as hand washing in cool water and line drying. To avoid excessive fiber damage, white items should be bleached with chlorine compounds (bleach) only when necessary, not routinely in each successive laundering, and an extra rinse should be used to ensure the complete removal of any residual chlorine. To avoid potential bleeding and staining problems, towels with intense, deep-toned colors should be laundered separately. To avoid excessive deposition of softening agents, which reduces moisture absorption, some liquid fabric softeners should be omitted every third or fourth time the items are laundered.

Bath Rugs and Mats

Soft floorcoverings are produced in various sizes and shapes for use in bathroom interiors. **Bath rugs** (Figure 27.10) are larger and normally heavier than **bath mats**, and are used continuously for decoration, softness underfoot, or insulation. Bath mats are used temporarily to protect the floor from moisture and to prevent bathers from slipping. Both floorcovering products are subject to a federal flammability mandate.

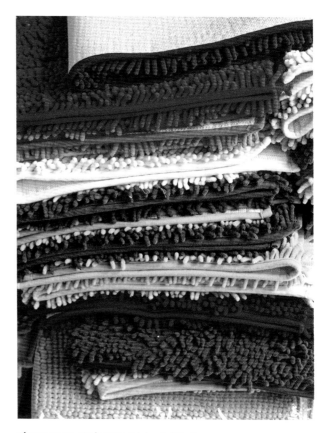

Figure 27.10 Bath rugs. Tatabrada/iStock.com.

Manufacturing Bath Rugs and Mats

Bath rugs are generally cut from tufted or knitted carpet that has a lower pile construction density and a greater pile height than carpet produced for other interior applications. For economy and ease of handling in use and care, no secondary backing is applied, but an adhesive is used to secure the tufts. For skid resistance, the adhesive compound is normally embossed. End-product producers cut various sizes of round, square, oval, and rectangular shapes from the wide carpet and finish the raw edges by hemming, serging, or binding with firmly woven tape. Frequently, rugs cut from solid colored greige goods are tufted a second time to introduce a distinctive design to the surface; no additional backcoating is applied to these items to secure the added pile yarns. Other rugs may be embellished with various types of trim, including rhinestone tape, braid, and fringe.

Pile fabric produced for use as a bath rug may also be used to construct such other items as toilet lid and tank covers. Lid covers have an elasticized edge or a drawstring run through a casing to secure them in use and permit their easy removal for laundering.

Bath mats may be woven in narrow widths, with the selvages as the side edges and small hems finishing the ends, or they may be cut from wide fabric and hemmed on all edges. Two different colors of warp pile yarns may be used to produce mats with different colors of loops on each side, or several colors of pile yarns may be used to produce richly patterned, Jacquard-woven mats.

Evaluating Flammability

16 CFR 1631 Standard for the Surface Flammability of Small Carpets and Rugs includes soft floorcovering items that have an area not greater than 24 square feet and no linear dimension greater than 6 feet; scatter rugs, bath rugs, bath mats, and smaller area rugs fall into this category.

Test Method and Acceptance Criteria

Items within the scope of 16 CFR 1631 are tested in accordance with the procedures outlined in the methenamine tablet test. This test method is also specified in the flammability standard established for large carpets and rugs, 16 CFR 1630 (see Chapter 12). The acceptance criteria, which are based on char length, are the same in both standards.

Labeling Requirements

Small rugs and mats that fail the tablet test may be marketed. They must, however, carry a permanently attached label bearing the following statement: "Flammable (fails U.S. Consumer Product Safety Commission Standard 16 CFR 1631, should not be used near sources of ignition)."

Shower Curtains

Shower curtains may be constructed of textile fabric or polymer film sheeting. Both types are often produced as part of a coordinated bath ensemble (Figure 27.11).

Polymer Film Shower Curtains

Various types of **polymer film sheeting** differ in gauge or thickness, in the level of transparency, and in color styling. Some films are relatively thin, others relatively thick; some are opaque, others transparent; some are solid colored, whereas others have contemporary designs printed with opaque pigments.

Figure 27.11 Fabric shower curtain with gromets. No liner is needed. WendellandCarolyn/iStock.com.

Textile Shower Curtains

With the exception of heavy, stiff structures, virtually any textile fabric may be used for a shower curtain. The fabric may be coated on the interior surface with a waterproofing compound to protect it from water and soap residue or the consumer may hang a thin film as a separate curtain lining. Many dense polyester fabrics, even very lightweight materials, do not need any treatment or a liner, and can be laundered frequently to remove soap residue. This is a popular solution in many hotels (Figure 27.12).

Evaluating Physical Performance Properties

Purchasers and suppliers may use ASTM D5378 Standard Performance Specification for Woven and Knitted Shower Curtains for Institutional and Household Use to establish specification requirements. The physical and structural property evaluations used with towelings are also those used with shower curtains, as shown in Table 27.4.

Breaking Force (Load)

The grab test procedure in ASTM D5034, described with towelings in this chapter and earlier in Chapter 19, is used to measure the breaking force (load) of household and institutional shower curtains. A minimum of 40 pounds of force is recommended for dry fabric strength; a minimum of 20 pounds of force is recommended for wet fabric strength.

Dimensional Change

AATCC Method 135 may be used to measure the dimensional stability of household shower curtains and AATCC Method 96 may be used for institutional products. A maximum of 3 percent change is recommended.

Bow and Skew

AATCC 179, discussed earlier in this chapter, is recommended for use in assessing the yarn alignment of shower curtains. ASTM D5378 includes a recommended maximum of 4 percent skew.

(a)

(b)

Figure 27.12 (a) Shower curtain with liner. (b) Hotel fabric shower curtain with liner. (a) Fotografia Inc./iStock.com. (b) Courtesy of Amy Willbanks, www.textilefabric.com.

TABLE 27.4

STANDARD PERFORMANCE SPECIFICATION FOR WOVEN AND KNITTED SHOWER CURTAINS FOR INSTITUTIONAL AND HOUSEHOLD USE

Characteristic	Test Method Number	Requirement
Breaking force (load)	ASTM D5034	
Dry		178 N (40 lbf), minimum
Wet		89 N (20 lbf), minimum
Bursting force (knits only)	ASTM D3786	178 N (40 lbf), minimum
Dimensional change (L × W)	AATCC 135 or AATCC 96	3.0% maximum
Bow and skew	AATCC 179	4.0% maximum
Colorfastness[a]		
Laundering	AATCC 61	
Shade change		Class 4[b] minimum
Staining		Class 3[c] minimum
Crocking	AATCC 8 for solids or AATCC 116 for prints	
Dry		Class 4[d] minimum
Wet		Class 4[d] minimum
Light (20 AATCC fading units), xenon	AATCC 16.3	Class 4[b] minimum
Water resistance	AATCC 35	
Categories based on minimum time for 1 g weight		
2 ft (600 mm)		30 s shower
2 ft (600 mm)		2 minute rain
3 ft (915 mm)		5 minute storm
Appearance retention	ASTM D5378, 7.2	Acceptable

[a] Class in the colorfastness requirements is based on a numerical scale from 5 for no color change or color transfer to 1 for severe color change or color transfer.
[b] AATCC Gray Scale for Color Change.
[c] AATCC Gray Scale for Staining.
[d] AATCC Chromatic Transference Scale.
Adapted, with permission from D5378 (2012) Standard Performance Specification for Woven and Knitted Shower Curtains for Institutional and Household Use, copyright ASTM International, 100 Barr Harbor Drive, West Conshohocken, PA 19428, www.astm.org. A copy of the complete standard may be obtained from ASTM International.

Appearance Retention

The appearance of the construction features of shower curtains (e.g., hems, ruffles, or other embellishments) may be evaluated before and after laundering. Purchaser and supplier should reach mutual appearance requirements.

Evaluating Colorfastness

ASTM D5378 specifies the same test methods for evaluating the colorfastness of shower curtains as is used

with towelings. These include colorfastness to laundering and to light.

Colorfastness to Laundering

The colorfastness of household and institutional shower curtains to laundering may be measured in accordance with AATCC Method 61 (see Chapter 19). As with toweling, the AATCC Gray Scale for Color Change is used, and AATCC Gray Scale for Staining is used to evaluate bleeding. Recommended minimum performance is Class 4 for shade change and Class 3 for staining.

Colorfastness to Crocking

AATCC Method 8 may be used to evaluate the fastness to crocking of solid-colored shower curtains, and AATCC Method 16 may be used for printed curtains. These methods are discussed in Chapter 19. The AATCC Color Transference Scale is used for the evaluation; recommended minimum performance is Class 4 for both dry and wet tests.

Colorfastness to Light

AATCC Method 16 (see Chapter 19) may be used to evaluate the colorfastness of household and institutional shower curtains to light. The AATCC Gray Scale for Color Change is used for the evaluation; recommended minimum performance is Class 4.

Evaluating Water Resistance

The **water resistance** of household and institutional shower curtains can be evaluated as directed in AATCC Method 35 Water Resistance: Rain Test. This test measures the resistance to the penetration of water by impact.

Test Specimens and Procedures

A minimum of three specimens 20 cm × 20 cm backed by a 15.2 × 15.2 cm of standard blotting paper is prepared. The backed specimen is clamped in the specimen holder and the assembly is mounted in a vertical rigid support frame. A horizontal water spray is directed at the specimen and allowed to continue for a period of five minutes (Figure 27.13).

Analysis of Results

Water penetration, as indicated by the increase in mass of the blotter paper, is calculated. An average for the three test specimens is reported.

Performance Guidelines

The performance recommendations listed may be agreed upon between purchaser and seller, or they may be

Figure 27.13 Rain tester. Courtesy of www.textiletestingequipment.com.

required by an agency having jurisdiction over an interior where shower curtains may be used.

Evaluating Microbe Resistance

Several test methods for the evaluation of microbe resistance are discussed earlier in the chapter. Again, because of the humid conditions in bathrooms, this test method is important to evaluate fungi and mold potential on shower curtains.

Key Terms

bath mats	microbes
bath rugs	polymer film sheeting
crash	terry toweling
disposable toweling	terry velour toweling
huck toweling (huckaback)	Turkish toweling
institutional toweling	water resistance

Review Questions

1. Why is cotton the most popular fiber used in the toweling market?
2. Given that linen has higher moisture absorbency than cotton, why hasn't linen captured a larger portion of the toweling market?
3. Describe the slack tension technique used for manufacturing terry toweling.
4. Why is the level of absorbency lower on the cut side of terry velour?
5. Why are stable colorants important to have with textile bath products?
6. Describe the procedures and calculations used in evaluating the absorbency of toweling.
7. Explain the cautionary labeling used with 16 CFR 1631.
8. Discuss why microbe resistance is important for bathroom products such as toweling and shower curtains.

28

Textile Bedding Products

The bedding products industry is an important segment of the interior textile industry: approximately 45 percent of the total fiber used for home textiles production (excluding soft floor-coverings) is channeled to the production of beddings. Whereas the primary function of bedcoverings is to provide warmth and comfort for sleeping, bedding products, like textiles for bath furnishings, also offer high visual impact.

The assortment of textile bedding products includes not only sheets and pillowcases, quilts, throws, comforters, blankets, bedspreads, and pillows, but also mattresses and box springs, mattress pads and mattress covers, and sleeping bags. All of these are produced in different sizes, and some have styling features as distinctive and varied as those typical of fashion apparel. Many of these items are made up of several components. For example, while most beddings are composed entirely of textile fibers, other products, including mattresses and box springs, contain essential nontextile components.

Fibers and Yarns for Bedding

Broadly speaking, cotton and synthetic fibers, primarily polyester, dominate the bedding market. A small percentage of wool is used for blankets and some mattress pads, rayon is sometimes used for sheets, and acrylic is sometimes used for blankets.

Since the bedding category covers such a wide array of products, from bedspreads and quilts to blankets and the outer fabric of mattresses and box-spring units, and from mattress-protector cloths to pillowcases and sheets, the fiber content is most meaningfully considered with regard to specific applications. Likewise, fiber preferences vary in the products used in homes, those used in commercial settings such as hotels, and those specified for healthcare facilities and other institutional settings. For example, while cotton is preferred for residential sheeting, while institutional applications rely on a higher content of polyester in blends. Mattress pads tend to utilize more synthetics than do top-of-the-bed materials.

Cotton is valued for its pleasing, soft hand, and because it is easy to clean and care for. Polyester has a harsher hand, but depending on the specific fabrication, polyester may

last longer, and is usually less expensive than cotton. Since it is a staple fiber, cotton is always spun, which contributes to its appealing surface texture. Most of the synthetic used in the market is in staple form that is then spun to simulate cotton, or is mixed with cotton in intimate blends. Staple fibers account for some 90 percent of today's market. Most fill used in bedding products is polyester or polypropylene, along with feather and down for pillows.

Disclosure of Fiber Composition

Most textile bedding products are subject to the labeling mandates set forth in the Textile Fiber Products Identification Act (TFPIA) and its accompanying set of rules and regulations. Specifically, the scope of the TFPIA includes all bedding, which is defined to include sheets, covers, blankets, comforters, pillows, pillowcases, quilts, bedspreads, pads, and all other textile fiber products used or intended to be used on or about a bed, not including furniture, mattresses, or box springs, or the outercoverings on these items. Fillings incorporated in bedding products primarily for warmth rather than for structural purposes are also included.

Mattress Foundations, Mattresses, and Mattress Protectors

Beds, sofa beds, convertible sofa beds, and futons have two basic units: a mattress and a mattress foundation. Because mattresses together with box springs are comparatively expensive, covers and pads are often used to protect them and prolong their use-life. Unlike other bedding products, mattresses and mattress pads are subject to a federal flammability standard. This information is discussed in Chapter 12.

Mattress Foundations

With the exception of air-filled mattresses, which are intended to be placed directly on the floor or ground, and water-filled mattresses, which are placed within a plastic-lined, boxlike frame, all mattresses are used with a resilient foundation.

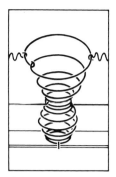 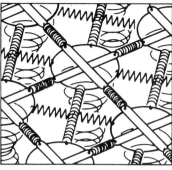 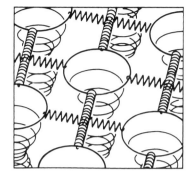

a) Tighter coiling in lower portion, looser in upper portion.

b) Flat metal bands provide a uniform surface.

c) Extra coils placed at top provide extra support.

Figure 28.1 Configurations of springs used in box springs and mattresses. Fairchild Books.

Bedspring Units

In bedspring units, flexible metal bands are anchored to the ends of the bed frame by tightly coiled springs. Additional springs, placed crosswise, stabilize the parallel bands. In other units, metal bands are interlaced and held to the sides and ends of the frame with spring units. Although these foundations are relatively inexpensive, they do not provide adequate support for everyday use and are normally used only with items intended for occasional use, such as cots and roll-away beds.

Box-Spring Units

In box-spring units, hundreds of coiled springs are anchored to wooden slats and framing boards and to each other. Because box springs and mattresses are offered as a coordinated set, the fabric that decorates the mattress also covers the exposed surfaces of the foundation. For economy, a fine, lightweight fabric such as batiste or spunbonded olefin (similar to the bottom fabric used in upholstered furniture) serves as a dustcover on the back (bottom) of the springs unit. Various types and amounts of filling are used for top cushioning, and an insulator fabric is placed over the springs to prevent them from penetrating into the filling materials.

Whereas the gauge of the wire used for the support springs in box springs is generally higher than that used for the support springs in mattresses, the configuration of the coils in the units may be identical. In double-deck springs, the tighter coiling of the lower portion is designed to provide firm support and the looser coiling of the upper portion is for resiliency (Figure 28.1a). The flat metal bands anchored over platform top springs (Figure 28.1b) provide a more uniform surface than that created by open-top springs. The extra coils placed at the top of convoluted springs provide increased support when the foundation is depressed by the weight of the body (Figure 28.1c). Individual manufacturers have distinctive variations of coil configurations, which they promote for various comfort levels.

The quality of box springs and innerspring mattresses depends on the gauge of the wires and the level of spring coiling. These features are the main determinants of the use-life of the units; they also help to determine the length of any warranty offered by the manufacturer.

Mattresses

Mattresses are available with different interior components and construction features. They are produced in several sizes and covered with a variety of fabrics.

Interior Components

Mattresses are available in several different types. The components in **innerspring mattresses** are illustrated in Figure 28.2. The spring units may be anchored to one another by coiled wires, metal clips, or flexible metal bands, or each spring may be encased within a fabric pocket and all pockets sewn together to minimize side sway. An insulator fabric like that on box springs

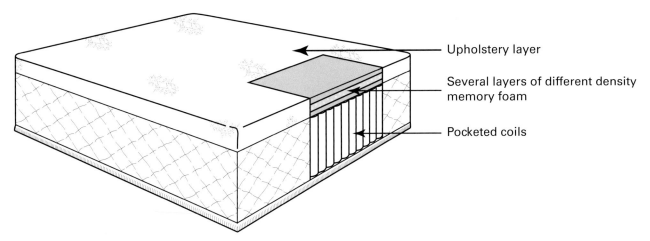

Figure 28.2 A hybrid mattress with springs and memory foam. Yelena Safronova/Fairchild Books.

Upholstery layer

Several layers of different density memory foam

Pocketed coils

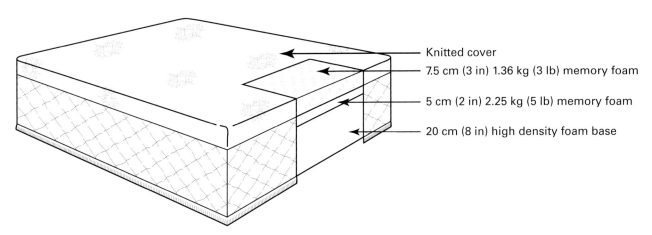

Figure 28.3 Memory foam mattress construction. Yelena Safronova/Fairchild Books.

Knitted cover

7.5 cm (3 in) 1.36 kg (3 lb) memory foam

5 cm (2 in) 2.25 kg (5 lb) memory foam

20 cm (8 in) high density foam base

prevents the springs from penetrating the upper filling layers. The degree of firmness can be increased by using a high gauge of wire for the spring units and by using resinated batting. Small holes should be built into the sides of mattresses to provide ventilation and preserve the freshness of the interior components.

Foam-core mattresses have a single interior component: a slab of expanded rubber or polyurethane foam (Figure 28.3). The level of support varies with the hardness and density of the foam in these mattresses. Some types of polyurethane foam are marketed as **memory foam**—such foam is slow to recover to its original shape after the load is removed. Memory foam is heat sensitive; it easily conforms to the shape of the body, without creating pressure on the hips, head, elbows, and

heels, while remaining very supportive. These qualities make it especially desirable for users who must spend long periods of time in bed. Foam-core mattresses tend to feel hotter than traditional innerspring mattresses. Memory foam is used not only in mattresses, but also in pillows and mattress pads.

Pillow-top mattresses have an extra layer of soft cushioning attached to the mattress surface. The toppers are made from a wide selection of luxury materials, from natural cotton and wool to advanced technology memory foams that conform to body shapes, and solid gels that have a cooling effect.

Latex foam mattresses, made from natural or synthetic rubber, offer firm, resilient support uniformly throughout the bed. Although latex foam provides greater support than memory foam, it is not as soft. The material is hypoallergenic and naturally resistant to bacteria, mildew, mold, and dust mites. It feels warm in the winter and cool in the summer.

Air mattresses, which are not the same as inflatable air mattresses, are designed to look like an innerspring mattress/box spring combination. Instead of innersprings or foam, these mattresses have air chambers that provide support. The air chambers are enclosed by foam and padding. An inflating/deflating device allows the firmness to be adjusted on each side of the mattress, and a foam top layer often covers these mattresses.

Gel mattresses have captured a significant market share. The gel is not a liquid, but a molded and highly flexible material used in conjunction with other mattress materials, such as memory foam. The gel is also used in mattress pads, and many consumers find the material emits a cooling sensation from the bed surface.

Exterior Coverings

Ticking is a generic term for any fabric used to cover the exterior of mattresses, box springs, and pillows. Tickings may be plain or highly decorative. Traditional tickings were ubiquitous as a narrow, navy blue or black stripe on a natural cotton ground, so that this pattern is commonly referred to as "ticking" even when used for other markets (Figure 28.4). Jacquard-woven damasks and other elaborate patterns (Figure 28.4a) have largely supplanted these basic stripes in the mattress ticking market. For long-term serviceability, tickings should be firmly woven of strong, smooth yarns. Less durable and less expensive coverings generally are made of coarse yarns and are constructed of low fabric counts.

Sizes

Mattresses are produced in a variety of sizes, with each size designated by name, rather than by dimensions. The names and characteristic dimensions of the more common mattresses are listed in Table 28.1.

Larger mattresses should have permanently attached side handles to facilitate the turning of the unit. As a precaution, consumers should measure their mattresses prior to purchasing bed coverings. The depth of mattresses can vary dramatically within the same length

Figure 28.4 Exterior mattress coverings: (a) pattern damask mattress covering, (b) twill-woven ticking mattress covering. Courtesy of Amy Willbanks, www.textilefabric.com.

TABLE 28.1
MATTRESS SIZES AND NAMES

Name	Inches (width × length)
Rollaway bed or cot	30 × 75
Studio couch or daybed	28 × 74
Single bed	33 × 75
Twin bed	39 × 75
Twin bed, extra long	39 × 80
Three-quarter bed	48 × 75
Double bed	54 × 75
Double bed, extra long	54 × 80
Queen-size bed	60 × 80
King-size bed	76 × 80
California king	72 × 84

and width category, as no standard depth has been adopted by the industry.

Mattress Covers and Pads

Mattress covers protect mattresses from dust, moisture, allergens, and abrasion. Mattress pads provide these features and increased cushioning as well.

Covers

Mattress covers, or encasements, may be designed and constructed to completely encase the mattress or to cover only the exposed surfaces. Zippers or elasticized edges ensure a smooth fit. When maximum protection against moisture is needed, a polypropylene (olefin) film sheeting bonded to a cotton fabric may be used as the covering fabric.

Dust mites, which thrive in pillows, mattresses, carpet, and upholstery fabrics found in most homes, are commonly cited as the most common trigger for patients suffering from allergies to household dust. Fully encasing pillow and mattress covers (of tightly woven cotton or cotton blend fabrics with zipper closings) helps control exposure to dust mites. Various bedding products claim to achieve filtration of up to 95 percent of particles as small as 1 micron. These particles would include allergens such as pollen, dust mites, dead skin, pet dander, and mold.

AATCC 194, Assessment of the Anti-House Dust Mite Properties of Textiles Under Long-Term Test Conditions, is used for the evaluation of the degree of anti-dust-mite activity for textiles treated at the manufacturing level for this purpose. The test and control samples are inoculated with the test organism and nutrients. After six weeks of incubation, sufficient time for mite colonies to flourish under optimal conditions, the dust mites are recovered from the specimens by heat extraction. Results are expressed as percent reduction on the treated sample versus the untreated control.

People all over the world are concerned by the growing outbreak of bedbugs. While a mattress covering will not protect your property from a bedbug infestation, it will effectively lock bedbugs out of your sleep system. However, only total encasement mattress protectors with a locking zipper provide protection against bedbugs.

Pads

Mattress pads are multicomponent structures that cushion and soften while they cover and protect the mattress. Most pads have a batting of polyester quilted between two woven or spunbonded fabrics. Some pads cover the sleeping surface only; others cover the sleeping surface and the vertical sides; and others completely encase the mattress. Memory foam, egg crate, and down are other types of mattress pads that are frequently used.

Mattress pads of wool have been used in hospitals and healthcare facilities for some time, but have only recently been promoted for residential use. These structures are produced by locking slivers of lambswool into a knitted base fabric composed of polyester. The fleece-like fabric is placed, pile up, under the bottom sheet, providing softness, warmth, and moisture absorption. The wool used in some of these **underblankets** has been treated with agents that minimize felting shrinkage, permitting the pad to be laundered. Care tag instructions indicate appropriate cleaning methods and should be carefully followed.

Microbe Resistance

The hospitality and healthcare industries and consumers are aware of problems associated with the presence of unwanted microbial organisms in bedding, coupled with the fact that most bedding is used multiple times between launderings. Interior designers, facility managers, and end-users can easily source bedding products that offer added antimicrobial finishes, including mattresses and mattress covers, pillows, sheeting, and outercoverings such as bedspreads and comforters.

Mattress covers and pads produced for use in hospitals and other healthcare facilities may be treated with agents that effectively reduce the action of microbes such as bacteria and fungi. Antimicrobial chemicals can be applied during finishing (see Chapter 10) and are becoming increasingly popular, although debate continues as to sustainability implication of all finishes and additives. Also, any added finish may change other properties of the material, from durability to cleanability.

Flammability Standard

The Standard for the Flammability of Mattresses, 16 CFR 1632, was established in an effort to protect the public against unreasonable risk of mattress fires leading to death, personal injury, or significant property damage. The most common mode of bedding ignition, a burning cigarette, is used as the ignition source in the test procedure.

In 2007 the Consumer Product Safety Commission established another test method: 16 CFR Part 1633, Standard Test Method for the Flammability (Open Flame) of Mattress Sets. Both of these standards are discussed in Chapter 12.

Fillings Used in Bedding Products

Filling components in bedding products may be composed of natural or manufactured materials. Some materials are used in loose, lofty masses; others, in stabilized battings; and still others, in well-defined, three-dimensional forms.

Natural Filling Materials

Natural filling materials include down, feathers, wool, and cotton. The low resiliency of cotton has prompted manufacturers to blend it with polyester. Although the use of wool as a filling material is limited, primarily because of its cost, some longer-staple wool fibers are occasionally used to produce lofty, three-dimensional battings for use in comforters.

Down and feathers are virtually always used loose in lofty masses. Down and feather products are lightweight, trapping the warmth of the body while wicking away moisture. Because it does not trap perspiration, it does not create the moist environment that dust mites need in order to survive. Down and feather pillows and comforters typically have a higher thread count and tighter seams (compared with synthetically filled comforters) in order to prevent the down and/or feathers from escaping. This quality construction creates a barrier to dust mites. Because of consumer demand for purely natural filling materials in bedding, down bedding is popular; nonetheless, people with asthma and allergies are usually intolerant of feathers and require synthetic bedding materials.

Standards for the Feather and Down Products Industry

The following organizations are involved in the development and enforcement of labeling laws and standards.

- The **International Association of Bedding and Furniture Law Officials (IABFLO)** is made up of state officials who are responsible for the enforcement of consumer-oriented bedding and furniture laws in their respective states.
- The **American Down and Feather Council (ADFC)** is a national trade organization of down- and feather-related companies such as down suppliers, processors, manufacturers, importers, retailers, and others.
- The **International Down and Feather Bureau (IDFB)** is the international trade association for the down and feather industry and promotes feather and down products worldwide as well as establishes international test methods and international standards.
- The **International Down and Feather Testing Laboratory (IDFL)** is a global leader in down and feather and textile product testing and inspecting and auditing down and feather and textile factories and supply chains worldwide.

Common terminology among these organizations includes:

- **Down**: The soft undercoating of waterfowl, which is composed of individual down fibers that are connected to one another at a central point.
- **Nestling down**: The underdeveloped down made up of soft fluffy barbs radiating from a sheath. Nestling down does not have quills.
- **Plumule**: Plumage consisting of soft quills and barbs.
- **Down cluster**: A group of components including down, nestling down, and plumules.
- **Feathers**: Two-dimensional in shape, feathers from ducks and geese provide lightweight support and are uniquely resilient.
- **Species identification**: Feathers are tested to determine bird species when they receive the ADFC Seal of Approval.
- **Fill power**: Fill power is a measure of loft, or the insulation ability of down products in cubic inches per ounce. The higher the number, the more fill power there is in the product.
- **Oxygen number**: Oxygen number indicates product cleanliness. Down and feathers are soaked and agitated in a solution of pure water, which is then measured for organic material. The lower the number, the better; the cleanest samples measure between 1.6 and 3.2, and the highest number allowed is 10.
- **Turbidity**: Turbidity helps determine if dust or dirt (organic and inorganic) is present in the

down and feather. A sample of down or feathers is soaked and agitated in pure water, the water is then measured for clarity. U.S. and European standards require a result of at least 300 mm. Very clean samples register at 550 mm or higher.

- **Filling weight**: The net filling weight of the down and feather is determined when given the ADFC Seal of Approval.
- **Thread count**: The thread count is the number of threads per square inch of fabric; it is measured at least five times and then the results are averaged together. Two-ply yarns are counted as one thread and may not be used to double thread count. Generally, the higher the thread count, the more down-proof the fabric.

Manufactured Filling Materials

Manufactured fillings include such materials as regenerated manufactured fibers, synthetic fibers, and polyurethane foam. Regenerated and synthetic fibers are virtually always in staple or tow forms for use as filling material. They may be used in loose, lofty masses, known as **fiberfill**, or organized into battings of various thicknesses. Today, fiberfill is almost exclusively composed of synthetic, usually polyester, fibers. A resin finish sprayed throughout **batting** structures stabilizes the layered polyester, or polyester and cotton, fibers.

Foamed synthetic rubber and urethane polymers may be molded into asymmetrical, three-dimensional shapes for use in pillows. Alternatively, they are cut from large foam blocks into thick slabs for use in mattresses, and into thin sheets for use in quilts.

Functions and Properties of Filling Materials

In mattresses, fillings provide support for the body; in bed pillows, they cushion the head; in decorative pillows, they impart and maintain a distinctive form. In most other bedding products, fillings are primarily intended for thermal insulation. Ideally, filling materials should be lofty or bulky without being heavy. They must be resilient in order to regain their original loftiness after being compressed, and they must be affordable.

To improve the loftiness and insulative value of fiberfill without increasing the weight, textile fiber chemists have engineered fibers with hollow interiors (Figure 28.5). The open interiors of the fibers and the air pockets surrounding them provide a great deal of insulation.

The insulative values of down, wool, polyester, and olefin are all effective, and each has advantages and disadvantages. Down and feathers offer the advantage of being inherently lofty and lightweight, but their limited supply in comparison to demand and the labor involved in their retrieval make them comparatively expensive.

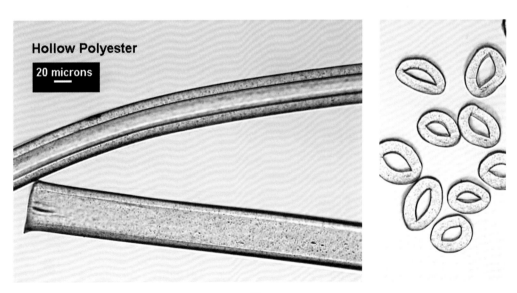

Figure 28.5 Photomicrographs of hollow polyester fibers. Courtesy of DAK Americas LLC.

Wool has excellent resiliency, but the fibers are comparatively heavy and expensive. Fiberfill is lofty, lightweight, and economical; unlike the natural filling materials, it is also non-allergenic.

Care of Fillings

Bedding products filled with wool batting must be dry-cleaned to avoid the agitation that can cause felting shrinkage. Some manufacturers recommend that down, feather, and polyester fillings be dry-cleaned to minimize shifting and clumping of the materials. Others recommend that the fillings be laundered and then tumble-dried to encourage the materials to regain their original loftiness. In every case, the care procedures performed on the filling must be appropriate for the outercovering and vice versa. To prevent care practices that could cause unnecessary product failure—a problem generally accompanied by the consumer losing confidence in the producer's name—many manufacturers voluntarily label their goods with care instructions.

Pillows

Bed pillows and decorative pillows, or *accent throws* in industry parlance, are the two types of pillows available in the bedding products market. The same filling materials and ticking fabrics may be used in both types of pillows, but decorative pillows are produced in a wider variety of sizes and forms and their outercoverings have more elaborate styling features.

Sizes and Forms

Bed pillows are basically rectangular in shape, and most are 20 to 21 inches wide. Their length varies: standard pillows, intended to be used with a twin or double mattress, are 26 to 27 inches long; queen-size pillows are 30 to 31 inches long; and king-size pillows are generally 37 to 38 inches long.

Decorative pillows are available in various sizes and forms. Pillows come in nearly any size. Traditionally, neckroll pillows are cylindrical forms 6 inches by 14 inches or a larger 7 inches by 17 inches; boudoir pillows, also called breakfast pillows, are 12 inches by 16 inches;

bolster pillows are cylindrical or lozenge-shaped and may be from 40 to 50 inches long; European pillows are 26 inches square; round pillows are often 12 inches in diameter; and a bedrest (or backrest, or husband) pillow has a back and arms. See Figure 28.6 for examples of pillow sizes and forms.

Fillings and Tickings

Bed pillows and decorative pillows may be filled with fiberfill, down, feathers, or foam. Down and feathers are ideal for pillows because they can provide a range of support options while adjusting to body movements. The pillow molds itself to the sleeper's head and neck, cradling them with comfort and support.

TABLE 11.1		
SELECTED DECORATIVE PILLOW SHAPES AND SIZES		
Shape	Centimeters	Inches
European size, sold in Europe and the United States	65 × 65	26 × 26
Common US sizes		20 × 20 18 × 18 16 × 16
Common European sizes	55 × 55 50 × 50 45 × 45	18 ×18
Common round sizes	Diameter 40	Diameter 12
Rectangular pillows, also known as Boudoir or breakfast pillows Common European sizes	20 × 60 30 ×45	
Common US sizes		12 × 16 11 × 15 11 × 22
Cylindrical	15–25 × 25–198	6–18 × 10–78

(a)

(b)

Figure 28.6 Examples of pillow sizes and forms. crazycroat/iStock.com.

Figure 28.7 Spunbonded hypoallergenic polypropylene (olefin) pillow ticking. Courtesy of Amy Willbanks, www.textilefabric.com.

Ideally, the filling material is enclosed in a non-removable casing that is then protected by a zippered casing. The interior casing fabric should have an extremely high fabric count, around 220 when fine down filling materials are used, and the fabrics used for the pillow protectors must be machine washable. Commonly used fabrics include **muslin**, **percale**, **ticking**, **pattern damask**, and for economy markets, **spunbonded ticking** composed of polypropylene olefin film. The hypoallergenic and inexpensive spunbonded ticking shown in Figure 28.7 is commonly used for complimentary pillows provided by airlines and in healthcare facilities, for example.

Decorative Coverings for Pillows

For nighttime use, bed pillows are inserted into the familiar pillowcases. These may be plain or have decorative hem treatments. For daytime display, bed pillows may be inserted into a **pillow sham**, a decorative casing, which often has contrasting piping and ruffles. Shams are generally styled to match decorative pillows placed on the bed.

An assortment of decorative pillows covered and trimmed to coordinate with a variety of products are included in ensembles. The pillows are covered with the fabric used in other items in the grouping, and they are finished with identical trimmings. The trimming may include such embellishments as monograms, contrasting piping or fabric banding, embroidery, appliqué, ribbons, and ruffles.

Besides decorative pillows, a coordinated ensemble may include a quilt, a bedspread or comforter, sheets, and pillowcases. It may also include round or square tablecloths, towels, curtain and drapery panels, and valances for windows and canopy beds.

Sheets and Pillowcases

The assortment of sheets and pillowcases offered includes items ranging from those of minimal aesthetic appeal to those with distinctive color styling and decorative border embellishments. Much of today's sheeting is stabilized and given a resin finish to improve end-use serviceability.

Manufacturing Sheeting

Fabric manufacturers produce the major portion of sheeting fabric for both residential and institutional use in a plain weave. For the residential market, however, the assortment has been expanded to include satin, Jacquard, and knitted sheeting, usually of spun yarns of cotton or cotton and polyester.

Fiber and Yarn Usage

Cotton has long been the most popular fiber for sheeting. For this purpose the fabric is usually treated with durable-press resins. As explained in Chapter 10, while these treatments improve the fabric's resiliency, they may also weaken the fibers and reduce their abrasion resistance. In order to prolong the use-life of resin-treated sheeting, manufacturers trended towards increasing the polyester content of sheeting, and thereby decreasing the cotton content. In recent years, consumers have expressed a preference for natural fibers, which reverses this trend; that is, consumers want to decrease the polyester content and increase the cotton content. Sheets of 100 percent cotton are widely available and popular.

The preference for cotton is driven by its soft and cool hand, ease of care, and affordable cost. Meanwhile, increasing interest in sustainable and environmental issues has resulted in the demand for organic and natural sheeting fabrics and other bedding materials. Environmental issues are discussed in Chapter 3, and each fiber's attributes are discussed in Chapter 4. Cotton's sustainability attributes require a complex evaluation, and depend largely on the specific growers' and processers' practices. Rayon (whether from pulp or bamboo) has been marketed as an environmentally preferable material. This information is incorrect and against TFPIA guidelines. Although rayon is processed from natural materials, the fiber must first be chemically processed to be usable, and it is not recyclable.

The predominance of spun yarns in all textile bedding products was mentioned earlier in this chapter. In sheets and other bedding, more than 90 percent of all fibers are used in staple form, which are typically spun on the cotton system.

Fabricating Sheeting

Most sheeting fabrics are plain-weave cloths, which vary in density (yarn count) and in yarn type, size, and content. **Yarn count** generally means the number of warp yarns by the number of filling yarns (e.g., 84 × 50). In sheeting, however, yarn count customarily represents the number of warp threads per inch added to the filling threads per inch. Advertising of higher thread count in sheets, which is equated with luxury and smoothness, has led the consumer to base purchases primarily on thread count. As has been discussed at many points in this text, fabric quality cannot be judged on any one characteristic alone. For example, a very high warp density with a very low filling density (pickage) could yield a high "yarn count," but the fabric would be unbalanced and not desirable as sheeting. Another example: a 300-count sheeting made up of 2-ply yarns is sometimes labeled as a 600-count fabric, which is misleading.

In general, finer and smoother yarns and higher fabric counts are characteristic of higher-quality sheets. **Muslin** sheeting contains carded yarns, and its fabric count may be as low as 112 or as high as 140 yarns per inch, although 128 is most common. (Figure 28.8a shows an enlarged view of an unbleached muslin. Figure 28.8b is a bleached muslin.) **Percale** sheeting's fabric count may be as low as 168 or as high as 220; 180 is common. Most percale sheeting is woven from fine, combed yarns. Figure 28.9a shows a low-thread-count, plain-weave percale sheeting.

(a)

(b)

Figure 28.8 Enlarged views of Muslin sheeting: (a) unbleached, (b) bleached. Courtesy of Amy Willbanks, www.textilefabric.com.

Warp sateen, which is a high-thread-count satin-weave, is also a common sheeting fabric. Warp sateen sheeting is usually fabricated of smooth, combed cotton yarns, and is usually calendered (Figure 28.9b). The floating warp yarns produce a smooth, luxurious sleeping surface and a lustrous appearance.

Weft knitting is used to produce knitted sheets in a jersey fabric similar to T-shirt fabric. Knitting offers inherent stretch, which helps to keep the sheets fitting smoothly. However, a broken loop in a jersey knit fabric can lead to runs, as in nylon stockings.

Coloring and Finishing Sheeting

Solid-colored sheets are currently preferred for sheeting; therefore, piece dyeing is the relevant coloring system.

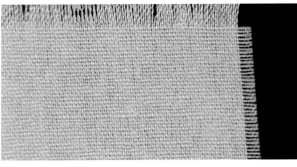

(a)

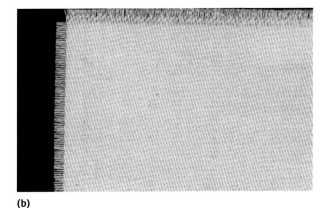

(b)

Figure 28.9 Enlarged views of low- and high-count sheetings: (a) low-yarn-count plain-weave percale sheeting, (b) high-yarn-count satin-weave sheeting. Courtesy of Amy Willbanks, www.textilefabric.com.

Rotary screen printing and digital printing are used to print sheeting. (These methods are explained in detail in Chapter 9.) Printed patterns range dramatically, and are especially popular in juvenile and other specialty markets. The bedding market is particularly active in licensing well-known fashion designers, film concepts, and celebrities, who offer their names or works to build a particular ensemble or lifestyle category for the manufacturer.

Sheeting greige goods may be preshrunk to relax the yarns, minimizing later shrinkage. Most sheeting greige goods are treated with durable press resins to avoid the need for ironing after laundering. (Durable press finishing is explained in Chapter 10.)

Napping treatments that raise fibers, entrap air, and provide thermal insulation are popular for cool climates where keeping warm while saving heating fuel is important. **Flannel** sheets are generally composed of 100 percent cotton or cotton blends, but brushed microfiber

polyester are also popular. Both provide softness, comfort, and warmth. Sheets that provide cooling sensations are also available. Various additives and processes help the fiber move heat away from skin and wick moisture so that it evaporates more quickly.

In a world that values youthful beauty, **cosmetotextiles** use nanotechnology to integrate materials into fibers at the molecular level that claim to have skin-smoothing properties. Among the marketing claims are that these fabrics make wrinkles disappear and smooth cellulite while the person works, sleeps, exercises, or goes about a daily routine![1]

Constructing Sheets and Pillowcases

Sheets and pillowcases have few specific construction requirements, but are produced in a variety of sizes and types. Decorative trimmings may embellish their hems.

Types and Sizes

Flat and fitted are the two types of sheets available in the United States. Flat sheets are hemmed at both ends and may be used as top or bottom sheets. Sheets with four contour corners, intended to be used as bottom sheets, are called **fitted sheets**. The sheeting selvedges provide a finished edge on the sides of all sheets; tape binding or elastic banding finishes the lower edges of contour corners.

Sheets and pillowcases are constructed in various sizes for use with various sizes of mattresses and pillows. Typical dimensions are listed in Table 28.2; actual dimensions vary among producers. It should be noted that the size of flat sheets that producers report is measured prior to hemming, and that the depth of fitted sheets is not standard and can vary dramatically.

Hems and Border Embellishments

The hems that finish flat sheets and pillowcases may be simple or highly decorative. A simple hem is normally 1 inch deep at the bottom of sheets and 3 to 4 inches deep at the top of sheets and the end of cases. Decorative hems have such border embellishments as delicate lace, scalloped eyelet trim, and contrasting piping.

TABLE 28.2
TYPES AND TRADITIONAL SIZES OF SHEETS AND PILLOWCASES

Type and Name	Inches (width × length)
Flat sheets	
Crib	45 × 68
Twin	66 × 104
Double or full	81 × 104
Queen	90 × 110
King	108 × 110
Fitted sheets	
Crib	29 × 54
Twin	39 × 75
Double or full	54 × 75
Queen	60 × 80
King	78 × 80
Pillowcases	
Standard	21 × 35
Queen	21 × 39
King	21 × 44

Coordinated Items

The sheeting fabric produced and used for a set of sheets and pillowcases frequently also appears in other items offered with the sheets and pillowcases in a coordinated ensemble, such as curtains, draperies, valences, tablecloths, duvet covers, and bed skirts (or dust ruffles). **Bed skirts**, also known as **dust ruffles** or platform skirts, are fabric panels that drape from the top of the foundation (box spring unit or bed frame) to the floor; the panels are normally pleated or gathered. Duvet covers protect comforters and duvets from soil accumulation and abrasion; their buttoned or Velcro® closures allow their easy removal for laundering.

Evaluating Sheeting Products

ASTM D5431, Standard Performance Specification for Woven and Knitted Sheeting Products for Institutional and Household Use, covers recommended levels of performance. The specifications include requirements for non-flannel sheeting of 100 percent cotton or polyester

and cotton blends, for flannel sheeting, and for knitted sheeting (see Table 28.3).

Blankets

Blankets provide warmth by reducing the loss of body heat; electric blankets provide warmth by generating heat. Blanketing fabrics may be woven, knit, tufted, flocked, or nonwoven.

Manufacturing Blanketing

Like most other bedding products, blankets are composed of cotton or synthetic fibers, though some are made of wool, and a limited number are composed of specialty wools. In the blanket market, synthetic fiber usage has been dropping and cotton increasing. Rayon is not popular because it is relatively weak, highly flammable, and generally requires dry-cleaning. Wool is relatively expensive and also requires dry-cleaning, but maintains a meaningful market category. Acrylic, because it insulates well and is lightweight but bulky, is a popular choice for blankets. It resembles wool, but without the problems of moths and dry-cleaning costs.

The growth of synthetic fiber usage in bedspreads and quilts is increasing slightly, at the expense of cotton. Virtually all fibers used in blankets and blanketing are staple length and are usually processed into yarns on the woolen or cotton spinning systems.

Woven Blanketing

Plain weaving and leno weaving are popular for blanketing. The leno-woven thermal blanket in Figure 28.10 is lightweight and lofty for thermal insulation.

Weaving one set of warp yarns and two sets of filling yarns together produces **double-faced blanketing**, or **reversible blanketing**, with different colors on each side. One set of filling yarns is carried to the face and one set to the back. The sets of filling yarns may have different colors or different fiber compositions. If the fiber compositions differ, cross dyeing can produce the two colors in one immersion procedure (see Chapter 9). The additional set of yarns adds strength, which compensates

TABLE 28.3

STANDARD PERFORMANCE SPECIFICATION FOR WOVEN AND KNITTED SHEETING PRODUCTS FOR INSTITUTIONAL AND HOUSEHOLD USE

Characteristic	Test Method Number	Requirements			
		Woven			Knitted
		Non-Flannel		Flannel	Flannel/Non-Flannel
		Polyester/Cotton	100% Cotton		
Breaking Force (Load)	ASTM D5034	222 N (50 lbf) min	178 N (40 lbf) min	156 N (35 lbf) min	NA
Bursting Force (Knits Only)	ASTM D3786 or 3787	NA	NA	NA	222 N (50 lbf) min
Tear Resistance	ASTM D1424	7 N (1.5 lbf) min	7 N (1.5 lbf) min	7 N (1.5 lbf) min	NA
Pilling	ASTM D3512	Class 4 min[f]	NA	NA	Class 4 min[f]
Dimensional Change					
Durable Press (in Each Direction)	AATCC 135 or AATCC 96	5% max	5% max	3.5% max	4% max
Nondurable Press (Nonpreshrunk)					
Length		8% max	8% max	8% max	
Width		6% max	6% max	6% max	
Preshrunk (in Each Direction)		2% max	3% max	3.5% max	
Laundered Appearance	AATCC 143	Acceptable	Acceptable	Acceptable	Acceptable
Fabric Appearance[a]	AATCC 124	SA 3.0 min[e]	SA 2.2 min[e]	NA	SA 3.0 min[e]
Bow and Skew	ASTM D3882	3% max	3% max	3% max	3% max
Colorfastness[a]					
Laundering	AATCC 61				
Alteration in Shade		Class 4 min[b]	Class 4 min[b]	Class 4 min[b]	Class 4 min[db]
Staining		Class 3 min[c]	Class 3 min[c]	Class 3 min[c]	Class 3 min[c]
Crocking	AATCC 8 for solids or AATCC 116 for prints				
Dry		Class 4 min[d]	Class 4 min[fd]	Class 4 min[d]	Class 4 min[d]
Wet		Class 3 min[d]	Class 3 min[d]	Class 3 min[d]	Class 3 min[d]
Light (20 AATCC Fading Units), Xenon	AATCC 16.3	Class 4 min[b]	Class 4 min[b]	Class 4 min[b]	Class 4 min[b]
Perspiration	AATCC 15	Class 4 min[b]	Class 4 min[d]	Class 4 min[d]	Class 4 min[d]
Alteration in Shade		Class 4 min[b]	Class 4 min[b]	Class 4 min[b]	Class 4 min[b]
Staining		Class 3 min[c]	Class 3 min[c]	Class 3 min[c]	Class 3 min[c]
Flammability	ASTM D1230	Class I	Class I	Class I	Class I

[a] Class in the colorfastness and fabric appearance requirements is based on a numerical scale from 5 for negligible color change, color transfer, or wrinkling to 1 for very severe color change, color transfer, or wrinkling.

[b] AATCC Gray Scale for Color Change.

[c] AATCC Gray Scale for Staining.

[d] AATCC Chromatic Transference Scale.

[e] AATCC 3D Smoothness Appearance Replicas.

[f] ASTM Photographic Pilling Replicas.

Adapted, with permission from D5431 (2008) Standard Performance Specification for Woven and Knitted Sheeting Products for Institutional and Household Use, copyright ASTM International, 100 Barr Harbor Drive, West Conshohocken, PA 19428, www.astm.org. A copy of the complete standard may be obtained from ASTM International.

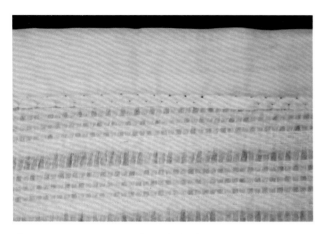

Figure 28.10 Leno-woven thermal blanket. Courtesy of Amy Willbanks, www.textilefabric.com.

for the weakening effect of the heavy napping used on both sides for warmth. Doublecloth (see Chapter 7) is the ideal vehicle for electric blanket fabric. Its pocket-like channels hold the wires and prevent them from shifting through the structure.

Knit Blanketing

Knit blanketing, which is generally constructed on a raschel knitting machine, may have a simple or a complex interlooping pattern. The thermal efficiency of this fabric can be engineered by varying the size of the yarns and the knitting gauge used. Napped, knit synthetic fleece fabrics, most of which are polyester, are very popular.

Tufted Blanketing

Tufting, used extensively for the production of soft floorcoverings and for some upholstery fabrics, has been adapted for the production of a small quantity of blanketing. The pile yarns are punched into the base fabric, and by napping the pile surface, the raised fibers have the effect of increasing the diameter of the pile yarns, helping to secure them in the fabric. The back is napped to soften the surface and further stabilize the pile yarns.

Needle-Punch Blanketing

Needle-punch (see Chapter 8) blanketing fabric is made by cross-layering a thick batt with webs of staple-length fibers on each side of a web of yarns. The batt is fed into a machine where pairs of closely spaced, barbed needles punch into the batt. Next, the material is chain-stitched to reduce the depth of the batt. Subsequent napping raises some surface fibers, softening the appearance and improving the thermal efficiency.

Flock Blanketing

Lightweight, warm blankets can be produced by flocking nylon over the surfaces of a thin slab of polyurethane foam. Together, the flocked fiber and the cellular foam serve to minimize heat transfer by restricting air flow, but the foam yields a stiff, rather than supple, character.

Coloring and Finishing

Blanketing may be yarn-dyed, piece-dyed, or printed. These fabrics are virtually all finished and napped. Blanket sizes vary considerably, but are normally finished to be wider than the mattress with which they are intended to pair. The side edges may be the fabric selvedges, machine overcast, or enclosed within satin-woven binding. The insulated wires of electric blankets are inserted into the blanket's interior channels before the edges are finished.

Caring for Blankets

Wool blankets must be stored with some type of moth repellent to protect the fibers from attack by moth larvae (see Chapter 10). The producer's voluntary care instructions should always take precedence, but usually wool blankets should be dry-cleaned in order to avoid felting shrinkage, while blankets composed of most other fibers can usually be laundered.

Evaluating Blankets

Two ASTM International standards are used to evaluate the performance of blankets. ASTM D4151, Standard Test Method for Flammability of Blankets, details the methodology for testing ignition and flame spread of blankets, and ASTM D5432, Standard Performance Specification for Blanket Products for Institutional and Household Use, is used to evaluate fabrics used in blankets (Table 28.4).

TABLE 28.4

STANDARD PERFORMANCE SPECIFICATION FOR BLANKET PRODUCTS FOR INSTITUTIONAL AND HOUSEHOLD USE

Characteristic	Test Method Number	Requirement	
		Knits/Flock	Woven/Nonwoven
Breaking force (load) each direction	ASTM D5034	NA	89 N (20 lbf) min
Bursting force (ball burst)	ASTM D3786	345 kpa (50 psi) min	NA
Dimensional change: After 5 launderings each direction	AATCC 135 or AATCC 96		
Wool (50% or more)		6.0% max	6.0% max
Cotton		5.0% max	5.0% max
All others		3.5% max	3.5% max
After 3 dry-cleanings each direction	ASTM D2724		
All fabrics		3.5% max	3.5% max
Colorfastness[a]			
Laundering	AATCC 61		
Shade change		Class 4[b] min	Class 4[b] min
Staining		Class 3[c] min	Class 3[c] min
Dry-cleaning	AATCC 132		
Shade change		Class 4[b] min	Class 4[b] min
Burnt gas fumes (2 cycles)	AATCC 23		
Shade change		Class 4[b] min	Class 4[b] min
Crocking	AATCC 8 for solids or AATCC 116 for prints		
Dry		Class 4[d] min	Class 4[d] min
Wet		Class 3[d] min	Class 3[d] min
Light (20 AATCC fading units), xenon	AATCC 16.3	Class 4[b] min	Class 4[b] min
Flammability	ASTM D4151	Class I	Class I
Thermal transmittance	ASTM D1518	Acceptable	Acceptable
Laundered appearance	ASTM D5432, 7.5	Acceptable	Acceptable

[a] Class rating for colorfastness requirements is based on a numerical scale from 5 for no color change or color transfer to 1 for severe color change or color transfer.

[b] AATCC Gray Scale for Color Change.

[c] AATCC Gray Scale for Staining.

[d] AATCC Chromatic Transference Scale.

Adapted, with permission from D5432 (2012) Standard Performance Specification for Blanket Products for Institutional and Household Use, copyright ASTM International, 100 Barr Harbor Drive, West Conshohocken, PA 19428, www.astm.org. A copy of the complete standard may be obtained from ASTM International.

Bedspreads and Comforters

ASTM D7023 Standard Terminology Related to Home Furnishings provides useful distinctions between bedspreads and comforters, the purpose of both of which is for appearance and warmth. **Bedspreads** are defined as a type of bedcovering that is placed over the blankets and sheets; a **comforter** is described as a bedcovering assembly consisting of an insulating filler secured between two layers of fabric.

Bedspreads

Most bedspreads are chosen primarily for their styling according to the purchaser's taste and preference. Warmth and insulative value may also be desired features.

Styles

Various styles of bedspread **drops**, ranging from tailored to ruffled styles, are illustrated in Figure 28.11. The appearance of any of these drops changes dramatically when executed in different fabrics. The qualities of the fabric must always be appropriate for the styling features of the spread. For example, although a heavy fabric would be suitable for use in a throw style, it would not drape properly in a style with gathered or shirred sides.

Fabrics

From smooth, plain-weave fabrics, to raised ribs and textures, to elaborate Jacquard patterns, to velvets, virtually any fabric may be used for a bedspread. Faux-fur fabrics are often used for throw-style coverings. (These pile fabrics are usually knit; combed fibers are incorporated into the base.) A tufting technique called *candlewicking* is used to produce chenille bedspreads, which do not actually contain chenille yarns. The pile tufts are spaced and cut, producing the caterpillar-like appearance of chenille yarns. (Fabrics woven or knit of chenille yarns can also be used as bedspreads, of course.) Current bedding trends lean towards using quilts or comforters as bed toppers, and bedspreads are less popular than in years gone by.

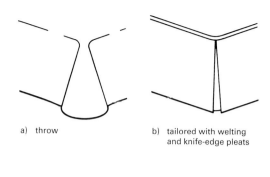

a) throw

b) tailored with welting
and knife-edge pleats

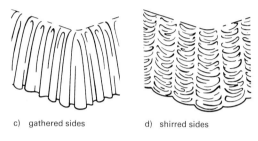

c) gathered sides

d) shirred sides

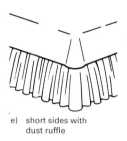

e) short sides with
dust ruffle

Figure 28.11 Typical bedspread drops. Fairchild Books.

Comforters

Comforters are multicomponent bed coverings and may be used in lieu of a bedspread or blanket (Figure 28.12). Comforters are usually filled with down, feathers, fiberfill, or a loose batting of polyester; those filled with down are frequently known as **duvets**, although the terms "duvet" and "comforter" are often used interchangeably.

Typical European bedding traditionally features comforters (or duvets) rather than blankets, with or without a top sheet. Most comforters are channel quilted to minimize shifting and clumping of the filling. Some products also use a system of crosswise baffles. Sleeping

Figure 28.12 Bedding ensemble: comforter in lieu of bedspread. laughingmango/iStock.com.

Figure 28.13 Quilted fabric with three quilting layers. Courtesy of Amy Willbanks, www.textilefabric.com.

bags are also often constructed in this manner, making them, in effect, folded comforters with zipper closures.

The close-up photograph in Figure 28.13 shows the use of a spunbonded backing fabric in a quilted fabric to prevent **fill leakage**, which is the migration or penetration of the filling material through the outercovering. Spunbonded fabric can also be used as an interior lining, allowing the use of decorative fabric on both sides of the comforter or bedspread.

Evaluating Bedspread Fabrics and Comforters

Established ASTM International standards may be used to evaluate the performance of bedspread fabrics and comforters. These include ASTM D4037, Standard Performance Specification for Woven, Knitted, or Flocked Bedspread Fabrics (Table 28.5), and ASTM D4769, Standard Specification for Woven and Warp Knitted Comforter Fabrics (Table 28.6).

TABLE 28.5

STANDARD PERFORMANCE SPECIFICATION FOR WOVEN, KNITTED, OR FLOCKED BEDSPREAD FABRICS

Characteristic	Test Method Number	Requirements	
		Woven	**Knit**
Breaking strength force (load)	ASTM D5034	25 lbf (111 N) min	NA
Bursting strength	ASTM D3786 or 3787	NA	35 psi (241 kPa) min
Tear strength	ASTM D2261	1.5 lbf (6.7 N) min	NA
Dimensional change: laundering and dry-cleaning each direction	AATCC 135 or 96 and ASTM D2724		
Tailored type		±3.5% max	±5.0% max
Throw type		±5.0% max	±5.0% max
Fabric appearance[a] (durable press)	AATCC 124	SA 3.5[e] min	SA 3.5[e] min
Retention of hand, character, and appearance	AATCC 135 and ASTM D2724	No significant change	No significant change
Durability of backcoating	ASTM D4037, 5.7	No significant change	No significant change
Colorfastness[a]			
Laundering	AATCC 61		
Shade change		Class 4 min[b]	Class 4 min[b]
Staining		Class 3 min[c]	Class 3 min[c]
Bleaching	AATCC 172 and AATCC 188		
Sodium hypochlorite		Class 4 min[b]	Class 4 min[b]
Nonchlorine		Class 4 min[b]	Class 4 min[b]
Dry-cleaning	AATCC 132		
Shade change		Class 4 min[b]	Class 4 min[b]
Burnt gas fumes (2 cycles)	AATCC 23		
Original shade change		Class 4 min[b]	Class 4 min[b]
After one laundering or one dry-cleaning shade change		Class 4 min[b]	Class 4 min[b]
Crocking	AATCC 8 for solids or AATCC 116 for prints		
Dry		Class 4 min[d]	Class 4 min[d]
Wet		Class 3 min[d]	Class 3 min[d]
Light (20 AATCC fading units), xenon	AATCC 16.3	Class 4 min[b]	Class 4 min[b]
Flammability	ASTM D4037, 5.9	Pass	Pass

[a] Class in the colorfastness and fabric appearance requirements is based on a numerical scale from 5 for no color change, color transfer, or wrinkling to 1 for very severe color change, color transfer, or wrinkling.

[b] AATCC Gray Scale for Color Change.

[c] AATCC Gray Scale for Staining.

[d] AATCC Chromatic Transference Scale.

[e] AATCC 3D Smoothness Appearance Replicas.

Adapted, with permission from D4037 (2008) Standard Performance Specification for Woven, Knitted, or Flocked Bedspread Fabrics, copyright ASTM International, 100 Barr Harbor Drive, West Conshohocken, PA 19428, www.astm.org. A copy of the complete standard may be obtained from ASTM International.

TABLE 28.6

STANDARD PERFORMANCE SPECIFICATION FOR WOVEN AND WARP KNITTED COMFORTER FABRICS

Characteristic	Test Method Number	Requirements	
		Woven Fabrics	**Warp Knit Fabrics**
Breaking strength (load)	ASTM D5034	133 N (30 lbf) min	NA
Bursting strength (motor-driven diaphragm tester)	ASTM D3786 or 3787	NA	35 psi (155 kPa)
Tear strength	ASTM D2261	6.7 N (1.5 lbf) min	NA
Dimensional change			
Laundering	AATCC 135 or 96	3% max	5% max
Dry-cleaning	ASTM D2724	3% max	5% max
Fabric appearance	AATCC 124	SA 3.5[e] min	SA 3.5[e] min
Colorfastness[a]			
Burnt gas fumes (2 cycles)	AATCC 23		
Shade change after one laundering or one dry-cleaning		Class 4[a] min	Class 4[a] min
Laundering	AATCC 61		
Shade change		Class 4[c] min	Class 4[b] min
Staining		Class 3[c] min	Class 3[c] min
Dry-cleaning	AATCC 132		
Shade change		Class 4[b] min	Class 4[b] min
Crocking	AATCC 8 for solids or AATCC 116 for prints		
Dry		Class 4[d] min	Class 4[d] min
Wet		Class 3[d] min	Class 3[d] min
Light (20 AATCC fading units), xenon	AATCC 16.3	Class 4[b] min	Class 4[b] min
Flammability		Pass	Pass
Fill leakage		Acceptable	Acceptable

[a] Class in the colorfastness and fabric appearance requirements is based on a numerical scale from 5 for no color change, color transfer, or wrinkling to 1 for very severe color change, color transfer, or wrinkling.
[b] AATCC Gray Scale for Color Change.
[c] AATCC Gray Scale for Staining.
[d] AATCC Chromatic Transference Scale.
[e] AATCC 3D Smoothness Appearance Replicas.

Adapted, with permission from D4769 (2012) Standard Performance Specification for Woven and Warp Knitted Comforter Fabrics, copyright ASTM International, 100 Barr Harbor Drive, West Conshohocken, PA 19428, www.astm.org. A copy of the complete standard may be obtained from ASTM International.

Key Terms

air mattress

American Down and
    Feather Council (ADFC)

batting

bed skirt

bedspread

comforter

cosmetotextiles

double-faced blanketing

down

down cluster

drops

dust ruffle

duvet

feathers

fiberfill

fill leakage

fill power

filling weight

fitted sheets

flannel

foam-core mattress

gel mattress

innerspring mattress

International Association
    of Bedding and
    Furniture Law Officials
    (IABFLO)

International Down and
    Feather Bureau (IDFB)

International Down
    and Feather Testing
    Laboratory (IDFL)

latex foam

mattress cover

mattress pad

memory foam

muslin

nestling down

oxygen number

pattern damask

percale

pillow sham

pillow-top mattress

plumule

reversible blanketing

species identification

spunbonded ticking

thread count

ticking

turbidity

underblanket

yarn count

Review Questions

1. Explain the importance of cotton in the bedding products industry.
2. Why is the usage of acrylic popular for blankets?
3. Identify bedding products included and excluded from the provisions of the TFPIA.
4. Why are spun yarns more widely used than filament yarns in bedding products?
5. Distinguish between down and feathers.
6. Discuss cosmetotextiles and how these materials are used in bedding.
7. Discuss the difference ways that blankets can be manufactured.
8. Explain why filling materials must retain their original loftiness in order to be effective.
9. Compare the positive and negative properties of down, wool, and polyester for use as filling materials.
10. Explain the use of wool underblankets in institutional settings.
11. Why are cigarettes used as the source of ignition in 16 CFR 1632?
12. Explain factors accounting for the changing market shares held by cotton and polyester in the sheeting market.
13. Distinguish between muslin and percale.
14. What is polyurethane foam used for? What are the advantages associated with its use?
15. Is flammability testing of blanketing mandatory or voluntary?
16. How is fill leakage minimized in comforters?
17. Observe the standard performance specification tables for woven and knitted sheeting products, comforters, blankets, bedspreads and comforters. Discuss one of these tables in terms of characteristic to be tested, test method used, and specification requirements.

Note

1. Glenna Musante. "The Fabric of Beauty." *AATCC Review*, vol. 13, no. 1, January/February 2013, p. 34.

GLOSSARY

AATCC Acronym for American Association of Textile Chemists and Colorists, a voluntary scientific association that develops standard test methods.

AATCC Chromatic Transference Scale Scale used in evaluations of staining.

AATCC Gray Scale for Color Change Scale used in evaluations of shade changes.

AATCC Gray Scale for Staining Scale used in evaluations of staining.

AATCC Review Monthly journal produced by AATCC which presents information concerning dyes and finishes.

AATCC Technical Manual Annual publication that includes AATCC test methods.

abaca Bast fiber used for cordage; also called Manila hemp.

abrasion Wearing away by friction or rubbing.

abrasion resistance Ability of a textile structure to resist damage and fiber loss by friction.

absorbency Ability of a fiber to take up moisture from the body or from the environment.

accelerated aging Premature aging of a material or product. Tests using heat and light exposure are used to evaluate how quickly items show signs of breakdown.

accordion-pleated shade Window treatment constructed of woven or knitted fabric that has been stiffened and set in a three-dimensional, folded configuration.

acetate Manufactured (regenerated) cellulose-based fiber made from trees, cotton linters, or bamboo.

acid print A process in which a weak sulfuric acid is printed on selected areas of a fabric composed of an acid-resistant fiber and an acid-degradable fiber. The acid destroys, or burns away, the acid-degradable fiber, which creates a higher level of transparency than in the untreated areas. Also called burn-out printing.

acoustical value The extent to which a structure prevents sound from becoming unwanted noise.

acrylic A manufactured synthetic fiber which imitates wool.

actual color Color characteristics of hue, value, and intensity are unaffected by such things as the light source, accumulated soil, and textural changes.

additives Agents or compounds added to polymer solutions prior to spinning, e.g., antistatic agents, delusterants, flame retardant agents, softeners, dye pigments, ultraviolet absorbers, optical brighteners.

advisory practices Labeling practices that are advisory in contrast to being mandatory.

affinity The dye is chemically compatible with the fiber so that it will accept dyestuffs.

after-flame time The time the specimen continues to flame after the burner flame is removed.

afterglow Smoldering combustion occurring after flames are extinguished.

airborne sounds Noise radiating directly into the air (e.g., people talking, telephones ringing).

air-jet texturing Filament yarns are fed over a tiny blast of air that forces the filaments into loops.

air mattress Mattress that has air chambers for support.

all-down Labeling term used when product contains only down; also known as pure down or 100 percent down.

alpaca Fiber obtained from alpacas, a domesticated animal of the camel family.

American Down and Feather Council (ADFC) National trade organization of down- and feather-related companies such as down suppliers, processors, manufacturers, importers, retailers, and others.

American National Standards Institute (ANSI) A private corporation that undertakes the development of standards only when so commissioned by an industry group or a government agency.

amorphous polymers Molecular arrangement in which the polymer chains are not aligned parallel to each other.

angora Hair fiber retrieved from Angora rabbits.

Annual Book of ASTM Standards Seventy-two volumes, divided among 16 sections, that contain approved ASTM standards, provisional standards, and related material.

antimicrobial agents Chemical agents used to kill or retard the growth of such microbes as bacteria and fungi; especially useful with mattress covers, mattress pads, and soft floorcoverings used in care-type facilities.

antique rugs Oriental rugs woven prior to the mid-1800s.

antique satin A satin weave fabric containing simple-warp yarns and slub-filling yarns.

antistatic finish Finish to help reduce static electricity.

apparent color Color characteristics of hue, value, and intensity are affected by such things as the light source, accumulated soil, and textural changes so they appear different than they actually are.

apparent color temperature Visual appearance of a light source expressed in degrees Kelvin (K). The higher the number, the cooler the color or the light.

apparent volume or bulk Apparent, but not actual, increase in volume or bulk created by texturizing multifilament yarns.

apparent whiteness or brightness Apparent, but not actual, increase in whiteness or brightness created by the presence of optical brighteners.

appearance retention How well a material maintains its original visual characteristics and quality after a period of use and exposure to environmental factors.

appliqué Shaped piece of fabric placed over a second fabric; raw edges are turned under and secured with blind stitches or embroidery stitches.

appliqué, reverse Needlework in which artisans layer fabrics and cut decreasing sizes of shaped areas from each fabric, turning the raw edges under and stitching the folded edge to each subsequent layer until the base fabric is reached; used in the production of molas.

aramid A manufactured synthetic fiber with high temperature and flame resistance.

area rugs Soft floorcoverings that range in size from 27 inches by 54 inches to 6 feet by 9 feet, and are available in a wide variety of shapes; moveable.

arm caps Accessories used to protect the arms of upholstered furniture; also called *arm covers* and *armettes*.

artificial silk Manufactured fiber first produced in the Unites Stated and later renamed rayon.

asbestos Natural mineral fiber; although fireproof, use of the fiber has been discontinued because it is a known carcinogen.

Association for Contract Textiles (ACT) A trade association created by members of the contract textile industry to address issues concerning contract upholstery fabrics, including performance guidelines and industry education.

ASTM International Acronym for American Society for Testing and Materials; a not-for-profit, voluntary scientific association having 132 committees that develop full-consensus standards for products, materials, or processes.

astrojets Dye-loaded needles.

athey shade Variation of the conventional Roman shade in which two shades are used, with one raised and one lowered for full closure.

atmospheric fading See *fume fading*.

Aubusson rugs French rugs characterized by classic designs, soft pastel colors, and a fine loop pile.

Austrian shade Window covering constructed of textile fabric that is vertically shirred to create lengthwise bands of horizontally draping folds.

auxochromes Components of dyestuffs that are responsible for the selective absorption and reflection of light waves; determine the hue.

average density Average density, D, considers pile height (finished thickness) and average pile weight to indicate the true density of floorcovering structures; calculated by multiplying the average pile weight in ounces per square yard by 36 and dividing the product by the average pile thickness in inches.

awnings Rigid structures that may be composed of metal or molded polymer sheeting or of textile fabric stretched and held over a rigid frame; generally mounted as exterior overhead treatments to provide protection from weather elements.

azlon A manufactured synthetic fiber composed of regenerated naturally occurring proteins.

backcoating Acrylic foam is applied to the back of upholstery fabrics to increase strength; used on low yarn count fabrics.

backfilled Use of a large amount of sizing on fabrics that generally have lower fabric counts; also known as loading.

bacteria Extremely simple vegetative plant forms that can react with perspiration to cause odor and can cause infection and slow the healing process; also referred to as a microbe.

balanced construction Weave structure in which there is approximately an equal number of warp and filling yarns.

balloon shades Window coverings composed of textile fabric that form balloon-like puffs when they are raised.

bamboo Family of fast-growing woody grasses found in warm climates and used for the production of rayon.

base yarn Foundation yarn in decorative yarns; determines yarn length.

basket weave Interlacing pattern in which two or more warp yarns, side by side, interlace with one or more filling yarns.

bast fiber Classifies cellulose fibers retrieved from stem portion of plants (e.g., jute, linen, ramie, and hemp).

batch dyeing Dyeing relatively small quantities or batches of carpet in a discontinuous-dyeing operations, using a carpet winch, a jet beck, or a horizontal beam-dyeing machine.

bath mat Relatively small textile floorcovering used temporarily to protect the floor from moisture and prevent bathers from slipping.

bath rug Larger and heavier than a bath mat, bath rugs are used continuously for decoration, softness underfoot, or insulation.

batik Hand print produced by artisans who apply melted wax to fabric areas that are to resist dye penetration.

batiste A plain weave, lightweight fabric. Typically made of cotton or cotton/polyester blend.

batons Rods used manually to open and close curtain and drapery panels; also known as curtain tenders.

battening In weaving, beating the filling picks against those already in place, aligning them parallel.

batting Three-dimensional fibrous structure that is bonded into a relatively flat nonwoven fabric; three-dimensional fibrous structure used as filling in quilts and comforters.

beam dyeing Immersing a beam wound with warp yarns or a full width of carpet into a dyebath when the dye liquor is forcibly circulated.

bearding Development of long fiber fuzz on loop pile floorcoverings; caused by snagging and poor penetration of pile yarn bundle by adhesive.

beater bar Loom device used in battening; also known as the lay.

beck dyeing A continuous dye process used for long pieces of cloth. Up to several thousand yards are loaded open width in rope form and passed through the dye bath in constant circular motion.

bedding Includes sheets, covers, blankets, comforters, pillows, pillowcases, quilts, bedspreads, pads, and all other textile fiber products used or intended to be used on or about a bed.

Bedford cord A dobby-woven fabric containing heavy warp cords, due to extra filling yarns floating on the back of the fabric.

bed skirts Fabric panels dropping from the top of box springs to the floor.

bedspread A decorative cloth used to cover a bed.

beetling Finish in which heavy wooden planks hammer the surface of linen fabric to flatten the cross section of the yarns to increase the surface reflection.

below-grade Below ground level.

bengaline A filling-rib-weave fabric containing equally sized and spaced ribs slightly larger than taffeta.

Berber yarn Speck yarn, hand-spun by peoples of northern Africa, composed of naturally colored wool; simulated by spinning fiber-dyed acrylic.

Better Cotton Initiative (BCI) Organization whose members promote the environmental, social, and economical sustainable cotton production around the world.

biaxial Interlacing in which the warp and filling yarns cross at right angles.

bicomponent fiber Fiber composed of two or more generically similar polymer compounds.

biconstituent fiber Fiber composed of two or more generically dissimilar polymer compounds.

binder yarn Yarn used to secure fancy yarn to base yarn in complex, decorative yarns.

biopolymer fiber Fibers that are made with petrochemicals and natural, renewably-sourced components

birdseye piqué Dobby woven curtain fabric with small, diamond-shaped designs.

bishop's sleeve treatment See *pouf or bishop's sleeve treatment.*

blackout shade Shade used when a total dark room is needed.

blanketing, double-faced Blanketing woven with one set of warp yarns and two sets of filling yarns, with one set of filling yarns carried to the face and one set of filling yarns carried to the back; often has different colors on each side.

blanketing, thermal Leno-woven blanket that is lightweight and lofty for thermal insulation.

bleaching agents Agents and compounds, such as sunlight, hydrogen peroxide and sodium hypochlorite, used to remove unwanted color.

bleeding Loss or migration of color when dye mixes with fluids.

blend Fabric or yarns composed of different fiber types.

blended yarns Yarns formed by combining two generically dissimilar filaments immediately after extrusion.

blind Window covering that typically opens horizontally.

block print Hand print produced by artisans who press a hand-carved, dye-covered block onto fabric surface.

blotch print Color style in which fabric background is printed, leaving undyed design motifs.

bobbin Device that holds the filling yarns when it is inserted by the shuttle.

bobbinet Transparent net with six-sided openings that appear round; produced by raschel stitching; used as a base for tambour-embroidered appliques.

bobbin lace Lace created by artisans manipulating multiple pairs of bobbins to twist and cross yarns.

BOCA Acronym for Building Officials and Code Administrators.

body cloth The main outer upholstery fabric that covers a sofa or chair.

boiling off Washing silk to remove the natural gum called sericin.

bonded polyurethane foam Carpet cushions made by bonding and compressing together chopped pieces of recycled prime polyurethane foam. The term *rebond* is sometimes used to identify these cushions.

bonded-web fabric Nonwoven fabric produced by applying adhesive or heat to webs of fibers.

bottom fabrics Fabrics used underneath the deck of upholstered furniture to conceal the interior components and give a finished look.

bouclé yarn Complex yarn with pronounced, closed loops that vary in size and spacing.

bow Indicates an off-grain problem.

boxing Wrapping strips of fabric around front and sides of upholstered cushions and throw pillows.

bracket Used in Axminster weaving; formed by linking three or four 3-foot spools that carry the pile yarns.

braiding Diagonal interlacing of three yarns.

breaking Process used in retrieving linen fibers from the flax plant; breaks up or crumbles the rotted woody core.

breaking force (load) Indicates the load required to rupture a fiber, yarn, or fabric.

breaking strength (tenacity) Strength reported as force per unit of linear density, for example, grams per denier (gpd or g/den) or grams per tex (gpt or g/tex).

broadloom Carpet produced 54 or more inches wide; does not identify a method of construction and carries no implication of quality.

brocade A Jacquard weave fabric woven from more than one set of filling yarns. The extra yarns are woven in a filling-faced twill or sateen interlacing pattern, creating a slightly raised effect. The ground is woven in a plain, twill, satin, or filling-rib interlacing pattern.

brocatelle A Jacquard weave fabric typically made from one set of fine warp yarns, one set of heavy warp yarns, and two sets of filling yarns. It contains a raised pattern, created by inserting filling stuffer yarns on the back of the fabric.

browning Staining of pile yarns as water wicks upward from overwetted jute carpet and rug backing yarns.

brushing Aligning pile surfaces using straight wires; introduces pronounced fabric nap or pile sweep.

Brussels Name used earlier for loop pile carpet woven on a Jacquard loom; now, all carpet woven on a Jacquard loom is called Wilton carpet.

Building Assessment Protocol for Commercial Buildings Developed as a rating system by The Green Building Initiative (GBI) for its Green Globes certification.

bulk continuous filament yarn (BCF) Yarn that has undergone a texturing process to introduce bulk and cohesiveness.

bulk or apparent volume See *apparent volume or bulk*.

bullion Fringe composed of metallic-colored strands; used as decorative trimming.

bundle penetration Adhesive penetration of the pile yarns in tufted constructions; helps to prevent individual staple or filament fibers from being pulled out of the yarns and rubbed into fuzz and pills on the carpet surface.

burlap A loosely woven plain weave fabric often made of heavy, coarse jute yarns.

burling Repair of imperfections in textile floorcoverings.

burn-out See *acid print*.

burnt gas fumes Such atmospheric gases as nitrogen dioxide and sulfur dioxide; may cause fading or color change with colored textiles.

bursting strength Force (load) required to rupture or burst a knitted fabric.

Business and Institutional Furniture Manufacturers Association (BIFMA) Nonprofit professional organization made up of business and institutional furniture manufacturers and other interested stakeholders. BIFMA creates voluntary standards for the furniture industry, including its LEVEL® certification for sustainability.

cable yarn Simple yarn formed by plying two or more cords

café curtains Unlined window coverings used alone or in combination with draperies; frequently constructed with scalloped headings and hung by rings looped over a rod.

calendering Industrial ironing using heated and highly polished cylinders.

calico Lightweight, plain-woven fabric characterized by small, colorful, printed motifs and solid-colored ground.

California Technical Bulletins California Bulletin #117 (CAL 117) is a small-scale upholstery fabric flammability test. California Bulletin #133 (CAL 133) is a full-scale upholstered seating flammability test.

camel hair Fiber obtained from the two-humped Bactrian camel.

cane Long, hollow, or pithy, bamboo-like grass retrieved from the rattan, a climbing palm; used in hand-woven chair seats and Roman shades.

cantonniére Rigid overhead window treatment mounted flush to the wall, framing the window; has a curved cornice and side panels that extend to the floor.

canvas See *duck*.

Cape Cod curtains Window treatment in which single-tier café curtains are combined with ruffled, tied-back panels; also known as cottage curtains.

carbonizing Using weak acid to degrade cellulosic matter (e.g., cockle burrs, twigs) in wool fleece.

carded yarns Yarns spun of both long and short cotton fibers and having a relatively low degree of fiber alignment.

carding Aligning fibers to partially straighten them in the yarn production process.

carpet Singular as well as plural form of term used to identify textile floorcovering securely attached to the floor; carpets and carpeting are incorrect forms.

Carpet America Recovery Effort (CARE) An organization that promotes recycling of post-consumer carpet and encourages carpet designed for recyclability.

Carpet and Rug Institute (CRI) The national trade association representing the carpet and rug industry. Membership consists of carpet manufacturers and suppliers to the industry of raw materials and services.

Carpet Cushion Council An organization that promotes recycling of post-consumer carpet and encourages that carpet be designed for recyclability.

carpet tiles Floorcoverings, generally 18-inches square, that are laid wall-to-wall; may be installed with no adhesive or with releasable or permanent adhesive.

carpet winch Vessel used for dyeing full widths of carpet which is folded or plaited and fed into the dye liquor; a type of batch dyeing.

cascade loop shade Window covering having horizontal tucks in the fabric panels; soft folds form when the shade is raised.

cascades Nonrigid side window treatments composed of gathered fabric falling in folds of graduated length; normally hung behind ends of swagged valance.

casement General term for curtain and drapery fabrics that have medium weight and some degree of transparency.

cashmere Fine, soft fiber retrieved from cashmere goats.

casing Opening formed by hemming the upper edge of window covering fabric and through which a rod is inserted.

cattlehair Natural material used earlier as a filling in upholstered furniture cushions and in carpet cushions.

cc system Cotton count system; used to indicate the size or count or number of yarns spun on the cotton yarn spinning system; gives the yarn count based on length per unit of weight; is an indirect yarn numbering system.

cellular rubber cushions Carpet cushions often referred to as foam rubber, sponge rubber, expanded rubber or latex rubber.

cellular shade See *honeycomb shade*.

cellulose A carbohydrate found in all plant life.

cellulosic fibers Fibers that are from plants.

certification marks Coined names and stylized logos that may be used on the labels of end products that conform with fiber content specifications or performance specifications established by the owner of the mark.

certifications Official document attesting that a product, process, service, or building has met specific criteria based on set standards.

chain warp yarns Warp yarns used in machine-woven floorcoverings.

challis A lightweight, soft, drapable, balanced plain weave fabric. It is typically made from rayon or cotton.

channel back tufting A style of tufting in which a series of straight seams along the cushion, either vertically or horizontally, pull through from the face of the outer fabric to sofa back.

char length The distance of fabric damage produced by flame in standard flammability test methods.

cheeses Yarn packages.

chemical washing Use of chlorine or acetic acid and glycerin to simulate the prized sheen and soft luster of older Oriental rugs that were dyed with natural rather than synthetic dyestuffs; also known as culturing and luster washing.

chenille carpet Soft floorcovering woven with chenille yarns as the pile yarns.

chenille spread Bedspread fabric produced with closely spaced pile tufts inserted by tufting.

chenille yarn Yarn-like strand cut from leno-woven fabric that has fine warp yarns and coarse filling yarns.

China grass See *ramie*.

chintz A balanced plain weave fabric that has been glazed to add luster.

chroma See *intensity*.

chromophores Components of dyestuffs that are responsible for the quantity of waves reflected, influencing the value of the hue.

circular braids Narrow, often decorative strands created by interlacing yarns or yarn-like strands around a textile cord.

Clean Air Act A United States federal law designed to control air pollution on a national level, effective 1963.

cleaning code Letter codes used with upholstery fabric to identify the recommended method of cleaning.

Clean Water Act The primary United States federal law governing water pollution. Became effective in 1972 with the objective of restoring and maintaining the chemical, physical, and biological quality of the nation's water resources.

clipped-dot or -spot fabric See *dot or spot weave*.

cloque A doublecloth fabric containing four sets of yarns that are woven in a pattern to simulate quilting stitches.

cloth beam Circular beam that holds the finished woven fabric.

coated fabrics A material typically comprised of a knit or nonwoven substrate with one or more added layers of a film-forming material such as vinyl, polyurethane, or silicone on the wear surface of the fabric.

Code of Federal Regulation (CFR) The codification of the general and permanent rules and regulations published in the Federal Register of the United States federal government.

codes Mandatory practices concerned with the safety and well-being of the general population; they are laws enacted by federal, state, and local governments.

cohesiveness Ability of fibers to adhere to one another; affected by such inherent features as the twist in cotton and the scales covering wool; may be introduced with texturing.

coir Fiber retrieved from husk of coconuts; used in pile layer of track-off mats.

collagen Protein compound in leather fibers.

colorants Dyestuffs used to color textiles.

color characteristics Distinguishing features of colors, including hue, value, and intensity.

colorfastness Ability of a colorant or dyestuff to retain its original color characteristics.

colorist A professional who determines appropriate colors in which a product will be offered to a given marketplace.

color rendering index (CRI) Scale of 0 to 100, indicating how accurately colors appear under a light source, with a CRI of 100 being the truest color rendering.

color sealed Term used to identify solution-dyed fibers.

COM See *customer's own material*.

combed yarns Yarns spun of long cotton fibers having a relatively high degree of fiber alignment.

combing Combing fibers to align them and to separate the shorter staple-length fibers in the yarn production process.

combustible Material capable of undergoing combustion.

combustion Chemical process in which combustible material combines with oxygen to produce heat and light (flame).

combustion, flameless Combustion in which no flames are evident (e.g., glowing, smoldering).

combustion, flaming Combustion in which flame and heat are being produced.

comforters Bed covering having a face fabric, lofty filling, and a backing fabric.

commercial interiors Includes stores, shopping centers, offices, schools, hospitals, hotels and motels, libraries and public buildings, religious buildings, restaurants, penal institutions, and the like.

commercial quilting See *quilting, machine stitching.*

common names Names of natural fibers (e.g., wool, silk, flax, cotton).

compacted selvage Selvage in which the number of warp yarns is relatively high to increase the compactness of construction.

completion Application of upholstery fabric so the pattern flows uninterrupted down the back pillows, the seat cushions, the seat boxing, the seat front, and the skirt.

complex cords Decorative yarns composed of two or more complex ply yarns.

complex plies Decorative yarns composed of two or more complex single or ply yarns.

complex single yarn Decorative yarn composed of one complex yarn.

complex yarn Decorative yarn having a base yarn, a fancy yarn, and/or a binder or tie yarn; may be single, ply, or cord.

compressibility The ease with which a textile structure can be crushed or reduced in thickness.

compressional loft Ability of a textile structure to recover from compression and regain its original loft; also known as compressional resiliency.

compressional resiliency See *compressional loft.*

compression deflection The extent to which a structure resists compression force.

compression force deflection (CFD) The force required to deflect or compress a specimen assembly a given percentage of its original thickness; reported as the average number of pounds per square inch.

compression loss The extent to which a structure fails to recover its original thickness after being compressed under a static load; also known as compression set.

compression set See *compression loss.*

compressive shrinkage treatment Mechanical treatment used to improve the dimensional stability of fabrics composed of cotton.

conditioning Placing test specimens in a controlled atmosphere of 70 + or - 2°F and 65 + or - 2% relative humidity for a minimum of 24 hours prior to measuring a given property.

conduction Mechanism by which heat energy, electrical charges, and sound waves are transmitted through solids, liquids, and gases.

conductors Materials, including textile fibers, that keep electrons flowing, minimizing their accumulation.

consumer The person or corporation who ultimately pays for a product or service.

Consumer Product Safety Commission (CPSC) Federal agency concerned with the safety of consumer products.

continental rod Flat curtain rod typically 2½ to 4½ inches wide and projecting from the wall surface.

continuous dyeing Dyeing operation that includes wetting the carpet, applying the dyestuff, steaming, washing, drying, and rolling up the dyed and dried goods; used for large quantities of greige goods.

continuous filament See *filament.*

contract design The design of commercial spaces.

contrast-welt Fabric-covered cord inserted in seam lines of upholstered furniture coverings that differs in color or material from the body cloth.

convection Transmission of heat energy by air movement.

conventional selvage Selvage formed by the continuous filling yarn being turned at each edge to produce a finished, nonraveling edge.

converters Textile finishers; convert greige goods into finished fabric.

convertible sofa bed An upholstered sofa with a mattress concealed under the cushions.

copolymer Fiber composed of two different monomer units (e.g., polyester, nylon).

corduroy A filling pile fabric containing a cut surface texture. Typically composed of cotton or cotton/polyester blends. Most corduroy upholstery fabric is characterized by wide, densely constructed wales.

cord yarn Simple yarn formed by plying two or more plied yarns.

core-spun yarn Yarn formed by spinning staple-length fibers around an elastomeric filament.

corium The central portion of hides and skins; composed of a network of interlaced bundles of tiny fibers.

cork The lightweight, durable, resilient substance obtained from the outer layer bark of cork oak trees.

corkscrew yarn See *spiral yarn.*

cork veneer Thin slices of natural materials that are laminated to paper or nonwoven backing.

cornice Rigid overhead treatment mounted over drapery heading and hardware.

cortex The central part of a wool fiber that contains cortical cells.

cosmetotextiles New development in the textile industry which adds compounds to bedding materials to keep a youthful appearance.

cottage curtains See *Cape Cod curtains.*

cotton A seed fiber from the boll of the cotton plant.

cotton batting Three-dimensional batting structure used as a filling in upholstered furniture.

cotton spinning system Spinning system used to spin cotton fibers into yarns.

courses Crosswise rows of loops in a knitted fabric.

covered-core yarn Yarn formed by wrapping or braiding filaments around an elastomeric filament.

covering power The ability of a textile structure to cover or conceal a surface without undue weight.

crackle effect Striated appearance seen with batik prints; created by cracking the wax to allow the dye liquor to run through the cracks.

cradle-to-cradle A textile certification process focusing on life-cycle characteristics.

Cradle to Cradle Products Innovation Institute A nonprofit organization that certifies products according to Cradle to Cradle® standards.

cradle-to-grave A way of evaluating how an item or method affects the environment throughout its life, from the time of creation to disposal.

crash A plain weave fabric composed of coarse, irregular yarns. Typically made from flax fiber.

creative director See *design director*.

crease resistance Misnomer: creases are planned, wrinkles are not.

creel frame Device used to hold the yarn cheeses as the warp yarns are wound onto the warp or loom beam.

crepe A fabric characterized by a random or irregular interlacing pattern. The floats are not uniform in length and in no distinct pattern.

crepe filament yarn A high-twist filament yarn.

cretonne A plain weave fabric characterized by coarse yarns, a stiff hand, dull finish and large printed motifs. It is infrequently used today.

crimp Bends and twists along the fiber length.

critical radiant flux (CRF) Numerical value determined by converting the distance of flame spread to watts per square centimeter after completion of the flooring radiant panel test; indicates the minimum heat energy necessary to sustain burning of a floorcovering that leads to flame propagation.

crocking Transfer of color from one material to another as a result of surface rubbing.

Crockmeter Machine used to measure the colorfastness to crocking.

cross dyeing Variation of piece dyeing in which a fabric composed of two or more different and strategically placed fibers is immersed into a dyebath formulated with dyestuffs that will be selectively accepted and rejected; produces a multicolored fabric from one immersion process; also known as differential dyeing.

cross-sectional shape Lateral shape of textile fibers (e.g., round, trilobal).

crushed velvet A warp pile fabric that has been mechanically twisted while wet to create a crushed, wrinkled surface.

crushing A treatment used on velvet fabrics; the pile yarns in some areas are flattened, whereas pile yarns in the adjacent areas are oriented in various directions; varying levels of luster are produced.

crystalline polymer chain Parallel arrangement of polymer chains anchored by lateral bonds.

cubicle curtains See *privacy curtains*.

culturing See *chemical washing*.

cuprammonium Conventional rayon fiber.

curing Salting the raw hides to retard bacterial action; initial process of converting hides and skins into leather.

curtains General term for textile window covering fabrics hung without linings.

curtain tender See *baton*.

customer's own material (COM) Textile or nontextile fabric supplied to end-product manufacturers by consumers.

cuticle Wax-like film that coats the primary wall of cotton.

cystine An amino acid found in wool fibers.

damask A two-dimensional, Jacquard-woven fabric containing one set of warp yarns and one set of filling yarns that incorporate one or two colors.

dead-and-buried yarns Yarns carried in the back portion of a Wilton carpet; contribute weight and resiliency.

deck Portion of furniture frame that supports the seat cushions.

degree of polymerization The extent to which monomers link to form polymers; the average number of monomer units in the polymer chains of a fiber.

delamination Separation of attached layers in a textile structure.

delamination strength The force required to separate the primary and secondary backings of tufted floorcoverings.

delusterants Titanium dioxide particles added to the polymer solutions of manufactured fibers.

denier Describes the fibers size or fineness; calculated by dividing the yarn size by the number of filaments.

denier system Direct yarn numbering system; gives weight per unit of length measurement of a fiber or yarn; weight of 9,000 meters of fiber or yarn.

den number Yarn number determined with the denier system; numerically equal to the weight in grams of 9,000 meters of the strand.

densified prime polyurethane cushions The cushion chemical structure is modified during the manufacturing process to produce a product with specific performance characteristics. Densified prime polyurethane foam cushions have a higher density than grafted prime foam.

density Mass or amount of matter per unit of volume of a fiber or other textile structure; reported as pounds per cubic inch or grams per cubic centimeter.

density factor Product resulting from the multiplication of yarn size, needle count, and stitches per inch used in a pile floorcovering.

density index See *density factor*.

dents Openings in the reed through which the warp yarns are threaded; help to keep the warp yarns aligned and ensure grain straightness.

dents per inch Number of openings per inch in a reed; determines compactness of the warp yarns.

design director The professional who is responsible for design decisions within an organization.

design elements Color, texture, pattern, light, form, and shape; provide a way to evaluate aesthetic considerations for an abstract problem.

design principles Balance, harmony, rhythm, emphasis, contrast, scale, and proportion; provide a way to evaluate aesthetic considerations for an abstract problem.

design professionals As used in this text, pertains primarily to professionally trained interior designers and architects.

dhurrie (durrie, durry) rugs Flat, hand-woven rugs having a plain, twill, or tapestry interlacing.

diameter The width of a fiber.

differential dyeing See *cross dyeing*.

digital printing Printing from a digital image onto a material such as a fabric. Large format, detailed prints, and small runs are possible.

dimensional stability The ability of a textile structure to maintain its size and shape after use and care.

dimity Sheer, warp-rib woven curtain fabric.

direct-glue The method of applying wallcovering material to walls using an adhesive.

directional pile lay See *nap*.

direct printing Printing in which the colors are applied directly to the fabric or yarns.

direct yarn numbering system Systems that give the yarn number as weight per unit of length; as yarn number increases, yarn size increases; examples include the denier and tex systems.

discharge printing Operation in which fabric is piece dyed before the selective application of an agent that will remove the dye, creating undyed motifs and a solid colored ground.

discontinuous dyeing Dyeing operation in which the wet carpet must be removed from the dyeing machine and dried elsewhere; also known as batch dyeing.

disposable toweling Toweling produced by bonding webs of fibers; may be reinforced with a scrim.

distortion of yarn See *yarn distortion*.

disulfide crosslinks Linkages (-S-S-) contained in cystine that are attractive to moth and carpet beetle larvae.

dobby Woven fabric with small, geometric motifs.

dobby weave Decorative weave requiring many harnesses; distinguished by small, geometric woven-in motifs.

doctor blade Squeegee-like metal blade used to clean nonengraved portion of metal-covered printing rollers or to transfer dye liquor from a roller to the surface of greige goods.

document fabrics Accurate reproduction of historic fabrics using true colors, replicated patterns, and the same fiber composition and fabric construction.

domestics A general term for household textiles, including bath and kitchen toweling and bedding.

dope Liquid spinning solution.

dope dyeing See *solution dyeing*.

dot or spot weave Surface figure weave in which extra yarns interlace with the base yarns to create a small motif; yarns floating between the motifs may be clipped away (unclipped dot or spot weave) or left in place (unclipped dot or spot weave).

dotted swiss A lightweight, sheer, plain weave fabric containing extra filling yarns woven in periodically and clipped. Flocked dotted swiss resembles dotted swiss but is created through localized flocking fibers to the surface of the fabric.

doublecloth Fabric woven of three or more sets of yarn.

double cloth construction technique Fabrication in which pile yarns are alternately interlaced in an upper fabric and a lower fabric; as the weaving progresses, the pile yarns joining the two fabrics are cut, resulting in two lengths of fabric.

double knit A term used to describe a category of filling knit fabrics created using two needle beds.

double rubs A forward and backward oscillation of the cylinder used in the Wyzenbeek test method; equivalent to one cycle.

down Soft undercoating of waterfowl, composed of individual down fibers that are connected to one another at a central point.

down cluster Group of components including down, nestling down and plumules.

drape The ability of a fabric to form graceful configurations, such as folds in curtain and drapery panels.

draperies Lined textile fabric panels hung to drape gracefully at windows.

draw curtains Unlined window treatment panels that are drawn in one direction, stacking on one side of the window, or in two directions, stacking on both sides of the window.

drawing Stretching a manufactured filament to improve its interior order, especially to increase the orientation of the polymer chains.

drawing out In yarn spinning, combining several slivers into one new sliver.

drill A fabric backing that weighs an average of 3.6 ounces per square yard used with Type III vinyl wallcoverings.

drop-match patterns Patterns that repeat themselves diagonally across the width of the carpet; may be half-drop or quarter-drop.

drops The portion of a bedspread that hangs vertically from the bed surface to the floor; may be tailored, ruffled, gathered, or shirred.

drop wire Device used on industrial looms to stop the weaving when a warp yarns ruptures.

drum dyeing Rotating leather in dye liquor rotating in large vessels.

dry extraction cleaning Absorbent powder that contains water-based cleaning fluids or detergents and a small amount of solvent is sprinkled on the carpet, releasing and absorbing the soil, which is subsequently removed by vacuuming.

dry foam cleaning Water-based shampoo in foam form is sprayed onto the carpet, mechanically worked in, and the soil-foam residue is subsequently removed by vacuuming.

dry spinning A volatile solvent is used to dissolve the polymer compound, then evaporated after extrusion to allow the filaments to solidify.

duck Basket woven fabric often used in slipcovers, outdoor furniture, and boat covers.

dupioni silk A type of silk that results when two silkworms spin their cocoons together.

duplex printing Printing on both sides of a fabric.

durable press finishing Chemical treatment used to improve the resiliency of fabrics composed of cellulose fibers; creates strong cross-links.

durable press resins Chemical compounds added to a fabric to help retain resiliency.

dust ruffles See *bed skirts*.

duvet Comforters filled with down.

dye beck Pressure cooker-like vessel used in dyeing.

dyed-in-the-wool Old adage meaning deeply ingrained and staunchly dedicated; arose from the observation that wool fibers dyed prior to spinning had richer and deeper colors than those produced by dyeing yarns or fabrics.

dyeing ranges Systems used in continuous dyeing operations, includes units for all stages of the dyeing and drying operation.

dye liquor Combination of dyestuff and relatively large quantities of water; used in immersion dyeing operation.

dye migration Movement of dye liquor through fabric; necessary for uniform application of the dye; creates uneven level of dye intensity if in-use cleaning agents or procedures promote such movement.

dye paste Combination of dyestuff and relatively small quantities of water; used in printing operations.

dye pigments Insoluble dyestuffs that may be added to polymer solutions prior to spinning.

dyes or dyestuffs Color-producing compounds that are normally soluble in water.

Ecolabel Index An organization that maintains a database of ecolabels.

ecolabels Common reference for certifications related to sustainability attributes.

Eco-Textile Labeling Guide A biennial publication of Ecotextile News (www.ecotextile.com).

Ecotextile News A periodical that publishes the biennial Eco-Textile Labeling Guide.

edge abrasion Wear caused by friction where the fabric is folded, as is the case at linen napkins.

editors Used in the interiors furnishings market, especially in Europe, as a label for firms that purchase fabrics from mills in order to sell an edited line of products to interior designers and architects. Also called wholesalers, jobbers, distributors.

effective face yarn weight Weight of the pile yarns in the wear layer of a textile floorcovering, not in the backing.

effect yarn Fancy or decorative yarn found in complex decorative yarns.

egress The act of leaving an interior in the event of fire; the exit way or means of egress should be free of obstructions.

Egyptian cotton Cotton fiber which originated in the Nile Valley; up to 1½ inches in length.

elastane An elastic polyurethane material.

elasticity The ability of a textile structure to be extended and to recover from the extension; also known as stretchability.

elastic modulus Initial resistance to deformation stress exhibited by a fiber or other textile structure.

elastic recovery The extent to which a fiber, yarn, or fabric recovers from extension.

electrical conductivity The relative ease with which a fiber conducts the flow of electrons.

electrical resistivity The relative ease with which a fiber resists the flow of electrons.

electromagnetic spectrum Range of waves of electromagnetic energy, from extremely short cosmic and gamma rays to relatively long radio waves.

electronic color meter Sophisticated meter used to detect differences in the color characteristics of fabrics.

electrostatic flocking Using an electrostatic field to induce flock to embed itself into a fabric coating.

elevator effect Euphemism for the sagging and shrinking of curtain and drapery panels composed of conventional rayon fibers when the level of relative humidity fluctuates; also known as hiking and yo-yo effect.

elongation The ability of a fiber, yarn, or other textile structure to extend or elongate; normally measured and reported as percent elongation at the rupture point.

embodied energy Total energy used in the production and delivery of a product.

embossing Mechanical treatment used to introduce convex and concave design forms to two-dimensional fabric.

embroidering Hand or machine stitching of colored yarns in decorative patterns on a portion of a base fabric.

Emergency Planning and Community Right-to-Know Act Passed in 1986 in response to concerns regarding the environmental and safety hazards posed by the storage and handling of toxic chemicals.

emerizing See *sueding*.

end One warp yarn.

end-product producers/designers Members of the interior textile industry who design and manufacture textile end products for use in residential or commercial interiors.

end-user The person, facility, or entity that purchases a material and ultimately uses it in their own environment. The end-user does not always make the purchasing decision for the material.

Energy Independence and Security Act U.S. federal law that supports production of clean renewable fuels and research on greenhouse gas capture and storage options.

Energy Policy Act Federal law that addresses energy production, energy efficiency, renewable energy, and climate change technology.

Environmentally Preferable Purchasing (EPP) Program An EPA-developed database of environmental information for products and services with reduced environmental impact.

Environmental Protection Agency (EPA) Government agency established to protect human health and safeguard the natural environment (air, water, and land), upon which life depends.

environmental stewardship Conversation of natural resources.

epidermis The top layer of hides and skins.

etched-out print See *acid print*.

even twill Twill fabric in which an equal amount of warp and filling are visible on the face of the fabric.

expanded polymer solutions Polymer solutions having air incorporated to increase the apparent volume and comfort.

extrusion Mechanical spinning of manufactured filaments; polymer solution is extruded or forced through openings in a spinneret.

eyelet An embroidered fabric containing thread stitched holes.

fabrication techniques Ways to make fabrics (e.g., weaving, knitting, felting, braiding, needle punching).

fabric designers Personnel who identify the aesthetic features preferred by contemporary consumers, interpret and forecast trends, and design fabrics that will meet end-use requirements and expectations.

fabric count Numerical indication of compactness of construction; equal to the number of warp and filling yarns per square inch of greige goods; also known as thread count or yarn count.

fabric nap See *nap*.

fabric openness The ration of the open areas between the yarns to the total area of the fabric.

fabric panel Portion of a window treatment in which a number of fabric widths, and, if necessary, a partial width are seamed together.

fabric weights Weights that are placed in the lower hem areas of fabric panels to improve the draping quality.

face yarns Yarns in the face or pile portion of a fabric or floorcovering.

Facts certification A certification authorized by the Association for Contract Textiles (ACT) that recognizes contract textiles that conform to the rigors of the multi-attribute standard NSF/ANSI 336 and are third-party certified.

Fade-Ometer® Equipment used in accelerated testing for lightfastness.

fading Loss of or weakening of the original color characteristics.

faille A filling-rib weave fabric containing slightly larger and flatter ribs than taffeta and rep. Typically contains filament warp yarns and heavier spun filling yarns.

false-twist coiling Texturing technique involving continuous twisting, heat setting, and untwisting; introduces apparent volume and bulk but little or no stretch.

feather fiber The detached barbs of feathers that are not joined or attached to each other.

feathers Two-dimensional appendage growing from a bird's skin and forming its plumage.

feathers, crushed, chopped, or broken Feathers that have been processed by a curling, crushing, or chopping machine, which has changed the original form of the feathers without removing the quill; the term also includes the fiber resulting from such processing.

feathers, damaged Feathers that have been damaged by insects, or otherwise materially injured.

feathers, land fowl Nonwaterfowl feathers derived from chickens, turkeys, and other land fowl.

feathers, nonwaterfowl See *feathers, land fowl*.

feathers, quill Feathers that are over 4 inches in length or that have a quill point exceeding 6/16 inch in length.

feathers, waterfowl Feathers derived from ducks and geese.

Federal Aviation Administration (FAA) Government agency that controls the flammability of items used in airplanes.

Federal Housing Administration (FHA) Government agency with jurisdiction over the materials used in the interiors of such places as elderly and care-type housing, low-rent public housing projects, and structures insured by FHA.

Federal Insecticide, Fungicide, and Rodenticide Act A U.S. federal law that set up the basic U.S. system of pesticide regulation to protect applicators, consumers, and the environment.

Federal Trade Commission (FTC) U.S. federal governmental agency empowered and directed to prevent unfair methods of competition in commerce.

felt Fabric made from wool fibers.

felted wool yarns Yarns produced by exposing loosely knitted strands of wool rovings to heat, agitation, and moisture, causing felting shrinkage and converting the strands to yarns.

felting Interlocking of the scales covering wool fiber that results in matting and shrinking of the yarns and fabric; caused by heat, agitation, and moisture.

fenestration Design, arrangement, and proportions of the windows and doors in an interior.

festoon Ornamental trimming draped over a valence or other overhead window treatment.

fiber A thin, threadlike structure from animal or plant tissue or made synthetically. A fiber is a distinct chemical unit.

fiber dyeing Immersing loose masses of fiber into dye liquor; frequently used with wool fiber; also known as stock dyeing.

fiberfill Loose, lofty masses of staple or tow used as filling for pillows; generally polyester.

fiber variant Manufactured fiber that is chemically related to other fibers in its generic class but distinguished by a structural feature, such as diameter or cross-sectional shape, or by the inclusion of a polymer additive.

fibrillation Breaking off of minute slivers of glass from high-denier glass filaments as a result of flexing and abrasion.

fibrous batts 1. Three-dimensional arrangement of webs of fibers that can be bonded with adhesive or heat into essentially flat structures (e.g., nonwoven interfacing fabric). 2. Three-dimensional arrangement of webs of fibers that are stabilized and used as filling or padding in upholstered furniture, quilts, or as carpet cushions.

fibrous cushions Carpet cushions produced by needle punching fibers into felt-like structures.

filament fiber An extremely long textile fiber, measured in yards, meters, miles, or kilometers; also known as a continuous filament.

filament yarn Yarn composed of filament fibers.

filling-faced satin weave Interlacing pattern in which the filling yarns float over four or more warp yarns.

filling knitting Fabrication in which fabric is produced by continuously interlooping one or more yarns from side to side, creating one course after another; also known as weft knitting.

filling or weft shots Crosswise yarns in woven carpet; used in pairs in Axminster carpet.

filling pile fabric Fabric in which the pile layer is created with extra filling yarns (e.g., velveteen and corduroy).

filling-rib weave Variation of the plain weave in which larger or grouped filling yarns create a ribbed or ridged effect in the crosswise fabric direction.

filling weight Net filling weight of the down and feather.

filling yarns Crosswise yarns in woven fabric; also known as weft yarns and woof yarns.

fill leakage The migration or penetration of the filling material through the outercovering; minimized by using a spunbonded interior lining fabric.

fill power Measure of loft, or the insulation ability of down products in cubic inches per ounce.

film Sheeting made directly from a polymer solution.

finials Decorative pieces attached to the ends of curtain and drapery rods.

finishers Companies whose main commercial activities are processing fabric material after it is fabricated.

finishes Processes that fabric may go through after it is woven, such as scouring, calendering, heatsetting, and adding features such as stain resistance or antimicrobial properties.

fireproof fiber A fiber that is unaffected by heat (e.g., asbestos).

fitted sheets Sheets constructed with four contour corners to fit the mattress.

flameless combustion See *combustion, flameless.*

flame propagation Flame spreading (e.g., from original source of ignition to other items within an interior).

flame-resistant fiber Fiber exhibiting relatively high decomposition and ignition temperatures.

flame retardant Agents added to fibers to increase their relative flame resistance.

flame spread Distance flame spreads from site of ignition; measured in several flammability test methods.

flame yarn Complex yarn produced by twisting a simple yarn around a single slub yarn that has large and elongated areas of low twist.

flaming combustion See *combustion, flaming.*

Flammable Fabrics Act (FFA) A U.S. federal law that regulates the manufacture of flammable clothing.

flammable fiber Fiber that is relatively easy to ignite and sustains combustion until it is consumed.

flannel Plain or twill weave fabric with a nap on both sides.

flannelette A plain weave fabric with napping on one side only.

flashover Situation in which all combustible materials burst into flame.

flat abrasion Abrasion of a textile while it is fairly flat, such as on the seat cushions of automobiles and interior furniture items.

flat-bed screen printing Printing the textile surface by forcing dye paste through openings in a screen mounted above the surface; screens have been treated to resist flow through of the paste wherever the fabric is not to be printed.

flat braid Narrow, often decorative strand formed by interlacing a minimum of three yarns or yarn-like strands.

flat rubber cushions Carpet cushion manufactured by converting liquid latex and fillers into flat, continuous sheets.

flax A natural cellulose fiber obtained from the stem of the flax plant.

flesh tissue The bottommost portion of hides and skins.

flex abrasion Abrasion of a textile while it is bent or curved, such as on the arms and curved portions of seat and back cushions, as well as with that covering prominent welts.

flexibility Pliability; improves with fiber fineness; needed for freedom of movement.

float Point where yarns cross over more than one yarn at a time.

flock Extremely short fibers.

flocked dotted Swiss A lightweight sheer fabric containing small dots created by adhering fibers in localized areas on the base fabric.

flocking Embedding extremely short fibers, known as flock, into an adhesive or resin compound.

flock or flake yarn Complex yarn having enlarged segments created by periodically binding thin bits of roving between plied single yarns.

flokati (flocati) rugs Long-pile wool floorcoverings woven in Greece; after the pile is formed, the rugs are immersed in a pool of water beyond a waterfall where the swirling waters cause felting of the pile tufts.

flossa stick Stick used in weaving rya rugs; pile is formed over the stick to ensure uniform pile height.

fluorescent compounds Agents that absorb invisible ultraviolet light and emit visible blue or violet light; used to neutralize the natural yellow hues of wool or yellowed laundered fabrics; create apparent whiteness and brightness; also known as optical brighteners.

fluorocarbon compounds Agents used to lower the critical surface energy of fibers so dirt and lint do not adhere to their surface and fluids bead up rather than pass into the fibers.

flying shuttle loom Loom having devices to hammer the canoe-like shuttle in the picking operation to send it "flying" through the shed.

foam-core See *mattress, foam-core.*

foot traffic units In floorcoverings testing, the number of passes by human walkers, not the number of times each specimen is stepped on.

FoxFibre® Trademark of naturally colored cotton.

FPLA Acronym for Fur Products Labeling Act.

frames The number of colors in a Wilton carpet is denoted by the number of frames (e.g., 3-frame, 4-frame).

free-lay installation Installation of carpet modules or squares in which the modules are held in place by gravity, not by adhesive.

frictional heat energy With floorcoverings, for example, the rubbing of the soles on carpet and rug fibers creates frictional heat energy, which causes negatively charged electrons to transfer from the fiber surfaces to the body.

frieze Level, uncut pile fabric made of multifilament yarns.

frieze (carpeting) Textured carpet constructed of yarns having maximum twist for high stability and wear-life. Each yarn is clearly visible.

frostiness Absence of dye on yarn tips; planned and executed by gum printing operations.

frosting Loss of color as a result of abrasion-induced fiber loss.

fugitive colorant Textile colorant exhibiting poor colorfastness.

full-consensus standards A standard developed with the participation of stakeholders with an interest in their development and use.

full-grain leather Leather having unaltered grain markings.

fulling Conversion process used to encourage yarns in fabrics composed of wool to relax and shrink, resulting in a more compact fabric.

fullness Yardage added when calculating the measurement of the fabric panels.

full-scale testing Flammability testing done in facilities constructed to replicate a room or a corridor.

full warranty See *warranty, full*.

fume fading Color change typically seen with acetate dyed blue, brown, or green with disperse dyestuffs and exposed to oxides of nitrogen or sulfur; blues turn pink, browns turn reddish, and greens turn brownish yellow; can be avoided by solution dyeing the fibers; also known as gas fading and atmospheric fading.

fungi Extremely simple vegetative plant forms, such as molds and mildew; they feed on cellulosic fibers and sizing, producing stains and odors.

Fur Products Labeling Act (FPLA) Governs the labeling and advertising of fur and fur products.

fused selvage Selvage in which the ends of the filling yarns, which must be composed of thermoplastic fibers, are heated to fuse them together; often used with water-jet looms.

fusion bonding Fabrication technique in which pile yarns are embedded into a vinyl compound coating a base fabric.

fusion printing Using heat to secure colored acrylic resins to the surface of glass fiber fabrics.

futons Flexible mattresses typically filled with cotton batting.

galloon Narrow, tape-like length of trimming; often contains metallic strands.

garneting A recycling process in which wool yarns and fabrics are shredded and converting them back to fibers.

gas fading See *fume fading*.

gasfastness Stability of colorants when exposed to gases.

gauge 1. Fractional distance between needles on tufting machines; reported in whole-number fractions. 2. Number of loops per inch of width in knitted constructions. 3. Thickness of polymer film sheeting.

gauze A balanced plain weave lightweight fabric. It has a slightly higher yarn count than cheesecloth.

gear crimping Texturing process in which intermeshing gears introduce a planar or two-dimensional crimp to filaments; used to improve fiber cohesiveness.

gel mattress Mattress composed of a molded and highly gel.

General Services Administration (GSA) Government agency that oversees the selection of materials for federal facilities.

generation Level of manufactured fiber development.

generic class Class or name of manufactured fibers; defined in terms of chemical composition (e.g., nylon, polyester, acetate, acrylic, spandex).

generic name Family of fibers that have the same chemical composition.

genetically modified cotton A cotton seed that has been genetically modified to resist natural pests.

genuine suede Suede produced by processing the flesh side of hides and skins.

Ghiordes knot Hand-tied knot used in the production of rya rugs and some Oriental rugs; also known as Turkish knot.

gimp yarn Yarn formed by spirally wrapping one yarn around another, or by braiding three or more strands around one central yarn; interior yarn is completely covered and outer yarns are often metallic strands.

gingham A lightweight, yarn-dyed plain weave fabric with a checked pattern.

ginning Mechanical process used to separate cotton fibers from the cotton seeds.

glass A manufactured synthetic fiber used in drapery for its flame resistance.

glass curtains Sheer curtains hung next to the window glass; may or may not be composed of glass fiber; also known as sheers.

glass transition temperature Temperature at which lateral bonds within a fiber are disturbed, allowing the position of the polymer chains to be shifted.

glazed chintz See *chintz*.

glazed finish Leather having a high gloss created by the application and polishing of resins, waxes, or lacquer-based compounds.

glazing Finishing treatment in which glue, shellac, or resin is added to fabric to create a hard, high shine.

Global Ecolabelling Network A nonprofit organization that maintains databases of ecolabels.

Global Organic Textile Standard (GOTS) A processing standard for organic fibers and covers the entire textile supply chain. The standard defines requirements to ensure organic textile claims.

glowing See *combustion, flameless*.

glue-down installation Installation of carpet or carpet modules in which a permanent or releasable adhesive is used; no pad is used; provides greater stability when rolling traffic is present.

goose-eye twill A dobby weave fabric with a woven-in design created by selectively reversing the direction of the visual diagonal. The small diamond shapes are said to resemble the eye of a goose.

governmental regulatory agencies A government agency responsible for exercising autonomous authority over some area of human activity in a regulatory or supervisory capacity.

grafted prime polyurethane cushions Cushions manufactured by a chemical mixing reaction process. They are flexible cushions formulated with additives that provide reinforcement for increased load-bearing.

grain The relationship of warp yarns to filling yarns.

grain markings The pores that are exposed when the hair is removed from hides and skins.

grain-straight Characteristic of woven fabric in which all warp yarns are parallel and all warp and filling yarns cross at right angles.

grams per denier Indicates force per unit of linear density necessary to rupture a fiber, yarn, or thread; also gpd and g/den.

grams per tex Indicates force per unit of linear density necessary to rupture a fiber, yarn, or thread; also gpt and g/tex.

grasscloth A wallcovering made by gluing woven native grasses (typically arrowroot) onto a paper backing. Often handwoven.

grassing Using sunshine to bleach fabrics of linen.

Green Building Initiative (GBI) An acronym for the Green Building Initiative, a nonprofit organization that promotes building practices resulting in energy-efficient, healthy, and environmentally sustainable buildings.

green building rating system A rating system based on guidelines or standards that rank construction practices, resulting in energy-efficient, healthier, and environmentally sustainable buildings.

green certification Third-party confirmation that environmental claims regarding products, processes, or services have met criteria based on recognized standards.

green cotton Cotton fabric that has not been bleached or treated with any other chemicals, finishes or dye products.

Green Globes A program developed by the Green Building Initiative (GBI), a sustainable whole building rating system.

Green Globes Assessor Technical experts who are certified by Green Globes Initiative to perform independent third-party assessments for prospective Green Globes building projects.

Green Globes Professional Industry professional trained in the Green Globes building assessment and certification process and are qualified to share insights on the program.

Greenguard Environmental Institute (GEI) The GEI is an ANSI authorized standards developer that establishes acceptable indoor air standards for products.

Greenguard Gold The highest-level certification offered by the Greenguard Environmental Institute (GEI) for indoor air standards for products.

Green Guides A Federal Trade Commission (FTC) publication that helps marketers avoid making environmental claims that mislead consumers.

Green Label; Green Label Plus Certifications developed and administered by the Carpet and Rug Institute that certifies to California Department of Public Health test CA01350 and aims to encourage specification of carpet, adhesive, and cushion products with the lowest possible VOC chemical emissions.

green standard Describes a specific performance, behavior, attribute, or test result regarding a product or process that affects the ecosystem.

greenwashing Making unsubstantiated or misleading claims about the environmental benefits of a product, service or technology.

greige goods Unfinished fabrics.

grin Exposure of the backing in floorcovering with low pile construction density.

grospoint A woven pile fabric that has a level surface with pronounced loops larger than those of frieze.

growth Unrecovered elongation.

guide bars Devices used in warp knitting to position the yarns around the hooks of the needles; as the number of guide bars is increased, the complexity of the interlooping can be increased.

guides Collection of labeling provisions issued by the FTC; serve to inform members of a limited portion of the interior textile industry how to avoid engaging in unfair and deceptive labeling practices; advisory in nature.

Guides for the Feather and Down Products Industry Labeling guidelines that include definitions of terms and recommended procedures for labeling products filled with feather and down.

gum printing Application of a gum compound to the tips of pile yarns prior to dyeing to prevent dye absorption and migration; develops a frosted appearance.

gypsum A high-density, uncrystallized plaster used to coat the back of open-weave burlap wallcovering.

hackling Aligning linen fibers prior to spinning.

half-drop-match patterns In pattern repeats, it is the complementing portion of a design located at a point up or down one-half the length of the repeat.

hand The tactile qualities of a fabric, perceived by touch.

hand embroidering See *embroidering*.

harnesses Devices on looms that support the heddles and form the shed.

Hawser yarn Simple yarn formed by twisting two or more ropes together.

head covers or head rests Fabric coverings that protect the upholstery fabric from neck and hair oils and hair coloring.

headings Treatments used at the top of curtain and drapery panels to finish the upper edge and distribute fullness evenly across the finished width.

heat conductivity Rate at which a material conducts heat; reported as K-value; synonymous with heat transmittance.

heather Color styling in which two or more colors of fibers are uniformly distributed along the length of a spun yarn or in which two or more colors of filaments have been thrown.

heat of combustion values Amount of heat energy generated by burning materials that could cause burn injuries as well as maintain the temperature required for further decomposition and combustion; reported as BTUs/lb.

heat resistivity Rate at which a material resists heat flow, that is, how effectively it insulates and prevents heat exchange; reported as R-value.

heat sensitivity See *thermoplasticity*.

heat setting Use of heat to stabilize thermoplastic fibers, improving their dimensional stability and that of yarns and fabrics composed of them; also improves resiliency.

heat transfer printing Transfer of dyestuff from printed paper to fabric surface; heat is used to cause the dyestuff to sublime, that is, change from a solid on the paper to a gas to a solid on the fabric.

heat transmittance See *heat conductivity*.

heddles Devices on looms through which the warp yarns are threaded; the threading and shedding patterns determine the interlacing pattern.

held-back panel Window treatment in which the panels are held to the side by such devices as cords, chains, and medallions.

hemp A natural cellulosic fiber produced from the stem of a hemp plant.

henequin A natural cellulosic fiber used for rope and twine.

herringbone 1. Variation of the basic twill weave in which the direction of the visual diagonal is continually reversed. 2. Upholstery fabric produced with a herringbone weave.

hides Animal hides retrieved from such large animals as deer, horses, and cattle.

high-frequency welding A method of joining layers of fabric together in which an electrical charge connects the top and bottom layers, following the form of a mold or embossed plate.

high-low Name given to some multilevel cut and loop carpet surface textures; the higher tufts may have the appearance of shag textures.

high surface tension The molecules in the fabric have a higher affinity for one other; similar to raindrops beading up on a waxed car surface.

hiking See *elevator effect*.

hoghair Natural material used earlier as a filling in upholstered furniture cushions and in carpet cushions.

hollow fibers Manufactured fibers engineered to have hollow interiors for insulation without undue weight.

homespun A balanced plain weave fabric made of heavy, coarse yarns that resemble hand-spun yarns.

honeycomb shade Window treatment composed of spunbonded polyester fabric which is permanently pleated and paired to create a single- or double-cell structure with an insulating layer of air.

hopsacking A balanced plain weave or basket weave fabric with coarse, irregular yarns.

horsehair Natural material used earlier as a filling in upholstered cushions.

hot water extraction cleaning Properly diluted shampoo is driven into the pile as a spray by high-pressure jets; it is then immediately extracted by the vacuum component of the machine; also called steam extraction.

houndstooth check Broken-check motif said to resemble the tooth of a dog; produced by interlacing different colors of strategically placed yarns in a twill weave.

huck toweling (huckaback) Toweling woven on a dobby loom and having small filling floats that improve the drying efficiency of the towel and decreasing lint.

hue Color (e.g., blue, red, green, yellow).

hydrophilic fiber Fiber having strong attraction for water; also known as water-loving fiber.

hydrophobic fiber Fiber having low attraction for water; also known as water-hating fiber.

hygroscopic Fibers that absorb moisture without feeling wet.

ignition temperature Temperature at which a combustible material combines with oxygen, igniting to produce heat and such other combustion by-products as light and smoke; also known as kindling temperature.

ikat Hand print produced by artisans who tie off selected areas of bundled warp yarns and dye them prior to weaving.

impact insulation class (IIC) Numerical value used to indicate the effectiveness of a floor, carpet, cushion, or combination in reducing noise transmission; IIC values are roughly equal to the INR values plus 51.

impact noise rating (INR) Numerical value used to indicate the effectiveness of a floor, carpet, cushion, or combination in reducing noise transmission; INR values are roughly equal to IIC values minus 51.

impact or structurally borne sounds Sounds generated by impacts, such as walking, jumping, dropping items on the floor, and so on; concern is for their transmission as noise to interior spaces below.

implied warranty See *warranty, implied*.

indirect light Light reflected from walls, ceilings, doors, and furnishings.

indirect yarn numbering systems Systems in which the yarn number is determined as the length per unit of weight; as yarn number increases, size decreases; examples include the cc system, ll system, wc system, and wr system.

indoor air quality (IAQ) The air quality within and around buildings and structures, especially as it relates to the health, safety, and comfort of building occupants.

inflation Demand exceeds supply and prices rise.

Ingeo™ Registered trademark of Cargill for natural flame-resistant PLA.

ingrain A colonial-era flat-woven, yarn-dyed, reversible rug.

inherent color Natural color of fibers; may be retained for their natural beauty or removed to avoid interference with fashion colors.

initial cost Includes such variables as product price, accessories prices, fees for design professional, delivery charges, and installation charges.

inkjet printing Using electronically controlled jets to precisely deliver dye liquor to create detailed designs and pattern repeats.

innerspring mattress See *mattress, innerspring*.

institutional textiles A general term for the fabrics that are used in healthcare facilities, schools, and other institutions, such as kitchen and bath towels and bedding.

institutional toweling Twill-woven toweling produced with brightly colored stripes on each long side and constructed into towels used in restaurants.

insulation See *R-value or R-factor*.

insulative value Numerical indication of the ability to prevent the transfer of heat.

insulators Materials, including textile fibers, that offer resistance to the flow of electrons, allowing them to "pool" on their surfaces, readily available for transfer.

intensity Terms used to describe the purity or strength of a color (e.g., strong, weak); also known as chroma.

interim maintenance Maintenance activities designed to assure a high level of appearance retention for an extended period of time and to delay the need for restorative procedures.

interior acid rain Formed when vapor-phase moisture reacts with such gases such as sulfur oxide and nitrogen oxide and forms weak sulfuric acid and weak nitric acid; may attack chemical bonds within fibers, rupturing the polymer chains and weakening the fibers.

interlacing Point at which a yarn changes its position from one side of the fabric to the other.

interlining The layer of fabric in a drapery that is between the outer decorative fabric and the lining.

interlock stitch Interlooping yarns to create the appearance of two interknitted fabrics.

International Association of Bedding and Furniture Law Officials (IABFLO) Association made up of state officials who are responsible for the enforcement of consumer-oriented bedding and furniture laws in their respective states.

International Building Code (IBC) A model building code developed by the International Code Council (ICC) that has been adopted for use as a base code standard by most jurisdictions in the United States.

International Code Council (ICC) Organization that seeks to establish a single coordinated set of national codes.

International Down and Feather Bureau (IDFB) International trade association for the down and feather industry; promotes feather and down products worldwide and establishes international test methods and international standards.

International Down and Feather Testing Laboratory (IDFL) Global leader in down and feather and textile product testing; inspects and audits down and feather and textile factories and supply chains worldwide.

International Energy Conservation Code (IECC) A model code that addresses energy efficiency developed by The International Code Council (ICC) and the U.S. Department of Energy (DOE) Building Energy Codes Program in collaboration.

International Green Construction Code (IgCC) A model building code developed by the ICC that includes sustainability measures for entire construction projects and sites.

International Living Future Institute A nonprofit that works to build an ecologically minded world.

International Organization for Standardization (ISO) Acronym for International Organization for Standardization; engages in the development of standards to help foster international textile trade.

Intertek An organization offering eco-testing, supply chain audits, certification services, and life-cycle assessments for a large number of industries including textiles.

in-the-muslin Furniture offered covered in muslin so it subsequently can be covered with a variety of decorative slipcovers.

in-use performance Level of serviceability of a textile product while being used by the customer or client.

jabots Nonrigid side window treatments composed of pleated fabric; lower end may be level or angled; normally hung in front of ends of swagged valance.

Jacquard Decorative weave in which independent control of each warp yarns provides for an infinite variety of sheds, and, thus, extremely complex interlacing patterns.

Jacquard-woven tapestry A Jacquard-woven fabric that utilizes a warp of various colors arranged in multicolor bands that can be brought to the face as desired in order to achieve machine-woven fabrics that simulate handwoven tapestry fabrics.

jersey stitch Filling knitting stitch distinguished by herringbone-like wales on the fabric face and crescents or half-moon courses on the fabric back; subject to running.

jet beck Vessel used in the discontinuous dyeing of carpet in rope form; dye is introduced by jets.

jet printing See *inkjet printing*.

jet spraying Using pressurized dye jets to spray dye liquor onto skeins of yarns.

jig dyeing Fabric is passed through a stationary dye bath (not immersed), then the fabric reverses is passed through the dye bath.

jute A natural cellulose fiber used in carpet backing.

kapok A cellulosic fiber obtained from the seed pods of the kapok tree; use as a filling material has diminished.

khilim (kelim, kilim) rugs Rugs woven in eastern European countries; may have stylized designs depicting flowers, animals, and other natural things; may have slits; reversible.

kindling temperature See *ignition temperature*.

knee kicker Device used to grip and anchor the edges of carpet over the pins in tackless strips.

knife-edge treatment Use of a plain seam to join the fabric pieces of upholstery cushions.

knit-de-knit crinkling Texturing technique in which multifilament yarns are first knitted into a fabric that is then heat set and, subsequently, de-knitted or unraveled; introduces a wavy configuration.

knit-de-knit space dyeing Combining jet spraying with knit-de-knit crinkling to produce a texturized, space dyed (variegated) yarn.

knit-sewing See *stitch-knitting*

knitted pile fabrics A pile fabric produced through a knitting process.

knitting Interlooping yarns to create a fabric.

knop or knot yarn Complex yarns in which bits of tightly compacted and contrastingly colored fibers are incorporated into nubs.

knotting and twisting A machine-knitting procedure used primarily for producing certain curtains.

kraftcord Heavy, cord-like strands used in the back layers of woven floorcoverings.

K-value or K-factor Numerical value that reports the rate at which a material conducts heat.

lace Twisting fine fibers around one another.

lambrequin Rigid overhead window treatment with a straight cornice and side panels that protrude some distance from the wall and extend some distance down the sides of the window.

lampas A Jacquard-woven fabric characterized by elaborate woven-in designs typical of the 17th and 18th centuries. The designs are created by combining satin and sateen interlacings. Typically made with two sets of identically colored warp yarns and one or more sets of variously colored filling yarns.

lanolin Byproduct of the wool scouring process; the grease from the fleece.

lappet weave Surface-figure weave in which extra warp yarns are shifted laterally to create a zigzag surface pattern that resembles hand embroidery.

large-scale test methods Laboratory procedures which require large test specimens, in contrast to small-scale testing which requires small test specimens.

lastrol A generic subclass of elastic olefin.

latex foam Natural rubber or synthesized rubber having tiny, air-filled cells; used as an upholstered cushion filling material and as a carpet cushion material.

latex mattress Mattress made from natural or synthetic rubber.

Launder-Ometer Equipment used in accelerated testing for colorfastness to laundry and dry-cleaning agents.

law labels Labels required by law identifying contents and materials.

lay See *beater bar*.

Leadership in Energy and Environmental Design (LEED) Green Building rating system for developing high performance, sustainable buildings.

leaf Classifies cellulose fibers retrieved from the leaf portion of plants (e.g., abaca, banana, sisal).

lea system Used to determine the yarn number of yarns produced on the linen spinning system.

leather The hide or skin of an animal that has been processed to prevent rotting. It is used extensively to upholster furniture.

LEED Accredited Professional Accredited design professionals who have the knowledge and skills to supervise the LEED certification process.

LEED Green Associate A credential that signifies core competency in the green building principles developed by the USGBC.

left-hand twill Twill interlacing in which the visual diagonal ascends from left to right.

leno Decorative weave in which paired warp yarns cross as they encircle and secure the filling yarns.

leno-reinforced selvage Selvage in which a leno weave is used in the selvage areas.

let off A term that describes the forwarding of warp yarn off the warp beam as the weaving process progresses.

LEVEL® certification A certification for furniture based on an ANSI standard developed by BIFMA to differentiate environmentally preferable office furniture that has been manufactured in a socially responsible manner.

level of light transmission Degree to which light can pass through a medium.

level of openness Relative opacity of fabric; see also *fabric openness*.

licensing programs Voluntary programs in which companies sell the right to use their company-owned processes.

life-cycle assessment (LCA) An evaluation process that aids in identifying products, processes, or services that are environmentally preferable.

life-cycle cost (LCC) The total cost of a product during its expected use-life; includes initial purchase costs, installation charges, and long-term maintenance expenses; the total LCC values of several products may be amortized according to their respective life expectancies to show the annual use-cost of each.

life-cycle inventory (LCI) An analysis that creates an inventory of flows from, and back to, nature for a product-making system.

lightfastness Colorfastness to light.

light reflectance factor (LRF) Numerical value indicating the percentage of incident light being reflected by a carpet surface; complement of the LRF indicates the percentage of incident light being absorbed.

light resistance The characteristic of a material to maintain its character and color after exposure to varying degrees of light.

light transmittance value Numerical value indicating the amount of light passing through smoke generated during flaming and nonflaming conditions; values are converted into specific optical density values.

limited warranty See *warranty, limited*.

limiting oxygen index (LOI) Numerical value identifying the amount of oxygen required to support the combustion of a textile fiber.

linear density Weight or mass per unit of length; denier and tex indicate linear density.

line fibers Extremely long linen fibers, ranging from 12 inches to more than 24 inches.

linen Fabric made from flax fibers.

linens In earlier years, used as a collective term for sheets, towels, table cloths, napkins, and related products composed entirely or primarily of linen fibers; although the use of linen fabric in these goods has declined significantly, the term continues to be used.

lint Cotton after it has been ginned.

linters Short fibers covering the cotton seed after the ginning process.

liquor ratio Ratio of pounds of dye liquor to pounds of greige goods.

liseré A Jacquard-woven fabric made from two sets of warp yarns and one set of filling yarns. One set of warp yarns is typically identical in color to the filling yarns. The second set of warp yarns are various colored. Liseré is commonly characterized by patterned bands interspersed with satin-woven stripes.

Living Building Challenge A sustainable building certification program created in 2006 by the nonprofit International Living Future Institute.

llama Hair fiber retrieved from the South American llama, a domesticated animal of the camel family.

LL system Linen lea yarn numbering system; used to determine number of yarns produced on the linen spinning system; the ll number is equal to the number of 300-yard hanks of yarn produced from one pound of fiber.

loft See *loftiness*.

loftiness Quality of bulk without weight.

longitudinal configuration Lengthwise shape and form of textile fibers.

loom Machine that produces a woven fabric.

loop or curl yarn Complex yarns with open, airy loops.

loose-pillow styles Style of upholstered furniture having pillows that can be shifted or removed.

lumen Central canal of cotton fibers that provides the nutrients to the fiber as it matures.

luminosity See *value*.

luster The brightness of a fiber, yarn, or fabric; affected by cross-sectional shape, surface texture, presence or absence of delusterants, finishing agents, directional pile lay, etc.

luster washing See *chemical washing*.

lyocell Manufactured cellulose-based fibers composed of cellulose derived from trees grown on managed tree farms.

machine embroidering See *embroidering*.

machine stitching See *quilting, machine stitching*.

Magnuson-Moss Warranty Act U.S. Congressional law governing product warranties.

malipol Mali technique in which pile yarns are incorporated into the chain-stitched layers of base yarns.

manufactured fiber Usable fiber forms produced from monomers extracted or synthesized from natural compounds.

manufactured fiber producers Members of the industry who manufacture usable fiber forms using monomers extracted or synthesized from natural compounds.

marled Descriptive of the color styling produced by spinning together two differently colored rovings.

marquisette A transparent leno-woven fabric composed of fine filament yarns.

Martindale Abrasion Test Method Method used to evaluate the flat abrasion resistance of fabric.

matelassé A doublecloth fabric that incorporates the multiple sets of yarns to simulate a quilted three dimensional look. Pockets are formed in the motif and typically, a third set of filling yarns floats in pockets to create a puffy appearance and enhance the quilted look.

Material Safety Data Sheet Documentation that identifies hazardous chemicals and the health hazards for individuals coming into contact with such items.

mattress covers Beddings designed to completely encase the mattress or to cover only the exposed surfaces; may have vinyl film sheeting to protect against moisture.

mattress, foam-core Mattresses filled with a slab of rubber or urethane foam; support determined by the foam density.

mattress, innerspring Mattress filled with metal springs that are anchored to one another with metal clips or encased in fabric and sewn together.

mattress pads Beddings designed to provide extra cushioning and to protect the mattress; generally a multicomponent quilted structure.

mattress, pillow-top Mattresses that are manufactured with an extra layer of soft cushioning attached to the mattress surface.

mechanical flocking Sifting flock through a screen to embed itself in a coated surface.

mechanically frothed polyurethane cushions Polyurethane chemicals combined with reinforcing fillers that are frothed with air while in a liquid state. The result is a denser, firmer type of foam that can be attached directly to the carpet or used as a separate cushion.

medulla Central part of a wool fiber that contains hollow, honeycombed-shaped cells.

melt spinning Heat is used to dissolve the polymer compound; cold causes the filaments to solidify following extrusion.

Memorandum of Understanding (MOU) for Carpet Stewardship Document that established a plan to increase the amount of recycling and reuse of post-consumer carpet and to reduce the amount of waste carpet going into landfills.

memory foam Foam that is slow to return to its original shape after weight is removed.

mercerization Treatment of cotton or linen fibers, yarns, or fabrics with NaOH and tension to improve the strength, absorption, or luster.

metallic fibers Fibers that have the appearance of, or are made from, metals.

metallic yarns Yarns made of colored particles or colored foil encased in clear sheeting that is then slit into thin, yarn-like strands.

methenamine tablet test Flammability test method in which a methenamine tablet is used as the ignition source, simulating a burning match, an ignited cigarette, or a glowing ember; also known as the pill test.

microbes See *bacteria* and *fungi*.

microencapsulation A substance is contained in nanosized capsules within the fiber structure; as the fabric moves against the skin, the capsules break and release the contents.

microfiber A fiber with denier of less than 1.

micrometer 1/1,000 millimeter or 1/25,400 inch

microscopic voids Minute tunnels or conduits that are lengthwise within fibers; deflect incident light waves, obscuring the appearance of soil.

migration Movement of dye through fabric; results in varied levels of intensity.

mildew Growth caused by spore-forming fungi; may result in discoloration, odor, and fiber degradation.

mineral fiber Fibers that come from the ground.

minor protein fiber A protein fiber that captures only a small percentage of market share.

modacrylic A manufactured synthetic fiber with relatively high flame resistance.

Modal® A registered trade name for a variety of rayon derived exclusively from beech trees.

model codes A code that is developed and maintained by a standards organization independent of the jurisdiction responsible for enacting the code.

modern rugs Oriental rugs produced during the twentieth century.

mohair Hair fiber retrieved from Angora goat; often used in loop yarns.

moiré Finish characterized by a wood-grain or water-marked effect.

moisture regain values Calculations of the ability of fibers to absorb vapor-phase moisture; % moisture regain is determined by subtracting the dry weight of a specimen from its conditioned weight, dividing the result by the dry weight, and multiplying by 100.

molas Textile accents created with a reverse appliqué technique.

momie weave Fabrics with a random or irregular, interlacing pattern and characterized by a rough, pebbly surface. These fabrics are also referred to as crepe weaves.

monk's cloth A basket-woven fabric typically produced in a 4 × 4 interlacing, but a 2 × 2 pattern may also be used.

monofilament yarn Simple yarn composed of a single filament; used in sheer curtain fabrics and as transparent sewing thread.

monomer Basic building block of textile fibers; several monomers are linked end-to-end to form polymers.

mordant Compound, usually metallic salt, used to increase the attraction between fibers and dyestuffs.

moresque Descriptive term used to identify color effect of ply yarn formed by twisting different colors of single yarns.

mosquito netting Transparent leno-weave fabric used as a curtain-like bed canopy in tropical climates, forming a barrier against mosquitoes.

moth resistance Ability of wool fibers to resist attack by moth larvae; may be permanently incorporated by introducing a methane group between the sulfur atoms.

MTS An acronym for the Institute for Market Transformation Sustainability, best known for their SMaRT certification program for building products, fabric, apparel, textiles, and flooring.

multifilament yarn Simple yarn composed of several filaments.

multi-tier café curtains Window treatment style in which tiers of café curtains overlap one another.

muslin An undyed, plain-woven fabric composed of carded cotton yarns.

MVSS 302 Acronym for Motor Vehicle Safety Standard No. 302; designed to reduce deaths and injuries to motor vehicle occupants caused by vehicle fires, especially those originating in the interior of the vehicle from sources such as matches or cigarettes.

nailhead trimming Using nails to secure heavier upholstery coverings, such as genuine leather to framework.

nanometer Unit of measure equal to one billionth of a meter.

nanotechnology The science and technology of manipulating structures at the molecular level.

nap Directional orientation of yarns in pile layers; also known as pile sweep, pile lay, and directional pile lay.

naphthalene Agents used to make wool moth resistant.

napping Conversion operation in which fiber ends are teased to the surface, making it fuzzy, soft, and warmer.

National Electronic Injury Surveillance System (NEISS) A surveillance and follow-up system administered by the U.S. Consumer Product Safety Commission for collecting data on consumer product-related injuries occurring in the United States.

National Fire Protection Association (NFPA) A voluntary scientific association concerned with fire safety.

National Highway Traffic Safety Administration (NHTSA) Government agency that oversees the flammability of items used in motor vehicles.

National Institute of Standards and Technology (NIST) A physical sciences laboratory that is a nonregulatory agency of the U.S. Department of Commerce with the mission of promoting innovation and industrial competitiveness.

natural-colored cotton Cotton grown naturally in colors of browns, greens, tans, green and rust.

natural fiber Fibers found in nature and used in the same form from which they are found.

natural fiber suppliers Businesses that provide already-formed or readymade fibers, principally from sheep, silk caterpillars, cotton bolls, and flax plants.

natural man-made fiber producer Members of the industry who manufacture usable fiber forms by synthesizing natural compounds through chemical and mechanical methods.

needle count Number of needles per crosswise inch on tufting machines.

needle punch Fabrication technique in which barbed needles are used to introduce a mechanical chain-stitch in a fibrous batting.

nestling down Underdeveloped down made up of soft fluffy barbs radiating from a sheath. Nestling down does not have quills.

net fabric A general term for fabrics that are openly knitted or woven.

new wool See *wool, virgin*.

NFPA 101® Life Safety Code Publication of the NFPA; includes recommendations to reduce the extent of injury, loss of life, and destruction of property from fire; includes the design of egress facilities permitting the prompt escape of occupants from burning buildings or into safe areas within the buildings.

NFPA 701 Standard methods of fire tests for flame-resistant textiles and films; includes Test Method 1 and 2.

ninon A plain-weave, sheer fabric characterized by omitting every third warp yarn.

nodes Markings similar to the cross marking on bamboo and corn plants; keeps the flax fiber from collapsing.

noil Relatively short cotton staples; separated and removed when producing combed cotton yarns.

noise Unwanted sound.

noise reduction coefficient (NRC) Numerical value that indicates the effectiveness of textile floor and wallcoverings at absorbing sound.

noise transmission Transmission of unwanted sound to other interior areas; especially important in multilevel structures, where impact sounds can be transmitted to the interior spaces below.

noncellulosic manufactured fibers Fibers manufactured from compounds other than cellulose; includes such fibers as nylon, polyester, acrylic, and spandex.

noncombustible fiber Fiber that does not burn or contribute significant amounts of smoke; may undergo pyrolysis.

nontraversing panel Stationary curtain or drapery treatments.

nonwaterfowl feathers Feathers derived from chickens, turkeys, and other land fowl.

nonwoven fabric Fabric produced by stabilizing fibrous batts.

Nottingham lace Flat lace or net with warp and filling yarns; machine-made.

novelty yarns Yarns that feature unusual features such as varying thicknesses, nubs, slubs, seeds, and multicolor effects.

NSF International NSF is an independent global organization committed to protecting public health and the environment through the development of standards and guidelines.

nub yarn Complex yarn with tightly compacted projections created at irregular intervals along its length; also known as spot or knot yarns.

nylon A manufactured synthetic fiber commonly used in carpeting and upholstery fabric.

nylon cap Web of nylon fibers needle punched into face of primary backing; color-coordinated with pile yarn.

Occupational Safety and Health Administration (OSHA) Agency with the goal of saving lives and preventing and controlling disease, injury, and disability.

Oeko-Tex 100 Standard A standard devised by the International Oeko-Tex Association used to evaluate textiles for harmful substances in processed textiles that come into direct or near contact with the skin.

off-gassing Refers to the release of volatile organic compounds (chemicals) into the air we breathe, both inside and outside.

off-grain Yarn alignment that exhibits filling bow or filling skew.

off-grain fabric A fabric in which the warp and filling yarns do not intersect at a right angle.

oil-borne stain Stain carried by an oily compound.

olefin A manufactured synthetic fiber used in wallcovering, rugs and upholstered furniture.

oleophilic fiber Fiber which exhibits a strong attraction to oily stains.

oleophobic Oil-hating; resistant to oily soil.

ombré Descriptive of the color styling produced by a gradual change in the level of intensity of a single hue.

one-way draw draperies Window treatment on a traverse rod that allows the movement of all of the fabric to one end of the rod.

opacity Level of fabric openness in which light is not permitted to pass through fabric.

opening and cleaning Initial operation in yarn spinning process; opening the bale of cotton and cleaning the fibers.

optical brighteners See *fluorescent compounds*.

optical density The amount of light capable of being transmitted through smoke.

optical properties Fiber characteristics such as color, luster, apparent whiteness and brightness, and soil hiding.

organdy A transparent, lightweight, plain weave, cotton fabric. It has a stiff hand that is created by exposing the fabric to a weak solution of sulfuric acid.

organically grown Fibers cultivated on land that has been chemical free for a minimum of three years, and without the use of chemicals.

organic cotton Cotton grown without synthetic chemicals.

organic wool Wool that is produced in accordance with federal standards for organic livestock production.

organza A lightweight, sheer, plain weave fabric with a crisp hand. Characterized by filament yarns, it is typically made from polyester, nylon, or silk.

Oriental design rugs Machine-made rugs having traditional Oriental patterns; generally woven on an Axminster loom.

Oriental rugs Hand-woven rugs having hand-knotted pile tufts; see also *Ghiordes knot* and *Sehna knot*.

oriented polymer chain Polymer arrangement in which the polymer chains are aligned in the direction of the long axis of the fiber.

Oscillatory Cylinder Method Test method used to measure the abrasion resistance of textile fabrics; also known as ASTM D 4157 and the Wyzenbeek test method.

osnaburg A fabric backing that weighs an average of 2.0 ounces per square yard, used with Type II wallcoverings.

ottoman Filling-rib woven upholstery fabric; has large, flat ribs of equal size and spacing or of unequal size and spacing.

out-of-register When rollers are improperly aligned in a roller print, resulting in a print that does not line up

overdraperies Draperies that are hung in combination with sheers.

overhead treatment Drapery treatment that covers and conceals panel headings and hardware.

overprinting Printing dye paste or pigments over an initial color application.

over-the-counter fabric Refers to lengths of piece goods or fabric sold by retail distributors; also called OTC fabric.

over-the-wire construction technique Fabrication in which the pile yarns are supported by wires during weaving; knives have smooth or sharp ends to leave the pile in loops or cut tufts as they are removed.

oxygen number Indicates product cleanliness. The lower the number the better, the cleaner samples.

ozone fading Color loss as a result of exposure to ozone.

package dyeing Immersing yarns wound on perforated cylinders, that is, packages, into dye liquor held in a dye beck.

package-injection technique Using astrojets to repeatedly "inject" packages of yarn with dye liquor.

packages The cone or tube that yarn is wound on in preparation for weaving or knitting.

pad dyeing Fabric passes through the dye bath, then through the rollers, where the dye solution is squeezed into the fabric.

palm grass A natural fiber often used for wooden frame chair seats.

panel fabrics Fabric that is developed primarily to be upholstered on moveable walls in office systems furniture.

panels The moveable walls in office systems furniture.

panné velvet Velvet fabric that has a pronounced nap.

Paragraph 25.853 (b) The Federal Aviation Administration (FAA) flammability regulation for textiles used in compartments occupied by the crew or passengers in airplanes.

partial blackout Reduction of the level of light transmission in which most of the incident rays are blocked.

pattern damask Damask fabric used in ticking.

pattern drafts Graphic representations of interlacing patterns; also known as point designs and print designs.

pattern repeat In patterned goods, a repetition of the full pattern of motifs and ground.

peace silk Cultivated silk that is obtained without destroying the silk worms.

pearl yarns Fine cords formed by plying three two-ply yarns composed of mercerized cotton; used in hand embroidering.

pentabromodiphenyl (PentaBDE) A type of polybrominated diphenyl ether flame retardant used extensively in foams.

percale A balanced, plain weave, sheeting fabric typically composed of fine, combed yarns. The fabric count ranges from 168 to 220.

permanent press See *durable press finishing*.

permeability With respect to the acoustic value of carpet, cushions, and carpet/cushion assemblies, the more permeable the structures, the more efficiently they will absorb sound, lessening the level of noise within an interior; at the same time, the more permeable the structures, the more likely they will allow noise to be transmitted to interior spaces below.

permethrin Compound used to modify the disulfide linkages in wool, making the fibers mothproof.

Persian knot Knot used in authentic Oriental rugs; can be tied to slant to the left or to the right; also known as the Sehna knot.

Persian yarns Loosely twisted three-ply strands composed of wool; used in needlepoint stitching.

pick One filling or weft yarn.

picking The second step in weaving in which the filling yarn or pick is inserted through the shed.

piece A bolt of fabric. Usually (approximately) 55 to 60 yards long for upholstery, 45 yards for heavy materials such as pile fabrics, and 75 to 80 yards for lightweight drapery.

piece dyeing Immersing piece goods into dye liquor.

pigment print Color styling in which opaque pigments are applied.

pigments Insoluble dyestuffs.

pile density Value indicating number of pile tufts per square inch; with tufted constructions, calculate by multiplying the needle count by the stitches per inch; with woven constructions, calculate by multiplying the pitch divided by 27 by the number of rows or wires per inch.

pile height The length of the pile tufts above the backing.

pile lay See *nap*.

pile reversal Pile yarns crushed to lay in opposing directions; area appears as a large stain; also known as watermarking, shading, and pooling.

pile sweep See *nap*.

pile thickness Average thickness of the pile material above the backing.

pile warp yarns Warp yarns used to form pile layer; used with velvet and most woven floorcoverings; also known as face yarns.

pile yarn integrity Ability of pile yarns to retain their original level of twist.

pile yarns See *face yarns*.

pile yarn weight The weight of the yarns used in the wear layer and those portions of the pile yarns that extend into the backing layer; expressed in ounces per square yard.

pilling The formation of balls of fiber on the surface of textile fabrics.

pillow sham A decorative casing for bed pillows which often has contrasting piping and ruffles.

pillow-top mattress See *mattress, pillow-top*.

pills Unsightly bunches or balls of fiber formed on fabric surfaces.

pima cotton Cotton grown in the American southwest; fine and up to 1⅝ inches in length.

piña A leaf fiber obtained from the pineapple plant.

pinned-up panels Window treatment style in which the fabric panels are held by two-piece, stylized magnets or by decorative pins that function like large tie-backs.

pinsonic melding See *quilting*.

pinwale piqué A dobby-woven fabric containing fine lengthwise ribs.

pitch Number of pile tufts per 27 inches of width in a woven floorcovering.

PLA A manufactured biopolymer fiber produced from corn (polylactic acid).

plaid twill Twill weave with linear patterns that intersect at right angles to each other.

plain weave Simple interlacing in which warp and filling yarns alternately cross one another; also known as tabby weave and homespun weave.

planting Periodically substituting a colored pile yarn for a basic pile yarn in Wilton carpet weaving; reduces quantity of buried yarns and, thus, yarn costs.

plied slub yarn Complex ply yarns have a decorative slub yarn plied with a simple ply yarn or with a second slub yarn.

plumule Plumage consisting of soft quills and barbs.

plush One level, cut pile surface texture; pile height ranges from 0.625 inch to 0.750 inch; also known as *velvet* and *velvet plush*.

ply yarn Yarn formed by twisting two or more single yarns.

pocket cloth A doublecloth fabric that contains two sets of warp yarns and two sets of filling yarns. The pockets are created by weaving two fabrics together on the same loom.

pollutant gases Atmospheric gases such as oxides of nitrogen and oxides of sulfur that react with vapor-phase moisture to form weak acids; cause shade changes and fiber tendering.

Pollution Prevention Act Enacted in 1990 to promote pollution prevention through hazardous substance reduction and increased efficiency.

polybrominated diphenyl ethers (PBDEs) Flame retardants containing certain bioaccumulative chemicals that are toxic to both humans and the environment.

polyester The most widely used manufactured synthetic fiber.

polyethylene terephthalate (PET) A clear, strong, and lightweight plastic that is widely used for textiles as well as packaged foods and beverages.

polymer Compound composed of extremely long, chain-like molecules.

polymer additives Compounds added to polymer solutions to engineer specific properties (e.g., reduced luster, reduced static propensity, colorfastness). See also *additives*.

polymer film sheeting Fabric produced by forming polymer solutions into a thin film.

polymerization Extent to which monomers link to form polymer chains.

polymer tape Yarn-like structures produced by slitting film sheeting into long strands of the desired width.

polypropylene Term commonly used in the interior design industry for olefin fibers and fabrics.

polyurethane foam See *memory foam*.

polyvinyl chloride (PVC) One of the most widely produced synthetic plastic polymers, used in many forms and many building and furnishing applications.

pooling Collecting of electrons on fiber surfaces, making them readily available for transfer to shoe soles or other surfaces.

post-consumer Products that have been used in the consumer marketplace. Most commonly used to refer to the recycling, or potential recycling, of these products.

post-industrial Materials that have not left the manufacturing facility and therefore have not been used in the consumer marketplace. Most commonly used to refer to the recycling, or potential recycling, of such materials.

pouf or bishop's sleeve treatment Drapery treatment in which tiers of bouffant or billowed-out areas are created by periodically gathering the fabric panels; also known as bishop's sleeve treatment.

power stretcher Device used to place uniform stretch over carpet in wall-to-wall installations.

preventive maintenance Protective cleaning procedures intended to capture soil and grit in track-off, funnel, and concentrated traffic areas.

primary backing Carpet base fabric into which pile yarns are tufted.

primary wall Outercovering of the cotton fiber.

print design Graphic representation of color positions in textile structures.

printing A technique in which color (usually dye) is applied only to certain areas of the surface of the cloth or other surface in order to create a design.

priscilla curtains Window treatment in which ruffled panels overlap at their upper edges and are held-back by ruffled tie-backs.

privacy curtains Curtains used as room dividers in healthcare facilities. Also called *cubicle curtains*.

project bid Detailed price listing of all products specified for a particular project.

project specification A listing of multiple performance criteria that should lead to a single product specification.

Proposition 65 A California law that aims to protect drinking water sources, and to eliminate exposure generally, from toxic substances. Formerly The Safe Drinking Water and Toxic Enforcement Act of 1986.

protein fibers Natural fibers of animal origin.

pure down See *all down*.

pure silk 100 percent silk fabric that does not contain any metallic weighting compounds.

pyrolysis Process in which high temperature causes the decomposition of textile fibers and other organic materials, which in turn produce combustible materials.

quality-control work Work undertaken by members of the industry to ensure the quality of their products; often use standard methods of testing and performance specifications.

quarter-drop-match pattern A pattern structure in which figures in one repeat unit match one-quarter of the repeat on the opposite edge so that successive pieces of carpet are shifted and aligned to create a diagonal pattern.

quill Device used to hold the filling yarns during weaving; also known as a bobbin.

quilting To stitch two pieces of fabric and a filling material together; stitches may create a decorative surface pattern.

quilting, machine stitching Commercial quilting using many needles to join separate components and to impart a surface pattern.

quilting, pinsonic melding Commercial quilting using heat and sound waves to meld separate components at specific points; meld points simulate the appearance of sewn quilting stitches.

quilts Multicomponent bed coverings usually having a face fabric, a fibrous or polyurethane batting, and a back fabric; layers are secured with hand or machine quilting stitches.

quivit Fine fiber obtained from the underbelly of the domesticated musk ox.

radiant energy Energy, such as heat or light, which is transmitted in waves.

radiant heat Heat that is transferred in the form of waves or rays.

radiation Mechanism by which heat is transferred in the form of waves or rays.

rag rug A rug made from small strips of fabric. The strips may be tufted into a base fabric or used as a filling in a woven fabric.

railroad Cutting upholstery fabric so that the lengthwise grain aligns crosswise on the cushions, given that the fabric motifs and repeats do not directional features.

raised fiber surfaces Fabric surfaces that have been napped or brushed to raise fibers from yarns to give a soft, fuzzy hand; examples are flannelette and flannel.

ramie Cellulosic fiber retrieved from stem portion of plants; also called China grass.

random shear Multilevel, cut and loop pile in which the uppermost portions of some of the higher yarn tufts are sheared.

rapier Device used in picking to carry the filling yarn to the center of the shed where it is picked up by a second rapier and carried to the opposite selvage.

raschel knitting Warp knit.

raschel stitching Versatile warp knitting operation using up to 30 guide bars which select and positions the various yarns in preparation of knitting.

ratiné yarn Complex yarn with small, uniformly spaced loops of equal size.

ratings Refers to how, based on a given scale, a product, service, or method ranks based on guidelines or standards. Environmental building ratings are typically used to evaluate construction practices that result in energy-efficient, healthier and environmentally sustainable buildings.

raveling Fraying at the cut edges of a woven or knitted fabric when threads start to come apart.

raw silk Silk from which the natural gum, sericin, has not been removed.

rayon A manufactured fiber composed of regenerated cellulose.

reclined diagonal Visual diagonal in a twill weave fabric that falls at an angle less than 45 degrees to the fabric grain.

recycled wool See *wool, recycled*.

recycling Major component of the environmental movement to reduce ecological damage.

reed Comb-like device held by the beater bar; has openings through which the warp yarns are threaded.

reeling Silk process in which the natural gum, sericin, is softened and skilled technicians collect the filaments and unwind the cocoons.

regenerated fibers Manufactured fiber that are produced using raw materials from nature.

regular diagonal Visual diagonal in a twill weave fabric that falls at an angle of 45 degrees to the fabric grain.

regulatory agencies Municipal, state, or federal agencies that have jurisdiction to oversee and power to regulate product selection and/or marketing.

reinforced rubber carpet cushions Carpet cushions made from ground tire scrap rubber granules bonded with latex.

relative humidity The proportion of vapor-phase moisture present in air to the maximum possible at a given temperature; expressed as a percentage.

relaxation shrinkage Shrinkage of yarns; occurs when yarns recover or relax from strains imposed by manufacturing stresses.

rep A filling-rib weave fabric with fine ribs that are slightly larger than those of taffeta.

reprocessed wool See *wool, reprocessed*.

repurposing Adapting an existing product for a different use.

residential interiors Interiors in private residences (e.g., mobile homes, apartments, condominiums, town homes, free-standing homes).

residual shrinkage Shrinkage of fibers; fibers become progressively shorter during use and care.

residue Matter that remains at the end of a burning test.

resiliency Ability of a textile structure to recover from folding, bending, crushing and twisting.

resilient batting Three-dimensional fibrous structure that springs back into its original shape after being compressed.

resin compounds Compounds used to improve the resiliency and dimensional stability of fabrics composed of cellulosic fibers.

resist printing Immersing a fabric that has been selectively printed with an agent that will resist penetration of the dye liquor.

Resource Conservation and Recovery Act The principal U.S. federal law that governs the disposal of solid waste and hazardous waste.

restorative maintenance Maintenance involving overall or wall-to-wall cleaning.

retting Process in which moisture and bacteria or chemicals are used to dissolve the binding agents, known as pectins, in the bark-like covering of flax stalks.

reverse appliqué See *appliqué, reverse.*

reversible blanketing See *blanketing, double-faced.*

ribcord A warp-rib weave fabric created by combining fine and coarse yarns.

rib weave A woven fabric with distinctive crosswise or lengthwise ribs or ridges.

right-hand twill Twill interlacing in which the visual diagonal ascends from right to left.

rippling Process in which flax stalks are pulled through a coarse metal comb to remove the seeds, which will be processed to retrieve linseed oil.

roller printing Using engraved copper-covered rollers to transfer dye paste to the surface of fabrics.

roller shade Fabric or other material mounted on a spring-loaded cylinder mounted on a window frame, allowing the fabric to be pulled down to cover the window or rolled up on the cylinder.

rollgoods Soft floorcoverings available in widths of 9, 12, and 15 feet and long lengths.

Roman shades Window coverings that hang flat at the window until pleats form when panels are raised; may be constructed of textile fabric or woven wood.

room-fit rugs Loose-laid rugs designed or cut to come within one or two inches of the walls.

room-size rugs Loose-laid rugs that are designed or cut to come within 12 inches of each wall.

rope Simple yarn formed by plying two or more cable yarns.

rotary screen printing Printing textile surfaces by forcing dye paste through openings in cylindrical-shaped screens; selected areas of the screens are treated to resist flow through of the dye paste.

routine maintenance Practices such as regular vacuuming to remove accumulated dust.

roving A strand of fibers that is only slightly twisted.

rows per inch The number of crosswise rows of pile tufts per lengthwise inch in Axminster and chenille floorcoverings.

ruffled, tie-back curtains Window treatments in which ruffled panels do not cross at their upper edges.

rug Soft floorcovering that is loose-laid on floor or over wall-to-wall carpet.

runner A long, narrow form of a room-fit rug installed in hallways and on stairs.

rush Strands produced by twisting two or three flat cattail leaves together used to make chair seats or backs.

R-value or R-factor Numerical value indicating how effectively a structure resists heat flow, that is, how effectively it insulates and prevents heat exchange; R-value equals the thickness of the structure divided by its K-value.

rya rugs Hand-knotted rugs; originated in Scandinavian countries; pile may be from one to three inches.

rya stick See *flossa stick.*

saddle (carpet term) A seam condition with parallel seams on each side of a doorway.

Safe Drinking Water Act The principal U.S. federal law that intends to ensure safe drinking water for the public.

Safety Data Sheets (SDS) A record, provided by a manufacturer, that provides comprehensive technical information about a substance or material. Also called *Material Safety Data Sheet.*

salvage maintenance Maintenance procedures used for extremely soiled carpet or for removing built-up residue.

sample labeling A producer or distributor's voluntary labeling on product samples that includes style, color, content, and design names.

saran A manufactured synthetic with excellent weathering properties.

sash curtains Window treatment in which the panels are anchored at their upper and lower edges; typically used on French doors.

sateen A filling-faced satin weave fabric with a soft luster. The majority of the filling yarns float across the face of the fabric. Characterized by spun yarns and typically made of cotton. Not as commonly used as warp sateen. See also *warp sateen.*

satin A warp-faced satin weave fabric created by floating each warp yarn over 4 or more filling yarns. Characterized by filament yarns and typically made of acetate, nylon or polyester. Most often produced with a high luster but is available with a matte appearance as well.

Savonnerie rugs French Oriental rugs originally made in a factory used earlier for the production of soap; distinguished by classic designs and soft pastel colors.

Saxony One level, cut pile surface texture; pile height ranges from 0.625 to 0.750 inches; yarn twist is stabilized by heat setting.

scales The outercovering of a wool fiber resembling fish scales.

scatter rugs Small rugs, often 2 feet by 3 feet; often decorative accents.

schreinering Calendering process in which etched rollers impart minute diagonal "hills and valleys" into the fabric surface; gives soft luster.

scouring The process of removing sand, dirt, plant material, and dried body excrement from the wool fiber.

screen printing See *flat-bed screen printing* and *rotary screen printing*.

screen shade See *solar shade*.

scrim Flat woven fabric with low fabric count; used as backing in tufted floorcoverings and as reinforcing layer in needle punched carpet, hair cushions, and spunbonded fabrics.

SCS Global A third-party provider of certification, auditing and testing services, and standards for specific environmental claims.

SCS Indoor Advantage Gold The highest-level certification offered by SCS Global Services for indoor air standards of products.

sculptured Multilevel cut and loop pile surface texture; in most cases, the higher loops are all cut and the lower loops are all uncut.

scutching Linen processing in which the degraded woody core of the flax plant is removed from the linen fiber bundles.

SeaCell® A modified lyocell fiber with a natural anti-inflammatory and skin protection additive.

sea grass Yarn-like structure produced by twisting plied strands of grass into a cord; used in wallcoverings.

Sea Island cotton Variety of cotton grown originally off the coast of Georgia; up to 2½ inches in length.

seams A line along which two pieces of fabric are sewn together.

seam slippage The pulling apart or separation of fabric at seams, which causes gaps or holes in the garment or upholstery.

secondary backing See *scrim*.

secondary wall Part of the wool fiber made up of layers of cellulose.

seed fibers Natural fibers retrieved from the seeds of plants.

seed yarn Complex yarn with tiny nubs.

Sehna (Senna) knot Hand-tied knot used in the production of some authentic Oriental rugs; also known as Persian knot.

self-deck treatment Use of the exposed outercovering fabric to cover the deck.

self-extinguishing Fiber that stops burning when the source of ignition heat is removed.

self-welt A fabric-covered cord inserted in seam lines of upholstered furniture coverings that matches the body cloth of the piece of furniture.

selvages, selvedges Narrow band on each side of a woven fabric; see also *compacted selvage, conventional selvage, leno-reinforced selvage,* and *tucked-in selvage*.

semi-antique rugs Oriental rugs woven during the latter part of the nineteenth century.

serging Machine overcasting.

sericin Natural gum binding silk filaments into a cocoon.

sericulture The growth of silkworms and the production of cultivated silk.

set-match patterns Patterns that repeat themselves across the width of carpet or wallpaper; the crosswise repeats may be fully completed or partially completed.

shade Color feature produced by adding a compound known to absorb all wavelengths, creating black, to a colorant, decreasing its value and luminosity.

shade changes Fading of original hue after exposure to such things as sunlight, laundry, and gases; may be evaluated, for example, with the AATCC Gray Scale for Color Change.

shading See *pile reversal*.

shading coefficient (S/C) Numerical rating that indicates light transmission in relation to temperature flow; calculated by dividing the total amount of heat transmitted by a window and window covering combination by the total amount of heat transmitted by a single pane of clear glass 1/8 inch in thickness.

shag One level, cut pile surface texture; pile height may be as high as 1.250 inches; pile density is lower than that of plush and Saxony textures.

shantung A filling-rib weave fabric characterized by filament warp yarns and an irregular surface due to spun thick and thin yarns in the filling direction.

shearing Conversion operation in which raised fiber and pile surfaces are cut to be level.

shed V-shaped opening of the warp yarns through which the filling pick is inserted.

shedding 1. Occurs with new carpet when short lengths of fibers that have accumulated during manufacturing work to the surface; fiber loss is not significant. 2. In weaving operations, using the harnesses to raise some warp yarns and lower others, creating the shed.

sheen A soft luster on a surface.

sheers Very thin window coverings typically used for privacy.

sheet casings Covers that protect comforters from soil accumulation and abrasion; their releasable closures permit easy removal for laundering.

sheets, flat Sheets constructed with hems at both ends; may be used as top or bottom sheets.

shift mark Distorted yarn group.

shirring Gathering fabric; seen with Austrian shades and bedspread drops.

shots Filling yarns used in machine-woven floorcoverings.

shrinkage See *relaxation shrinkage* and *residual shrinkage*.

shrinkage resistance The ability of a fiber to retain its original shape during care procedures.

shutters Decorative panels hung at the sides of windows; may be stationary or unfolded to cover the glass to reduce heat exchange.

shuttle Canoe-shaped device used to carry the filling picks through the shed.

shuttleless looms Looms which have devices other than shuttles to carry the filling picks through the shed (e.g., grippers, rapiers, jets of water, jets of air).

shuttle loom Conventional loom that has a shuttle attachment.

silencers Felt or heavily napped fabric placed under tablecloths; cushion the impact force of dishes, artifacts, and so on.

silicone A specific class of synthetic polymer materials that are typically resistant to chemical attack and insensitive to temperature changes.

silicone compounds Agents used to impart water repellency.

silk A natural protein fiber produced by the larva of silk moths; used in apparel and home furnishings.

Silk Latte® A registered trade name for an azlon fiber; made from milk protein.

simple cord yarns Simple yarns formed by twisting or plying together two or more simple ply yarns.

simple ply yarns Simple yarns formed by twisting or plying together two or more simple single yarns.

simple single yarns Simple yarns formed by spinning staple fibers into a simple yarn or by combining several filaments into a simple yarn with or without twist.

simple yarns Yarns having a smooth appearance and a uniform diameter along their length.

simulated fur fabrics Pile fabrics formed by incorporating fibers or yarns among base yarns, creating a three-dimensional structure; fiber composition is often acrylic or modacrylic.

simulated leather Fabric manufactured by coating a base structure with foam or bonding a base structure with film sheeting; often embossed to impart grain markings.

simulated suede Fabric manufactured by emerizing a coated fabric to roughen the surface, imparting a suede-like hand and appearance.

singeing The burning of fiber ends projecting from the surface of a fabric to reduce pilling.

sisal A natural cellulosic, relatively stiff fiber retrieved from the leaves of the agave or yucca plant; used for ropes and placemats.

skein dyeing Immersing skeins of yarns into a dyebath.

skew Distorted yarn alignment in woven fabric; filling yarns slant below straight crosswise grain.

skins Animal skins retrieved from such small animals as lambs, goats, and calves.

skirt Fabric added to the base of an upholstered furniture item to conceal the legs.

slab cushions Three-dimensional foam structures used in upholstered furniture.

slabs Three-dimensional structure generally composed of synthesized rubber or polyurethane foam; used as filling layer in mattresses and quilts.

slack tension technique Weaving technique in which the base warp yarns are held under regular (high) tension and the pile warp yarns are held under slackened tension; used to produce terry toweling.

slashing Adding starch or sizing to the warp yarns prior to weaving to make them smoother and stronger.

slipcovers Furniture coverings that are cut, seamed, and fitted over the permanently attached coverings; used for protection and/or decorative purposes.

sliver A small, thin, narrow piece of fiber.

slub yarn Complex single yarn with fine and coarse segments along its length, which are produced by varying the level of twist used in spinning.

small-scale test methods Tests used in the laboratory to measure specific flammability characteristics. See also *large-scale test methods*.

smoke density Concentration of smoke passing through light measured numerically as the light transmission value and reported as optical density value.

smoke generation The amount of airborne solid materials under flaming and nonflaming (smoldering) conditions. The purpose of such testing is to identify materials that would generate large volumes of dense smoke.

smoldering Flameless combustion.

smoothing Laying pile yarns in one direction after the surface has been brushed.

snarl yarn See *spike yarn*.

Social Security Administration (SSA) Government agency that administers the Medicare and Medicaid programs.

sofa bed An upholstered sofa with a hinged back that swings down flat with the seating cushions to form the sleeping surface.

soil Dirt or other foreign matter that is mechanically held and comparatively easy to remove.

soil hiding The ability of a fiber or coloration to hide or camouflage dirt; carpet, for example, will look cleaner than it is.

soil magnification Occurs when soil particles reflect incident light waves through round, nondelustered fiber; carpet, for example, will look dirtier than it is.

soil reduction Reduction of the quantity of soil accumulated; achieved by chemical finishing agents or by using an extra-large denier per filament.

soil release compounds Fluorocarbon-based compounds increase the surface energy of the fibers, making them more hydrophilic so the water can more readily carry the detergent molecules into the fiber crevices and emulsify and remove the soil material.

soil repellency Fluorocarbon compounds make textile compounds more oleophobic or oil-hating, as well as more hydrophobic.

soil shedding Reduction of the quantity of soil accumulated; achieved by using a trilobal fiber that has a microrough surface.

solar shade Shade of synthetic mesh fabric that filters light while allowing a view.

solar transmittance The amount of solar energy and visible light which passes through a solar shade.

solid foam mattress See *latex mattress*.

solution dyeing Adding dye pigments to the spinning solution of manufactured fibers prior to spinning; also known as dope dyeing and producer colored.

solvent spinning Manufactured fiber spinning technique in which a solvent is used to dissolve the polymer and the solution is extruded into a solvent that is recovered for continued use; used to produce lyocell fibers.

SoySilk® A trade name for Azlon; made from the soybean waste from the tofu manufacturing project.

space dyeing Dyeing spaces or segments of yarns; produces variegated color styling.

spandex A manufactured synthetic fiber with excellent elongation and elastic recovery.

specialty wools Wool fiber from the goat, camel, and rabbit families.

species identification Identification of bird species as part of feather testing.

specification listing A listing of preferred or required features of a product, including such things as appearance, composition, construction features, functional benefits, and performance properties.

specific gravity The density of a fiber relative to that of water at 4°C, which is 1.

specify To select and precisely stipulate in a comprehensive document the products and materials to be used in a specific building project.

speck yarn Complex single yarn having small tufts of differently colored fibers incorporated along its length; also known as tweed or flock yarn.

spectrum The array of microorganisms vulnerable to a particular antimicrobial.

spike yarn Complex, loop-type yarns composed of yarns having different levels of twist; the more highly twisted yarn is introduced at a faster rate, causing the extra length to form well-defined kinks or loops; also known as snarl yarns.

spillover Refers to the migration of fire from the room of origination to other rooms and/or corridors.

spinneret Shower head-like device used for mechanically spinning manufactured fibers.

spinners Members of the industry who align and spin staple fibers into spun yarns.

spinning and twisting Process in yarn spinning in which fibers that are aligned in yarn-like structures are spun and twisted into a yarn; twisting introduces strength.

spiral yarn Complex yarn formed by twisting a heavy yarn around a fine yarn; also known as a corkscrew yarn.

splash yarn Complex yarn having elongated nubs along its length.

split leather Leather fabric produced from an inner layer of hide; lacks natural grain markings.

spoken warranties See *warranties*, *spoken*.

spontaneous combustion Combustion process initiated by heat rather than flame.

spools Three-foot-long spools that are linked end-to-end to form a bracket; used in Axminster carpet weaving.

spot yarn See *nub yarn*.

sprouting The protrusion of a tuft above the surface of the wear layer of carpet.

spunbonded ticking Ticking composed of spunbonded polypropylene olefin film.

spunbonding Fabrication technique in which a web of filaments is stabilized with heat or adhesive binders.

spunlacing Fabrication technique in which webs of fibers are mechanically entangled.

spun yarn Yarn composed of short, staple fibers.

stackback space Distance on one or both sides of a window that is allowed for the panels to remain when drawn open.

Stage 1 Fire Characterizes a fire when only the ignited item is burning.

Stage 2 Fire Characterizes a fire when all combustible items in a room burst into flames, producing a situation known as flashover.

Stage 3 Fire Characterizes a fire when the flames spread beyond the burning room into the corridor or passageway.

stain Dirt or other foreign matter that is chemically bonded to the fiber surfaces and is comparatively difficult to remove.

stair tread test A long-term, service exposure test; carpet specimens are installed without a cushion on heavily used stairs.

standard fading units (SFU) The number of hours a specimens is exposed to light in a Fade-Ometer®.

standard performance specification A performance specification established by, for example, a voluntary scientific association; see also *performance specification*.

standards Written descriptions of specific performance, behaviors, attributes, or results.

standard test method A prescribed procedure for measuring a property; established by, for example, a voluntary scientific association.

staple fiber A relatively short textile fiber; measured in inches or centimeters.

static electricity Frictional electric charge caused by the rubbing together of two dissimilar objects.

static propensity Ease with which materials such as textile fibers accumulate electrons and develop electrostatic charges.

stationary casement panels Window treatments made of open weave fabric which are not designed to be opened and closed.

steep diagonal Visual diagonal in a twill weave fabric that falls at an angle greater than 45 degrees to the fabric grain.

Steiner Tunnel Test Method See *tunnel test*.

stiffness Degree of flexibility exhibited by fibers; affects fabric draping quality.

stitch-bonding Fabrication technique in which knitting stitches are used to stabilize webs of fibers.

stitch-knitting Fabrication technique in which knitting stitches are used to anchor webs of yarns; also known as *knit-sewing*.

stock dyeing See *fiber dyeing*.

stretch-in installation Technique used to install rollgoods wall-to-wall; see also *power stretcher*.

strié (striaé) Descriptive of color style in which yarns of various shades of the same hue are woven in narrow, lengthwise bands to produce the effect of irregularly placed stripes.

strikethrough When adhesive used to apply wallcovering to a surface seeps through to the surface of the wallcovering.

stuffer-box crimping Texturing technique in which yarns are rapidly stuffed into a heated, box-like chamber, backing up on themselves; develops a three-dimensional crimp.

stuffer yarns 1. Extra warp yarns running in a plane and supporting wales or other woven-in dobby designs. 2. Extra warp yarns running in a plane in the back of woven floorcoverings, adding weight, strength, dimensional stability, and thickness.

S twist A left-handed or counterclockwise direction of yarn twist.

stylist A professional who is responsible for developing design and aesthetic directions within a company.

sublime The process of heat causing a dyestuff to change from a solid to a gas to a solid; occurs in heat transfer printing.

sublistatic printing See *heat transfer printing*.

suede Leather with a velvety surface, achieved by rubbing the flesh side of the material.

sueding Revolving sandpaper-covered disks against a flocked surface; also known as emerizing.

sunlight resistance The ability of a fabric to withstand deterioration by sunlight.

surface dyeing Staining the surface of leather to impart a fashion color.

surface noise radiation Noise created by the activities of walking, running, and shuffling, and by the shifting of furniture and equipment.

surface sounds Movement of surface noise created by such activities as walking, running, and shuffling throughout an interior space.

surface tension Determined by the affinity that molecules in a compound have for one another, in contrast for a second surface.

surface texture Visual and textural characteristics of a textile surface (e.g., smooth, rough, short pile, fuzzy, and so on).

susceptibility to heat Characteristic of being affected by heat (e.g., scorches).

sustainability Describes practices and policies that reduce environmental pollution.

swags Softly draping lengths of fabrics hanging at the sides of windows.

swivel weave Surface-figure weave in which extra yarns encircle the base yarns to create a motif.

synthetic fiber Fibers that are derived from such materials as natural gas, oil, and coal.

synthetic manufactured fiber producers Manufacturers that produce acrylic, nylon, polyester, polypropylene (olefin), and PVC (polyvinyl chloride, also known as vinyon) from synthetic polymers derived from petroleum.

synthetic yarn producers Manufacturers that produce yarns of synthetic polymer fibers derived from petroleum.

tabby weave See *plain weave*.

tackless strips Pin-holding strip used in stretch-in tackless installation projects.

taffeta A filling-rib weave fabric characterized by fine, thin ribs.

taken up Said of the winding of woven fabric onto the loom's cloth beam as it is woven.

taking up and letting off In the weaving operation, taking up woven fabric and letting off warp yarns.

TAK printing Adding droplets of intense color to the already-colored pile surfaces.

tambour embroidering Machine stitching that resembles hand chain-stitching.

tanning Leather processing in which selected mineral substances react with the collagen, rendering the fibers insoluble.

tapestry A Jacquard-woven fabric typically characterized by floral patterns or picture-like motifs; may be woven with multiple sets of yarns.

tear strength Force required to continue or propagate a tear in a fabric; can be used to predict the likelihood that a small cut or puncture would become a large tear with continued use of the fabric.

tenacity The force per unit of linear density necessary to rupture a fiber, yarn, or thread; reported as grams per denier (gpd or g/den) or grams per tex (gpt or g/tex).

Tencel® Registered trade name for lyocell by Lenzing Fibers Inc.

tendering Weakening of fibers by, for example, sunlight or chemicals.

tensile strength The force per unit of cross-sectional area necessary to rupture a fabric; reported as pounds per square inch (psi) or grams per square centimeter.

tentering Mechanical treatment used to improve the grain of woven fabrics.

terry toweling Toweling having a loop pile on one or both sides of the fabric; also known as Turkish toweling.

terry velour toweling Toweling having a loop pile on one side and a cut pile on the other side of the fabric.

tex number Weight per unit of length measurement of a fiber of yarn; numerically equal to the weight in grams of 1,000 meters of the strand.

textile Formerly used only in reference to woven fabrics; now applied to fibers, yarns, and fibrous fabrics manufactured in various ways; not applicable to leather and film fabrics.

textile colorists Members of the industry who add fashion colors to textiles.

textile cords Thick string used to hand tie or hand knot spring used in upholstered furniture.

textile designers Members of the industry who design textile fabrics.

textile end products Goods that are ready for consumer purchase and use; includes such items as apparel, apparel fabric, upholstery fabric, upholstered furniture, curtains and draperies and curtain and drapery fabrics; soft floorcoverings, household and institutional textiles, and wallcoverings.

Textile Fiber Products Identification Act (TFPIA) A U.S. federal act administered by the FTC that requires manufacturers to attach a label to stipulated textile products that provides (1) the generic name and percentage by weight of each fiber in the product; (2) the manufacturer or supplier's name; and (3) the country in which the product was manufactured. Also called *Textile Labeling Rule* or *Label Law*.

texture Nature of the fiber or fabric surface.

textured filament yarn See *bulk continuous filament*.

texturing Introducing multidimensional configurations to otherwise parallel and smooth filaments.

thermal blanketing See *blanketing, thermal*.

thermal insulation Heat insulation.

thermoplasticity Property that allows a fiber to be softened and stabilized with controlled heat and that results in melting at higher temperatures; also known as heat sensitivity.

thick-and-thin yarn Complex single yarn characterized by variations in diameter that are created by varying extrusion pressure.

third-party certification A certification achieved after an independent organization (that has no stake in the success of the product, process, or service being evaluated) has reviewed the manufacturing or other related processes and has independently determined that the final product complies with specific standards for safety, quality, or performance.

thread count The number of individual yarns within a given sized unit of fabric (usually an inch or centimeter) in either warp or filling direction. Usually listed as number of warp yarns by number of filling yarns, e.g. 82 × 60.

threshold of human sensitivity The level of static voltage that produces a noticeable shock for most people when it discharges from their bodies; the level is normally 2,500 static volts.

throwing In yarn production, plying or twisting monofilaments into multifilaments.

throwsters Members of the industry who work in yarn throwing production.

ticking A generic term used for any fabric used to cover the exterior of mattresses, box springs, and pillows. Ticking is constructed in a variety of weaves, including Jacquard and twill weaves.

tie-back curtain Curtain tied back to the sides of the window by fabric of the same curtain material.

tied-back draperies Drapery panels tied back to the sides of the window by such items as cords, chains, and medallions.

tie-dye Print produced by artisans who tie off selected areas of fabric so that they resist penetration of dye liquor.

tight-pillow styles Style of upholstered furniture having pillows that cannot be shifted or removed.

tint Color feature created by adding a compound known to reflect all wavelengths, creating white, to colorants, increasing its value and luminosity.

tinting Adding colorants that neutralize the natural color (e.g., violet tints may be used to neutralize the natural yellow hues of wool fiber).

tippiness Unwanted concentration of dye on yarn tips; result of poor dye migration.

tip shear One level, cut pile surface texture produced by selectively shearing the uppermost portion of some yarn loops.

titanium dioxide Minute white particles used to deluster manufactured fibers.

tjanting A Javanese term for a wax resist dyeing technique in which wax is applied in fine lines with a fine metal tube that is attached to a reed or bamboo handle (tjanting tool).

Toile de Jouy A fabric that is printed with a monochromatic color styling. The motifs are typically large and have a picture-like quality. The base fabric is most often a plain weave or duck fabric.

tone-on-tone effect A type of dyeing that produces light and dark shades of the same color on a fabric containing two different types of one generic fiber.

top-grain leather Leather having minor corrections of the natural grain markings.

total blackout Complete blockage of light transmission.

total weight The total weight of a floorcovering including the weight of the pile yarns as well as the weight of the backing yarns, backing fabrics, and backcoatings.

tow 1. A rope-like bundle of manufactured filaments having crimp but no twist.

tow fibers Linen fibers approximately 12 inches long.

toxic gases Gases that are hazardous when inhaled; generated in the combustion of such things as fibers.

Toxic Substance Control Act A U.S. federal law administered by the United States EPA that regulates the introduction of new or existing chemicals.

trade associations Organizations that represent, protect, and promote the interests of their members who provide financial support for the operation and activities of the associations.

trade discount A discount off retail pricing customarily given by suppliers to other members of the trade that would not be offered to retail customers.

trademarks Distinctive names, words, phrases, and stylized logos that are used to promote product recognition and selection.

trade name Name given a fiber by a particular company.

trade practice rules Collection of labeling provisions issued by the FTC in response to requests by members of a limited segment of the industry; advisory in nature; several trade practice rules have been superseded by guides.

trade regulation rules Collection of mandatory labeling provisions issued by the FTC.

transfer printing See *heat transfer printing*.

traversing panel Curtain or drapery treatments that can be opened and closed as desired.

triacetate A regenerated cellulosic fiber; no longer produced in the United States.

triaxial weaving Fabrication technique in which two sets of warp yarns and one set of filling yarns are interlaced at 60-degree angles.

tricot stitch Warp knitting stitch produced with spring needles and one or two guide bars; nonrun and stable; distinguished by herringbone-like wales on the face of the fabric and herringbone-like courses on the back of the fabric.

triexta Generic subclass of polyester made in part from renewable sourced ingredients.

trimmings Ornamental trimmings used on drapery and curtain treatments.

true bias Fabric position falling at 45 degrees to the lengthwise and crosswise grains of woven fabric; position of highest stretch.

tucked-in selvage Fabric edge finish in which the ends of the cut filling picks are turned back into the next shed; creates a finished edge that resembles that of a conventional selvage.

tuft bind Average force required to remove a pile tuft from tufted structures.

tufted trimming Using buttons to secure the outercovering and filling tightly in a deeply indented three-dimensional pattern.

tufted upholstery fabric Pile fabric produced by tufting machines rather than weaving.

tufting Fabrication technique in which pile yarns are inserted into a preformed base fabric.

tufts per square inch Indicates pile construction density; calculated by multiplying the needle count by the number of stitches per inch in tufted constructions and by multiplying the number of rows or wires per inch by the pitch divided by 27 in woven constructions.

tunnel test Flammability test method that measures the surface burning characteristics of building materials; assesses flame spread and smoke generation; also known as the Steiner tunnel test method.

turbidity Percentage of dust or dirt present in down and feather.

Turkish knot See *Ghiordes knot*.

Turkish toweling See *terry toweling*.

turns per inch (tpi) Numerical indication of the level of yarn twist.

Tussah silk A type of wild silk.

tweed A fabric containing speck or tweed yarns.

tweed yarn Yarns which have small tufts of contrasting colored fibers during spinning; also called speck or tweed yarns.

twill weave Basic weaving pattern in which the warp and filling yarns are interlaced to create a visual diagonal.

twisting Used to introduce strength to spun yarns; used to combine monofilaments into multifilaments.

two-way draw draperies Window treatment style in which the drapery panels are drawn to stack on both sides of the window.

Type I Vinyl A wallcovering with a total face weight of 7 to 13 ounces per square yard and used in residential and light commercial applications.

Type II Vinyl A wallcovering with a total face weight of 15 to 22 ounces per square yard and used in medium-use commercial applications.

Type III Vinyl A wallcovering with a total face weight greater than 22 ounces per square yard and used in high-service commercial applications.

UFAC Voluntary Action Program A series of upholstered furniture tests designed to improve the ability of residential upholstered furniture to resist catching fire from a burning cigarette.

ugly out Due to improper maintenance, carpet shows wearing, soiling, matting, and loss of color before it is worn out.

ultraviolet transmission The amount of UV rays that can penetrate a material.

unclipped-dot or -spot fabric See *dot or spot weave*.

underblankets Fleece-like mattress pad having a knitted base and pile of lamb's wool; placed under the bottom bed sheet to provide softness, warmth, and moisture absorption.

uneven filling-faced twill Twill fabric in which more filling yarn than warp yarn shows on the face of the fabric.

uneven warp-faced twill Twill fabric in which more warp yarn than filling yarn shows on the face of the fabric.

union dyeing Variation of piece dyeing in which a fabric composed of two or more different and strategically placed fibers is immersed into a dyebath formulated with dyestuffs that will be selectively accepted and rejected; produces a single, uniform color from one immersion process.

Upholstered Furniture Action Council (UFAC) A voluntary program designed to encourage development of residential upholstered furniture that resists catching fire from a burning cigarette.

upholstered wall Unbacked or lightly backed fabric stapled over a layer of batting either directly to the wall surface over a batting or to lath strips nailed to the top, bottom, and sides of the wall and next to the framework of the doors and windows.

upland cotton Variety of cotton ground inland, in contrast to on an island; most fibers are a relatively short 13/16 inch in length.

up-the-bolt Cutting upholstery fabric so that the lengthwise grain runs vertically on the cushions, given that the motifs and repeats have a directional feature.

usable fiber form Relatively long and thin form, in contrast to being relatively short and thick; affects flexibility.

U.S. Green Building Council (USGBC) Non-profit organization providing green building resources, educational courses, research, statistical information, and the Leadership in Energy and Environmental Design (LEED).

U-values Numerical indications of how much heat actually does pass outward through windows in winter and inward in summer.

valance Fabric window treatment at the top of the window which may stand alone or serve to cover drapery hardware; usually pleated or shirred.

value Color characteristic referring to the quantity of light being reflected from a textile or other surface; also known as luminosity.

vapor-phase moisture Water vapor held in the air.

variegated yarns Space-dyed yarns having a variety of colors along their lengths.

velour A warp pile weave fabric in which the pile layer is created with extra warp yarns; characterized by a deeper pile and a more pronounced nap than velvet.

velour (carpeting) A soft floorcovering of fine, short, and dense construction.

velvet A warp pile weave fabric in which the pile layer is created with extra warp yarns.

velvet carpet weaving Weaving floorcoverings using an over-the-wire-construction technique; pile may be conventional or woven-through-the-back.

velveteen A filling pile weave fabric with a short nap. Typically made of cotton or cotton blend.

velvet plush See *plush*.

Venetian blinds Window coverings made up of horizontal slats or louvers laced together with textile cords.

vertical blinds Window coverings in which the louvers or vanes are suspended vertically and may be rotated 180 degrees.

vertical manufacturers A textile company that produces or handles most but not all of the manufacturing steps from fiber to end product.

vicuna Fiber obtained from the hair of the vicuna, a rare wild animal of the camel family.

vinyl Vinal in film form.

vinylized fabric Fabric given a vinyl coating to protect it from such things as soil and spilled fluids.

vinyon A manufactured synthetic fiber also known as polyvinyl chloride or PVC.

virgin wool See *wool, virgin*.

viscoelastic polyurethane foam Open cell foam of polyurethane which has a slow recovery time when compressed and is sensitive to heat; commonly known as "memory foam."

visible spectrum Portion of the electromagnetic spectrum containing wavelengths that can be interpreted by the eye when reflected.

visible transmittance Amount of solar energy and visible light.

visual diagonal Surface feature created with twill interlacing patterns.

voided velvet A velvet fabric that contains patterns created by omitting selected pile yarns and exposing areas of the base fabric.

voile A transparent, balanced plain weave fabric. It is characterized by highly twisted cotton or cotton blend yarns.

volatile organic compounds (VOC) Chemicals that contain carbon, which, during evaporation, gives off gases and can cause health problems.

V pattern Pile interlacing in which the pile yarn is anchored by one base filling yarn.

vulcanizing Heating latex with sulfur to introduce strong chemical cross links that stabilize the shape and add strength.

waffled rubber cushion Carpet cushion with a bubbled or rippled surface.

waffle piqué A dobby-woven fabric with a three dimensional surface that resembles a waffle or honeycomb.

wales Ridge-like features created in filling pile weaving (e.g., pinwale corduroy) or dobby weaving (e.g., pinwale piqué); diagonal lines in a twill weave.

walk-off mat Floorcovering used in entrance areas subjected to high traffic levels to capture tracked-in dirt and grit, protecting the carpet from abrasion and apparent changes in color.

wall system An installation system that uses specialized wall-mounted channels with locking clips or loop-and-hook fasteners to hold fabric panels over walls to achieve the appearance of upholstered walls. A polyester batting is usually placed within the mounting frame to increase acoustical features.

wall-to-wall installation Installation of carpet to cover the entire floor space, baseboard to baseboard.

warp knitting Simultaneous interlooping of adjacent yarns in a vertical direction.

warp laminates A wallcovering in which yarns are lined up vertically, parallel, next to each other and laminated to a backing that is usually colored or sometimes printed.

warp pile fabric Fabric in which the pile layer is created with extra warp yarns (e.g., velvet, terry, terry velour, friezé, grospoint).

warp print Color style produced by printing the warp yarns prior to weaving; distinguished by striated or blurred appearance; used for draperies.

warp-rib weave Variation of the plain weave in which larger or grouped warp yarns create a ribbed or ridged effect in the lengthwise fabric direction.

warp sateen A satin-woven fabric characterized by spun yarns.

warp yarns Lengthwise yarns in a woven fabric; also known as ends.

warranty, full Guarantee program designation that indicates what the warrantor agrees to do for the purchaser, as well as what is expected of the purchaser; gives more than a limited warranty.

warranty, implied Guarantees that come automatically with every sale unless the product is sold "as is"; rights are provided by state law.

warranty, limited Guarantee program designation that indicates what the warrantor agrees to do for the purchaser, as well as what is expected of the purchaser; gives less than a full warranty.

warranty programs Program offering some level of protection from defective or faulty merchandise; most warranties are legally binding. See also *warranty, full*; *warranty, implied*; *warranty, limited*; *warranty, spoken*; and *warranty, written*.

warranty, spoken Verbal promise; virtually impossible to enforce.

warranty, written Legally binding promise that the warrantor is ensuring quality and performance; subject to the provisions of the Magnuson-Moss Warranty Act.

washfastness Resistance of colored textiles to fading, bleeding, migration, and/or color change when laundered.

water-borne stain Stain carried by water.

waterfowl feathers Feathers derived from ducks and geese.

watermarking See *pile reversal*.

waterproof fabric A fabric that will not be wet regardless of the amount of time it is exposed to water or the force with which the water strikes the fabric.

water resistance Characteristic of repelling water, delaying absorption.

wc system Worsted count (wc) yarn numbering system.

wear layer The face or pile yarns above the backing in pile floorcoverings.

Weather-Ometer Apparatus used for the accelerated laboratory testing of textile fabrics to be installed outdoors.

weaving The process of making fabric on a loom.

weft insertion Fabrication technique in which weft or filling yarns are inserted through loops of a tricot-stitched fabric.

weft knitting See *filling knitting*.

weft yarns Another name for filling yarns; also known as woof.

weight density Product of the average pile weight in ounces per square yard and the average density of soft floorcoverings.

weighting Adding metallic salts in silk to add body, luster, and physical weight.

welt Fabric-covered cord inserted in seam lines of upholstered furniture coverings.

wet shampoo cleaning Restorative maintenance procedure in which a diluted detergent solution or foam is driven into the pile with rotating brushes, followed by a thorough vacuuming.

wet spinning Manufactured fiber spinning technique in which a basic solvent is used to dissolve the polymer and the solution is extruded into a weak acid bath where filaments coagulate.

wicking The ability of a textile fiber to transport moisture along its surface by capillary action.

wild silk Fiber obtained from the cocoons of silk moths found in the wild.

Wilton Carpet woven on a Jacquard loom; distinguished by having buried pile yarns.

wires per inch The number of wires used per lengthwise inch in the construction of Wilton and velvet carpet; also the number of crosswise rows of tufts per lengthwise inch in Wilton and velvet carpet, since one wire is used per row of tufts.

wood veneer Thin slices of wood that are laminated to paper or nonwoven backing.

woof yarns See *weft yarns*.

wool Labeling term that means the fiber from the fleece of the sheep or lamb has never been reclaimed from any woven or felted wool product.

woolen yarn Yarn spun of both long and short wool fibers and exhibiting a relatively low degree of fiber alignment.

wool, new See *wool, virgin*.

Wool Products Labeling Act (WPLA) Thin slices of wood that are laminated to paper or nonwoven backing.

wool, recycled Labeling term used to identify the resulting fiber when wool or reprocessed wool had been spun, woven, knitted, or felted into a wool product that, without ever having been used or after having been used by a consumer, subsequently had been returned to a fibrous state; replaced in 1980 by the term "recycled wool."

wool, reprocessed Wool yarn made from captured, post-industrial or post-consumer waste wool yarn or fiber.

wool, virgin Labeling term that means the constituent fibers have undergone manufacturing only once; they have not been reclaimed from any spun, woven, knitted, felted, braided, bonded, or otherwise manufactured or used product; synonymous with "new wool."

worsted yarn Yarn spun of long wool fibers and exhibiting a relatively high degree of fiber alignment.

woven-through-the-back Velvet carpet in which the pile yarns are anchored by both the upper and lower filling shots.

W pattern Pile interlacing in which the pile yarn is anchored by three base filling yarns.

wrinkle recovery Recovery from folding and bending deformations, minimizing fabric mussiness; see *resiliency*.

written warranty See *warranty, written*.

wr system Woolen run (wr); yarn numbering system used to determine number of yarns spun on the woolen spinning system.

Wyzenbeek Test Method See *Oscillatory Cylinder Method*.

yak Fiber obtained from a large Tibetan ox; used for blanketing.

yarn alignment In woven fabric when vertical (warp) yarns and horizontal (weft) yarns are at right angles to each other.

yarn balance The ratio of warp yarns to filling yarns.

yarn beam Circular beam that holds the supply of warp yarns.

yarn count See *yarn number*.

yarn distortion A condition in which the symmetrical surface appearance of a fabric is altered by the shifting or sliding of filling or warp yarns.

yarn dyeing Dyeing in the yarn stage. See also *package dyeing*, *beam dyeing*, *skein dyeing*, and *space dyeing*.

yarn number Numerical designation of the fineness or size of a yarn; based on length per unit of mass (weight) or mass (weight) per unit of length; also known as yarn count.

yarn raveling Yarn falling from a raw edge of fabric.

yarn slippage See *yarn distortion*.

yarn splay Untwisting of yarns, resulting in a loss of tuft definition.

yarn tip The end of a cut yarn, especially in cut-pile carpet.

yo-yo effect See *elevator effect*.

Z twist A right-handed or clockwise direction of yarn twist.

BIBLIOGRAPHY

American Association of Textile Chemists and Colorists. 2017. *AATCC Technical Manual*. Research Triangle Park, North Carolina: AATCC. www.aatcc.org.

Anton-Katzenbach, Sabine. 2012. "Stain Repellants: Safety vs. Performance." *AATCC Review*, Vol. 12, No. 1, 31–36.

ASTM International. 2017. *Annual Book of ASTM Standards*. West Conshohocken, Pennsylvania: ASTM International. www.astm .org.

Axelson, Kirk B., and Barbara Talmadge. 2006. *Elements of Soft Treatments*. Denver: Precision Draperies Education.

Binggeli, Corky. 2013. *Materials for Interior Environments*, 2nd ed. Hoboken, New Jersey: John Wiley and Sons, Inc.

Bonda, Penny, and Katie Sosnowchik. 2007. *Sustainable Commercial Interiors*. Hoboken, New Jersey: John Wiley and Sons, Inc.

Braddock, Sarah E. and Marie O'Mahony. 1998. *Techno Textiles*. New York: Thames and Hudson Inc.

Brentin, Robert. 2012. "Protecting Carpets with Antimicrobials." *SpecialChem*, March 20. http://www. specialchem4polymers.com/resources/articles/article. aspx?id=7209&q=protecting%20carpets%20with%20 antimicrobials.

Carpet America Recovery Effort. 2017. *CARE 2017 Annual Report*. Dalton, Georgia: Carpet America Recovery Effort.

Carpet and Rug Institute. 2003. *The Carpet Primer*. Dalton, Georgia: Carpet and Rug Institute.

Carpet and Rug Institute. 2008. *The Carpet Industry's Sustainability Report*. Dalton, Georgia: Carpet and Rug Institute.

Carpet and Rug Institute. 2011. *CRI Carpet Installation Standard*. Dalton, Georgia: Carpet and Rug Institute.

Carpet and Rug Institute. 2018. *CRI Technical Bulletin: Acoustical Characteristics of Carpet*. Dalton, Georgia: Carpet and Rug Institute.

Carpet and Rug Institute. 2018. *CRI Technical Bulletin: Antimicrobial Carpet Treatments*. Dalton, Georgia: Carpet and Rug Institute.

Carpet and Rug Institute. 2018. *CRI Technical Bulletin: Carpet and Indoor Air Quality* Dalton, Georgia: Carpet and Rug Institute.

Carpet and Rug Institute. 2018. *CRI Technical Bulletin: Static Control*. Dalton, Georgia: Carpet and Rug Institute.

Cohen, Allen C. and Ingrid Johnson. 2010. *J. J. Pizzuto's Fabric Science*, 9th ed. New York: Fairchild Books.

Constantine, Mildred, and Laurel Reuter. 1997. *Whole Cloth*. New York: Monacelli Press, Inc.

Elsasser, Virginia H. 2004. *Know Your Home Furnishings*. New York: Fairchild Books.

Elsasser, Virginia H. 2011. *Textiles: Concepts & Principles*, 3rd ed. New York: Fairchild Books.

Emery, Irene. 1966. *The Primary Structure of Fabrics*. Washington, D.C.: The Textile Museum.

Environmental Protection Agency. 1998. Executive Order 13101, Section 201—*Greening the Government Through Waste Prevention, Recycling, and Federal Acquisition*.

Environmental Protection Agency. 2006. *Life Cycle Assessment: Principles and Practice*.

Environmental Protection Agency. 2016. *Final Guidance on Environmentally Preferable Purchasing*. www.epa.gov/ greenerproducts/final-pilot-assessment-guidelines-epas- recommendations-standards-and-ecolabels.

Fiber Economics Bureau. 2006. "Carpet Fiber Trends: Carpet Face Fiber Analysis: 2001 to 2011, Table 2." *Fiber Organon*, Volume 77, No. 9, September, 171.

Fiber Economics Bureau. 2012. "U.S. End Use Survey: 2007– 2011, Table 5." *Fiber Organon*, Volume 83, No. 10, October 2012, 193.

Godsey, Lisa. 2017. *Interior Design Materials and Specifications*, 3rd ed. New York: Fairchild Books.

Gordon, Beverly. 2011. *Textiles: The Whole Story*, New York: Thames and Hudson.

Gorga, Russell. 2010. "Nanotechnology in Textiles." *Textile World*. November/December, 33–35.

Harmon, Sharon K., and Katherine E. Kennon. 2011. *The Codes Guidebook for Interiors*, 5th ed. Hoboken, New Jersey: John Wiley & Sons, Inc.

International Association of Bedding and Furniture Law Officials. 2013. *Classification of Filling Materials, Section 10: Wool*. Mechanicsville, Virginia: International Association of Bedding and Furniture Law Officials.

Ireland, Jeannie. 2009. *History of Interior Design*. New York: Fairchild Books.

Jackman, Dianne, M. Dixon, and J. Condra. 2003. *The Guide to Textiles for Interiors*, 3rd ed. Winnipeg: Portage and Main Press.

Johnston, Meda P., and Glen Kaufman. 1981. *Design on Fabrics*. New York: Van Nostrand Reinhold Co.

Joint Industry Fabric Standards and Guidelines Committee. 2010. *Woven & Knit Residential Upholstery Fabric Standards and Guidelines*. www.ahfa.us/wp-content/uploads/2014/05/FabricStdsGuideline.pdf.

Jones, Louise. 2008. *Environmentally Responsible Design*. Hoboken, New Jersey: John Wiley & Sons, Inc.

Jones, Lynn, and Phyllis S. Allen. 2009. *Beginnings of Interior Environments*, 10th ed. Upper Saddle River, New Jersey: Pearson Education, Inc.

Juracek, Judy. 1996. *Surfaces*. New York: W. W. Norton and Co., Inc.

Juracek, Judy. 1999. *Soft Surfaces*. New York: W. W. Norton and Co., Inc.

Kadolph, Sara J. 2011. *Textiles*, 11th ed. Upper Saddle River, NJ: Pearson Education, Inc.

Kadolph, Sara J. 2013. *Textile Basics*. Upper Saddle River, NJ: Pearson Education, Inc.

Kopec, Dak. 2009. *Health, Sustainability, and the Built Environment*. New York: Fairchild Books.

Koe, Frank T. 2017. *Fabrics for the Designed Interior*, 3rd ed. New York: Fairchild Books.

Kolander, Cheryl. 1985. *A Silk Worker's Notebook*, rev. ed. Loveland, Colorado: Interweave Press, Inc.

Larsen, Jack Lenor, and Jeanne Weeks. 1975. *Fabrics for Interiors*. New York: Van Nostrand Reinhold Co.

Mandal, Jyotshna, and Helmut Brandl. 2011. "Bioaerosols in Indoor Environment—A Review with Special Reference to Residential and Occupational Locations." *The Open Environmental & Biological Monitoring Journal*, 4, 83–96.

McGowan, Maryrose. 2005. *Specifying Interiors: A Guide to Construction and FF & E for Commercial Interior Products*, 2nd ed. Hoboken, New Jersey: John Wiley & Sons, Inc.

Musante, Glenna. 2012. "Bridging the Chasm." *AATCC Review*, Vol. 12, No. 6, 22–29.

Musante, Glenna. 2012. "Fighting Fungi." *AATCC Review*, Vol. 12, No. 3, 24–30.

Musante, Glenna. 2013. "The Fabric of Beauty." *AATCC Review*, Vol. 13, No. 1, 34–38.

National Fire Protection Association. 2015. *NFPA 701: Standard Methods of Fire Tests for Flame Propagation of Textiles and Films*. Quincy, Massachusetts: National Fire Protection Association. https://www.nfpa.org/codes-and-standards/all-codes-and-standards/list-of-codes-and-standards/detail?code=701.

National Fire Protection Association. 2018. *NFPA 10®1: Life Safety Code*. Quincy, Massachusetts: National Fire Protection Association. https://www.nfpa.org/codes-and-standards/all-codes-and-standards/list-of-codes-and-standards/detail?code=101.

Neilson, Karla J. 2007. *Interior Textiles: Fabrics, Applications & Historic Style*. Hoboken, New Jersey: John Wiley & Sons, Inc.

Office of Environmental Health Hazard Assessment (OEHHA). 1986. *California Proposition 65: Safe Drinking Water and Toxic Enforcement Act of 1986*. https://oehha.ca.gov/proposition-65.

Pegler, Martin. 2006. *The Fairchild Dictionary of Interior Design*, 2nd ed. New York: Fairchild Books.

Pile, John. 2005. *A History of Interior Design*, 2nd ed. Hoboken, New Jersey: John Wiley & Sons, Inc.

Polyurethane Foam Association. 1994. *Joint Industry Foam Standards and Guidelines*. Loudon, Tennessee: Polyurethane Foam Association.

Randall, Charles T. 2012. *The Encyclopedia of Window Fashions*, 7th ed. San Clemente, California: Randall International.

Reichard, Robert. 2013. "Textiles 2013: The Turnaround." *Textile World*, January/February, 24–33.

Raskauskas, Barbara. *How to Choose the Right Upholstery Foam*. Retrieved August 2013, www.ehow.com.

Rodie, Janet B. 2008. "Going Green: Beyond Marketing Hype." *Textile World*, November/December, 28–32.

Rodie, Janet B. 2013. "What's in a Brand?" *Textile World*, March/April, 26–29.

Rosenfield, Jeffery and Wid Chapman. 2008. *Home Design in an Aging World*. New York: Fairchild Books.

Rupp, Jurg. 2008. "Manmade Fibers: New Attitude." *Textile World*, November/December, 33–37.

Rupp, Jurg. 2011. "Sustainable Dyeing and Finishing." *Textile World*, March/April, 38–40.

Slotkis, Susan. 2013. *Foundations of Interior Design*, 2nd ed. New York: Fairchild Books.

State of California Department of Consumer Affairs. 1980. *California Technical Bulletin 116: Requirements, Test Procedure and Apparatus for Testing the Flame Retardance of Upholstered Furniture*. North Highlands, California: State of California Department of Consumer Affairs, Bureau of Home Furnishings and Thermal Insulation.

State of California Department of Consumer Affairs. 1991. *California Technical Bulletin 133: Flammability Test Procedure for Seating Furniture for Use in Public Occupancies*, North Highlands CA: State of California Department of

Consumer Affairs, Bureau of Home Furnishings and Thermal Insulation. www.bearhfti.ca.gov/industry/bulletin.shtml.

State of California Department of Consumer Affairs. 2013. *California Technical Bulletin 117-2013: Requirements, Test Procedure and Apparatus for Testing the Flame Retardance of Resilient Filling Materials Used in Upholstered Furniture.* Sacramento, California: State of California Bureau of Electronic & Appliance Repair, Home Furnishings and Thermal Insulation. www.bearhfti.ca.gov/industry/bulletin.shtml.

Thiry, Maria C. 2006. "Smarter Than You Think." *AATCC Review*, Vol. 6, No. 12, 18–23.

Thiry, Maria C. 2008. "Tag, You're It." *AATCC Review*, Vol. 9, No. 5, 22–28.

Thiry, Maria C. 2009. "Unsung Heroes: Antimicrobials Save the Day." *AATCC Review*, Vol. 9, No. 5, 20–27.

Thiry, Maria C. 2009. "Everything Old is New Again: Recycling, Recycled, and Recyclable Fibers." *AATCC Review*, Vol. 9, No. 3, 20–26.

Thiry, Maria C. 2011. "Naturally Good." *AATCC Review*, Vol. 11, No. 3, 22–30.

Thiry, Maria C. 2011. "Made to Order." *AATCC Review*, Vol. 11, No. 3, 31–34.

Thiry, Maria C. 2011. "Staying Alive: Making Textiles Sustainable." *AATCC Review*, Vol. 11, No. 6, 26–32.

U.S. Code of Federal Regulations (CFR). 2013. Title 16 – Commercial Practices, Chapter 1, FTC Part 260 – Guides for the Use of Environmental Marketing Claims.

U.S. Department of Commerce. 2013. *Guide to United States Furniture Compliance Requirements.*

Weibel, Adèle Coulin. 1952. *Two Thousand Years of Textiles.* New York: Pantheon Books.

Weiner, Annette B. and Jane Schneider (eds). 1989. *Cloth and the Human Experience.* Washington D.C.: Smithsonian Institution Press.

Von Tobel, Jackie. 2007. *The Design Directory of Window Treatments.* Salt Lake City, Utah: Gibbs Smith.

White, Christine. 2007. *Uniquely Felt.* North Adams, Massachusetts: Storey Publishing.

Winchip, Susan. 2011. *Fundamentals of Lighting*, 2nd ed. New York: Fairchild Books.

Winchip, Susan. 2011. *Sustainable Design for Interior Environments*, 2nd ed. New York: Fairchild Books.

Wingate, Dr. Isabel B. *Fairchild's Dictionary of Textiles*, 6th ed. New York: Fairchild Publications, 1979.

Yates, MaryPaul. *Fabrics: A Guide for Interior Designers and Architects.* New York: W. W. Norton and Co., Inc., 2003.

Yates, MaryPaul. *Textiles: A Handbook for Designers*, rev. ed. New York: W. W. Norton and Co., Inc., 1996.

RESOURCES

Periodicals

AATCC Review
www.aatcc.org/pub/aatcc-review/

Fiber Organon
www.fibersource.com/feb/fiber-organon/

Furniture Today
www.furnituretoday.com/

Furniture World
www.furninfo.com/

Interior Design
www.interiordesign.net/

Interiors Magazine
http://interiorsmagazine.com/

Interiors + Sources
www.interiorsandsources.com

Nonwovens Industry
www.nonwovens-industry.com/

Textile Institute
www.textileinstitute.org/

Textile World
www.textileworld.com/

Window Fashion Vision
www.wf-vision.com/

Scientific Organizations

American Association of Textile Chemists and Colorists (AATCC)
www.aatcc.org

American National Standards Institute, Inc. (ANSI)
www.ansi.org

ASTM International (American Society for Testing and Materials)
www.ASTM.org

Cradle to Cradle Products Innovation Institute
www.c2ccertified.org

Efficient Windows Collaborative
www.efficientwindows.org

Global Organic Textile Standard (GOTS)
www.global-standard.org

Green Building Initiative (GBI)
www.thegbi.org

Greenguard Environmental Institute (GEI) (UL Environment)
www.greenguard.org

Institute for Market Transformation Sustainability (MTS)
www.imt.org

International Down and Feather Testing and Laboratory
www.idfl.com

International Living Future Institute
www.living-future.org

International Organization for Standardization (ISO)
www.iso.org

National Center for Sustainability Standards, NSF International
www.nsf.org

National Fire Protection Association, Inc. (NFPA)
www.nfpa.org

National Institute of Standards and Technology (NIST)
www.nist.gov

Oeko-Tex® Association
www.oeko-tex.com

SCS Global Services (Scientific Certification Systems)
www.sgsglobalservices.com

Underwriters Laboratories
www.ul.com

U.S. Green Building Council (USGBC)
www.usgbc.org

Government Agencies

Architectural and Transportation Barriers Compliance Board, Office of the Federal Register (NF)
www.access-board.gov/

Federal Aviation and Administration (FAA), U.S. Department of Transportation
www.faa.gov

Federal Emergency Management Agency (FEMA)
www.fema.gov

Federal Housing Administration (FHA), U.S. Department of Housing and Urban Development
www.fha.gov

Federal Trade Commission (FTC)
www.ftc.gov

General Services Administration (GSA)
www.gsa.gov

National Highway Traffic Safety Administration (NHTSA)
www.nhtsa.gov

U.S. Department of Transportation
www.transportation.gov

Office of Energy Efficiency and Renewable Energy (EERE)
www.energy.gov/eere/office-energy-efficiency-renewable-energy

State of California Department of Consumer Affairs, Bureau of Home Furnishings and Thermal Insulation
www.dca.ca.gov

United States Access Board
www.access-board.gov

U.S. Consumer Product Safety Commission (CPSC)
www.cpsc.gov

U.S. Department of Commerce
www.commerce.gov

U.S. Department of Energy
www.energy.gov

U.S. Department of Labor
www.dol.gov

U.S. Department of Veterans Affairs
www.va.gov

U.S. Environmental Protection Agency (EPA)
www.epa.gov

U.S. Social Security Administration
www.ssa.gov

Trade Associations

The Academy of Textiles and Flooring
www.atfinfo.com

American Fiber Manufacturers Association, Inc.
www.fibersource.com

American Home Furnishings Alliance (formerly American Furniture Manufacturers Association)
www.ahfa.us

American Law Label, Inc.
www.americanlawlabel.com

Association for Contract Textiles
www.contracttextiles.org

Association for Linen Management
www.almnet.org

Australian Wool Innovation Limited
www.wool.com

BIFMA International
www.bifma.org

California Furniture Manufacturers Association
www.cfma.com

Canadian Carpet Institute
www.canadiancarpet.org

Carpet America Recovery Effort (CARE)
www.carpetrecovery.org

Carpet and Rug Institute (CRI)
www.carpet-rug.org

Carpet Cushion Council
www.carpetcushion.org

CELC—Masters Of Linen
www.mastersoflinencom

Cotton Incorporated
www.cottoninc.com

Cycle-Tex, Inc.
www.cycletex.com

Drycleaning and Laundry Institute International
www.dlionline.org

GreenGuard Environmental Institute
www.greenguard.org

Industrial Fabrics Association International
www.ifai.com

Institute of Inspection Cleaning and Restoration Certification
www.iicrc.org

International Furnishings and Design Association
www.ifda.com

National Association of Decorative Fabrics Distributors
www.nadfd.com

National Cotton Council of America
www.cotton.org

National Fenestration Rating Council
www.nfrc.org

National Home Furnishings Association
www.myhfa.org

North American Association of Floor Covering Distributors
www.nafcd.org

Polyurethane Foam Association
www.pfa.org

The Society of the Plastics Industry, Inc.
www.plasticindustry.org

Synthetic Yarn and Fiber Association
www.thesyfa.org

Upholstered Furniture Action Council (UFAC)
www.ufac.org

Vinyl Institute
www.vinylinfo.org

Wallcovering Association (WA)
www.wallcovering.org

Window Coverings Association of America (WCAA)
www.wcaa.org

Appendix A

Federal Trade Commission Generic Fiber Names

Acetate	Nytril
Acrylic	Olefin
Anidex	PBI
Aramid	PLA
Azlon	Polyester
Fluoropolymer	Rayon
Glass	Rubber
Lastrile	Saran
Lyocell	Spandex
Melamine	Sulfar
Metallic	Triacetate
Modacrylic	Vinal
Novoloid	Vinyon
Nylon	

Note: Listed fibers are produced in many countries globally, and few are currently produced domestically in the United States.

Appendix B

ACT Voluntary Performance Guidelines

act.

association
for contract
textiles

ACT Voluntary Performance Guidelines for Flammability and four aspects of fabric durability—Wet & Dry Crocking, Colorfastness to Light, Physical Properties, and Abrasion—make fabric specification easier.

To give architects, designers, and end-users a vast amount of performance information in a succinct visual way, ACT developed icons to indicate that a fabric meets or exceeds guideline requirements. Look for these Registered Certification Marks on ACT Member Company sampling to assure that the fabrics you specify perform up to contract standards and pass all applicable testing.

All ACT Voluntary Performance Guidelines cover woven and coated fabrics for indoor use. "Woven Fabrics" consist of two sets of yarns, warp and filling, formed by weaving, which is the process of interlacing these sets of yarns. "Coated Fabrics" typically include a fabric or similar substrate with one or more layers of a film-forming polymer such as vinyl or polyurethane on the wear surface of the fabric.

Test methods included in the Guidelines measure fabric performance under standard laboratory conditions and are intended to represent the most current test version. Note: Individual ACT Member product information may represent a different version of a test method depending on the date the product was introduced to market.

Important: These tests represent minimum requirements, which are subject to change without notice and may not reflect requirements or laws in all locations.

Flammability

The measurement of a fabric's performance when it is exposed to specific sources of ignition.

Note: ACT guidelines specify different flammability tests dictated by the intended end use for the fabric.

Upholstery
California Technical Bulletin 117-2013 Section 1 – Pass

Direct Glue Wallcoverings and Adhered Panels
ASTM E84 (Adhered Mounting Method) – Class A or Class 1

Wrapped Wall Panels and Upholstered Walls
ASTM E84 (Unadhered Mounting Method) – Class A or Class 1

Panel System Furniture
Any one or combination of the following: UL recognized component under Office Panel Fabrics category, UL 1286 Listed, ASTM E84 (Adhered or Unadhered Mounting Method) –
Class A or Class 1

Drapery
NFPA 701 Method 1 or 2 as appropriate – Pass

P.O. Box 101981 Fort Worth, TX 76185 817.924.8048 www.contracttextiles.org

association
for contract
textiles

Wet & Dry Crocking

Transfer of dye from the surface of a dyed or printed fabric onto another surface by rubbing.

Upholstery – Woven Fabrics

| AATCC 8 | Dry Crocking, Grade 4 minimum |
| | Wet Crocking, Grade 3 minimum |

Upholstery – Coated Fabrics

| AATCC 8 | Dry Crocking, Grade 4 minimum |
| | Wet Crocking, Grade 4 minimum |

Direct Glue Wallcoverings

| AATCC 8 | Dry Crocking, Grade 3 minimum |
| | Wet Crocking, Grade 3 minimum |

Wrapped Panels and Upholstered Walls

| AATCC 8 | Dry Crocking, Grade 3 minimum |
| | Wet Crocking, Grade 3 minimum |

Drapery

AATCC 8 (Solids)	Dry Crocking, Grade 3 minimum
	Wet Crocking, Grade 3 minimum
AATCC 116 (Prints)	Dry Crocking, Grade 3 minimum
	Wet Crocking, Grade 3 minimum

association
for contract
textiles

Colorfastness to Light

A material's degree of resistance to the fading effect of light.

Upholstery – Woven Fabrics

AATCC 16 Option 1 or 3	Grade 4 minimum at 40 hours*

Upholstery – Coated Fabrics

AATCC 16 Option 1 or 3	Grade 4 minimum at 200 hours*
Or	
ASTM D4329	No appreciable color change at 150 hours*

Direct Glue Wallcoverings

AATCC 16 Option 1 or 3	Grade 4 minimum at 40 hours*

Wrapped Panels and Upholstered Walls

AATCC 16 Option 1 or 3	Grade 4 minimum at 40 hours*

Drapery

AATCC 16 Option 1 or 3	Grade 4 minimum at 60 hours*

Note: There is no direct correlation between the numbers of testing hours and hours of service in the field.

association
for contract
textiles

Physical Properties

Key factors in assessing overall durability of a fabric vary depending on the fabric construction.

Upholstery – Woven Fabrics
Pilling
ASTM D3511 (Brush Pill), Class 3 minimum
Or
ASTM D4970, (Martindale Tester), Class 3 minimum
Pilling is the formation of fuzzy balls of fiber on the surface of a fabric that remain attached to the fabric.

Breaking Strength
ASTM D5034 (Grab Test), 50 lbs. minimum in warp and weft
Breaking strength is the measurement of stress exerted to pull a fabric apart under tension.

Seam Slippage
ASTM D4034, 25 lbs. minimum in warp and weft
Seam Slippage is the movement of yarns in a fabric that occurs when it is pulled apart at a seam.

Upholstery – Coated Fabrics
Adhesion of Coating
ASTM D751 Sections 45-48, 3 lbf/in minimum
Adhesion of coating is the measurement of the force required to separate the coatings from the substrate.

Tear Strength
ASTM D2261 (Tongue Tear) – Knits & Woven Substrates, 4 x 4 lbs
ASTM D5733 (Trap Tear) – Nonwoven Substrates & Nonwoven Composites, 15 x 15 lbs
Tear Strength is the measurement of stress exerted to rip the fabric under tension.

Hydrolysis Resistance – Applicable to Polyurethanes Only
ISO 1419 (Tropical Test Method C), 5 weeks
Visual Evaluation for no cracking, peeling or delamination
Hydrolysis resistance is the evaluation of a polyurethane fabric's ability to withstand exposure to extended periods of heat and humidity.

Note: There is no direct correlation of testing weeks to years of service in the field.

Stretch & Set
ACT has chosen not to establish a minimum requirement for this performance characteristic since the ability of a fabric to return to its initial state is strongly impacted by factors that are attributed to furniture construction and fabrication such as the density of foam. The SAE J855 test can be used to evaluate the stretch and set of a coated fabric; however, ACT suggests that you consult with both your fabric supplier and furniture manufacturer to determine if there are any potential issues.

Wrapped Panels and Upholstered Walls
Breaking Strength
ASTM D5034 (Grab Test), 35 lbs. minimum in warp and weft

Drapery
Seam Slippage
ASTM D434 for fabrics over 6 oz./sq. yard, 25 lbs. minimum in warp and weft

January 2015
Page 4

association
for contract
textiles

Abrasion

*Low Traffic /
Private Spaces –
Woven Upholstery Fabrics*

*High Traffic /
Public Spaces –
Woven Upholstery Fabrics*

*High Traffic /
Public Spaces –
Coated Upholstery Fabrics*

The surface wear of a fabric caused by friction.

Low Traffic / Private Spaces – Woven Upholstery Fabrics
ASTM D4157 (ACT approved #10 Cotton Duck)
15,000 double rubs Wyzenbeek method

ASTM D4966 (12 KPa pressure)
20,000 cycles Martindale method

High Traffic / Public Spaces – Woven Upholstery Fabrics
ASTM D4157 (ACT approved #10 Cotton Duck)
30,000 double rubs Wyzenbeek method

ASTM D4966 (12 KPa pressure)
40,000 cycles Martindale method

High Traffic / Public Spaces – Coated Upholstery Fabrics
ASTM D4157 (ACT approved #10 Cotton Duck or Wire Screen)
50,000 double rubs Wyzenbeek method

Print Retention – Applicable for Printed Coated Upholstery Fabrics
ASTM D3389 (modified to evaluate visual determination of print loss), Rating of 3 or higher*
H-18 Wheel, 250 grams, 250 cycles Taber Tester method
*Using the ACT photographic scale of approved replicas

Disclaimer:

Wyzenbeek test results are not necessarily a reliable indicator of fabric lifespan. Comparative laboratory testing results on the same textiles frequently differ and testing methods do not necessarily correlate well with the variables encountered in actual use by the end-user. Licensees using the ACT performance certification marks and publishing test results in excess of 100,000 double rubs are required, at a minimum, to provide in their sampling, marketing materials and Website, the following statement:

> *Multiple factors affect fabric durability and appearance retention, including end-user application and proper maintenance. Wyzenbeek results above 100,000 double rubs have not been shown to be a reliable indicator of increased fabric lifespan.*

Notes:

ACT studies indicate that results of multiple abrasion tests performed on some woven fabric structures may vary significantly – as much as 60 percent or more.

There is no correlation between Wyzenbeek and Martindale results.

For more information please refer to abrasion white papers on the ACT website:
http://www.contracttextiles.org/index.php?page=research

January 2015
Page 5

**IMPORTANT INFORMATION AND DISCLAIMERS REGARDING ACT'S
VOLUNTARY PERFORMANCE GUIDELINES**

As noted above, ACT's Voluntary Performance Guidelines ("Guidelines") and associated symbols ("Marks") are for information purposes only and are made available to help assist specifiers and end-users in evaluating certain characteristics of contract textiles.

Neither the Guidelines, nor the Marks constitute any promise, representation or warranty that a product or sample that bears or to which a Mark is referenced will in fact comply with applicable federal, state, or municipal laws, codes, rules and regulations concerning the intended use of such product ("Laws"), nor any assurance, representation or guarantee regarding or relating in any manner to the safety of any product or sample that bears or, to which a Mark is referenced.

Whenever appropriate, specifiers and end users should seek the advice of professionals or other knowledgeable persons to ascertain whether a product will in fact comply with applicable Laws.

Understand that the testing and standards ("Standards") referenced in the Guidelines are developed and promulgated by third parties not associated with ACT, and that these Standards often change or are supplemented by such third parties. Accordingly, the fact that a particular Standard is referenced in the Guidelines (and/or associated with any Mark) does not mean, nor is it intended to be a representation that Standard is the most current one.

It is the responsibility of the contract textile vendor and/or the manufacturer (not ACT) to determine in all instances whether or not a textile meets each of the Standards to which a particular Mark is referenced.

THE ASSOCIATION FOR CONTRACT TEXTILES EXPRESSLY DISCLAIMS LIABILITY TO ANY AND ALL PERSONS AND ENTITIES FOR PERSONAL INJURY, PROPERTY DAMAGE, AND ANY OTHER DAMAGE OF ANY KIND OR NATURE, (WHETHER OR NOT SUCH DAMAGES ARE DIRECT, INDIRECT, CONSEQUENTIAL OR COMPENSATORY) RESULTING FROM, OR IN ANY WAY RELATING TO THE GUIDELINES AND MARKS.

The marks ♥, ✿, ☀, ☆, A, ▢, are Registered Certification Marks at the US Patent and Trademark Office and are owned by the Association for Contract Textiles, Inc.

INDEX

diameter, 43–44
digital printing, 121
dimensional stability, 48, 133, 250–51
dimity, 226
Diné rug, 311
direct-glue installation, 238
directional pile lay, 129
direct printing, 114–16
direct yarn numbering systems, 80
discharge printing, 119
discontinuous brocade, 227
discontinuous-dyeing operations, 111
discontinuous weft, 189
disposable toweling, 356
distributors, 4
dobbies, 187
dobby loom, parts of, 85–86
dobby weave, 89, 90
doctor blade, 115
domestics, 5
dope dyeing, 108
dot/spot weaves, 189
dotted swiss, 227, 228
doublecloth, 190
double cloth construction, 91, 92
double-faced blanketing, 379
double-knit fabric, 101
down, 181, 373
drape, 44
draperies, 208, 225
drapery panel, 45
draw curtains, 209
drawing out, 74
drill, 244
drop, 383
drop-match patterns, 340
drop wire, 85
drum dyeing, 193
Dry Cleaning and Laundry Institute International, 11
dry extraction cleaning, 350
dry foam cleaning, 350
duck, 185, 229
Duette® honeycomb shade, 219
dupioni silk, 60, 78, 226, 227
durable press finishing, 137
durable press resins, 253
dust ruffles, 378
duvets, 383
dye, 3, 107
    colorants and color perception, 106–8
    dyeing fabrics and fabric components, 108–14
    factors affecting apparent color, 122–23

printing greige goods, 114–21
    techniques, 113–14
dye beck, 109
dyeing ranges, 113
dye liquor, 108
dye paste, 114
dyestuffs, 107

E
ecolabels, 30
economic factors, 10
editors, 5
effective face yarn weight, 292
egress, 153
elastane, 67
elastic recovery, 47
electrical conductivity, 51
electromagnetic spectrum, 106
electronic color meters, 254
electrostatic flocking operations, 131, 194
elongation, 46, 250, 321
embellishment, 129–32
embodied energy, 29
embossed vinyl wallcovering, 237
embossing, 128, 194
embroidered fabric, 65
embroidered grasscloth, 244
embroidery, 232
Emergency Planning and Community Right-to-Know Act, 27
emerizing, 194
end, 85
end-product designers, 5
end-product producers, 5
end products, 2
end-users, 6
Energy and Product Information Division, 141
Energy Independence and Security Act, 27
Energy Policy Act, 27
Environmentally Preferable Purchasing (EPP) Program, 26
environmentally related building codes, 27–28
Environmental Protection Agency (EPA), 25, 329
environmental regulations, 26–27
environmental stewardship, 69
epinglé, 192
etched-out print, 121
European rugs, 307–8
expanded polymer solution, 194
expanded vinyl, 194
eyelet, 232

F
fabric and sustainability. *See* sustainability
fabrications, 240–43
    combined fiber fabrications, 102–4
    films and coated fabrics, 96–98
    knits, 98–101
    knotted and twisted fabrics and braided yarns, 101–2
    pile fabrics, 101
fabric designers, 4
fabric manufacturers, 3
fabric nap, 129
fabric openness, 200
fabric panel, 216
fabric performance and evaluation
    building codes and regulations, 18
    codes, 18
    organizations, 16–19
    regulatory agencies, 19
    revisions of standards, 17–18
    standards, certifications, ratings and guidelines, 15–16
    standard test method, 16
fabric producers, 10
fabric weights, 213
face yarn fibers, 264–66
facts, 12, 32
faille, 185, 229
feathers, 181, 373
Federal Aviation Administration (FAA), 19, 160
Federal Insecticide, Fungicide, and Rodenticide Act, 26
Federal Trade Commission (FTC), 25, 39, 141
    investigative and rulemaking procedures, 141–42
    responsibilities and powers, 141
felted wool yarns, 82
felting, 3, 61
felting fibrous batts, 103
fenestration, 198
FHA (Federal Housing Administration), 19
fiber, 2, 39
    aesthetic properties, 44–45
    appearance retention properties, 45–48
    classification, 39–41
    comfort properties, 48–49
    composition, 42
    composition labeling, 266
    developments, 69
    external physical features, 43–44

health, safety and protection properties, 49, 51
    identification, 42
    molecular structure, 42–43
    pyrolytic characteristics of, 50
    sheets and pillowcases, 376–77
    textile bedding products, 368
    trade names, 146
fiber dyeing, 108
fiberfill, 181, 374
fiber producers, 10
fibers and yarns, 240
fiber suppliers, 2
fiber variants, 64
fibrous battings, 179–80
fibrous batts, 103
fibrous cushions, 314
filament, 2
filament fibers, 43
filament slub, 78
filament yarns, 74–75
filling, 85, 296
filling-faced satin weave, 89
filling pile fabrics, 91
filling-rib weaves, 185–86
filling weight, 374
fill leakage, 384
fill power, 373
film, 3
    knits, 98
    polypropylene, 97
    polyurethane, 97, 98
    PVC, 96–97
    silicone, 98
finials, 214
finished commercial carpet, 324–25
finishers, 3
finishes, 3, 23, 243–45
    engineering service-related features, 135–38
    functional, 132–34
    transforming surface appearance, 126–32
finishing, 193–94
fireproof fiber, 49
firmness, 180
fitted sheets, 378
flameless combustion, 152
flame propagation, 154
flame resistance, 135
flame-resistant fiber, 49
flame retardants, 135
flame spread, 154, 156
flaming combustion, 151
flammability, 179, 329–30
    characteristics, 49
Flammable Fabrics Act (FFA), 150
    1967 Amendment, 150–51

monofilament yarns, 74
monomers, 42
mordants, 108
mosquito netting, 231
multifilament yarns, 74
multilevel cut-pile styles, 274–76
multilevel loop-pile styles, 274
muslin, 376, 377

N

nailhead trimming, 178
nanofibers, 44
nanofinishes, 138
nanometers (nm), 106
nanotechnology, 69, 138
nap, 272
napping, 135
National Electronic Injury
    Surveillance System
    (NEISS), 150
National Fenestration Rating
    Council (NFRC), 202
National Fire Protection Association
    (NFPA), 18–19
National Highway Traffic Safety
    Administration (NHTSA), 19
National Institute of Standards and
    Technology (NIST), 150
natural cellulosic fibers, 54
    cork, 54
    cotton, 54–55
    flax, 55–56
    hemp, 56–58
    jute, 58
    ramie, 58
    sisal, 59
natural-colored cotton, 55
natural fiber, 39, 240
    batting, 179–80
    suppliers, 2
natural filling, materials, 373–74
natural man-made fiber producers, 2
natural materials, 44
natural protein fibers
    silk, 59–60
    wool, 60–62
needle count, 288
needle-punch blanketing, 381
needle-punched carpeting, 103
needle punching, 3, 104, 303
needle punching fibrous batts, 103–4
nestling down, 373
net fabric, 231
new wool, 143
NFPA 101®, 157–59
NFPA 701 test method, 160–61
nodes, 56
noil, 60

noise reduction, 236
noise reduction coefficient (NRC),
    202, 236, 326
noise transmission, 327
noncombustible fibers, 49
nontraversing panels, 208
nonwovens, 3, 103, 230–32
North American Free Trade
    Agreement (NAFTA), 144
novelty yarns, 78–79
nub yarns, 78
nylon fibers, 66, 348–49

O

Occupational Safety and Health
    Administration (OSHA),
    26, 328
Odette, 61
OEKO-TEX®, 33
OEKO-TEX's STeP (Sustainable
    Textile Production), 33
OEKO-TEX Standard 100, 33
O-fading, 255
off-gassing period, 23
off-grain fabrics, 93, 132, 248
office system workstation, 240
olefin fiber, 66–67
oleophilic propensity, 48
oleophobic, 136
Ombré, 109
one-level cut-pile styles, 273–74
one-level loop-pile styles, 274
one-way draw draperies, 209
opacity, 233
opaque fabrics, 228–30
opening and cleaning, 74
open weaves, 230–32
optical brighteners, 135
optical density values, 159
organdy, 226
organic cotton, 55
organic fiber, 25
organic wool, 62
organizations, 16–19
    sustainability, 30–31
oriental rugs, 306–7
oriented crystalline, 42
osnaburg, 230, 244
ottoman weave, 186
out-of-register print, 115
outward vision, modification of, 201
overdraperies, 209
overhead treatments, 210–13
overprinting, 114
over-the-wire construction
    technique, 93
oxygen number, 373
ozone, 255

P

package, 109
package dyeing, 109
package-injection technique, 10
pad, 314, 372
pad dyeing, 112
panel fabric, 239–40
    component materials and
        constructions, 240–45
    functional attributes, 236–37
    wallcovering installation
        methods, 238, 239–40
panels, 337, 338
panel width, 216, 217
Paragraph 25.853 (b), 160
Parkland Venetian blinds, 218
partial blackout, 233
pattern damask, 376
pattern distortion, 249–50
patterned fabric applications,
    174–75
pattern repeat, 250
PentaBDF, 318
pentabromodiphenyl, 318
percale, 376, 377
performance and safety product
    selection, 7, 8
permanently attached lining
    materials, 233–34
permeability, 326
Persian knot, 306
PET (polyethylene
    terephthalate), 24
picking, 74
piece, 3
piece-dyeing, 3, 111
pigment printing, 114, 228
pigments, 107
pile construction density, 301
pile density, 272
pile direction, 272
pile fabrics, 101
pile height, 272
pile or face yarns, 286
pile reversal, 272
pile sweep, 128
pile thickness, 272
pile warp yarns, 296
pile-weave fabrics, 91–93, 191–92
pile yarn, 339
    integrity, 268
    orientation of, 128–29
    weight, 292
pilling, 48, 134, 253
pillow
    decorative coverings for, 376
    fillings and tickings, 375–76
    sizes and forms, 375

pillowcases
    construction, 378–79
    manufacturing, 376–78
    product evaluation, 379
pillow sham, 376
pillow-top mattresses, 370
piña fiber, 59
pinned-up styles, 209
pinsonic melding, 131
pinsonic quilted fabric, 132
pitch, 297
PLA (polylactic acid), 68–69
plaid fabric, 185
plains, 226–27
plain weave fabric, 87, 185–86
plain-woven jute, 287
plain-woven lining fabrics, 233
plain-woven olefin, 287
planting, 299
plied yarn, 78
plumage, 373
plush, 192, 273, 274
ply yarns, 77
pocket cloth, 190
Pollution Prevention Act, 27
polyester, 24, 67, 225, 240
polyethylene terephthalate
    (PET), 281
polymer, 42
polymer film sheeting fabrics, 96
polymer film shower curtains, 362
polymerization, 42
polymer tapes, 82
polypropylene, 66, 97, 266
polyurethane, 67, 96–98, 180
polyurethane foam cushions, 316–17
    bonded polyurethane foam,
        317–18
    frothed polyurethane
        structures, 317
    prime polyurethane foam
        structures, 317
pooling, 272
post-consumer materials, 24
postindustrial materials, 24
pouf treatments, 209
power stretcher, 335
preventive maintenance, 346–49
primary backing fabrics, 286
prime polyurethane foam
    structures, 317
print design, 296
printing, 3
printing greige goods
    acid printing, 121
    digital printing, 121
    direct printing, 114–16
    discharge printing, 119

upholstery coverings
  backcoating, 184
  coated fabrics, 194
  flat-weave upholstery fabrics, 184–91
  leather, 192–94
  pile upholstery fabrics, 191–92
  upholstery fibers and yarns, 184
upholstery fabrics, 250
  cleaning codes, 259
  emergency action, 259
  maintenance, 258, 259
  routine care, 258–59
upholstery fibers and yarns, 184
up-the-bolt, 174
use groups, 330
U.S. Green Building Council (USGBC), 34
U-values, 203

V

valances, 210
value, 107
variegated yarns, 10
Vellux® blanket, 131
velour, 192
velour surfaces, 273, 274
velvet, 91, 191, 273
velvet carpet weaving, 301
velveteen, 91, 191
velvet plush, 273
venetian blinds, 216–17
vertical blinds, 218
vertical manufacturers, 3
vertical process, 3
Vignette® shades, 220
vinyl, 96, 194
vinyon, 68
virgin wool, 143
viscoelastic, 180
visible spectrum, 106
visible transmittance, 221
voided velvet, 191
voile, 226, 227
volatile organic compounds (VOCs), 23
voluntary labeling programs
  certification marks, 146

fiber trade names, 146
licensing programs, 147
sample labeling, 148
TM and ®, use of, 145–46
warranty programs, 147–48
V pattern, 91, 92

W

waffled rubber cushions, 315
wales, 91, 98
walk-off mat, 271
wallcovering
  component materials and constructions, 240–45
  fabrics, 260
  functional attributes, 236–37
  installation methods, 238–40
wallpaper, 242, 243
wall protection, 236–37
wall systems, 239
wall-to-wall carpet, 268, 270
wall-to-wall installation, 334–37
warp-faced satin weave, 89
warp knitting, 98–100
warp laminate, 242
warp printing, 115–16
warp sateen, 187, 229, 377
warp yarns, 85
warranty programs, 147–48
waste-to-energy (WTE) processes, 282
watermarking, 272
waterproof fabric, 138
water resistance, shower curtains, 365
4-way match, 174
wear resistance, 330–31
Weather-Ometer®, 256
weaving, 3
  decorative interlacing patterns, 89–94
  interlacing patterns, 87–89
  loom and fundamentals, 85–87
weft insertion, 99–100
weft knitting, 100–101, 377
weft yarns, 85
weight density, 293
weight-related factors, 292–93

welting, 175
wet shampoo method, 350–51
whole-building environmental standards, 34
wild silk, 60
wilton carpet, 299–300
window covering
  drapery lining materials, 233–34
  fibers and yarns, 225–26
  hard window covering materials, 233
  structures, 259–60
  surface embellishments, 232
  woven window covering fabrics, 226–32
window-covering fabrics, 251
window treatment selection
  appearance, 198, 199
  budgets, 205
  function, 199–205
window treatment styles
  awnings, 221–22
  blinds, 216–18
  calculating yardage required, 214–16
  curtain and drapery treatments, 208–14
  shades, 218–21
  shutters, 222
wire loom, 93
wires per inch, 300
wood veneer, 243
wool, 60–62, 143, 264, 185
woolen run (wr) system, 80
woolen yarns, 74
wool fabrics, 185
Woolmark Company, 146
Wool Products Labeling Act (WPLA), 61, 142–43
worsted count (wc) system, 80
worsted yarns, 61, 74
woven, 240–42
woven blanketing, 379, 381
woven grasscloth, 241
woven pile floorcoverings
  axminster carpet, 296–99
  basic components, 296

chenille carpet, 301
pile construction density, 301
velvet carpet, 301
wilton carpet, 299–300
woven-through-the-back velvet, 301
woven window covering fabrics
  decorative fabrics, 226
  opaque fabrics, 228–30
  open weaves, knits, knotted fabrics and nonwovens, 230–32
  plains and sheers, 226–27
  privacy curtains, 230
  sheer variations, 227–28
W pattern, 91, 92
written warranty, 147
Wyzenbeek test method, 251

Y

yarn, 39
  sheets and pillowcases, 376–77
  textile bedding products, 368
yarn alignment, 248
yarn beams, 85
yarn count, 377
yarn distortion, 248, 249
yarn-dyed, 3, 109
yarn-like structures
  classification and nomenclature, 78–80
  construction, designation of, 80–81
  formation of, 81–82
yarn number, 80
yarn numbering systems, 80–81
yarn producers, 3
yarn splay, 268
yarn twist, 273

Z

Z twist, 77